Ethics and World Politics

Ethics and
World Politics

Edited by

Duncan Bell

OXFORD
UNIVERSITY PRESS

OXFORD
UNIVERSITY PRESS

Great Clarendon Street, Oxford OX2 6DP

Oxford University Press is a department of the University of Oxford.
It furthers the University's objective of excellence in research, scholarship,
and education by publishing worldwide in

Oxford New York

Auckland Cape Town Dar es Salaam Hong Kong Karachi
Kuala Lumpur Madrid Melbourne Mexico City Nairobi
New Delhi Shanghai Taipei Toronto

With offices in

Argentina Austria Brazil Chile Czech Republic France Greece
Guatemala Hungary Italy Japan Poland Portugal Singapore
South Korea Switzerland Thailand Turkey Ukraine Vietnam

Oxford is a registered trade mark of Oxford University Press
in the UK and in certain other countries

Published in the United States
by Oxford University Press Inc., New York

British Library Cataloguing in Publication Data
Data available

Library of Congress Cataloging-in-Publication Data
Data available

Typeset by MPS Limited, A Macmillan Company
Printed in Great Britain on acid-free paper by CPI Group (UK) Ltd, Croydon, CR0 4YY

ISBN 978–0–19–954862–0

5 7 9 10 8 6 4

■ ACKNOWLEDGEMENTS

This book could not have been completed without the valuable support of numerous individuals and institutions, and I would like to record my gratitude to them. First, I would like to thank the contributors to the book for their time, patience, and intellectual energy. Joe Hoover and Christian Schemmel did stellar work on the website, the glossary, and the bibliography. The following people provided very helpful advice on different aspects of the project: Michael Boyle, Sarah Fine, Mathew Humphrey, Margaret Kohn, Patricia Owens, Casper Sylvest, Mette Eilstrup Sangiovanni, Nick Rengger, and Leif Wenar. Sarah has been a source of fine judgments and wonderful company throughout. Catriona McKinnon kindly gave permission to use some of the glossary terms from her excellent textbook, *Issues in Political Theory* (Oxford University Press, 2008). I have benefitted greatly from working with three superb editors at Oxford University Press: Ruth Anderson, Claire Brewer, and Catherine Page. Finally, the Department of Politics and International Studies, University of Cambridge, Christ's College, Cambridge, and the Leverhulme Trust, provided welcome resources.

Oxford University Press acknowledges that Arash Abizadeh has written a chapter titled 'Closed borders, human rights, and democratic legitimation' in *Driven from Home: Protecting the Rights of Forced Migrants*, edited by David Hollenbach, SJ, to be published by Georgetown University Press.

◼ BRIEF CONTENTS

PART THREE Issues

■ DETAILED CONTENTS

PART THREE Issues

LIST OF CASE STUDIES

NOTES ON THE CONTRIBUTORS

Arash Abizadeh is Associate Professor of Political Theory at McGill University. His research focuses on democratic theory and questions of identity, nationalism, and cosmopolitanism; immigration, and border control; Habermas and discourse ethics; and seventeenth- and eighteenth-century philosophy, particularly Hobbes and Rousseau. His publications have appeared in journals including *American Political Science Review, History of Political Thought, Journal of Political Philosophy, Nations and Nationalism, Philosophical Studies, Philosophy & Public Affairs, Political Theory*, and *Review of Metaphysics*.

Amy Allen is Professor of Philosophy and Parents Distinguished Research Professor in the Humanities at Dartmouth College. She is the author of *The Power of Feminist Theory: Domination, Resistance, Solidarity* (Westview, 1999) and *The Politics of Our Selves: Power, Autonomy, and Gender in Contemporary Critical Theory* (Columbia University Press, 2008). Her current research focuses on the relationship between power and reason in the critical theory tradition and in contemporary debates about cosmopolitanism.

Duncan Bell is a Lecturer in the Department of Politics and International Studies at the University of Cambridge, and a Fellow of Christ's College. He works on assorted topics in the history of modern European and American political thought, and contemporary international political theory. He is the author of *The Idea of Greater Britain: Empire and the Future of World Order, 1860–1900* (Princeton University Press, 2007), and the editor of various books, including *Memory, Trauma, and World Politics: Reflections on the Relationship Between Past and Present* (Palgrave, 2006), and *Political Thought and International Relations: Variations on a Realist Theme* (Oxford University Press, 2009).

Colin Bird is Associate Professor of Politics at the University of Virginia. He received his PhD in Political Theory at Columbia University and is the author of *The Myth of Liberal Individualism* (Cambridge University Press, 1999) and *An Introduction to Political Philosophy* (Cambridge University Press, 2006).

James Bohman is Danforth Professor of Philosophy and Professor of International Studies at Saint Louis University, Missouri. He is author of *Democracy across Borders: From Dêmos to Dêmoi* (MIT Press, 2007), *Public Deliberation: Pluralism, Complexity and Democracy* (MIT Press, 1996) and *New Philosophy of Social Science: Problems of Indeterminacy* (MIT Press, 1991).

Simon Caney is Professor in Political Theory at the University of Oxford. He is the author of *Justice Beyond Borders: A Global Political Theory* (Oxford University Press, 2005). He has also published articles in philosophy, law, and politics journals on issues in contemporary political philosophy, especially on questions of global justice. He currently holds an ESRC Climate Change Leadership Fellowship and is completing two books for Oxford University Press: *Global Justice and Climate Change* (with Derek Bell) and *On Cosmopolitanism*. He is a co-editor (with Stephen Gardiner, Dale Jamieson, and Henry Shue) of *Climate Ethics: Essential Readings* (Oxford University Press, 2009).

Anthony Carty is the Sir Y. K. Pao Professor of Public Law at the Faculty of Law, the University of Hong Kong. Previously he was Professor of Public Law at the University of Aberdeen; Visiting Professor at the Politics Departments of the Free University of Berlin and Laval University, Quebec; also Visiting Professor at the Law Faculties of the Universities of Paris I and II, and Tokyo. His books include *Sir Gerald Fitzmaurice and the World Crisis: A Legal Adviser in the Foreign Office, 1932–1945* (Kluwer International, 2000), *The Decay of International Law? A Reappraisal of the Limits of Legal Imagination in International Affairs* (Manchester University Press, 1986) and *The Philosophy of International Law* (Edinburgh University Press, 2007).

Andrew Gamble is Professor of Politics and Head of the Department of Politics and International Studies at the University of Cambridge. He is a Fellow of Queens' College and was formerly Professor of Politics and Pro Vice-Chancellor at the University of Sheffield. He is a Fellow of the British Academy and joint editor of *The Political Quarterly*. He has published widely on British politics, public policy, and political economy, and his recent books include *The Spectre at the Feast: Capitalist Crisis and the Politics of Recession* (Palgrave, 2009) and *Between Europe and America: The Future of British Politics* (Palgrave, 2003). In 2005 he was awarded the Political Studies Association Isaiah Berlin prize for Lifetime Contribution to Political Studies.

Christopher Goto-Jones is Professor of Comparative Philosophy and Political Thought, and Director of the Modern East Asia Research Centre at Leiden University in the Netherlands. His publications include *Political Philosophy in Japan: Nishida, the Kyoto School and Co-Prosperity* (Routledge, 2005) and an edited volume on *Re-Politicising the Kyoto School as Philosophy* (Routledge, 2007). He heads a major 'VICI' research project on comparative political thought, funded by the NOW (Netherlands Organization for Scientific Research), focused on understanding political ideas outside of Europe and in non-conventional media.

Virginia Held is Distinguished Professor of Philosophy at the City University of New York, Graduate School, and Professor Emerita at Hunter College. She is the author of *How Terrorism Is Wrong: Morality and Political Violence* (Oxford University Press, 2008). Among her other books are *The Ethics of Care: Personal, Political, and Global* (Oxford University Press, 2006), *Feminist Morality: Transforming Culture, Society, and Politics* (University of Chicago Press, 1993), *Rights and Goods: Justifying Social Action* (Free Press, 1984), and the co-edited collection *Philosophy, Morality, and International Affairs* (Oxford University Press, 1974). In 2001–2002 she was President of the Eastern Division of the American Philosophical Association. She has also taught at Yale, Dartmouth, UCLA, and Hamilton, and has five grandchildren.

Mathew Humphrey is Reader in Political Philosophy at the University of Nottingham. He is the author of *Preservation versus the People: Nature, Humanity, and Political Philosophy* (Oxford University Press, 2002) and *Ecological Politics and Democratic Theory: The Challenge to the Deliberative Ideal* (Routledge, 2007).

Kimberly Hutchings is Professor of International Relations at the London School of Economics and Political Science. Her research interests include: global ethics; political violence; feminist ethical and political theory; and theories of time and history in world politics. Her books include: *Kant, Critique and Politics* (Routledge, 1995), *International Political Theory: Re-thinking Ethics in a Global Era* (Sage, 1999), *Hegel and Feminist Philosophy* (Polity, 2003), *Time and World Politics: Thinking the Present* (Manchester University Press, 2008), and *Introduction to Global Ethics* (Polity, 2009).

Duncan Ivison is Professor of Political Philosophy at the University of Sydney. He is the author of *Rights* (Acumen, 2008); *Postcolonial Liberalism* (Cambridge University Press, 2002); *The Self at Liberty: Political Argument and the Arts of Government* (Cornell University Press, 1997); and co-editor of *Political Theory and the Rights of Indigenous Peoples* (Cambridge University Press, 2000).

Peter Jones is Professor of Political Philosophy at Newcastle University. He has authored and edited books on rights and his other published work includes articles on human rights, group rights, cultural diversity, value pluralism, toleration and recognition, freedom of belief and expression, global justice, democracy, and liberalism.

Margaret Kohn is Associate Professor of Political Science at the University of Toronto. She is the author of *Radical Space: Building the House of the People* (Cornell University Press, 2003) and *Brave New Neighborhoods: The Privatization of Public Space* (Routledge, 2004). She has published several articles on the issue of colonialism in European and non-Western political theory. She is currently completing a book entitled *Colonial Critique and Postcolonial Power* (with Keally McBride).

Anthony F. Lang, Jr is a Senior Lecturer in the School of International Relations at the University of St Andrews. He has taught at the American University in Cairo, Yale University, Bard College, and Albright College and served as a program officer at the Carnegie Council on Ethics and International Affairs. His research and teaching focus on international political theory. He has written two books, *Agency and Ethics: The Politics of Military Intervention* (SUNY Press, 2002) and *Punishment, Justice, and International Relations: Ethics and Order after the Cold War* (Routledge 2008), and edited or co-edited five others. He has also published a number of articles and book chapters on political responsibility, the just war tradition, punishment, humanitarian intervention, and international political theory. His current work focuses on global constitutionalism.

Margaret Moore is the Sir Edward Peacock Professor of Political Theory at Queens University, Kingston, Canada. She is the author of *Foundations of Liberalism* (Oxford University Press, 1993) and *The Ethics of Nationalism* (Oxford University Press, 2001). She has also published two edited collections on state borders and secession: *National Self-Determination and Secession* (Oxford University Press, 1998) and a volume using comparative political theory, (co-edited with Allen Buchanan), *Nations, States and Borders: Diverse Ethical Theories* (Cambridge University Press, 2003). She is currently working on issues connected to global justice theory and the normative status of land or territory.

Patricia Owens is Senior Lecturer in Politics at Queen Mary, University of London. She is the author of *Between War and Politics: International Relations and the Thought of Hannah Arendt* (Oxford University Press, 2007), a book tentatively called *War, Politics and Security* (Polity, forthcoming) and co-editor of *The Globalization of World Politics* (4th edn, Oxford University Press, 2008). She has published in *Review of International Studies, International Affairs, International Politics, International Relations, Alternatives*, and *Millennium*. She has held research positions at Princeton, Berkeley, the University of Southern California UCLA, and Oxford.

Max Pensky is Professor of Philosophy at Binghamton University, the State University of New York. He has published widely on critical theory, contemporary political philosophy, and German culture and politics. He is the author of several books on critical theory, including a study of Habermas, *The Ends of Solidarity: Discourse Theory in Ethics and Politics* (SUNY Press, 2008). His edited books include *Globalizing Critical Theory* (Rowman & Littlefield, 2005). He has held fellowships at Cornell, Frankfurt and Oxford.

Nicholas Rengger is Professor of Political Theory and International Relations at the University of St Andrews, and Editor of the *Review of International Studies*. He has published on many aspects of political thought, international political theory and ethics, philosophical and political theology and intellectual history. He is the author of *Political Theory, Modernity, and Postmodernity: Beyond Enlightenment and Critique* (Blackwell, 1995); *International Relations, Political Theory and the Problem of Order* (Routledge, 1999); and *Judgments of War: The Just War Tradition and the Uncivil Condition* (Routledge, 2010). He is currently finishing a study titled *Between Progressivisms, Pessimism and Pluralism: Conversations in International Political Theory*.

Kok-Chor Tan is Associate Professor of Philosophy at the University of Pennsylvania. He specializes in political philosophy, and is especially interested in problems of global justice, nationalism and human rights. His publications include *Toleration, Diversity and Global Justice* (Penn State Press, 2000) and *Justice without Borders: Cosmopolitanism, Nationalism, and Patriotism* (Cambridge University Press, 2004).

■ GUIDED TOUR OF THE ONLINE RESOURCE CENTRE

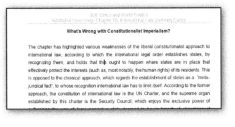

The Online Resource Centre that accompanies this book provides students and instructors with ready-to-use teaching and learning materials. These resources are free of charge and designed to maximize the learning experience.
www.oxfordtextbooks.co.uk/orc/bell_ethics/

For students:

Additional Case Studies

Additional case studies are provided to reinforce your understanding of the complex issues involved. These case studies often present a different perspective from the chapter in the book, highlighting the various ways in which ethical issues in world politics can be approached.

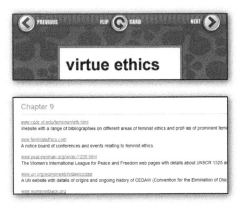

Flashcard Glossary

A series of interactive flashcards containing key terms and concepts has been provided to test your understanding of terminology.

Web Links

A series of annotated web links has been provided to point you in the direction of different theoretical debates, important documents and organizations, articles, and other relevant sources of information.

For Instructors:

PowerPoint® Slides

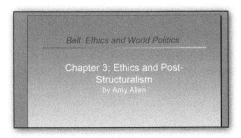

These complement each chapter of the book and are a useful resource for preparing lectures and handouts. They allow lecturers to guide students through the key concepts and can be fully customized to meet the needs of the course.

■ GUIDED TOUR OF LEARNING FEATURES

This book is enriched with a range of learning tools to help you navigate the text and reinforce your knowledge of ethics and world politics. This guided tour shows you how to get the most out of your textbook package.

Reader's Guides

Reader's guides at the beginning of every chapter set the scene for upcoming themes and issues to be discussed, and indicate the scope of coverage in each chapter.

Cross-References

Cross-reference icons, which appear in the margin, emphasize the links between thinkers and ideas throughout the book.

Questions

A set of carefully devised questions has been provided to help assess your comprehension of core themes, and may be used as the basis of seminar discussion and coursework.

Further Reading

At the end of each chapter, the contributors identify some of the most important or interesting texts on a particular topic. These readings will help to extend and deepen your engagement with the issues.

Web Links

Each chapter contains an annotated summary of useful websites which will help you to explore the topic further.

> ▓ **WEB LINKS**
>
> **http://plato.stanford.edu** An excellent on-line encyclopaedia of philosophy range of thinkers and topics.
>
> **http://publicreason.net** A site dedicated to issues in contemporary political discussion of thinkers and ideas, and includes listings for journals and up
>
> **http://leiterlegalphilosophy.typepad.com/** This is a blog dedicated to discussi philosophy, run by a leading scholar in the field.
>
> **http://crookedtimber.org/books/** Crooked Timber is a popular multi-author

Glossary Terms

Key terms appear in bold in the text and are defined in the glossary at the end of the book.

> **nism and justice**
>
> kinds of contemporary cosmopolitanism this chapter will now tail. Cosmopolitan theories of **distributive justice** are discussed 14 and for that reason will receive a relatively short treatment tice-based cosmopolitanism bears on the two other kinds of cosy political cosmopolitanism) and, since it also includes more short discussion here of the nature and varieties of justice-based ropriate. In what follows I shall, therefore, describe the nature

Case Studies

The chapters in Part III of the book all include case studies that aim to stimulate debate by exploring how challenging theoretical arguments can illuminate concrete cases.

> **20.7 Case study: fortress Europe?**
>
> Today, most countries are, to varying degrees, simultaneously coun and destination for interstate migrants. This contrasts with half a ce countries of origin were European, and only a small number of indi such as Australia, Canada, and the United States—were countries of for several centuries Europeans systematically migrated, whether as or refugees, to the Earth's four corners, today the tide has reversed a major destination for interstate migrants. By 2005, Europe was

Ethics and world politics: Introduction

Duncan Bell

1 Introduction

Let us start with some statistics on human suffering:

- According to a recent report from the United Nations Development Programme (UNDP), approximately 1 billion people around the world are living 'at the margins of survival' on less than $1 per day; 2.6 billion people, or 40% of the world's population, live on less than $2 per day. Around 10 million children under the age of five die each year as a result of preventable causes, while 28% of all children in 'developing' countries are malnourished. The world is marked not only by poverty, but also by huge inequalities between rich and poor. While the poorest 40% earn only 5% of total global income between them, the richest 20% earn 75% of income. More than 80% of people live in countries where the gap between rich and poor is growing (UNDP, 2008, p. 25).

- The World Health Organization (WHO) estimates that at least 150,000 people per year die as a result of global climate change, chiefly through increased levels of malnutrition and preventable diseases (such as malaria) in vulnerable geographical areas (WHO, 2003, 2005). This figure only looks set to increase in the future.

- Finally, we can turn to war. The twentieth century was the most destructive in human history, with approximately 231 million people dying as a result of armed conflict or political violence (Leitenberg, 2006). The twenty-first century has got off to a bloody start. According to conservative estimates, the 2003 invasion of Iraq and the subsequent conflict in that country have killed around 100,000 people, although the actual figure is likely to be considerably higher. Hundreds of thousands have died in Darfur in Sudan, millions in the Democratic Republic of Congo. These are only three examples from a much longer list of recent or ongoing conflicts.

The statistics bear witness to a vast amount of misery. They speak directly to the ethical dimensions of world politics, the subject matter of this book. In all of the cases, things could have turned out differently. Wars might have been avoided or fought in less destructive ways. Poverty could be alleviated, even eliminated. Inequality could be reduced. Climate change could be averted or slowed down. Where choices like this arise—where the actions of humans, either individually or collectively, can alter the course of events—we enter into the realm of ethical deliberation. This is the realm in which we evaluate and judge human action, where we begin to think about what is wrong (and what is right) with the world, and how things might be improved.

Thinking in this manner generates a wide range of difficult questions. These include:

- Do the rich states (and citizens) of the global North have an obligation to distribute wealth to the poor states (and citizens) of the global South, and, if so, who should bear the costs—states, corporations, or individuals?

- Does the onset of anthropogenic (human-created) climate change mean that we should be forced to alter our way of life? And who are the 'we' here?

- Under what conditions, if any, is war justified? What sort of rules should govern how war is actually fought? Should countries increase the risk to their soldiers if it decreases the risk to civilian populations, and should certain types of weapon—for example land mines—be outlawed?

- Should democratic states intervene militarily to protect the **human rights** of people in other countries? If so, were the interventions in Bosnia and Kosovo during the 1990s legitimate? Was the invasion of Iraq in 2003 justifiable on humanitarian grounds?

- Are human rights simply a new form of Western imperialism? What exactly is wrong with imperialism in the first place?

- Can **terrorism** ever be a legitimate political tactic? Can states be guilty of terrorism?

- Should we care more for our fellow citizens than for distant strangers? Is patriotism a virtue or a vice? Do **cultural identities** have moral value, and if so, why? How does gender impact on the frequency and form of political violence?

- Is global democracy desirable? How might it work?

These questions, and many like them, stir up passionate debate. They help to structure the deliberations of governments throughout the world. They inform and motivate the activities of many international organizations (IOs), including the United Nations (UN), and non-governmental organizations (NGOs), such as Amnesty International and Human Rights Watch. They are the catalyst of political activism and of protest on the streets. They are the subject of conversations over dinner tables and in classrooms. *Ethics and World Politics* outlines the latest scholarly thinking about some of the most important and complex ethical issues in world politics. It offers no easy answers, but it will provide the reader with a good sense of the types of questions that arise, and the very different ways in which they can be addressed.

The remainder of this introduction outlines some of the key theoretical issues at stake in thinking about ethics and world politics (section 2), and then discusses the scope and content of the book (sections 3 and 4).

2 Debating the ethical dimensions of world politics

Before proceeding, it is worth reflecting on both parts of the title of this book: 'ethics' and 'world politics'.

The type of material that is explored in the following chapters is sometimes called 'international ethics', or is seen as a subset of the academic field of International Relations (IR).[1] The problem with both of these expressions, however, is that the word 'international' implies a quite narrow focus—the relations between (nation) states. While this is a very important subject, and one which features prominently in this book, it does not exhaust the range of political or ethical issues facing the world today. The study of world politics, including the analysis of its ethical dimensions, needs to encompass a wide range of non-state actors, including NGOs, terrorist organizations, cultural or religious communities, multinational corporations, even individual human beings. 'World politics', then, has been chosen as a more inclusive, open category. It includes reflection on 'international' themes, but it also moves well beyond them.

In recent years there has been a resurgence of scholarly interest in the ethical dimensions of world politics. This boom began in the 1990s and continues to this day. Political theorists and IR specialists of the previous generation had tended to downplay the topic. They concentrated on ethical issues arising in the context of domestic politics, looking within (or taking for granted) the state, rather than discussing questions that arose about the relations between political communities.[2] Meanwhile IR scholars, and especially those based in the United States, focused their intellectual energy on trying to explain how the states in the international system interacted with each other—what causes wars to break out, what conditions are necessary for co-operation between states, why some states are rich and others poor—while paying little explicit attention to ethical concerns.[3] While there were always exceptions to these trends, it is fair to say that in general the ethical dimensions of world politics were marginalized.

Today, however, ethical issues have moved to the forefront of debates in several overlapping academic fields. Arguments about 'global justice' stand at the very heart of political theory. Thomas Nagel, a leading philosopher, writes that the 'need for workable ideas about the global or international case presents political theory with its most important current task' (2005, p. 113). Few would disagree with him. Moreover, while many IR scholars continue to focus on empirical topics, the field is currently witnessing a renaissance of interest in ethical questions. *Ethics and World Politics* draws on and seeks to provide a map of these exciting developments. In doing so, it stands at the intersection of IR and political theory.

---

[1] It is common to distinguish between International Relations (IR) as an academic field and international relations (lower case) as the actual processes that are studied by scholars.

[2] However, for pioneering examples of work addressing global poverty, see Singer (1972), Beitz (1979), Shue (1980), Sen (1982), and O'Neill (1986). The Cold War also spawned a significant literature on the ethics of war, including Ramsey (1968), Walzer (1977), and Finnis et al. (1987). For an important study of totalitarian politics, see Arendt (1973 [1951]).

[3] There were, of course, exceptions to this general trend (e.g. Hoffmann, 1981). Early work in the discipline of IR, in the two decades before and after World War II (1939–45), was often concerned with ethical issues (Long & Wilson, 1995; Schmidt, 1998; Bell, 2009b).

The reasons for this shift towards addressing ethics in a global context are many and varied. One of the most significant is the changing character of world politics itself. The end of the Cold War in 1989–90 opened up a new range of political possibilities, generating wide-ranging debates over the character of the 'new world order'. During the 1990s violent conflicts in Iraq, Bosnia, Rwanda, and Kosovo, raised a host of complex questions about the ethics of war, and in particular about whether or not Western states should employ military force to protect human rights in other countries. At the same time the idea of 'globalization' came to dominate much public and scholarly discourse. For many politicians, journalists, and academic commentators, it seemed that increasing economic interconnection and the rise of new technologies (such as the Internet) were transforming the conditions of modern political life. This was joined by growing fears about the potential consequences of climate change and horror at the continuing existence of global poverty. Such phenomena, it was increasingly realized, could only be tackled effectively by the co-ordinated action of people and political communities across the world. By the start of the new millennium, the shift towards addressing global questions was in full swing. It was further reinforced by the terrorist attacks on 9/11, the 2003 invasion of Iraq, the subsequent war in Afghanistan, and the so-called 'war on terror'. In combination, these developments widened the horizons of many political thinkers, generating a sophisticated and growing literature on the ethics of world politics.

Theoretical pluralism

Despite this surge of interest, however, scholars remain deeply divided over how best to approach the study of ethics in a global context. This divide takes different forms. Like politicians and citizens in general, scholars disagree sharply over how to answer the types of question that I outlined at the beginning of this introduction. Some think that the rich have a moral obligation to redistribute wealth to the poor, while others argue that redistribution is unrealistic or unnecessary, or that it would subvert the operating principles of the free market economic system. Some insist that Western states should intervene to protect human rights around the world, while others think that this should be condemned as a contemporary form of imperialism. Some celebrate the ethical virtues of nationality and cultural identity, others worry that identity politics undermines the quest for global equality and justice. These kinds of disagreement are hardly surprising—they are the very stuff of politics. There are no uncontroversial or uncontested arguments about complex moral and political problems.

However, the disagreements between scholars often go deeper than this. They diverge over the very terms of the debate—over how we should even begin to think about the meaning of ethics, politics, and the relations between them. This is because they draw on ideas from a variety of schools of thought—or intellectual traditions—that offer diverse ways of understanding these issues. One way to think about this is to imagine the various theoretical approaches as acting like the lenses in a pair of sunglasses. The world looks both the same and different when viewed through red or green lenses. They filter the light in distinctive ways, offering contrasting perspectives on the world.

Some aspects of the world will look the same in some senses, e.g. shapes, but many other features, such as light and shade of colour, will look very different, so different in fact that they seem to show alternative worlds. (Smith, 2007, p. 11)

Scholars working in these traditions often focus on different topics, and argue about them in divergent ways. Three of these traditions—**analytic political theory**, post-structuralism, and critical theory—are introduced in more depth in Part One.

It is quite common to reduce the diversity of theoretical approaches available to a crude distinction between 'Continental' and 'Anglo-American' (or 'Analytic') philosophy. According to this view, 'Continental' philosophy draws its inspiration and arguments from a range of modern European thinkers, mainly French and German, including Georg Hegel, Friedrich Nietzsche, Jürgen Habermas, Michel Foucault, and Jacques Derrida. Pitched against this position, it is then claimed, is an alternative and radically different Anglo-Saxon school, which draws its inspiration and arguments from other sources, including John Locke, David Hume, John Stuart Mill, Ronald Dworkin, and John Rawls. Textbooks are often written in ways that reinforce this purported divide, focusing only on debates *within* a tradition, while ignoring or downplaying alternative approaches.

However, this is an unhelpful way of carving up the scholarly field. It both exaggerates the similarities between scholars who are lumped together into these two camps and implies falsely that you have to make a choice between them, that you should only be interested in (or know about) one particular approach. This misses the fact that much interesting work in political theory draws on ideas and arguments that straddle various traditions. Moreover, it can lead to an impoverished and often distorted understanding of the nature and scope of political theorizing, and of the range of arguments available.

Ethics and World Politics deliberately avoids this polarized way of presenting work on ethics and political theory. Instead, it is designed to offer readers insights into some of the diverse ways in which ethical issues can be approached. In order to do so, it examines a range of different types of theorizing and draws together contributors working in assorted intellectual traditions and academic disciplines.

Normative theorizing

The term ethics can be confusing, for it is used in a wide variety of ways. In this book it is employed in a very broad sense. Much of the material that is discussed in the following chapters travels under different names in different academic contexts. These include, 'international ethics', 'global ethics', 'international political theory', 'normative IR theory', or simply 'political theory and international relations'. Although subtle distinctions can be drawn between these formulations, in practice they are often used interchangeably. All of them can be seen as forms of 'normative' theory—theory that, among other things, *evaluates* the rightness or wrongness of actions, policies, institutions, or practices. These assessments are often made in relation to how theorists interpret the meaning and implication of values like freedom, justice, or equality. Normative theories are often (but not always) *prescriptive*—that is, they seek to identify the best (or better) ways of organizing human collective life.

A distinction is often drawn between *normative* and *descriptive* theory.[4] Normative work is, as mentioned above, usually concerned with questions about how the world *ought to be*. It focuses on questions of value. Descriptive work, on the other hand, is usually understood to focus on identifying how the world *actually is*. It aims to accurately describe (or explain) the processes and dynamics of world politics. In order to do so, scholars utilize a wide array of social scientific methodologies.

The distinction certainly picks out something important—different types of theory are designed to answer different types of question. It is one thing to ask why the Second World War started, another to ask whether the war was morally justified. Yet the apparent strict divide between normative and descriptive scholarship can also be misleading. This is because these two dimensions are interwoven:

- First, descriptive work is usually motivated by normative concerns. Many attempts to explain the causes of war or of poverty have been generated by a desire to try to limit the frequency of violence and suffering. These are normative goals. This position is neatly summarized by Robert Keohane, a leading IR scholar, in a discussion about how young political scientists should choose topics to work on.

  We should choose normatively important problems because we care about improving human behaviour, we should explain these choices to our students and our readers, and we should not apologize for making value-laden choices even as we seek to search unflinchingly for the truth, as unpleasant or unpopular as that may be. (Keohane, 2009, p. 363)

- Secondly, descriptive work in the social sciences contains within it all sorts of normative assumptions, whether its practitioners admit this or not. There are no non-value-laden choices to make. It is impossible to analyse politics, or any other aspect of human activity, without bringing value-judgements to bear, not least because the very language and concepts we use to study politics—democracy, liberty, security, and so forth—are themselves always value-laden.[5] The types of questions that are asked, and the ways in which people go about answering them, are invariably saturated with normative assumptions. There is much to be said for Christian Reus-Smit and Duncan Snidal's argument (2008b) that all theories of international politics, of whatever kind, represent 'contending practical discourses' which offer answers to the question 'how should we act?'[6]

- Finally, normative theorizing always contains empirical (descriptive) assumptions. These assumptions might concern human nature, or accounts of the workings of political institutions, or of the way in which cultures and other group identities are formed. Sometimes these empirical assumptions play only a minor role in the theory, but in other instances they are very important, and the success or failure of the theory will

---

[4] Other terms are sometimes used instead of 'descriptive', including 'explanatory', 'empirical', or 'positive'.
[5] This type of issue is widely discussed in literature on the philosophy of social science. See, for example, Flyvbjerg (2001); Hollis (1994); Baert (2005); Jackson (2009).
[6] For good introductions to IR theory see: Sterling-Folker (2005); Dunne et al. (2007); Burchill et al. (2009).

partly depend on how accurate the empirical assumptions are. For example, if a theory relies on an account of politics that ignores economic factors, and yet it can be shown that such factors are vital in understanding modern political life, then the theory would be of limited value. In Chapter 4 Andrew Gamble analyses how empirical assumptions about the character of globalization play an important role in debates over global justice.

It is a mistake, then, to see 'normative' and 'descriptive' work as completely different. All types of theory contain elements of both.

The purposes of normative theorizing: prescription and understanding

There are different ways of viewing the purposes of normative theorizing and, once again, these differences can be seen in the chapters in this book.

For many scholars, political theory is 'a branch or application of moral philosophy' (Simmons, 2007, p. 2). According to this view, the main job of the political philosopher is to identify how things *ought to be*—the kinds of political communities we should live in, how they should relate to each other, the types of laws we should create and the policies governments should adopt. It should be, in other words, chiefly a prescriptive exercise. This conception is the dominant one among 'Anglo-American' (or analytic) theorists.

Yet other scholars disagree. The main job of the political philosopher, they argue, should not be to posit rules and principles to govern how people should live. Instead, they point to a different conception, one in which political theory should be 'primarily concerned to understand rather than to prescribe' and that, as such, it should not be seen as a 'practical philosophy' aimed at 'recommending specific institutions and policies' (Parekh, 1996, pp. 505–6). The main role of the theorist is instead to try and understand important features of the world, and in particular to identify and criticize the various ways that groups of people hold and use power. Here, political theory necessarily engages with concrete social and political circumstances, drawing heavily on insights from sociology, history, anthropology, and politics (e.g. Geuss, 2001). Proponents of this view argue that only by systematically analysing the nature of political life—the way institutions work to enable and constrain action, how cultural beliefs shape the way people interpret the world, how political ideas actually work in practice—can we even begin to think about changing things. It is for this reason that some types of theory focus mainly on identifying the ways in which humans are shaped and constrained by language, culture, and political institutions. For example, post-colonial theory, which is examined by Margaret Kohn in Chapter 11, traces the highly damaging ways in which Western cultural (and especially racial) stereotypes about other societies have had a profound impact on political life, most notably by providing justifications for imperialism—for the conquest of, and rule over, other peoples. These types of theory are normative insofar as they focus on questions of value, and on the ways in which ethical arguments are constructed and employed, but they are not primarily prescriptive.

Should normative theories be realistic?

It is a long-standing criticism of political theory that it is often *utopian*—that it identifies political ideals, or types of social and political order, that are simply beyond the reach of humans as we know them. Utopianism of this kind, the critics continue, is either *pointless* (because it will not change anything) or alternatively, *dangerous* (because ambitious schemes for social transformation often result in disaster). The violence that followed the French Revolution at the end of the eighteenth century, or the suffering inflicted by Soviet Communism in the twentieth century, are often held up as examples of the dangers of utopian thinking when it is put into practice.

There are various ways that 'utopophobia' (Estlund, 2008, pp. 263–75) can be challenged. The first is to defend, or even celebrate, the role of utopianism. The argument here, in short, is that utopian theory—whether about justice or peace or other values—can help us to think systematically and cogently about our own world, and how we might seek to change it. Only by working out what society, or world order, should look like in highly idealized terms can we (1) have a basis for assessing and criticizing our existing arrangements, or (2) work out the direction in which we should be heading. 'We can properly understand what we should do here and now only after we have understood where we are trying to go from here' (Simmons, 2007, p. 13).

One common way of thinking about this issue, indebted to the influential political philosopher John Rawls, is to distinguish between **ideal** and **non-ideal theory**.

The aim of ideal theory is to formulate principles for the governance of a society in which everybody complies with those principles, and that compliance is common knowledge. The aim of non-ideal theory, by contrast, is to articulate lower-level principles, precepts, and rules to guide decision-making in circumstances—our own—in which there is only partial compliance with the principles (Sangiovanni, 2009, p. 221).

Ideal theory is, in a sense, deliberately unrealistic. It makes assumptions about the way people act—for example, in Rawls's own account, that they will all comply with the rules governing their society—that are not plausible. Yet for many political philosophers, ideal theorizing provides a way of thinking rigorously about how we should structure political institutions if we take seriously the demands of, for example, justice or equality. It is designed to help us to think about how the world can be changed for the better. If we always resort to what seems practical or achievable in a particular context, little would ever change. It is, therefore, important to step back from day-to-day life, and to reflect on fundamental ideas about how individuals and communities should relate to each other. Ideal visions provide important resources for the imagination, opening up new horizons that can help to guide us as we navigate the complexities of the world. While Rawls recognizes the 'pressing and urgent matters' that arise in the non-ideal world, he argues that ideal theory provides 'the only basis for the systematic grasp of these more pressing problems' (Rawls, 1971, p. 8). We must start, in other words, with ideal theory. This argument has been very popular among political theorists influenced by Rawls. In Chapter 4, Andrew Gamble outlines some of the arguments for and against viewing political theory in this manner.

There are many examples of ideal theorizing. One that plays a significant role in this book emerges from the debates about **cosmopolitanism**, a topic discussed by Simon Caney in Chapter 8. Many cosmopolitans argue that the states, and other political and economic institutions that dominate our world, act in ways that are deeply unjust, for they fail to take account of the fundamental moral equality of human beings. Consequently, the cosmopolitans offer a wide range of suggestions for alternative ways in which we could organize our communal life. Some go as far as calling for the abolition of states and the creation of new forms of political community. Of course, they recognize that these radical demands are not likely to be met any time soon, but they insist that if we are to take seriously claims about equality and justice, then this is what must ultimately be done. From this 'ideal' starting point, they derive arguments that can be applied to the 'non-ideal' world in which we live. They argue, for example, that the rich have an obligation to redistribute far greater amounts of wealth to the poor than is currently the case and they have come up with a range of proposals for how to do so. These arguments are discussed by Kok-Chor Tan in Chapter 14.

A second answer to the charge of utopianism is to deny that the schemes identified by normative theorists are necessarily utopian in the pejorative sense. In other words, we could argue that while they might be very ambitious it is not impossible to imagine them being realized at some stage in the future. This argument can be strengthened by pointing to the differences between the past and the present. History provides an illuminating range of cases that show how ideas that once seemed impossible or outlandish have come to appear uncontroversial. Take the example of slavery. Two-hundred years ago many people in the West regarded slavery as part of the natural condition of humankind. Yet today the vast majority of people think that slavery is indefensible. Things can change, and change on a very large scale, and it is therefore important to recognize the power of idealism and imagination in history and politics. The lesson to draw from this is that just because something seems far-fetched today does not mean that it will always be so.

Another way of challenging the critique of utopianism is to propose alternatives that are feasible under current conditions. These alternatives would involve some changes to the existing order of things, but not a radical transformation of political life. This is the domain of the non-ideal, and it is where many political theorists focus their attention, arguing that while morality may actually demand very ambitious changes in the way we live (as identified in ideal theorizing), in order to have a realistic chance of improving things it is essential to offer more limited proposals. Thus, Thomas Pogge (2002, p. 205), a leading advocate of cosmopolitanism, argues for the importance of 'modesty' in prescribing political and economic institutions on a global scale. This type of work often draws heavily on relevant empirical scholarship in the social sciences, whether in sociology, economics, or politics, in order to work out the best way to proceed. This has been an especially significant phenomenon in recent debates over global wealth inequality, and scholars have turned their attention to identifying feasible policy options, for example innovative forms of global taxation (e.g. Pogge, 2002; Caney, 2006b; Brock, 2009).

Finally, we might return to the criticism of utopianism, but come at it from a different angle. It can be argued that certain forms of idealistic (or utopian) theorizing are actually very conservative (Geuss, 2008). They distract attention away from radical change. Carole Pateman and Charles Mills, for example, argue that the kind of 'ideal' theorizing propounded by Rawls and his followers has led political theorists, especially in the United States, to ignore or downplay issues of racial and gender injustice (Mills & Pateman, 2007). The problem is not abstraction itself. After all, some kind of abstraction is essential for any form of systematic social and political theorizing. It is rather that the kind of ideal theory which dominates much contemporary political philosophy is abstract in the wrong way—it abstracts '*away* from relations of structural domination, exploitation, coercion, and oppression' (Mills, 2005, p. 168). It presents a highly unrealistic picture of human beings and social institutions, and says little or nothing about the historic forces of oppression and their continuing pervasive impact. This means that ideal theory cannot adequately understand (or even see) the very things which it is supposed to address. The 'fact- and reality-avoidance' of ideal theory, Mills suggests, actually diverts attention away from the best ways to engage properly with urgent problems (Mills, 2005, p. 179). He concludes that political theorists should focus their attention on understanding the structures of power and domination, and how best to challenge them, in the non-ideal world in which we live.

When assessing a political theory, it is important to think about who would benefit from it if it was actually successful—if the world ended up being arranged according to its principles. Robert Cox, a leading critical IR theorist, puts the point concisely: 'Theories are always *for* some one and *for* some purpose' (Cox, 1981, p. 128). Cox is arguing that the vision of society or world order articulated in theories always serves particular interests, benefitting some groups at the expense of others. It is important, then, to identify who the winners and losers would be—the rich or poor within a society, the members of the global North (the wealthy industrialized countries) or the global South (the poorer countries), men or women, young or old. It may well be the case that the consequences were unforeseen by those who constructed the theory in the first place. In other words, a scholar might think that they are designing a theory to alleviate poverty, but if put into practice it would actually end up making the situation worse. A different example, which is explored further by Anthony Lang in Chapter 18, concerns **humanitarian intervention**. In recent years, many political theorists have argued that it is legitimate for states to intervene militarily in the domestic affairs of other states in order to protect the human rights of vulnerable populations. Yet critics argue that whatever the intentions behind these arguments, the consequences have been deeply problematic. Some argue that it has increased the amount of violence in the world while failing to stop human rights abuses. Others claim that even if the theory is good, it is impossible to put into practice—that politics is always too complicated for the mission to be accomplished properly. Another argument is that the popularity of humanitarian arguments allows aggressive states to cloak their selfish (non-humanitarian) ambitions in the language of justice, thus providing ideological support for imperial domination. I leave it to the reader to assess whether these arguments are compelling, but whatever conclusion you reach there is an important lesson here: while it is useful to know the aims of various types of theorizing, it is also important to try to work out the political consequences that would follow from the practical application of the theory.

3 The scope of the book

Every textbook is the product of choices made by the editor and the contributors about what to include and what to leave out, which issues to emphasize, and how best to discuss them. The design of *Ethics and World Politics* is motivated by the belief that it is valuable to introduce readers to a wide range of different, and often conflicting, ways of understanding the ethical issues that confront our world.

The book is designed to be used in various ways. It can serve as a general introduction to the rich assortment of methods and perspectives available for studying normative questions in world politics. As such, it can be employed as a general course text, with individual chapters introducing readers to important lines of argument about a diverse range of issues. However, it can also serve as a resource for focusing on particular topics. Clusters of chapters, when read in conjunction, act as detailed introductions to specific debates. For example, for those with interests in—or taking a course on—the ethics of political violence, Chapters 5, 9, 11, 15, 16, 17, 18, and 19 offer analyses of, among other things, the **just war** tradition, critical approaches to the ethics of war, humanitarian intervention, and terrorism. Likewise, for those seeking an introduction to the debates around **distributive justice** in a global context, Chapters 1, 6, 7, 8, 13, and 14 provide a state of the art survey of the arguments. For those with an interest in how feminist theorists interpret world politics, Chapters 9, 11, 16, and 19 provide a useful entry point. Various pathways can be traced through the book.

The chapters should not be read as definitive statements on a subject, or as covering each and every available topic or position. There is no completely neutral or objective position from which to write a chapter about ethical issues in world politics. Some of the authors explicitly defend particular lines of argument, while most of them provide criticisms of approaches that they find unpersuasive. The chapters are best read, then, as *invitations to further reflection, debate, and intellectual exploration*.

While this book surveys a wide selection of methods, perspectives, and issues, it does not claim to be exhaustive. In particular, it does not provide a systematic overview of three major areas: the historical development of moral and political thought about international relations; religious accounts of world politics; and approaches to political ethics developed outside of Europe and North America. This is not because these subjects are unimportant, but rather the opposite—they are too important to be given only superficial treatment. Existing textbooks often start with a perfunctory historical survey, or include a chapter or two dealing with religion. Yet this seems inadequate in light of the sheer complexity of these topics.

Before moving on to discuss the content of *Ethics and World Politics*, it is worth highlighting why these topics are of general importance and how exploring them further can complement, or challenge, the type of work discussed in this volume.

- *The history of (international) political thought.* The last 20 years has seen a blossoming interest in tracing the historical development of ideas about international politics, focusing in particular on questions of war, empire, and commerce.[7] These studies

---

[7] Historical studies include: Tuck (1998); Armitage (2000); Hont (2005); Bell (2007); Tully (1995). Introductory surveys include: Doyle (1997); Boucher (1998); Keene (2005). Extracts from important primary texts can be found in Brown et al. (2002).

often focus on thinkers who remain central to debates in contemporary normative theorizing, including Thomas Hobbes, John Locke, Immanuel Kant, Adam Smith, G. W. F. Hegel, Karl Marx, and John Stuart Mill. Aside from its historical value, scholarship of this kind can highlight how many issues—including globalization and humanitarian intervention, for example—have their intellectual roots deep in the history of political reflection. Sophisticated thinkers have been discussing them for a very long time. Historical analyses, then, can serve as a useful antidote to claims about the uniqueness of the world in which we live, offering historical perspective on complex moral and political issues. Moreover, exploring the arguments of past thinkers can provide intellectual resources—arguments, concepts, styles of thinking—that can (at least sometimes) be employed to think through contemporary issues. Although none of the chapters in this book are primarily historical in character, a number of them—notably Chapters 2, 4, 5, 8, 9, 11, and 16—do touch on significant historical themes.

- *Religious ethics.* The importance of religion in contemporary world politics hardly needs emphasizing. In recent years, and especially in the post-9/11 era, it has assumed new and pressing forms. Yet much contemporary political theory is secular—while it frequently discusses the role that religion should play in society, it rarely does so using theological forms of argument. Whether this is a strength or a weakness is for the reader to judge. This situation may well change in the next few years, in particular as citizens and scholars try and work out how secular and religious value systems can be accommodated to each other across linguistic and cultural boundaries (Connolly, 2000; Kymlicka & Sullivan, 2007; Taylor, 2007). Some theorists have responded to the heightened prominence of religion by embarking on studies in comparative political theory (which I discuss below) or by revisiting the importance of religious concepts and styles of thinking. For example, the question of the meaning and nature of 'evil' has generated a lively recent literature.[8] As with the history of political thought, religion is not completely absent from this volume—the Christian origins of the Just War tradition, for example, is a leading theme in Chapter 16. However, none of the chapters is specifically dedicated to religion, because any attempt to do justice to the vast range of competing perspectives available within and between religious world views would take up a large volume in itself.

- *Non-Western thought.* This book focuses primarily on those approaches that have played an important role in shaping scholarly and public political debates in the Western, and in particular, the English-speaking, world. This reflects the way in which the fields of political theory and IR have developed over the last few decades. Once again, it seems likely that both 'comparative political theory'—which encompasses the study of non-Western political theory, as well as assessments of how diverse political and religious traditions can interact with each other—and non-Western IR theory will play increasingly prominent roles in years to come.[9] Non-Western themes and approaches are not completely absent, however, and Chapter 12 is explicitly dedicated to exploring

---

[8] See, for example, Bernstein, 2002, 2005; Jeffrey, 2008a, b; Neiman, 2002.
[9] For non-western approaches to IR theory, see Tickner & Waever (2009); Acharya & Buzan (2009). See also Connell (2008).

the tricky issue of how we can compare and contrast political and ethical ideas across different cultural contexts, and the benefits (as well as the costs) of attempting to do so.

After having identified what the *Ethics and World Politics* does not address, or addresses only briefly, let us now turn to what it does include.

4 The structure of the book

The book is divided into three main parts.

● Part One: Methods and approaches

The chapters in Part One provide incisive introductions to different ways of thinking about the nature and role of ethics and political theory. Chapters 1–3 introduce some of the basic themes and arguments in analytic political theory, critical theory, and post-structuralism. As the authors note, these widely employed labels can be misleading, implying a commonality between the different authors covered by the labels, where there actually exists a diverse range of views. This cautionary note is important, but it is also important to understand how the terms are employed by scholars and, more significantly, the kinds of arguments that are developed by those who are associated with the different approaches. One of the main purposes of this book is to provide readers with some of the basic tools to make up their own minds about the strengths and weakness of different forms of theorizing. The chapters in Part One, then, are not only helpful for understanding the later chapters in the book, but also for approaching other reading assignments. The final chapter in this section—Chapter 4—addresses the complicated question of the role that 'empirical' politics (and descriptive theory) plays in debates over ethics and world politics. It focuses in particular on how the processes of globalization are changing the way in which scholars argue about the ethical dimensions of world politics.

● Part Two: Perspectives

The chapters in Part Two introduce a series of *general perspectives* on ethics and world politics. These can be seen as broad frameworks—or, to return to an earlier metaphor, as wide-angle lenses—for evaluating the landscape of world politics. The opening chapter explores political **realism**, an approach that focuses on the centrality of power in politics, and consequently stresses the limits of ethical action in a turbulent world. Peter Jones and Margaret Moore then outline two prominent types of argument which defend the moral value of bounded political communities. Jones focuses on arguments, including those of the '**English School**' and John Rawls, that give special moral status to the state (or other kinds of political institution) and which defend the value of an international society. Moore discusses theories that focus on the moral value of national and cultural identity. This is followed by Simon Caney's chapter on cosmopolitanism, which surveys a range of arguments that view humans as 'citizens of the world'. Kimberley Hutchings addresses the numerous ways in which feminist analysis can illuminate important topics in international ethics. Mathew Humphrey then outlines how environmental concerns reshape our understanding of the nature of political theorizing. Margaret Kohn introduces work on post-colonial theory, drawing on both literary scholarship about how representations of other cultures help to structure political action, and Marxist-inspired accounts of global economic inequality. Finally, Christopher Goto-Jones explores the potential of comparative political theory.

● Part Three: Issues

The chapters in Part Three focus on more narrowly conceived *issues*, each of which can be approached from a variety of different *general perspectives*, using diverse *methods and approaches*. Duncan Ivison provides a concise overview of debates about the character of human rights. Kok-Chor Tan analyses some of the most prominent ways in which scholars have addressed questions of global poverty and inequality. Anthony Carty then discusses different ways of understanding the nature and purpose of international law. Nicholas Rengger and Patricia Owens explore contrasting accounts of the ethics of war, with Rengger focusing on the Just War tradition and Owens sketching out some critical alternatives to it. This is followed by two other chapters on political violence. Anthony Lang examines the meaning and **legitimacy** of humanitarian intervention, while Virginia Held probes the political and ethical complexities of terrorism. This is followed by Arash Abizadeh's account of the ethics of immigration and citizenship, and, to round off the volume, James Bohman's discussion of diverse ways of understanding democracy in a global age. Each of the chapters in Part Three includes a brief case study, which draws together and helps to illuminate the general arguments that have been outlined. The *Online Resource* website includes further case studies for readers to browse, all of which offer different perspectives on the issues covered in the chapters.

PART ONE

Methods and approaches

<table>
<tr><td>1</td><td>Ethics and analytic political philosophy</td></tr>
</table>

Ethics and analytic political philosophy

Colin Bird

READER'S GUIDE

The most influential recent contributions to Anglophone political philosophy are often characterized as 'analytic'. This chapter outlines and assesses these contributions, with particular attention to the work of John Rawls and his critics. It dispels some misconceptions encouraged by the 'analytic' label in two ways: first, by considering the history of analytic philosophy more generally; and secondly, by identifying and evaluating the most serious objections that those forms of political philosophy conventionally classified as 'analytic' frequently invite.

1.1 Introduction

Many today would say that the modes of political thought currently dominant in the English-speaking world exemplify **'analytic political philosophy'**. However, this label is problematic, and trying to define it is like trying to define 'sentimental music' or 'vulgar literature'. The Blues, Elgar's Cello concerto, and the songs of Dolly Parton could all be described as 'sentimental', yet the expectation that they are all 'sentimental' in the same way for the same reasons is naive. 'Sentimentality' and 'vulgarity' have several different senses, and exist much more in the (usually disapproving) eye of the beholder than as independent properties of the literature or music in question. Something similar holds for 'analytic political philosophy'. When commentators today identify the work of a political philosopher as 'analytic' they are more often accusing her of something than dispassionately describing her approach. Furthermore, the very notion that there is a distinctively 'analytic' approach to political philosophy is a myth.

This is not to deny the existence of '**analytic philosophy**' itself. There is unquestionably such a tradition, one that enjoyed its heyday in the middle years of the twentieth century and that dominates the academic study of philosophy in the English-speaking world to this day (Soames, 2003; Glock, 2008). As we shall see, however, the link between the characteristic concerns of this tradition and those of recently influential *political* philosophers is circumstantial at best. To be sure, contemporary political philosophy, as it has developed within the English-speaking academy, shares certain common features, and these have attracted criticism, but neither those common features, nor the objections they invite, can be adequately understood as reflecting the 'analytic' character of contemporary Anglophone political philosophy. Instead, they reflect its characteristic commitment to the centrality of specifically *moral* or *ethical* categories in political argument. By steering newcomers away from some long-standing misconceptions about a distinctively 'analytic' approach to political philosophy, this chapter hopes to guide them to a clearer perception of the actual character, strengths, and weaknesses of the forms of political philosophy that dominate the contemporary scene.

1.2 Twentieth century analytic philosophy

However, to unravel all this, we need first to understand the nature of analytic philosophy itself. Two connected traits capture its enduring character. First, analytic philosophers have typically construed the basic philosophical task as the rather modest one of conceptual clarification. This intellectual modesty emerged as a reaction to what the early pioneers in the analytic movement (especially Bertrand Russell and G. E. Moore) saw as the excesses of the then dominant school of idealism in British philosophy. Idealism was a philosophical paradigm that originated in Europe under the influence of the early nineteenth century German philosopher G. W. F. Hegel. Idealism is committed to the metaphysical thesis that reality is ultimately constituted by certain ideas, not physical matter, and hence that the truth about the world can be disclosed only by philosophical contemplation, rather than through a scientific investigation of observable phenomena. For idealists, then, science offers, at best, a superficial picture of the world; only philosophical speculation of a very rarefied, metaphysical, kind can apprehend its deeper truth. Moore and Russell repudiated this grandiose image of the philosophical project. In their view, philosophy should emphasize loyalty to common sense, use language clearly, stress the limits of philosophical argument, cultivate suspicion of metaphysical speculation, and defer willingly to researchers working in other, non-philosophical fields (especially the natural sciences).

In part, the break with idealism was a matter of style—a distinctive feature of much writing in the analytic tradition is its emphasis on precise expression, perspicuous definition, transparent argumentation, and the careful drawing of pertinent distinctions. For the analytic philosopher, vagueness and obscurantism have always been cardinal sins;

this partly explains why analytic philosophers so often complain about the self-indulgent mystification they perceive in some continental European philosophical traditions (not coincidentally, because often heavily influenced by Hegelian models). However, it also reflected a substantive view about the proper scope and limits of philosophical inquiry. On an analytic account, philosophical reflection is inevitably entangled in questions about language and its capacities. This is not because analytic philosophers think that the only important philosophical questions are about language, but rather because they are impressed by the way that language permeates our efforts to understand the world, to form concepts, and to engage in reflection and argument about what to think. This led Moore, Russell, and their followers to the conclusion that linguistic analysis should replace metaphysical speculation as the central vehicle for philosophical inquiry.

Secondly, the analytic philosophical tradition is closely associated with the effort to vindicate the credentials of modern science as a privileged mode of inquiry, uniquely equipped to disclose the true nature of the world. This distinctive orientation has led analytic philosophers to take a special interest in:

- Questions of epistemology, that is, questions about the sense in which scientific conclusions count as 'knowledge' of some kind, how they represent, or 'refer' to the world they purport to describe, and whether and in what sense scientific methods can adjudicate on the truth or falsehood of possible beliefs, etc.
- The structure and operation of the formal systems (especially mathematics and logic) by which scientists analyse data and formulate theories about the phenomena they study.

By clarifying these matters, analytic philosophers thought of themselves as clearing the way for scientific inquiry to proceed with (as it were) a clear philosophical conscience.

The interest in formal systems like logic and mathematics connects naturally with the stress on precision and clarity in philosophical argumentation mentioned earlier. For a period, some analytic philosophers nursed the ambition of specifying an 'ideal language' that would, by means of a sophisticated logical schema, allow the precise and complete specification of every possible meaningful proposition. This ideal, which was taken seriously by Russell, Wittgenstein (in his early writings), A. J. Ayer, and the so-called 'logical positivists' was motivated by a desire to replace (what these thinkers saw as) the unrigorous vagueness of ordinary language with the more exact mode of expression demanded by rigorous scientific inquiry (see Ayer, 1946). However, this ambition quickly faded and, under the influence of J. L. Austin, Gilbert Ryle, and the later Wittgenstein, analytic philosophy in the 1950s and 60s increasingly looked to precise articulations of ordinary language use to provide the conceptual clarifications they sought (Ryle, 1949; Wittgenstein, 1958; Austin, 1961, 1962). In many ways, this turn away from Russell's more mathematically orientated approach to philosophy was a retrieval of Moore's original interest in 'common sense' as a source of philosophical insight (Moore, 1925).

Since the 1960s, Anglophone philosophers have felt increasingly confined by, and have gradually thrown off, the narrowly linguistic focus of mid-twentieth century analytic philosophy. Although conceptual precision and clarity in argument are still recognized as cardinal virtues by philosophers teaching in Britain, North America and Australasia, the intellectual modesty and aversion to metaphysical inquiry that marked earlier phases of the tradition are no longer universally regarded as virtues (Williamson, 2005). This recent repudiation of the 'linguistic turn' horrifies some loyalists (Hacker, 2006). It also puts the continued integrity of an analytic tradition in doubt. However, I want to leave these later developments aside and to keep the focus on the earlier, classical phase of the tradition. In particular, I want to explain why interest in political philosophy withered away as the analytic paradigm achieved dominance in the mid-twentieth century.

1.3 The 'death' of political philosophy

However one conceives it, political philosophy engages prescriptive and evaluative questions. The political writings of such philosophers as Plato, Aristotle, Cicero, Hobbes, Locke, Rousseau, Kant, Bentham, Mill, Hegel, and Marx defend a bewildering variety of political views. However, they all at least tacitly accept the idea that it is possible and desirable to evaluate, criticize, and recommend alternative political arrangements from some putatively rational standpoint. Viewed through the lens of classical analytic philosophy, however, this idea of rational political criticism came to seem problematic.

Analytic philosophers writing in the mid-twentieth century tended to follow the eighteenth-century Scottish philosopher David Hume's lead in sharply distinguishing the logical status of propositions purporting to describe the world empirically, or to assert what is the case ('the cat is on the mat', 'Jupiter orbits the sun', etc.) and utterances that express value judgements of various sorts ('Down with democracy!', 'The Holocaust was an abomination', 'free, uncoerced economic exchange is just', etc.). Not only did analytic philosophers maintain that factual and evaluative claims are formally *distinct*, they also often held, more controversially, that they are logically *insulated* from each other. They denied, that is, both that value judgements can be used to support claims about what is the case, and that value judgements can follow logically from true descriptions of the world. On this view, for example, explanations of how atomic bombs work, descriptions of their effects, measurements of their power, or historical accounts of their role in international conflict, express factual claims and so cannot entail that we should celebrate or regret their invention, or regard their use as morally permissible or impermissible. These value judgements about nuclear weapons stand apart from empirically verifiable propositions about their properties, operation, or deployment under particular political circumstances.

This doctrine interacted with the effort to validate the pretensions of modern empirical science in a way that left little room for political philosophy. As I have already hinted, that effort frequently insinuated that the methods of the empirical sciences, in tandem with analytic philosophy, jointly exhaust the scope of rational human inquiry. Taken to an extreme, this 'logical positivist' thesis implies that any field of study that involves neither the logical analysis of concepts (analytic philosophy), nor empirically informed investigations of factual questions (the sciences) must fall outside the scope of rational inquiry. It can only be a pseudo-science or (perhaps) a pseudo-philosophy. When combined with the view that value judgements are logically insulated from propositions stating facts, this implies that political philosophy (along with idealist metaphysics, theology, aesthetics, and ethics) must be a pseudo-discipline of this sort, at least insofar as it aims to defend value judgements about alternative forms of organized public life. On this view, the claims advanced by political theorists can become legitimate objects of intellectual inquiry only if we convert them into hypotheses that social and political scientists can then subject to empirical testing. As the Oxford analytic philosopher T. D. Weldon concluded in 1953, 'the questions of traditional political philosophy' are little more than 'confused formulations of purely empirical difficulties' (1953, p. 192).

Those who took this view did not think that the evaluation of political institutions should cease or that it is somehow pointless. They just denied that philosophical reflection has any special role in furthering it, except perhaps the very minimal one of clarifying the meaning and logical relations between the concepts used in political criticism. Nor did they suppose that empirical research is entirely irrelevant to political judgement. For example, suppose we accept the principle that a just society must try to eliminate poverty, and that we are tempted to pursue some policy intended to improve the condition of the poor. Economists, however, provide good empirical evidence for thinking that the policy will have predictably self-defeating results. In this case, the empirical findings of social science should lead us to drop the policy in question. Acknowledging this, however, does not establish that either philosophy or scientific inquiry can justify the application of the ethical principles that make such information relevant in the first place.

Nor, finally, did analytic philosophers of the period deny that value-judgement can be the object of philosophical inquiry when approached in the right way. For example, some developed quite sophisticated theories intended to explicate the meaning and nature of ethical utterance. However, they denied that clarifying the *meaning* of ethical discourse in this way either did, or could commit them to *endorsing* or *justifying* any particular ethical judgements. Rather, they regarded themselves as merely clarifying the logical status of ethical judgement in relation to other forms of utterance. The philosophical investigation of ethical utterance along these lines came to be called 'meta-ethics'. It's also worth noting that the meta-ethical theory most favoured by analytic philosophers during this period was one that (again following Hume) characterized moral utterance as a species of emotive expression (Stevenson, 1944). On this view, calling something a 'gross injustice' is not (despite appearances) to describe a state of affairs; rather, it is to express an aversive reaction akin to 'yuck!' Obviously, however, this idea that ethical judgement is fundamentally a matter of emotive expression rather than rational judgement was cold comfort to anyone inclined to take the idea of *reasoned* evaluation of political institutions seriously.

Fortunately, by the 1950s, analytic philosophers had moved away from strict 'logical positivism' and were taking the ordinary use of natural language increasingly seriously. The resulting thaw in philosophical attitudes prepared the ground for a revival of political philosophy. Most sophisticated 'ordinary language' philosophers (like the later Wittgenstein, J. L. Austin, Stephen Toulmin, and H. L. A. Hart) happily acknowledged that hard and fast distinctions between 'facts' and 'values' cannot be sustained in the face of our everyday practices of mutual criticism, of reason-giving, and of justification. This more supple understanding is well illustrated by Hart's *The Concept of Law* (1961), still recognized as a landmark in modern legal theory. Although Hart rejected the classical natural law thesis that we can only certify rules as legally valid by evaluating them from a moral standpoint, and did not attempt to prescribe an ideal legal system, he nevertheless emphasized the way in which judgements about legal validity supply agents with reasons to evaluate and criticize conduct. A legal order, he suggested, was a complex social practice in which social rules are taken to provide distinctive reasons for and against certain sorts of actions, judgements, and evaluations, much as players in a game recognize violations of the rules as reasons for criticism and complaint. Hart also insisted that the practical force of these and other normative rules is not a simple function of our 'feelings' of obligation, of our fear of punishment, or of other non-rational dispositions. It is also a matter of the way in which recognized norms and rules structure reasoned critical reflection about how to behave.

By the 1950s, then, there was a general recognition that the reasons we have for criticizing or recommending political institutions are themselves objects of philosophical interest in their own right. However, this did not lead immediately to the re-invigoration of serious political philosophy, although there were already some early pioneers (Benn & Peters, 1959; Hart, 1963, 1968; Barry, 1965; Berlin, 1969). As is often the case in intellectual history, political philosophy had to wait for a seminal contribution from a highly original thinker to show a way forward.

1.4 Rawls and the great revival

The breakthrough came in 1971, with the publication of John Rawls's *A Theory of Justice*. Rawls had spent some time at Oxford in the 1950s, where he was influenced and befriended by Hart, so it is not surprising that his reflections about **social justice** originated in part in reflection about the status of normative rules in public life. However, it's difficult to trace the origins of his 1971 masterpiece to anything in the climate of analytic philosophy in the immediately prior decades. The book is without obvious precedent.

Rawls tackled an extremely ambitious question: what would an ideally just political society look like? He offered a remarkably comprehensive answer, detailing two principles of justice. Roughly, these require, first, that all citizens should enjoy, as a matter of right, certain carefully defined basic political liberties and, secondly, that economic distribution should be configured so that those in the least advantaged social positions can expect to fare as well as possible, regardless of how well others do (the notorious '**difference principle**'). Rawls saw this as an exercise in '**ideal theory**', in that his argument made the simplifying assumption that agents will comply willingly with principles of justice as a matter of course. While this assumption of 'perfect compliance' conflicts with political reality as we know it, Rawls believed that we should resolve disagreements about this ideal case first, before thinking about how we might move toward that ideal from our present, far from ideal, circumstances.

Rawls mounted an intriguing defence of his ideal. He claimed that if you and your fellow citizens had met in advance to irrevocably choose principles of justice that will regulate the institutional framework within which you will later live, you and they would all have agreed on the principles Rawls recommends. Of course, you were not (and will not ever be) asked to participate in such a meeting, but Rawls reasoned as follows—if you were prepared to admit that such a meeting was set up fairly, on terms that all participants could see as reasonable, and you conceded that Rawls's principles would, indeed, be agreed to in that situation, then you should consider the principles justified.

Rawls called this conjectural initial situation the '**original position**', and conceived it, along with the hypothesized agreement on principles of justice to which it leads, as an adaptation of the classical theory of the **social contract** found in the writings of Locke, Rousseau, and Kant. His amendments to this old theory were, however, very substantial; his most important innovation was the idea that the individuals in the original position deliberate behind a '**veil of ignorance**' that deprives them of specific information about themselves and the sort of society they are about to enter. Although individuals in the original position know certain general facts about human psychology and the forms of political association that can exist, they are unaware of their personal characteristics (e.g. their membership in particular political societies, their tastes, their psychological propensities, their religious sensibilities, their sex or sexual orientation, etc.). Rawls reasoned that this restriction renders the original position fair because it guarantees a desirable sort of impartiality. For example, it prevents agents who know that they will be in a socially favoured position (e.g. members of an aristocratic elite, people with talents that happen to be highly valued in their society, adherents of a majority religion) from holding out for principles that would allow them to exploit these advantages for narrow personal or class gain.

More often than not, those who today target 'analytic political philosophy' have Rawls and his followers in their cross-hairs. Yet, as should by now be clear, Rawls's book was as much a break with prior analytic philosophy as a continuation of it. No-one in the analytic tradition had confronted a question about the ethical requirements of political association so directly or rigorously as did Rawls in *A Theory of Justice*. The book's grand and synoptic architecture is entirely out of character with the more piecemeal approaches that analytic philosophers preferred. Its leading ideas either reflect innovations introduced in a wholly original fashion by Rawls himself or leapfrog the analytic tradition entirely and engage much older lines of thought, especially classical **utilitarianism**, Kant's ethics and early modern social contract theory. The only uncontroversial point of continuity between Rawls and his immediate analytic predecessors is the lucidity of expression that one finds in the text of *A Theory of Justice*. However, while this is certainly characteristic of the analytic tradition, it's not exclusively so. Bentham, Hume, and Hobbes were no less insistent on clarity in philosophical argument, but it would be anachronistic to view them as analytic philosophers just for that reason.

1.5 Foundationalism

Rawls started from the assumption that human agents possess what he called a 'sense of justice', a set of moral dispositions that include a desire to act rightly, to co-operate on reasonable terms with others, and to resent conduct that offends their understandings of how important social goods, responsibilities, and entitlements should be allocated. He simply took for granted that his readers would recognize this 'sense of justice' as a settled feature of their own moral psychology. He took little interest in the question of the *basis* of this 'sense of justice', whether as an empirical question about how it arose and then developed in modern civilized societies, or as a philosophical question about the rationality of endorsing the particular ethical point of view it represents.

This last point is often overlooked. The failure to appreciate it lends false credence to the common charge that Rawls's theory, and therefore the (supposedly) 'analytic' political philosophy it inspired, displays a problematically 'foundationalist' orientation (e.g. Connolly, 1995, p. 73; Ankersmit, 2002, pp. 11, 169, 173). 'Foundationalism' is generally ill-defined, but here it refers to the effort to supply a rational basis for the traditional ethical expectations (those associated with norms of justice, and with the requirements of moral rightness or of virtuous rather vicious conduct, etc.). Imagine a sceptic who questions these expectations, perhaps acknowledging only reasons of self-interest, and who asks why she should care about them nonetheless. **Foundationalism** about ethics involves taking seriously, and trying to answer, this sort of sceptical challenge. It seeks to establish that everyone has reasons to recognize the authority of familiar ethical duties and expectations, even when compliance runs counter to one's interests. Today it has become fashionable, especially among those so-called 'postmodernists' or 'post-structuralists' hostile to the ideas of the **Enlightenment,** to view such demands for a rational foundation for ethics as unsatisfiable and, hence, misconceived. Yet, although this anti-foundationalist charge is often made against 'analytic' political philosophy in general and Rawls's theory in particular, there is little reason to think that it applies to either.

It is true that classical analytic philosophy was often 'foundationalist' about scientific knowledge in that it continued the 'modern' enlightenment project of providing a warrant for the epistemic claims of science. However, trying to ground science is one thing and trying to rationally ground ethics is another. None of the analytic philosophers of the mid-twentieth century was committed to the idea that ethics or morality are susceptible of a rational grounding in a foundationalist sense. Those who agreed with Hume that ethical utterance was a matter of emotive expression, not reasoned argument, certainly did not think so, but nor did more subtle later thinkers like Austin, Hart, and the later Wittgenstein. To be sure, they accepted that our ethical reflection involves a certain sensitivity to reasons. However, in acknowledging that ethical discourse is in this way a matter of canvassing reasons for and against actions and value judgements, they were not suggesting that ethics and morality are, or must be, somehow *grounded externally* on some set of non-moral considerations, such as those of rational self-interest. They were saying merely that ethical discourse is partly *constituted internally* by practices of reason-giving and so amounts to more than just an exchange of emotional outbursts. To illustrate, consider soccer players who make certain appeals to the referee ('Foul!', 'Offside!', 'Handball!') during a game. Such complaints are more than just emotive ejaculations, for when David Beckham commits a foul, he gives opposing players a valid *reason* for appealing to the referee. All participants presuppose that the referee has reasons to impose penalties where such appeals have merit. However, no-one thinks that these reasons for complaint and redress are valid only insofar as we convince sceptics on the sidelines to abandon their conviction that soccer is a worthless activity. Such external misgivings are normally irrelevant to the question of whether (say) Beckham should be sent off.

For more on post-structuralism, see Chapter 3.

What of Rawls? Does his theory go further than this, and seek an external foundation for the activity of upholding and enforcing publicly recognized rules of justice? Does it try to answer a sceptic on the sidelines who asks, 'what is justice to me?' Those who depict Rawls's theory as 'foundationalist' in this way often point to the original position argument and to the role that self-interest plays in it. They see Rawls's argument as attempting to derive the value of justice itself from considerations of rational self-interest.

However, here care is needed. It's true that self-interest plays a crucial role in Rawls's original position. The individuals at Rawls's hypothetical meeting are not asked to select principles by directly considering whether they correspond to their philosophical convictions about justice. Their preferences over alternative principles depend on their appreciation of the way that different principles, once enacted, would distribute a set of basic goods in which they all take a rational interest. Rawls called these goods the 'social primary goods', and they include: liberties, opportunities, income and wealth, and the 'social bases of self-respect'. Rawls took the individuals in the original position to be motivated to secure for themselves as large a share of these social primary goods as possible and he argued that they would select his principles of justice on this basis.

Rawls's case for his controversial 'difference principle', according to which inequalities in the distribution of income and wealth are acceptable only if they work to the greatest benefit of the least advantaged, illustrates the logic of this approach. Behind the veil of ignorance, individuals in the original position will not know whether they are in positions of economic advantage or disadvantage. This uncertainty will lead them to worry that, once the veil is lifted, they will find themselves in ill-favoured positions, lacking the economic resources needed to sustain their sense of self-worth (Rawls regarded 'the social bases of self-respect' as the most important of his social primary goods). They will, therefore, reject any scheme of principles that would permit better-advantaged others to ignore, perpetuate, or exploit the least-advantaged, fearing that they may turn out to be among the victims.

According to Rawls, these considerations rule out any principles (like those recommended by classical utilitarianism) that would require society to maximize overall welfare. Individuals in the original position will understand that this goal might sometimes require the impoverishment and exploitation of the few for the sake of the many, and will worry that this might turn out to be their fate. Repelled by that prospect, they will instead opt for principles that provide maximum protection to those most vulnerable, like Rawls's difference principle. By requiring that the share of income and wealth enjoyed by members of the least advantaged social group be as large as feasible, that principle provides everyone with a reasonable assurance of a life free of indignity and exploitation.

Do arguments along these lines indulge 'foundationalism' about ethics? Do they purport to identify a non-moral reason to take justice seriously?

There have been philosophers in recent years who have mobilized contractualist ideas to attempt to ground ethics and justice (e.g. Gauthier, 1986), but Rawls was not one of them. As I have said, Rawls simply presupposed the 'sense of justice'. He did not set out to address someone who lacks it or who questions whether it is worth having. Rather, his theory addresses people whose commitment to justice is unwavering, but who are, nevertheless, uncertain about what it specifically implies about social and distributive arrangements. As it stands, our concept of justice comprises various bare-bones commitments to impartiality, fairness, and the general idea of reasonable terms of social co-operation. However, these requirements might be elaborated in sharply conflicting ways. That is why there is so much conscientious disagreement about justice between people from different cultures, religious traditions, and social backgrounds. These disagreements are not over whether we should care about justice *at all*; they are about how best to articulate our commitment to it.

Rawls provided a framework through which we can think through our intuitions about justice in a systematic way and (he hoped) eventually construct a detailed account that meshes with our settled intuitions about justice as far as possible. The resulting theory is, as Rawls acknowledged, an artificial construct, but he maintained that insofar as it successfully reconciles the relevant intuitions into one integrated schema, we have good reasons to agree that it properly expresses our 'sense of justice'. Such a reconciliation would display the property of (what Rawls called) 'reflective equilibrium' in that it would, at all relevant points, fit with our intuitive convictions about justice. At the same time it provides fine-grained recommendations about what just societies must do. The aim here is not to get us to care about justice in the first place, but to flesh out the implications of a concept Rawls thinks we already accept.

Why, then, is self-interest involved in the original position argument? *Not* because Rawls sought to explain the underlying rationality of a commitment to justice itself, but rather because he believed it effectively modelled a key component of our basic 'sense of justice'. According to Rawls, that is, principles of social justice are concerned fundamentally with settling the terms on which individuals' competing interests can be fairly reconciled within an overall scheme of social co-operation. How far should self-interested complaints be recognized and upheld in a just society? Rawls thought that they should be recognized insofar as they reflect citizens' interest in the social primary goods and no further. So, when Rawls depicts individuals in the original position as motivated to secure for themselves as high a share of these goods as they can, he is trying to set a limit on self-interested claims in discourse about just social co-operation. The implication of Rawls's argument is that it's not unjust for the least advantaged groups to demand (say) that society provide them with as large a share of income and wealth as it can afford, even though that demand is self-interested. Conversely, it establishes that economically privileged individuals who resist any redistribution of their income required by the difference principle unjustly put their own interests ahead of the requirements of justice. *This* sort of self-interest Rawls's theory marks as unjust.

Rawls thus partly identifies social justice with the effort to balance, as exactly and as plausibly as possible, legitimate self-concern and proper respect for the just claims of others. Of course, Rawls's conclusions about how to strike a just balance are controversial, but if they are wrong, it is not due to the 'analytic' character of Rawls's argument, nor to a misguided 'foundationalist' effort to ground justice on self-interest.

1.6 Political philosophy after Rawls

We can divide the genres of Anglophone political philosophy that developed after Rawls into three rough categories, although, like any such summary, this classification is far from perfect. A first group of theorists accepts that Rawls was asking the right sort of questions, but argues over whether his conclusions about justice, and his distinctive way of defending them, are satisfactory. Discussion within this first group has taken off from six general criticisms of Rawls's theory:

Rawls underestimates liberty

Rawls claimed to defend the inviolability of the individual and argued that this gives the preservation of individuals' liberties a special priority. They are not to be traded off for the sake of economic benefits, for example. At the same time, Rawls denied that individuals' liberties include an immunity to any redistributive taxation needed to satisfy the Difference Principle. Rawls's position depends on a sharp distinction between principles that allocate and define the liberties to which all individuals are entitled, and those that determine economic shares. However, **libertarians**, following Robert Nozick, deny that this distinction can be drawn clearly without compromising a commitment to liberty. For Nozick, liberty is meaningful only if it includes the right to engage in gainful economic activity and, concomitantly, a right to keep the profits one reaps from it. From this libertarian standpoint, coerced redistribution of earned income in the form of taxation is fundamentally unjust, because unless it's necessary to secure liberty itself (rather than to promote some valuable goal like 'maximizing overall welfare' or Rawls's 'ensuring that the least advantaged do as well as possible'), it violates agents' fundamental right to natural liberty. Rawls's insensitivity to this sort of injustice undermines his own avowed effort to give individual liberty inviolable priority, or so libertarian critics maintain (Nozick, 1974; Lomasky, 1986). Whether they are right about this remains a hotly disputed issue (Freeman, 2001).

Rawls and equality

Some critics complain that Rawls's difference principle objectionably ignores differences in the degree to which individuals take responsibility for their own prospects. For example, under Rawls's proposal, members of the least advantaged group receive the same whether they are lazy or industrious. Surely, the critics say, an adequately egalitarian distributive standard should take this into account. Furthermore, Rawls's index of social primary goods ignores natural differences in needs; the disabled, for example, may need more resources than able-bodied people to enjoy comparable levels of well-being or opportunity (Nussbaum, 2006). Arguments along these lines were pioneered especially by Ronald Dworkin (2000), but have been followed up by many others (Sen, 1981; Arneson, 1999; Cohen, 1989, 2001, 2008; Temkin, 2002; Anderson, 1999). Such arguments are resisted by those who doubt that equality is required by justice. They claim that what matters is '**sufficiency**' (everyone receiving enough for a decent life; Frankfurt, 1988), or (adapting one of Rawls's ideas) giving 'priority' to those least advantaged (Parfit, 1997; Arneson, 1999). Neither 'sufficiency' nor 'priority' require any commitment to the *equalization* of any goods, and so the status of distributive equality as a requirement of justice (both within and between nations) continues to be a live issue in contemporary debate.

For further discussion of equality see chapter 14.

Rawls underestimates community

Partly because it tracks a certain strand of liberalism so closely, Rawls's theory has acquired a reputation as problematically 'individualistic'. The veil of ignorance requires us to imagine ourselves with our particular characteristics stripped away; although individuals in the original position know *that* they have particular social ties and affiliations, they do not know what they are and must choose principles of justice without reference to them. Many have doubted that this feat of detachment is psychologically possible. Even if it is, critics have questioned whether thinking about social justice in this 'individualist' and a-contextual fashion is desirable. These so-called 'communitarians' argue that discourse about justice and other **social norms** makes sense only with the particular communities, histories, and traditions that constitute agents' identity fully in view.

 For more on communitarianism, see Chapter 7.

In the mid-1980s a wave of communitarian criticism swept over the Rawlsian breakwater and, for a while, threatened to deluge its precincts (Sandel, 1982; MacIntyre, 1981; Walzer, 1983, 1994; Taylor, 1985, 1995; Bell, 1993). In retrospect, however, many of these criticisms have been shown to be misdirected (Gutmann, 1985; Kymlicka, 1991). As early as 1975, Rawls had stressed that 'what sorts of persons we are is shaped by how we think of ourselves and this is, in turn, influenced by the social forms we live under' (Rawls, 1975, p. 300). His later writings emphasized ever more explicitly that his theory was never intended as a completely universal account of justice, designed to apply to all communities equally, but as an elaboration of a conception peculiar to late modern Western liberal societies. Since Rawls conceded all of this, it became unclear what, exactly, the communitarian critics were actually complaining about (apart from registering dissatisfaction with the rather competitive, alienating circumstances of modern capitalist life, something for which Rawls and the philosophers can hardly be blamed). Still, a lasting outcome of the 'liberal-communitarian' exchange has been a general acknowledgment that questions about the proper public recognition of identity groups (whether defined by religion, culture, ethnicity, nationality or language) raise important issues of social justice in their own right (Gutmann, 1994; Kymlicka, 1995, 2002).

Rawls botches gender

On feminism and world politics, see Chapter 9.

Should the internal organization of the family fall within the remit of a theory of justice? Feminists, who have long recognized the family as a site of gender oppression, insist that it must be. Liberals, however, have often cordoned the family off in a protected **private sphere** beyond the reach of public regulation and have thereby seemed to exclude it from the purview of public justice. Rawls vacillated on this issue, as feminist critics have been quick to point out (Pateman, 1988; Okin, 1989; Young, 1990a). He said that his theory applied to the '**basic structure** of society', which he characterized in terms of 'the way in which the major social institutions distribute fundamental rights and duties to determine the distribution of advantages from social co-operation'. It's not clear whether the 'family' is, or should be, counted among these 'major social institutions', and whether, if so, Rawls' approach can adequately handle the distinctive questions about gender justice that arise there.

Anti-perfectionism?

Rawls's contractualism requires that principles of justice be acceptable to every reasonable person subjected to them. However, he also thought that reasonable people inevitably differ in their conceptions of a good life (e.g. their religious proclivities, their moral sensibilities, their ideological commitments, political sympathies, etc.). This led him to insist that the framework of public institutions that would ideally realize his principles, as well as the argument he gave for them, must avoid taking a stance on any particular **conception of the good** life. Were they to do so, he reasoned, they would immediately alienate those who quite reasonably reject the conceptions involved. For example, a theory incompatible with biblical ideals of love could not expect to command the willing assent of Christians, so a theory of justice must remain silent on such matters as far as it can. In taking this position, however, Rawls abandoned an old tradition of 'perfectionist' political thought, which stretches right back to Plato and the ancient Greeks. Perfectionists hold that claims about the just or good society must ultimately rest on some true conception of human flourishing or the good life. Rawls claimed, however, that even if one or more perfectionist ideal(s) are sound, they remain too controversial for the purposes of political justice. This implies that a state that publicly endorses a controversial perfectionist view unjustly trespasses beyond its legitimate sphere of action. While some perfectionist views may be better than others, it's not the state's business to declare an allegiance on such issues. It must cultivate neutrality with respect to controversial conceptions of the good.

Critics find this anti-perfectionist position unnecessarily restrictive (MacIntyre, 1981; Raz, 1986; Sher, 1997; Wall, 1998; Chan, 2000). Some deny that any systematic vision of social justice can coherently avoid some appeal, if only tacit, to perfectionist ideals. Others ask: why, if individuals' lives will only be enhanced by policies intended to realize perfectionist goods, we should accept a principled prohibition on pursuing them? A vigorous debate over the possibility and desirability of Rawlsian state neutrality has ensued (see, e.g. Audi & Wolterstorff, 1997).

Rawls narrowly nationalist

Rawls restricted the application of his theory to a political community like a modern nation state, and thus denied that his principles should be applied to assess justice at a global, international, level. However, many of his readers have found this restriction philosophically arbitrary and anyway superseded by the reality of an ever more integrated international order. Against Rawls's **statist** instincts, they urge that justice become a cosmopolitan concern. At the end of his career, Rawls extended his theory to deal with global affairs, but he continued to resist a full-blown cosmopolitanism about justice. The resulting debates are dealt with at much greater length in several of the chapters in this volume.

 On Rawls's theory of international justice, see Chapter 6.

Non-ideal casuistry

A second group is agnostic about the value of Rawls's quest to specify an ideally just society, but sees the success of his work as an opportunity to pursue parallel questions about political ethics with the same sort of clarity that his writings exemplified. Writers in this group have pursued a very wide range of questions without sharing a single theoretical paradigm. Indeed, perhaps the only thing that unites them at all is a disinterest in (though not necessarily hostility to) Rawls's commitment to 'ideal theory'. Rather than specify ideals to aim for, these writers mobilize ethical arguments to address political topics as they arise in the non-ideal world in which we actually live.

Considerations of space prevent a comprehensive review of all the work that falls into this genre; the relevant literature is vast. However, any such survey would have to cite the debates that have developed around the following topics:

On the ethics of war, see Chapters 16–19.

- The ethics of war, inspired especially by Michael Walzer's *Just and Unjust Wars* (Walzer, 1977).

- The question of *political obligation,* i.e. that of whether, apart from a general moral obligation to support basically just and decent institutions, citizens have a special duty to submit to the authority of their states (Wolff, 1970; Simmons, 1979; Green, 1990; Klosko, 1992, 2005).

- Debates over the proper purposes of criminal punishment, whether deterrent (intended to discourage future crime), retributive (intended to give offenders what they deserve), or rehabilitative (intended to reform offenders) (Simmons, Cohen, Cohen, & Beitz, 1995).

See especially Chapters 6–8, and 14.

- The question of the extent of our responsibilities as members of affluent societies to alleviate poverty overseas, a topic raised pointedly by Peter Singer's seminal article, 'Famine, Affluence and Morality' (Singer 1972), and discussed in a number of chapters in this volume.

On the ethics of immigration, see Chapter 20.

- The ethics of immigration, and more particularly the question of whether we should adopt a policy of 'open borders' (Carens, 1987).

On the problem of 'dirty hands', see Chapter 5.

- The problem of '**dirty hands**', which asks whether government officials enjoy a partial immunity from moral restrictions that otherwise apply to agents in ordinary circumstances (Walzer, 1973).

- Questions about the legitimacy of programmes (like 'affirmative action' in the United States) intended to assist groups victimized by past discrimination (Nagel et al., 1985).

Criticisms

A third group rejects Rawls's starting point outright, and disparages the quest for an ideal account of social justice as fundamentally misconceived. Members of this third group are most likely to complain about 'analytic political philosophy'—they direct their objections mainly to political philosophers whose work falls in the first two categories. The philosophers who write in this vein form a diverse group and draw their inspiration from several important figures from European philosophical traditions, including especially Marx, Nietzsche, Max Weber, Martin Heidegger, Hannah Arendt, Carl Schmitt, the Frankfurt School, Michel Foucault, and Jacques Derrida. Whatever their other differences, however, they tend to agree that the genres of political philosophy we have surveyed to this point problematically displace *politics* by fixating on *ethics* and *morality* (Barber, 1989; Connolly, 1995; Honig, 1996; Mouffe, 1999; Wolin, 2004; Geuss, 2008).

On Derrida, Foucault, and the Frankfurt School, see Chapters 2 and 3.

This objection rests on the accurate observation that philosophers in the first two groups particularly emphasize ethical and moral categories in their arguments. They assume, that is, that reflection about what *moral* principles apply, which *duties* control our conduct, or which political *virtues* (e.g. justice) are at stake should be fundamental to political philosophy. This characterization holds true, moreover, whether they are discussing ideal theories of justice (first group), or more local 'non-ideal' questions about (say) what we owe the global poor in the here and now (second group).

According to their critics, however, this 'moralization' of politics is deeply problematic in either case. Attaching so much weight to moral and ethical concepts, they claim, prevents these writers from reckoning honestly with the real circumstances of political interaction. The objection is not so much that ethical discourse is too cerebral or idealistic, for those who lodge it often grant that moral and ethical commitment is an important feature of real-world political engagement. Rather, the critics see these writers' heavy investment in moral and ethical concepts as based on a delusion, that by settling intellectual questions about the relative weight of different moral requirements in different settings, the deep sources of political conflict can be dissolved philosophically. According to the critics, that political philosophers in these groups indulge this delusion is shown by their interest in two things: first, their emphasis on achieving reasoned consensus about the implications of moral concepts, whether in ideal or non-ideal cases; and second, their interest in reconciling our ethical intuitions with each other as far as possible ('reflective equilibrium') by means of constructive thought-experiments (like Rawls's Original Position).

The critics contend that such aspirations underestimate the recalcitrance of political conflict and disagreement. To them, the implausibility of the idea that politics can be reduced to intellectually resolvable disputes about the implications of shared moral intuitions is shown by the conspicuous failure of philosophers in the first two groups to actually achieve a reasoned consensus about the implications of justice, or about any of the other topics they have addressed. The critics diagnose this ongoing philosophical dissensus as itself an unrecognized symptom of irreconcilable underlying conflicts over power, interests, and values, conflicts that they, in turn, regard as the real substance of politics. Rather than continuing to pursue the vain fantasy of rational consensus about political ethics, then, we do better to reflect in a critical, historically aware, way on the fractured and contested field of political values, or so the critics urge. Here, the aim will not be to fabricate ethical consensus where there is none, but to properly map the terrain of dissensus, and in this way bring to light the latent political conflicts that hide beneath moral discourse.

Viewed from this angle, apparent conflicts among 'our' ethical intuitions (about justice, punishment, political obligation, etc.) need not mask an underlying coherence that philosophers are in a position to disclose by means of theories that aim for 'reflective equilibrium'. The idea that our moral concepts and intuitions are axioms belonging to some crystalline formal system certainly lacks plausibility. They have their own (often messy) history, one that often bears the imprint of political struggles to establish the concrete institutions and practices against whose background the concepts make sense. As Raymond Geuss has asked, why 'think that an appropriate point of departure for understanding the political world is *our* intuitions of what is "just", *without* reflecting on where those intuitions came from, how they are maintained, and what interests they might serve …[?]' (Geuss, 2008, p. 90). On such grounds, those in the third group claim that theorizing about such moral concepts as justice is rarely a suitable basis for serious social criticism.

Assessment

Arguments along these lines raise important doubts about political philosophy pursued in the first two modes, but readers should keep two points in mind as they assess them.

First, it's one thing to deny that the field of 'our' normative intuitions is in principle coherent and seamless, but another to claim that distinctively ethical or moral claims can never motivate serious social and political criticism. Political philosophers writing in the first two genres can acknowledge the former claim without being driven to accept the latter. For arguments based on moral intuitions to give rise to valid social criticism it is sufficient that the operative intuitions are accepted by the targets of social criticism. For example, suppose that a state claims to treat citizens justly. Suppose further that it is officially committed to a conception of justice that we can show implies that it ought to uphold some claim (racial equality, say). Yet in practice the institution fails to guarantee racial equality, while continuing to boast of its justness. This at least convicts the institution of hypocrisy. For such charges of hypocrisy to be accepted it's not necessary that the pertinent 'intuitions' about justice also be shown to be part of some seamless conceptual whole displaying 'reflective equilibrium'.

Secondly, critics in the third group sometimes caricature their interlocutors' commitment to ethical consensus in politics. Bonnie Honig, for example, characterizes this commitment as a fanciful 'yearning' for political 'closure'. She writes that Rawls and others in my first two groups 'converge in their assumption that success [in philosophical argument about politics] lies in the elimination ... of dissonance, resistance, conflict, or struggle ... They assume that the task of political theory is to resolve institutional questions, to get politics right, over, and done with' (Honig, 1996, p. 2). On this depiction, Rawls and others suppose that once one gets the ethical arguments right, the need for political conflict simply vanishes. The search for ethical consensus is here equated with the effort to somehow supersede all political conflict by philosophical means alone.

However, no reputable political philosopher writing in any genre has (to my knowledge) ever described their aims in these terms. This is not, for example, what Rawls meant when he set out to specify the requirements of justice by means of an 'ideal theory'. He would never have said that his ideal of a just society enforces itself to the extent that the arguments he provided for them are philosophically sound. He was quite aware that the effort to realize and then maintain his ideal, from our present non-ideal position, must overcome resistance, and may also require compromises with competing ethical expectations. For example, Rawls did not deny that under some non-ideal circumstances (e.g. a national emergency or natural disaster), the quest for justice must be postponed in order to meet more immediately pressing needs (security, saving lives). Nevertheless, he would have insisted that by elaborating an ideal of the just society, we clarify something that people think worth fighting for, something that structures their own understanding of the point of political struggle: social justice. In this view, philosophical argument is not a substitute for or a way of evading political conflict. Rather, it sharpens our understanding of what such conflict is and should be about. Of course, Rawls's particular account of justice may be unsatisfactory and he may have exaggerated the political significance of justice relative to other pertinent requirements of a good society. However, that does not show that any effort to reach informed agreement about such requirements and their relationships automatically indulges the misguided delusion that political conflict can somehow be terminated by means of philosophical argument.

1.7 Conclusion

When commentators today speak of 'analytic political philosophy' they mainly have in mind the first two genres reviewed here. Those who use the term in a pejorative way, in order to lodge some sort of criticism, usually intend the sort of reproaches made by philosophers in my third category. However, as I hope is now clear, the 'analytic' label does not helpfully specify either the categories or the reproaches. As I have emphasized, neither of the first two genres has much in common with classical analytic philosophy from the middle of last century. Critics sometimes identify 'analytic political philosophy' with a commitment to 'foundationalism' about ethics, but we have seen that this characterization is also implausible. Nor can we simply say that their 'analytic' quality consists in the fact that they are all in some sense 'Rawlsians'. This plainly will not work for political philosophy in the second genre, which often proceeds without reference to Rawlsian categories. However, even those in the first group, who take Rawls's questions seriously, often reject both his conclusions and his contractualist arguments for them, as we have seen.

To be sure, philosophers in both camps have aimed for clarity and conceptual precision in argument, but this is obviously a superficial stylistic point on which nothing important hinges. Anyway, many of those in the third group, who wish to reject the approaches taken by the first two, would also regard these as virtues. Their chief objection is not that political philosophy is insufficiently obscure, but that viewing politics through an ethical lens bleaches out the harsher realities of political conflict and disagreement. This remains the major challenge to the modes of Anglophone political philosophy that dominate the contemporary scene, but it's a mistake to see it as an issue about their supposedly 'analytic' character.

▓ QUESTIONS

1. Why was classical analytic philosophy so inhospitable to political philosophy as a serious intellectual enterprise?

2. How did Rawls attempt to justify his principles of justice?

3. Why (according to Rawls) would the 'difference principle' be selected in the 'Original Position'?

4. What are the advantages and disadvantages of Rawls's idea of a 'veil of ignorance'?

5. Should political theorists be concerned with the internal politics of the family, or should they avoid sticking their noses into this and other areas of 'personal life'?

6. Can we inquire into the justice of particular practices like affirmative action, restrictive immigration policies, redistributive taxation, etc., without first constructing a systematic ideal of a just society?

7. In what ways (if any) is Rawls's difference principle an 'egalitarian' requirement?

8. Is a naivety about the realities of political disagreement a necessary consequence of emphasizing the ethical dimensions of politics?

9. Can (or should) political philosophers avoid appealing to ethical intuitions in critical argument about the merits and demerits of political arrangements?

10. Should we agree with Rawls that 'justice is the first virtue of social institutions, as truth is of systems of thought'?

■ FURTHER READING

Alexander, L. & Beitz, C. (eds) (1985) *International Ethics: A Philosophy and Public Affairs Reader.* Princeton: Princeton University Press. Gives a good flavour of the second genre of political philosophy discussed above. The other titles in the *Philosophy and Public Affairs Readers* series are also recommended.

Bird, C. (2006) *An Introduction to Political Philosophy.* Cambridge: Cambridge University Press. Offers expanded discussions of most of the topics covered here.

Geuss, R. (2009) *Philosophy and Real Politics.* Princeton: Princeton University Press. The most sophisticated recent attack on the Rawlsian paradigm.

Honig, B. (1996) *Political Theory and the Displacement of Politics.* Ithaca: Cornell University Press. An influential, if overdrawn, statement of the view that political philosophers who focus on morality and ethics are fated to ignore the specifically *political* dimension of social co-operation.

Kymlicka, W. (2002) *An Introduction to Contemporary Political Philosophy.* Oxford: Oxford University Press. Provides highly detailed and sophisticated coverage of the debates constituting what I have categorized here as the first genre of post-Rawlsian political philosophy.

Rawls, J. (1999) *A Theory of Justice*, revised edn. Cambridge: Harvard University Press. Still the work that defines the field.

■ WEB LINKS

http://plato.stanford.edu An excellent online encyclopaedia of philosophy, with entries on a wide range of thinkers and topics.

http://publicreason.net A site dedicated to issues in contemporary political philosophy. It contains discussion of thinkers and ideas, and includes listings for journals and upcoming conferences.

http://leiterlegalphilosophy.typepad.com/ This is a blog dedicated to discussion of topics in legal philosophy, run by a leading scholar in the field.

http://crookedtimber.org/books/ Crooked Timber is a popular multi-author blog, with regular discussions of philosophy, politics, sociology, economics, and literature.

http://philosophybites.com/ Links and podcasts on a wide range of philosophical topics, including Raymond Geuss discussing 'philosophy and real politics' and Joshua Cohen on the ideas of John Rawls.

Visit the Online Resource Centre that accompanies this book to access more learning resources: www.oxfordtextbooks.co.uk/orc/bell_ethics/

2 Ethics and critical theory

Max Pensky

READER'S GUIDE

This chapter examines the development of 'Critical Theory', a position associated chiefly with a group of predominantly German theorists, mostly working at the Institute for Social Research in Frankfurt in the decades prior to the Second World War. They sought to develop a multi-disciplinary, collaborative, critical analysis of the forms of irrationality besetting modern capitalist societies. Today critical theory is largely represented by the work of Jürgen Habermas, who transformed the earlier work of the Institute and developed a distinctive philosophy of communication. Habermas's 'discourse theory' argues that rationality is a basic feature of intersubjective communication and that discourse, as a special form of communication, can serve as a critical standard for judging the rationality of political institutions. His work continues to influence current critical theorists, who argue for the discursive dimension of contemporary democratic society and politics.

2.1 Introduction

This chapter explores the tradition of 'critical theory', the work of an (initially) German group of social and political theorists. Beginning in the 1920s, they set out to craft a Marxist-inspired, interdisciplinary, and penetrating critical analysis of the bases of crisis and injustice in modern, capitalist societies. This project of the 'first generation' of critical theory was the foundation for the later work of the influential philosopher

Jürgen Habermas who, from the 1960s to the present, has developed an intricate theory of 'communicative rationality' and 'discourse', categories he employs to identify and address the structural forms of domination and irrationality inherent in contemporary complex societies. Habermas's work has been very influential in the study of **transnational** politics and global justice.

This chapter begins with a brief account of the origins, methods, and projects of the early critical theorists, the 'Frankfurt School'. It then turns to the work of Habermas, offering an outline of his theory of rationality as 'embedded' in social practices of communication and argumentation. After a brief consideration of the relevant similarities and differences between Habermas's discourse theory of contemporary politics and the liberal political theory of John Rawls, the chapter discusses some of the most significant implications of critical theory for contemporary debates in global politics.

2.2 **Background and early years**

Critical theory, in its most concrete sense (the term has been more or less broadly used) refers to the works, methodologies, and personalities comprising the 'Frankfurt School', centred upon the Institute for Social Research founded in the early 1920s in association with the Johann Wolfgang Goethe University in Frankfurt, Germany. From its inception, but in particular after 1930 under the directorship of Max Horkheimer, the Institute engaged in a multidisciplinary study of the various forms of social and political problems and crises that they diagnosed in modern capitalist societies. Even though 'theory' was what the critical theorists were doing, the collaborative and interdisciplinary nature of their work lay at the foundation of their own sense of mission. Horkheimer brought to the Institute a number of scholars and intellectuals—philosophers, economists, sociologists, political scientists, and theorists of law, literature, and the then-popular Freudian psychoanalytic theory—including Theodor W. Adorno, Herbert Marcuse, Leo Löwenthal, Erich Fromm, Franz Neumann, and (as something of an associate member) the cultural critic Walter Benjamin (Wiggershaus, 1994, pp. 41–105; Jay, 1996, pp. 3–41). Drawing from multiple intellectual traditions and equipped with multiple forms of training and methodology, the members of the original Institute for Social Research proposed that only such a transdisciplinary approach, above all a collaborative effort amongst political philosophy and the empirically grounded social sciences, was adequate for the systematic analysis of modern society and its characteristic problems.

Not surprisingly, the work of the Institute in Europe, and then America in the 1930s and 1940s, focused on creating a theory of crisis. Members designed empirical studies to document the rise of what they later termed the 'authoritarian personality': a new personality structure of unreflective compliance and docility in the face of authoritarian politics and the collapse of the democratic rule of law (Adorno et al., 1993). Convinced that liberal political theory's ideals of individual freedom and social equality were rendered meaningless in the face of mass capitalism, the Institute members controversially regarded mass democracy and political authoritarianism—and ultimately **totalitarianism** and **fascism**—as aspects of one and the same political phenomenon. They saw the collaboration of capitalism and fascism as evidence of the failure of the project of the eighteenth-century European **Enlightenment**, which had promised a rise in freedom and equality to match the rise of rationality in social, economic, and political institutions and practices. In fact, they argued, rationality yielded less freedom for individuals and less equality amongst them; worse still, the supposed rationality of Enlightenment thought was inseparable from the evident irrationality of fascist rule. Rationality, which had promised to fulfil human needs and increase human happiness, had in fact done just the opposite.

This increasingly bleak diagnosis culminated in the classic 1944 work by Horkheimer and Adorno, *Dialectic of Enlightenment* (2002). The book argued that the very core concept of enlightenment itself had been refuted by the rise of mass culture, and the unholy alliance of advanced capitalism and political authoritarianism. Rational enlightenment, once achieved, reverted back into new forms of the very constraints, superstitions, and collective irrationality that it had supposedly conquered (Honneth, 2009).

The Institute and its core members emigrated to the United States prior to the outbreak of the Second World War. Reinstalled in New York and California, they continued to produce interdisciplinary studies of aspects of social crisis, including detailed studies of the psychological and political features of anti-Semitism, the rise and influence of what they termed the 'culture industry'—the industrial production and distribution of entertainment—and the link between cultural consumption and political compliance (Adorno, 2001). Returning to Frankfurt relatively soon after the war's end, Horkheimer and Adorno re-established the Institute for Social Research. Throughout the 1950s and 1960s, both men, but Adorno in particular, became outspoken and highly visible public intellectuals, arguing for a liberalized academic culture, for a concerted effort at national collective self-examination and self-criticism in the wake of war and genocide, and for expanded conceptions of political education as Germany adapted itself to a democratic political culture (Mueller-Doohm, 2004, pp. 366–98).

2.3 The critique of capitalist society in the 'first generation' of critical theory

Whilst many of the Institute's members were heavily influenced by Marx and Marxism, and worked to develop a broadly Marxist critique of contemporary capitalist society, none of its members could be called orthodox Marxists, and the impact and influence of Marx on the Institute's work is best described as a complex and transformative appropriation (Kellner, 1989). Critical theory broadly accepted Marx's double-edged observation about the destructive and creative aspects of capitalism. Capitalism had destroyed all traditional, pre-modern political and cultural conditions, and in doing so had set off a process of modernization where efficiency, control, and technological innovation, rather than values, became the pace-setters not just for economies but for social relations and political institutions as well (Marx, 2002). For Marx, modernity meant the inauguration of a new model of reasonable and effective governance, the emancipation of the individual from traditional forms of identity and political belonging, and the institutionalization of the new political values of freedom and equality. However, like Marx, the early critical theorists also observed the double-sided nature of capitalist modernity. Whilst modern political and social institutions offered emancipation from traditional forms of servitude, they also depended on an economic system, based on industrial labour, which generated new and severe forms of inequality, drudgery, and domination.

Capitalism demanded continuously expanded production and consumption, and the regimentation and rationalization of productive and social relationships. Capitalist economies' tendencies toward over-production required compensations for capitalism's own internal instabilities, whether through the manufacture of popular consent and satisfaction or by means of a 'culture industry' of planned, manufactured distraction, and entertainment, paired with new powerful forms of advertising and aided by new technology, which produced such products as Hollywood cinema, popular radio music, magazines, and television. Where capitalism could not maintain control by such indirect means, it ultimately had to resort to more crude ones: international wars as means to manufacture political solidarity and, ultimately, mechanisms of outright domination and oppression, such as the rejection of democratic rule and the introduction of a police state. The economic instabilities of capitalism, in other words, could only be counteracted by economic or cultural means for so long. Eventually, democratic institutions would convert to authoritarian ones under the pressure of persistent economic crises.

The early critical theorists focused much of their attention on the overt movements toward the curtailment of individual liberties and social solidarity in European (and later American) political culture over the course of the 1930s. But they also examined the less overt modes of political domination, the function of ideology, which Marx had (for them) under-theorized and underestimated. This resulted in a broad shift in attention, from a Marxist focus on *material* reproduction (the making and distributing of commodities and the cycle of commodities) to *symbolic* reproduction (the making and distribution of ideas, emotions, attitudes, even forms of consciousness). This led critical theory to a new conception of the nature and uses of 'bourgeois ideology' that went far beyond what Marx had accomplished in his original version.

Ideology, at least in the sense we are using it here, refers essentially to a network of shared beliefs and attitudes which unjustly legitimate the domination of one part of a society by another. This is a normative or, as Raymond Geuss has put it, a pejorative sense of ideology (Geuss, 1980, pp. 25–40). Ideology is a form of consciousness, adopted by those dominated, as well as those dominating, in which changeable and contingent relations of power in a society are falsely perceived as natural, immutable, and justified. 'Bourgeois ideology', the form of consciousness justifying relations of domination between a capital-owning class and a working class within capitalist societies, thus functions as a set of assumptions, ideas, and values justifying this domination by generating the false consciousness that capital, classes, and relations of deep material inequality in society are natural and inevitable. The chief inheritance of critical theory from Marx and Marxist political thought is that theory must dedicate itself to the revelation of ideology; that is, theory must criticize ideology by disclosing its contents and functions. Like Marx, the critical theorists saw the history of modern political theory itself as part of the very bourgeois ideology that demanded criticism.

On one level, the early critical theorists largely accepted Marx's theory of bourgeois ideology. Capitalist social and economic institutions were engaged in a complex causal relationship with forms of intellectual production—political theory included. As parts of the very society that they study, normative theories understood as ideology had a dual function. They translated into clear, theoretical language the basic ideals of freedom and equality underlying modern political and social institutions, but simultaneously contributed to making those ideals unrealizable. They did this by taking what were actually highly historically contingent and changeable conditions, and making them appear as though they were inevitable and natural. 'Man', for instance, could be portrayed as 'naturally' acquisitive and self-interested, as in the social **contract theory** of Thomas Hobbes. Freedom could be explained as a 'universal' feature of autonomous individuals, as in Immanuel Kant's moral philosophy, rather than an ideal that had arisen in a particular historical context for identifiable reasons.

Borrowing from the earlier work of the Hungarian philosopher Georg Lukács, critical theory observed a process of 'reification' in the way political theory worked: literally 'turning into things', reification implies the transformation of living, dynamic human relationships into objects, and, conversely, the tendency to take abstract concepts or objects and endow them with human characteristics. The latter half of this reification process was most painfully clear in capitalist economies in the way that manufactured commodities such as cars are granted human qualities in advertising and thence in peoples' consciousnesses. These human qualities not only make the commodities more desirable, but also mask their status as human products, as expressions of human creativity and unmet human needs. However, the former side, wherein real human products such as political theories, become alien, thing-like, and supposedly fixed and inevitable, is another and perhaps just as insidious a way, the critical theorists argued, that ideology transforms real resources for political change into their very opposites (Lukács, 1972, pp. 83–148; Held, 1980, pp. 22–6). 'Traditional' theory, then, from the social contract theory of Hobbes through the nineteenth century works of Kant and Hegel, needed a double-sided form of reading appropriate to its dual status: revealing how theory itself functioned as ideology was part of recovering the unmet demands for freedom, equality, and happiness that traditional theories contained.

This more complex relation to political theory was what Max Horkheimer described in his programmatic 1937 essay on 'Traditional and Critical Theory' (Horkheimer, 1972). 'Traditional' theory, Horkheimer claimed, whether in politics, sociology, or philosophy, presupposed an artificial detachment of the theorist from their own society, a distorting observer-perspective that made critical insight into the social and economic bases for the production of theory itself impossible. Traditional theory, in other words, was by its very design incapable of self-reflection and unable to theorize about its own role in the reproduction of the social conditions it described.

Under the same premises, the young Marx had demanded that 'theory' itself be overcome, in favour of a new science of political economy that could connect up directly with organized political (revolutionary) action. The critical theorists were not prepared to make that leap. Instead, Horkheimer proposed a transformation of the bases, nature, and purpose of political theory. Unlike traditional theory, *critical* theory would incorporate a form of continuous self-reflection about its relation to the society it takes as its object of study. This implies, at an initial level, a kind of persistent self-criticism and seems to threaten a form of infinite regress or paralysis. However, critical theory, Horkheimer argued, also rejected the image of scientific objectivity that the social sciences offered as the model that political theory and political sociology should emulate. Neither purely social science nor purely philosophy, critical theory was instead meant as a form of ongoing reflection on the relation between these two. Always with an eye to the double-sided nature of rational enlightenment, the critical theorists hoped to recover the enlightenment conception of the emancipatory power of reason: the capacity of persons to criticize and reject unjust or oppressive social institutions and practices by declaring them irrational, contradicting humans' inherent claims to live as rationally autonomous agents. Critical theory's particular version of 'critique' can be traced in large part back to Marx's notion of criticism as revealing, not just indicting, forms of irrationality in society, on the assumption that such forms maintain their **legitimacy** by hiding their status *as* irrational. Critique thus operates by unmasking forms of domination and oppression in society that illegitimately take on the form of reason, manufacturing various kinds of justification and taking on the appearance of being rational, right, and without obvious alternative.

Just as Marx in his 'Theses on Feuerbach' had famously called for a new theory that would change the world rather than merely interpret it (Marx, 1998), critical theory called for the end of traditional philosophy, or at least an end to the traditional aloofness of philosophy from the empirical social sciences. But their interdisciplinary mission was, in contrast to the autodidact and solitary Marx, truly extraordinary and highly demanding.

Horkheimer's chief claim for a new form of post-traditional critical theory was that theorists abandon a number of assumptions on which an outmoded and unreflective model of political and social theory rested. The form of disciplinary separation of autonomous academic disciplines, each with its own jealously guarded area of theoretical, methodological, and empirical expertise, was itself a piece of ideology, and Horkheimer insisted that these disciplinary walls be pulled down.

Doing so required that one reject yet another persistent and unnecessary dualism, one that had made the split between philosophy and the social sciences possible in the first place. In this dualism, the isolated philosophical theorist, on the one side, carefully builds up an adequate vision of their contemporary world, dealing in abstract normative terms, and communicating largely to other theorists. On the other, empirically orientated social scientists happily work on a group or collaborative model, but remain deeply suspicious of normative analysis, contenting themselves with building up observably verifiable, statistically uniform knowledge with little or no interest in what practical normative use can be made of these facts. To replace this dualism, critical theory proposed an ongoing interdisciplinary (or maybe better, meta-disciplinary) research collaborative, where both theoretical and methodological boundaries would be themselves the objects of critical inquiry. Traditional theory—and in this context, Rawlsian **ideal theory** serves as an excellent example—can no longer maintain the pretension of aloofness from its own material conditions. The hypothetical thought experiments that both early modern and contemporary social contract theory depends on presuppose a kind of 'view from nowhere'. A supposedly *minimal* conception of rationality—the means-ends rationality of the isolated utility-maximizer, choosing from a situation of limited information in a way that

On Rawls and ideal theory, see Chapters 1 and 4.

will intelligently fulfil, or at least minimally harm, their own interests—turns out to be highly historically contingent and filled with important yet unarticulated presuppositions about the nature of social life.

In a moment, we will see how this basic orientation of critical theory comes to play a key role as its most influential current member, Jürgen Habermas, criticizes John Rawls' theory of justice and political liberalism.

First-generation critical theory's various methodological innovations proved highly productive, leading to a series of classic studies of new modes of material and non-material domination in modern societies. At the same time, the work of the Institute for Social Research was consistently hindered by a number of ultimately insurmountable obstacles. Many of these were external. Forced into American exile in the 1930s, the Institute, once reconstituted in New York, shifted its focus from the enabling conditions for the triumph of European fascism to the hegemonic nature of American popular culture. The return to Germany in the late 1940s left many behind. The Institute's key members, Horkheimer and Adorno, the most philosophically orientated of the original Frankfurt School, retained this philosophical focus in their individual writings as well, even as they plunged into the chaotic public intellectual culture of the post-war Federal Republic of Germany.

Critical theory's project of developing a practically orientated, multidisciplinary critique of the irrationality of contemporary culture was also beset by internal difficulties. Perhaps not so surprisingly, the intensive interdisciplinary work that was critical theory's core methodological commitment proved far more demanding than had been envisaged. Moreover, Horkheimer and Adorno's *Dialectic of Enlightenment*, the most influential of all the first generation's works, had broken dramatically from this interdisciplinary model—it was a work of philosophy, not of 'theory' as a team effort. The book delivered an unrelentingly bleak assessment of the totalizing nature of 'instrumental rationality', that seemed incompatible with the very idea that critical theory can help to change, rather than just indict, an irrational and unjust social order.

Dialectic of Enlightenment understood rationality not so much as an exalted or quasi-divine human faculty meant to liberate us from our shackles, but rather as a cold procedure for calculating efficiencies, of devising the appropriate means for any end whatever. No substantive moral or political value can ultimately be derived from rationality itself, they argued. If rationality is nothing other than the systematic discovery of efficient means to any goal, then there is no longer any way to declare one goal 'more rational' or 'less rational' than any other: the same efficiency that can make industrial production into a powerhouse strong enough to satisfy human material wants can just as easily be applied to the industrial killing of millions of people.

Worse still, instrumental rationality is itself a distant descendant of basic human aggression and appetite; indeed, of a kind of coldness and indifference to suffering or vulnerability. What appears so irrational in the appearance of fascism, the book argues, is in fact nothing more than the final victory of a form of means-ends reason that must be indifferent to what it brings about in the world. This famous indictment of the destructive violence within instrumental reason had important precedents in thinkers such as Friedrich Nietzsche and the sociologist Max Weber, and would later re-appear in different guise in the work of Michel Foucault (Nietzsche, 1989; Weber, 1993; Foucault, 2000). However, this 'globalizing critique' came to a kind of climax—and perhaps dead-end—in

On Foucault, see Chapter 3.

the first generation of critical theory. Their vision of the total predominance of instrumental reason appeared to leave little room for any utopian dream of an internal connection between reason and emancipation. For Horkheimer and Adorno, there is no escape from the dialectic of enlightenment, and no clear avenue for disclosing a kind of rationality that would make the promises of **autonomy**, freedom, and political equality anything more than new modes of more subtle and effective domination (Habermas, 1984–87, pp. 339–402). The critical theorists became increasingly unable to use the language of philosophy or social science to describe what kind of rationality they appealed to themselves, in order to indict the global dominance of instrumental reason, and point toward a better, reasonable, emancipated society. Perhaps not surprisingly, most of Adorno's post-war work, notably his massive unfinished *Aesthetic Theory*, concerned identifying the fugitive traces of emancipatory promise left in stubborn pockets of modern life resistant to the pull of popular culture: primarily philosophy and modernist works of music, literature, and theatre (Adorno, 1996).

The first generation of critical theory is widely seen to have run into a 'dead end' in the task of defending a notion of rationality in the name of a larger project of a critique of social domination. Certainly, their political philosophy did not finally manage such a consistent critique. Nevertheless, in concluding this discussion it is vital to bear in mind an area where they did have a decisive impact. Especially following their return to Germany after the Second World War, the critical theorists, above all Horkheimer and Adorno, were deeply committed and engaged public intellectuals, arguing passionately for a transformation of Germany's political culture in the wake of moral and political catastrophe. Their interventions were influential, and often decisive, across a broad spectrum of public controversies. They were at the centre of discussions of Germans' collective responsibility for war and genocide, the status of the new public universities, and the disciplines of philosophy and sociology within them, reform of secondary school curricula, and above all the nature, purpose and tenor of political life—the very 'public sphere' which, as we will see in a moment, was to become the chief focus of their main inheritor, Jürgen Habermas. This vital and ongoing engagement in public political life is perhaps the most important legacy of the first generation of critical theory and offers a sharp (and ongoing) contrast to the role of the political theorist in the **analytic** tradition, which still remains very much a 'traditional' one.

2.4 The discourse theory of Jürgen Habermas

Jürgen Habermas, by far the most influential successor to the first-generation critical theorists, preserved some key elements of the Frankfurt School's methodological programme, while breaking dramatically with many of its substantive claims about the role and fate of rationality in modern societies. Habermas was born in 1929. After working briefly as a journalist he served for several years in the late 1950s as Adorno's assistant in Frankfurt. Unlike Adorno and Horkheimer, however, Habermas became keenly interested in forms of philosophy that had been introduced in Germany in the decade following the Second World War, specifically Anglo-American **analytic philosophy** and the philosophical pragmatism of American philosophers, such as John Dewey. He became increasingly unsatisfied with the results of Horkheimer and Adorno's account of the fate of Enlightenment rationality and grew convinced that their own earlier programme of a collaboration of philosophy and the social sciences remained to be fulfilled. With this motivation Habermas began to develop a broad-based theory of socially embedded reason, and self-consciously resolved to depend less on the titans of eighteenth-and nineteenth-century European philosophy and more on a diverse, even patchwork amalgam of theoretical approaches borrowed from philosophy, the theory of language and communication, political sociology, anthropology, human development, and social history.

At the core of Habermas's new approach was a strikingly humble claim regarding the everyday character of reason or rationality. It is lodged, Habermas argued, in the ways that persons co-ordinate their joint behaviour through linguistic communication. Rationality is a feature of how people successfully communicate, and is best found in the *forms* of relationship people must adopt toward one another in order to communicate successfully, rather than the *content* of what they happen to be saying. Interpersonal communication carried out in everyday natural language, Habermas claimed, contained within itself the normative kernel of the Enlightenment promise of individual autonomy and interpersonal equality. Persons who choose to co-ordinate what they do via speech are not acting instrumentally, since the implicit goal of communication-guided action is not efficiency, but agreement. Agreement, unlike other kinds of success, cannot be ascertained apart from the unforced assent of all those involved in communication. If a group resolves to come up with a consensus on how they ought to solve a problem collectively, we cannot confuse the solution that they collectively agree to with the most efficient possible solution given all the evidence—we hope these two coincide, but we see the difference. Moreover, we also know the difference between a solution that is produced on the basis of a consensus, and an outcome based on lying, or pressuring, or excluding, or some other means of frustrating a consensus.

When problems have to be solved by agreement, rather than force or mere considerations of efficiency, then communicative competence—the ability to use language well in order to generate agreements—does, in fact, exhibit a kind of rationality with a normative dimension missing from instrumental reason. Communicative competence requires that persons grasp and employ rules of *procedural equality*, *symmetry*, and *reciprocity*. That is, in order to reach an agreement, competent persons must be able to treat other communication partners as equal, in the sense that each partner counts as equally entitled to be given reasons, and to respond with agreement or disagreement. They must be capable of grasping what it is to convince another through reasons rather than overwhelming them by force or tricking them. They must be open to receiving and judging the reasons and interests of others; in other words, to communicate and agree people must have a capacity for 'reversibility', or taking the perspective of another person, seeing why a reason may not be convincing to them, or seeing why she might be convinced by a reason other than one's own.

These basic rules are procedural (that is, process-based, rather than substantive) norms that comprise the pragmatic conditions for successful communication. On a more advanced level, successful communication partners are capable of communicating or arguing with one another *about* the rules and procedures of successful communication. They can make the rules and procedures themselves into a subject of argumentation; in other words, they can (either by mutual agreement or by a pre-established rule) make a transition from 'everyday' communication about whatever topic, to a *discourse* in which they consciously set out to resolve, by consensus, disputed values, norms, and procedures. And discourses can be, and have been, *institutionalized* in modern societies. Whilst the earlier critical theorists focused largely on how capitalism institutionalized instrumental rationality in the form of technical control, Habermas concentrates instead on how the rationality inherent in communication and discourse has been institutionalized in the parliamentary procedures of modern democratic forms of governance.

The story of political and social modernity, for Habermas, is a fragile but irreversible process in which very basic communicative competences have acquired a durable institutional form. Discourse, as a form of rationality, is a dramatic alternative to Horkheimer and Adorno's bleak conclusions about the fate of reason in the modern world. From the early 1960s until the present, Habermas has successively expanded and refined a discourse theory of modern subjectivity, democracy, and society.

In 1962, Habermas published his first substantial work, *The Structural Transformation of the Public Sphere* (Habermas, 1992). The book would establish a consistent research programme for the half-century to follow. True to his Frankfurt School heritage of interdisciplinarity Habermas drew on political theory, sociology, and social history to chart the rise of a liberal 'public sphere' of citizen-debaters in the bourgeois society of eighteenth-century France, England, and Germany. Largely independent of governmental oversight and lightly anchored in new non-governmental institutions, such as salons, coffee houses, debating clubs, and journals, this unofficial sphere comprised a loose circle capable of 'democratic opinion- and will-formation', that is, of identifying, discussing, clarifying, and transmitting to state authorities the topics of relevance for a population of citizens. In this way, the public sphere arose as a new form of political agency, both communicating its interests and positions to state power, and holding state power accountable for its responsiveness, thus establishing a new basis for the legitimacy of state authority itself.

Habermas argues that the emergence of a bourgeois public sphere in the eighteenth century represented a social embodiment of enlightenment rationality with an immediate practical, political role, one that was seriously underestimated by Marxist theories of the ideological function of bourgeois political institutions. The inherently intersubjective structure of the public sphere is an open, unfettered debate amongst a group of equals, each prepared to be persuaded by the force of the better argument, and each alert to the demands of reasonable co-operation in a political society. This offers a clear alternative to the narrow conception of self-interested, instrumental rational calculation as the primary mode of practical reason in democratic politics. Public spheres transmit public agreements to the more formal institutions of parliamentary democracy. Public spheres communicate to formal legislatures, which are expected to respond to input from the public sphere with the appropriate kinds of legislative output. Political legitimacy, accordingly, consists of an interaction between informal and formal procedures for producing consensus and mutual understanding. Together with the modern state bureaucracy and the modern market economy, such processes of fair and open deliberation, reason-giving and reason-taking together form a vital mechanism of social co-ordination and integration in modern complex societies.

Despite this far more optimistic alternative to the vision of total instrumental reason developed by the first generation of critical theory, Habermas inherited the older theorists' concern with a diagnosis of social dysfunction. *The Structural Transformation of the*

Public Sphere was also a theory of crisis. Tracing the rise of a public sphere to a loose constellation of voluntary associations, the book also described how the public sphere came to be increasingly circumscribed and, ultimately, nearly shut down over the course of the nineteenth and twentieth centuries. As the book's title already indicated, this slowly evolving crisis of legitimacy was due to tensions within the very structure of the public sphere itself. The values of egalitarian, open, unfettered debate and unforced agreement that the public sphere meant to embody, values that justified the rise of a regime of equal basic rights for all citizens, came into increasing conflict with exclusionary trends toward inequality within bourgeois society itself. This was most visible in the growing antagonism of classes. The social welfare states of the twentieth century mark the effective end of the liberal public sphere, as capitalist economies and power-based administrative state apparatuses increasingly shut down the narrow space between state, economy, and democratic citizenry that the public sphere had opened up.

The Structural Transformation of the Public Sphere ends on a sombre note, offering little in the way of a positive recommendation for countering this decline. But the book also provides a blueprint for a discourse-based critical theory to which Habermas has remained faithful. It established the important claim that political modernity comprises a foundational tension between two very different dynamics of modernization and two competing modes of rational co-ordination of social life: on the one hand, a form of reason orientated toward technical success in the explanation and control of things—instrumental rationality. On the other, however, Habermas observed a communicative form of rationality orientated at consensus based on intersubjective reason-giving and reason-taking. While nothing internal to these two forms of rationality destines them to come into conflict with one another, the actual history of modernization in Western societies—the basic subject-matter of sociology—is the story of the gradual, worsening tension between them. The democratic, indeed radically egalitarian, potential inherent in processes of reaching mutual understanding and agreement is gradually hijacked by instrumental forms of economic and bureaucratic power.

A reconstructive critical social theory takes on the task of identifying the specific mechanisms and episodes of this history, as a form of diagnosis of the crisis of modernity, but it also has the practical intent of identifying the potential for emancipation from power, and for collective freedom and equality, that persist within modern forms of social life. Describing modernity as an ongoing struggle over how two different forms of rationality are institutionalized draws attention to the contingent and changeable nature of modern social crises, and to the untapped potential for transformative social agency lodged in everyday forms of social behaviour.

2.5 Habermas and normative political theory

Habermas has produced a series of works developing a discourse theory based on his original insights into the nature of communicative reason. This theory is highly normative—that is, it makes strong claims for how discourse *ought* to work, on both everyday levels of moral reasoning, and in the institutions of democratic life. On the first, everyday level,

Habermas develops a '**discourse ethics**', a purely procedural account of how moral rules can be justified (Habermas, 2001a). Rather than argue for a transcendent or foundational rationality to which we have some private access through reflection, Habermas argues that moral rules—indeed, any moral claim—are justifiable only through public processes of giving and taking reasons. The solution to any moral controversy is to be looked for less in some objective answer than in the appropriate (reasonable) procedure that governs the behaviour of those involved in the controversy as they jointly argue toward a possible solution. Moral rules are liable to justification through agreement by all those affected by them in a discourse situation characterized by symmetry, reciprocity, and mutual perspective-taking. The capacity of those engaged in deliberation to take one another's perspective on the problem is a way of understanding why reasons for or against a disputed norm may be convincing for them. As Habermas puts it,

… everyone is required to take the perspective of everyone else and thus to project herself into the understandings of self and world of all others; from this interlocking of perspectives there emerges an ideally extended 'we-perspective' from which all can test in common whether they wish to make a controversial norm the basis of their shared practice … (Habermas, 2000, p. 58).

This 'discourse principle'—the rule that norms are justified via unforced agreement amongst those involved—is just as relevant in politics as in interpersonal morality. Indeed, proceduralism—the idea that normative rightness consists in the appropriate process for settling disputes, rather than the correct outcome preordained in advance—captures something of the rational essence of democratic governance. This is especially true in modern democratic societies, where diversity and the pluralism of different cultural ways of life virtually guarantee deep and irresolvable differences on many norms.

Habermas thus regards his proceduralist discourse theory as the best expression of the quintessentially universalistic nature of modern morality, politics, and law. To include all moral agents, with their diverse conceptions of ethical life, under a single moral point of view requires that morality consist in a procedure for settling conflicting norms that no one involved could reasonably reject. Moreover, as societies grow in complexity and diversity of lifestyles, and of substantive conceptions of the good, morality plays a decreasing role in everyday life as a way of regulating social interaction. The procedural parameters for moral discourse are institutionalized far more effectively in modern positive law and in democratic politics, both of which are, or at least are meant to be, highly tolerant of a plurality of different conceptions of the good. We do not expect morality to judge amongst different kinds of religious claims, for instance. However, we do expect laws to lay down religious rights so that, regardless of what our values are, we and fellow-citizens have equal legal rights to formulate and pursue our values. Democratic pluralism demands a mode of universalism that offers individual persons essentially abstract legal guarantees in the form of legal rights, while simultaneously offering the resources for all citizens to make up a single polity in order to practice collective or popular sovereignty—a tall order indeed.

Democracy, of course, often gets things very wrong, but substantively wrong outcomes of procedurally correct deliberations are 'wrong' in a different sense than the normative one of justice. Factual or substantive errors generally emerge only when the application of a deliberative decision yields results different from what was expected, retrospectively revealing insufficient and/or incorrect information. Democratic deliberation is (and must be) fallible for just this reason. Normatively, however, the discourse principle does rule out procedurally correct decisions that knowingly and forseeably adversely affect some constituency that was properly included in deliberations.

On Rawls's theory of justice, see Chapter 1.

The astute reader will by now have noticed how Habermas's discourse theory comes remarkably close to some of the most basic conclusions of John Rawls's theory of justice (Rawls, 1971). This is a claim worth analysing for a moment.

It is undeniable that Rawls and Habermas arrive at strongly comparable views of a modern conception of what could count as justice under conditions of diversity and permanent disagreements within societies about how one ought to live. Both contemporary critical theory (Habermas) and contemporary political liberalism (Rawls) begin with the view that such deep disagreements over morality, ethics, and values are permanent features of modern societies, to be embraced rather than cured. Both men defend a strong form of proceduralism; both intend to use their theories to capture the most basic normative intuitions concerning the irreducible value of the freedom and equality of individuals contained in the European enlightenment. Yet, on the crucial question of the nature of the rational foundation for freedom and equality of persons, Habermas and Rawls actually differ quite sharply.

For one thing, we should notice that Rawls's reconstruction of principles of justice via a careful account of an '**original position**' is a hypothetical situation—a thought experiment—whereas the symmetry and reciprocity conditions from which Habermas derives his discourse principle is an idealization of what we are already doing in everyday communication. There is nothing hypothetical about it.

Habermas, for his part, is troubled that Rawls's original position succeeds in clarifying the basic terms of modern political justice—the equal autonomy of citizens—only by denying to hypothetical choosers in the original position that very autonomy (in the sense of reciprocal access to *one another's* higher-order desires and beliefs). Rawls sees persons in the 'original position' under a '**veil of ignorance**' as solitary egoists. They act only according to a narrow conception of rational choice, maximizing their own (unknown) scenario (or minimizing their worst-case scenario). They employ a mode of rationality that requires efficiency of outcomes above all else. However, for Habermas, this condition that Rawls imposes on his hypothetical choosers denies them the very forms of reason that would qualify them as autonomous, which on Habermas's terms involve the capacity to engage as full and equal members in discursive justification processes, and to engage in the kind of ideal role-taking or perspective-changing that is part and parcel of what we mean by rationality. Rawls simply brackets off the very mode of intersubjective reason that lies at the heart of the political justice he wants to reconstruct by means of philosophy.

In a move that can be traced back to the ideology critique of Horkheimer and Adorno, Habermas insists that *A Theory of Justice* adopts a methodology, a conception of rationality, artificially removed from the rationality that is already, actually, embedded in the everyday modes of social life. Rawls's dependence on an economistic conception of rational choice, far from a neutral methodological choice, actually introduces quite substantive prejudices into his theory.

At the same time, it is also worth noting that, despite some rather serious disagreement between Habermas and Rawls on the nature of rationality, a far sharper difference exists between Habermas and practitioners of what is often called post-structural political theory; specifically authors such as Jacques Derrida and Michel Foucault. Although these authors will be discussed in detail in the next chapter, they are important inheritors of the tradition of 'radical' critique associated with Marx and then with Horkheimer, Adorno, and the 'first generation' of critical theory. Habermas's sharp disagreements with post-structuralist political theorists rests on his claim that reason, even though a far more modest, procedural, and intersubjective conception of reason than is found in the philosophical tradition, is a real force within modern democratic societies, and still provides a normative criterion for indicting irrational political institutions and practices through theoretical criticism. Power can be exerted in rational and justifiable, or irrational and unjust ways (Habermas, 1987, 1990).

 On post-structuralism, see Chapter 3.

2.6 **Critical theory and transnational politics**

Critical theory is in many respects at heart a theory of transnational justice. In its first generation, certainly, the writings of the members of the Institute for Social Research set out to explain the rise of essentially post-national economic and political phenomena: global capitalism and, more controversially, a corresponding outbreak of totalitarianism and fascism that the critical theorists generally regarded less as a specifically German evil than as one linked internally to the dialectic of enlightenment itself. Thus, whilst continuing the basically Marxist project of regarding nation states as functional parts of an international capitalist economy and nationalism as bourgeois ideology, the early critical theorists did not offer anything resembling Marx's vision of a post-capitalist (communist), post-national politics.

In its current forms, however, critical theory has been highly productive on topics of transnational politics and global justice. Habermas's discourse theory of modern morality, democracy and law is, not surprisingly, also a theory about global ethics and politics. This section offers a brief and necessarily incomplete account of Habermas's conception of global justice—incomplete since Habermas remains a highly productive thinker, and his views on global justice and international relations continue to evolve.

Habermas describes what he terms the 'post-national constellation' that currently characterizes the global political situation (Habermas, 2001b). The traditional sovereign nation state arose in the modern era as a kind of institutional response to the problems of modernization and the increase in social complexity. Concentrating administrative and bureaucratic functions in state agencies provided huge gains in efficiency, but at the cost of a crucial loss of solidarity, the vital resource of collective belonging and willingness of persons to include one another as citizens in a shared project of self-governance.

This loss of solidarity threatened dysfunction if members were unable or unwilling to affirm membership or make sacrifices, whether dramatic (military service) or not (voting, paying taxes). The nation state provided a kind of institutional hybrid, combining otherwise separate functions as a way of mobilizing, and stabilizing, relatively large populations. Nation states succeeded in this, however, only at the cost of an internal contradiction, what Habermas terms the double or 'Janus face' of the nation state. The nation state offers not just relative stability and efficiency for self-interested individuals, but also a powerful compensation for the solidarity lost in the process of modernization.

Nation states combine these otherwise very different goods (abstract legal rights for individuals; powerful forms of group identity for a collective) in the status of citizenship. However, the economic and social interaction that large, complex nation states make possible, and the values of individual freedom and equality that citizens' civil rights enshrine, unleash a developmental dynamic that eventually comes to outstrip what the geographically and politically bounded nation state can provide. National constitutions generally offer rights only to their citizens, even as the underlying justifications for bearing such rights against their state and one another, refer not to one's status as a Briton or Finn, but to rational human beings irrespective of national borders.

For this reason, the universalistic normative basis of individual legal rights become increasingly hard to reconcile with the morally arbitrary geographical boundaries of the nation state and the historically arbitrary conception of 'the nation' as the carriers of such universalistic rights. This contradiction becomes a real problem under the pressure of new volumes and intensities of migration flows, as well as the nascent regime of international law. Habermas, therefore, sees nation states as coming under increasing stress both on functional and on normative grounds. Nation states are increasingly unable to handle the intensity and volume of flows of persons, information, capital, and problems that cross their borders. At they same time, they are also less and less able to remain true to the universalistic normative values of equal freedom for all that they promise along with citizenship status.

Both on normative and strictly pragmatic, functional grounds, then, the nation state finds itself less and less able to fulfil the traditional demands of political **sovereignty**: a foreign policy that maintains effective control over a delimited geographical territory within fixed borders, and pursues an identifiable national interest in relation to similarly bounded nation states and a domestic policy that maintains effective policy control over a delimited group of people sharing some pertinent conception of political identity.

These considerations make Habermas's discourse theory of global politics a distinctly cosmopolitan one. Looking to a future beyond the national-state system, Habermas argues that the dynamic of democratization is leading to new transnational and ultimately global forms of governance appropriate to the universal, border-crossing aspect of democratic legitimacy. Cosmopolitanism in the legal sense demands a gradual transition from international to cosmopolitan law with a constitutional basis (Habermas, 2006).

On cosmo-politanism see Chapter 8.

What is needed, Habermas argues, is some functional equivalent of a world constitution, with a global schedule of basic **human rights**, beyond the current patchwork of treaty-based and **customary international law**, and its dependence on the imperatives of national-state sovereignty. A 'global domestic politics' alone can satisfy the demands of global **distributive justice**, and respond to the growing inequality between regions of the world and the risks that inequality brings with it. Moreover, political solidarity manufactured by the classical nation state, self-contradictory as we have seen, must give way to

On distributive justice and global inequality, see Chapter 14.

a mode of *cosmopolitan* solidarity in which persons can regard one another mutually as fellow world citizens irrespective of nationality. Law can in some senses prepare the way for this form of cosmopolitan solidarity, and domestic politics can provide a necessary adjunct to it. However, Habermas ultimately believes it is up to the populations of democratic states to make a historic next step to a form of mutual political and even moral inclusion that will finally live up to the unbounded modes of accommodation of difference already promised in the ideals of the Enlightenment.

 See Chapters 6 and 7.

Discourse theory therefore implies a robust form of legal, political, and even moral cosmopolitanism. It offers a powerful response to contemporary liberal political theory, whether in the form of Rawls's *Law of Peoples* (1999) or other contemporary variants of 'liberal nationalism', which maintains the relevance of ethically substantive categories such as 'the people' or 'the nation' for deciding on questions of global economic justice. For Habermas, as for the first-generation critical theorists, the universalistic claims of Enlightenment are simply not, in the long run, compatible with the modern conception of the nation state.

Nevertheless, despite its many robust aspects, Habermas's cosmopolitan vision of a future, post-national global order is in important respects far more cautious and qualified than many of contemporary cosmopolitanism's more energetic defenders. He does not and has never advocated a world state, observing that global governance requires the dispersion, rather than the concentration of sovereign power. He carefully avoids any suggestion that a global public sphere, effacing and transcending cultural diversity and difference, is either possible or desirable. Instead, Habermas describes a complex, multilevel model, with a hierarchy of institutional forms of cosmopolitan governance at subnational, national, transnational, and **supranational** levels, as a form of distribution of labour.

On Habermas and global governance, see also Chapter 21.

At the supranational or global level, Habermas sees the basic tasks of world security and the protection and promotion of basic **human rights**. At the regional or transnational level, however, international politics and new regional negotiation regimes would continue to pursue a global domestic policy aimed at countering massive economic inequalities and ecological threats. This would effectively disburden existing nation states from the huge task of managing regional and global problems from the realist perspective of national interest, and free them to address nationally bounded or local problems.

On human rights, see Chapter 13.

On realism, see Chapter 5.

Moreover, whilst Habermas has welcomed developments in popular and political culture and in communication technology that have promoted more and faster communicative links between different cultures, he has also been careful to note the potential dangers of a homogenization of cultural differences. A single, undifferentiated global public sphere would not necessarily represent an advance, in normative terms, over a model of linked public spheres, maximally inclusive, commensurate with the complex function of multiple sovereignties in a new post-national order. Habermas is concerned that globalization also might result in the loss of diversity in ethical life, the varying 'conceptions of the good' that provide the necessary shared vocabulary for people to understand, articulate, and argue for their own interests and goals.

Habermas's position is quite different from a **communitarian** notion of 'a people' or nation bearing its own internal justification for political **self-determination**. However, he is also wary of a form of cosmopolitanism that would merely eradicate ethical and cultural differences. Cosmopolitan solidarity requires an embrace of universalistic value orientations through, not instead of, local attachments and commitments.

In addition to the ongoing work of Habermas, a range of younger theorists continue to pursue the project of critical theory, and their work is often particularly influential in contemporary debates concerning global justice and transnational politics. Axel Honneth carries on the work of critical theory with his own theory of intersubjective recognition and the origins of social disrespect (Honneth, 2007). True to the critical theory tradition, Honneth continues to see theory as a tool for identifying and correcting the pathological dimension of socially embedded rationality, under the premise that a freer and more just society is one that has better institutionalized forms of rationality already inherent in everyday human intersubjectivity (Honneth, 2009). In the field of international relations, critical theory in general and Habermasian discourse theory in particular have influenced Seyla Benhabib in her work on the transformations of citizenship status in modern **multicultural** democracies (Benhabib, 2004). Benhabib has also written extensively on how cultural conflicts over such flash-points as constitutional protections for religious minorities, multiple citizenships and new immigration dynamics, or claims for group-based **cultural identity**, can be reconciled with modern principles of democratic citizenship through a modified version of Habermas's discourse theory (Benhabib, 2002). Nancy Fraser has contributed widely to questions of political justice in the post-national era, and both continue to offer discourse theory-based descriptions of political cosmopolitanism (Benhabib, 2006; Fraser, 2008). Both Benhabib and Fraser have also contributed important work on extending critical theory to questions of gender and sexism (Fraser, 1989; Benhabib, 1992).

The British theorist Andrew Linklater, meanwhile, has worked to develop a theory of international relations that takes its bearings directly from (Habermasian) critical theory, offering what Linklater argues is a vital next step beyond the outmoded alternatives of Marxism and realism (Linklater, 1990). He has followed this programmatic study with a highly influential work, *The Transformation of Political Community* (Linklater, 1998), drawing on discourse theory to imagine new, post-national forms of civic identity and political belonging.

2.7 Conclusion

From its origins as a multidisciplinary, Marxist-inspired programme of the critique of bourgeois ideology to its current form as a broad-based project of reformulating and clarifying the philosophical bases of contemporary transnational politics, critical theory has remained true to its name: it is a form of normative theory that takes seriously the need to criticize—to reveal, describe, and condemn—forms of thought, institutions, and practices that perpetuate domination. Whether this domination is construed as an ideology that demands the false consciousness of an unsuspecting population, or subtle modes of exclusion from discursive practices where they ought to have a voice, critical theory insists that more just and equitable forms of collective life are also more reasonable ones.

▨ QUESTIONS

1. In what ways were the 'first generation' critical theorists influenced by Karl Marx? What were some significant differences and disagreements they had with Marxism?

2. What were some important innovations that critical theory proposed in order to break with 'traditional' philosophical theories?

3. Discuss the role of the European Enlightenment, and the Enlightenment conception of rational autonomy, in critical theory.

4. What is meant by 'instrumental rationality'? What role does this concept play in critical theory's view of modern capitalist societies?

5. How does Habermas's conception of 'communicative rationality' address the problems encountered by the 'first generation' of critical theorists?

6. What is the 'public sphere' and what is its importance for Habermas's critical theory?

7. What is Habermas's 'proceduralist' theory of rationality?

8. What are some differences between Habermas's and John Rawls's theories of political justice?

9. What criticisms does Habermas offer of the nation state?

10. Describe the form(s) of political cosmopolitanism that Habermas supports.

▨ FURTHER READING

Benhabib, S. (1986) *Critique, Norm, Utopia: A Study of the Foundations of Critical Theory*. New York: Columbia University Press. Offers an in-depth exploration of the foundations of the Frankfurt School, including Habermas.

Bronner, S. E. (ed.) (1989) *Critical Theory and Society: A Reader*. London: Routledge. A helpful anthology of essays and excerpts, offering a representative sample of the works of the Frankfurt School.

Finlayson, G. (2005) *Habermas: A Very Short Introduction*. Oxford: Oxford University Press. A good short introduction and overview.

Habermas, J. (1984–1987) *The Theory of Communicative Action* (transl. McCarthy, T.). Cambridge: Polity. Habermas's theoretical masterwork, the massive two-volume work lays out the foundations of his discourse theory.

Habermas, J. (1996) *Between Facts and Norms: Contributions to a Discourse Theory of Law and Democracy* (transl. Rehg, W.), Cambridge: Polity. Habermas's major work on the relation between democracy and law.

Jay, M. (1996) *The Dialectical Imagination: A History of the Frankfurt School and the Institute of Social Research 1923–1950*. Los Angeles: University of California Press. The classic study of the history of the early Frankfurt School.

McCarthy, T. (1981) *The Critical Theory of Jürgen Habermas*. Cambridge: MIT Press. A good comprehensive introduction to Habermas's early work.

Wiggershaus, R. (1994) *The Frankfurt School: Its History, Theories, and Political Significance*. Cambridge: MIT Press. A comprehensive history of the first generation of critical theorists.

■ WEB LINKS

http://www.uta.edu/huma/illuminations/ *Illuminations: The Critical Theory Website*, based at the University of Texas, is dedicated to archiving important works of the Frankfurt School.

http://pegasus.cc.ucf.edu/~janzb/crittheory/ The 'Critical Theory Resources' site, where numerous online texts by critical theorists are available.

http://www.msu.edu/user/robins11/habermas/ The Jürgen Habermas Web Resource, where works by or about Habermas can be accessed.

http://www.marxists.org/ A site containing a very extensive range of primary texts, scholarly articles, and links about different aspects of Marxism. It includes much commentary on critical theory.

Visit the Online Resource Centre that accompanies this book to access more learning resources: **www.oxfordtextbooks.co.uk/orc/bell_ethics/**

3 Ethics and post-structuralism

Amy Allen

READER'S GUIDE

This chapter surveys the two main 'post-structuralist' approaches to ethics and politics, exemplified by the work of Michel Foucault and Jacques Derrida, respectively. The chapter introduces the reader to core concepts in Foucault's ethical-political thought—including his analytics of power, his understanding of subjection, the account of ethics in his late work, and his notion of governmentality—and in Derrida's ethical-political thought—including his concept of deconstruction, his account of ethical responsibility, his understanding of justice as undeconstructible, and his analysis of democracy as always *à-venir* (to come). The chapter also places the work of these theorists in the context of their shared inheritance of the Kantian notion of critique and briefly considers the connections between their work and contemporary critical theory, in particular the work of Jürgen Habermas.

3.1 Introduction

As a label, 'post-structuralism' is problematic. Although it is more specific than its close cousin 'postmodernism', it is perhaps a bit too specific to fit all of the figures to whom it typically refers. The term 'post-structuralism' at its most basic refers to the movement in French philosophy that comes after the heyday of structuralism, a movement that started in linguistics (with the work of the Swiss linguist Ferdinand de Saussure) and spread to psychoanalysis (with the work of the French psychoanalyst Jacques Lacan) and anthropology (with the work of French anthropologist Claude Lévi-Strauss). Whereas structuralism focused on the unconscious linguistic, cultural and social codes that 'structure' our experience of the world, 'post-structuralism' rejects the very idea of static, unchanging 'structures' on which structuralism is based. However, the term 'post-structuralism' is rejected by the very thinkers to whom it is most often applied. For example, Jacques Derrida specifically refuses this label when he writes: 'I do not consider myself either a post-structuralist or a post-modernist. I have often explained why I never use these words, except to say that they are inadequate to what I am trying to do' (Derrida, 1999, p. 229). Similarly, although Michel Foucault denies vehemently that he is a structuralist, he refrains from describing his work as 'post-structuralist', preferring instead to call his approach a 'genealogy of the modern subject' (Foucault, 1993, p. 202). Not only is the term 'post-structuralism' rejected by two of the most prominent 'post-structuralists', it also covers over or obscures the important philosophical differences between thinkers who are grouped together under this label.

Still, labels have their utility and this one can responsibly be used to refer to a broad current of thought, one that has important implications for thinking about ethics and politics. This chapter will draw out those implications. However, rather than trying to talk about 'post-structuralism' in general, I will instead focus on the ethical and political implications of the work of the two 'post-structuralist' thinkers mentioned in the previous paragraph. The diversity of these implications is indicative of the diversity of currents of thought that are contained under this heading.

Foucault and Derrida are, first and foremost, philosophers, not scholars of international relations; hence, the bulk of their work deals with philosophical issues, rather than world politics per se. (Of course, there are exceptions to this rule, particularly in the case of Derrida. See, for example, his compelling discussion of political sovereignty in a post-9/11 world [Derrida, 2005]). However, each philosopher advances a theoretical method or paradigm for thinking about ethics and politics—through a rethinking of such core ethical-political notions as power, **autonomy**, government, responsibility, and justice—that has been widely employed by those interested in understanding contemporary world politics (Der Derian & Shapiro, 1989; Edkins, 1999; Campbell & Shapiro, 1999; Burke, 2008). This chapter begins with the work of Michel Foucault, focusing on his analyses of the concepts of power, subjectivity, ethics, and **governmentality**. It then turns to a discussion of Derrida's political thought, with an emphasis on his concepts of **deconstruction**, ethical responsibility, justice-to-come, and democracy. After a brief discussion of the critique of post-structuralism offered by the critical theorist Jürgen Habermas, the chapter closes with a consideration of the post-structuralist conception of critique. Along the way, I will offer some examples of how the post-structuralist ideas explained here have been employed in contemporary debates about world politics.

On Habermas, see Chapter 2.

3.2 Power, subjectivity, and ethics: Michel Foucault

Michel Foucault wrote on a wide variety of topics, including the history of psychiatry and psychoanalysis, the emergence of modern clinical practice in medicine, and the history of sexuality, including sexual practices and sexual identity. However, he is probably best known for the provocative and complicated analyses of power that he developed during the 1970s. During this time period, Foucault began to write what he calls genealogies. Foucault borrows the term genealogy from Nietzsche, and uses it to refer to a historical and philosophical method that analyses how systems of thought, institutional structures, and social practices that appear to be natural and inevitable emerge out of contingent historical events. Foucault's genealogies of modern power relations and of the modern ethical subject are the most relevant for contemporary discussions of world politics (for examples of recent work on world politics that draws heavily on Foucault, see Ferguson, 1994; Bartelson, 1995; Lynn Doty, 1996; Campbell, 1998b; Dillon & Reid, 2007; Dillon & Neal, 2008). The next few sections will explain:

- Foucault's analysis of power as relational and strategic;
- his account of how the individual subject is constituted by power, a process that he terms 'subjection';
- his notion of governmentality as the point that links individuals and broader relations of power;
- his understanding of ethics as rooted in what he calls practices of the self.

Foucault's analysis of power

Unlike many theorists in the Western political theory tradition, Foucault understands power not as a substance, but as a relation (Foucault, 2003, p. 168). This means that power is not some stuff that can be possessed or had. Rather, the term power refers to a particular kind of social or political relationship between individuals. However, what kind of relationship counts as a power relationship? Once again, contrary to traditional understandings of power, Foucault insists that power relations are not first and foremost repressive relationships, where one individual or group of individuals thwarts, censors, or represses the desires of another individual or group. Foucault does not deny that power relationships can sometimes take repressive forms—as he might say, power sometimes functions by saying no—but he also claims that power is fundamentally a productive relationship (Foucault, 1978, pp. 3–13). What, then, do power relationships produce? The short answer is, almost everything in our social world—institutions, social practices, cultural discourses, and so on. For example, Foucault argues that the new form of **disciplinary power** that emerged in the modern era produced new modes of criminal punishment centred on imprisonment, rather than spectacular corporal punishment, new types of educational institutions organized by hierarchical examinations, and new ways of organizing workers and soldiers by controlling their physical movements down to the smallest detail (Foucault, 1977). Even more provocatively, Foucault maintains that power relationships produce our systems of knowledge, including both objects to be known and knowing subjects. Hence, they produce or construct our reality (Foucault, 1977, p. 194; for a discussion of this idea in relation to post-colonialism, see Lynn Doty, 1996).

Power relationships are not only productive, they are also strategic in two senses. First, power relationships involve a struggle or confrontation between two opposing forces and, secondly, each party to that relational struggle aims to get the other to do what he/she wants. As Foucault puts it:

power must be understood in the first instance as the multiplicity of force relations immanent in the sphere in which they operate and which constitute their own organization; as the process which, through ceaseless struggles and confrontations, transforms, strengthens, or reverses them; as the support which these force relations find in one another, thus forming a chain or a system, or on the contrary, the disjunctions and contradictions which isolate them from one another; and lastly, as the strategies in which they take effect, whose general design or institutional crystallization is embodied in the state apparatus, in the formulation of law, in the various social hegemonies. (Foucault, 1978, pp. 92–3)

The references to the 'state apparatus' and the 'formulation of law' in the last part of this passage brings us to the contrast between Foucault's strategic, relational model of power and what he calls the juridical model of power. The juridical model understands power in terms of law and views power as invested in the sovereign. For the juridical model of power, the main questions regarding power concern whether and how an exercise of power on the part of the sovereign can be regarded as legitimate. Foucault rejects the juridical model of power for several reasons. First, the juridical model assumes that power is a stuff that can be possessed or transferred, for example, from individuals in the **state of nature** to the sovereign through the mechanism of the **social contract**. As we have seen, Foucault thinks that it is a mistake to understand power as a substance. Secondly, the talk of legitimate or illegitimate uses of the sovereign's power obscures what Foucault regards as a crucial issue: namely, how broader relations of domination undergird **sovereignty** by making possible the social cohesion that sovereign states need in order to function. As Foucault sees it, without what he calls 'disciplinary power', there would be no cohesive social body that could either delegate its rights to self-governance to a sovereign or that could engage in the practice of collective will-formation and self-governance. Finally, Foucault argues on historical grounds that the more diffuse and decentralized form of power known as disciplinary power comes to the fore in the modern West, and that the juridical model of power is insufficient for analysing it.

   On the basis of this critique of the juridical model of power, Foucault proposes the following methodological propositions for analysing modern disciplinary power. First, power should be understood as invested not solely in the centralized institutions of the state, but as spread throughout the capillaries of the social body (Foucault, 2003, p. 27). Secondly, power should be studied via a bottom-up, ascending analysis that starts with a fine-grained investigation of local and specific power relations, rather than a top-down, descending analysis of power that presupposes broad structures of domination and reads those structures into specific social relations (Foucault, 1978, p. 94). This does not mean that Foucault thinks it is illegitimate to talk about broad, systematic power relationships, such as the oppression of women or class domination—it just means that we have to think of such broad power structures as the end result of a complicated network of specific, local, and capillary power relations. Thirdly, Foucault maintains that power relations are intentional, but non-subjective (Foucault, 1978). By 'intentional', Foucault means that power relations have a point or aim, that they are directed toward certain ends that can be understood and analysed. By 'non-subjective', however, he means that those ends are neither controlled, nor can they necessarily be anticipated by individual subjects (or groups of subjects). Foucault's claim that power relations are non-subjective is closely related to his contention that the individual is constituted by power, an idea that he refers to with the notion of subjection.

Subjectivity and subjection

When Foucault uses the term 'subjection', he always means it in a dual sense. Subjection refers simultaneously to the process through which individuals are turned into subjects who are capable of thought and action by being subjected to power relations (Foucault, 1978, p. 60). Essentially, this is what Foucault means by saying that the individual is constituted by, or is an effect of, power. For Foucault, the subject is constituted by power, but it is constituted as a subject who is capable of action and even of acts of self-constitution, as we will see below. As Foucault puts it in a well-known passage:

It is..., I think, a mistake to think of the individual as a sort of elementary nucleus, a primitive atom or some multiple, inert matter to which power is applied, or which is struck by a power that subordinates or destroys individuals. In actual fact, one of the first effects of power is that it allows bodies, gestures, discourses, and desires to be identified and constituted as something individual. The individual is not, in other words, power's opposite number; the individual is one of power's first effects. The individual is in fact a power-effect, and at the same time, to the extent that he is a power-effect, the individual is a relay: power passes through the individuals it has constituted. (Foucault, 2003, pp. 29-30)

This passage contains an implicit contrast with the notion of the individual presupposed by the juridical conception of power, according to which the individual is in and of itself unsullied by power relations; it is an 'elementary nucleus' or 'primitive atom' that can be distorted when power relations are applied to it. For Foucault, power shapes and constitutes our very individuality. A primary example of this process, for Foucault, is the way that power relations in modern Western societies compel us to adopt a particular sexual identity, to think of ourselves as essentially either hetero- or homosexual, and to bind ourselves to that way of being (Foucault, 1978). However, this does not mean that Foucault regards individuals as nothing more than the power relations that constitute them (notice how he says in the above quoted passage that individuals are not 'inert'). If the individual is always the 'relay' of power, then this suggests that she plays an active role in maintaining and reproducing the power relations that shape her. Foucault uses the term 'government' to describe the intersection between the power relations that shape individuals—what he calls 'technologies of domination'—and the ways in which individuals constitute themselves through ethical practices—what he calls 'technologies of the self' (Foucault, 1993, p. 203).

Foucault's analysis of subjection has been applied on a broader scale to rethink the relationship between political identity and the state. For example, drawing on Foucault's analysis of subjectivity, David Campbell has argued that the foreign policy of the United States is a practice that is central to the constitution and maintenance of American political identity. Rather than viewing states as pre-existing sovereign individuals whose foreign policies are constructed in response to objectively existing dangers, Campbell views both sovereign states and the dangers that shape their foreign policies as socially constituted realities that are produced by complex global power relations. Moreover, Campbell argues that the threat of external danger is necessary for securing the internal identity of the state; far from being a threat to the stability and identity of the state, 'external' dangers are among the state's conditions of possibility (Campbell, 1998b).

Governmentalization and governmentality

Up to this point, I have discussed only one of the two modes of modern power that Foucault identifies: disciplinary power. This is because Foucault initially presents disciplinary power as the distinctive form of power that emerges in modernity. Later on, however, he identifies a second distinctively modern form of power, which he calls '**biopower**' (Foucault, 1978, pp. 135–59; Foucault, 2003, pp. 239–64). Understanding these two forms of modern power and how they are interrelated is crucial for understanding Foucault's account of governmentality. Disciplinary power emerges first, in the seventeenth- and early-eighteenth centuries, and it targets individual bodies. Biopower emerges somewhat later, in the latter half of the eighteenth century, and it targets not individuals, but populations or, in the extreme, the species as a whole. These two forms of power intertwine in modern Western societies to produce a mode of power that is simultaneously individualizing and totalizing.

   The intertwining of disciplinary and biopower is crucial to understanding Foucault's critique of the modern state. For Foucault, the modern state both individualizes—through the disciplining of individuals—and totalizes—through the **biopolitical** management and regulation of populations. In the eighteenth century, the state begins to concern itself not just with the control of individual citizens but also with a new target: the population. This also gives the state a new task: the management of populations, which encompasses such goals as regulating and optimizing rates of reproduction, disease, accidents, and mortality (Foucault, 2007). This task gives rise to new domains of knowledge, including statistics and demographics (Hacking, 1990), that enable states to manage risk through such mechanisms as insurance programmes, public health, and the welfare state, all in the name of governing their populations (Burchell et al., 1991, chapters 10, 11, and 14).

   Foucault uses the term 'governmentalization' to refer to the historical process through which the modern state—a state that is both individualizing and totalizing—emerges. Despite an apparent tension between the aim of improving the lives of individuals and that of fostering the unity of the state, Foucault maintains that the modern state integrates these two aims by disciplining individuals in such as a way as to strengthen the state (Foucault, 2000, p. 322). According to Foucault, this analysis shows that the modern state is not only individualizing and totalizing, but individualizing and *totalitarian* (Foucault, 2000, p. 325). Thus, the lesson to be learned by anyone who wishes to critique or oppose the modern state is that 'opposing the individual and his interests to [the modern state] is just as hazardous as opposing it with the community and its requirements … Liberation can come only from attacking not just one of these two effects but political rationality's very roots' (Foucault, 2000, p. 325). That is to say, 'liberation' from the governmentalization of the modern state can come only through an attack on the entwinement of disciplinary power and biopower.

What does such an attack entail? Foucault highlights what he calls 'struggles against subjection' (Foucault, 1983, p. 212). The intertwining of disciplinary and biopower in modern Western states has resulted in what Foucault calls a 'government of individualization', a form of power that

categorizes the individual, marks him by his own individuality, attaches him to his own identity, imposes a law of truth on him which he must recognize and which other have to recognize in him. It is a form of power which makes individuals subjects. (Foucault, 1983, p. 212)

Struggles against subjection are not struggles against the modern state in the name of the individual; rather, they are struggles against the modern state's government of individualization (Foucault, 1983, p. 212). Foucault offers the feminist movement and the anti-psychiatry movement as examples of such struggles. Given that subjection is one of the principal mechanisms through which disciplinary power and biopower operate, resistance to modern power will involve refusing our subjection and promoting new forms of subjectivity.

The goal of promoting new forms of subjectivity leads us to the emphasis in Foucault's late work (from the early 1980s) on ethical practices of the self. The thread that connects Foucault's late work on the self to his earlier analysis of power is the concept of 'governmentality'. As Foucault uses the term, 'government' refers not (or at least not only) to the institutions or structures of the state; rather, it refers primarily to a way of understanding the conduct of individuals. For Foucault, to govern is, in a broad sense, 'to structure the possible field of action of others' (Foucault, 1983, p. 221). Governmentality in this sense concerns the intersection of the relationship of the self to itself and of the self to others (Foucault, 1997b, p. 300). The notion of governmentality thus provides Foucault with a way of understanding power—which involves both determining the conduct of others and having ones' conduct determined by others' conduct—while preserving a space for freedom—which is implicit in the idea of ethical practices of the self. Government, the conduct of conduct, is a matter not only of the state's management of its citizenry, but also of the parent's management of children and the household, the priest's shepherding of his flock, and the individual's control and care of themself. This notion has inspired a great deal of research in what is now called 'governmentality studies' (Rose et al., 2006) and some work in disability studies (Tremain, 2005) and post-colonial theory as well (Chakrabarty, 2000; Mahmood, 2005).

On feminism, see Chapter 9.

On post-colonial theory, see Chapter 11.

Foucault's ethics

Foucault's account of ethical practices of the self consists of detailed explorations of ancient Greek and Greco-Roman ethical texts. His aim in developing this account is to provide some resources for challenging the government of individualization that holds sway in contemporary Western societies. However, we must be very careful here. Foucault is not claiming that those engaged in contemporary struggles against subjection should live their lives by or organize their social movements around the precepts of ancient Greek or Roman ethics. Greek ethics is not the solution to the problems posed by modern disciplinary and biopolitical power relations. Nevertheless, Foucault finds these ancient notions of practices of the self appealing inasmuch as they focus on living a beautiful, noble, and memorable life rather than, as in modern ethical views, following some moral law or being governed by some disciplinary norm.

Foucault begins his study of ancient ethics by distinguishing between moral codes, or rules for right action, and ethical forms of subjectivation, which concern the proper modes of self-formation of the ethical subject in relation to those codes (Foucault, 1984, p. 26). Foucault maintains that every morality (in the broad sense of that term) consists of both moral codes and ethical forms of subjectivation, but each morality tends to foreground one or the other of these elements. Whereas morality in modern Western societies tends to be more code-orientated (and this is true not only of Christian morality, which Foucault has in mind, but also of much work in analytic moral philosophy, which tends to focus on providing justification for specific moral rules or principles), morality in ancient Greece and Rome was focused more on ethical subjectivation or practices of the self. Although the relative importance of moral codes has become more pronounced over time, Foucault maintains that the content of those moral codes themselves has remained strikingly consistent. He identifies three moral rules relating to sexuality common to Greek and Greco-Roman antiquity, the Christian middle ages, and modern Western societies: the prohibitions on excessive sexual activity, extra-marital sexual relationships, and homosexual acts. Despite the continuity of these moral codes, however, there are significant shifts from antiquity through Christianity up to the present in the forms of ethical subjectivation. In volumes 2 and 3 of his *History of Sexuality*, Foucault charts these shifts.

Foucault identifies four aspects of these forms of ethical subjectivation. The first is the ethical substance, which refers to that aspect of ourselves or our behaviour that is relevant for ethical judgement. During Greek and Greco-Roman antiquity, Foucault maintains that the ethical substance is 'aphrodisiac', which centres on the sexual act (Foucault, 1997a, p. 263); thus, ethical judgement concerns what one does. This aspect of ethics undergoes a significant shift in the Christian era from aphrodisia to desire; with this shift, ethical judgement comes to focus not on what one does but on what—or whom—one desires. The second aspect is the mode of subjection, or the way in which the individual subjects himself to the moral rule and recognizes himself as bound by it (Foucault, 1985, p. 26). For the Greeks, the mode of subjection is both political and aesthetic: if one rules over others, one must live a beautiful life, and in order to live a beautiful life, one is obliged to follow the moral codes regarding sexuality. In the Christian period, the mode of subjection shifts from the conditions for living a beautiful life to the obligation to follow divine law. The third aspect is the ascetic practices of the self, practices through which one transforms oneself into an ethical subject (Foucault, 1985, p. 26). For the Greeks, ascetic practices are practices of self-mastery and self-control. The specific ascetic practices of Greco-Roman antiquity, such as self-examination and conscience-guiding, are later taken up by the medieval Christians, and transformed into self-deciphering, confessional techniques that reveal the inner workings of one's soul. The final aspect is the *telos* or goal of ethical forms of subjectivation, or the kind of being that we aspire to become when we act ethically (Foucault, 1997a, p. 265). For Greek and Greco-Roman antiquity, the *telos* of ethics is self-mastery; for Christianity, the telos of ethics is moral purity and immortality.

What does this account of the transformations of forms of ethical subjectivation in the ancient world and the Middle Ages have to do with Foucault's analysis of contemporary power relations? Foucault notes that the aesthetic dimension of ancient ethics—the focus on living a beautiful life—makes the ancients' conception of the self very different from our own (Foucault, 1997a, p. 271). According to Foucault's diagnosis, medieval Christianity replaced the emphasis on ethical self-creation in antiquity with a self-renunciation designed to enable one to attain spiritual purity and immortality. Thus, he explains,

the problem of ethics as an aesthetics of existence is covered over by the problem of purification. This new Christian self had to be constantly examined because in this self were lodged concupiscence and desires of the flesh. From that moment on, the self was no longer something to be made but something to be renounced and deciphered. (Foucault, 1997a, p. 274)

In the modern era, despite the relative decline in the influence of Christianity, these themes of self-renunciation and self-deciphering have not disappeared. Instead, they have been incorporated into the juridical and disciplinary apparatus of the modern secular state. As a result, our own practices of the self are markedly different from the ancient aesthetics of existence.

However, Foucault does not think that the ancient forms of self-relation have completely disappeared. Instead they have been taken up and transformed in Christianity (Foucault, 1997a, pp. 277–8). As I discussed in the previous paragraph, the Christian pastorate adopted certain techniques of self-examination and conscience-guiding from the Stoics, Epicureans, and Pythagoreans, and transformed them into techniques for deciphering the souls of their flock. Something akin to these self-examination techniques survives in our own, modern, secular confessional practices, for example, in contemporary psychotherapy (Foucault, 1993, pp. 200–1). What is central for Foucault is that these practices of the self are neither dominating nor freedom-enhancing in themselves; everything depends on how they are used, to what ends, in what sorts of circumstances. Such practices can be used to reinforce modern disciplinary power and biopower (as Foucault tends to view the practice of modern psychiatry), but they can also be turned against themselves and taken up in transformative ways. Indeed, if, as Foucault argues, power is co-extensive with the social body, then there is no way of escaping power altogether. Thus, resistance for Foucault will have to take the form of working through existing relations of power and subjection in a transformative way. As Foucault sees it, resistance to what we referred to above as the government of individualization involves transforming modern relations of subjection from within. If our own modes of subjection are related, however distantly, to ancient technologies of the self, then this continuity makes it possible for us to recover certain elements of ancient practices of the self and to marshal those resources in our contemporary struggles against subjection.

3.3 Deconstruction, justice, and democracy: Jacques Derrida

Jacques Derrida was a prolific philosopher whose work had a profound influence on philosophy, literary theory and criticism, and cultural studies. He is perhaps best known as the founding father of 'deconstruction', an approach to language and meaning that radically changed the way that many people read literary and philosophical texts. In the late 1980s and early 1990s, he began explicitly highlighting the ethical and political dimensions of deconstruction. These writings are the most relevant for students of world politics (for some examples of recent work in world politics that draws heavily on Derrida's work, see Bulley, 2009; Campbell, 1998a; Edkins, 2000; Zehfuss, 2002, 2007). The following sections will explain:

- the term 'deconstruction' and its relation to différance;
- the 'ethical-political' turn in Derrida's work;
- Derrida's account of ethical responsibility;
- his understanding of justice;
- his analysis of democracy.

Deconstruction and différance

The term deconstruction is open to much misunderstanding. Derrida himself preferred to think of it as an activity or a process of reading, rather than a method, since method implies that deconstruction is a unified concept, whereas deconstruction itself calls into question precisely the assumption that concepts are unified. Deconstruction is a way of reading texts—for Derrida, those texts were primarily the philosophical texts of the Western tradition, although later in his career he also became interested in religious texts—that reveals the fundamental contradictions in the text and what the text leaves unsaid. A basic assumption of Derrida's is that there is no outside-the-text (Derrida, 1998, p. 158), by which he means that reality cannot be known independently of our representations of it. Although this is one of Derrida's more controversial claims, it has been used productively in international relations theory as the basis for an argument against social constructivism (Zehfuss, 2002).

Deconstruction offers a critique of Western metaphysics (the philosophical study of the ultimate nature of reality), with Plato's metaphysics being the primary point of reference. Platonic metaphysics is based on the assumption that reality is structured in terms of a basic hierarchical opposition between the timeless, universal essences of things—known as the forms—and the ever-changing, contingent, sensible particulars that we experience in the world around us—the realm of appearances. Related to this basic opposition between essence and appearance are a whole host of other binary, hierarchical oppositions that also undergird Western philosophical thought, including truth versus falsity, being versus nothingness, same versus other, one versus many, and masculine versus feminine. The important point for Derrida is that these are not just philosophical distinctions, they are also hierarchical oppositions, according to which essence is privileged over appearance, truth over falsity, and so on. Derrida suggests that deconstruction proceeds in two phases (Derrida, 1981, pp. 4–6). In its first phase, deconstruction attacks the belief in these rigid hierarchies by reversing them. For example, deconstruction privileges appearance over essence, by arguing that all of our knowledge of essences is actually grounded in our experience of appearances. In its second phase, deconstruction re-inscribes the previously inferior term as the source of the original opposition. So, appearance is not only more fundamental than essence, it is also the source of the very distinction between appearance and essence. At some point, the philosophical tradition made a decision to try to separate essence from appearance and established this hierarchy. However, this is ultimately an impossible decision because these rigid hierarchical oppositions cannot be maintained; one term of the opposition always and necessarily infects the other. Derrida's deconstructions of philosophical texts show how oppositions, such as essence/appearance, cannot be sustained and ultimately break down.[1]

In one of Derrida's most famous essays, he uses the term **'différance'** to demonstrate this deconstructive logic (Derrida, 1982). As a term, différance is designed to destabilize the binary oppositions fundamental to Western metaphysical thought, to reveal the ways in which such oppositions dissolve and their opposing terms reverse and slide into one another. Derrida claims that 'différance is literally neither a word nor a concept' (Derrida, 1982, p. 3). Différance is a neologism—the French word for difference is spelled différence; Derrida substitutes an 'a' for the second 'e'—hence, it is, strictly speaking, not a word at all. Nor is différance simply a concept like any other concept; rather, Derrida claims, it is the condition of possibility of all conceptuality inasmuch as it refers to the process of signification whereby concepts are able to mean anything at all. The term différance is derived from the French verb différer, which means both to differ and to defer. The meaning of any concept necessarily differs from—that is, fails to match exactly—the thing to which it refers and, thus, its meaning is endlessly deferred, made sense of only through its relation to other concepts. Because it is the condition of possibility of all conceptuality and, thus, of all meaning, différance produces all binary oppositions; as such, it necessarily exceeds these binary oppositions. Yet, Derrida believes that we have no way of thinking apart from these binaries. Derrida uses the term différance to indicate the limitations of our concepts and our language, but not to overcome them, for this is, in his view, impossible.

Derrida's 'ethical-political turn'

Although it may not be obvious from the above definition, the deconstructive critique of metaphysics has political implications (for a discussion of those implications in the context of Bosnian national identity, see Campbell [1998a]). This is not so easy to see with the example of essence/appearance opposition, but it is more evident if we consider the masculine/feminine opposition. Derridean feminists have used deconstruction to reverse the standard hierarchical opposition between masculine and feminine, and to re-inscribe the feminine as the source and origin of that opposition, thereby destabilizing that binary (Holland, 1997). To be sure, Derrida insists that

there never was in the 1980s or 1990s, as has sometimes been claimed, a *political turn* or *ethical turn* in 'deconstruction', at least not as I experience it. The thinking of the political has always been a thinking of différance and the thinking of différance always a thinking *of* the political, of the contour and limits of the political ... (Derrida, 2005, p. 39).

Nevertheless, it is the case that the ethical and political dimensions became much more prominent in this later phase of his work.

---

[1] For helpful discussion of the different definitions of 'deconstruction' in Derrida's work, see Lawlor (2006).

In his essay, 'The Force of Law', Derrida frames the ethical and political dimensions of deconstruction in terms of its relation to justice (Derrida, 1989–90, pp. 921–23). Indeed, one of the aims of the essay is 'to show why and how what is now called Deconstruction, while seeming not to "address" the problem of justice, has done nothing but address it, if only obliquely, unable to do so directly' (Derrida, 1989–90, p. 935). In response to those critics who assume that deconstruction must undermine or destabilize the distinction between justice and injustice, thus resulting in moral nihilism, Derrida offers another definition of deconstruction, this time emphasizing its political rather than its metaphysical aspects. Here, he distinguishes two styles (rather than phases) of deconstruction. The first style focuses on uncovering the history of our concepts, such as the concept of justice (Derrida, 1989–90, p. 955). Here, one might draw interesting connections between Derrida and Foucault, who was also committed to offering a genealogical history of our concepts. The second style has more in common with Derrida's earlier definition of deconstruction, and it focuses on the formal task of examining the paradoxes or aporias—the unresolvable, but also unavoidable logical contradictions—that emerge as we try to pin down the meaning of our concepts. Derrida's focus in this essay is on the unstable aporia between law understood as a specific and calculable system of rules that we are obliged to follow and justice as an infinite and incalculable ethical-political demand (Derrida, 1989–90, p. 957). As Derrida puts it,

it turns out that *droit* [law or right] claims to exercise itself in the name of justice and that justice is required to establish itself in the name of a law that must be "enforced". Deconstruction always finds itself between these two poles. (Derrida, 1989–90, pp. 959–61)

Ethical responsibility

Derrida's account of the ethical-political dimensions of deconstruction draws a good deal of inspiration from the ethical work of the French philosopher Emmanuel Levinas.[2] In particular, Derrida draws on Levinas's notion of ethical responsibility, understood as an infinite, asymmetrical, non-reciprocal demand placed on us by the other in the face-to-face encounter. For Levinas, this demand is asymmetrical and non-reciprocal because it is rooted in the absolute transcendence of the other, that is, in the fact that the other lies wholly beyond me. This means that her world cannot be assimilated to or contained within my own. Levinas understands the face-to-face encounter as first and foremost an ethical, affective encounter, and only secondarily or derivatively a cognitive one. The face of the other issues to me an ethical demand—'do not kill me'—and calls on me to be responsive to that demand (Bergo, 2007). Derrida draws on Levinas to analyse what he calls the aporia or paradox of responsibility. Responsibility is paradoxical because it has *both* a moment of universality or generality—a general demand that one answer for oneself—*and* a moment of absolute uniqueness and singularity—a responsibility to or for this unique, irreplaceable other (Derrida, 2008, p. 62).

---

[2] For a helpful discussion of Levinas and Derrida's understandings of ethical responsibility in the context of international relations, see Campbell (1999).

As an illustration of this paradox, Derrida offers a reading of the biblical story of Abraham and Isaac.[3] If we think about this story from the point of view of Abraham's responsibility to his son, his willingness to sacrifice Isaac seems to be, at best, an extreme expression of his faith and, at worst, a monstrous disregard for his son's welfare. Either way, the story seems exceptional and extraordinary. However, Derrida insists, if we think about it from the point of view of Abraham's responsibility to God, the story reveals something that is basic to our common, everyday experience of ethical responsibility. As he puts it,

As soon as I enter into a relation with the absolute other [God], my singularity enters into relation with his on the level of obligation and duty. I am responsible before the other as other; I answer to him and I answer for what I do before him. But of course, what binds me thus in my singularity to the absolute singularity of the other immediately propels me into the space or risk of absolute sacrifice....I cannot respond to the call, the request, the obligation, or even the love of another without sacrificing the other other, the other others (Derrida, 2008, pp. 68–69).

Abraham cannot respond to God's command, cannot fulfil his responsibility to God, without sacrificing the other other, represented in this story by his son Isaac. Moreover, Derrida suggests that our everyday ethical relationship to the other is structurally the same as Abraham's relationship to God. Following Levinas, Derrida maintains that, like God, the other is absolutely and infinitely transcendent, it lies wholly beyond my own consciousness or experience (Derrida, 2008, p. 78). In this sense, the experience of the other is akin to the experience of the divine. Derrida sums this up with this phrase: '*Every other (one) is every (bit) other [tout autre est tout autre]*' (Derrida, 2008, p. 69). Every other is wholly other, hence, my relationship to the other is like Abraham's relationship to God, and it demands of me an infinite, asymmetrical, non-reciprocal ethical responsibility.

Justice

Derrida's account of justice is grounded in his Levinasian analysis of ethical responsibility. For Derrida, as for Levinas, at its most fundamental level, justice is simply the incalculable, infinite, ethical relationship to others (Derrida, 1994, p. 23). Hence, Derrida uses the term 'justice' quite differently than liberal political philosophers such as Rawls or critical theorists such as Habermas. Justice for Derrida refers to an infinite ethical demand, rather than to a set of principles that govern the **basic structure** of society or a set of procedures by means of which norms can be justified. Derrida also relates his notion of justice to his understanding of deconstruction, but in a way that is perhaps surprising. Whereas his earlier work on deconstruction might be interpreted as suggesting that all hierarchical oppositions or distinctions, including that between justice and injustice, can be shown ultimately to break down, Derrida himself claims that justice is what makes the practice of deconstruction possible. Hence, he writes, 'justice in itself, if such a thing exists, outside or beyond law, is not deconstructible. No more than deconstruction itself, if such a thing exists. Deconstruction is justice ...' (Derrida, 1989–90, p. 945; see also Derrida, 1994, pp. 27–28). The claim that justice is undeconstructible only makes sense when one

On Rawls's theory of justice, see Chapter 1.

[3] See Genesis 22: 1–24. God commands Abraham to sacrifice his son Isaac. Abraham sets out to obey God's command and binds Isaac to the altar, but before he can carry out the sacrifice, the angel of the Lord steps in and stops him. Abraham sacrifices a ram that he finds nearby instead.

appreciates the complexity of Derrida's notion of justice. First of all, Derrida distinguishes justice from law or right (*droit*). Law refers to the specific, calculable, juridical norms that govern our social and political lives. Justice, by contrast, is an infinite, incalculable demand rooted in the absolute, asymmetrical, non-reciprocal ethical relationship to the other. Secondly, for Derrida, justice, unlike law, is not something that actually exists or ever can actually exist in a determinate future. Rather, it is always on the way, thus, it is always, necessarily, a justice-to-come (*à venir*) (Derrida, 1989–90, p. 969).

The idea of justice to come distinguishes Derrida's political thought from various strains of utopian political thinking. Derrida does not presuppose the possibility of achieving a just social and political order at some point in the determinate future. Rather, for Derrida, justice is of necessity infinitely deferred, and the idea of justice-to-come serves as the principle for a radical and ongoing critique of the present (Derrida, 1994, p. 90). Derrida uses the phrase 'messianicity without messianism' to refer to this future-oriented but non-utopian conception of justice. The notion of messianicity refers to the experience of emancipatory promise that is necessarily implicit in the notion of justice-to-come; by saying that it is a messianicity without messianism, Derrida signals that this is not a religious notion (Derrida, 1994, p. 59). Like the notion of justice, messianicity without messianism is undeconstructible. As Derrida puts it, messianicity without messianism 'remains undeconstructible because the movement of any deconstruction presupposes it' (Derrida, 1999, p. 253).

Democracy-to-come

Related to these notions of justice-to-come and messianicity without messianism is Derrida's conception of democracy. Derrida understands democracy in terms of its fundamental promise, which is the promise of an infinite hospitality or absolute openness toward the other. Derrida calls this absolute openness toward the other 'hospitality without reserve' (Derrida, 1994, p. 65). Derrida acknowledges that such an absolute openness to the singularity of the other is impossible to attain, but he also insists that its very impossibility is the condition of possibility of the democratic. Thus, as with justice, Derrida always speaks not simply of democracy, but of democracy-to-come. The idea of democracy-to-come refers to the ineliminable gap between democracy's infinite promise and the determinate, but necessarily inadequate forms that democracy takes (Derrida, 1994, p. 65).

Derrida insists that democracy is related to the notion of différance that has such prominence in his earlier work. Like différance, democracy both defers itself and differs from itself. It defers itself in that it is always to come, it always refers to a future that is not a future present but an indefinite future. It differs from itself in that it contains within itself the ineliminable gap between its infinite promise and its determinate forms. Democracy thus refers us back to différance, but Derrida maintains,

… not only to différance as deferral, as the turn of a detour, as a path that is turned aside, as adjournment in the economy of the same. For what is also and at the same time at stake—and marked by this same word in *différance*—is différance as reference or referral to the other, that is, as the undeniable, and I underscore *undeniable*, experience of the alterity [otherness] of the other, of heterogeneity, of the singular, the not-same, the different, the dissymmetric, the heteronomous. (Derrida, 1994, p. 38)

Here, Derrida claims that implicit in the notion of différance is not only the infinite deferral and slippage of meaning that was a prominent theme in his early work, but also the ethical responsibility that structures our relationship to the other that is a prominent theme in his later work.

What makes democracy distinctive as a form of political organization, for Derrida, is that its very structure draws attention to this gap. That is to say, Derrida views democracy as uniquely open to internal criticism, dissent, and self-transformation, thus, as uniquely concerned with its own perfectibility (Derrida, 2005, p. 25). Democracy is the only political system that is intrinsically open to a radical form of self-criticism in which everything is fair game, including the core ideals of democracy themselves, such as the rule of law and the value of freedom. Even the value of democracy itself can be questioned within a democratic context. Thus, democracy is 'the only system that welcomes in itself, in its very concept, that expression of autoimmunity called the right to self-critique and perfectibility ... It is thus the only paradigm that is universalizable, whence its chance and its fragility' (Derrida, 2005, pp. 86–7).

As with the notion of justice-to-come, the 'to-come' in democracy-to-come signals that democracy as such will never have a determinate existence because the structure of democracy is internally aporetic or paradoxical. It entails, as Derrida says, 'force *without* force, incalculable singularity *and* calculable equality, commensurability *and* incommensurability, heteronomy *and* autonomy, indivisible sovereignty *and* divisible or shared sovereignty, an empty name, a despairing messianicity or a messianicity in despair, and so on' (Derrida, 2005, p. 86). Thus, the notion of democracy-to-come is also related to the necessity of an ongoing, radical critique of the present.

3.4 Post-structuralism as critique

Foucault and Derrida did not develop their ideas about ethics and politics in isolation. Not only were they in conversation with each other, they also engaged in important debates with thinkers who were influenced by different traditions. In particular, the German critical theorist, Jürgen Habermas, proved to be an important interlocutor for both Foucault and Derrida. In this final section, I will:

On Habermas, see Chapter 2.

- discuss the core of Habermas's criticisms of Foucault and Derrida;
- identify the similarities between post-structuralism and Habermasian critical theory.

Habermas and other critical theorists have raised a number of incisive criticisms of post-structuralism (Habermas, 1987/1990; McCarthy, 1991; Fraser, 1989). In general, Habermas understands post-structuralism as a rejection of the project of modernity, with its emphasis on **Enlightenment** reason and universal morality. He fears that this rejection leads at best to relativism, at worst to an anti-modern conservatism. With respect to Foucault, Habermas argues that Foucault's genealogy treats both truth and normative validity as nothing more than relations of power. As a result, Foucault's analysis of power is, on Habermas's view, mired in relativism and 'crypto-normative'—in other words, it is unable to defend consistently its own implicit normative position (Habermas, 1987/1990, p. 282). Habermas contends that because he presents normative validity as nothing more than a certain kind of power relation, Foucault cannot explain how social order is possible, since valid social norms play a crucial role in creating and maintaining a stable social world. Nor can he explain how individual and society are related, since his account of subjection views individuals as copies 'mechanically punched out' by disciplinary power (Habermas, 1987/1990, p. 293). Although he does not discuss Foucault's late work on ethics and the Enlightenment in detail, Habermas suggests that this work stands in stark contradiction to his earlier work (Habermas, 1989, p. 179; McCarthy, 1991).

With respect to Derrida, Habermas claims that Derrida's deconstruction offers a radical critique of reason and logic, arguing instead for the primacy of rhetoric and poetry. The problem, as Habermas sees it, is that in order to critique reason and logic, Derrida has to rely on the tools of reason and logic. This means that Derrida's deconstruction is guilty, in Habermas's eyes, of a 'performative contradiction', which means that the performance of the critique relies on the very rational and logical tools that are being criticized and rejected. As Habermas sees it, Derrida's emphasis on the primacy of the poetic dimensions of language also leads him to neglect the rational potential inherent in linguistic communication, its ability to help us solve problems and to co-ordinate our interactions.

Contra Habermas, however, it is possible to read Foucault as a thinker who aims not to reject, but rather to transform the Enlightenment project from within (Allen, 2008). This is, in fact, how Foucault presents his own philosophical work in an important late essay (Foucault, 1997b). This reading complicates considerably Habermas's interpretation of Foucault as an anti-modern young conservative who sets out to abstractly negate the Enlightenment project only to find himself unwittingly drawn back into its orbit. It is also possible to question Habermas's portrayal of Foucault's genealogical analysis of the subject as a 'mechanically punched out' copy (Allen, 2008). Indeed, challenging this reading is particularly important in light of Foucault's late work on practices of the self, which presuppose a degree of autonomy and deliberate self-transformation that would seem impossible if Habermas's reading of Foucault's earlier work is correct. The fuller picture of Foucault's account of the self that emerges from his late work is that of a self who engages in practices of self-formation and self-discipline, although these do not take place outside of power relations. Although Foucault himself may not have given a completely satisfactory account of how his late work on self-constituting ethical practices and his earlier genealogical analysis of the disciplined subject are compatible, the existence of the former once again calls into question Habermas's account of the latter. It is also possible to rethink the normative stance of Foucault's critique, by uncovering an implicit norm of freedom at work in Foucault's texts (Oksala, 2005). This reading calls into question Habermas's charge that Foucault thinks of moral or political norms as nothing more than power relations. Each of these reinterpretations makes it possible to challenge the received view of the Foucault–Habermas debate, according to which Foucault and Habermas offer diametrically opposed approaches to ethical and political theory.

Habermas's critique of Derrida, like his critique of Foucault, is predicated on presenting Derrida as an anti-modern, anti-Enlightenment thinker who rejects reason in favour of its rhetorical and poetic Other. Yet, as with Foucault, it is possible to read Derrida as a philosopher who is self-consciously transforming the Enlightenment from within. On this reading, Derrida's aim is not to collapse or dissolve the distinctions between rhetoric and logic, or literature and philosophy. Rather, the aim is to problematize such distinctions, to demonstrate their impurity by showing how one side of the opposition necessarily infects the other, and to reflect on the philosophical and political implications of such impurity. This reading of Derrida complicates Habermas's portrayal of him as an anti-modern young conservative. Further complicating Habermas's critique is the fact that it is based entirely on Derrida's early work. As such, it does not take into account the ethical-political 'turn' of his late work. This is a pity, because in that ethical and political work, a good deal more common ground emerges between Derrida and Habermas than is evident in Habermas's critique.[4] Derrida's embrace of our infinite ethical responsibility toward the other, his gestures toward an impossible and necessary justice to come, and his embrace of an inherently open, contestable and self-critical form of democracy bring his work into closer contact with Habermas's central concerns. In fact, toward the end of Derrida's life, he and Habermas collaborated on a few projects that bring to light some of those shared concerns (Borradori, 2003; Habermas & Derrida, 2003).

If Habermas, Foucault, and Derrida can all be productively understood as transforming the critical project of the Enlightenment from within, albeit in different ways, then their disagreements look less like a war between entrenched philosophical camps and more like a family quarrel. This quarrel will be resolved only when we are no longer held captive by the picture of Habermas as the pro-modern, pro-Enlightenment, progressive hero, and Foucault and Derrida as the anti-modern, counter-Enlightenment, young conservative villains. As that picture loses its ability to captivate us, productive new visions of a simultaneously deconstructive and reconstructive critical theory may begin to emerge.

3.5 Conclusion

As was stated at the outset of this chapter, there is no uniform 'post-structuralist' position on ethics and politics. Rather, the two main 'post-structuralist' ethical and political thinkers discussed here offer diverse and internally heterogeneous perspectives on some fundamental issues in ethical and political theory, including the constitution of the ethical subject, the nature of ethical responsibility, and how best to understand the notions of power, government, justice, and democracy. These perspectives offer productive starting points for contemporary students of ethics and world politics.

---

[4] For an exploration of that common ground in the context of the post-9/11 political landscape, see Borradori (2003).

■ QUESTIONS

1. What does it mean to say that Foucault understands power as relational and strategic? Explain how Foucault's view of power differs from the juridical conception of power.

2. What does Foucault mean by the term 'subjection'? What role does this concept play in Foucault's analysis of power?

3. What does Foucault mean by the term 'governmentality'? What role does this concept play in Foucault's work?

4. How does Foucault understand the term ethics? How does this understanding differ from the other understandings of ethics presented in this book?

5. Explain what Derrida means by deconstruction, and how this is related to the term 'différance'.

6. What is Derrida's account of the relationship between deconstruction and justice? How does Derrida's understanding of justice differ from that of liberal political philosophers, such as Rawls, or critical theorists, such as Habermas?

7. How does Derrida understand ethical responsibility?

8. Explain Derrida's account of democracy-to-come. What are some similarities and differences between Derrida and Habermas's understandings of democracy?

9. What criticisms does Habermas offer of Foucault, and how might one respond to them on Foucault's behalf?

10. What criticisms does Habermas offer of Derrida, and how might one respond to them on Derrida's behalf?

■ FURTHER READING

Beardsworth, R. (1996) *Derrida and the Political*. New York: Routledge. This is the first book to consider the political implications of Derrida's notion of deconstruction.

Borradori, G. (2003) *Philosophy in a Time of Terror: Dialogues with Jürgen Habermas and Jacques Derrida*. Chicago: University of Chicago Press. This book contains interviews with Habermas and Derrida in which they reflect on the role of political philosophy in the context of the 'war on terror', as well as helpful critical discussions of the work of each philosopher.

Campbell, D., & Shapiro, M.J. (eds) (1999) *Moral Spaces: Rethinking Ethics and World Politics*. Minneapolis: University of Minnesota Press. This edited collection reconsiders the relationship between ethics and world politics, and the normative underpinnings of international relations. Editors and contributors to the volume draw extensively, but not uncritically, on the work of Foucault, Derrida, and Levinas.

Critchley, S. (2000) *The Ethics of Deconstruction: Derrida and Levinas*, Edinburgh: Edinburgh University Press. This influential book was the first to argue for the ethical turn in Derrida's work and to show the ethical implications of deconstruction.

Dillon, M., & Neal, A. (eds) (2008) *Foucault on Politics, Security and War*. New York: Palgrave. This edited collection considers the relevance of Foucault's work for questions of international politics, security, and war, with particular focus on such topics as the 'war on terror', biosecurity, and the global AIDS epidemic.

Edkins, J. (1999) *Post-structuralism and International Relations: Bringing the Political Back In*. Boulder: Lynne Rienner Press. This book offers a clear introduction to post-structuralist theory (including the work of Foucault and Derrida) and argues for the importance of post-structuralism to international relations.

Kelly, M. (1994) *Critique and Power: Recasting the Foucault/Habermas Debate*, Cambridge: MIT Press. This collection combines critical chapters by Habermas on Foucault and vice versa with critical commentaries on the Foucault–Habermas debate by distinguished philosophers and political theorists.

Simons, J. (1995) *Foucault and the Political*. New York: Routledge. This book offers a clear overview of the implications of Foucault's thought for political theory and brings Foucault's work into conversation with thinkers in the liberal, feminist, communitarian, and critical theory traditions.

■ WEB LINKS

http://www.foucault.qut.edu.au/ This site offers a variety of resources related to Foucault, including bibliographies of his writings and critical commentaries on his work.

http://hydra.humanities.uci.edu/derrida/ This site offers a variety of resources related to Derrida, including bibliographies, excerpts from his work, and audio clips of some interviews with Derrida.

http://plato.stanford.edu/entries/foucault A clear, comprehensive overview of Foucault's life and work from *The Stanford Encyclopedia of Philosophy*.

http://plato.stanford.edu/entries/derrida An excellent short overview of Derrida's life and work, including a helpful discussion of the political implications of deconstruction, from *The Stanford Encyclopedia of Philosophy*.

http://www.rienner.com/title/Alternatives_Global_Local_Political The website for the journal *Alternatives*, which publishes work in political theory and international politics, much of which is influenced by post-structuralist theory.

Visit the Online Resource Centre that accompanies this book to access more learning resources: **www.oxfordtextbooks.co.uk/orc/bell_ethics/**

4 Ethics and politics

Andrew Gamble

READER'S GUIDE

The relationship between ethics and politics has been understood in different ways, giving rise to different conceptions of politics, and of the relationship between theory and practice. A central issue is whether ethical rules apply universally or whether different rules apply as far as politics is concerned. Three particular approaches are explored here; deontological, consequentialist, and contextualist. Each understands the relation of ethics to politics in different ways. Deontological ethics reasons from first principles and the notion of an ideal community, and judges politics by how far it reaches the ideal. Consequentialist ethics reasons from outcomes, and judges politics by how far it maximizes the public good. Contextualist ethics reasons from circumstances and judges politics by its own internal criteria, rather than some external standard. The implications of these approaches are brought out by considering debates over globalization.

4.1 Introduction

There have always been different ways of understanding the relationship between ethics and politics. They go to the heart of what is understood by politics and by ethics, and by the relationship between theory and practice. What role does ethics play in politics and what role should it play? The dominant tradition in Western political theory, first set out by Plato, makes the claim that reflecting on the principles and ethical ideals that should guide political action is the most important task of the political philosopher. Immanuel

Kant provided the most influential modern expression of this standpoint, and inaugurated a way of thinking about ethics in terms of first principles that has recently been revived by John Rawls. The main rival to this way of thinking within liberalism has been the **consequentialist** ethics associated with **utilitarianism**, arguing that it is outcomes that should be used to judge whether an action is right or not, rather than conformity to first principles. Various critiques that propose some kind of contextualist ethics offer alternatives to both **deontological** and consequentialist positions. These argue that political philosophers should concentrate on understanding how politics works and how the world is actually ordered, rather than speculate about ideal orders or use abstract concepts of the public good to judge politics. This contrast has been expressed by the distinction between idealism and materialism, and between idealism and **realism**, but many other terms have been also employed.

Within the idealist tradition there is also a more recent contrast in contemporary liberal political theory between **ideal** and **non-ideal theory**, associated with the work of Rawls. This chapter considers the nature of ideal and non-ideal theory, and then looks at other forms of rationalism in politics, before turning to some of the critics, particularly those who employ realist and contextualist arguments, which emphasize power, interests, and agency, to argue for alternative ways of understanding the relationship between ethics and politics, and more generally the part which theory should play in politics (Dunn, 1990). Some of these issues are then considered in relation to the debate about the possibility of a cosmopolitan legal order and its implications for the international state system.

4.2 Ideal and non-ideal theory

Ethics denotes moral systems, or even more simply, rules of conduct. As such, it is inseparable from how we understand human activity, and from politics. It defines what is good and what is bad, what is to be prized and what shunned. No area of human activity, including politics, could be without ethics in this sense. The debate about the relationship between ethics and politics is about what kind of ethics should apply. Part of the confusion arises because we have come to think of ethics as something outside practice. Ethics is, however, embedded in practices. It is the reflection on those practices that allows ethics to be codified and, once codified, ethics then takes on a life of its own. It can be abstracted and purified, providing universal, timeless and absolute criteria, which are used to judge behaviour. The debate in political theory about the right relationship between ethics and politics is about whether the various ethical codes that are available to us, including the abstract discourse about ethics that has developed in contemporary Anglo-American political philosophy, has any relationship to how people in politics actually behave. Should we rely on the internal, embedded ethical codes of politics, which are inextricably interwined with interest and circumstance? Or does it help to have abstract, external codes as well, which can then be made binding in some way, or at least provide criteria which politicians can be expected to follow in making their decisions and which can be used for holding them to account?

Many of the most powerful ethical codes had their origins in religion, which provided precise injunctions, such as 'Thou shalt not kill', as well as more general standards of behaviour. Philosophers have always been interested in these codes, what underpins them, and how conflicts between the various principles and the underlying assumptions of such codes can be clarified and resolved. Many philosophers have set out their own accounts of first principles, as did John Rawls in *A Theory of Justice* in 1971. Rawls was critical of utilitarian ethics and defended what he called ideal theory, a return to thinking about justice in terms of first principles. Such a theory seeks to 'resolve moral disagreement by demonstrating that alternative theories and principles should be rejected' (Gutmann & Thompson, 2004, p. 13). He argued that this would allow us to develop a better account of justice than utilitarianism. The purpose of ideal theory was to develop a political conception of justice that relied on ideals to specify a reasonable and just society, and was therefore in the strict sense utopian, because these ideals are realized nowhere. He rejected the idea that justice could be based on a comprehensive doctrine of how individuals should live their lives, a substantive **conception of the good**. Instead he argued that justice should be based on a set of rules which could be justified to all citizens.

On Rawls's theory of justice, see Chapter 1.

The purpose of political theory was to elucidate what justice is by imagining the best possible conditions for its realization. He later described this as a 'realistic utopia', because it relies on taking human beings as they are, and constitutional and civil laws as they might be, and because its principles must be capable of being applied to existing political and social arrangements (Rawls, 1999), what the eighteenth-century philosopher David Hume had called the 'circumstances of justice'. Such a realistic utopia was still part of ideal theory. Arguing against one of the supreme 'realist' theorists of international relations, E. H. Carr, Rawls maintained that a realistic utopia did not mean a compromise between power and political right and justice, but should 'set limits to the reasonable exercise of power'. Otherwise power would determine what the compromise would be (Rawls, 1999, p. 6, fn 8). He contrasted this idea of ideal theory with non-ideal theory, which explicitly introduced conditions that were not the best possible. Such non-ideal conditions might include the fact that many citizens might be unwilling to comply with the rules of justice, and that societies might be open rather than closed. These were 'non-ideal' because they would make it much more difficult to sustain the kind of agreement on values and criteria that is possible in settled, closed, solidaristic communities.

On realism, see Chapter 5.

Proponents of ideal theory, such as G. A. Cohen and Andrew Mason, have argued that Rawls concedes too much to his critics (Cohen, 2003; Mason, 2004). They argue that there is no need for the theorist to take into account questions of feasibility when constructing theories of justice. To do so risks losing the power to imagine genuine and radical alternatives to the status quo. There is no reason why the debate on alternatives should be closed off in this way. The value of political philosophy is precisely that it can go far beyond what is feasible or acceptable in today's politics. There is no harm if the utopias it proposes are 'unreasonable', provided the argument is cogent enough. What such arguments may do is elucidate truths about our ethical principles that otherwise might be hidden. Mason also suggests that the position Rawls adopts in his later writings can be reformulated. Instead of the two stages of ideal and non-ideal theory, there are really three. The first is the level of pure abstract ideal theory. The second is ideal theory modified by considerations of feasibility and institutional design, Rawls's realistic utopia.

The third stage incorporates non-ideal conditions into the theory. For Mason all three are legitimate areas in which political philosophers should be engaged, but he thinks in practice they are often confused (Mason, 2004).

Other critics of Rawls have wanted to develop non-ideal theory while rejecting ideal theory. For them, realistic utopia is a mirage that is more of a hindrance than a help in developing an effective non-ideal theory. The starting point has to be the non-ideal conditions of the real world, in order to understand the true costs and benefits of different courses of action, and the necessary trade-offs between different principles. Non-ideal theory is still interested in exploring ethical principles and how these might relate to politics. However, it thinks these principles are best clarified within non-ideal theory, rather than arrived at through a thought experiment in which none of these constraints exist (Stears, 2005; Sen, 2009). Adam Swift and Stuart White (2008) highlight the difference between the policies that would be justified in an ideally just society and those that can be justified in societies that fall short of the ideal, the societies in which we live.

Ideal theory remains potent, however, because its advocates, like Cohen and Mason, argue that there is no good reason why thought should be restricted in the way its critics seem to want. Why place restrictions on what we can hope for, just because we cannot immediately see our way to achieving it? (Sangiovanni, 2009). There have been many forms of ideal theory, which differ amongst themselves, but the common thread is the belief that principles for a just or a free or an equal social order can be identified through rational reflection. Kantian and deontological approaches assert that there are principles of conduct, which all individuals at some level acknowledge as valid, and which in some accounts reflect fundamental features of human beings. These principles of conduct may then be distilled to form the basis of a discourse of rights. Robert Nozick's work provides an influential example of this. His starting point in *Anarchy, State and Utopia* takes this form: 'Individuals have rights and there are things no person or group may do to them without violating their rights' (Nozick, 1974, p. ix). This principle governs the argument of the book and is used to evaluate existing political arrangements. If the opening statement about individuals and rights is valid, then any political arrangement which can be shown to violate individuals' rights stands condemned. Nozick deploys the technique to great effect, arguing that a **minimal state** can be justified, but very little beyond it, since from his ethical standpoint all forms of government taxation that redistribute income and wealth and provide services must violate individual rights.

The internal coherence of Nozick's argument is strong and it is hard to fault his objections to the modern extended state if we accept his starting principles. The main weakness of his approach is that there is no easy way to validate this starting point, and if the initial assumptions are challenged, as many have done, the argument collapses. To take one example, Nozick has often been held up as a **libertarian**, but many libertarians have criticized his defence of a minimal state, on the grounds that, in doing so, he has to justify coercion and, therefore, the violation of rights, since to a thorough-going libertarian, taxes raised by the state to fund a police force or external defence are just as much a violation of individuals' rights as taxes raised to fund education and health programmes (Rothbard, 1977). If the only ethical rules of conduct that are legitimate are voluntary unforced exchanges between individuals, it follows that all state action must be illegitimate.

Nozick's libertarian blast against American liberalism is a perfect example of what Raymond Geuss (2008) calls 'politics as applied ethics'. It provides a searing indictment of the way Western democracies have organized their affairs for the last 60 years, and reads like a political manifesto for the dismantling of the extended state, particularly the welfare state, that has grown up during that time. The ethical rules it endorses are crystal clear, but the social conditions in which they are to be applied have been idealized. Nozick is not interested in the circumstances that might make the rolling back of the state not viable or not desirable. His only concession to circumstances and to context is his acceptance of the case for some coercion of citizens as far as defence, and law and order, are concerned. However, in all other areas Nozick's 'entitlement' theory means that the state has to be completely dismantled if the individual is to be free, and individual rights not violated. All existing state services must either be provided by voluntary exchange or not at all.

Such libertarian ethical arguments are an example of ideal theory, and the way in which it can be applied to politics, although the mainstream in the Anglo-American academy has been much more concerned with the defence of various forms of egalitarian, rather than libertarian, ethics. Nozick wrote his entitlement theory of justice in part as a rejoinder to the patterned theory of justice developed by Rawls. Both acknowledged the importance of the principle of justice and both presented their theory as ideal theory. Rawls's influential attempt to restate a theory of justice by rethinking the idea of the **social contract** was very different from Nozick, but what they had in common was the belief that the way to proceed was to develop an ideal theory—idealizing the conditions in which the theory would be applied, and abstracting from history and from actual politics in order to set out their favoured principle of justice in the sharpest and most consistent manner possible.

A great deal of contemporary normative theory, even when it is not explicitly Rawlsian, has proceeded in this manner, although currently there is something of a reaction against it, and the case for non-ideal theory is being made more strongly (Stears, 2005; Swift & White, 2008; Sen, 2009). Critics of Rawls have long argued that to abstract from all the determinants that make choice possible means that the '**veil of ignorance**' transports us to a realm which is outside human experience. Does it then have anything much to tell us about real politics? If Rawls's conception was so far removed from any political experience as to make it unintelligible to us, it would not be interesting. However, Rawls can be understood as making a similar move to John Locke. The **state of nature** that Locke imagined to exist before the formation of the state was already highly social, full of institutions that promoted social co-operation and social solidarity. Similarly, Rawls has suggested in his later work that what he was trying to do was to make the existing arrangements of American society intelligible to its citizens, bringing out the logic of the existing principles of justice that underlay the pattern of inequalities and the pattern of distribution, and showing how their character could be better understood. If a patterned theory of justice was the one that best expressed American arrangements, then it might be used to judge proposals to change or improve those arrangements in the future, and help determine the extent to which the society was just.

In doing this Rawls consciously did not seek to claim **universality** for his theory. He restricted his attention to the kind of society that had been established in the United States in the second half of the twentieth century. His principles of justice were specific to a particular kind of society. Only if other societies became liberal like the United States would the same principles of justice apply to them. In his writings on international affairs, Rawls carefully distinguishes between liberal peoples and non-liberal peoples, and divides the latter into two classes: 'decent hierarchical' peoples, who can be tolerated by liberal peoples, and outlaw states and societies burdened by unfavourable conditions. Both pose problems for a liberal world order (Rawls, 1999, p. 4).

On Rawls's international theory, see Chapter 6.

Rawls sets out this position most clearly in *The Law of Peoples* (1999), which develops Kant's ideas of the conditions for a liberal peace. It dismayed many Rawlsians and some have tried to go beyond it. The solution Rawls adopts to the problem of international justice is strongly influenced by his conception of a realistic utopia. The principles of **social justice** that emerge from the ideal conditions arrived at under the veil of ignorance for a national society can become principles of international justice, through a second contract made between the representatives of justly constituted societies. This would be a league of liberal peoples. This second contract encompasses such principles as equal rights, **self-determination**, the right of self-defence and non-intervention. The veil of ignorance is substantially modified. The body of global citizens is split up into a number of national communities with separate and often competing interests. This still allows the principles of justice set out by Rawls to be extended at least in part to the international sphere. States achieve social justice within their own jurisdictions and this provides the basis for it to be generalized. This approach is similar to that of Kant who accepted the division of the world into separate national jurisdictions, but still maintained that there was an appropriate set of rules for each level of the global order. Politics as applied ethics meant ensuring that human beings lived in a legal constitutional order. Achieving a legal constitutional order at the national level was the passport to membership of the legal constitutional order at the next level. A league of republican states, all observing the same ethical rules of conduct, is the best hope for embedding norms of international justice.

Kant and Rawls were both sceptical about the possibilities of world government and, therefore, deliberately narrowed the application of their principles to the international sphere, while not giving up all hope of making progress. Rawls saw strict practical limits to the universalizing of the principles of justice, but argued that, nevertheless, they were advancing in the contemporary world as more peoples became liberal peoples. A contemporary example of this process in operation is the European Union (EU), membership of which is dependent on fulfilling certain criteria in respect of **human rights**, and political and civic freedoms. This obliges all applicants to achieve a legal constitutional order in their domestic political arrangements, which meets the criteria that the EU has set. The threshold is much higher than that for membership of the United Nations (UN) for example. It makes the EU a Kantian league in a way that the UN is not.

On human rights, see Chapter 13.

One of the consequences of treating politics as applied ethics is that political practice is almost by definition found wanting. The American Declaration of Independence (1776) began with the claim 'We hold these truths to be self-evident, that all men are created equal, that they are endowed by their Creator with certain unalienable Rights, that among these are Life, Liberty and the pursuit of Happiness'. Despite the apparent universal character of these rights in the political practice of the time they did not extend to slaves, indigenous peoples, or women. The proclamation by the French Revolutionaries of 'Liberty, Equality, and Fraternity' was similarly flawed in political practice. The aspirations of the eighteenth-century revolutions ran far ahead of what was politically practicable, but advocates of this rationalist strain of liberalism have defended the proclamation of universal ethical principles that treat all human beings the same, and challenge all societies and states to fulfil these aspirations.

The creation of abstract standards, either in political theory or in political manifestos, is intended to raise the bar for what is possible politically, and the argument is made that notwithstanding all the shortcomings and all the disasters of the last 200 years, there has been substantial progress. One piece of evidence that is often adduced is the increasing number of states that are formally considered to be democracies, and the empirical fact that democracies do not fight one another (Doyle, 1997). The number of democracies has risen sharply since 1945 and currently stands at an all-time high, almost half of all states according to one estimate (Freedom House, 2009). Against that critics point to the huge inequalities which still exist throughout the global economy and the difficulty of reconciling them with principles of justice, and the lack of meaningful international forums where these issues can be addressed substantively, rather than rhetorically. It is this disjunction between a world of ideal theory and ideal distributions and the reality of world politics that makes many question the value of much contemporary normative theory. The gulf between theory and practice just seems too wide.

4.3 Utilitarianism

Treating politics as applied ethics is not anything particularly new. Although it has been given a new and powerful impulse by the kind of normative theory which has flourished particularly in parts of the Anglo-American academy in the last 40 years, its roots lie much further back. It is closely connected with a particular strand of **Enlightenment** liberalism, which was much in evidence in the American and French Revolutions at the end of the eighteenth century and has been a powerful current ever since. Apart from the deontological liberalism of Kant and his followers, the other main strand has been the consequentialism of Bentham and the utilitarians (Quinton, 1989; Rosen, 2006). Utilitarianism is very different in its methods and its approach from Kantianism, but it shares the view that politics should be applied ethics, while disagreeing on what the content of the ethics should be.

Utilitarianism puts the emphasis always on *consequences*, not on first principles. Employing the criterion of the 'greatest happiness of the greatest number'—made famous originally by the philosopher Jeremy Bentham (Schofield, 2006)—as a criterion for judging public policy becomes the means for deciding whether a particular policy is good or bad, and allows it to be judged retrospectively in accordance with whether it achieved its goals. Justifying decisions by their outcomes is a hallmark of this style of thinking, and it was liberating in the nineteenth century in pushing aside numerous vested interests and political obstacles that prevented reform. Asking whether something was useful or not gave utilitarianism its reputation for philistinism but also its radicalism. As an ethical principle it has proved to be extremely powerful (Goodin, 1995).

Utilitarianism is a different kind of ideal theory from a Rawlsian account of social justice, because it is concerned with substantive outcomes, rather than procedural principles. Utilitarianism derives its account of the good from a highly abstract account of human nature, which isolates the pursuit of pleasure and the avoidance of pain as the main drivers of human behaviour and forms the basis for the utilitarian account of self-interest. This abstract ideal theory formed the basis for the modern discipline of economics and it has become one of the most influential methods in the social sciences. It leads to a focus on that aspect of human behaviour which is rational in so far as it is concerned to maximize utility. This approach, as developed by adherents of the 'rational choice' school, has come to dominate much contemporary political science, especially in the United States (Green & Shapiro, 1994). Techniques like cost–benefit analysis and game theory are contemporary manifestations of utilitarianism, as is the discourse on efficiency that pervades so much public policy debate. This is an ideal conception, abstracted from real politics and from social circumstances, and is used to frame choices by comparing outcomes and determining which outcomes are good and which are bad. This form of ideal theory has become embedded in everyday institutions, rather than floating above them in the manner of the ethical principles of cosmopolitanism, and this makes it omnipresent and also harder to detect. It has become common sense, but it is a very strange kind of common sense, resting on very abstract foundations.

On cosmopolitanism, see Chapter 8.

Utilitarianism and Kantianism offer different ethical principles, but they are not wholly irreconcilable, and in some liberal thinkers, such as Friedrich Hayek, Kantian and utilitarian arguments are combined to advocate the kind of society based on free market principles that Hayek favours (Hayek, 1960; Gamble, 1996; Shearmur, 1996). Hayek's mode of argument is another illustration of a conception of the political, which treats politics as applied ethics. Hayek first establishes the principles and procedures of a liberal order, which in his earlier writings are set out in Kantian form, with an emphasis on the general rules that are necessary for such an order to come into existence and be maintained. Hayek envisages what he calls (following Adam Smith) the 'Great Society' as an abstract ideal order, which is not the product of human intention or human design and whose outcomes cannot be controlled by human reason. The shape of this order and its requirements can, however, be grasped by the human mind, which allows political action to prevent others from destabilizing it or interfering with its spontaneous mechanisms. As the philosopher Michael Oakeshott once commented on Hayek: 'a plan to resist all planning may be better than its opposite but it belongs to the same style of politics' (Oakeshott, 1962, p. 21). Despite his powerful critique of rationalism and what he terms the false kind of liberalism, Hayek remains a rationalist himself. He creates an ideal which he counterposes to real politics and which real politics is constantly in danger of subverting.

Hayek did not start from the enunciation of first principles as Nozick did. He was much more sympathetic to Rawls. He disliked the term 'social justice', but he approved of the emphasis Rawls placed on general rules and, therefore, on procedures, rather than on substantive outcomes. Where he diverged from Rawls was that although the general cast of Hayek's thought was Kantian he was increasingly drawn to utilitarianism to provide ethical justifications for the kind of social and economic arrangements that he favoured. In his later writings he used the argument that only the liberal market order with its advanced division of labour and advanced division of knowledge could support the much enlarged population of the world that had grown up in the previous 200 years (Hayek, 1983). Capitalism was the most ethical economic system because only capitalism could feed the world's population. Far from capitalism being the cause of the poverty and the suffering of several billion of the world's poor, as many critics argue, it was indispensable to keeping them alive. Spreading capitalist institutions to all parts of the world was therefore not unethical, but the most ethical policy that could be pursued.

Utilitarian ethics are less discussed in the academy than they once were, but they still pervade most aspects of everyday life. Despite their differences, utilitarians approach politics in the same manner as many Rawlsians, treating it as a realm to which ethics should be applied, the content of the ethics having been determined by a rational process of deliberation divorced from practice. It is this assumption that is challenged by contextualist approaches.

4.4 **Real politics**

The main alternative to understanding politics as applied ethics in the Western tradition has been various kinds of realist and contextualist understandings of politics. One influential strand has argued that politics has its own ethics, and that invoking external ethical criteria or the taking of abstract moral positions has no relevance to real politics. In the realist tradition that runs through Machiavelli, Hobbes, Mandeville, and Marx, the realm of politics and political action is seen as separate from moral discourse, which applies in other spheres. The moral rules that govern private life do not apply, or should be set aside if political action is to be effective and achieve its goals. From this perspective, all forms of ideal theory and the ethics to which they give rise, whether deontological or consequentialist, are regarded as failing to understand the realities of politics and, as a consequence, guilty of purveying illusions and aspirations that will never be realized. The point is not that the political realm is a world without morals and rules of conduct, but that it is significantly different from other realms, because the rules that emerge and are upheld depend on the distribution of power and the way in which power is exercised. A similar distinction is drawn in this tradition between the domestic and the international. States are often bound by different rules in their internal dealings with their citizens than they are in their dealings with one another in the international state system or with the citizens of other states. A recent example of this distinction is the policy of the Bush Administration towards those it interned in the detention centre at Guantanamo Bay suspected of terrorist activities. By labelling them 'enemy combatants' and holding them outside the United States, the Administration was able, for a long time, to deny those detained due process, which it would not have been able to do had they been held in the United States itself. Cosmopolitans wish to deny that distinction and to close the gap. States and foreign nationals should be subject to the same ethical principles as private citizens, both internally and externally. These ethical principles should be enshrined in international law and obeyed by all governments. The realist answer is that this mistakes the nature of politics, and the constraints under which politicians are obliged to operate.

On realism, see also Chapter 5.

The contextualist position advanced by Raymond Geuss (2008) among others asserts that politics is about action and the context of action, rather than about unanchored beliefs and propositions. In thinking about politics in any particular time or place, it is necessary always to think about it historically. The institutional locations in which politics takes place are created by human interaction and change over time, and are only ever partially understood. Gaining a fuller understanding of the circumstances and characteristics of a location is a minimal precondition, according to Geuss, for having sensible human desires and projects. This makes politics a *craft*, and not something to which you can apply a theory, ethical or otherwise. Theoretical understanding is always involved in practical politics, however this is not an abstract, a priori theory, but theory that is grounded in the particular circumstances of a specific time and place, and is part of the reality that it seeks to understand.

This position can be compared with that of Oakeshott (1962) who strongly criticized what he called 'rationalism' in politics, arguing that politics had to be understood as an activity and not as something that could be distilled into a set of maxims or principles. Possessing a cookbook on this view is not the same as cooking, because there are certain things involved in any practical activity that can only be understood by taking part in the activity, and not by abstract reflection upon it. Rationalism in politics always involves abridgement of the experience of politics and, therefore, its distortion, and leads to attempts to make politics depend on rational plans, rather than pursuing 'intimations', which are a form of tacit knowledge, dependent on experience, rather than abstract reflection. Practical affairs for Oakeshott are about understanding traditions of behaviour, and the more a tradition of behaviour is grasped by participating in it, the more well-grounded are the intimations for how to adjust and modify it in the light of experience.

Oakeshott's argument derives in part from the eighteenth-century politician and philosopher Edmund Burke and, while not shutting the door to all reform and change, he is very hostile to any change determined on abstract rational principles. The kind of ideal theory of contemporary liberalism intended to be applied to politics and guide political action is for Oakeshottians an example of such rationalism. Rawls believed that the pressing problems of a particular society could only be fully understood and engaged with by first imagining what a perfectly just society would be like. Oakeshott's objection to this way of proceeding is not to theory as such, but to theory divorced from its practical context where it alone can make sense. Understanding a tradition of behaviour, with the ethical ideas inherent in that tradition, is very different from either proclaiming universal ethical principles which are not subject to time and chance, as liberal revolutionaries were prone to do, or attempting like Rawls to distil the essence of a society's understanding of justice in a rationalist form. Oakeshott has no objection to other forms of experience, whether philosophical, scientific, historical, or aesthetic, indeed he celebrates them, but he warns against any of them being mistaken for practical experience or being used to substitute for practical experience. The others belong in a world of theoretical and intellectual activity. All forms of practical activity, including politics, involve a special relationship between theory and practice, and it is not one in which theory is superior to practice, rather it is embedded in that practice and helps to constitute it (Greenleaf, 1966; Franco, 2004).

Contextualist accounts of politics lead to very particular views of the nature of politics and political action. Geuss again is particularly illuminating on what it involves, more so than Oakeshott who is mainly concerned with keeping rationalism out of politics, rather than exploring politics itself. Geuss starts from the position that while human interaction and co-operation are both essential to politics as an activity, neither can be taken for granted. There is always huge potential in human affairs for conflict, instability, and disruption. He draws on the Hobbesian insight about the nature of politics, and the consequent fragility of order, however stable and solid any particular state of affairs may appear to be. One of the profound implications of such an approach is that there is considerable variation in what counts as either freedom or as order. There are no universal ethical principles that can be applied, only a changing set of meanings.

Geuss sharpens this analysis further by arguing that there are three basic questions to be asked about politics. These are the questions of Lenin, Nietzsche, and Weber. Lenin's question is 'Who Whom?' or as Geuss elaborates it, 'who does what to whom for whose benefit'? For several important theoretical approaches, including many strands of Marxism, the answers to these questions supply the key to understanding politics (Haugaard, 2002; Lukes, 2005). There are ethical issues involved, but they are integral to the focus on power, on interests and on agency which this approach encourages. This, for Geuss, is the essence of thinking politically, rather than abstract reasoning about ethics. Much ideal theory seems uninterested in power and, therefore, in most of the things with which politics is concerned. Geuss does not want to limit power to coercion and domination, rather he seeks to understand different forms of power, including power as the ability to do, as well as the ability to constrain. This means that we should focus on empirical examination of the different forms that power can take: coercive, persuasive, charismatic, and strategic powers among them. The familiar contrasts between coercion and consent, between domination and hegemony, between hard power and soft power are here swept up in a broader, and more differentiated account of how we should study power and its effects. The point Geuss makes is that we cannot begin to understand how politics works unless we understand different forms of power and how they are utilized in different contexts.

The second question about politics is Nietzsche's and it, too, is related to a particular conception of politics. For Nietzsche, the most striking feature of human existence is its finitude, so the question that must always be asked about politics is what do individuals value and what, in consequence, are the choices that they make in their everyday lives? Politics appears as a constant process of evaluating and choosing between alternatives, because choosing to pursue one thing means not being able to pursue another. All values have a radical contingency and there has always to be an act of will to choose one value over another. There are no reliable foundations in politics to lay the basis for a universal and unchanging ethics, only the ceaseless activity of evaluating and choosing between alternatives. For Niezsche, as also for Michel Foucault, an agent could well choose the ethical principles of ideal theory but these would not have any greater intrinsic **authority** than any other set of values. Their authority would rest on their practical efficacy, not on their theoretical coherence.

On Foucault, see Chapter 3.

The third question is Max Weber's and concerns **legitimacy**. What gives legitimacy to politics, and makes order and obedience possible? What makes legitimacy so important for politics is that without it collective action would be impossible. There are many different kinds of collective action and one of the most important functions of politics as an activity is to provide legitimacy for them. Weber's particular definition of legitimacy has been controversial because his main interest is in examining what is accepted unquestioningly in everyday life as legitimate, rather than attempting to relate legitimacy to any particular set of values or principles. It is an empirical, rather than a normative account of legitimacy. Legitimacy can, therefore, be conferred as easily on a dictatorship as on a democracy and on a regime that violates human rights as much as on one that upholds them. Politics as applied ethics has no meaning in this world. Ethics are only relevant if they have practical efficacy and in being valued by citizens are imposed as a standard for evaluating the government. However, the core meaning of legitimacy is here lawful authority, and there are many different ways by which lawful authority can be recognized and sustained.

These hard-edged conceptions lie at the heart of the contextualist approach and have often seemed to its critics to imply a relativism in ethical judgements. If legitimacy depends on the power to enforce a claim to rule, then changes of loyalty can be justified on grounds of political expediency. When a leader or a regime loses legitimacy it becomes acceptable to transfer loyalty to the successor. This comes close to saying that might is right, but in the history of states that has generally been the case. Once power has been lost legitimacy disappears also and those that are displaced, like the Shah of Iran after he was overthrown in the revolution of 1979, have no means of enforcing their claims, and legitimacy comes to be defined in a new way.

The main objection to making these three questions the heart of our understanding of politics is that it elevates context above principles, and downplays the importance of values and ethical imperatives. David Beetham (1991) has argued that Weber's definition is deficient because it fails to allow for the way in which certain ethical beliefs widely held in the population create a means to judge government policies, instead of simply accepting that whoever has power has legitimacy. Contextualists do not deny that there can be a number of different beliefs about legitimacy, but they observe as a matter of fact that what counts is the way such beliefs are related to the motives for action, and to the political and social institutions that are established. This is treated as a far superior way to understanding politics than elaborating a set of abstract concepts of justice or abstract concepts of the public good to determine what is legitimate and what is not. Politics, according to this account, is about power, its acquisition, distribution and use (Geuss, 2008, p. 96).

4.5 Globalization and the global community

What are the implications of these different approaches applied to actual political problems? A relevant example is the writing on globalization, global community, and global **civil society** that has become so prevalent in the last 30 years. One of the characteristics of normative theorizing about politics has been to push beyond the national and even the regional, taking the whole world and the entire human species as the object of enquiry. This is the subject of many of the chapters in this book. A strong version of this approach would be to argue that a certain kind of global political community already exists which supplies the criteria for judging policies and institutions (Slaughter, 2004). Yet not all cosmopolitan theorists argue in this way. Most do not think that the world is yet a single political community, but they do argue that it can be considered a single moral community. If every individual is considered to be of equal moral worth then certain consequences follow for the way we think about international politics and make political judgements about international issues.

On cosmo-politanism, see Chapter 7.

The recent interest in globalization has made it seem that there might be a reconciliation between normative theorizing and empirical studies of world politics, because the world appears to be evolving in a direction that the normative theorists since Kant have assumed in their theories, namely the possibility of a genuine international community observing universal norms and standards. The earlier part of the twentieth century was not kind to normative liberal theories or to universal theories of any kind. Belief in progress collapsed. During the nineteenth century some liberals had believed that the creation of universal interdependence through trade would make possible a peaceful world order, and that if there were sufficient common interests that cut across nations, there would be strong reasons for nations to cease to fight one another and to adopt a set of legal principles, which could resolve differences peacefully (Bell & Sylvest, 2006; Sylvest, 2009). A universal community could be built on the foundation of universal commerce and a community of nations. This was liberal internationalism, rather than cosmopolitanism. Similarly socialists believed that the unity of all working people of all nations and races could be forged, which would create a true international community and could prevent nations fighting one another. The norms of universal brotherhood and solidarity could be invoked to prevent worker fighting worker.

These hopes were to prove illusory with the outbreak of the First World War in 1914. Nationalism proved a much stronger force than internationalism. Representatives of the working class in the major states for the most part supported their nation and voted for the war, rather than declaring class solidarity across borders. The foundations of the liberal economic order collapsed and international class solidarity perished in 1914. Yet the dream of international co-operation and of transcending competitive nationalism in an international community remained strong, not least in the rhetoric of the American President Woodrow Wilson who on the conclusion of hostilities attempted to broker a far-reaching settlement based on the assumption that the world could come together as an international community and agree principles for the ordering of its affairs which would outlaw certain types of behaviour and make possible a perpetual peace (Gardner, 1976). The League of Nations and the principles of national self-determination were essential parts of this vision. It foundered from the first, partly because no other nation was prepared to sign up to it fully, partly because the United States Senate refused to endorse it, partly because many Americans suspected they would bear much of the cost, while the European powers would refuse to co-operate, by for example dismantling their colonial empires. The League of Nations was established, without US participation, but never achieved the authority or the capacity required to institute an international rule of law.

The inability of the League to prevent the Second World War (1939–45), and the rise of **totalitarian** regimes in both Russia and Germany seemed to mark the nadir of liberal fortunes and the hopes for a universal community. The Second World War was more extensive and more destructive than the First, and although those states most committed to international liberalism, the United States and Britain, were victors, and the United States moved to establish a new liberal world order, a large part of the world did not participate, and a cold war developed between West and East, both armed with weapons that threatened the survival of the human species itself. The UN, which the United States this time did support, was hampered from the start by the need to accommodate the interests of the victors, and to give vetoes to the United States and the USSR, which both proved ready to wield in defence of their national interests.

On this revival, see also Chapter 1.

Against this background it might be thought that the twentieth century should have been the graveyard of normative liberal theory, but in the last quarter of the twentieth century it experienced a remarkable revival, centred on the Anglo-American world. The connection with globalization is not a direct one, although it is a remarkable co-incidence that the floating of the American dollar in 1971, which marked the end of the Bretton Woods system of managed exchange rates and the beginning of a new era of freedom for financial markets, took place in the same year as the publication of *A Theory of Justice*. What does seem to be true is that progress towards the creation of a liberal world order and the evident economic progress of Western liberal societies during the long boom of the 1950s and 1960s reawakened liberal hopes about the possibility of advancing once again towards a universal community. The progress of globalization in the 1970s and 1980s led to speculation about the creation of a set of connections which were **transnational** and undermined the capacities and the jurisdictions of nation states. The opening of the Berlin Wall in 1989 and the collapse of the Soviet Union in 1991 reunited the world economy in a way which it had not been since before 1914 (Held & McGrew, 2007). This return to 'One World' and the end of superpower rivalry was hailed as the dawn of a new world order and as the triumph of the West, and the adoption of a common set of institutions and policies and ethical principles for conducting world affairs.

This era of liberal peace has since been interrupted by new wars, new security threats and, most recently, financial collapse (Gamble, 2009), but it has allowed the discourse of rights and justice to flourish as the dominant way of thinking about global political issues. Many of these theories make little attempt to show how their theorizing is connected to empirical realities; they tend to postulate the existence of a single political community, or a single moral community and reason on that basis. However, as the previous discussion showed, this is not necessarily wild utopian speculation, since the progress towards the construction of a liberal world order since 1945, based on the rule of law, has been considerable. There have been a growing number of international agencies, many instances of pooled or shared **sovereignty**, the establishment of new policy regimes encouraging collaborative arrangements, new social movements, and pressure groups and think tanks in global civil society, and many campaigns on global issues, such as poverty and climate change (Slaughter, 2004). There is, in many ways, a greater basis for a universal community than at any previous time in human history. There are more countries that are classified as democracies and a greater degree of acceptance of certain universal concepts, such as human rights. Even if this liberal order and universal community are far from perfect, there are reasonable grounds for arguing that such an order does seem to be emerging, and this makes viable an ethics-based discourse that assumes the tendencies towards a universal community based on the ethical principles of freedom and justice will continue.

From within liberalism this position is strongly criticized by Hayek and many '**neo-liberals**' (Turner, 2008). They accept the global liberal *economic* order, but argue that a global liberal *political* order is unachievable, and that trying to achieve social justice by applying ethical principles would have catastrophic consequences, because it could only be done by giving authority to international government agencies to intervene to redistribute income and resources, or impose a low carbon economy. On Hayekian principles the pursuit of social justice is a chimera because it involves interfering with free market exchange, which is the basis of the liberal order. To preserve that liberal order the ethical principles that are required are those that are involved in the process of market exchange itself—such as honesty, consistency, and trust. Ethical principles derived from a discourse of the ideal community lead to interventions that misunderstand the nature of the real community, which for Hayek is the spontaneous order of the Great Society.

From realist and contextualist perspectives, however, the argument is still back to front. The universal market of free exchange and the universal community of social justice are utopian aspirations which cannot be realized because of the nature of politics. Hayek is still the prisoner of an ideal conception; he merely displaces it from the state to the market. Advocates of the analysis of international politics in terms of power—which among others include Marxists and also those influenced by Carl Schmitt (Schmitt, 1996; Odysseos & Petito, 2007)—argue that international law and cosmopolitan principles simply disguise the interests of powerful states. Critics of Britain in the nineteenth century argued that the doctrine of free trade purported to benefit all the peoples of the world, but in reality benefited the British because of their superior productivity. On this view, abstract ethical conceptions have no claim at all upon international politics, and simply obscure the reality, which is one of national interest.

A different line of argument is taken by those who accept that the conception of the international system as based on sovereign nation states has changed and acknowledge the growing strength of certain kinds of cosmopolitanism, particularly the growth of horizontal and vertical transgovernmental networks. This directs attention to the gradual growth of international law, but still based on the consent of states. What is much less clear is whether there is also the emergence of a cosmopolitan legal order which allows the state-based system of international law, resting as it does on the principles of self-determination and non-interference, to be overridden. As Jean Cohen has argued, the problem with asserting that there is such a cosmopolitan legal order and that potentially it overrides national jurisdictions if, for example, there are serious violations of human rights, is that it legitimizes actions by powerful states whose purpose may be to extend their empire, rather than to contribute to international justice (Cohen, 2004a). It is in the discussion of such contemporary questions of international politics as whether intervention in the affairs of other states can ever be justified, that some of the most complex problems of the relationship of ethics and politics are raised.

On international law, see Chapter 15.

On humanitarian intervention, see Chapter 18.

4.6 **Conclusion**

The relationship between politics and ethics has been explored in this chapter by considering three important approaches—deontological, consequentialist, and contextualist. Deontological approaches have been very influential in the last 40 years, and they have a practical resonance also, particularly in the emphasis that is placed on human rights. Consequentialist ethics, however, are much more pervasive in shaping public discourse and the evaluation of public actions. Both these two approaches are examples of politics as applied ethics and, at times, they seem to crowd out all other approaches. Practitioners of many disciplines think it appropriate to adopt abstract external criteria to judge political actions and outcomes. As such they have become part of our politics and embedded within it. However, they are not the whole of politics and the contextualist approach, in its many diverse manifestations, is a reminder of older and more subtle ways of thinking about the relationship between ethics and politics. By thinking about politics in terms of power and conflict, it does not discard considerations of right and wrong, or treat all ethical values as equivalent, but relates them to the contexts in which politics arises and in which their significance can be understood.

▦ QUESTIONS

1. Explain the distinction between ideal and non-ideal theory.

2. Do politics and ethics inhabit separate realms?

3. Can a contextualist approach avoid relativism?

4. How do utilitarians relate ethics to politics?

5. What does a contextualist understand by politics?

6. Is a realistic Utopia a contradiction in terms?

7. Does legitimacy always rest on power?

8. Do ethical considerations apply in politics?

9. Is cosmopolitanism a feasible ideal?

10. Write a defence of ideal theory.

▦ FURTHER READING

Beetham, D. (1991) *The Legitimation of Power*. London: Macmillan. Provides a very clear exposition and critique of Weber's theory of power and legitimation.

Cohen, J. (2004) Whose sovereignty? Empire versus international law. *Ethics and International Affairs*, **18**(3):1–24. Analyses competing interpretations of power and law in international politics.

Geuss, R. (2008) *Philosophy and Real Politics*. Princeton: Princeton University Press. Provides a searching critique of ideal theory and argues for the superiority of the contextualist approach.

Goodin, R. (1995) *Utilitarianism as a Public Philosophy*. Cambridge: Cambridge University Press. Examines the nature of utilitarianism and its approach to public policy.

Oakeshott, M. (1962) *Rationalism in Politics*. London: Methuen. Provides a critique of rationalism, and argues for understanding politics as a tradition of behaviour.

Rawls, J. (1999) *The Law of Peoples*. Cambridge: Harvard University Press. Applies the approach of ideal theory and realistic Utopia to the relations between peoples.

Schmitt, C. (1996) *The Concept of the Political*, transl. J. H. Lomax. Chicago: University of Chicago Press. A strong conservative polemic against all forms of ideal theory.

Swift, A., & White, S. (2008) Political science, social science and real politics, in: D. Leopold & M. Stears (eds), *Political Theory: Methods and Approaches*. Oxford: Oxford University Press, pp. 49–69. Argues for political theory that takes account of empirical politics and addresses real political problems.

WEB LINKS

http://plato.stanford.edu/ A comprehensive philosophical encyclopaedia, which contains longer entries on many of the themes addressed in this chapter.

http://www.e-ir.info/ A wide-ranging website aimed principally at students, containing news, essays, podcasts, and commentary on international politics.

http://www.opendemocracy.net/ An excellent resource for debates over democracy and world politics.

http://globetrotter.berkeley.edu/conversations/ Video interviews with leading scholars and public figures talking about their life and work, hosted at the Institute of International Studies, University of California, Berkeley.

http://www2.etown.edu/vl/ The 'WWW Virtual Library: International Affairs Resources' site provides links to numerous international organizations, media outlets, academic journals, government agencies, and much more.

Visit the Online Resource Centre that accompanies this book to access more learning resources: **www.oxfordtextbooks.co.uk/orc/bell_ethics/**

PART TWO

General perspectives

5 | Political realism and the limits of ethics

Duncan Bell

READER'S GUIDE

It is often claimed that realists deny any role for morality in international politics. While some realists have made this argument, many others have defended assorted ethical positions. This chapter starts by arguing that realist social scientific scholarship has implications for how we think about the feasibility of normative theorizing. I then suggest that realist political theory is not opposed to morality, but rather to 'moralism'—a distorted kind of moral argument. I also distinguish between three realist positions: conservative realism, liberal realism, and realism as radical critique. I finish with a discussion of the problem of 'dirty hands'—of when it is right to do wrong—and Max Weber's 'ethics of responsibility'. In summary, realism is not opposed to ethical arguments in international affairs, but, in all of its different variants, it highlights the limits of ethics.

5.1 Introduction

The terms **realism** and realist are employed in diverse ways in the study of ethics, politics, literature, and art. In everyday language, to be a realist is to assume a certain attitude towards the world, to focus on the most significant aspects of a given situation, whether or not they conform to our preferences or desires. Realism implies the will and the ability to grasp 'reality'—however this might be understood—and not to be misled by trivial aspects of it. It also suggests wariness of easy answers and of unreflective optimism. This sense carries over into its usage in politics, where realism is usually employed as a term to describe approaches that focus on the centrality of power and conflict.

Realism might seem an odd theme to include in a book on ethics and world politics. Many political theorists view realism as a tradition of political thought that denies the role of ethics or morality (I use the two terms interchangeably in this chapter). Charles Beitz suggests that one of the 'foundations' of realism is the view that 'moral judgments have no place in discussions of international affairs or foreign policy' (Beitz, 1979, p. 15). Realists, Allen Buchanan maintains, insist that 'the nature of international relations rules out morality in that sphere' (Buchanan, 2004, p. 29). According to Marshall Cohen, meanwhile, realists 'argue that ... the conduct of nations is, and should be, guided and judged exclusively by the amoral requirements of the national interest' (Cohen, 1985, p. 4).

The belief that realism denies space for morality—or at best grants it a very minor role—makes it an easy target for political theorists. First, even if normative concerns were largely irrelevant in shaping international politics (an empirical argument) it does not follow that we should avoid thinking about how the world should be organized (a normative argument). Secondly, it is straightforward to point to numerous cases where normative arguments *do* play important roles in political life. Think, for example, about the contemporary significance of **human rights** discourse, or about the role of anti-imperial campaigns in ending European imperialism in the mid-twentieth century, or about the success of the abolitionist crusade to eradicate slavery in the eighteenth and nineteenth centuries (Crawford, 2002; Price, 2008). Yet while some realists have made implausible claims about the irrelevance of morality, they are the exception not the rule. Realist theorizing encompasses a diverse range of ethical arguments.

The label 'realism' is used to describe two discrete, although often intersecting, bodies of political thought. The first emerges from the field of International Relations (IR) and, in particular, the writings of the so-called 'classical realists' of the mid-twentieth century, a group that includes the British historian E. H. Carr, the German émigré scholar Hans Morgenthau, and the American theologian Reinhold Niebuhr (reputedly Barack Obama's favourite thinker). The other literature is more varied. Rather than addressing questions of international politics directly, its 'realism' resides in its account of the nature of politics, and in particular the relationship between politics and morality. Here, we find reference to a wide array of thinkers, including Thucydides, Niccolò Machiavelli, Jean-Jacques Rousseau, Thomas Hobbes, and Max Weber. Classical realism in IR can be seen, in part, as an attempt to employ (some of) their insights to understand the character of modern international politics.

Scholars disagree over how best to interpret the history of realism. One common argument is that realism embodies 'timeless wisdom' about politics (Buzan, 1996). From this perspective, the ancient Greek historian Thucydides is often seen as the patron saint of realism (Doyle, 1997; Lebow, 2003). Other scholars prefer to trace realism to the politics of the Renaissance or early modern Europe (Haslam, 2002; Williams, 2005a). The key figures in this account are usually Machiavelli and Hobbes. Realism, on this view, emerges out of the incessant warfare of the Italian city-states and reaches maturity in the '**Westphalian**' inter-state system—the modern system of territorial states that originated in western Europe and spread, often via the imperialism of the European powers, until it encompassed the whole world in the second half of the twentieth century. As such, realism is sometimes seen as the dominant political theory of the modern inter-state order. An extreme version of this position is called *raison d'etat*, or 'reason of state' (Meinecke,

1957). It preaches that the role of political leaders is to advance the interests of their own state above all other considerations. When critics lambast realism for its amorality, they often have this narrow version in mind.

Still other scholars prefer to interpret political realism primarily as an ideological product of the twentieth century, albeit one that draws extensively on the assorted insights of the 'Thucydidean' and 'Westphalian' interpretations (Smith, 1986; Rosenthal, 1991; Bell, 2009a). On this view, political realism is best understood as a body of thought that was shaped by the political, social, and technological forces of what the historian Eric Hobsbawm (1994) calls the 'Age of Extremes' (1914–1991). The rise of **totalitarian** forms of government, the advent of nuclear weapons, and the horrors of the Holocaust, all assume fundamental roles in this narrative. The key figures shaping it are chiefly German (or German-speaking), including Karl Marx, Friedrich Nietzsche, Max Weber, Sigmund Freud, and Carl Schmitt. All of the historical interpretations also note a distinct break in the character of IR theory during the 1960s and 1970s, when 'classical realism' of the kind associated with Morgenthau and Niebuhr was increasingly supplanted by a new kind of realist analysis that claimed scientific status. Realist political thought gave way to realist 'political science', especially in the United States (Bell, 2009b; Schmidt, 1998; Waltz, 2008, pp. 67–83).

Whatever historical interpretation you prefer, it is important to recognize that realism—of one kind or another, and often in its crudest forms—continues to 'dominate foreign policy communities on a nearly world-wide basis' (Lebow, 2007, p. 424). It remains central to public discourse about world politics. It is therefore essential to understand the strengths and weaknesses of realist arguments.

While the historical debate over realism is lively, this chapter focuses instead on what realism can add to contemporary discussions of global ethics. Two important types of question arise and, although they are related (and often conflated), it is important to distinguish them. The first concerns the relationship between realism as a social scientific enterprise and normative theory. The second concerns realist accounts of ethics. The first question relates to the character of realist scholarship. Most chapters in this book focus on normative theories—theories designed to assess the value of, or to prescribe, various forms of human collective action. Those that are not easily classified as straightforwardly normative—such as post-**colonialism** and post-structuralism—are nevertheless explicit about their value-orientation, their ethical content. Yet most contemporary realist IR scholarship is produced by academics seeking to describe the actual operation of international politics, and who frequently deny that their work is normative in any important sense. A question therefore arises: does realist IR theory of this kind say anything important about ethical issues? The second type of question asks what, if anything, is distinctive about a realist conception of political ethics? Here, we need to look beyond contemporary social science and revisit the kinds of arguments developed by the 'classical' realists.

On post-structuralism and post-colonialism, see Chapters 3 and 11.

Section 5.2 outlines the basic features of contemporary realist IR theory and asks what it can contribute to normative debates. Section 5.3 argues that the key to realist ethics lies in a critique of *moralism*—a particular kind of moral argument—not of morality itself. Section 5.4 delineates three contrasting realist normative positions. Finally, section 5.5 discusses Weber's account of the '**ethics of responsibility**' and the 'problem of dirty hands'—the issue of whether it is ever right to do wrong.

5.2 The limits of ethics: realism as social science

On social science and political theory, see also Chapter 4.

Contemporary realist scholarship is mainly dedicated to explaining how states interact with each other in an 'anarchical' international system—a system, that is, without an overarching political **authority**. Above all, realists focus on questions of power, which they usually define in terms of the military and economic capacity of political actors. 'In analysing international relations, realists thus look for where the power is, for what the group interests are, and to the role power relations play in reconciling clashing interests' (Wohlforth, 2008, p. 134).

Realist IR theory is composed of different strands (Elman, 2010; Wohlforth, 2008). Yet while realists disagree over many issues, they are committed to at least four general propositions:

- Politics is a domain of human activity structured by power and coercion. The ever-present potential of conflict, including but not limited to lethal violence, accounts for much of the intensity of political life.

- Within political communities power and the possibility of conflict can usually be constrained by political institutions, although they can never be eliminated entirely. In contrast, relations between political communities—today primarily territorial states—unfold largely in a context of **'anarchy'** (a context defined by the lack of an overarching political authority).

- Governments adopt a hierarchy of priorities, almost always placing the 'national interest' above other considerations. At the core of the 'national interest' lies 'national security'. Although ideas about the content of the national interest vary, this ranking of priorities is found in all types of regime, from democracies to dictatorships.

- The most powerful states set the terms of global interaction and dominate international institutions (e.g. the United Nations and the International Monetary Fund). Relationships between these 'great powers' are frequently marked by fierce competition, even war. Although such states voluntarily enter arrangements that constrain their behaviour, they will not adopt policies that fail to conform with their interpretation of the national interest. It follows that binding agreements (including international law) and international institutions are limited in their scope and effects, at least where they are seen to challenge the interests of the powerful.

The realist vision is pessimistic: international politics is marked by constant power struggles and conflict, and it presents a wide range of obstacles to achieving greater levels of peaceful co-operation. While realists do not necessarily deny the possibility of limited forms of progress, they are, in general, sceptical of the likelihood of fundamental changes in the international system, at least for the foreseeable future. They tend to see international politics as a 'realm of recurrence and repetition' (Wight, 1966, p. 26; Waltz, 1979).

What does this have to do with normative theorizing?

First, even when couched in the supposedly objective language of social science, realist arguments contain significant normative *assumptions*. A typical realist argument runs as follows: because the world works in the way that realists describe, it is necessary to pursue certain foreign policy options *in order to secure the safety of the state and the stability of the international system*. Note, however, that this argument presupposes a normative defence of (1) the priority of system stability and (2) state security. Implicit in the argument, then, is a set of ethical claims about what people should value. The same is true of arguments about the 'national interest'. Realist IR scholars often suggest that the national interest trumps the pursuit of values in international affairs. This position seems to contrast 'interests' to 'ethics', and it underpins the argument that realists preach the necessity of acting immorally. This is misleading. The argument that politicians should prioritize the national interest already implies an ethical position: it suggests that the national interest (however that might be defined) takes moral priority over the claims of other agents (individual persons, cultures, other states) in the international system. It is, in short, an argument about the normative priority of the state. I return to this issue in section 5.3.

Secondly, realist arguments have significant normative *implications*. This is most apparent in terms of foreign policy prescriptions. Think of the two recent American-led wars against Iraq. Most realists—like most **just war** theorists —supported Operation Desert Storm, the campaign to eject Saddam Hussein from Kuwait in 1990–1991. They argued that the situation presented a clear threat to American interests. By invading Kuwait, Iraq destabilized the fragile international order, and endangered Israel and Saudi Arabia, close allies of the US. It also threatened vital oil supplies. However, most realists opposed the 2003 war, arguing that there were no essential US interests at stake. They predicted that the war would entangle the US in a bloody conflict, undermine American power, and help destabilize the region (Payne, 2007; Schmidt & Williams, 2008). Realist opposition to the war was unsurprising— for similar reasons the classical realists were harsh critics of the Vietnam war.

On the just war tradition, see Chapter 16.

In the public debates in the lead up the 2003 invasion of Iraq realists were pitched into a losing battle with the 'neo-conservatives', an influential group of thinkers and politicians (such as Paul Wolfowitz and Robert Kagan) who supported a much more assertive role for the US in the world.[1] Realists and neo-conservatives have long presented divergent views of the nature and purposes of American power and foreign policy. On both normative and practical grounds, realists have been very critical of neo-conservative ambitions to spread Western capitalist democracy around the world.

Realist empirical scholarship also addresses questions of feasibility. Should political theories be realistic, either in their assumptions or their prescriptions? Scholars are deeply divided over the issue. For some, feasibility should play little or no role in the development of normative theories. For others, however, feasibility is paramount. It is here that realism can play an important cautionary role, pinpointing the kinds of policy prescriptions that are politically salient. Realists argue, for example, that existing political constraints place

On feasibility, see the Introduction and Chapter 4.

---

[1] On neo-conservatism, see Ehrman, 1995; Halper & Clarke, 2004; Williams, 2005d; Friedman, 2006; Fukuyama, 2006.

On cosmo-
politanism,
see Chapter 8.

formidable barriers in the way of transforming the norms and institutions of international politics in ways that would help to realize **cosmopolitan** goals. These constraints include:

- The way in which state leaders routinely prioritize the 'national interest' above international or global justice. Moreover, claims about 'national security' are often invoked to justify the denial of civil rights and the use of political violence (Holmes, 2007; Burke, 2008).

- The overriding importance accorded to state **sovereignty** by the most powerful states. This position is hypocritical, as the dominant states often deny autonomy to weaker states by repeatedly interfering in their domestic affairs (Krasner, 1999).

On interna-
tional law,
see Chapter 15.

- The general weakness of international law in constraining the actions of the most powerful states. Historically, indeed, international law has often been utilized by the 'great powers' to justify their military actions, including imperialism (Nabulsi, 1999; Simpson, 2004).

- The way in which the major international institutions—including the UN, IMF, World Bank, and so forth—are controlled by the most powerful states.

For realists, then, the global system is dominated by a small number of powerful states, and it is not clear to them how this situation can be transcended. Yet as their disagreements with the neo-conservatives highlights, it does not follow that the normative implications of realist arguments are inconsequential—far from it. Indeed they argue that in light of existing political constraints it is both practically and normatively desirable that politicians act prudentially and avoid the arrogant temptation to radically transform the world.

Other realists focus on more specific topics. Jack Snyder and Leslie Vinjamuri, for example, employ realist insights to challenge a common line of argument among advocates of global justice. They contend that the post-conflict prosecution of human rights abusers, including war criminals, 'risks causing more atrocities than it would prevent, because it pays insufficient attention to political realities' (Snyder & Vinjamuri, 2004, p. 5). They argue that if political and military leaders know they will be prosecuted they will not make the compromises and bargains necessary to end hostilities. The rule of law does not lead to political stability—only once stability has been created can a legal system operate effectively. Stability and peace may only be possible at the expense of bringing the perpetrators of crimes to justice. As such, the creation of war crimes tribunals and international courts might serve as a potential source of further violence and death. Indeed, it may be best to offer the perpetrators amnesty, however unjust this might seem.

Realist social scientific work is open to a variety of criticisms. For example, realist accounts of 'power' are arguably under-developed (Guzzini, 1993, 2004). Many scholars also suggest that realism underestimates the effects of globalization on the international system. Others maintain that realists are too quick to deny the possibility of progressive normative change. Jack Donnelly, for example, argues that realists 'regularly, sometimes spectacularly, overstate the nature and significance of the "facts" that constrain the pursuit of moral objectives in (international) politics' (Donnelly, 2008, p. 153). Despite these concerns, however, realist empirical work can play an important cautionary role in normative debates.

5.3 Against moralism: the nature of realist ethics

We can now turn to the conception of ethics found in realist thinking. Realism is best seen as a position that challenges *moralism*, not *morality*. As C. A. J. Coady observes, the 'realist target is, or should be, not morality but certain distortions of morality, distortions that deserve the name moralism' (Coady, 2008a, p. 14). Coady's qualifier 'or should be' points to the fact that realist writings in IR often lack clarity on this issue, collapsing together moralism (as a special case of morality) and morality itself. When discussing ethics, realists sometimes 'shoot pretty indiscriminately, and from the hip' (Coady, 2008a, p. 48). This has provided ammunition for their critics, who highlight contradictions in realist arguments (e.g. Donnelly, 2000, 2008). Despite the confusions of individual thinkers, however, Coady is right to argue that realism is seen best as a challenge to moralism.

What, then, is moralism? It is 'a kind of vice involved in certain ways of practising morality or in exercising moral judgement, or thinking that you are doing so' (Coady, 2008a, p. 15).

… moralism often involves an inappropriate set of emotions or attitudes in making or acting upon moral judgements, or in judging others in light of moral considerations. The moralizer is typically thought to lack self-awareness and a breadth of understanding of others and of the situations in which she and they find themselves. In addition, or in consequence, the moralizer is subject to an often-delusional sense of moral superiority over those coming under his or her judgement. (Coady, 2008a, p. 17)

Moralism is a form of moral reasoning that can (and often does) lead to practical consequences that are normatively problematic. It can take various forms, which are often combined. Three are of particular significance.

The moralism of unbalanced focus

This arises from ascribing 'an unbalanced weighting to one set of moral concerns over others that are just as or more relevant' (Coady, 2008a, p. 29). In virtually all practical situations there are a variety of competing moral considerations, and the problem here resides in emphasizing one of them to the exclusion of others. This can sometimes generate dangerous results. The problem is encapsulated in the Roman maxim *Fiat justitia ruat caelum*—let justice be done though the heavens fall. Following this advice can be interpreted as courageous, as doing the right thing despite the costs involved, but in other situations—such as the cases studied by Snyder and Vinjamuri (2004)—pursuing one value (criminal justice) above all others can result in serious problems.

Realists have warned repeatedly against this kind of thinking. Raymond Aron, for example, stated that the 'criticism of idealist illusion is not only pragmatic, it is also moral. Idealist diplomacy slips too often into fanaticism' (Aron, 1966, p. 307). Coady argues that much well-intentioned support for **humanitarian intervention** represents an 'unbalanced focus', which leads to a misguided form of 'militant humanitarianism' (Coady, 2003). Supporters of the humanitarian mission, he argues, often focus on the idea of helping others—of saving distant strangers—at the expense of other vital

On humanitarian intervention, see Chapter 18.

considerations. They are, in short, 'often blind to the prudential considerations that can militate against' intervention, including knowledge of the relevant cultural, religious or political circumstances, recognition of the limits of military action, and of the pernicious consequences of employing force (Coady, 2008a, p. 32). None of these concerns rule out humanitarian intervention in principle, but they do highlight the need to be more aware of the complexities of politics than is often the case with moralizers.

The moralism of imposition

The 'error' of the moralism of imposition (or interference) is 'to insist that what may well be valid moral judgements on their subject matter be imposed inappropriately on other people' (Coady, 2008a, pp. 35–6). This is not an argument about cultural or moral relativism—of whether we can or should make moral judgements about other ways of life.[2] While some realists, including Carr, have defended versions of relativism (Carr, 1939), this point is a different one. It concerns whether or not we should seek to impose values (even if we think they are universally applicable in principle) on other people and communities. This type of imposition almost always requires the use of coercion, disrespect or force (Coady, 2008a, pp. 38–9).

The moralism of abstraction

This refers to what Stanley Hoffmann calls 'excessive moralizing in the abstract' (1981, p. 26). According to this view discussion about political morality, perhaps especially in global politics, is often alienated from the messy realities of the world. It takes different forms, four of which are especially salient (Coady, 2008a, p. 30):

- Moralism is too *universalistic*—it ignores normatively and politically important issues of cultural and political diversity, too often assuming a 'one size fits all' model.

- It is too *rationalistic*—as a consequence it ignores or downplays the emotions, including the (often dangerous) role of political passions. The classical realists, in particular, frequently highlighted the unavoidable role of irrationality in political action.

- It is too *simplistic*—it misses many important aspects of moral and political life, meaning that it is incapable of motivating people to act in appropriate ways.

- It is *unfeasible*—because its prescriptions are overly utopian, they are incapable of being realized.

These criticisms are all variations on a single theme: 'the abstract apparatus of morality … cannot satisfactorily fit the world it is supposedly made for' (Coady, 2008a, p. 39). Note that this is not an argument against abstraction, reason, or **universalism**, but only against excesses, or crude articulations, of them. The moralism of abstraction leads to two main dangers. The first is that moralizing arguments are irrelevant—because they fail to capture pertinent aspects of reality, or because they are so detached from existing conditions, they

---

[2] For further discussion of relativism see Blackburn (2001); Lukes (2009).

cannot motivate people to act in ways the moralizer demands. The second is that this level of abstraction is actually dangerous: it can lead to forms of action—remember the example of Iraq—that are deeply counter-productive. To avoid moralism it is advisable to display greater sensitivity to other ways of life and recognize that in international politics it is necessary (if not always palatable) to coexist with other political systems shaped by often very different values.

The structure of realist ethical argument

Realists do not deny the importance of normative considerations in global politics, but they are highly sensitive to the constraints on ethical action and wary of the dangers of moralism. Rather than elaborating 'ideal' theories, realists usually start from a pessimistic account of how world politics operates (as outlined in section 5.2) and then proceed to explore the ethical possibilities available to political actors. On this view, normative commitments are shaped by recognition of the constraints placed on action by the character of politics in general and inter-state politics in particular. This constitutes a specific account of the relationship between political theory and political practice, where the former is structured by the possibilities compatible with the latter.

Typically realists identify the state as the key actor in international politics—for good or ill—and focus their attention on how states should interact with each other. This leads to an emphasis on questions of political leadership, judgement, and foreign policy. Realism rarely involves the elaboration of fully-fledged normative theories, encompassing all or most dimensions of human social and political life—for example, realists have had little to say about questions of **distributive justice**. Instead, they usually concentrate on how states, and in particular the United States, should act in the world (e.g. Ikenberry & Kupchan, 2004; Lieven & Hulsman, 2006). This means that much realist ethical reflection can be seen as the elaboration of a political theory of 'responsible power' (Rosenthal, 1991)—of how to use power in a normatively defensible manner, and in particular how to channel its use to secure order and stability in the international system.

On global distributive justice, see Chapter 14.

The importance of the 'national interest' lies at the heart of many (although not all) accounts of realism. The concept is employed in different ways (Burchill, 2005), and it can be prioritized for various reasons. These include:

- Claims that it is best always to place the interests of your own state above all other considerations (**realpolitik**).

- More subtle arguments that stress the moral importance of nationality or legal and political institutions.

On these arguments, see Chapters 6 and 7.

- It might simply be based on a calculation of prudence, suggesting that in a dangerous world it would be counterproductive to pursue policies that undermined state stability. Here prudence is regarded as an element of morality, indeed as a virtuous form of political judgement (Coady, 2008a, pp. 21–2).

In general, contemporary political science realists do not provide systematic justifications for the prioritization of the national interest; they simply assume its value. Yet in normative terms, 'unless the national interest is in some sense good, there is no obvious reason to follow it' (Donnelly, 2008, p. 152).

Some of the classical realists, notably Morgenthau (1952), provide more sophisticated accounts. He regarded the national interest as an ethical idea, arguing that

[the] equation of political moralizing with morality and of political realism with immorality is itself untenable. The choice is not between moral principles and the national interest, devoid of moral dignity, but between one set of principles divorced from political reality and another set of principles derived from political reality. (Morgenthau, 1952, p. 34)

Michael Williams provides a compelling interpretation of this position. He argues that for Morgenthau the idea of the 'national interest' performed an important ethical and political role that many contemporary IR realists would not recognize. The national interest is a 'rhetorical device that seeks to use the political power of this concept to encourage critical reflection and dialogue about interests and their relation to identity—to how a society sees itself and wishes to be seen by others' (Williams, 2005c, p. 169). This dialogue over the **legitimacy** of the state and its activities—this encouragement to reflect on the value and purpose of the policies pursued in the name of the citizens—can serve 'to mobilize civic virtue and support a politics of limits' (Williams, 2005c, p. 11). Here, realism overlaps with strands of **republican** political theory in seeking to foster certain critical virtues, including active political participation, among the citizens.[3]

Realists have often viewed politics as tragic, although they interpret the term in different ways. John Mearsheimer, for example, argues that international politics is tragic because the anarchical structure of the system leads inevitably to violent conflict between great powers. It 'forces states which seek only to be secure to act aggressively toward each other' (Mearsheimer, 2001, p. 3). Richard Ned Lebow elaborates a richer understanding drawn from the ancient Greeks. This 'tragic vision', he suggests, infuses the writings of the classical realists. For Lebow, tragedy is not simply a function of the structural ordering of states, but is inherent in the human condition. It identifies the complexity of human motives and desires, and the inability of people to fully grasp and control the circumstances in which they live. It also points to the dangers of agents—whether individuals or states—believing they can transcend their environments. 'Tragedy confronts us with our frailties and limits, and the disastrous consequences of trying to exceed them' (Lebow, 2003, p. 20). The attempt to exceed limits leads to *hubris*, a form of arrogance which often ends in disaster (or *nemesis*). In Greek tragedy, hubris usually results in the death of the protagonists. In international politics, it encourages unjust and aggressive behaviour—Lebow identifies the invasion of Iraq in 2003 as an archetypal moment of imperial hubris. Adopting a 'tragic vision' provides no easy answers to the questions that confront us, but it induces a certain kind of attitude to the world, one that 'encourages us to develop and use our analytical facilities, but to be equally attentive to our imagination and feelings, to balance inference with prophecy and to recognize that the world is full of contradictions that we cannot resolve' (Lebow, 2003, p. 20). This, in turn, leads to recognition of the virtues of prudence, self-knowledge, modesty, and restraint.

Realists, then, tend to argue that while radical political change might be desirable, it is nevertheless often *utopian* to pursue it. This position can underpin a gradualist defence of

---

[3] The links between republicanism and realism are discussed in: Deudney (2007); Williams (2005a); Shapiro (2007); Tjalve (2008).

reform; it need not serve as a simple rationalization of the status quo. The argument comes in two basic forms. First, that the extreme difficulty of securing global political transformation means that limited resources are better spent on limited reforms (*utopianism as distraction*). Secondly, that given the character of international politics attempts to transform the system are fundamentally perilous, threatening some of the norms—for example, state sovereignty—that are essential for the stability of the system (*utopianism as danger*).

5.4 The ethics of limits: three varieties of realism

In this section I outline three distinct realist positions. Some classical realists, perhaps especially Morgenthau, oscillated between them, but they can point in different directions.

Conservative realism

Realism of this kind defends the existing order of things. It stresses the primacy of the 'national interest', and argues that leaders of states should pay minimal attention to the demands of those residing outside their borders. This severely limits the scope of justice. Conservative realists prioritize stability and order in the international system above the pursuit of other values. An arch-example of this kind of realism is provided by the American statesman Henry Kissinger (Kissinger, 1994; Kuklick, 2006, pp. 182–204). This kind of realism finds few admirers among political theorists, but it is arguable that it has played, and continues to play, a very significant role in public debates about the means and ends of foreign policy.

Liberal realism

It is a common mistake to view realism as *inherently* conservative. Many conservatives have been realists—indeed, it is arguable that a coherent conservatism demands adherence to some form of realism—but not all realists are conservative. Indeed, many are liberal political thinkers. To some, this may sound peculiar, for it is often suggested that realism is an alternative to liberalism, that they are opposing political traditions. This is a mistake. As John Herz, a self-described 'liberal realist', wrote once 'there is no essential opposition of realism and idealism' (Herz, 1981, p. 203).

Liberal realists also emphasize the importance of order, but do so to secure the conditions necessary for liberal states and values to flourish in a brutally competitive world. They navigate a middle course between conservative versions of realism and ambitious visions for transforming the international system. Both Herz (1951) and Aron (1966) were liberal realists. Arguably, some of the '**English School**' writers, including Hedley Bull (2002), R.J. Vincent (1986), and James Mayall (2000), can also be viewed in this way.

 On the English School, see Chapter 6.

Liberal realism can be seen as an international variant of the 'liberalism of fear', a position that focuses on how to avoid cruelty and violence, not on specifying ideal conditions for human flourishing (Shklar, 1989). Tempered by the cataclysmic violence of the twentieth century, and shaped by scepticism about the desire or the will of humans to radically transform their circumstances, its advocates seek instead to ameliorate human suffering in the present. Eschewing the 'intense moralism' of much contemporary political philosophy, they insist that political theorists should attend first of all to the 'only certainly universal material of politics: power, powerlessness, fear, cruelty'—in short, the 'universalism of negative capabilities' (Williams, 2005b, pp. 22, 59).

Stanley Hoffmann is an exponent of liberal realism, criticizing both narrow realists and liberal 'utopians' (1981, 1998b). Narrow realists, he suggests, present a picture of the world that is both descriptively inaccurate and normatively undesirable. It is descriptively inaccurate because, among other things, it fails to recognize that values and norms help shape international affairs. It is normatively inadequate because it either denies the role of morality or, through insisting on the absolute priority of the 'national interest', it defends a perverted form of it. Yet he also argues that many liberal visions of global order are implausible and that 'ideal' theorizing about international affairs has 'little relevance to reality' (1981, p. 2).

In contrast, liberal realism 'acknowledges the constraints of international politics, the realities of competition in uncertainty, and yet it aims at changing quite thoroughly the traditional rules of the game' (Hoffmann, 1981, p. xii). Hoffmann prescribes a non-utopian liberalism of fear which 'modestly aims at damage control', but today, he insists, 'that in itself is a revolutionary aspiration' (Hoffmann, 1998b, pp. 51–3). He does not construct an overarching normative theory, but rather sketches various reformist proposals for how states (and other organizations) should act to limit interstate violence, uphold human rights, protect vulnerable peoples, and ameliorate economic inequalities.

In contrast to the 'moralism of abstraction', Hoffmann argues that it is essential to locate ethical concerns in context. 'All ethical judgements in politics', he argues, 'are historical judgements. They are ... contextual or situational: they are not separable from the concrete circumstances, from the actual cases' (1981, p. 27). Moreover, his argument is premised, in typical realist fashion, on a distinct (but not absolute) break between domestic politics and international politics. The realm of domestic politics, presided over by a central government and uniting citizens through certain minimal forms of national solidarity, is more amenable to ethical arguments. It provides better material for the liberal reformer to work on. International politics is a different matter—it is an anarchical order populated by societies embodying very different, and often antagonistic, value systems. This constrains the scope of ethical action.

Realism as radical critique

While many realists are liberals, realism also offers intellectual resources for more radical forms of political thought. Craig Murphy (2001), for example, identifies the classical realism of Carr and Niebuhr as an 'international theory of the left'. Morgenthau started his career as a left-wing lawyer (Scheuerman, 2009). Noam Chomsky, one of the most radical commentators on contemporary world politics, can be interpreted as a realist (Osborn, 2009).

The *critical* dimension in realism is generated by its ability to unmask the dynamics of existing power relations, and to expose the self-interest and hypocrisy behind the practices of political actors. Realism of this kind expresses scepticism about the scope of reason and the influence of morality in a world in which power, and the relentless pursuit of power, is a pervasive feature. This position is 'inevitably antagonistic toward political power ... [a] rebellion against the seduction of prevailing structures of power, identity, and knowledge' (Williams 2005a, p. 179). It faces up to the folly and perversity of political life, without illusion or false hope. This dimension of realist thought has some affinities with critical theory and post-structuralism (Geuss, 2008; Williams, 2005c).

On critical theory and post-structuralism, see Chapters 2 and 3.

Moreover, critical realism is not committed to defending the existing institutions and operating principles of the international system. If we understand realism as a political and ethical position attuned to the realities of the world, then it can actually be used to challenge many of the central pillars of contemporary IR realism. Realism about the world may well demand an end to the way in which we organize political life on a global scale. For example, if empirical conditions have changed enough, new forms of politics may be necessary. Yet realism also warns against easy answers, highlighting the extreme difficulties of transforming global politics in ways that might be necessary, but which conflict with the perceived self-interest of the most powerful agents in the system.

We can even find intimations of this kind of transformative argument in classical realism. Morgenthau once wrote that

[n]othing in the realist position militates against the assumption that the present division of the political world into nation states will be replaced by units of a quite different character, more in keeping with the technical potentialities and the moral requirements of the contemporary world. (Morgenthau, 1985, p. 10)

Morgenthau and Herz argued in the 1950s that the advent of the nuclear age fundamentally changed global politics. The fact that humans had developed the technical ability to annihilate their own species meant that the main rationale for the state—its ability to protect its citizens—was called into question. This led both thinkers, albeit rather hesitantly, to argue that the nation state model was obsolete and to suggest the necessity of a global state, although neither thought this was realizable (Craig, 2003; Deudney, 2007). The point here is simple: realism is often thought to justify particular kinds of political association, and especially the state, yet it can also be employed to challenge existing political forms in the name of human survival.

A further radical possibility is available to realists, although it is one that most do not explore. As I discussed earlier, realists typically derive their normative prescriptions from their empirical account of international politics. However, these two aspects can be pulled apart—one can accept realist empirical arguments about how the world works, while also affirming a much more radical normative vision about how the world should be structured. It is thus theoretically possible, for example, to be both a realist and a cosmopolitan.

5.5 The 'ethics of responsibility' and the problem of 'dirty hands'

What form of ethical reasoning is most appropriate for political life? One important answer, termed the 'ethics of responsibility', was developed by Max Weber (1864–1920).[4] His work has exercised a profound influence on realist writers of different kinds, including

---

[4]For those who want to learn more about Weber, see Mommsen (1984); Kelly (2003); Kim (2004); Radkau (2009).

On Weber, see also Chapters 4 and 17.

Morgenthau (Turner, 2009) and Geuss (2001, 2008).[5] He developed his argument in 'Politics as a Vocation', a lecture delivered in 1919, where he suggested that in politics 'ethically oriented activity can follow two fundamentally different, irreconcilably opposed maxims' (Weber, 1919, 1984, p. 359). The first he called the 'ethics of responsibility', the second the **'ethics of principled conviction'.**

The adherent of the 'ethic of principled conviction' acts without taking into account the possible consequences. What matters is the quality of the intention guiding the action: if the intentions are good, then it is praiseworthy. Like the Sermon on the Mount or the biblical injunction to 'turn the other cheek' this form of ethical prescription is 'unconditional and unambiguous' (Weber, 1919, 1984, p. 358). It represents an absolutist form of morality, allowing no exceptions. While Weber expresses some admiration for principled conviction, he argues that it is inappropriate for politics. The failure to consider consequences points to the problems with *moralism* discussed earlier. Tony Blair, the Prime Minister who led Britain into the Iraq war in 2003, provides a striking example. His justification of his role gave pride of place to his good intentions, to doing what seemed right (Runciman, 2006).

Weber then turned to the 'ethics of responsibility'. Here individual agents 'must answer for the (foreseeable) consequences' of their actions (Weber, 1919, 1984, p. 360).

If evil consequences flow from an action done out of pure conviction, this type of person holds the world, not the doer, responsible, or the stupidity of others, or the will of God who made them thus. A man who subscribes to the ethic of responsibility, by contrast, will make allowances for precisely these everyday shortcomings in people. He has no right … to presuppose goodness and perfection in human beings. He does not feel that he can shuffle off the consequences of his own actions, as far as he could foresee them, and place the burden on the shoulders of others. He will say, 'These consequences are to be attributed to my actions' (Weber, 1919, p. 360).

For Weber, politics is ultimately characterized by the use or threat of violence as a means to pursue diverse and often conflicting ends (happiness, wealth, social equality, national glory, etc.). This is what marks it out as a distinctive domain of human activity, and it has profound consequences for those who hold or seek political power. He warned that 'anyone who gets involved with politics, which is to say with the means of power and violence, is making a pact with diabolical powers' (p. 362). It is arguable that Weber exaggerated the pervasiveness of violence, but his general point is compelling. Politics is often a messy business, saturated with moral ambiguity, and ultimately we should be wary of the moral absolutism of the conviction politician. Yet, Weber concludes, the true politician—the person who has a proper 'vocation' for politics—somehow manages to combine conviction and responsibility in ways that it is not possible to prescribe beforehand. The ability to know when it is right to prioritize one or the other, or in what ways to unite them, is a mark of sound political judgement, even wisdom, and it is a very rare quality. This explains why realists have put so much energy into studying successful political leaders like Winston Churchill and Abraham Lincoln (e.g. Morgenthau, 1946).

---

[5] Looking back on his career, Morgenthau wrote, 'Weber's political thought possessed all the intellectual and moral qualities I had looked for in vain' (Morgenthau, 1978, p. 64).

Realists often argue that the peculiar character of politics—and above all the centrality of violence within it—gives rise to a distinctive set of ethical issues. One of these is called the 'problem of the dirty hands'. (While realists are sensitive to issues like this, it is important to note that you do not have to be a realist to recognize their significance.) The problem can be stated succinctly: in politics it is sometimes right to do wrong. Or, more precisely: in certain circumstances it is permissible or necessary to act in ways contrary to regular codes of morality. This idea has deep historical roots (Parrish, 2007), finding its most famous expression in Machiavelli's injunction in *The Prince* (1513) that political leaders, while pretending to be virtuous, should, if necessary, act in ways that contravene ordinary morality. He suggests that good leaders need to learn how to do wrong for the sake of the political community. This idea is also implied by Weber's account of the 'ethics of responsibility'.

The problem was posed in its current form by Michael Walzer, in a famous essay published in 1973 (Walzer, 2007).[6] Walzer's position has mutated over the years. In his original formulation, he characterized the problem of dirty hands as a 'central feature of political life' (p. 280). 'It means', he argued, 'that a particular act of government (in a political party or in the state) may be exactly the right thing to do', yet it would leave the person responsible for the action 'guilty of a moral wrong' (p. 279). He gave two examples. In one, a candidate in an important election does a deal with a dishonest local politician in order to secure victory. The second example is more extreme: a politician orders the torture of a terrorist suspect to extract information about the location of a bomb, thus saving the lives of hundreds of people. The contemporary relevance of this kind of case is obvious.[7] In special circumstances, Walzer argues, we should accept that these (hypothetical) politicians were justified in acting as they did. Underlying this view is the idea that politics is a sphere of human activity different from, although still related to, everyday life. In this domain, it is vital to weigh up a variety of competing considerations, and in particular to pay attention to the specificities of time and place, to history and context. This is, as noted above, a theme that runs throughout the writings of realist authors.

The dilemma only arises, however, if we recognize that the actor is actually doing something wrong in the first place. Two other ways of looking at the situation dissolve the dilemma. On one account, which Walzer calls 'absolutist', an agent would simply refuse to act 'badly'—they would not torture or lie or betray under any circumstances. The problem with this **deontological** view is that it can lead to perverse consequences. In the case of the ticking bomb, hundreds of people might die in order to avoid inflicting non-lethal pain on one person. This is another example of the dangers of the maxim 'let justice be done or the heavens fall'. On the other view, which Walzer calls **utilitarian**, to torture or lie or betray would not, in the right circumstances, be seen as a bad thing—indeed, they would be morally praiseworthy, because they helped to bring about a greater good of some kind. There would be nothing to be guilty about. (Some conservative realists have adopted this view, although it is certainly not intrinsic to a realist account of ethics.) The problem here, as Walzer suggests, is that this position is too permissive: it encourages the view that any means are justifiable to secure particular ends. This is why he thinks it is

 On utilitarianism, see Chapter 4.

---

[6] Note that Walzer does not consider himself a realist.
[7] On the psychology, legality, and morality of torture, see Brecher (2007); Meisels (2008); Rejali (2008); Sands (2008).

vital to recognize that the dilemma encodes a paradox—it is sometimes right to act in ways that are (recognized as) wrong. 'Here is the moral politician: it is by his dirty hands that we know him. If he were a moral man and nothing else, his hands would not be dirty; if he were a politician and nothing else, he would pretend that they were clean' (Walzer, 2007, p. 284). As Weber warned, politics is no place for saints; yet we should also condemn those who do not recognize that the lesser evil is still an evil.

On the just war tradition, see Chapter 16.

Over time, however, Walzer has restricted the scope of the 'dirty hands' argument. In particular, he has linked it to another of his ideas, that of 'supreme emergency'. In *Just and Unjust Wars* (1977) Walzer argued that the prohibitions of the just war could be over-ridden in certain extreme situations where the existence of the political community was threatened. In such situations, it was legitimate to act in ways that would normally be impermissible. His main example was the terror bombing of German cities in the Second World War. He argued that this was justified when Britain was in imminent danger, but that it constituted a crime against humanity after it became clear that the British and their allies were winning the war (Walzer, 1977). It is important to recognize that 'supreme emergency' conditions are extremely rare.[8] The attacks of 9/11, for example, do not constitute such an emergency for the United States. In the 1980s Walzer modified his earlier argument by claiming that 'dirty hands aren't permissible (or necessary) when anything less than the ongoingness of the community is at stake, or when the danger that we face is anything less than communal death' (1988, p. 46). In other words, the transgression of regular moral norms was only permissible in situations of 'supreme emergency'.

The shift in Walzer's view seems to push him in the direction of interpreting most of the domain of politics in the absolutist terms he (and Weber) originally criticized. In other words, he suggests that only in situations so rare that most people will never experience them can political leaders be right to do wrong. Yet if we are to take the dilemma seriously, as realists argue we should, then this seems implausible. The realist would concur with Walzer's earlier formulation that dirty hands are a 'central feature' of political life. It is because of issues like this that realists have often characterized politics as tragic—such dilemmas are inevitable and the choice to be made is often between a variety of unsatisfying, even deadly, options.

However, it is also vital to recognize the need for caution in thinking about this kind of issue (Walzer, 1988, p. 33). One of the main reasons is that the thought-experiments of philosophers—like that of the ticking bomb—are often 'comically remote from the reasoning and psychology of the spooks and politicians that actually get their hands, arms, and shoulders dirty' (Coady, 2008a, p. 87).[9] We should therefore avoid basing moral arguments solely on extreme examples (like torture), or using 'dirty hands' arguments as a simple justification for every wrong done by those who govern us. Despite these dangers, the idea of dirty hands captures something important about the complex character of political action and the activity of passing moral judgement on it.

---

[8] Walzer's account of supreme emergency is based on a **communitarian** defence of the moral value of political community (on which see Chapter 7 in this volume, and Walzer, 1988, p. 44–5). For many non-communitarians, Walzer places undue emphasis on the value of community, and they would reject the argument that moral principles could be overridden in emergency situations.

[9] For further reflections on 'dirty hands' see Hollis (1982); Rynard & Shugarman (2000); Parrish (2007); Coady (2008a, pp. 76–104).

5.6 **Conclusion**

While they share much in common, realists differ in many important respects. Realism is perhaps best understood negatively—in terms of what realists fear, what they seek to avoid, and what they criticize as dangerous or misguided. Suspicious of utopianism and moralism, realists of different stripes concentrate on power, violence, and conflicts over meaning and value. However, the conclusions they draw from this focus—and their political projects—vary greatly, ranging from conservative defences of the existing order through to radical forms of political critique.

The main value of realism is that it can sensitize us to the importance of limits. This takes two main forms. The first concerns the limits on feasibility identified by realist IR scholars. They provide a valuable service by delineating some of the constraints facing actors in international politics, as well as the dangers of ignoring the complexity of political life in the pursuit of moral ideals. This can help to identify possibilities for realistic action in a world pervaded by conflict and divided between groups of people with clashing values and political projects. The second type of limit concerns the scope of ethical theorizing itself. Realists warn us against the dangers of *moralism*, of approaching moral questions in the wrong way. Among other things, this draws attention to the importance of culture, politics and history in thinking about ethics in a global context.

QUESTIONS

1. Is realism inherently conservative?

2. What is wrong with moralism in international ethics?

3. What is the relationship between realist IR theory and realist political ethics?

4. Are realism and utopianism compatible?

5. Can realism be seen as a form of critical theory?

6. Should political theorists be concerned with questions of feasibility?

7. Why did many realists oppose the invasion of Iraq in 2003?

8. Is political realism obsolete in an age of globalization?

9. What are the main differences between the 'classical realism' of Morgenthau, Carr, and Niebuhr, and the contemporary realism of Waltz, Mearsheimer, and Snyder?

10. What are the problems with Walzer's account of 'dirty hands'?

FURTHER READING

Bell, D. (ed.) (2009) *Political Thought and International Relations: Variations on a Realist Theme*. Oxford: Oxford University Press. Contains essays on a wide variety of approaches to realist political thinking.

Coady, C. A. J. (2008) *Messy Morality: The Challenge of Politics*. Oxford: Oxford University Press. An illuminating discussion of the problems of moralism.

Geuss, R. (2008) *Philosophy and Real Politics*. Princeton: Princeton University Press. A hard-hitting defence of the necessity of realism in political philosophy.

Lebow, R. N. (2003) *The Tragic Vision of Politics: Ethics, Interests, and Orders*. Cambridge: Cambridge University Press. A bold reinterpretation of classical realism, focusing on the idea of tragedy.

Morgenthau, H. (1946) *Scientific Man versus Power Politics*. Chicago: University of Chicago Press. Morgenthau's most interesting book. His most popular book, *Politics Among Nations* (1948), is also worth reading.

Scheuerman, W. E. (2009) *Morgenthau*. Cambridge: Polity. An insightful account of Morgenthau's complex body of work.

Smith, M. J. (1986) *Realist Thought from Weber to Kissinger*. Baton Rouge: Louisiana State University Press. A good overview of twentieth-century realism.

Walzer, M. (1973) Political action: the problem of dirty hands. In: Walzer, M. (2007) *Thinking Politically: Essays in Political Theory*, ed. D. Miller. New Haven: Yale University Press, pp. 278–96. A provocative essay on why it is sometimes right to do wrong.

Weber, M. (1919) The profession and vocation of politics. In: Weber, M. (1984) *Political Writings*, P. Lassman and R. Speirs (eds). Cambridge: Cambridge University Press. A seminal discussion of the 'ethics of responsibility'.

Williams, M. C. (2005) *The Realist Tradition and the Limits of International Relations*, Cambridge: Cambridge University Press. An innovative reinterpretation of realist political thinking, highlighting its critical potential.

WEB LINKS

http://www.opendemocracy.net/democracy-americanpower/morgenthau_2522.jsp An essay by John Mearsheimer, a leading realist scholar, discussing Hans Morgenthau, and the differences between realism and neo-conservatism in relation to the war in Iraq.

http://classics.mit.edu/Thucydides/pelopwar.html The text of Thucydides' *History of the Peloponnesian War*, which many realists see as a classic statement of realism.

http://www.theory-talks.org/2008/07/theory-talk-12.html An interview with Robert Jervis, a leading realist scholar, on aspects of IR theory, American foreign policy, and nuclear weapons.

http://www.realisticforeignpolicy.org The website of the Coalition for a Realistic Foreign Policy, which promotes a realist policy.

http://walt.foreignpolicy.com/blog The blog of a prominent realist scholar, dedicated to discussion of foreign policy and IR theory.

Visit the Online Resource Centre that accompanies this book to access more learning resources: www.oxfordtextbooks.co.uk/orc/bell_ethics/

6 The ethics of international society

Peter Jones

READER'S GUIDE

The idea of 'international society' embodies two claims: that the main actors in international politics are states, and that states can and should constitute a society. This chapter analyses both the idea and the reality of international society, drawing especially on the work of Hedley Bull. It considers how states can be moral agents and patients, and how the current states system might be defended against alternative ways of organizing the international world. It also examines the debate between 'pluralists' and 'solidarists' on what our ambitions for international society should be. Finally, it turns to John Rawls's moral theory of international society and considers why he and others believe that international justice should take the form of a just society of peoples rather than a cosmopolitan order.

6.1 The idea of international society

'International society' is a society of states. Just as citizens constitute the members of a domestic society, so states constitute the members of international society. International society is not, therefore, the same as 'global' or 'world' society, terms that normally convey a conception of all humanity as a single community. 'International' means 'inter-state' and 'international society' describes a community of states. There are, of course, many actors in the international world besides states, such as non-governmental organizations and multinational corporations, but those non-state actors are not usually considered members of international society.[1]

International 'society' describes more than the existence of a plurality of states that interact with one another; geographical proximity and interaction are not enough to constitute a society of either states or individuals. International 'society' indicates that states possess common values and interests, and comply with common rules and institutions. Hedley Bull famously distinguished between a 'system of states' and a 'society of states'. States form an international 'system' when they have sufficient contact and impact upon one another to behave as parts of a whole. However, they form an international 'society' only when they are 'conscious of certain common interests and common values' and conceive themselves as 'bound by a common set of rules in their relations with one another, and share in the working of common institutions' (Bull, 2002, pp. 9, 13).

The idea of an international 'society' clearly draws upon that of a domestic society, but domestic societies normally have governments that create, oversee, and uphold their society's rules and institutions. International society, as we know it, has no such common government and is, therefore, in the literal sense, an **anarchy**. Its being an anarchy has led many to conclude we should understand international relations on the model of Hobbes's **state of nature**—a state of war, cold if not hot, which is bereft of anything we might describe as 'society'. The thesis of Bull and other proponents of international society is that the absence of a world government does not preclude either the possibility or the reality of states' developing rules and relationships in virtue of which they constitute a society, albeit an 'anarchical society'.

International society, therefore, has two preconditions. First, there must be states. The state is a political form that emerged in Europe during the modern era and that has gradually become the normal unit of political life for most of humanity. It is usually defined as an independent political community that has a government, and a territory and population over which it wields sovereign **authority**. That simple definition is too simple to describe the reality of contemporary states, but it suffices to distinguish the state from other political arrangements, such as those of Europe during the medieval era or of populations who have been subjected to imperial rule. The states system is not therefore a general feature of human existence. It is possible to identify pre-modern arrangements that share some similarity with it, such as the poleis system of Ancient Greece and the city-states of medieval Italy. However, strictly speaking, states did not exist before the modern era and they became a world-wide phenomenon only during the second half of the twentieth century.

Secondly, states form a society only when they recognize common rules and institutions and conduct themselves accordingly. An international society need not be universal in scope. An international society, facilitated by a common culture and nested within a larger international system, existed within Christendom during the sixteenth

---

[1] There may be a case for interpreting 'international society' more inclusively, particularly if we substitute 'participants' for 'members', but in this chapter I keep faith with the orthodoxy that understands it to be a society of states. Non-state actors can be assigned to 'world society' or 'transnational society' (Buzan, 2004).

and seventeenth centuries, and amongst European states during the eighteenth and nine-teenth centuries (Bull, 2002, pp. 26–36). International society became global only in the twentieth century, and it remains more fully developed amongst some states and within some regions than across the world as a whole.

The ethics of international society describes the morality appropriate to a society of states. It concerns the moral status of states, the principles and values that should govern their dealings with one another, and the aims that international society should pursue. It differs from cosmopolitan moralities in the moral significance it gives to states. A cos-mopolitan morality holds that the ultimate units of concern are human individuals, that all human individuals enjoy that status equally, and that all individuals (rather than, for example, only one's fellow-citizens) should be of ultimate concern to everyone (Pogge, 1992, pp. 48–9). Cosmopolitans do not necessarily reject the state as an institution, but they regard it as properly no more than a vehicle for securing justice amongst all of humanity.

On cosmo-politanism, see Chapter 8.

Exponents of international society can also—although they do not have to—regard human individuals as the ultimate units of moral concern; they may treat the moral claims of states as ultimately those of the individuals who constitute their members. How-ever, they hold that the existence of states fundamentally alters the moral landscape. In-dividuals who are fellow members of a state possess moral rights and duties in relation to one another that are different from and more extensive than those they have in relation to 'outsiders'. Moreover, at the international level, moral relationships between individu-als are mediated by states: individuals belonging to different states relate to one another as different bodies of citizens, rather than as individual members of the human race.

An ethic of international society is also distinct from a morality that gives fundamental significance to nationhood, where nationhood means something different from state-hood. The idea of a society of states need not compete with that of a society of nations in quite the way that it competes with cosmopolitan visions. Traditionally, nationalists have sought national **self-determination** in the form of independent states, so that each nation will constitute a state and all states will be nation states. That vision is consist-ent with a society of states, provided that each nation state's aspirations are consistent with the rules of international society. However, proponents of international society take the political fact of statehood, rather than a distinct and prior notion of nationhood, as their starting point, and they may take little or no account of the claims of nations and nationalism.

On the ethics of nationhood, see Chapter 7.

6.2 Ideas and realities

Concern with the ethics of international society can be of two sorts. We might examine the ethic of an actually existing international society in an entirely empirical spirit. The values to which people and institutions are committed, and that they manifest in their conduct, are matters of fact, and they are no less so for being facts about values. The morality, which as a matter of fact prevails in a society, is sometimes described as its 'positive' morality. Much of the effort of international relations scholars in examining international society has aimed simply to identify and document the norms and rules that constitute its positive morality.

Alternatively, we might examine the ethic that *ought* to govern international society. Our concern will then be normative rather than empirical and will focus on 'critical', rather than 'positive' morality. The relevant morality will be 'critical' not because it must find fault with the conduct of states or their values, but because it will not depend for its content upon what, as a matter of fact, states do or people believe; it can, therefore, assess actions and beliefs as right or wrong, good or bad, praiseworthy or blameworthy.

A well-known adage of moral philosophy observes that we cannot derive an 'ought' from an 'is': we cannot validly derive value conclusions—conclusions about how we ought to behave—from purely factual premises. However, that adage does not mean that our normative thinking need take no account of facts. On the contrary, there are many ways in which empirical questions bear upon normative concerns and many ways in which the realities of international politics have significance for normative thought about international society. For one thing, if the states system did not already exist, it is most unlikely that anyone would argue for its invention. We grapple with the issues raised by that system, not because it is a moral ideal, but because it is a contemporary reality. Similarly, there is a point in making international society central to our thought, only so long as states remain the principal players in the international world. If states were to be overtaken by business firms and other non-state organizations as the principal actors in international life (a process that some argue is already well advanced), it would be idle to make international society the focus of our moral thought.

 See also Chapter 4.

Another well-known adage relating the normative to the empirical is 'ought implies can'. There is no point in prescribing the impossible, so argument about what there ought to be must take account of what there can be. More sceptical forms of **realism** have doubted the reality and possibility of rule-governed behaviour amongst states in the anarchical circumstances of international politics: states will be disinclined to observe constraints when they have no assurance that other states will do—or will be made to do—the same. The claim that there is an international society is a counter to that scepticism. Those who have made it, principally the English School, have done so primarily because they have sought to dispel a misconception of the realities of international politics.[2] However, establishing the reality of international society is also important as an antidote to suggestions that normative aspirations for international society are misplaced because there can be no such society.

On realism, see Chapter 5.

Finally, there is the question of what we should understand international society itself to be. We might adopt a simple idealized model of that society, which accords all states an equal status and the same rights of self-determination. Within this model, each state will respect the principle of state **sovereignty** and so not interfere in the internal affairs of other states. In their dealings with one another, states will act in good faith, honour treaties and agreements, and contribute to and play their allotted role in the institutions

---

[2] In this chapter, I focus on the work of Hedley Bull, but other leading figures of the original English School included Martin Wight, Herbert Butterfield, and Charles Manning. On the English School, see Dunne (1998); Roberson (1998); Bellamy (2005); Hall (2006a); Linklater & Sugunami (2006). On the ethics of the English School, see Cochran (2008a, 2009).

of the society of states. Later in this chapter, we shall see a close approximation to this model in John Rawls's portrait of a just society of peoples.

Rawls sees his model as utopian yet realistic, but it is clearly at some distance from the world as we know it. Others' conceptions of international society have been shaped more by the world as it is. So Hedley Bull (2002), for example, identified the principal institutions of international society as the balance of power, international law, diplomacy, war, and the great powers. Of these, international law and diplomacy are unsurprising, but why should international society include a balance of power, war, and great powers?

Although states possess a formally equal status, they differ greatly in their actual power. That inequality raises the prospect of one state achieving a hegemony that will enable it to dominate all others. Bull saw a balance of power as essential to fending off that possibility and maintaining the plurality of sovereign states that is essential for international society. Maintaining that balance may require resort to war; for Bull, the chief purpose of a balance of power was not to secure peace, but to preserve the states system, although a stable balance of power would help to promote peace. War itself may seem the antithesis of international society, less the manifestation of a society than a symptom of its breakdown. In one respect, that is clearly so, but 'war' describes not any act of violence, but only a conflict between sovereign states; it has a legal status and is governed by the rules and norms of international society.

The idea of 'great powers' is also out of kilter with a conception of states as equal members of international society, yet Bull saw those powers not merely as facts of life but also as essential for the functioning of international society. They were distinguished not merely by their superior strength but also by their special rights and duties to manage the affairs of international society. They promoted order by preventing, managing, and containing conflicts amongst other states. Great powers pursued their own interests and their impact on international society was not always benign but, Bull suggested, their dominance simplified international relations and secured a greater measure of order than we might find in a society of states that were more equal in power.

Bull gave significant roles, as one might expect, to international law and diplomacy in the society of states. Unlike some legal theorists, he did not doubt that international law was really law and he observed that the great majority of states recognized and complied with it for most of the time. Equally, the practice of diplomacy both promoted and symbolized international society. Yet Bull argued that international society might exist without either; international norms did not have to take the form of laws and states could communicate without diplomacy. Moreover, both presupposed the existence of international society since neither could function without it, and sometimes the good of international society might require that they be set aside; for example, when maintaining the balance of power required the overriding of international law (Bull, 2002, p. 138).

Thus, Bull's conception of international society was far from utopian; it was inspired not by a moral ideal, but by what he found in the world.[3] It took issue with the Hobbesian conception of international politics, but it also bore the hallmarks of realism. Bull did not suppose that states subordinated their interests to moral principle; rather they saw their

---

[3] For a study of international society in its contemporary form, that has a scope similar to Bull's account, see Hurrell (2007); see also Buzan (2004); Little & Williams (2006).

interests as served by their compliance with international society. We can, of course, detach the normative ethic that should govern international society from the past and present reality of that society. But Bull was interested in providing for the world as it was and saw little point in moral fantasies that had no purchase on it. Moreover, while it is reasonable to enjoin states to discharge their obligations as members of the international society of which they are actually a part, it is unreasonable as well as unrealistic to enjoin them to behave as if they already belonged to an international society of a more idealized sort.

6.3 The moral standing of states

If states are the members of international society, can we really speak of an ethic of that society? Are states capable of moral conduct? Can they bear moral, as well as legal, rights, duties, and responsibilities?

Those questions may seem unnecessary. States do not decide or act; it is politicians and officials who declare war, conclude peace, enter into negotiations, and so on. Nevertheless, they do these things in the name of their states so that we speak, for example, of Britain going to war, or France concluding peace, or the US entering into negotiations with Russia. When individuals act on behalf of states, what they do has moral and political significance beyond themselves. States can be patients, as well as agents and if, for example, a state's rights are violated, we cannot translate that violation as a harm suffered by particular politicians or officials. Thus, we still need to conceive states as the bearers of rights, duties and responsibilities. That is not especially problematic. States are created institutions, but once these 'artificial persons' exist, they can be ascribed rights, duties, and responsibilities in the way that we ascribe those to commercial companies, churches, universities, and other such bodies.

We do not, however, have to give ultimate moral significance to states. We might hold that their moral standing is reducible to that of the people whom they represent and for whom they act. We can then conceive that 'people' in either of two ways. We might think of it is as a unitary entity, 'a people', that it is more than a set of individuals at any particular moment. If, for example, we think of a people or a nation as having an identity that is continuous across successive generations of individuals, we seem to conceive it in that way. When John Rawls (1999) reinterprets the society of states as a society of peoples, he conceives peoples according to that 'corporate' model.

Alternatively, we can think of 'the people' as the set of individuals who constitute a state's population. Those individuals cannot intelligibly hold their state's rights and duties as separate individuals, but they can hold them together, collectively or jointly. According to this 'collective' model, a people is no more than the members of a political community who, in virtue of their shared interests as members of that community, hold collective rights against, and owe collective duties to, other political communities (Jones, 1999b). Michael Walzer, for example, holds that

the idea of communal integrity derives its moral and political force from the rights of contemporary men and women to live as members of a historic community, and to express their inherited culture through political forms worked out among themselves. (Walzer, 1980, p. 211; see also Bull, 2002, pp. 21, 308; Charvet, 1998)

6.4 **Defending the states system**

We live in a world of states, but do we have reason to endorse that condition? There may seem little point in defending the states system. Humanity has lived without states in the past and may do so again in the future, but states have existed for centuries and are unlikely to disappear very soon. So we may view the states system as merely a fact of modern life. Bull himself remarked that there was 'nothing historically inevitable or morally sacrosanct' about a society of sovereign states (2002, pp. 65, 135). However, even if we take that view, the fact that humanity is organized into separate, more or less self-governing, political communities may be a fact that our moral thinking should still take into account. Arguably, that fact should affect our thinking on the rights and duties people possess, in relation to whom they possess them, and how they relate morally to one another at the global level. Our moral thinking should not ignore the fact that people are citizens as well as humans.

On citizenship, see Chapter 26.

If we move to defend the states system, we might do so in largely negative terms. That is, we might take a poor view of the feasibility or desirability of the alternatives (e.g. Bull, 2002, Part 3). Rather than strive for peace and co-operation amongst states, it might seem desirable to move towards global government so that the world becomes, in effect, one domestic society. However, many believe that concentrating political power in a single world government, from whose jurisdiction there could be no escape, would be unacceptably dangerous and oppressive. Moreover, the substitution of world government for the states system may do little to enhance peace; it may simply substitute internal for external conflict—civil conflicts are already more common than wars between states. We also have reason to doubt the efficacy with which a world state would discharge the functions and provide the services we expect from governments.

However, rather than faulting all the possible alternatives, we might defend the state system in more positive terms. There is a long tradition of valuing civic life, a form of life made possible by states and state membership (e.g. Frost, 1996; Pettit, 1997, 2010). If states disappear, so will citizenship as we know it and all that we value in citizenship. People might, of course, become world citizens, but membership of a vast community encompassing all of humanity may prove a poor substitute for state-citizenship. Democracy, popular participation, and collective self-determination would also become less meaningful if we move from states to world government. However, these issues are far from simple. The extent to which people's lives are shaped by influences external to their state already detracts from the authenticity of intra-state democracy, and large differences in the size, character, and power of modern states (compare Iceland with China) impair the credibility of general defences of the current system of states. Nor is the choice simply between state or world government. Supra-state organizations can complement, rather than obliterate, the states system; consider, for example, the United Nations and the European Union.

On democracy, see Chapter 21.

A different, if related, defence focuses upon people's affective ties to their state, particularly national identity. Nationalism has received a bad press because of the aggressive and xenophobic forms it has sometimes taken. Doubt has also been cast upon the credibility of ethnic nationhood and the project of using that idea to determine statehood. It has

On the ethics of national identity, see Chapter 7.

now become common among academic writers on nationalism to accept that nationality is largely a matter of who people believe themselves to be. Nevertheless, people's sense of nationhood and of national belonging remains a real and potent feature of our world. It is strongly associated with statehood, simply because the experience of shared state-hood plays a major role in generating it and is presupposed by the phenomenon of 'civic' nationalism. Once again things are not entirely simple. National identities do not always map onto states, nor should they always—or so many people think. However, in so far as there is value in communal ties of national identity, and the trust, mutual concern, and sense of belonging they generate, we may think they should be recognized and fostered through the states system (Walzer, 1983, 1994; Margalit & Raz, 1990; Miller, 1995).

Differences in national identity relate to a further defence. Human beings are diverse; they are committed to different values, beliefs, cultures, and ways of life. The states system enables different communities to live and to organize themselves according to their different allegiances. It obviously does not provide comprehensively for human diversity, since virtually all states have internally diverse populations. However, it does contribute to the accommodation of human diversity and to people's freedom to pursue different forms of collective life (Nardin, 1983; Williams, 2002; Frost, 2009).

6.5 Pluralism or solidarism?

Justifying international society is much more straightforward than defending the states system. If there are to be states, it is obviously preferable that they should share rules and institutions that enable them to coexist peacefully and co-operatively, rather than live in a condition of mistrust, insecurity, and incipient or actual conflict. Moreover, many norms of international society simply translate our beliefs about right conduct from persons to states: states should, for example, refrain from inflicting gratuitous harm, respect one another's possessions, and honour their undertakings. People may quarrel about how far an international society does or can exist, but they can hardly prefer its absence to its presence.

That still leaves room for differences of view on the proper role of international society. How ambitious should that role be? Hedley Bull (1966) coined two terms that have structured subsequent argument on that issue: **solidarism** and **pluralism**. Solidarism describes the belief that states as members of international society can and should unite in the pursuit of shared goals that aim for more than merely their own coexistence. Pluralism rejects that aspiration and holds that international society should limit itself to maintaining the minimal rules necessary for its own continuance. Although the idea of solidarity amongst states is neutral with respect to the goals around which states might unite, solidarism has come to be associated with a strong commitment to **human rights** and the pursuit of justice amongst humanity as a whole. It often, therefore, connotes two different sorts of solidarity: solidarity amongst states and solidarity with the human race.

 On human rights, see Chapter 13.

Pluralists and solidarists usually divide over an empirical question: are states capable of agreement on more than the minimal rules necessary for their coexistence? Solidarists typically answer that question more optimistically than pluralists. The two camps may also disagree morally: are there goals beyond mere coexistence that international society has moral reason to pursue? Solidarists often have more expansive moral ideals than pluralists and are willing to concede more to the claims of cosmopolitan moral thinking.[4]

Pluralists combine empirical and moral considerations into a single reason for rejecting solidarism: if we set more than minimal goals for international society, those goals will be a source of dispute and conflict amongst states and that, in turn, will undermine international society. We should not impose on international society 'a strain which it cannot bear' (Bull, 1966, p. 70).

One of the clearest exponents of pluralism is Terry Nardin (1983). Drawing on the work of Michael Oakeshott, he distinguishes between two types of association: purposive and practical. A purposive association exists to pursue a particular end as, for example, a business pursues profit, a university promotes knowledge and a hospital provides health-care. A practical association is committed to no such end; it aspires only to provide a framework within which its members can pursue their own ends, which can be different and conflicting ends. Nardin argues that international society, properly conceived, is a form of practical association. It provides rules that enable its member states to coexist and to interact with one another in a peaceful and orderly fashion, even though they are committed to different cultures, ways of life, and political systems. States have different goals and international society provides for that fact, not by arbitrating amongst those goals itself, but by establishing arrangements that leave states free to pursue their own goals. Various interested parties have sought to transform international society into a purposive association, but their aspirations have been at odds with its essential character and principal merit.

Nardin does not understand his pluralism to sacrifice justice for order, since he takes international justice to consist in compliance with the laws and moral norms of international society conceived as a practical association, and rejects attempts to redefine justice as a purposive value directed at goals such as economic development and the global redistribution of resources (Nardin, 1983, pp. 255–77; Nardin, 2005). He does, however, embrace a modest list of human rights, and argues that the obligation of states to recognize and respect those rights is consistent with international society as a practical association.

Hedley Bull was more ambivalent about the relation between justice and order. He saw order as the principal good secured by international society. Order is no mean good once we take account of all the other goods it makes possible which, for Bull, included three basic social goods: securing life, maintaining agreements, and stabilizing possessions. However, he recognized justice as a value separate from order and identified three of its forms: justice among states, justice for human individuals, particularly human rights, and cosmopolitan or world justice. He feared that the pursuit of any of these might disrupt international order. Cosmopolitan justice was at odds with the constitution of international society. Human rights could license states' interference in one another's internal affairs, which would be a rich source of conflict, especially given dissensus on the content of human rights. Even justice between states might militate against order, since order

---

[4] Some significant discussions of the pluralist-solidarist issue are Wheeler & Dunne (1996); Almeida (2003, 2006); Buzan (2004); Linklater & Suganami (2006); Hurrell (2007).

may require unjust acts, for example, action against an innocent, but over-mighty state to restore the balance of power. In *The Anarchical Society* he refused consistently to rank order ahead of justice, but the burden of much of his argument was to prioritize order over justice in the spirit of pluralism. In later work, he moved more towards solidarism, but still worried about the impact of justice upon order (Bull, 1984, esp. pp. 17–18).

It would be rare now for a proponent of international society to reject the idea of human rights. There is little open support for the principle that sovereignty should entitle a regime to treat its population in any way it likes and respect for human rights has become a well-entrenched norm of international society. Yet human rights are not without complication for the idea of international society. Recognizing human rights seems to entail ascribing international moral standing to individuals, as well as to states. We might hold that people possess human rights only if and because the society of states recognizes those rights, but it is hard to find a *reason* for that recognition that does not give independent moral standing to human individuals. If the rights of individuals are to limit the powers of states, the morality of that condition is captured most satisfactorily by an ethic that gives international standing to both parties. International society can remain a society of states only, but it will be a society that recognizes the independent standing of persons and the duties it owes them.

On human rights, see Chapter 13.

Another problem is widespread dispute over the content of human rights. The more substantial we make those rights, the more we curtail the authority of states. Since pluralists are anxious to accommodate international diversity, the human rights they recognize are often more modest than those favoured by solidarists. Yet both parties can claim that the idea and reality of human rights is consistent with international society, since the chief purpose of those rights is to stipulate what states may not do to, or what they must do for, their own citizens. As currently conceived, human rights are principally the rights of individuals living in states.

On humanitarianism, see Chapter 18.

International society must also face the vexed question of what it should do if states violate human rights. How readily should it set aside its prohibitions on intervention and the use of force in order to protect human rights? Nicholas Wheeler (2000) has formulated a powerful solidarist case for **humanitarian intervention**, which includes the claim that humanitarian intervention, of the right sort and in the right circumstances, is now an established norm of international society. He also argues that international society can and should go further in sanctioning humanitarian intervention. Humanitarian intervention keeps faith with the idea of international society to the extent that it acknowledges non-intervention as the prevailing norm, breach of which requires special justification. Moreover, justifications of humanitarian intervention typically advocate its use not for any human rights violation but only when violations become 'grave', amounting to a 'supreme humanitarian emergency' (Wheeler, 2000, pp. 34, 50). However, given disagreement over the content and weight of human rights, the propensity of states to interpret moral reasons to suit their interests, and the hazardous and uncertain consequences of intervention, pluralists remain reluctant to relax the norm of non-intervention very much (Vincent, 1974; Slater & Nardin, 1986; Jackson, 2000; Mayall, 2000). They are not indifferent to human suffering; they simply believe that misrule has often to be tolerated because the costs and consequences (long- as well as short-term) of not tolerating it are likely to be much worse.

Solidarism can go only so far if it is to remain consistent with international society. Bull sometimes elided human rights with cosmopolitanism, but he also distinguished them, in part, because he thought the realization of cosmopolitan ideas of justice, unlike human rights, required abandoning international society for cosmopolitan society (Bull, 2002, pp. 80–4). Adherents of international society can endorse international action to eliminate poverty (e.g. Vincent, 1986), but, as we shall see, they have reason to baulk at more ambitious ideas of global **distributive justice**.

6.6 John Rawls and the law of peoples

While Hedley Bull has provided the most influential analysis of international society as a political reality, John Rawls (1999) has produced the fullest moral theory of international society. Bull, fearing that justice might undermine order, was inclined to prioritize order over justice. Rawls, by contrast, gives primacy to justice and sees it as essential for order. Only when the members of international society endorse it as just will we have genuine international stability grounded in 'the right reasons', rather than a mere balance of power (Rawls, 1999, pp. 44–54).

Rawls describes his ideal of international society as a 'realistic utopia' (Rawls, 1999, pp. 11–23). It is utopian because it envisages a society whose members enjoy entirely just and peaceful relations. It is realistic because it remains sufficiently close to our world to be attainable.

While Rawls writes about international relations squarely within the international society tradition, he characterizes the members of international society as peoples, rather than states (Rawls, 1999, pp. 25–29). He does so to dissociate himself from the traditional view that states possess unlimited sovereignty and may use war in pursuit of their interests. For Rawls, a state's sovereignty is curtailed by human rights, and the use and conduct of war is closely circumscribed by principles of justice. He also wants to conceive the members of international society as moral agents who are capable of reasonableness, as well as rationality, and able therefore to offer fair terms of co-operation to one another. How, then, does he identify a 'people'? He describes it as united by 'common sympathies', such as those that might arise from a common language, history, or political culture; yet he shows little inclination to separate nationhood from statehood and, for the most part, conceives a people as a political entity defined by common state-membership.

Rawls aims to work out the principles that should govern a society of peoples. In working out principles for a domestic liberal society, he famously deploys his notions of an '**original position**' and a '**veil of ignorance**' along with the traditional idea of **social contract** (1971, 1993, 2001b). We imagine individuals situated in an original position in which they have to agree upon the principles that are to govern their own society; but they have to reach agreement behind a veil of ignorance, which prevents their knowing features of themselves such as their gender, race, IQ, and their likely economic position in the society. They also do not know to which 'comprehensive doctrine' (religious, philosophical or moral) they subscribe or what is their

On Rawls's theory of justice, see Chapter 1.

'**conception of the good**' (what ends they wish to pursue in life). The point of the veil of ignorance is to ensure that principles agreed in the original position will be fair. People cannot favour themselves unfairly if they do not know what kind of people they will be.

Rawls investigates international justice initially by asking what principles should guide the foreign policy of liberal peoples in their relations with one another (1999, pp. 30–5). His answer uses the same conceptual apparatus as he deploys for domestic political arrangements. This time, we imagine an original position in which representatives of liberal peoples have to agree on the rules that are to govern their international relations. Behind the veil of ignorance, representatives do not know details of the state they represent, such as the size of its population and territory, its relative strength, and its specific political system; they cannot, therefore, be biased by that information in deciding upon the rules that should govern relationships between peoples.[5]

Rawls supposes that this imaginary international decision-making process would yield the following eight principles, which he describes as the '**law of peoples**' (Rawls, 1999, pp. 35–43). Peoples:

- are free and independent, and must respect one another's freedom and independence;
- must observe treaties and undertakings;
- have an equal status and are parties to agreements that bind them;
- must observe a duty of non-intervention;
- have a right of self-defence, but no right to instigate war for other reasons;
- must honour human rights;
- must observe specified restrictions in their conduct of war;
- have a duty to assist other peoples who live under unfavourable conditions that prevent their having a just or decent political and social regime.

Rawls believes that the rightness of these principles would be readily apparent to the representatives and they would need to debate only alternative formulations or interpretations of them.

The eight principles are not 'laws' in the ordinary sense. They are moral principles that should govern the conduct of international life. Nor do they exhaust the content of the law of peoples. Additional principles will provide for fair international trade, the formation and regulation of international federations, and mutual assistance during times of famine and drought. However, the eight principles constitute the 'basic charter' of the law of peoples.

Rawls's conception of justice amongst peoples mimics his conception of justice amongst the citizens of a liberal society. Peoples as members of international society, like the citizens of a liberal society, possess a free and equal status. Given their free and equal status, it would be unjust if some peoples used political power to impose their preferred form of domestic society upon other peoples, just as it would be unjust for some liberal citizens to use political power to impose their preferred comprehensive doctrine upon others.

---

[5] For a different contractual account of international society, see Charvet (1998).

In both cases, however, Rawls allows that members' equal status can permit certain 'functional' inequalities, provided those inequalities work to the common advantage (Rawls, 1999, pp. 41, 43).

Justice does not require peoples to behave entirely selflessly. Each people has an interest in its safety and security, its independence and political institutions, its territorial integrity, and the well-being of its citizens (Rawls, 1999, pp. 34–5). It can also exhibit the 'proper patriotism' that accompanies self-respect (Rawls, 1999, pp. 44–5). A people may legitimately pursue these interests, but it must do so justly, that is, in compliance with the law of peoples. Just peoples will pursue their ends 'reasonably', as well as 'rationally'.

Although Rawls begins by considering relations amongst liberal peoples only, he also includes 'decent non-liberal' peoples in international society. He outlines a decent hierarchical society, exemplified by an imaginary Muslim society, to indicate the type of non-liberal society that is legitimately a member of the society of peoples (Rawls, 1999, pp. 62–78). That hierarchical society qualifies as decent on several counts. Externally, it is not aggressive, but pursues its aims through diplomacy and other peaceful means. Internally, it is guided by a common good idea of justice, which recognizes human rights and imposes duties upon all persons within its territory. It is not a democracy and its members do not possess the equal basic rights enjoyed by liberal citizens. But it does possess a consultation hierarchy in which individuals participate through their membership of groups. Individuals have the right to dissent and, although there is a state religion, they enjoy a measure of religious freedom. Finally, the society's judges and officials possess 'a sincere and not unreasonable' belief that their legal system is guided by a common good idea of justice rather than supported by mere force. Decent hierarchical peoples, like liberal peoples, are 'well-ordered'.

Suppose, now, that we place representatives of decent hierarchical peoples in an original position behind a suitable veil of ignorance, and ask them to agree upon the rules that should govern their international relations. Rawls argues that they would embrace the same law as would liberal peoples (Rawls, 1999, pp. 68–70). Thus, both types of people can belong to the same international society and can recognize the same law of peoples. In particular, even though decent peoples do not accord a free and equal status to individuals within their societies, they can accord a free and equal status to peoples.

Given their differences, liberal and decent non-liberal peoples will need to tolerate one another, but that toleration is a matter of justice rather than grace. It requires each to recognize and respect other peoples as equal members of international society, possessing the same rights and duties as itself (Rawls, 1999, pp. 122–30). While Rawls believes decent non-liberal societies to be internally less just than liberal societies (Rawls, 1999, pp. 62, 78, 83), he holds that they are due no less international respect. If liberal societies sought to transform decent non-liberal societies into liberal societies by using military force, or economic or diplomatic sanctions, or even financial incentives, they would act unjustly. Liberal societies can encourage decent non-liberal societies to become liberal, but only in ways that respect their free and equal status.

Decent peoples therefore figure alongside liberal peoples in the '**ideal theory**' of international society. That theory is 'ideal' in that it sets out the moral constitution of international society without concession to imperfection. The inclusion of decent non-liberal peoples in the society of peoples is a requirement of justice, not a second-best arrangement.

Rawls does, however, identify three other types of society: outlaw states, burdened societies, and benevolent despotisms (Rawls, 1999, pp. 4, 90). Outlaw states are aggressive and refuse to comply with the law of peoples. Burdened societies suffer unfavourable historical, social, or economic conditions that prevent their establishing well-ordered regimes. Benevolent despotisms honour human rights, but are not well-ordered because they deny their members any meaningful role in political decision-making. In examining how liberal and decent peoples should deal with these societies, we enter the realm of '**non-ideal theory**', since in a fully just world these defective societies would not exist. The goal of the law of peoples is to transform them into decent or liberal societies so that international society will be universal in scope: all peoples will be genuine members of the society of peoples (Rawls, 1999, pp. 105–6).

How should decent and liberal peoples respond to outlaw states? Decent and liberal peoples will not wage war against one another, since they comply with the law of peoples, which gives them a right of self-defence, but no right to instigate war for other reasons. However, their right of self-defence may justify their going to war against aggressive and expansionist outlaw states. Other means of curbing outlaw states may be available; war would be a weapon of last resort and, if used, would observe the principles for conduct found in the **just war** tradition (Rawls, 1999, pp. 94–7).

On the just war tradition, see Chapter 16.

Rawls also suggests that violations of human rights may justify intervention, either military or non-military (Rawls, 1999, pp. 81, 93–4). Once again, intervention would not be needed amongst decent and liberal peoples since they honour human rights, but it may be needed to prevent grave human rights violations by outlaw states.

Rawls's position on human rights has attracted much critical comment (e.g. Buchanan, 2006; Macleod, 2006; Tasioulas, 2002). In part, that is because he presents a very limited list of human rights, which includes rights to personal security and the means of subsistence; freedom from slavery and serfdom; sufficient liberty of conscience to ensure freedom of religion; personal property; and the formal equality required by natural justice (Rawls, 1999, pp. 65, 78–9). Compared with the human rights now recognized in UN declarations and conventions, that is a highly attenuated list. It does not include, for example, rights to freedom of expression or association, or democratic rights. Rawls distinguishes the rights of liberal democratic citizens from human rights, which he conceives as a 'special class of urgent rights' (p. 79). Clearly, he has to make that distinction if respect for human rights is to be a condition of international **legitimacy** and if decent non-liberal societies are to qualify as legitimate.

Rawls's modest list of human rights may look like a moral compromise designed to facilitate the inclusiveness of international society. However, for Rawls human rights do not merely set moral limits to a regime's autonomy; they also indicate when external intervention is justified, if only in principle. While he might wish individuals to enjoy a set of rights that is more extensive than human rights, the crucial question is whether a society's failure to provide those additional rights would justify intervention. He thinks not.

6.7 **World poverty and global distributive justice**

Rawls's just liberal domestic society would distribute resources amongst its citizens according to his '**difference principle**': resources would be distributed equally, unless an unequal distribution would work to the advantage of all, especially the worst-off group. Several philosophers have used Rawls's ideas to develop theories of global distributive justice (e.g. Beitz; 1999, Pogge, 1989). If we place the world's population in an original position and behind a veil of ignorance, and ask what principle of distribution they would adopt, arguably the answer would be a global version of Rawls's 'difference principle', a principle that would seem to require a radical redistribution of the world's resources.

On Rawls's 'difference principle', see Chapter 1.

On global wealth redistribution, see also Chapters 8, 14.

Proponents of international society, including Rawls himself, reject this approach to distributive justice, since it takes no account of the fact that people live in states. They could apply his difference principle to societies, rather than to individuals, but there is little moral appeal in worrying about how resources are distributed amongst societies, but not within them. Generally, proponents of international society apply the concept of distributive justice only within state boundaries. That may be no more than a consequence of their recognizing the legitimacy of the state system. Traditionally, the jurisdiction of a state extends to the resources that fall within its territory. One society may decide to give aid to another, but no society has a just entitlement to another society's resources. However, rather than rely only on the status quo, defenders of international society do give more reasoned arguments for resisting theories of global distributive justice.

Rawls, as we have seen, holds that liberal and decent peoples have a duty to assist burdened societies (Rawls, 1999, pp. 106–113). Burdened societies 'lack the political and cultural traditions, the human capital and know-how and, often, the material and technological resources needed to be well-ordered' (Rawls, 1999, p. 106). However, Rawls does not conceive the duty to assist these societies as a duty to relieve poverty as such, nor as a duty owed directly to the world's poor. Rather it is duty to assist burdened societies to become well-ordered so that they can become members in good standing of the society of peoples. The duty is really, therefore, a duty to promote international society. Certainly transforming burdened societies into well-ordered societies will benefit their populations, since well-ordered societies honour human rights, including the right to subsistence. However, for Rawls, the duty to provide for an individual's basic needs really falls upon the people to whom that individual belongs; the duty of other peoples is only to assist burdened societies to achieve conditions that will enable them to discharge their duties to their populations (Rawls, 1999, pp. 118–20).

Underlying Rawls's view is his belief that the causes of poverty, including famines, lie typically not in natural circumstances, but in social and political failings. He believes too that failure to develop a well-ordered regime usually owes more to a society's political culture than to its economic circumstances (Rawls, 1999, pp. 108–9; see also Risse, 2005a, b). With the possible exception of some indigenous peoples, no society is so lacking in natural resources and human talent that it cannot sustain a well-ordered regime (Rawls, 1999, pp. 108, 119).

Once all duties of assistance have been discharged, significant economic inequalities amongst peoples may well remain; but, unless those inequalities undermine the free and equal status of peoples, they do not, for Rawls, constitute injustices (Rawls, 1999, pp. 113–15). Why not?

Since Rawls believes that a country's fate, including its economic fate, is really determined by its political culture, he is unmoved by complaints that nature has distributed its resources unevenly and arbitrarily amongst societies (Rawls, 1999, pp. 116–17). What then of inequalities in created wealth? Rawls conceives societies as schemes of co-operation that function for the mutual benefit of their members, so that the fruits of co-operation belong only to the co-operators. That is why distributive justice applies within societies, but not beyond them (Rawls, 1999, p. 14). Moreover, societies opt for different economic policies and, as a consequence, some are likely over time to become wealthier than others. Given the origins of those inequalities in societies' different choices, it would be wrong to eradicate them through redistribution (Rawls, 1999, pp. 117–18).

Rawls's position here seems oblivious to changes wrought by globalization, but it does connect with a more general difficulty confronting principles of global distributive justice in current political circumstances. In the current states system each society claims, and in some measure enjoys, a right of self-determination. Can we reasonably hold the world at large responsible for everyone's material condition if it can exert little or no control over the way each society conducts its affairs (Benhabib, 2006)?

As for his difference principle, Rawls conceives that as a specifically liberal principle (Rawls, 1999, p. 70). If we applied it globally, we would treat decent non-liberal peoples unjustly by subjecting them to a liberal principle. We would also treat liberal peoples unjustly, since the difference principle properly governs their internal arrangements, but not their external relations.

See also Chapter 14.
Several philosophers have added to Rawls's objections to cosmopolitan theories of distributive justice. Typically, they accept that, if world government were to replace state government, distributive justice could become global in scope; but, as long as the states system persists, principles of distributive justice should apply within states, but not beyond them. Typically, too, they endorse international action to eliminate global poverty conceived as an 'absolute' bad, but they distinguish that humanitarian obligation from suggestions that justice requires us to attend to people's 'relative' wealth across humanity as a whole.

Taking the value of individual autonomy as fundamental, Michael Blake (2002) argues that a state's coercion needs to be justified to all who are subject to it, since it restricts their autonomy. The state's coercion includes legal arrangements, such as taxation and property laws, which shape the distribution of a society's resources. It is the limiting of citizens' autonomy by a common state authority that provides the moral imperative for securing distributive justice amongst a body of citizens. No such autonomy-limiting authority exists at the international level, so there is no similar case for distributive justice at that level. The value of individual autonomy does provide a case for international action to eliminate poverty, since poverty deprives people of autonomy, but it provides no case for global theories of distributive justice.

Thomas Nagel (2005) also finds the coercive character of the state significant. Socio-economic justice requires the co-ordinated conduct of large numbers of people and, he argues, in our world only the coercive authority of the sovereign state is able to secure that co-ordination, even amongst morally well-motivated people. As long as there is no global state, there can be no global distributive justice. In addition, individuals as fellow members of a state rightly owe special economic obligations to one another. Their state makes unique demands upon their wills and they, through their state, make unique demands upon one another. Those exceptional demands bring with them mutual obligations of distributive justice. Thus, Nagel's claim is not only that, in current circumstances, distributive justice *can* exist only within states, but also that, *morally*, distributive justice arises only as a special associative responsibility of citizens and not as a general human obligation.

Andrea Sangiovanni (2007) agrees, but shifts the focus away from coercion and closer to Rawls's own thinking. The members of a state owe obligations of egalitarian justice to one another because each plays a part in supporting and maintaining the basic collective goods of their society, such as protection from physical attack and the maintenance of a stable system of property rights. While state coercion is instrumental in securing collective goods, it is the reciprocal relationship of a state's members as participants in, and contributors to, a joint undertaking that explains why there should be distributive justice amongst them rather than amongst humanity at large. People do, of course, interact directly and indirectly with more than their fellow citizens. However, Sangiovanni argues, the basic extractive, regulative, and distributive functions performed by the state are still sufficiently different in character and scale from anything that takes place at the global level for the state to remain the proper arena for distributive justice.[6]

6.8 Conclusion

The great strength of the international society approach is that it recognizes and seeks to provide for the existing world of states. That gives it a purchase upon the realities of the international world, but still leaves scope for thought about how that world might be improved. International society, as we have seen, can be an ideal as well as a reality. Proponents of international society are often more optimistic than realists about what states might achieve together, but are sceptical of or resistant to cosmopolitan ambitions for a world in which states either disappear or cease to count morally. Realism and cosmopolitanism present the two main challenges that defenders of international society have to face, but they are also challenges that intrude into thinking about international society itself: how great can our ambitions for international society reasonably be, and how far should they become global ambitions for humanity, rather than only international ambitions for states? As long as we live in a world of states, those two questions will press for answers.

---

[6] For further argument against global distributive justice, see Freeman (2007); Miller (2007). For cosmopolitan replies to state-based objections to global distributive justice, see Caney, 2008; Pevnick, 2008a.

▨ QUESTIONS

1. What is international society?

2. How does the international society approach to global ethics differ from cosmopolitan and nationalist approaches?

3. How did Hedley Bull conceive the character and make-up of international society?

4. Can we conceive of states as moral agents and patients?

5. How might the current states system be defended?

6. What are pluralism and solidarism, and why have theorists of international society divided between those two positions?

7. How might international society accommodate the idea of human rights?

8. How does Rawls arrive at his 'law of peoples'?

9. Is Rawls justified in including liberal and decent non-liberal peoples in a just international society, while excluding other sorts of state?

10. Why do Rawls and others resist the idea of global distributive justice favoured by many of Rawls's disciples?

▨ FURTHER READING

Bellamy, A. (ed.) (2005) *International Society and its Critics*. Oxford: Oxford University Press. Critical studies, from a variety of perspectives, of the English School and its idea of international society.

Bull, H. (2002) *The Anarchical Society: A Study of Order in World Politics*, 3rd edn. Basingstoke: Palgrave. Bull's influential account of international society, published originally in 1977.

Dunne, T. (1998) *Inventing International Society: A History of the English School*, London: Palgrave. A scholarly account of the development of the English School and the work of its leading figures.

Hurrell, A. (2007) *On Global Order: Power, Values, and the Constitution of International Society*. Oxford: Oxford University Press. A comprehensive assessment of international society taking account of the globalized character of the contemporary world.

Linklater, A., & Suganami, H. (2006) *The English School of International Relations: A Contemporary Reassessment*. Cambridge: Cambridge University Press. A wide-ranging critical assessment of the work of the English School.

Mapel, D., & Nardin, T. (eds) (1998) *International Society: Diverse Ethical Perspectives*. Princeton: Princeton University Press. Essays adopting different moral approaches to international society.

Martin, R., & Reidy, D. (eds) (2006) *Rawls's Law of Peoples: A Realistic Utopia?* Oxford: Blackwell. Critical essays on Rawls's international political thought.

Rawls, J. (1999) *The Law of Peoples*. Cambridge: Harvard University Press. Rawls's influential account of a just society of peoples.

▓ WEB LINKS

http://www.polis.leeds.ac.uk/research/international-relations-security/english-school/ A website dedicated to the 'English School' of international relations, containing a wide variety of links to articles.

http://plato.stanford.edu/entries/international-justice/ A good short overview of the theoretical debates over international/global justice, from *The Stanford Encyclopaedia of Philosophy*.

http://plato.stanford.edu/entries/sovereignty/ An analysis of the idea of sovereignty, both past and present, from *The Stanford Encyclopaedia of Philosophy*.

http://plato.stanford.edu/entries/rawls/ An excellent account of the life and work of John Rawls, including a discussion of his ideas about international politics.

Visit the Online Resource Centre that accompanies this book to access more learning resources: **www.oxfordtextbooks.co.uk/orc/bell_ethics/**

7 Defending community: nationalism, patriotism, and culture

Margaret Moore

READER'S GUIDE

This chapter offers reasons why cosmopolitanism is not compatible with treating cultural affiliations and political self-determination seriously. Section 7.1 outlines the basic cosmopolitan position, while section 7.2 sketches two reasons for thinking that cultural attachments warrant protection by jurisdictional authorities. It argues that there are important moral goods embedded in collective self-determination. Section 7.4 explores four criticisms of cosmopolitan egalitarianism, focusing on the idea that it fails to take seriously these attachments and aspirations. In general, the chapter is critical of the extension of domestic justice theory across the globe, and focuses on cultural or broadly communitarian considerations.

7.1 Introduction

This chapter will outline, from a somewhat sympathetic perspective, a broadly **communitarian** position on the current global justice debate. It will focus on two arguments that have been offered for protecting political or cultural communities, and then explain why these should call into question strong variants of cosmopolitanism.

The chapter identifies the basic cosmopolitan position—which is discussed in detail in Chapter 8—as a form of global egalitarianism. Although the term 'cosmopolitanism' means literally, from the Greek, 'world state' or 'world polis', most contemporary cosmopolitans do not argue for a world state or think it is implied in their argument. They are concerned, instead, with ensuring that justice applies universally (across the globe) and this includes the demands of redistributive justice, from the wealthy to the poorest regions of the world.

In section 7.2, the chapter provides a background discussion of cosmopolitanism and the responses to it, focusing mainly on the justificatory arguments underlying cosmopolitan ideals. Section 7.3 puts forward two reasons why we should take seriously cultural affiliations and collective **self-determination** over the relatively local conditions of one's existence. Section 7.4 then discusses four reasons why communitarianism is preferable to cosmopolitanism:

- the responsibility argument;
- the challenge of cultural disagreement about goods argument;
- an argument that political communities are themselves justice-creating, which challenges the assumption of universality in justice theory;
- an argument raising concerns about the potential for imperialism in cosmopolitan justice theory.

Underlying some of these worries is a concern that global justice actually implies taking over many of the functions of the contemporary state, so that, despite their protestations to the contrary, cosmopolitan justice theorists are, in fact, committed to something that takes on many of the functions of a true 'cosmo polis' (world state). To explore this claim, section 7.4 assesses four interrelated arguments that explain why the cosmopolitan ideal, either theoretically or in practice, is in tension with cultural commitments and political **autonomy**.

7.2 The state of the debate

Normative political theory's initial preoccupation with justice within a state has been replaced by a concern for global justice, largely based on the increasingly globalized character of the world. In traditional liberal-democratic political theory, *morality* is conceived of as interested in the appropriate rules, practices, and behaviour of individuals in their dealings with other people and possibly occupants of the life-world (animals, the environment, and so on). It is much broader than, but inclusive of, *justice* and includes such things as **virtue ethics**, and the actions and attitudes that individuals should express towards each other. Justice, by contrast, is typically narrower; it is concerned with the principles that ought to govern the basic institutional structure of the society. In *A Theory of Justice* (1971) John Rawls is quite explicit that justice is concerned primarily with the justice of institutions, or what he calls the '**basic structure**' of domestic society (the institutions of the state), which are characterized by the presence of two features: (1) they have a pervasive impact on people's lives, and (2) they are coercive.

On Rawls's theory of justice, see Chapter 1.

The cosmopolitan project largely grows out of this Rawlsian argument. Those influenced by Rawls—many of them his former students—argued that the principles of justice should not be limited to the state, but were properly conceived as universal; accordingly, they put forward a theory of global justice (Beitz, 1979; Pogge, 2002). They disagreed with Rawls about limiting the scope of justice to the state, and have suggested that the global realm is not simply an arena where the strictures of morality apply, but rules of justice too. On this (cosmopolitan) view, the increasingly globalized character of the world has meant that the global order comprises a set of institutions within which people interact, and membership in this institutional system is of moral relevance. Globalization, then, has meant that justice cannot be confined to a single state (domestic justice): we need to extend the principles of justice globally.

Many cosmopolitan theorists have also supplemented the globalization argument with another argument, which appeals to a basic intuition about fairness (also articulated in Rawlsian terms). This argument for cosmopolitan justice rests on an intuitive idea that there is something wrong or fundamentally unfair about a situation where some people fare much worse than others through no fault of their own. On this view of the requirements of justice—a view that is usually put forward for the domestic sphere—people are compensated for undeserved bad luck (and 'bad luck' in this context could mean lacking some fundamental natural endowments, suffering from accidents or illness, and/or being disadvantaged by social class). Distributive justice involves redistribution with an aim to mitigate the effects of these undeserved advantages, just as Rawls's '**difference principle**' is, in part, justified by the idea that talent is undeserved. This idea of the undeserved character of our well-being seems particularly relevant to global justice in the sense that one of our core intuitions is that it is unfair that some people are born into poor societies, and, through no fault of their own, fare worse than those born into rich societies. As Thomas Nagel argues, the 'accident of being born in a poor rather than a rich country is as arbitrary a determinant of one's fate as the accident of being born in to a poor rather than a rich family in the same country' (Nagel, 2005, p. 126).

This move to describing the world as a sphere in which justice claims apply simply extends the argument for justice in the state in a global direction. It does so by saying either that the world now meets the conditions that were once thought to be confined only to the state—the world is like the state writ large—or that the basic normative argument that was applied to domestic justice can simply be extended, unproblematically, to the global arena. In the sections that follow, I argue that this tendency to theorize global justice as simply a larger or more extensive version of the contemporary state has missed a real opportunity to re-think what a just global order would look like, especially from the point of view of groups with diverse cultures and collective identities.

On defences of the state, see Chapters 6 and 14. Before moving on to the main body of the chapter, it is perhaps worth mentioning that the main response to the extension project—the project to extend (Rawlsian) justice across the globe—has been a defence of the *state* as an arena for justice theory (Blake, 2001; Nagel, 2005; Miller, 1998a). Defenders of the state have accepted Rawls's argument in the *Law of Peoples* (1999), where he explicitly rejects the extension of his account of domestic justice across the globe. They focus on the idea that there is something special about the state that triggers the requirements of justice. The fact of *state* coercion triggers demanding requirements of legitimacy, and necessitates a concern for distributive equality. In short, the arguments between defenders of cosmopolitan justice and its critics have largely been undertaken in Rawlsian terms: between those Rawlsians who think that the argument of *A Theory of Justice* should be extended across the globe; and other Rawlsians who are more influenced by *The Law of Peoples* and various aspects of his original theory of justice that support the idea that justice should be confined to the domestic state.

The argument of this chapter departs from the largely Rawlsian terms of the debate. In the sections that follow, I outline arguments that focus mainly on cultural and national identity diversity, to suggest that it is deeply problematic to theorize global justice as simply a larger, or more extensive, version of the contemporary state.

7.3 Culture, political communities, and cosmopolitanism

In this section, I will offer two reasons why we should care about culture and about political communities. This is an important step in the argument, which continues into section 7.4, that strong versions of cosmopolitanism may not protect people's culture and fails to respect their political identities.

The culture and jurisdictional control argument

The general outline of an argument for jurisdictional **authority** (for territorially concentrated cultural groups) is well-known and articulated in different ways by both David Miller (1995, 2007) and Will Kymlicka (1995). The term 'jurisdictional authority' denotes an area of jurisdiction—either a state or sub-state unit that has devolved authority in which the community can exercise self-government. This argument focuses on the connection between political authority, culture, and a rich understanding of the conditions for the exercise of personal autonomy. The most influential versions of this are developed in relation to the protection of minority groups, but because this argument rests on a particular account of the relationship of jurisdictional authority to the protection of group culture (not specifically minority group culture), it is best understood as about the appropriate and justified relationship between jurisdictional authority and cultural group identity.

The most prominent contemporary version of this argument involves essentially three claims:

- The first move in the argument attempts to establish a link between the collective good of culture and the exercise of personal autonomy.

- The second move relates the good of culture to mechanisms for protection, especially the capacity to make collective decisions about culture.

- The third move is an equality claim, which is typically applied to minorities for the protection of their culture.

In its more influential versions, the argument involves identifying a range of interests that are at stake in the recognition of people's culture and relating these interests to an expansive understanding of the conditions that are necessary for the exercise of individual autonomy. Crucially, it turns out that there are a number of public goods including a shared public culture—as well as a good education system, ensuring literacy and numeracy for all (Taylor, 1995)—that are necessary conditions for the exercise of autonomy. The claim that there is an internal relationship between culture and autonomy is developed by examining the conditions under which individuals can be said to be autonomous. According to Miller, 'A common culture … gives its bearers … a background against which meaningful choices can be made' (Miller, 1995, pp. 85–6). In Kymlicka's view, '[i]ndividual choice is dependent on the presence of a societal culture, defined by language and history' (Kymlicka, 1995, pp. 82–3). Not only does the culture provide the options from which the individual chooses but it infuses them with meaning. This is important to the argument: the autonomous ideal of a self-choosing, self-forming person presupposes some conception of value according to which a human life is constituted, and this conception of value is provided by a national or societal culture.

At this stage of the argument the emphasis is on providing a coherent conception of value—a 'societal culture' in Kymlicka's terms. By 'a societal culture', they mean an integrating culture, across a whole society, within which people can choose amongst a variety of options or ways of life, and which also has its own conception of value that makes these choices valuable ones. For example, a religious culture or an indigenous culture, or even the Canadian or French culture contains particular conceptions of value; in the case of an indigenous culture, for example, there might be particular emphasis on an environmentally sustainable way of life and so on. Because the 'societal culture' has to be large enough to contain a whole range of options, the concept mainly seems to apply to what we might think of as 'national communities'—people in Quebec (within Canada), or the Mohawk people, or the Catalans in Spain, or Kurds in Turkey or Iraq, all represent such societal cultures, which should be given political autonomy to protect their own culture. This might mean the power to protect areas of jurisdiction that are particularly important to them—e.g. authority over their own education system—or jurisdictional control over a territory, or geographical domain, in which the group constitutes a majority (e.g. a province or unit in a federation, such as Quebec in Canada or the Basque region within Spain). It does not apply to subcultures within society—such as Goths or rockers or Rastafarians—who might form a culture in some sense, but one which cannot provide a range of options among which to choose or an overall conception of what is valuable.

The next step in the argument is the claim that, since a rich flourishing culture is an essential condition of the exercise of autonomy, liberals have good reason to adopt measures that would protect culture. At this point, the argument has only shown that the existence of (some) flourishing cultural structure is necessary to the exercise of autonomy, but not a specific culture. Proponents of this argument then go on to claim that the particular cultures to which people are attached should be protected because they provide the context in which autonomy is exercised. Although they do not provide an explanatory argument for the nature of this attachment, there are such empirical arguments, derived from modernist theories of the emergence and persistence of nationalism (Gellner, 1983; Hobsbawm, 1990). The crucial point here is that, on a full understanding of the exercise of autonomy, there is an important cultural dimension, which requires that we take seriously those things that threaten people's overarching cultural framework.

Kymlicka then points to the equality principle to justify rights for minority groups: it is unfair for majorities to have the protection of their culture which comes from being a majority in the state, for this places an unfair burden on minorities, who find that they have to bear the costs for maintaining their culture. Drawing on 'the legitimate interests' that people have in ensuring 'access to a societal culture' and the 'deep bond [that most people have] to their own culture', Kymlicka argues in favour of poly-ethnic rights for ethnic groups. He means by this rights that permit **multicultural** groups in society to continue to practice their own language or religion, and integrate into the larger society on fairer terms; and self-government rights for national minorities, which in practice might mean jurisdictional authority over their collective life for aboriginal peoples, federalism in Spain for Catalans and Galicians and Basque people, and so on (Kymlicka, 1995, p. 107).

This argument has been extensively discussed in terms of its reconciliation of liberal autonomy with the protection of culture. Because, according to this argument, culture is valuable in so far as it contributes to the exercise of autonomy, rights to the protection of culture are justified as long as these are consistent with the protection of personal autonomy. Kymlicka proposes that external protections, which allow the group to protect their culture vis-à-vis majority groups in the state, are justified; but not internal restrictions on the autonomy of the members of that culture. In other words, it is justified for indigenous people to have authority over their language and education and communities for the purposes of preventing assimilation and gaining control over their lives, but not for indigenous elites to use this jurisdictional authority to oppress people inside the community, such as homosexuals or women or dissenters. The internal–external distinction is intended to reconcile concern with the fairness of access to culture and protection of culture with protection for individuals in the exercise of their autonomy.

This argument provides an important justification for ensuring that jurisdictional authority is held by members of a particular cultural group. It argues that there is an important link between jurisdictional authority, protection of culture, and the background conditions for the exercise of autonomy. It also suggests a mechanism for drawing the boundaries of such communities, namely, that borders should be drawn consistent with people's cultural identifications. Although this is usually classified as a 'minority protection' argument for borders and is viewed in the context of an argument for minority rights, what is interesting is its recognition that people have a range of legitimate cultural identities and attachments, including attachments to a particular political community. It suggests that political boundaries should be drawn *around* such groups, to enable them to be collectively self-governing.

The collective self-determination argument

One important moral good that is threatened by strong versions of cosmopolitanism is that of collective self-determination over the conditions of one's existence. This argument focuses more directly on the kind of collective control and identification that people might have for smaller associations, in contrast to a global governmental order. One fairly straightforward concern here appeals to the idea of scale: the larger the unit, the less control the individual has in relation to it. One might think that democracy on an

On theories of democracy, see Chapter 21.

immense scale (e.g. global democracy or even very large democracies) would not really be democratic, because the individual could not see the laws of the polity as in any sense an expression of his or her own will. This is the point Benjamin Constant made in the early nineteenth century against the French Revolutionaries who tried to apply Jean-Jacques Rousseau's ideas to France, and it is relevant today when thinking about institutional forms of cosmopolitanism (Constant, 1988). After all, if the central point of democracy is to allow people to have collective control over the conditions of their existence—to feel that they are agents, rather than passive subjects in making decisions over their collective future—then global democracy is somewhat wanting.

The main worry, however, which is only obliquely connected with the issue of scale, presupposes an understanding of political communities as centrally involved in the creation of a common life, in which people are co-participants and co-creators. In addition to the various goods that political authority can secure, there is also value in the particular community being collectively self-determining.

This thought—about the value of collective self-determination—is consonant with our central moral and political principles. It helps to explain what is wrong with imperialism: the evils of imperialism and undemocratic governance are not explained simply in terms of their consequences (e.g. that they lead to bad government) for this may or may not obtain. It is explained directly in terms of the violation of the collective autonomy of the people in question. The value of collective autonomy helps to explain the injustice involved in colonizing people, annexing their states, and dismantling their legitimate democracies (Wellman, 2005). If we properly value collective autonomy then we can give a non-**consequentialist** explanation of the wrongs involved in forcibly colonizing others, as well as why we should value democratic governance.

The value of the common life that we share and the autonomy that is exercised through our collectively self-determining political association also explains why we might think that certain attitudes are appropriate—respect towards people who work to improve the lot of the community, patriotism towards the central values or tenets of it, and why we might think that certain actions constitute legitimate forms of dissent, while others seem to be objectionable disrespect. If we think that there is value in protecting a common life, and ensuring that the political community can be collectively self-determining over the conditions of its existence, then we can also justify or explain duties to protect and promote the interests of the community. On this view, political communities not only enable collective self-determination over the common life that members share, participants are also engaged in a project of creating justice together. The political project in which they are engaged is essentially a project of justice-creation and justice-maintenance, for it is through their political communities that people establish the rules of justice that govern their collective life.

7.4 Four worries about cosmopolitanism

This section of the chapter assumes that either one or both arguments outlined in the previous section are valid and that there are good moral reasons (1) why we want to ensure that cultures are protected and (2) why political communities might be valuable.

If we assume that cultural difference does not simply involve thin linguistic or religious diversity, but diversity in what people think is valuable or good in life, and especially in preferential ranking of what counts as a good life, it is reasonable that different communities will come to value and use political authority to protect different things. Obviously, cosmopolitans do not explicitly object to this. Indeed, the various arguments for distributive justice they put forward purport to involve a simple, unproblematic redistribution (of goods) from the affluent parts of the globe to the poorer parts. It is possible to imagine such redistribution occurring at the same time as allowing different political communities to reach different social choices in the exercise of their collective self-determination and different cultures to flourish. However, there are a number of reasons to think that the two are not that compatible. In this section, I will explore some of these worries, and also suggest that underlying some of these arguments is a more general concern that cosmopolitan principles seem to require for their implementation something approximating a state, which would interfere with meaningful political autonomy.

The responsibility argument

First, there is a straightforward problem of responsibility that comes with making choices and decisions. Political communities that have some form of self-government, and so can make choices, should be responsible for the (social) choices that they make. It is counter-intuitive to combine both strong autonomy and strong egalitarianism without considering the question of responsibility. Let us imagine, say, that country A, let us call it Frankia, prefers to have strong protections for workers, but the price for this, in a capitalist economy, is higher levels of unemployment. This is a trade-off that the society is willing to make, as can be seen by support in society for the various governments that implement and/or maintain this policy. Country B, let us call it Amerikada, has less worker protection and this more flexible labour market leads to lower levels of unemployment. This seems like a legitimate social choice (as long as the people who are worse off in both situations are protected from serious deprivation). These are social choices connected to how to organize a society, and it seems that part of having jurisdictional authority or control over certain areas of life involves also the responsibility to bear the cost of one's choice.

Let us accept the principle of responsibility for social choices, but change the example. Suppose that society A prefers a relatively leisurely existence, protection of the environment, and strict controls on various kinds of capitalist development. This is a legitimate social choice; indeed, it sounds like a very attractive society. Society B, on the other hand, has a more laissez-faire approach to capitalism that generates rapid growth and, as a result, it incurs various kinds of costs—both social and environmental—for its choice to develop fairly rapidly. It would seem unfair that, having made the choice to prefer wealth over a better quality of life (in some senses of that term), the society that opted for greater wealth (society B) would then have to transfer some of that wealth to society A. I am not suggesting that most deprived states in the global South have made the decision to be poor, but rather to point out that there is a danger of conceiving of poor countries as pure victims.

In *National Responsibility and Global Justice* (2007), David Miller focuses on the issue of responsibility, which is a key component in his theory of global justice. According to Miller, an acceptable theory of global justice has to strike the right balance between two aspects of the human condition: between regarding people as needy and vulnerable creatures who may not be able to live decently without the help of others; and regarding them as responsible agents who should be allowed to enjoy the benefits, but also bear the costs, of their choices and actions. He distinguishes between two senses of responsibility: the responsibility we bear for our own actions and decisions (which he calls 'outcome responsibility') and the responsibility we have to come to the aid of those who need help (which he calls 'remedial responsibility'). A theory of global justice, he argues, should be sensitive to both kinds of responsibility—as well as responsibility for goods and harms.

As in the argument above, Miller considers communities of people as responsible and as capable of agency. The collective agent here is not necessarily a political state, understood as an organized political entity that has structures to make laws and enter into agreements with other political communities. Rather, he argues that the nation, on whose behalf the state is operating, is responsible. This is the most controversial aspect of his theory. Obviously, as Miller notes, where nations are subject to external or autocratic rule, it is difficult to identify acts undertaken by individual members, even in concert, or by the state as genuinely national acts, and so it is inappropriate to spread responsibility throughout the nation. However, it also means that in cases where the state is democratic, and there is general support for the practice or policy it is not simply the state or the government to whom responsibility can be ascribed, but the nation. This provides support for a theory of remedial responsibility: for apologizing for past wrongs or compensation for past exploitation. However, it also suggests that people can be responsible for creating goods (like more wealth) and this implies some entitlement to it. Clearly, a strong account of responsibility that tries to trace the effects of collective decisions is in tension with cosmopolitan egalitarianism, since it suggests that some inequalities between societies can be justified, if they are the product of decisions or practices that the nation (in Miller's case) or the state (in the argument above) has made.

There is, then, a danger inherent in a-historical approaches to redistributive justice (Young, 2007), for these fail to track responsibility (for the bad state of affairs) and particularly responsibility for the kinds of social choices that societies make when they have the institutional or jurisdictional capacity to do so.

The challenge of (cultural) disagreement about goods

In many arguments for cosmopolitan justice, theorists make non-neutral or culturally biased assumptions about what counts as a 'good' that confers 'advantages'. It is necessary for a theory of justice to have some conception of 'goods' or 'advantages' for these are what theories of distributive justice argue need to be redistributed. Reflection on these goods reveals the ways in which cosmopolitan arguments are insufficiently sensitive to cultural differences.

Consider, for example, Charles Beitz's cosmopolitan argument, which rests on the view that the distribution of natural resources amongst countries is morally arbitrary and unfair, and therefore analogous, but even more powerful, than arguments premised on the arbitrary distribution of talents among people. He writes that 'the fact that someone happens to be located advantageously with respect to natural resources does not provide a reason why he or she should be entitled to exclude others from the benefits that might be derived from them' (Beitz, 1999, p. 138). Therefore, the parties (to the international '**original position**') from which principles of international justice are derived would think that the resources, or the benefits derived from them, 'should be subject to a resource redistribution principle' (Beitz, 1999, p. 138) and argue for the redistribution of (benefits to) natural resources.

The difficulty here is *not* with the idea of a resource distribution tax, understood as a way to raise money for international governance organizations and redistribution across countries, but, rather, the entitlement assumption that lurks behind that principle. It is difficult to plausibly maintain that each person really has equal entitlement to each resource, because it fails to take into account the various ways in which specific people are related to the land, or to the territory, as well as to particular natural resources. There are a number of different, morally important ways in which we might think that resources are related to people, and these ways might justify differential control over the land or territory or resource in question. Natural resources do not just fall like manna from heaven: typically, they stem from material, pre-existing in the world, and are transformed into *resources*, from which value can be derived, by human beings (Miller, 2007).

Beitz's cosmopolitan argument assumes that the only relationship between land and the people is an instrumental one, where the land is viewed, potentially, as a source of wealth, as material to be worked or exploited, or otherwise transformed into economic use-value. However, this instrumental conception is not how all people view the land on which they live. Consider the case of the Lakota Sioux in South Dakota, USA. The Lakota Sioux refused to sell or accept any financial compensation for mining in the Black Hills, which they want stopped, because they view the land as sacred. The same is true of Maori land in New Zealand, which cannot be sold now, precisely because, when they realized what selling the land actually meant, the Maoris stopped the practice (Spinner-Halev, 2007, pp. 574–97). It is hard to see how any group that sees itself as a spiritual guardian of the land would have sold it voluntarily or adopted the instrumental view that land is simply a source of wealth, a stock of resources to be used to fulfil one's own particular **conception of the good** (to use Rawlsian language).

Avery Kolers has pointed out that all nomadic people seek to use the land to sustain their nomadic way of life, and that this involves a hostile relationship to attempts to extract resources from the land, which requires building and transportation networks at odds with the Bedouin and Inuit way of life (Kolers, 2009). Nor is this non-instrumental view typical of marginalized (indigenous and/or nomadic) peoples only, who some might object are a relatively small group of people in the world. Even in modern industrialized societies, the use to which land is put—and the relationship of land to resource-extraction—is, and should be, a hotly contested issue. The instrumental conception is not necessarily the right one, or the dominant one, when we are considering whether to allow strip mining in a wetlands area, or oil drilling in the fragile High Arctic, or whether an old cemetery should be ploughed over to make room for a shopping complex. There are other values here, not least environmental sustainability and the kind of society the collective self-determining group wants to become. This is why it is wrong to simply assume that land is of purely instrumental value, that it is a stock of resources from which value can be derived and equalized to all people in the world.

 On the environment, see Chapter 10.

The assumption of universal justice

On the argument above, political communities are themselves *sites of justice*, valuable precisely because they are the sites in which co-members create and maintain justice, and are thereby collectively self-determining (Walzer, 1983). This idea is in tension with an ideal that is implicit in much cosmopolitan justice theory, namely, that justice is **universal** in scope and that, therefore, the site of justice is universal. Indeed, a typical cosmopolitan argumentative strategy is to put forward (universal) principles of justice and then argue that these, being universal, ought also to apply at the global level.

Consider, for example, Simon Caney's cosmopolitan argument for a global equality of opportunity principle, which states that 'persons of different nations should enjoy equal opportunities: no one should face worse opportunities because of their nationality' (Caney, 2005a, p. 122). In his major work on global justice, in which he endorses the global equality of opportunity principle, Caney draws on an argument for equality of opportunity at the domestic level:

If one thinks, as egalitarian liberals do, that it is unjust if persons fare worse because of their class or ethnic identity one should surely also think that it is unjust if persons fare worse because of their nationality. The logic underpinning equality of opportunity entails that it should be globalized. (Caney, 2005a, p. 123)

Caney emphasizes the point in terms of an arbitrariness objection:

It is difficult to see why such arbitrary facts about people should determine their prospects in life. Given that it is an injustice that some face worse opportunities because of their class or their ethnicity, is it not an injustice that some face worse opportunities because of their nationality? (Caney, 2005a, p. 123)

It should be noted that the argument here works only if we agree that nationality is analogous to class and ethnic identity in being an unacceptable basis for unequal opportunities. However, a person's national or political community is not an unchosen aspect of the person's identity and this makes the analogy that Caney relies on (between nation and ethnicity, or nation and class position) unpersuasive. Contemporary liberal nationalists do not have in mind racist or ethnically exclusive 'nations' along the lines of Hitler's 'national socialist' movement. Rather, following David Miller, they view 'nations' in much more normatively neutral terms. Miller lists five elements that together constitute a nation: it is. It must be:

(1) constituted by shared beliefs and mutual commitments, (2) extended in history, (3) active in character, (4) connected to a particular territory, and (5) marked off from other communities by its distinct public culture. (Miller, 1995, p. 27)

The second, third and fifth criteria all refer in different ways to the fact that, while nations do have some 'objective' features—such as a shared language or religion—they also include an element of subjective identification between co-members, who are engaged in, or aspire to be engaged in, a common political project. As a group, they either are, or aspire to be, collectively self-determining; to make decisions over the collective conditions of their lives, and to establish justice (the rule of law, the potential for the exercise of collective self-determination, security for all). As they are engaged in a political project of creating justice together, they owe duties to other co-members as well as to the political project that creates benefits for them.

On Caney's view, the site of justice and the scope of justice are identical; since justice is, by definition, universal, the rules or principles should be universalized. This is the formal structure of his argument. While he does not explicitly argue that this requires a world state, it does seem to suggest that political authorities below the level of the world must at least be consistent with universal justice. This is a very common position. It is also expressed by viewing projects of collective self-determination as purely instrumental to the achievement of universal duties. Consider, for example, Robert Goodin's view that local duties are merely instruments for the achievement of cosmopolitan duties, that they have no independent moral weight (Goodin, 1988, pp. 663–86; Tan, 2004, p. 144). On this view, dividing up our duties along the lines of our national affiliation is an effective or efficient way of co-ordinating the achievement of our universal duties, that is, our duties to individuals in general. The problem with this instrumental account is that it mis-describes the source of these duties and thereby morally impoverishes them. It treats the duties that arise in political associations and, by extension, any kind of association, as merely instrumental to the achievement of the requirement of the impartial principle, but not as themselves arising from morally valuable relationships.

The fundamental point which most cosmopolitans make—about the universality of justice theorizing—is either assumed or presupposed in cosmopolitan thought. However, this might not be the right way to look at things. While it makes sense to think of injustice as universal— indeed, we can often identify what injustice is (for example, torture, murder, and slavery)—it is less clear what counts as a just ordering of the basic institutions of society. We can at least imagine reasonable disagreement on whether the appropriate principle of justice should be *prioritarian* (giving priority to the worse off), *egalitarian* (strict equality), or a *threshold concep-tion* (where the most important goal is to avoid serious forms of deprivation, understood not relationally, but in absolute terms). One can argue that these sorts of principles of distributive justice are subject to reasonable disagreement, and that different people and different po-litical communities might arrive at different answers to the question of what a just political ordering consists in, or what principles should be institutionalized in a just society.

The basic insight here is that it's relatively easy to recognize injustice and to agree to what constitutes serious injustices, but less obvious what particular rules or practices might count as uniquely just. For this reason, we might think that what makes collective self-gov-ernment so valuable, so important, is precisely that political communities allow people to co-create and implement justice amongst themselves. Justice here is not fully determinate from a universal perspective. It is possible to think that there are different sites of justice, a conception that is at odds with the assumptions of most cosmopolitan theorists, who seek to extend Rawlsian justice (from the domestic sphere) to the whole world.

Cosmopolitanism as imperialism

There is a more postmodernist version of the multiplicity of justice arguments advanced above, which I will rehearse here, as it is also in opposition to the universal theorizing of much cosmopolitan writing. This view emphasizes not merely the fact of reasonable disagreement about the basic principles of justice, but the origins of justice theory in

Enlightenment reason and the West's colonization of much of the world (Tully, 1995; Ivison, 2002). On this view, the problem with cosmopolitan justice is that it assumes the Truth of Western Reason, and represents a universal theory that can be extended across the globe and further entrench the West's hegemony over the poorer regions in the Global South. This argument begins by noting that much of the global South has experienced the dark side of Western modernity—**colonialism**—and that this colonial project was supported and maintained by (false) claims to universal reason. The cosmopolitan project, too, emanates from the West, and offers a universal theory, based on Enlightenment Reason, which is presented as singular and monolithic.

On colonialism, see also Chapter 11.

The problem is not simply that the origins of universalism are linked to the history of Western aggression, but that some contemporary arguments about universal (cosmopolitan) justice seem to replicate the logic of imperialism. Liberal imperialist arguments about 'civilizing' natives and spreading 'civilization' to backward corners of the earth, common throughout the history of imperialism, have been updated, and are now characterized in terms of the necessity of universalizing Western norms and values, including **human rights**, democracy, and (Rawlsian) justice. To put it another way, the language of liberal universalism is today often just a dressed-up version of a centuries-old tradition of liberal imperialism. Cosmopolitans would of course deny this charge, pointing out that their intentions are very different from aggressive imperialists. Yet liberal imperialists in the past, like John Stuart Mill (Mehta, 1999), also thought that they were engaged in an enlightened mission to help eradicate human suffering. From this perspective, cosmopolitan justice principles are likely to curtail, rather than enable, emancipatory possibilities.

This objection is arguably guilty of committing a 'genetic fallacy'—of assuming that the suspect origins of a theory damage its credentials as a valid theory. The origin of a viewpoint or theory or tradition does not tell us very much about its validity. The institution of the family, for example, may have its origins in sexual conquest and violence, but that does not mean that the family could not be re-constituted on some other (morally acceptable) ground, like love.

This argument does, however, offer an important historically nuanced perspective and points out that a similar well-intentioned attempt at extending values to other people was a crucial component of the West's imperial project. It reminds us to be modest about our aims and capacities for reason, and to limit the ambition of 'universal' principles to those people who accept the principles, rather than for all people. There is a kind of attractive modesty that reflection on the history of colonialism should engender and which should give cosmopolitans pause while they are articulating principles for everyone.

7.5 Conclusion

For defences of the state, see Chapters 6 and 14.

In this chapter, I have tried to do three things. First, I have offered cultural and national identity-based reasons to be suspicious of cosmopolitanism in the global justice debate—and these reasons are different from the reasons offered by defenders of the state, who focus on the coerciveness of the state and the increased demands on **legitimacy** engendered by it.

Underlying some of the worries elaborated above is a concern that the principles endorsed by cosmopolitans have been developed by reasoning within a domestic context that has then been extended to the world as a whole. However, it may be that the principles endorsed by cosmopolitans require for their operation something approximating a state. The global equality of opportunity principle, for example, requires that we treat the international sphere as the domestic sphere writ large:

- it presupposes a single authoritative political structure, which regulates individuals' opportunities;
- it presupposes a single economic market, and a political and bureaucratic order to regulate income and labour rights (and presumably, to make this fair, all economic transactions).

This version of cosmopolitanism is not a departure from **statism**: it treats the globe as if it is a single state, with a single economy, and a single, harmonized regulatory system (Kolers, 2004).

More specifically, this chapter has argued that the principles put forward by cosmopolitanism fail to track responsibility appropriately, in so far as they are largely a-historical, and that they tend to offer culturally biased conceptions of the appropriate goods, subject to the concerns of distributive justice. It also offered methodological reasons to be suspicious of the general tendency to view justice as easily or straightforwardly extendable across the globe.

The debate considered here is in many ways a mainly academic one, about the appropriateness of 'justice' principles in the global realm, because the current world is so far from being morally ideal that, in practice, there is a substantial amount of agreement between the two positions. Those who criticize cosmopolitan principles from a cultural or national self-determination perspective (section 7.3) do not think—and cannot justifiably think—that others (strangers/people beyond their borders) have no moral claims on them. The question at issue is not whether moral principles apply, but whether universal justice principles apply uniformly across the globe. Both traditions agree on some moral principles—for example, a no-harm principle to govern individual interactions, and a non-exploitation principle. Similarly, most non-cosmopolitans argue that there are duties of humanitarian assistance; these are moral duties to assist people in situations of severe deprivation (who are willing to accept assistance), regardless of the relationships (or lack of them) that bind the deprived and the affluent together.

Those who argue for the importance of national self-determination cannot ignore the fact that this is a right that must be held by other similarly situated peoples, and that there might be certain conditions or thresholds that must be in place for collective self-determination to be possible at all. For example, it might be argued that it is counter to the self-determination of community X if it were so poor, and so unequal in relation to other political communities, that it could not plausibly be seen as the author of its own future. Relations of severe inequality or deprivation also threaten the capacity to protect one's own culture and the capacity to be collectively self-determining. This does not justify intervention—if by that we mean something that would violate the self-determination of the oppressed or deprived group of people—but it could justify duties to assist the deprived group, as long as the duties were discharged in a way that was consistent with viewing the group as a people, capable of agency and entitled to their own self-determination. All this means, of course, that the central issue between the cosmopolitans and their critics is whether the requirements of justice should be viewed as uniform universal substantive principles of justice.

On the view advanced here, by contrast, political communities should be viewed as sites of justice (the self-determination argument) and this permits each political community to protect those aspects of its culture that are important to the people in that community, and co-create their own institutions of justice. This is a quite different approach from the standard cosmopolitan argument, which seeks to apply substantive principles to govern people across the globe.

QUESTIONS

1. Do we have a duty to assist the global poor?

2. What duties do you think are associated with the cosmopolitan perspective? What duties are associated with the cultural and national self-determination perspectives?

3. Do nations have a right to self-determination?

4. Can the right to self-determination be justified in cosmopolitan terms?

5. What universal duties does the right to national self-determination or cultural protection give rise to?

6. Are the two (cultural and self-determination) arguments compatible? Do they give rise to different rights or obligations?

7. Do cosmopolitan and cultural/national arguments generate different accounts of responsibility?

8. How could the cosmopolitan theorist respond to these four criticisms?

9. What different kinds of meanings attach to land and how does this challenge cosmopolitanism?

10. What are the parallels between the earlier imperial project and the current wave of cosmopolitan theory?

FURTHER READING

Brooks, T. (ed.) (2008) *The Global Justice Reader*. Oxford: Wiley-Blackwell. A very useful collection that includes many of the most influential articles relevant to global justice, both historical and contemporary.

Kymlicka, W. (1995) *Multicultural Citizenship: A Liberal Theory of Minority Rights*. Oxford: Oxford University Press. Kymlicka outlines his multicultural theory and offers an influential argument for why liberals need to consider particular cultures and commitments.

Mandle, J. (2006) *Global Justice*. Cambridge: Polity Press. This offers a clear discussion of the main cosmopolitan/anti-cosmopolitan perspectives and of the influence of Rawls in this debate.

Mehta, U.S. (1999) *Liberalism and Empire: A Study in Nineteenth-Century British Liberal Thought*. Chicago: University of Chicago Press. An account of the relations between universalist liberal theory and imperialism.

Miller, D. (1995) *On Nationality*. Oxford: Oxford University Press. Miller puts forward a normative argument for taking nations and national sentiments seriously, and shows how the idea of a 'nation' can be distinguished from its darker, ethnically exclusive meanings.

Miller, D. (2007) *National Responsibility and Global Justice*. Oxford: Oxford University Press. Offers a thorough discussion of the issue of 'responsibility' and the problems attached to identifying responsible agents in the global context. It also provides a clear discussion of why cosmopolitan theory should not ignore nations.

Moore, M. (2001) *The Ethics of Nationalism*. Oxford: Oxford University Press. Discusses the basic ethical issues at stake in nationalism, including national self-determination and nation-building projects. It offers a perspective from which to challenge the assumption that political communities have no value or meaning for people beyond being means to the realization of universal justice.

Rawls, J. (2001) *The Law of Peoples with 'The Idea of Public Reason Revisited'*, Cambridge: Harvard University Press. Rawls identifies principles to govern the relationship between different societies and rejects the extension of his liberal principles across the globe.

Taylor, C. (1995) *Philosophy and the Human Sciences: Philosophical Papers*, Vol. II. Cambridge: Harvard University Press. The relational concept of autonomy discussed here has been influential both as a critique of individualist liberal theory and as a way of thinking about societies.

Tan, K-C. (2004) *Justice without Borders: Cosmopolitanism, Nationalism and Patriotism*. Cambridge: Cambridge University Press. This book seeks to bring together two distinct sets of debates: the debate among liberal multiculturalists and the debate amongst liberal cosmopolitans. Despite its claims to offer a 'reconciliation' of the debates, it is wedded to a very egalitarian (between individuals) view of global justice.

▥ WEB LINKS

http://www.nationalismproject.org/ The Nationalism Project at the University of Wisconsin-Madison is a resource intended to help forward the online study of nationalism. It contains a wide variety of links to books, articles, and documents.

http://www.cwis.org/ The 'Fourth World Documentation Project', run by the Centre for World Indigenous Studies in Olympia, Washington, includes useful information about indigenous peoples around the world.

http://www.eurac.edu/miris The Minority Rights Information System (MIRIS) promotes minority rights standards by providing researchers, officials, NGOs, and minority representatives with access to legal documents and information on minority rights regimes around the world.

http://plato.stanford.edu/entries/patriotism/ The *Stanford Encyclopedia of Philosophy* entry on 'patriotism'.

http://philosophybites.com/past_programmes.html Podcast interviews with leading philosophers on a wide range of topics, including Will Kymlicka discussing minority rights and Anne Phillips on multiculturalism.

Visit the Online Resource Centre that accompanies this book to access more learning resources: **www.oxfordtextbooks.co.uk/orc/bell_ethics/**

8 Cosmopolitanism

Simon Caney

READER'S GUIDE

The key idea of cosmopolitanism is that persons are citizens of the world. This chapter analyses the various ways in which this concept has been employed—ranging from the ancient Greeks to the present day. It then focuses on three types of cosmopolitanism: cosmopolitanism as an account of the scope of principles of justice; cosmopolitanism as an account of the nature of the good life; and cosmopolitanism as an account of what political institutions there should be. It examines each of these types in turn, exploring the arguments for and against, and, where applicable, traces their implications for political practice.

8.1 Introduction

The meanings of cosmopolitanism

The cosmopolitan ideal has been invoked in a variety of ways by very different political thinkers, ranging from Cynic and Stoic philosophers in the ancient world to modern-day thinkers like Charles Beitz, David Held, Thomas Pogge, and Jeremy Waldron. The literal meaning of a cosmopolitan (or a cosmopolite) is one who is a citizen of the world. However, different thinkers in different times have interpreted this core idea to refer to a variety of ideas and ideals.

We can get a sense of this diversity if we turn to the earliest exponents of a cosmopolitan viewpoint. An early, perhaps the earliest, usage of it is that by Diogenes the Cynic. As Diogenes Laërtius writes, when 'Asked where he came from, he [Diogenes the Cynic] said,

"I am a citizen of the world'" (2005, p. 65). The cosmopolitan ideal was also affirmed and developed by subsequent Stoic thinkers like Cicero, Epictetus, Plutarch, Seneca, and Marcus Aurelius. For example, Marcus Aurelius defended the ideal of world citizenship in his *Meditations*. He argues that all humans are subject to a common law and, therefore, are fellow members of the same city: it follows then that they are all fellow citizens of the world (Aurelius, 1998, p. 24). Seneca too gives eloquent expression to the ideal of world citizenship. In a justly famous passage in his essay 'On Leisure' ('*de Otio*') he argues that persons are citizens not only of their own *polis*, but also of the world as a whole. As he writes:

> there are two commonwealths—the one, a vast and truly common state, which embraces alike gods and men, in which we look neither to this corner of earth nor to that, but measure the bounds of our citizenship by the path of the sun; the other, the one to which we have been assigned by the accident of birth. (Seneca, 2001a, pp.187–9)

Cosmopolitan ideas also flourished during the **Enlightenment** in the eighteenth century. Again, they took a diversity of forms, but what they had in common was a commitment to the notion that persons are all citizens of the world. Cosmopolitan commitments can, for example, be found in the work of Immanuel Kant. His essay on 'Perpetual Peace', written in 1795, articulates a cosmopolitan commitment to certain rights. He asserts three Definitive Articles, the third of which affirms a principle of 'Cosmopolitan Right', which includes 'Conditions of Universal Hospitality' (Kant, 1991, pp. 105–8). Kant's **deontological** perspective can be contrasted with the **utilitarian** approach adopted by another cosmopolitan, Jeremy Bentham. Bentham's cosmopolitanism is apparent in his four essays on international law. In the first, 'Objects of International Law', he enquires what kind of international law would be chosen by a 'citizen of the world' (Bentham, 1843a, p. 537). His answer is that 'the end that a disinterested legislator upon international law would propose to himself, would ... be the greatest happiness of all nations taken together' (p. 538). Like Kant and other eighteenth century philosophers, Bentham also wrote an essay on perpetual peace ('A Plan for an Universal and Perpetual Peace', Bentham, 1843b). In this essay Bentham defends a cosmopolitan legal framework, one which calls for the creation of an international 'court of judicature, for the decision of differences between the several nations' (Bentham, 1843b, p. 552; see also pp. 552–54). In addition to Bentham and Kant, other prominent Enlightenment cosmopolitans include Denis Diderot, Voltaire, Thomas Paine, Friedrich Schiller, and Gottfried Wilhelm Leibniz.[1]

On utilitarianism, see Chapter 4.

Most of those referred to so far see cosmopolitanism as representing a normative ideal. It therefore bears noting that some employ the term in a straightforwardly descriptive sense. Two good examples are John Stuart Mill and Karl Marx. Mill, for example, writes that

On descriptive and normative theories, see the Introduction.

> capital is becoming more and more cosmopolitan; there is so much greater similarity of manners and institutions than formerly, and so much less alienation of feeling, among the more civilized countries, that both population and capital now move from one of those countries to another on much less temptation than heretofore. (Mill, 1866, p. 348)

By this, Mill means simply that capital and human interactions more generally transcend national boundaries. Marx too uses the term 'cosmopolitan' to refer to

---

[1] In the famous *Encyclopédie* (1751–1772) that he co-edited with Jean D'Alembert, Diderot provided a memorable definition of the cosmopolitan as someone who is not a stranger anywhere (1754, p. 297). On Enlightenment cosmopolitanism see Schlereth (1977).

phenomena which cross national boundaries. For example, in his *Contribution to a Critique of Political Economy* he writes that:

[a]s money develops into international money, so the commodity-owner becomes a cosmopolitan. The cosmopolitan relations of men to one another originally comprise only their relations as commodity-owners. Commodities as such are indifferent to all religious, political, national and linguistic barriers. Their universal language is price and their common bond is money. But together with the development of international money as against national coins, there develops the commodity-owner's cosmopolitanism, a cult of practical reason, in opposition to the traditional religious, national and other prejudices which impede the metabolic process of mankind. (Marx, 1981 [1859], p.152)

For Marx and Mill, then, the concept of cosmopolitanism is an empirical concept, referring to phenomena which are not confined within national boundaries, but are instead global in their nature and reach.

More recently, the sociologist Ulrich Beck has also employed the term 'cosmopolitanism' is this descriptive sense. In his work *The Cosmopolitan Vision* (2006), he argues that the contemporary world is undergoing a process of 'cosmopolitanization' (2006, p. 8). That is, territorial boundaries are becoming less and less significant, societies are becoming more open, and persons' horizons are increasingly shaped by factors outside their own societies. Persons in the modern world, Beck argues, experience what he terms a 'banal cosmopolitanism' (2006, p. 10): that is, all aspects of their everyday existence (what they eat, how they dress, what lifestyles they pursue) are infused with influences from a variety of cultures across the world. For Beck this process is irreversible and requires us to reject methodological analyses which operate within the terms of the nation state (what he terms 'methodological nationalism') (2006, pp. 73–4).

8.2 Three kinds of contemporary cosmopolitanism

In this chapter I shall, however, concentrate on cosmopolitanism as a normative project and within that my focus will be on contemporary cosmopolitanism.[2] Again, there is a wide variety of different usages of the term 'cosmopolitan'. It is helpful to distinguish between several well-known versions of modern cosmopolitanism. These offer three different interpretations of the concept of being a 'citizen of the world' (Tan, 2004, pp. 10–12; Caney, 2005a, pp. 3–7).

The first is what I shall term 'justice-based' cosmopolitanism.[3] This holds that there are global principles of (civil, political, or economic) justice that apply to all individuals

---

[2] Contemporary cosmopolitans rarely draw on the arguments of the original Greek and Roman cosmopolitans. Martha Nussbaum is an important exception (Nussbaum et al., 1996; Nussbaum, 1997, 2006).

[3] This includes what Samuel Scheffler terms 'cosmopolitanism about justice' (Scheffler, 2001, p. 111). Scheffler, however, seems to employ this term to refer solely to a 'cosmopolitan' conception of *distributive* justice and, as I make clear above, I am using the term 'justice-based' cosmopolitanism to refer to a cosmopolitan approach to civil and political justice, as well as to distributive justice. Justice-based cosmopolitanism thus includes Scheffler's 'cosmopolitanism about justice', but is more inclusive than his conception.

of the world. Persons are citizens of the world, according to this first conception, in the sense that they belong to a system of justice that includes all persons within its scope. Their global citizenship exists in the sense that they have entitlements as members of this universal set of principles of justice and they may also have responsibilities as citizens of the world. The key features of this kind of cosmopolitanism are well captured by Thomas Pogge who writes that cosmopolitanism has three key components—what he terms 'individualism' ('the ultimate units of concern are *human beings*, or *persons*'), 'universality' ('the status of ultimate unit of concern attaches to *every* living human being *equally*'), and 'generality' ('persons are ultimate units of concern *for everyone*') (Pogge, 2008, p. 175).[4] It is in virtue of these three tenets that there are, so cosmopolitans argue, global principles of justice that apply to all individuals.

This first kind of cosmopolitanism can be contrasted with a second kind—what I shall refer to as 'cosmopolitanism about the good life'. This view maintains that the good life can, or perhaps must, draw on and combine ideas from different cultures. On this view, to say that persons are citizens of the world is to say that their good does not necessarily lie simply with the ways of life practiced in their local community. To flourish, persons may draw on ideals and practices pursued by others in other parts of the world. This view rejects a parochial account of the good that maintains that one's good lies in following the established practices of one's traditional community. This second kind of cosmopolitanism is more often called 'cosmopolitanism about culture' (Scheffler, 2001, pp.112–14; see also Waldron, 1992, 2000), but I think that that is an unhelpfully broad term because it can cover two separate, albeit connected, phenomena. A culture can comprise both (1) beliefs about the good life and human flourishing (what I am terming cosmopolitanism about the good), and also (2) beliefs about and attitudes to one's political institutions (what is often termed 'political culture'). Now those who refer to cosmopolitanism about culture tend to mean it to refer to issues about the good life—do people have a need to belong to a rooted community? Is a lifestyle drawing eclectically on different cultures fulfilling?[5] However, these should not be confused with the idea of a political culture. A cosmopolitan culture in sense (1) is one that is orientated to a wide variety of different conceptions of the good. A cosmopolitan culture in sense (2) is a political culture that is supportive of cosmopolitan principles of justice and the institutions needed to realize them.

We may turn now to a third kind of cosmopolitanism—that often termed 'political cosmopolitanism'. It is also sometimes named 'legal' cosmopolitanism (Pogge, 2008, p. 175) or 'institutional' cosmopolitanism (Beitz, 1994, p. 120). This offers a different interpretation of what it means to be a citizen of the world. It makes a claim about what kind of political and legal institutions there should be, and it holds that there must be global political institutions. Some past cosmopolitans have held that there should be a

---

[4] Pogge maintains that these three tenets are 'shared by *all* cosmopolitan positions' (2008, p. 175). I think, however, that it is best understood as a characterization of justice-based cosmopolitanism in particular, and works less well as an account of the two other types of cosmopolitanism, especially what I term 'cosmopolitanism about the good life'.

[5] For example, Scheffler explicitly employs the term 'cosmopolitanism about culture' (2001, p. 111) to refer to a view about whether people require the preservation of their culture to 'flourish' (2001, pp. 113, 114, 116). What he terms 'cosmopolitanism about culture' is a thesis about the nature of 'individuals' well-being or their identity or their capacity for effective human agency' (2001, p. 112).

world state, but very few modern cosmopolitans accept this. They may favour instead a system in which power and **authority** is divided between global and state level, and local bodies (Pogge, 2008, chapter 7). Political cosmopolitans are critical of a wholly **statist** order and see it as being either undemocratic (Held, 1995a), or hostile to the realization of cosmopolitan principles of justice, or both (Pogge, 2008).

Having introduced three kinds of contemporary cosmopolitanism, two further comments are in order. First, many have pointed out that each of these kinds of cosmopolitanism can be given an ambitious or a modest interpretation (e.g. Scheffler, 2001, p. 114). The modest form of justice-based cosmopolitanism asserts only that there are some global principles of justice, whereas a more ambitious version affirms this, but also denies that there are any state-level or national-level principles of justice. Consider now 'political cosmopolitanism'. Again, we can distinguish between a modest and an ambitious form. The modest version calls for the existence of supra-state institutions, but allows the continued existence of states. An ambitious kind affirms the need for supra-state institutions, but also rejects states. As such, it calls for some kind of world state. The distinction between modest and ambitious cosmopolitanism can also be applied to cosmopolitanism about the good life. In this case, the modest version asserts that some may flourish by leading a cosmopolitan lifestyle (but also accepts that some may flourish only if they live according to the ideals and values of their own national culture). The ambitious version, by contrast, holds that it is true of all persons that they can flourish only if they lead a cosmopolitan lifestyle (Scheffler, 2001, pp. 116–17).

Secondly, it is worth commenting on the relationships between the three kinds of cosmopolitanism. Two extreme accounts of how the three cosmopolitanisms are related—what one might term the 'logical inseparability' view and the 'no connection' view—can be rejected. According to the former, those who subscribe to one kind of cosmopolitan claim (say justice-based cosmopolitanism) are logically committed to endorsing the two other kinds of cosmopolitanism. This view holds then that the three kinds of cosmopolitanism are logically inseparable. Such an extreme view is, however, unsustainable. There is nothing logically incoherent in, say, affirming a cosmopolitan conception of the scope of justice, but also affirming a non-cosmopolitan **conception of the good** life. Someone might hold, for example, that everyone has an interest in the preservation of their own culture(s) and, as such, repudiate cosmopolitanism about the good life, but also believe in the redistribution of wealth globally (and, as such, affirm a cosmopolitan conception of distributive justice). So the idea that the three views logically entail each other is mistaken (see also Tan, 2004, chapter 5).

Consider now a second opposite extreme—what I have termed the 'no connection' view. This maintains that there are no interconnections at all between the three kinds of cosmopolitanism and so one can affirm any particular combination. This view is, however, also unsustainable. One primary reason for this is that there are likely to be empirical links between the three views. To give one example discussed at greater length below: one might argue that implementation of a cosmopolitan conception of justice requires—for various theoretical and empirical reasons—the creation of accountable international political institutions. Now if this is the case then it would, other things being equal, be incoherent to affirm a cosmopolitan conception of justice and yet repudiate a political cosmopolitan approach. A commitment to cosmopolitan ideals of justice may then provide strong support for cosmopolitan political institutions.

In short, then, there may be links between the three kinds of cosmopolitanism (contra the 'no connections' view), but it does not follow that the three views are logically inseparable (contra the 'logical inseparability' view). The precise links will be explored below and, as we shall see, they depend, in part, on the precise claims made by the particular kinds of cosmopolitanism and, in part, on empirical assumptions.

8.3 **Cosmopolitanism and justice**

Having introduced three kinds of contemporary cosmopolitanism this chapter will now explore each in more detail. Cosmopolitan theories of **distributive justice** are discussed extensively in Chapter 14 and for that reason will receive a relatively short treatment here. However, since justice-based cosmopolitanism bears on the two other kinds of cosmopolitanism (especially political cosmopolitanism) and, since it also includes more than *distributive* justice, a short discussion here of the nature and varieties of justice-based cosmopolitanism is appropriate. In what follows I shall, therefore, describe the nature of justice-based cosmopolitanism in greater detail, draw attention to the reasons for and against it, and conclude by noting the implications it has for other areas of global political theory.

Justice-based cosmopolitanism

As was noted above, justice-based cosmopolitans hold that there are global principles of *civil*, *political*, and/or *economic* justice. To gain a fuller understanding of what this entails, it is important to unpack these separate component parts. Consider first the 'civic' aspect. Justice-based cosmopolitans may hold, for example, that all persons—no matter what their nationality or citizenship—have **human rights** to various civil liberties. Consider the human rights proclaimed by the Universal Declaration of Human Rights (UDHR). Justice-based cosmopolitans may, for example, follow the UDHR in affirming human rights to life and liberty (Article 3), and human rights not to be enslaved (Article 4) or tortured (Article 5). They might also affirm human rights to **freedom of movement** (Article 13), freedom of thought and expression (Article 19), and freedom of association (Article 20). To the extent that one affirms these as *human* rights, and not as rights that persons have as members of political communities, then one is affirming a cosmopolitan principle of civil justice. In this sense, very many people embrace some kind of cosmopolitanism.

 On human rights, see Chapter 13.

Consider now 'political' justice. Some justice-based cosmopolitans do not restrict themselves to the affirmation of universal principles of civil liberties, but also affirm a set of universal political rights as well, most notably the right to democratic government. If, then, one holds that persons have a human right to democratic government then one is affirming a cosmopolitan conception of political justice.

Consider finally cosmopolitan ideals of distributive justice. Many contemporary cosmopolitan thinkers have developed cosmopolitan principles of distributive justice.

On distributive justice and the 'difference principle', see Chapter 1.

An important example is the theory of justice developed by Charles Beitz in his justly influential work *Political Theory and International Relations* (1999). Beitz argued that Rawls's '**difference principle**' (the view that inequalities should be organized so as to maximize the condition of the least advantaged) should be applied to the population of the whole planet. Others argue that principles of equality of opportunity should be applied globally (Caney, 2001). It is worth observing, however, that although many contemporary cosmopolitans affirm liberal egalitarian views, justice-based cosmopolitanism is not in itself committed to global redistribution. Justice-based cosmopolitanism is a claim about the *scope* of distributive justice and not about its *content*. To see this, note that one might apply **libertarian** principles of economic justice to the global realm. A good example of a market-based theory of justice which is cosmopolitan in the sense that I have defined it is that advanced by Friedrich Hayek. He maintains that national borders do not have relevance for the scope of justice. For example, in *The Constitution of Liberty* he repudiates 'the contention that membership in a particular community or nation entitles the individual to a particular material standard that is determined by the general wealth of the group to which he belongs' (Hayek, 1960, p. 100). As he writes, '[t]here is clearly no merit in being born into a particular community, and no argument of justice can be based on the accident of a particular individual's being born in one place rather than another' (Hayek, 1960, p. 100). One might, indeed, go further and hold that libertarian views must, to be consistent with their key commitment to liberty, deny the relevance of national borders. It would be wrong to interfere with freely chosen contracts engaged in by members of different nations. There are, then, a variety of different proposed cosmopolitan principles of distributive justice.

On Hayek, see also Chapter 4.

It is important to note at this point that justice-based cosmopolitanism does not simply claim that there are global principles of justice. It claims that there are global principles of justice that apply to *individuals*. One might, for example, affirm some global principles of distributive justice that are not to be applied to individuals but to states—holding, say, that there should be a redistribution of wealth among states. This affirms a global principle of redistribution, but it is not a cosmopolitan claim, for unlike the latter it is not defined in terms of the application of global principles of justice to *individuals*. It is a key feature of cosmopolitanism that it is fundamentally committed to the rights and interests of individuals.

Arguments for and against

If we turn now from the nature of justice-based cosmopolitanism to the arguments mustered in its defence it is worth recording *both* the variety of different kinds of arguments given for justice-based cosmopolitanism and *yet at the same time* the fact that they share a common core. Arguments for a cosmopolitan conception of justice have, for example, been given by Kantians like Onora O'Neill (1996). She employs the Kantian notion of universalizability (broadly, the notion that one must act on those principles that one would be willing to make into a universal law) to derive a commitment not to injure others (O'Neill, 1996, pp.163–6). She further argues that this principle (not to injure others) should have a universal scope (O'Neill, 1996, pp.113–21). Other cosmopolitan thinkers, such as Peter Singer (2002) and Robert Goodin (1988), take a broadly **consequentialist** approach, arguing that persons have a duty to alleviate suffering and promote well-being. At the heart of their theories is a commitment to promoting desirable outcomes or states of affairs. Another broadly consequentialist approach is taken by Martha Nussbaum. On her approach, justice requires that persons enjoy various '**capabilities**' in order to flourish: this, on her view, should be applied to all persons across the globe (Nussbaum, 2006).[6]

For further discussion of O'Neill and Singer, see Chapter 14.

In addition to Kantian and consequentialist vindications of cosmopolitanism, some adopt a third approach and ground their cosmopolitanism in an account of rights. For example, Henry Shue (1996) and Charles Jones (1999a) defend a set of basic rights, which they argue should be held by all persons. Thomas Pogge also adopts a human rights approach—although unlike Jones and Shue, he eschews any appeal to **positive duties** (2008).

For further discussion of Pogge, see Chapter 14.

Finally, in addition to duty-based, consequentialist and rights-based derivations of cosmopolitanism, some other cosmopolitan thinkers, such as Beitz (1999) and, more recently, Moellendorf (2002), have employed a contractarian method. That is, they have argued that parties in a suitably characterized **social contract** would select cosmopolitan principles of distributive justice. Some of these arguments are explored in much greater depth in Chapter 14, but it is worth mentioning them here for it illustrates the great variety of justifications of cosmopolitanism.

Note, however, that underlying this diversity is a common conviction—namely that membership of a nation or state is not morally relevant to a person's entitlements, and the distribution of burdens and benefits. From a utilitarian point of view, for example, the starting point is that all that matters is utility. Whether someone is Swedish or Nigerian or American is morally irrelevant. The same thesis applies to the 'human rights' approach: this holds that persons have entitlements as human beings and their national identity is not germane. All cosmopolitan conceptions of justice share a common scepticism toward the claim that nationality or civic allegiance bears on one's fundamental entitlements.

We can gain a fuller understanding of the case for cosmopolitanism by considering the different ways in which one might reject it. One can distinguish between two kinds of non-cosmopolitan approach. The first more radical response rejects cosmopolitan principles of justice because it rejects all universal values and endorses a kind of **cultural relativism**. Proponents of this approach often object, for example, that human rights are a Western ideal and have no place in non-Western cultures. This extreme anti-cosmopolitanism can be contrasted with a second more moderate view, one which holds that while there are some universal values they are very minimal ones (Walzer, 1987, p. 24). A moderate anti-cosmopolitan might thus affirm a basic set of human rights, but deny the full cosmopolitan package. One very influential version of this more moderate anti-cosmopolitanism is John Rawls's *The Law of Peoples* (1999). While it affirms some human rights, it explicitly rejects the proposal made by many liberal cosmopolitans to accord the full set of liberal rights to all human beings. In Rawls's view, for liberal societies to impose liberal values on the remainder of the world would be for them to act in an intolerant

For further discussion of Rawls's law of peoples, see Chapter 6.

---

[6] The idea that justice requires promoting persons' capabilities has long been advanced by Martha Nussbaum (2000) and Amartya Sen (e. g. 2009, part III).

fashion. They are under a duty to respect what he terms 'decent societies'. These are societies that satisfy some fundamental moral constraints even if they do not meet liberal criteria of justice. One kind of decent society is what Rawls terms a 'decent hierarchical society': this is not aggressive, respects some fundamental human rights, and is animated by a conception of the common good (1999, pp. 64-67).

At the heart of the disagreement between cosmopolitans and their critics here is a disagreement about what reasons one has for affirming civil, political, and economic rights. The cosmopolitan response to both the extreme and the moderate anti-cosmopolitan positions is that the very reasons that we think that people in our own society have certain entitlements (say their capacity for **autonomy**, or the fact each individual is best at knowing what is for his or her own good) entail, as a matter of logic, that all persons who have these properties have these same entitlements (Caney, 2005a, chapters 2, 3, and 4). On this view it would be bad faith, for example, to affirm that women in one's own society have a right to an abortion (on the grounds, say, that persons own their own body) and yet to deny this right to women who live in other cultures. In order to sustain an anti-cosmopolitan position here one has to show that the justifications of the principles of justice that one affirms within one's society do *not* entail that those same principles apply globally.

Political implications

Any analysis of cosmopolitan ideals of justice would be incomplete without drawing attention to the implications that the affirmation of cosmopolitan principles have for a number of other concepts such as **humanitarian intervention**, **just war**, and institutional design. Consider, for example, humanitarian intervention. The endorsement of cosmopolitan principles of justice has considerable relevance to the question as to whether states or other political actors may intervene in other states. If one strongly affirms cosmopolitan principles of civic, economic, and political justice then one is more likely to be sceptical than others of the claim that states have a moral entitlement to non-intervention. This does *not* mean that cosmopolitan theorists will necessarily endorse humanitarian intervention for they may hold, on empirical grounds, that interventions may not succeed, or may make matters worse, or that the idea of a 'humanitarian' intervention may be used by unjust states simply to promote their own interests through imperialist usurpation of other countries. It does, however, mean that cosmopolitan thinkers will adopt a less reverential attitude to state **sovereignty** and will accept a state's sovereignty, only to the extent that respecting it best promotes persons' fundamental human rights.

Cosmopolitan ideals also have considerable implications for delineating and justifying principles of just war. If, for example, one affirms cosmopolitan ideals of rights then this will bear on one's account of when states are entitled to wage war (*jus ad bellum*). It is not clear, for example, why states that violate their own citizens' fundamental rights have a moral right to wage war to perpetuate themselves. On a cosmopolitan conception of just war what rights states possess, including whether they can wage war, will depend on whether they respect human rights. In addition to this, cosmopolitan ideals of justice will also have relevance for the question of how states may wage war (*jus in bello*). If one

On humanitarian intervention, see Chapter 18.

On the just war tradition, see Chapter 16.

embraces a strong set of inviolable human rights then this will rule out some courses of action (such as torture or some cases of attacking civilians) that might otherwise be pursued (Caney, 2005a, chapter 6).

Finally, one might note that justice-based cosmopolitanism can have considerable implications for institutional design. That is, it will bear on the question of what role and powers we wish to accord to international institutions including, for example, international courts. (This point will be developed further in section 8.5 and so the discussion will be postponed until then.)

8.4 Cosmopolitanism, culture, and the good life

Having discussed justice-based cosmopolitanism, we may now turn to cosmopolitanism about the good life. This view, recall, rejects an extreme **communitarianism**, which holds that one can flourish only by conforming to the ideals and practices of one's traditional culture(s). It emphasizes the value of living a life in which one draws on a multiplicity of different cultural traditions and norms. As was noted in section 8.2, one can distinguish between what Scheffler terms the 'moderate' view, which holds that it is possible to flourish by drawing in an eclectic way on the ideas of other cultures, and the more 'extreme' view that it is *only* possible to flourish by drawing on the ideas of other cultures (Scheffler, 2001, pp. 116–17).

This section will further explore the nature of this kind of cosmopolitanism, examine the reasoning underpinning it and misgivings voiced about it, and finally draw attention to its implications.

Cosmopolitanism about the good life

Cosmopolitanism about the good life has been defended by a variety of different scholars— including Kwame Anthony Appiah, Jeremy Waldron, and David Hollinger. Appiah, for example, provides a rousing defence in *Cosmopolitanism: Ethics in a World of Strangers* (2006), where he endorses what he terms 'cosmopolitan contamination' (2006, chapter 7). Appiah objects to proposals to keep cultures pure from interaction with other cultures, arguing in favour of borrowing between cultures, mixing different traditions, multiple allegiances, and hybrid identities. It is in this sense that he writes 'in praise of contamination' (Appiah, 2006, p. 111). A similar approach is taken by Waldron (1992). In his influential critique of **multiculturalism** he articulates a cosmopolitan conception of the good life. Finally, we can find a similar (but not identical) account in the work of the historian David Hollinger, who defends an explicitly 'cosmopolitan' approach in his *Postethnic America* (2000). Hollinger focuses his attention on how states should respond to cultural diversity. He distinguishes between a 'pluralist' and a 'cosmopolitan' approach to cultural difference, where the former seeks to maintain and preserve existing cultural traditions and the latter 'promotes multiple identities, [and] emphasizes the dynamic and changing character of many groups' (2000, p. 3). Hollinger argues that the cosmopolitan perspective is the most appropriate to the complex social identities that people possess.

This type of cosmopolitanism arguably has roots in much earlier kinds of cosmopolitanism. Stoic cosmopolitans, for example, rejected the claim that persons must live in their own traditional cultural community in order to flourish. This can be seen in their analyses of exile. Both Plutarch (2000) and Seneca (2001b), for example, argue that exile is not the great evil it is supposed to be and they do so by challenging the thesis that persons can lead a fulfilling life only if they inhabit the community into which they were born. Furthermore, the cosmopolitans of the Enlightenment celebrated international communication and the exchange of ideas between people from different cultures (Schlereth, 1977). As Hollinger notes, the contemporary cosmopolitanism he and others affirm 'is an impulse toward worldly breadth associated especially with the Enlightenment of the eighteenth century' (2000, p. 5).

Arguments for and against

Having analysed what cosmopolitanism about the good entails, let us turn now to consider the reasons offered in its defence. Why adopt a cosmopolitan perspective on the good life?

One of the best-known answers is given by Waldron. He argues that to adhere to anything other than a cosmopolitan approach to the good life is to fail to recognize the eclectic and hybrid nature of modern social existence. Cultures, Waldron argues, are not hermetically sealed for they always interact with each. Furthermore, they are always changing. His argument is worth quoting at length. Waldron writes:

… the hybrid lifestyle of the true cosmopolitan is in fact the only appropriate response to the modern world in which we live. We live in a world formed by technology and trade; by economic, religious, and political imperialism and their offspring; by mass migration and the dispersion of cultural influences. In this context, to immerse oneself in the traditional practices of, say, an aboriginal culture might be a fascinating anthropological experiment, but it involves an artificial dislocation from what actually is going on in the world. That it is an artifice is evidenced by the fact that such immersion often requires special subsidization and extraordinary provision by those who live in the real world, where cultures and practices are not so sealed off from one another. The charge, in other words, is one of *inauthenticity*. Let me state it provocatively. From a cosmopolitan point of view, immersion in the traditions of a particular community in the modern world is like living in Disneyland and thinking that one's surroundings epitomize what it is for a culture really to exist. Worse still, it is like demanding the funds to live in Disneyland and the protection of modern society for the boundaries of Disneyland, while still managing to convince oneself that what happens inside Disneyland is all there is to an adequate and fulfilling life. (Waldron, 1992, p. 763)

Waldron's claim then is that cultures are, by their nature, constantly evolving through interaction with other cultures. Hence, trying to preserve a culture misunderstands their fundamentally dynamic character.

Waldron also advances a second challenge to those who hold that some need the preservation of their culture. Some people, Waldron argues, clearly flourish in adopting a cosmopolitan lifestyle. Given this, however, it follows that others do not actually need the preservation of their own culture. They might want their culture to persist but they do not have a 'need' that must be met. As Waldron writes:

Suppose first, that a freewheeling cosmopolitan life, lived in a kaleidoscope of cultures, is both possible and fulfilling. Suppose such a life turns out to be rich and creative, and with no more unhappiness than one expects to find anywhere in human existence. Immediately, one argument for the protection of minority cultures is undercut. It can no longer be said that all people *need* their rootedness in the particular culture in which they and their ancestors were reared in the way that they need food, clothing, and shelter. People used to think they *needed* red meat in their diet. It turns out not to be true: vegetarian alternatives are available. Now some still may prefer and enjoy a carnivorous diet, but it is no longer a matter of necessity. The same—if the cosmopolitan alternative can be sustained—is true for immersion in the culture of a particular community. Such immersion may be something that particular people like and enjoy. But they no longer can claim that it is something that they need. (Waldron, 1992, p. 762)

We may now turn to consider misgivings about cosmopolitan ideals of the good. Some, for example, may find Waldron's arguments unpersuasive. In response to the first argument, one might argue that it overlooks the distinction between, on the one hand, preventing any change at all and, on the other hand, seeking to slow the rate of change. Those who call for cultural protection may wish not to freeze a culture as it currently is in perpetuity, but, more modestly, to minimize abrupt and sudden upheaval. For example, those who favour language rights for cultural minorities can accept that languages evolve. What they want to prevent, however, is the obliteration of a minority language (Kymlicka, 1995, pp. 103–5; Caney, 2009).

> For ethical defences of culture, see Chapter 7.

Consider now Waldron's second argument. A critic might argue that just because some can flourish without immersion in their culture does not mean that immersion in one's own culture is not a 'need' for others. I can currently flourish without a wheelchair but that does not entail that others cannot have a 'need' for one: clearly some do. Different people can and do have different needs (Scheffler, 2001, p. 117).

More generally, some may simply argue that cosmopolitanism about the good is insufficiently sensitive to the harmful effects that profound upheaval and dislocation can wreak on people's lives. For those strongly attached to a pre-existing culture, social changes that lead to a more 'cosmopolitan' culture may result in a sense of alienation and estrangement.

Political implications

What implications does this have for political practice? The tenability or otherwise of cosmopolitanism about the good life has considerable importance for a number of practical issues. These include: the desirability of national **self-determination** and **secession**, the rights of cultural minorities, language rights, and the defensibility of immigration controls. It also has implications for educational policy, affecting what should be taught: national culture, world culture? (Nussbaum, 1997). In all of these cases what policy should be adopted depends, in part, on how important it is to preserve existing communal traditions and practices. Thus, both the extreme and the more moderate kinds of cosmopolitanism about the good life will have policy implications. Note, however, that they will have subtly different implications. If Waldron is right that flourishing requires a cosmopolitan lifestyle then this would straightforwardly undermine the case for cultural protection in all of the examples given above. The more moderate kind of cosmopolitanism has more complex implications. For if it is the case that some flourish by adopting a cosmopolitan approach and that others flourish by leading a more traditional lifestyle, then political actors will have to try to find some way of jointly respecting the interests of both. This can be especially difficult when states face a binary choice between protecting a culture or not and when cosmopolitans and traditionalists are intermingled.

When considering the policy implications of cosmopolitanism about the good life it is also worth considering its relationship to other kinds of cosmopolitanism (such as justice-based cosmopolitanism). For example, if one adheres to cosmopolitan principles of justice which include a strong commitment to free movement then this is likely to have the effect of eroding traditional cultures, and bringing about a world in which more people adopt a cosmopolitan conception of the good. Some may welcome this, but others who reject cosmopolitanism about the good life may re-think their commitment to the particular cosmopolitan principles of justice in question.

On free movement and migration, see Chapter 20.

8.5 Cosmopolitanism and political institutions

Having introduced two types of contemporary cosmopolitanism, we can now turn to the third kind mentioned earlier—so-called 'political' cosmopolitanism. I shall first provide a fuller description of the nature of this kind of cosmopolitanism, outline a number of different kinds of argument for this approach, and then turn to the misgivings some have about it.

Political cosmopolitanism

Political cosmopolitanism is committed to the claim that there should be global political institutions. As was noted above, this does *not* necessarily mean that there should be a world state. Some cosmopolitanism have indeed affirmed such an ideal (Lu, 2006), but others are quite explicit that this is not required (Caney, 2006b). Thomas Pogge, for example, rejects a world state and defends a multilevel system of governance in *World Poverty and Human Rights* (Pogge, 2008, chapter 7). He envisages a system of supra-state institutions, state-level institutions and sub-state political institutions. None possesses final authority and so none is sovereign. This is a post-sovereign political framework. Another important statement of political cosmopolitanism is given by David Held in his seminal *Democracy and the Global Order* (1995a). There Held argues that there should be a 'global parliament', more accountable regional and global political institutions, and the 'permanent shift of a growing proportion of a nation state's coercive capability to regional and global institutions' (1995a, p. 279). Held, and others like Daniele Archibugi, have defended what they term 'cosmopolitan democracy' (Archibugi & Held, 1995; Archibugi et al., 1998; Archibugi, 2008).

On cosmopolitanism and democracy, see Chapter 21.

Political cosmopolitanism can be fruitfully contrasted with a number of alternative political perspectives. In the first place, it rejects the ideal of a 'society of states' that has been defended by a number of international relations scholars. For many, like Terry Nardin (1983), international justice requires an international system comprised of free

On the society of states, see Chapter 6.

and equal political communities. In its purist form this rejects the idea of any supra-state authority standing over states and locates all authority within states. Secondly, political cosmopolitanism clearly differs from conventional '**realism**'. Realists are likely to be highly sceptical of the capacity of international institutions to act in the ways that cosmopolitan theorists wish. They will emphasize the immense role of power and will doubt the possibility of international institutions that are both effective and motivated by the moral considerations that cosmopolitans posit. Thirdly, political cosmopolitanism may be rejected by nationalist thinkers like David Miller (1995). Nationalists place emphasis on the value of a self-governing national community and reject calls for extensive supranational governance.

 On realism, see Chapter 5.

On nationalism, see Chapter 7.

Arguments for

On what grounds might one defend political cosmopolitanism? Here, it is worth distinguishing between two different kinds of justification—'instrumental' arguments and democracy-based arguments. Both draw on cosmopolitan principles of justice but do so in very different ways.

Consider the instrumental arguments first. These arguments make two central claims. First, they start by defending some cosmopolitan principles of justice. They might, for example, be committed to some principles of global distributive justice (defending, say, a principle of global equality or a global 'difference principle'). Or they might defend global civil and political principles—arguing that all persons possess some fundamental human rights to civil and political liberties. Or they might defend global principles of environmental justice—arguing, for example, that anthropogenic climate change requires global principles of justice to distribute the burdens associated with combating climate change.

Having defended some cosmopolitan principles of justice, instrumental arguments for political cosmopolitanism then claim (and this is the second step) that global political institutions are necessary to realize these principles of justice. The second step thus holds that a system of states, for example, is on its own inadequate. A number of reasons are given for the necessity of global political institutions. First, one might argue that a system of states is prone to **collective action problem**s and is unable to achieve the necessary coordination and cooperation. Consider, for example, global environmental problems (like biodiversity loss and global climate change). It is often said that a system of states is ill-equipped to deal with these, and it is for this reason, among others, that a binding, powerful international agreement to combat climate change remains elusive. In addition to this, it is suggested that global institutions can curb powerful actors and can provide a rule-governed institutional structure which protects the weak and the vulnerable. One might also, in this vein, defend strong supra-national courts to which citizens can appeal if they think that justice is not being done within their own state. Similarly, one might defend the role and importance of the **International Criminal Court** in these terms. Note, in addition to this, that international institutions can sometimes offer incentives for compliance with human rights. To take one example, the European Union imposes certain conditions on membership, requiring member states to honour some fundamental human rights. Through this kind of mechanism, international institutions may foster and encourage a greater realization of cosmopolitan principles of justice.

On ethics and the environment, see Chapter 10.

In short, then, one kind of defence of political cosmopolitanism justifies global institutions on the grounds that they are needed to realize cosmopolitan principles of justice. At this point, it is worth stressing that this argument is dependent on some empirical assumptions about the likely effects of supra-state institutions. Given this, justice-based cosmopolitans can quite consistently reject political cosmopolitanism and favour a wholly statist order if they reject these empirical assumptions (Beitz, 1994, p. 121).

Let us turn now to consider the democracy-based argument. This rejects the instrumental approach and argues instead that a system of democratic international institutions is needed if people are to enjoy democratic control over their own lives. Stated more fully, the democracy-based argument rests on two key claims. First, it holds that where people's lives are determined by social, economic, and legal processes, then they have a democratic right to take part in the governance of those processes. Pogge, for example, writes that 'persons have a right to an institutional order under which those significantly and legitimately affected by a political decision have a roughly equal opportunity to influence the making of this decision—directly or through elected delegates or representatives' (Pogge, 2008, p. 190). In a similar spirit, Held writes that 'those whose life expectancy and life chances are significantly affected by social forces and processes ought to have a stake in the determination of the conditions and regulation of these, either directly or indirectly through political representatives' (2004, p. 100).

Proponents of the democracy-based argument then make the empirical claim that we are living in a globalized world: the social and economic processes that significantly affect people's fundamental interests are global in nature.

From this, it follows that persons have a right to democratically accountable supra-state institutions. It is only with such institutions that people can exercise democratic control over the processes that determine people's lives.

Arguments against

Having set out the case for political cosmopolitanism, let us turn now to consider the misgivings. These are many and varied. Three are particularly pressing. Let us call these the tyranny argument, the redundancy argument, and the social unity argument (Caney, 2005a, chapter 5; Lu, 2006). First, many worry that strengthened international institutions will be tyrannical. Kant, for example, rejects world government on precisely these grounds (1991, p. 113). Relatedly, some (particularly those sympathetic to realism) may worry that international institutions will be 'captured' by powerful states and political actors and so not embody the cosmopolitan ideals that they are intended to embody. Nationalists might also worry that this gives insufficient room to national self-determination. A second line of criticism holds that international institutions are superfluous because a society of states can cooperate and provide the goods that the instrumental argument claims require international institutions. It might thus be argued that cooperation does not always require an overarching coercive agent and can evolve through repeated interaction. Thirdly, nationalists are critical of political cosmopolitanism on the grounds that global political institutions will lack the social unity needed for them to function properly (Miller, 1995). Political institutions, on this argument, require a supportive political culture and an ethos of co-operation and compliance. This culture, nationalists argue, can exist within nation states, but is entirely absent at the global level. Hence, global political institutions cannot operate in the way cosmopolitans claim.

Clearly, more can be said about each of these objections and the resources available to cosmopolitans to respond to them. The above, though, should provide some sense of where political cosmopolitans and their critics disagree.

8.6 **Conclusion**

As the preceding analysis has illustrated, the term 'cosmopolitanism' is employed to refer to a diverse set of doctrines, including both empirical claims about the nature of the world (Beck), as well as three kinds of normative claim. Underlying these three normative ideals is a shared conviction—namely, that persons' normative horizons (be it their obligations of justice, their source of ideals of the good or their political membership) should not be circumscribed by existing boundaries. It offers an ideal in which people transcend the local and the particular, and it problematizes existing borders. As such cosmopolitanism poses a radical challenge to existing political practice.

The radical nature of this challenge often prompts two different kinds of concern. The first is that cosmopolitanism is undesirable because it fails to recognize the deep importance of local ties and loyalties. Cosmopolitans will, however, respond that this claim is misconceived. Justice-based cosmopolitanism can, for example, recognize that friends, families, and colleagues have special duties to one another. Furthermore, those who subscribe to 'modest' cosmopolitanism also affirm nation-level or state-level principles of justice. Even those who think that national membership has no relevance for people's entitlements may think that it bears on people's duties. Some may think, for example, that no one is entitled to more than anyone else because of their nationality, and thus affirm a wholly cosmopolitan account of people's entitlements. However, they may also hold that persons have a special responsibility to uphold the cosmopolitan entitlements of their fellow citizens. In this way, they may combine a cosmopolitan account of persons' entitlements with an endorsement of the role of particularistic attachments.[7] To this we should also add that political cosmopolitans need not deny a role for national self-determination.

The second concern prompted by the radical nature of the cosmopolitan perspective is that it is utopian. The world as it is currently constituted falls radically short of even the most modest cosmopolitan ideals of distributive justice. Furthermore, basic civil and political human rights are systematically violated in many countries. To this we should add that global political institutions of the kind favoured by political cosmopolitans seem a distant dream. In light of all this some might object that cosmopolitanism has little relevance and is unduly idealistic. Again, cosmopolitans will respond that this objection is too quick. In the first place, they can observe that the status quo is not writ in stone, but is subject to human agency and, as such, change is possible. Secondly, however, they can

On utopianism, see the Introduction and Chapter 4.

---

[7] For a related (but non-identical) point see Miller (1995, pp. 75–77). For a comprehensive discussion of the compatibility of cosmopolitanism with nationalism see Tan (2004).

argue that it is a mistake to reject cosmopolitan principles of justice and cosmopolitan accounts of political **legitimacy** simply on the grounds that they will not be realized. Cosmopolitan ideals are intended to provide a benchmark by which to judge current and past practices and institutions (Beitz, 1999, pp. 156 and 170), not as predictions as to how humans will behave. That we do not currently live up to them, and indeed may never do so, does not in any way invalidate them or call into question their validity as standards by which to evaluate human conduct and institutions. Rather what it shows is just how far short we fall of living in a just and legitimate world.

QUESTIONS

1. How can one best define 'cosmopolitanism'?
2. What reasons, if any, are there to affirm a cosmopolitan account of justice?
3. How persuasive is Rawls's argument against applying liberal egalitarian principles of justice to the global realm?
4. What implications do cosmopolitan ideals of justice have for the use of force?
5. How persuasive is Waldron's defence of cosmopolitanism about the good life?
6. What implications does cosmopolitanism about the good life have for how the state should treat minority cultures?
7. Assess the claim that in a globalized world a commitment to democratic decision-making entails a commitment to a cosmopolitan democracy.
8. Is political cosmopolitanism a realistic and desirable ideal?
9. Can one consistently endorse cosmopolitan ideals of distributive justice without also endorsing some kind of political cosmopolitanism?
10. How vulnerable is cosmopolitanism to the objection that its ideals are utopian and unrealistic?

FURTHER READING

Beitz, C. (1999) *Political Theory and International Relations*. Princeton: Princeton University Press. An influential defence of a cosmopolitan theory of justice.

Brock, G. & Brighouse, H. (eds) (2005) *The Political Philosophy of Cosmopolitanism*. Cambridge: Cambridge University Press. A collection by eminent contemporary political philosophers on the nature and justifiability of cosmopolitanism.

Buchanan, A. (2004) *Justice, Legitimacy, and Self-Determination: Moral Foundations for International Law*. Oxford: Oxford University Press. An interesting application of cosmopolitan political morality to international law.

Caney, S. (2005) *Justice Beyond Borders: A Global Political Theory*. Oxford: Oxford University Press. A defence of a liberal egalitarian cosmopolitan theory of justice.

Held, D. (1995) *Democracy and the Global Order: From the Modern State to Cosmopolitan Governance*. Cambridge: Polity. A leading defence of cosmopolitan democracy.

Miller, D. (2007) *National Responsibility and Global Justice*. Oxford: Oxford University Press. A critique of egalitarian cosmopolitanism from a leading nationalist thinker.

Rawls, J. (1999) *The Law of Peoples*. Cambridge: Harvard University Press. A defence of a non-cosmopolitan international political theory.

Pogge, T. (2008) *World Poverty and Human Rights: Cosmopolitan Responsibilities and Reforms*, 2nd edn. Cambridge: Polity. A powerful defence of a cosmopolitan theory of justice centred around human rights.

Schlereth, T.J. (1977) *The Cosmopolitan Ideal in Enlightenment Thought: Its Form and Function in the Ideas of Franklin, Hume, and Voltaire 1694–1790*. South Bend: University of Notre Dame Press. An excellent intellectual history of Enlightenment cosmopolitanism.

Tan, K-C. (2004) *Justice without Borders: Cosmopolitanism, Nationalism, and Patriotism*. Cambridge: Cambridge University Press. A defence of a cosmopolitanism that can accommodate nationalist concerns.

■ WEB LINKS

http://www.un.org/en/documents/udhr/ The text of the Universal Declaration of Human Rights.

http://plato.stanford.edu/entries/cosmopolitanism/ An essay surveying the different forms of cosmopolitanism from the excellent *Stanford Encyclopedia of Philosophy*.

http://plato.stanford.edu/entries/world-government/ An essay on the idea of 'World Government', also from *The Stanford Encyclopaedia of Philosophy*.

http://international-political-theory.net/ipt-articles.htm The International Political Theory Beacon is an excellent source for accessing some of the latest research on cosmopolitanism and related topics. Among other things, it contains links to important academic articles, video interviews with leading scholars, and book reviews.

http://philosophybites.com/past_programmes.html Podcast interviews with leading philosophers on a wide range of topics, including Anthony Appiah on cosmopolitanism.

Visit the Online Resource Centre that accompanies this book to access more learning resources: www.oxfordtextbooks.co.uk/orc/bell_ethics/

9 Feminism

Kimberly Hutchings

READER'S GUIDE

The aim of this chapter is to introduce the reader to feminist ethical perspectives on world politics. We will begin by looking at the history of feminist politics in the international context. Following on from this, we will identify three main traditions of ethical thinking arising out of feminist politics—justice, care, and postmodernist. The chapter will examine the implications of these different types of feminist ethics for thinking about moral questions in world politics, in contrast to alternative ethical perspectives as well as to each other. In conclusion, we will consider the common ground between distinct feminist ethical traditions.

9.1 Introduction

As with green or post-colonial ethics, feminist ethics emerged out of a movement (or, more accurately, a set of movements in different historical contexts) of political resistance that was committed to radical change and promoted new ways of analysing the world. Feminists pursue the goal of redressing ways in which *women* are disadvantaged by current social, cultural, economic, and political arrangements in specific contexts. In doing this, feminists draw attention to the centrality of *gender* as a hierarchical principle for organizing social, cultural, economic, and political dimensions of human existence. *Gender* is usually defined, in contrast to biological sex, as the socially constructed identities, roles, and characteristics assigned to ideas about what it means to be or to act as a man (masculine) or a woman (feminine).

As a politically inspired perspective, we would expect feminist ethics to share ground with critical theory and post-structuralist methods and to oppose itself to mainstream ethical positions on world politics, such as those of **realism, cosmopolitanism**, international society, or **communitarianism**. However, neither feminist politics nor feminist ethics can be categorized as a single way of approaching the world. Different strands within **feminism** relate differently to the methods and the theories discussed elsewhere in this book. Some examples of feminist ethics follow an **'analytic'** approach, some are fundamentally critical of it. Some examples of feminist ethics share ground with cosmopolitan or communitarian arguments, some are fundamentally opposed to them. Feminism as an international or global ethical theory takes distinct and not always compatible forms. The reasons for this are embedded in feminism's history as a political movement and we will begin with a brief overview of this history.

On 'analytic' political theory, see Chapter 1.

On cosmopolitanism and communitarianism, see Chapters 7 and 8.

9.2 Feminist politics

Feminist politics in historical context

Feminist political ideology, like other modern political ideologies, such as liberalism, nationalism, and socialism, originated in response to the French Revolution and developed during the nineteenth century (Wollstonecraft, 1992). By the end of the nineteenth century, there were well-established organizations campaigning for equal legal and political rights for women in Europe and the USA. These focused on issues such as women's suffrage, women's property rights, women's legal independence from fathers or husbands, and women's access to education and the professions. They were predominantly middle-class movements. In addition, socialist, trades union, and anti-slavery movements all included feminist activists who fought for women's interests as part of those struggles. Over time, membership of feminist organizations broadened to include other categories of women. Nevertheless, at the time of the First World War, formally organized feminist groups remained overwhelmingly middle class and overwhelmingly focused on issues of legal equality, in particular in relation to property and the vote.

The First World War inspired a somewhat different type of feminist politics, one that argued for a link between feminist politics and peace. This line of argument shifted feminist argument away from a focus on demonstrating that women were essentially the same as men as a basis for their legal and political equality. Instead, it built on a critique of masculine aggression as the source of both women's subordination and war, and argued that the pacific qualities traditionally associated with women in the **private sphere** could become the basis of an alternative political order in which both peace and women's equality would be established. The *Women's International League for Peace and Freedom* was inaugurated in 1915, and was actively involved in debates about the League of Nations and in the movements that supported pacifism in the inter-war period.

The 1918–1939 period was characterized by two different types of feminist politics concentrated in Europe and the USA. First, feminists continued to campaign for equality on the grounds of sameness to men. Secondly, feminists campaigned for different, non-violent ways of doing politics as a prerequisite for fundamentally improving the position of women, building on women's difference from, rather than women's sameness to, men. At the same time, the USSR proclaimed the equality of men and women, and that the overcoming of a need for feminist politics in a socialist state and nascent anti-colonial struggles, in some cases, included feminist aims within their broader fight for national **self-determination**.

Feminist politics revived again in the 1960s and 1970s in liberal states. What is now often referred to as 'Second Wave' feminism was inspired by the experience of women's continued inequality and subordination, even in states where most of the battles for legal equality had been won. In its initial phases, Second Wave feminism echoed the earlier movement, including a mixture of both 'sameness' and 'difference' type politics. Increasingly, however, in the 1980s and beyond, feminist politics of both the 'sameness' and 'difference' kinds was challenged by a 'Third Wave' of critical feminists who argued that both strands of feminist thinking illegitimately universalized an undifferentiated understanding of both women and men. In particular, it was argued, both these kinds of feminist politics modelled their understanding of women on white, middle class, first world and heterosexual women. This meant that they failed to address the position of women who did not fall into this category and sidelined ways in which, for instance, many women *and* men were oppressed by hierarchies of power, around race, class, nationality, and sexuality, from which some women as well as men benefited (hooks, 1982; Mohanty et al., 1991; Basu & McGrory, 1995).

In the decades since these critiques gained ground, feminism as a political movement has become much more complicated and fractured, and a third 'intersectional' mode of feminist politics, which emphasizes the interrelations between gender and other hierarchical markers of identity (such as race, class, sexuality) has taken its place alongside the 'sameness' and 'difference' modes that dominated in the early years of the Second Wave. In practice, feminist campaigning, both national and international, is now often characterized by coalition politics in which groups that have different views about the basis of gender subordination and about what the constituency of women means, link up with each other in relation to specific issues (Basu & McGrory, 1995; Snyder, 2003). Crudely speaking, I suggest that, in contemporary feminism as a **transnational** or international movement, we can identify three types of feminist politics in relation to transnational or international issues—equality feminism, radical feminism, and post-colonial feminism.

Equality feminism

Equality feminism has many variants, but is most closely linked to either liberal or socialist political ideologies. Liberal and socialist feminists regard the prevailing gender order in world politics as based on a false devaluation of women as human individuals, which denies their equal worth to men. From an equality feminist point of view the key problem in the current world is that women are treated differently and worse than men, whereas they should be treated equally. The key issues that need addressing in contemporary world politics are women's legal, political, and economic subordinate status in different parts of the world. Different equality feminisms envisage equality differently (e.g. equality of opportunity versus equality of outcome), but share the assumption that *all* women have the *same* interest in bringing this equality about.

In the last 20 years, with the dominance of liberalism and capitalism within the global political and economic order, this kind of feminist politics can be found in international campaigns around **gender mainstreaming** (in international policy formation, implementation, and delivery), women's equal access to healthcare, work and education, as well as democratization processes aimed at institutionalizing equal legal and political rights for women. Equality feminism is perhaps best summed up in the 1979 International Convention for the Elimination of Discrimination Against Women (CEDAW). For equality feminists, the aim has to be ultimately to make gender irrelevant to how women are treated.

Radical feminism

I am using the label 'radical feminists' to refer to feminist politics that bases itself on the fundamental difference, as opposed to the sameness, of women to men. Radical feminists do not necessarily disagree with equality feminisms' pursuit of equal rights for women. However, because their understanding of the situation of women in the current world order is different from that of equality feminists, it focuses on a different range of policy priorities, as well as a different feminist vision of what a future world order should look like. Radical feminists argue that equality feminism's emphasis on the sameness of women to men actually *disadvantages* women. For example, the international **human rights** regime sees the vulnerability of individuals to state power as the ground of primary protections against arbitrary violence. However, for many women, their key vulnerability to violence is not in relation to the state, but in relation to violence inflicted in the domestic sphere. For radical feminists this demonstrates that it is men, rather than women, that act as the model for the 'human' in documents like the Universal Declaration of Human Rights (Mackinnon, 2006).

Radical feminist politics politicizes issues such as sexual and domestic violence, motherhood, sex-trafficking, sex-tourism, and pornography in addition to supplementing equality feminist issues by campaigning for women to be treated differently from men where their needs and vulnerabilities are different. This involves a fundamental revaluation of characteristics and roles traditionally associated with women, and it is often linked to an argument that those characteristics and roles could work as a positive counter-weight to dominant masculine priorities in world politics. The area where this position is most widely used and accepted in international discourse is in relation to war and peace. UN Resolution 1325 (United Nations, 2000), which reflects consistent lobbying from feminist peace activists, requires that women take an equal role in peace-making and **peace-building** processes. It justifies this requirement in part by reference to the particular pacific skills and values that women, as women, bring to the negotiating table.

Post-colonial feminism

Both equality and radical feminisms offer a general diagnosis and prescription for the plight of women and what should be done about it. Post-colonial feminism takes issue with both of these positions, seeing them as tied up with an essentially imperialist

On post-colonialism, see Chapter 11.

politics. Both forms of feminism are accused of imposing a political agenda peculiar to the experience of middle class women in liberal, capitalist states on women in general. In the international context, from the post-colonial point of view, it is equality and radical feminisms that have exerted most influence on ideas about women's development and women's human rights. This has resulted in privileged Western feminists setting the agenda for transnational feminist politics more generally. Post-colonial feminists have sought to resist a 'top-down' international policy process in which, too often, the recipients of development aid or campaigns around topics such as female circumcision (also known as female genital mutilation or FGM) have not been involved in policy formation or delivery (Mohanty et al., 1991).

UN Women's conferences, such as in Nairobi 1985 or Beijing 1995, are contexts in which deep tensions emerge between the political priorities of different feminist groups, and in which the idea of both 'human' and 'woman' as distinct, inclusive identities is put into question (Snyder, 2003). Two examples of this might be equality feminism's championing of women's right to abortion and radical feminism's championing of campaigns against Internet pornography. From the point of view of feminist movements in countries where sex-selective abortion is a growing trend, and where there is strong state control of population growth, the politics of the debate over women's rights over their own bodies is quite different from the politics surrounding the issue in a rich liberal state. Similarly, from the point of view of feminist movements in countries that are desperately poor, the denigration of women in pornography is a much less significant issue than women's access to clean water. In the 1990s, feminists active within the emergent states in the break-up of Yugoslavia, found some Western feminists' reaction to the systematic sexual violence involved in those conflicts unhelpful, because it demonized particular national groups, and tended to racialize and essentialize victims, as well as perpetrators.

In response to post-colonial critiques of hegemonic forms of transnational feminism, both equality and difference feminisms have changed in both theory and practice over time. Most feminists involved in transnational campaigning are committed to taking the differences between different women seriously, and to democratizing transnational feminist practice in the formation and delivery of policy. Nevertheless, the discourses of either liberal equality or radical difference feminism are the ones that predominate in discussions of global 'women's' issues (Engle Merry, 2006).

Different types of feminist political activism are grounded in different experiences and understandings of the sources of gendered oppression. Within the academy, a range of feminist scholarship has grown up that builds, in diverse ways, on the insights of different types of feminism to develop critiques of existing ways of thinking, and to construct alternative feminist approaches to understanding and judging the world. In the following sections, we will examine three types of *ethical* theory that emerge out of feminist argument, and that correlate to the types of feminist politics outlined above—feminist justice ethics, feminist care ethics, and feminist postmodernist ethics. In each case we will examine the kinds of conclusions that follow for thinking about the ethics of world politics (Hutchings, 2000, 2007a).

9.3 Feminist justice ethics

The feminist justice critique

Feminist justice ethics takes its cue from the politics of equality feminism. It begins from the assumption of the *moral equality* of all human beings. From this perspective it is critical of communitarianism. The problem with communitarian approaches for feminist justice ethics is that, in giving moral privilege to the values inherent in culture or community, they provide no ground on which to criticize the ways that cultures and communities may exclude and exploit women. Susan Moller Okin famously raised the question of whether **multiculturalism** was bad for women, and drew attention to a range of cultural practices by which women were injured and subordinated (Okin, 1994). For this reason she, and a range of other feminist theorists, have argued that there have to be moral limits to cultural diversity which reflect giving equal weight to women's needs and interests (Nussbaum, 2000; Benhabib, 2002). For similar reasons, feminists are sceptical of any international society ethics that includes a significant degree of autonomy for states, and does not take seriously enough the dependence of states on inequitable gender arrangements, in which women's interests are rarely identified as a central concern.

On communitarian ethics, see Chapter 7.

On international society, see Chapter 6.

The grounds of justice feminism clearly overlap with those of different versions of cosmopolitanism, in particular those of a **deontological** or rights-based kind. From the point of view of justice feminism, however, much cosmopolitan theorizing does not live up to its claims to take the human as such as its starting point, because it tends to conflate what it means to be human with the position of individuals located in the **public sphere**, and to neglect questions of justice in relation to the private sphere on which the public sphere depends. In addition to criticizing communitarian ethical arguments, Okin also criticized the theory that has been most influential on contemporary cosmopolitan theories of justice, John Rawls's *A Theory of Justice* (Okin, 1989). She pointed out that Rawls's theory was set up in such a way that the participants in the '**original position**' were entirely orientated in relation to their position within the public sphere, and that **social justice** was assumed to apply only within that sphere. Questions about the division of labour within the household, childcare and so on, were presumed to be matters to which principles of justice did not apply. For justice feminists, this tendency to privatize and naturalize areas of life of particular significance in relation to gender subordination undermines the claims to universality made by many deontological, rights-based theories. In the case of feminist justice ethics, however, the response is not to abandon universal moral theories, but to make them genuinely inclusive and universal.

On cosmopolitanism, see Chapter 8.

On Rawls's theory of justice, see Chapter 1.

On this view, the problem with Rawls's theory of justice is not that he thinks about justice in the wrong way, but that he fails to include women's work within his thinking. The way to put this right, Okin argues, is to extend the scope of his analysis and add women and the family in, but this does not involve abandoning the universal pertinence of his principles of justice. Underlying this kind of move is the concern, shared by many feminists, that to abandon the universal status of certain moral principles of justice and rights is to fall into the communitarian trap, which will undermine the possibility of criticism of 'cultures' with moral norms that devalue women and the feminine (Benhabib, 1992, 2002). However, if feminists are to articulate justice ethics in a way that also does not discriminate against women and the feminine, then they clearly need to find a way of grounding moral claims in terms of justice and rights that does not rely on masculine-biased accounts of moral reasoning, as well as being able to be valid universally, across boundaries of culture and power.

Feminist justice ethics of world politics

One example of a feminist moral theory that develops this kind of universal account of ethics is the argument put forward by Martha Nussbaum in her book *Women and Human Development* (2000). In this book, Nussbaum finds the grounds for certain (limited) universal ethical values and claims in a set of human '**capabilities**' that she argues are foundational for the flourishing of any human life. She then uses the example of the lives of women in developing countries as a way to exemplify how the capabilities approach can be used as a kind of yardstick to critique existing practice in different national contexts and to provide fundamental principles for progress, in particular progress for women. In her argument, Nussbaum puts forward a robust defence of feminist moral **universalism**, but she also argues that her specific form of feminist justice ethics allows considerable space for cultural sensitivity and difference (Nussbaum, 2000, pp. 7, 70–71).

At the heart of Nussbaum's feminist justice ethics is a commitment to the intrinsic value of humanity and the right of every individual to be enabled to live in such a way that they are not simply subordinated to the ends of other people. At present, according to Nussbaum, women in developing countries are particularly likely to experience their lives as subordinated to others, including the demands of patriarchal cultures and of exploitative conditions of work. For this reason, she argues against approaches to morality that base themselves in cultural difference, since, in her view, communitarianism would justify local norms that subordinate and harm women. In addition, however, she argues that the premises of communitarianism are problematic sociologically and philosophically. They are problematic sociologically because they treat 'culture' as monolithic, and ignore the complex and contradictory nature of actual cultural contexts (see Benhabib, 2002, for a similar argument). They are problematic philosophically because moral relativism is an incoherent position, insofar as it wants to ground universal principles of toleration of different cultures in world politics, whilst arguing that there are no grounds on which such universal claims can be made.

In spite of her critique of communitarianism, however, Nussbaum's particular version of moral universalism is, she argues, less prone to problems associated with other kinds of justice ethics because it does not elaborate a substantive set of moral principles that all must follow, but rather specifies 'human capabilities' that are inherently enabling rather than prescriptive, and that can be the ongoing subject of debate. This still allows room for culture to play an important ethical role. The capabilities that Nussbaum outlines as of universal ethical significance are as follows and each of them suggests a range of requirements that need to be in place in terms of cultural assumptions and social and political institutions if they are to be realizable (Nussbaum, 2000, pp. 78–81).

- Life—the ability to live out a natural life span.
- Bodily health—the ability to have good health including reproductive health, adequate nourishment, shelter.
- Bodily integrity—**freedom of movement**, security from physical violation, sexual and reproductive autonomy.
- Senses, imagination, thought—the ability to use all of these fully in an educated way.
- Emotions—the ability to be attached to others, to have a capacity for love and affection.
- Practical reason—to be able to reflect rationally, identify one's own conception of the good life and plan for it.
- Affiliation—the ability to live with others in personal relationships and social communities.
- Other species—the ability to live in relation to nature.
- Play—the ability to enjoy recreation.
- Control over one's material and political environment—the ability to participate in political choices, ability to hold property, to work on equal terms with others.

Nussbaum uses the above list as a reference point for making judgements about the actual lives and conditions of women in developing countries, employing India as her specific example. In the light of this list she examines issues to do with property, work, the family, religion, and so on, and shows how capabilities are either sustained or undercut by these social institutions in practice. Nussbaum examines examples of how social institutions might be challenged or reformulated in order to provide better support for women's flourishing. It becomes clear very quickly that the capabilities approach is ethically very demanding, in that it requires the institutionalization of equality across a range of domains even to live up to threshold conditions. For example, the capability to live in affiliation with others is, in Nussbaum's view, fatally undermined by status-based discrimination on grounds of 'race, sex, sexual orientation, religion, caste, ethnicity, or national origin' (p. 79). Although her argument claims to make room for 'culture', it is clear that the universalization of certain fundamental rights trumps culture as a source of value in Nussbaum's account (Jaggar, 2005).

Nussbaum bases her argument on ideas of human need and human flourishing that owe a debt to Aristotelian **virtue ethics**, as well as to a more Kantian, deontological position. There are other examples of justice feminism that draw on different kinds of ethical argument, such as Okin's adaptation of Rawls's theory or justice (Okin, 1989), or Benhabib's adaptation of Habermasian **discourse ethics** (Benhabib 2002, 2006). In all cases, however, justice feminism insists on the idea that there are limits in principle on what can count as a morally valid account of justice for women in the international domain. These limits link to the key values of **autonomy** and equality that are embedded in justice feminism's view of what it means to be human. The implications of these values are strongly prescriptive. In the case of Nussbaum, for instance, morality requires a major redistribution of global wealth from rich to poor (particularly to poor women), and it also

On Habermas, see Chapter 2.

requires the institutionalization of human rights, including rights to bodily integrity, freedom of speech, political participation, and so on. From this perspective, justice feminism calls attention to customary practices that violate the human rights of women, such as female circumcision (FGM), and claims to provide a rational basis for the abolition of such practices in general, regardless of cultural context.

9.4 Feminist care ethics

Care as critique

On the ethics of care, see also Chapter 19.

The form of ethical thinking most commonly identified with feminism is the so-called 'ethic of care'. This tradition of feminist ethics was prompted by Carol Gilligan's argument in her book, *In A Different Voice: Psychological Theory and Women's Development* (1982). Gilligan was a social psychologist investigating theories about what we should count as appropriate mature moral reasoning in response to moral dilemmas. At the time she was writing, the predominant view was that the height of moral maturity was signified by the capacity of a moral agent to detach him or herself from the context of the specific moral dilemma, and make a judgement in terms of what general moral rules or values ought to apply to any similar situation. This reflected the predominant rationalism of much ethical theory, and also typifies the path taken by many cosmopolitan 'justice' theories of international ethics. In empirical work, social psychologists had found that men were more likely to rely on abstract procedures when faced with making a decision about a moral dilemma (e.g. reference back to a universal moral principle, such as 'it is always wrong to lie') as a basis for judgement. Women, in contrast, were more likely to make contextual judgements (e.g. asking for more information about the reasons for a particular lie, and how these related to the liar's relationships with and responsibilities to others). Because of this, social psychologists had identified women as less morally mature than men. In opposition to this, Gilligan argued that the rational, detached, autonomous characteristics supposedly significant of moral maturity in fact reflected the priorities of an ethic of justice that privileged masculinity over femininity.

Gilligan went on to argue that the supposedly inferior modes of moral reasoning more typical of women (ethics of care) were, in fact, equally reflective and sophisticated as those of an ethic of justice, and should be taken as equally indicative of moral maturity. For her the ethic of care and the ethic of justice were *both* essential to adequate moral reasoning. In many ways, however, her argument, and the ways in which it was taken up, reflected the politics of radical feminism. This was because of Gilligan's focus on revaluing (normally denigrated) skills and qualities specific to women, and her argument that mainstream theories tended to take male/masculine as norm. This meant that feminist care ethics formed a critique of communitarian as well as cosmopolitan thinking, since it sought to reverse the denigration of women and the feminine built in to both modern and traditional cultures, as well as criticizing the abstraction of much universalist moral theory. The idea of a feminist ethic of care inspired a whole literature that has taken issue with feminist justice ethics in a variety of ways (Card, 1991; Browning-Cole & Coultrap-McQuin, 1992; Held, 1995b). In broad terms, those feminists trying to take forward the idea of an ethic of care have sought to ground ethical value in the relations and responsibilities associated with caring practices most frequently carried out by women, and often exemplified by the relationship between mother and child (Noddings, 1984; Ruddick, 1989; Held, 1993, 2006).

Care ethics of world politics

Work on the feminist ethic of care developed in the 1980s connected closely with contemporary debates on the ethics of world politics in arguments about pacifism and the justice of war. In her book, *Maternal Thinking: Towards a Politics of Peace*, Sara Ruddick draws on the idea of an ethic of care as a central part of her argument for a feminist moral orientation in the context of international politics (Gilligan, 1982; Ruddick, 1989). The book involves a rejection of realist arguments as to the tragic inevitability or structural necessity of war and communitarian claims about the special ethical status of the collective group or nation. In addition, it develops a critique of traditional moral justifications for war—in both **utilitarian** and deontological variants—as well as a positive characterization of how a different kind of moral judgement and political practice is possible in relation to war. There are essentially two stages to Ruddick's argument. In the first stage she develops a feminist approach to moral judgement through the idea of 'maternal thinking', while in the second stage she explores the implications of 'maternal thinking' for making moral judgements about war.

'Maternal thinking', according to Ruddick, 'is a discipline in attentive love', a discipline that is rooted in the demands of a particular relation of care, that between mother and child, and which reflects a particular range of metaphysical attitudes, cognitive capacities and virtues (Ruddick, 1989, p. 123). Maternal thinking represents a kind of ideal type of mothering practice, but you do not have to be either a mother or a woman in order to do it. The key point about maternal thinking is that it does not rely on abstract moral principles, but on the recognition of the specificity of the moral agent's responsibilities and the needs of others in particular contexts. This recognition, Ruddick argues, works against the kind of thinking about others that is necessary to legitimate war as a practice: 'The analytic fictions of just war theory require a closure of moral issues final enough to justify killing and "enemies" abstract enough to be killable' (Ruddick, 1989, p. 150). What follows from care ethics, according to Ruddick, is a commitment to non-violent mechanisms of dialogue, mediation or non-violent confrontation for resolving political disputes (Ruddick, 1989, pp. 141–59).

On the just war tradition, see Chapters 16 and 17.

From the standpoint of maternal thinking, the appropriate stance to take in ethical judgement is to attempt to build on particular experiences of the practice of care to help to identify with and take responsibility for the needs and suffering of others. Ruddick frequently cites the example of the women in Argentina and Chile, whose sons, daughters, and grandchildren had 'disappeared', that is to say, been arbitrarily imprisoned, tortured, or killed by the ruling regime, without anyone being told. The women started staging demonstrations in public places, displaying the photographs of their missing children and grandchildren, and putting pressure on the government to admit its crimes (pp. 225–34). The movement gradually expanded to embrace concerns with children across the world who had suffered harm: 'This is not transcendent impartiality but a sympathetic apprehension of another grounded in one's own particular suffering' (Ruddick,

1993, p. 123). In addition, however, maternal thinking is sensitive to the specific contexts in which ethical dilemmas are embedded, and the importance of appreciating the ethical weight of the perspectives of all parties to any dispute or conflict. For Ruddick, ethical judgement, in strong contrast to the universalism of feminist justice ethics, has to be on a case-by-case basis, but without ready-made principles of adjudication.

In her book, *Globalizing Care: Ethics, Feminist Theory and International Relations* (1999), Fiona Robinson follows Ruddick in arguing for an approach to international ethics derived from 'care'. Her 'critical' care approach develops an international ethics that encompasses not only questions about the morality of war, but also about international human rights, development, and global **distributive justice**. Unlike Ruddick, Robinson does not rely on a concept of 'maternal thinking', but more generally on the idea of care as an everyday practice and moral orientation, embedded in a number of actual contexts. Moreover, Robinson places more emphasis than Ruddick on the significance for care ethics of the broader political, social, and economic context of the international sphere, and the ways in which particular patterns of advantage and disadvantage, power and oppression, sameness and difference are institutionalized within it. Nevertheless, although Robinson's work is broader in focus, and elaborates a more flexible account and defence of care ethics than Ruddick, what is morally 'wrong' is defined similarly to Ruddick as that which serves 'to undermine the ability of moral agents to identify and understand others as "real" individuals—with real, special, unique lives' (Robinson, 1999, p. 47).

In terms of ethical issues in world politics surrounding development, distributive justice or human rights, the ethic of care does not offer a settled set of prescriptions for outcomes. Instead it insists on giving ethical priority to a proper understanding of contexts and to the need for 'bottom-up' rather than 'top-down' approaches to addressing such issues. For example, Robinson sees recent changes in development policy in which decision-making power is shifted towards the recipient communities as reflecting good care practice. Similarly, rather than simply condemning practices, such as female circumcision (FGM) in terms of abstract, universal rights, a care ethics approach would seek to understand how such practices are integrated into a particular cultural and socio-economic context. From a care ethics point of view, such practices are embedded in systems in which women are denigrated rather than cared for, and they need to be challenged (Robinson, 2003). However, in order to challenge them it has to be understood how female circumcision has come to be construed as being compatible with caring practice in the first place. Those practicing female circumcision do not see themselves as inflicting pain for no good reason, or as acting against the interests of women in general. It is therefore inappropriate to legislate against the practice without engaging with its conditions. In this respect, care ethics shares ground with communitarianism, but is also opposed to it. Whereas, for the communitarian, the mere fact that a practice is embedded in a particular cultural context gives reason to respect it, from a care ethics perspective, this gives a reason to respect the practitioners, but not necessarily the practice. Care ethics may therefore have radical implications for cultures and ways of life, but would see transformations in the light of caring virtues as taking time and needing to make sense to those currently committed to patriarchal practices.

Feminist critiques of an ethics of world politics based on care typically come from two perspectives. Unsurprisingly, justice feminists, such as Nussbaum or Benhabib, identify problems for feminism with care ethics' abandonment of reliance on universal principle. They argue that this means both that care ethics lacks a critical edge and that it is forced to rely on feelings of responsibility and connection that may simply not be there in a global context. The second perspective is the postmodernist critique, which argues, contrary to the justice critics, that the ethic of care remains too close to the logic of traditional ethical paradigms in the context of international politics, because it treats the feminist standpoint for judgement in an overly universalized way. Both critiques worry about the incapacity of an ethics based on an idea of care to further the goals of feminism, goals broadly conceived as those of redressing gendered inequalities of power across the international arena. Nevertheless, the arguments of justice and postmodernist critics against care ethics are distinct. This will become clearer as we look at the postmodernist approach in more detail.

9.5 Feminist postmodernist ethics

Postmodernist critique

Feminist postmodernist ethics derives its inspiration from two directions: on the one hand, it is influenced by post-structuralist and postmodernist critiques of cosmopolitan and communitarian ethical methods and theories; on the other hand, it is influenced by the history of feminist politics and post-colonial feminism's challenge to both equality and radical feminisms. Postmodernist thinkers object to the claims of both cosmopolitanism and communitarianism on the basis that neither approach can sustain the grounds on which they lay claim to the source of moral truth. In the case of different types of cosmopolitanism, postmodernists argue that these are always based on supposedly universal truths about either human nature or reason that cannot be accounted for without arbitrary assumptions, and cannot be expressed except in concrete terms that identify the universal with the particular. This means that the supposed universality of cosmopolitan claims actually turns out always to exclude certain ways of being human or rational, in a way that is both unjustifiable and has actual, violently exclusive effects in practice. This can be exemplified by the ways in which the universal discourse of human rights has repeatedly been challenged by those, such as women, indigenous people or children, who claim recognition as human, but who have been excluded or marginalized in how the meaning of humanity in universal human rights has been understood.

On 'postmodernism', see Chapter 3.

On cosmopolitanism and communitarianism, see Chapters 7 & 8.

From the postmodernist point of view, communitarian arguments that locate moral **authority** in community and culture are equally vulnerable to the critique of unsustainable **foundationalism** and universalism. Communitarianism claims a universal validity to its location of morality within community, but it is unable to account for the basis on which it makes this claim, given its own commitment to locating ethical truth relative to culture and community. Moreover, in order to sustain this claim, it has to define community in a way that essentializes its meaning, and ignores the fragmented and contested nature of actual communities and cultures. Just as cosmopolitanism relies on essentializing certain models of humanity or reason, so communitarianism relies on essentializing the idea of community. When you define what it means to be British, you are simultaneously defining what it is and what it is not. If, for instance, to be British, is to be white and English speaking then to be British is also not to be black or non-English speaking. Postmodernist ethics sees all claims to what *is* as being haunted by constitutive exclusions with major ethical implications.

This philosophical critique of mainstream ethical theories resonates with the practical and political critique made by post-colonial feminists of equality (justice) and radical (care) feminisms. Postmodernist feminists argue that justice feminists fall into the same traps as cosmopolitan arguments more generally, and tend to conflate the universal with Western, liberal ideals of human rights for women. In an analogous way, care ethics is argued to essentialize a specific idea of women and femininity that is grounded in the history and culture of Western societies, and its model of familial and community relations. This means that care ethics treats both 'women' and 'care' as universal and undifferentiated categories, and is insufficiently sensitive to the ethical significance of major differences and inequalities between women.

Feminist postmodernist ethics of world politics

Postmodernist feminists insist on the ethical significance of the fact that all women are not the same, either in virtue of being *women* or in virtue of being *human* (Peterson, 1990; Jabri, 1999). As has already been noted, they are suspicious of both care and justice ethics precisely because those approaches are grounded on the universalization of either 'human' or 'feminine' qualities and attributes. This is not simply a theoretical dispute. For postmodernist feminists the prescriptive implications of care in relation to peace, and of justice in relation to human rights and development, have been shown to be ethically problematic for women who do not fit with standard Western liberal assumptions about either women or humans. It seems, therefore, as if postmodern feminist ethics may take us back to a more communitarian line of argument, and the cultural specificity of both the ways we defend our moral judgements and the judgements that we make. However, this is not the case. For postmodernist feminists, 'context' is not equivalent to a monolithic account of 'culture'. For postmodernists, culture and identity, like all other facets of social and political life, are sites of power relations and struggles, and there is therefore always a *political* dimension to ethics, and this, according to postmodernists, is the dimension that care and justice feminists, in different ways, neglect.

For postmodernist ethics it is ethical principles of respect for difference and radical democracy that are fundamental to feminism. Although they share with care and justice feminisms a commitment to challenging gendered relations of power, for postmodernists specific questions about what moral values should guide human conduct at a global level are incapable of being satisfactorily answered unless and until the world has changed in such a way that the voices of those currently most excluded from moral debate can be heard (Spivak, 1999; Mohanty, 2003; Hutchings, 2004). In the meantime, moral priority must be given to those ethical values that do most to support struggles to change the world to include the excluded and that do least to further repress the voices of the least powerful actors in current world politics. The problem with this ethical project is that, as postmodernists themselves point out, any explicitly articulated universal ethical claim in international ethics always carries its own exclusions with it, intended or unintended. This is typified by the Universal Declaration of Human Rights, which, for example, in speaking of all human beings' fundamental right to marriage and family life, necessarily excludes those human beings who do not fit with heterosexual norms, or with the assumption of a humanity split into two genders (Butler, 2004a, pp. 102–30).

One of the feminist ethical theorists who has attempted to address what postmodernist ethics implies in an international context is Judith Butler. Focusing on the concept of universal human rights, Butler has shown how the concept of the human in human rights, by setting up a norm of what it means to be human, consistently operates so as to situate certain categories of people as 'less than' human, rendering their lives in crucial respects 'unliveable' and 'ungrievable' (Butler, 2004a, pp. 225–27; Butler, 2004b, pp. 18–49). Thus, she directly challenges Nussbaum's claim that it is through an inclusive account of what it means to be human that a genuinely universal international ethics can be articulated as a yardstick for the judgement of practice. At the same time, Butler does not advocate the abandonment of the idea of universal rights, but rather argues that the meaning of 'universal' should always be open to challenge and re-negotiation, and that we should never assume that our claims to universality actually live up to their promise (2004a, p. 33).

There are no obituaries for the war casualties that the United State inflicts, and there cannot be. If there were to be an obituary, there would have to have been a life, a life worth noting, a life worth valuing and preserving, a life that qualifies for recognition. (Butler, 2004b, p. 34)

The above quotation, in which Butler reflects on the 2003 war following the US and allied invasion of Iraq, recalls Ruddick's argument about the ease with which militarist and just war theorists dismiss the value of enemy lives and suggests some overlap between postmodernist and care ethics in the emphasis on the problems of exclusion inherent in both cosmopolitan and communitarian moralities. Unlike Ruddick, however, it is not clear that postmodernist ethics could ever endorse pacifism as such, or the idea that there is a definable set of virtues that are morally superior (Hutchings, 2007b). Somewhat paradoxically, postmodernist ethics is universalist in its orientation towards giving moral priority to the excluded in general, but sees this universalism as always failing. For postmodernist ethics, ethical priorities will differ depending on context, so that there is (and ought to be) no feminist consensus on the ethics of war or the nature of fundamental human being. It is therefore inappropriate to condemn practices such as female circumcision (FGM) in the abstract, without a full understanding of the context of the practice and the ethical investments of the different parties to it. Moreover, the postmodernist ethical theorist needs to take responsibility for his or her own judgement and actions and recognize that well-intended policies may have unforeseen effects when implemented in a top-down way.

In terms of its substantive implications for issues such as global distributive justice or international human rights, postmodernist feminist ethics emphasizes the importance of the ways in which ethical judgements are made and implemented. In *Whose Hunger? Concepts of Famine, Practices of Aid* (2000), Jenny Edkins argues that there are two international discourses of response to famine: the first is a technical, scientific discourse that sees famine as a problem amenable to expert solution; the second is a moral humanitarian discourse, which claims to be grounded in universal truths. In both cases, according to Edkins, the claim to knowledge of what should be done is bogus. This is because there is no *general* answer to the ethically appropriate response to famine. As contemporary research into complex emergencies has shown, famines are constructed in a variety of ways, some people in famine affected areas, as well as outsiders, *profit* from famine, and international aid sometimes exacerbates rather than resolves the problem.

In place of a justice ethics position, Edkins argues that we need to approach the issue of famine contextually, in terms of the complex web of relations that connect the actors involved, and the causal and constitutive role of a range of local and global political and economic factors. We cannot know in advance what is the right thing to do, and we cannot assume that we know who the appropriate agents to do the right thing might be, but we still are responsible for acting. She argues that this kind of ethical approach echoes that recommended in the feminist ethic of care (p. 150). Where it differs from the ethic of care, however, is that for thinkers such as Edkins (or Butler), the question of justice is fundamentally undecidable. A feminist ethic of care offers criteria, in terms of caring virtues, by which we can be guided in working out our moral responses to global ethical issues. However, for postmodernist feminists, we bear responsibility for our relationships to others, but do not have settled criteria by which we can judge whether we have fulfilled that responsibility in the right way. A kind of deep ethical humility is therefore at the heart of feminist postmodernist ethics.

9.6 Conclusion

It is clear from the above discussion that feminist approaches to the ethics of world politics differ both from alternative ethical theories and from each other. They differ from alternative ethical theories because they all bring gender to the centre of the ethical stage, in a way that is systematically ignored by other theories. This means that, for instance, feminist justice ethics, although clearly sharing ground with cosmopolitan theories, never takes quite the same shape as such theories. Thinkers such as Nussbaum or Benhabib make much greater efforts to be sensitive to difference within their universalist approaches than their non-feminist counterparts, and are more inclined to draw on traditions of virtue or discourse ethics than to adopt a straightforwardly deontological approach to moral thinking. Feminist care and postmodernist ethics shares ground with communitarianism, in taking the embedded and embodied nature of ethical life as a crucial reference point for their thinking. Nevertheless, thinkers such as Ruddick, Robinson, Butler, or Edkins, are much more careful than mainstream communitarianism in acknowledging the complexity and hierarchies involved in cultural contexts, and recognizing how claims of cultural difference may actually reflect the power agenda of those who currently enjoy cultural privilege.

However, even if feminist theories are distinctive in relation to other ethical perspectives, it's not clear whether the term 'feminist' signifies anything more substantive that ties the different feminist approaches together. Does it actually make sense to use the same term to encompass the quite different arguments we have explored in this chapter? In my view, there is a common thread that ties these approaches together. The reasons why feminist universalist and contextualist ethical arguments do not precisely replicate other kinds of universalism and contextualism goes back to the roots of feminism. Feminism was inspired by the vulnerabilities suffered by women on account of an entrenched gender order that excluded them from moral status. Over time, this inspiration has led feminism to take seriously the ways in which that gender order is intertwined with other systematic modes of exclusion from moral status. What links the different forms of feminist ethics together is the aspiration (which is not always achieved) of de-centring moral judgement from the standpoint of the powerful to that of the vulnerable and excluded.

▦ QUESTIONS

1. What kinds of ethical assumptions can you identify underpinning CEDAW and UN Resolution 1325. Are they the same or different?

2. Is the issue of abortion morally equivalent in the UK and in India?

3. Does international justice need to extend to the private sphere of the family?

4. Is Nussbaum's account of human capabilities genuinely universal?

5. Is multiculturalism bad for women?

6. Is there an inherent connection between feminism and pacifism?

7. Assess the strengths and weaknesses of the feminist ethic of care.

8. MacKinnon claims that, in traditional human rights discourse, women are always either too female to be human or too human to be female—do you agree?

9. Assess the post-colonial critique of equality and radical feminisms.

10. Are postmodernist feminists ethical relativists?

▦ FURTHER READING

Benhabib, S. (1992) The debate over women and moral theory revisited, in: *Situating the Self: Gender, Community and Postmodernism in Contemporary Ethics*. Cambridge: Polity Press. A nuanced 'justice' critique of care ethics that tries to find a middle way between abstract universalism and respecting concrete differences between people.

Butler, J. (2004) *Precarious Life: The Powers of Mourning and Violence*. London: Verso. A good example of post-modernist ethical theorizing applied to recent issues in the war in Iraq and the war on terror.

Held, V. (ed.) (1995) *Justice and Care: Essential Readings in Feminist Ethics*, Boulder: Westview Press. An excellent collection of literature inspired by Gilligan's identification of a feminist ethic of care.

MacKinnon, C. (2006) *Are Women Human? And Other International Dialogues*, Cambridge: Harvard University Press. Inspired by radical feminism, includes critical articles about the gendered nature of contemporary human rights norms.

Mohanty, C.T. (2003) *Feminism Without Borders: Decolonizing Theory, Practicing Solidarity*. Durham: Duke University Press. An example of post-colonial theorizing that argues for an inclusive, non-essentialist feminism.

Nussbaum, M. (2000) *Women and Human Development.* Cambridge: Cambridge University Press. A justice feminist argument, applies the idea of human capability to the specific experience of poor women in India.

Okin, S.M. (1994) Gender inequality and cultural differences. *Political Theory*, **22**:5–24. Asks the question whether multiculturalism is bad for women from a justice feminism perspective.

Robinson, F. (1999) *Globalizing Care: Ethics, Feminist Theory and International Relations*, Boulder: Westview Press. The first fully-fledged application of feminist care ethics to the sphere of world politics.

Ruddick, S. (1989) *Maternal Thinking: Towards a Politics of Peace*, London: Women's Press. An influential care ethics argument for pacifism and non-violence in world politics.

Sjoberg, L. (2006) *Gender, Justice and the Wars in Iraq: A Feminist Reformulation of Just War Theory.* Lanham: Rowman & Littlefield. The first fully-fledged attempt to construct a just war theory for feminism.

▨ WEB LINKS

http://www.cddc.vt.edu/feminism/eth.html Website with a range of bibliographies on different areas of feminist ethics and profiles of prominent feminist ethical theorists.

http://www.feministethics.com A notice board of conferences and events relating to feminist ethics.

http://www.peacewoman.org/un/sc/1235.html The Women's International League for Peace and Freedom web pages with details about UNSCR 1325 and the rationale for its introduction.

http://www.un.org/womenwatch/daw/cedaw A UN website with details of the origins and ongoing history of CEDAW (Convention for the Elimination of Discrimination Against Women).

http://www.womeninblack.org The website for the worldwide 'Women in Black' peace demonstrations.

Visit the Online Resource Centre that accompanies this book to access more learning resources: www.oxfordtextbooks.co.uk/orc/bell_ethics/

Green political theory

Mathew Humphrey

READER'S GUIDE

The opening section explores the important analytical distinction between environmental and ecological forms of green political theory, as well as taking a brief look at the history of environmental thinking. There follows an account of the main strands of green political thought, explaining what they have in common and what divides them. This section makes clear that there is no single 'green' perspective on global politics. The subsequent section looks at how our existing conceptions of justice, democracy, and citizenship have been challenged by green political theorists, and explores how green political theory has been applied to one of the leading problems of the early twenty-first century—global climate change. This leads into discussion of the 'sceptical environmentalism' of Bjørn Lomborg and his very different recommendations for climate change action, before concluding.

10.1 Introduction

A preliminary: environment/ecology

When considering green political theory in relation to ethics it is important to bear some distinctions in mind. One of the most important that has emerged in the analysis of green political thought is that between 'environmentalism' and 'ecologism', which is sometimes framed as 'environmental' versus 'green' political thought and sometimes as 'shallow' versus 'deep' ecology (Naess, 1973; Dobson, 2007). These various dichotomies may emphasize different elements in the field of environmental thought (for example the 'deep' versus 'shallow' distinction takes great account of how we understand the nature of the physical universe), but all make some distinction between (1) responses to the perceived global environmental crisis that seek to adapt our existing economic and political systems (environmentalism/shallow ecology) and (2) responses that constitute a more fundamental challenge to those systems (ecologism/green/deep ecology). In particular, for those who place themselves at the deep/green/ecological end of the spectrum, the fundamental flaw of shallow, environmental approaches to ecological problems is that they fail to get to the root of the problem and seek instead to alleviate only the *symptoms* of a deeper malaise. Analytically, such dichotomies reveal something, but inevitably obscure as much as they enlighten. Environmental political thought is neither single-issue thinking nor dichotomous, and different versions clash across a range of questions. (Is 'industrialism' the problem or just the private ownership of the means of production? Is the state a necessary part of a solution or an inherently anti-ecological institution? Do women have a connection to the natural world that men lack, or is that proposition itself an essentializing myth?) This adapt/challenge distinction (which echoes the reformist/revolutionary split in much radical political thought) is useful for some studies of environmental thought, but can be put aside for those with a different purpose (Humphrey, 2007).

The stress placed upon this distinction in contemporary accounts can be somewhat disabling, partly because we lack an all-encompassing concept for green/environmental political thought, thus whatever label we use we appear to take a stance in the debate. If this chapter is about 'environmental' political thought does it merely consider ways of 'tinkering' with the existing economic and political systems? If it is entitled 'green' or 'ecological' political thought does it only review those forms of thought that seek fundamental change in those systems? We will use 'green' political theory as a broad category encompassing all forms of political thought that have as a high priority the conservation or preservation of the natural environment. 'Ecological' will refer to those forms of green thought that seek the dissolution of contemporary political and economic institutions, and 'environmental' is reserved for approaches that would specifically adapt existing institutions.

Context

Thinking about politics and the environment has a long history (Wall, 1994). This has generally taken the form of concern about particular environmental problems, or with the preservation of particular landscapes or features of the natural world at specific localities. One example here is concern about London smoke and smog, captured in John Evelyn's *Fumifugium* of 1661:

It is this horrid Smoake which obscures our Churches, and makes our Palaces look old, which fouls our Clothes, and corrupts the Waters, so as the very Rain, and refreshing Dews which fall in the several Seasons, precipitate this impure vapour, which, with its black and tenacious quality, spots and contaminates whatever is exposed to it. (Wall, 1994, p. 46)

The late twentieth century saw concern for the environment become truly global. The rise in consciousness of global environmental problems is often dated to the publication of some key popular books including Rachel Carson's *Silent Spring* (1962), the report for the Club of Rome entitled *Limits to Growth* (Meadows et al., 1972), Barry Commoner's *The Closing Circle* (1971) and *The Population Bomb* (1968) by Paul Ehrlich. These publications formed part of the 'first wave' of global environmental concern, and they also fostered further research into and political campaigning on behalf of the natural environment. In relation to environmental campaigning this period saw the development of (in addition to many local and specific groups and campaigns) **transnational** environmental campaigning organizations such as Friends of the Earth (1969), Greenpeace (1972), and Sea Shepherd (1981).

Green political thought makes the connection between ethics and world politics in a very clear way, although the details of the story differ between different examples of the genre. Most green thinking sees the question of humanity's relationship with the natural world in ethical terms. On this view human societies have been overly instrumental in their exploitation of the natural world, and have failed to treat it as a repository of value in an appropriate way. This 'instrumental' valuation of nature means that we see it only in terms of what it can offer us—for example nature as a store of raw materials, as a depository for our waste, or as a place for human recreation. At its weakest this amounts to the allegation that (Western industrial societies at least) have been imprudent and inefficient in their use of natural resources, and need to moderate their behaviour in order to ensure the long-term viability of industrial society. At its strongest, it amounts to the demand that we see the natural world as possessing intrinsic value, and that we engage in a comprehensive restructuring and deindustrialization of society in order to allow the flourishing of the non-human natural world on an equal basis with human society. On either version, and for those views that lie between, it is not taken to be feasible for any individual nation to achieve very much on their own. The global environmental crisis constitutes a worldwide **collective action problem**: the only route to effective remedy lies with international cooperation. This is not to deny that some environmental problems are, of course, still local, as when there is opposition to a road-building proposal or airport runway extension, but even these campaigns are likely to be linked to the global perspective. For the 'big' environmental problems, such as climate change, biodiversity loss, or oceanic acidification, there is no escaping the global perspective. Environmental problems are inherently problems for world politics.

10.2 Environmental political theory

There is no singular form of green political theory, but rather several interrelated views on the politics of the relationship between humanity and its environment, which can be usefully categorized into different 'strands' of environmental thought. This is, of course, a heuristic exercise, the categories will inevitably have fuzzy boundaries, and any individual theorist may seem to belong only somewhat awkwardly in one camp or another. Such caveats aside, the following are some of the main strands of environmental and ecological political theory, taking the former first.

Eco-authoritarianism

In the wake of the publication of books such as *Silent Spring* (Carson, 1962) and *Limits to Growth* (Meadows et al., 1972) one response was a sense, if not of panic, then certainly of extreme urgency. A certain catastrophism emerged in the early 1970s, in that looming environmental disaster was taken to justify fairly draconian political change. This school of thought became known as 'eco-authoritarianism' or 'survivalism' and is particularly associated with William Ophuls (1977), Robert Heilbroner (1974) and Garrett Hardin (1968); a more recent variation on the theme has been pursued by Laura Westra (1998). The eco-authoritarians operated with three core assumptions:

• The combination of resource depletion, pollution, and human population growth mean that ecological disaster is imminent.

• This places us in a collective action problem, where societies have to co-ordinate changes in the behaviour of the mass of citizens.

• People are attached to the 'wrong' values and will not change their behaviour without coercion.

This school of thought is also labelled 'neo-Hobbesian' as the problem is identified as one of assuring that people do not defect from the 'co-operative' strategy. One way of doing this might be to ensure that people are motivated by appropriate values, and certainly value change is seen as part of the long-term solution. However, in the absence of a long period of time in which to inculcate such a change, we have instead to rely upon what Hardin called 'mutual coercion, mutually agreed upon', and the most effective agent for achieving such coercion is the state. The liberal-democratic state is, however, unlikely to achieve this, as citizens in industrialized nations have shown no sign of changing their behaviour in an environmental direction. They are already wedded to the 'wrong' values associated with assumptions of material abundance, whereas we need values that are compatible with notions of ecological scarcity. Given that people cannot be expected to change their behaviour voluntarily, we need to (at least temporarily, until values do change) give up on democratic politics, and impose upon ourselves an 'expertocracy' of ecologists and scientists who can determine the policies that will be necessary to ensure the survival of human civilization.

The overriding concern of the eco-authoritarians was the survival of human societies under conditions of dire ecological danger, and they were willing to see the constitutional conventions of liberal democratic states put aside in pursuit of that goal. Human social and political rights count for little in the face of such an existential threat. This survivalist literature has been criticized on a number of grounds, for example in its reading of our ecological situation as one of dire crisis and for a view of an authoritarian state that is both overly benign, and that makes some large assumptions about state effectiveness. Centrally imposed, authoritarian 'solutions' to ecological problems may be as likely to instil resistance and non-co-operation from citizens as they are to get them to change their behaviour in the anticipated direction.

Whilst many of these criticisms are justified, one aspect of the eco-authoritarian literature worth preserving is its framework of analysis for environmental problems. Many environmental problems take the form that Garrett Hardin famously called the 'tragedy of the commons'. This applies when many individual, rational actions combine to degrade a common (strictly 'unowned', rather than 'owned in common') asset. Hardin's example was cattle over-grazing a pasture, but we might also think of the exploitation of fisheries or atmospheric pollution in the same way. Each trawler crew (for example) has an incentive to take as many fish as they can, even when every crew has full knowledge that in doing so they will deplete and ultimately destroy the fish stocks. This is why it is a 'tragedy', as the incentives facing everyone bring about the bad outcome even when all are aware that this is what they are doing. If any crew were to voluntarily refrain from taking their full catch, they would merely make those fish available to other crews, and the gesture would make no practical difference to the ultimate outcome. Better then to take the catch, for which one gets the full private benefit, whilst the costs of depletion are distributed across all crews. For trawling, international treaties, such as the European Union (EU) quotas, represent the 'mutual coercion, mutually agreed upon' that Hardin sees as the solution to the tragedy, although this 'solution' is only partial as the collective action problem is replayed at the EU level, with individual nation states competing for the largest possible share of resources.

Ecological modernization theory

Despite its title, ecological modernization theory (EMT) appears to belong on the 'environmental' side of Dobson's divide. EMT (Mol & Sonnenfeld, 2000) seeks to employ the incentives of the market and taxation in order to foster the development of environmentally benign technology and behaviour, whilst not giving up on the aspiration for economic growth. In its pursuit of benign growth, EMT ties in closely with ideas about sustainable development, which is most usually described as a development that 'meets the needs of the present without compromising the ability of future generations to meet their own needs' (United Nations, 1987). The substitution of existing employment taxes (such as National Insurance in the United Kingdom or Social Security Tax in the United States) with carbon taxes would be a typical EMT policy prescription, using the taxation system to encourage necessary behavioural change, whilst relieving taxes on another 'good'—employment. The overall aim is to, as far as practicable, 'decouple' economic growth from growth in environmental 'bads', such as pollution and resource depletion. EMT, particularly in its earlier 'weak' forms, has been viewed with some scepticism by many green political theorists. It is seen as an attempt to both have one's cake and eat it, an exercise in tinkering with the existing economic and political systems when fundamental reform is required. Empirically, evidence of 'decoupling' is viewed with suspicion when industrial jobs have been moving from Western nations to rapidly developing countries such as China and India. Unless the imputed ecological footprints of imported goods are also taken into account, 'decoupling' at the national level can appear as something of a mirage as developed nations move towards having economies dominated by service and high-tech sectors, whilst importing basic manufactured goods. This is one of the ways in which the development of a global economy complicates the attribution of important indicators, such as national levels of greenhouse gas (GHG) emissions.

10.3 Ecological political theory

Deep ecology

One of the early versions of the environmental/ecological divide was that made by the Norwegian philosopher Arne Naess, who distinguished 'shallow' and 'deep' ecology. The potential problems with definitional bias here are clear—who would not prefer to be 'deep', rather than 'shallow'? For Naess, however, the 'depth' of an ecological outlook refers to the extent to which it seeks to get to the roots of our environmental problems. 'Shallow' ecology accepts the dominant ways of thinking about the world, and is concerned merely with specific problems such as reducing pollution and resource depletion. 'Deep' ecology, on the other hand, sees our environmental problems as being intimately connected with dominant world views, which need to be challenged by and ultimately replaced with, an 'ecological' world view that sees all elements of the natural world as intrinsically connected. Ecologism is perhaps unusual amongst patterns of political thought in drawing so directly upon a specific science in its self-justification. One can think how odd it would seem for chemistry or physics to have a political movement bear its name. The recommended view of the world, as a 'biospherical net' in which all things are related—a world that is too complex for us to ever understand fully—is proposed to us in the name of science. However, as historians of ecological science such as Donald Worster (1994) remind us, ecology is more fragmented than that, there is not a single 'ecological worldview' and, indeed, the holistic version offered up by deep ecology represents a subordinate scientific strand. Much scientific work in ecology looks like 'ordinary', 'reductive' science, and whether any scientist would want to accept the proposition that nature is 'more complex than we *can* know' is highly debatable. That the world *must* remain a mystery seems to reflect a religious, rather than scientific mindset.

The extent to which deep ecology is an ethical system is contested. It can be seen to embody an 'ecocentric' ethic; the contrast here is with 'anthropocentric' (or 'human-centred') ethics. The latter takes human beings as the appropriate agents and recipients of moral concern. The demand to act rightly applies to human beings, and those whose rights are protected or whose welfare is to be improved through the application of ethical principles are also human. By contrast deep ecology posits a 'biospherical egalitarianism' in which the interests of all of nature are given prima facie moral equality. On the ethical imperatives of biospherical egalitarianism human beings would only be allowed to exploit nature in order to satisfy their essential needs, and this should be done in such a way as to minimize our impact on the non-human natural world. Naess also suggests the need to reduce radically the total number of human beings on the planet in an 'ethically acceptable' way. He assumed this would be a long process, taking place over hundreds of years, with improved education playing a key role. If taken seriously, this ethical system would imply enormous changes to existing Western lifestyles, for example universal vegetarianism would allow us to meet our nutritional needs with far less impact on the non-human world than diets that include meat.

Others, however, reject the view that deep ecology is an *ethical* system at all. For Warwick Fox (1995), what is uniquely 'deep' about deep ecology is its psychological aspect—the 'invitation' to a form of 'self-realization' that incorporates the rest of the natural world into an expanded, non-egotistical conception of selfhood. Deep ecology thus becomes a doctrine of self-realization, from which certain actions in the world are taken to flow quite naturally. If one sees defence of the natural world as a form of *self*-defence, then one does not need an ethical imperative at all, as care for nature will follow as naturally as breathing or eating.

Social ecology

An alternative current of green thought, known as 'social ecology' and particularly associated with the late activist and writer Murray Bookchin, has a very different view of humanity, nature, and the relationship between the two. Far from seeking the sense of identity with the non-human world suggested by deep ecology, it suggests that we should instead see that world as an 'other' for whom we have ethical responsibility. Borrowing explicitly from the German philosopher G. W. F. Hegel, Bookchin (1996) sees the development of the natural world in teleological terms, in which nature develops towards its *telos* or ultimate end. We can conceive of this development in terms of 'first-nature' and 'second-nature'. First-nature refers to that part of nature that has not developed reflective consciousness. That entails all of nature up to the point at which self-conscious humanoids emerge and to the non-human part of nature thereafter. We humans embody second nature or nature rendered self-aware.

What are the ethical implications of this view? With the reflexivity of second nature comes *responsibility*. We cannot uninvent self-consciousness, nor put the genie of human development back into the bottle and nor should we want to. What we can and should do is develop an 'ethics of complementarity'—we should see the non-human world as 'other' (contra deep ecology), but not in an antagonistic sense. We should accept that we have a responsibility for the continued flourishing of non-human nature and that the non-human natural world now has to be managed. Even the putting aside of areas of wilderness constitutes a form of conscious management—borders have to be established and decisions have to be made about elements, such as invasive species. To date, by contrast, human actions towards the non-human world have not been marked by ethical constraints. To the contrary, we have exploited nature quite ruthlessly, and Bookchin sees the institutions of the state and corporations, and the capitalist economic architecture of the developed world, as being an integral part of the problem. The politics of social ecology therefore generates a call to a return to local participatory democracy, what Bookchin refers to as 'libertarian municipalism', which looks back to an idealized version of the early New England town meetings. Today, this would involve communities governing themselves via direct democracy, joined together by a confederal system to which each community sends 'strictly mandated, recallable, and responsible' delegates (Bookchin, 1995, p. 253).

Eco-Marxism

The distrust of the state and capitalism is also articulated in the various strands of green political thought that have taken inspiration from Karl Marx. This generally takes one of two forms. In one version the work of Marx himself is mined for ecological insight, such as in his discussions of the 'metabolism' between humanity and nature, and his account of nature as man's 'inorganic body' in the '1844 Manuscripts'. Alternatively, Marx is adapted and applied to contemporary environmental problems, as with the thesis of the 'second contradiction' in capitalism (the undermining of capitalism's conditions of production through, for example, unsustainable resource use). Eco-Marxism (e.g. O'Connor,

1998) holds to Marx's general materialist understanding of the world. The view remains that we have to change our material practices and socialize the means of production if we are going to change humanity's relationship with non-human nature. The institutions and incentives of liberal-capitalism, with the non-stop search for profit and economic growth, are fundamental causes of environmental crisis. On this view ethics is superfluous or, at best, merely follows from material preconditions. Ethics is part of the superstructure of society, along with religion and other forms of ideology that emerge from the formation of the material base. Appeals for ethical change are in themselves always doomed to be ineffective unless they are combined with changes in our material practices. You cannot expect capitalists to behave ethically when their very survival means playing the game of competitive markets where, as a rule of thumb, the cheapest goods will be the most successful. Individual capitalists will always look to cut costs and increase profits, and if that entails environmentally destructive activity then we cannot expect them to hold back in the interests of something like 'biospherical egalitarianism'. Indeed, from this perspective the whole deep ecological project looks hopelessly idealistic and utopian.

Ecofeminism

On feminism, see also Chapter 9.

The fundamental claim of ecofeminists is that the domination over and exploitation of nature by humanity, and of women by men, are facets of the same problem: the supremacy of **patriarchy** in contemporary society. 'Patriarchy' can be seen as both the *ideology* that justifies male domination, and the *instantiation* of that ideology in the institutions and practices of contemporary society. Patriarchy distinguishes rationality, logic, science, technology, and progress from irrationality, emotion, intuition, nature, and caring. Patriarchy constructs a value dichotomy between these two sets of attributes, and within that dualism women are placed on the same disvalued side as nature and the irrational. Traditional female roles of childbearing, motherhood, and nurture are seen as relatively worthless. By contrast 'masculine' activities, such as scientific enquiry, technological development, logical thinking, and employing reason rather than emotion in defining and solving problems, are highly valued.

While ecofeminists may unite against the values of patriarchy, their response to it is more fragmented. Some argue for a revaluation of these female roles, and a celebration of the fact that women are somehow 'closer to nature' than men (even if they recognize that role as being socially created within patriarchy). Once the value of the duality between nature and artefact is reversed, these 'female' attributes will be allotted their rightful place. We need this transformation of values in order to save the world from the cold, abstract, technological and war-like qualities of patriarchy (Plant, 1991). Other ecofeminists, however, see a danger in this kind of approach of 'essentializing' the patriarchal view of women—that is, of seeing women as inherently close to nature, as having a rightful role as mothers and carers. This, it is argued, is precisely the view of women that feminists have been trying to break and, whilst we need to eliminate patriarchy to achieve ecological ends, we also need to move away from stereotyped notions of what women are 'really' like (Davion, 1994).

Anarcho-primitivism

There is one other strand of green thinking that is worth exploring, not least because it has had apparent influence amongst some of the more radical groups engaged in contemporary environmental activism. This is anarcho-primitivism, so called because it combines an idealization of the lives of 'primitive' hunter-gatherer societies with the stress on individual liberty and freedom from government that all forms of anarchism share. Anarcho-primitivists do not merely oppose the state and capitalism, they stand against 'civilization' entirely (Zerzan, 2005). This stance is sufficiently uncommon to warrant an explanation, as most people take civilization as one of humanity's crowning achievements, and to call someone 'civilized' is usually a compliment, not an insult. For anarcho-primitivists civilization is embodied in two spheres, a set of institutions and an accompanying set of legitimating ideas. The institutions render us unfree and the ideas make us believe that this unfreedom is natural, or at least a price worth paying for the benefits that civilization brings. The major historical mis-step came long ago with the development of agriculture and the accompanying emergence of static communities that required agricultural land. The entailments of the move to an agricultural form of life are an increasing intensity of workload as crops have to be planted, tended, and harvested, but more importantly the development of specialization and the division of labour. Fixed amounts of land upon which people are crucially dependent for food require defending from rival groups, and this leads to the emergence of a specialist class of soldiers. The warriors need feeding and so require part of the harvest, and we then need a class of people to undertake the transfer of food from farmers to soldiers, and so book-keeping, accounting, taxing, and so on all develop along with the agricultural form of life. These propensities are developed all the more with the Industrial Revolution, which gives us, along with a yet more intense division of labour, the modern state, and contemporary capitalism.

The main ideology of civilization is progress, the fiction, for anarcho-primitivists, that the world we live in today is a better world, a world that has made progress, when compared with the 'uncivilized' state that we have left behind. This is a world that has more wealth and material goods, but that side of civilization has brought about an ecological crisis that it cannot resolve. The main scorn, however, is reserved for the idea that the development of civilization has been marked by moral progress. Anarcho-primitivists see civilization as morally corrupt and corrupting. Not only is it marked by a lack of freedom, as we toil at pointless tasks to satisfy manufactured desires for consumer goods, but it is ethically bankrupt. Civilization brings nuclear conflict, war, the Holocaust, disease, an overweening state, and a mass of legislation against forms of human behaviour that are seen as 'deviant' or outside of civilized norms. Primitive societies, on the other hand, are lionized as offering a world of leisure and freedom, where food is gathered with little physical exertion, and wars are absent because bands of people are not trying to defend fixed territory.

As some critics have pointed out, anarcho-primitivists such as John Zerzan rely upon a rather selective reading of anthropology in developing their view of primitive societies. The 'primitive' has long stood as an empty receptacle, ready to be filled by the opposite of whatever we happen to dislike about life in civilization. Is civilization repressive, immoral, corrupt, enslaving, unfree, aggressive? Not primitive society. Whatever qualities are disvalued, we can project their opposites into a conception of the 'primitive'.

All of these versions of environmental or ecological political thought have their own conceptions of the causes of and solution to the environmental crisis, and they each have their own conception of ethics and the role of ethics in politics as well. This varies from the explicitly ethical approach of ecocentrism, which seeks a fundamental transformation of dominant ethical systems, to the materialism of eco-Marxism that sees ethics as being determined, to a greater or lesser extent, by the forces of production and accompanying relations of production involved in the human interaction with nature.

10.4 **The greening of political concepts**

In recent years, the attention of those working in the field of green political theory has shifted somewhat, away from the positing of comprehensive 'green' alternatives to existing sets of political and ethical ideas, towards work on particular and familiar political concepts, such as justice, the state, sovereignty, democracy, and citizenship. This, arguably, shows a maturing of the field (although some may see it as a deradicalization as well) as it becomes less focused on the comprehensive overturning of existing values and behaviour, and seeks instead to work immanently, exploiting existing political discourses and concepts and turning them to green ends. The next section will explore work in three of these areas, which are of particular importance for global politics—justice, democracy, and citizenship. In each case we will see how green theorists seek to disrupt established understandings of these concepts and open up a 'space' for developing the concept in an 'ecological' direction.

Justice in green political theory

Work on **distributive justice** revolves around three questions.

On distributive justice, see also Chapters 1 and 14.

- Who are the agents and recipients of justice? In other words, who owes justice to whom?

- What are the goods of justice? What, that is, are things that get distributed? They could be 'good goods', such as liberties or material wealth, but they also might be 'bads', such as environmental pollution.

- What are the principles of justice? By what notions do we decide who gets what from whom? Equality? Desert? Need? And so on.

Green political theorists give particular answers to these questions, informed by their more general theories about the principles that should govern human–human and human–nature relationships. Green work on justice is an area where the environmentalism/ecologism distinction is especially important and carries with it a particular meaning. 'Environmental justice' refers to the distribution of environmental goods and bads between different human individuals and communities. 'Ecological justice' refers to the idea that principles of justice should be applied beyond the normal boundaries of the human species. Thus, a book on 'environmental justice' will have a very different subject matter to one on 'ecological justice', although both will be concerned with a particular set of answers to the three questions posed above.

Recent years have seen the growth of an 'environmental justice movement', especially in the United States, which is largely a grassroots form of political activism. Environmental justice has, however, also been developed in theoretical terms and the answers to questions one and two for its advocates are relatively straightforward. The givers and recipients of justice are human agents, and part of the problem is that some of these agents have been invisible to those holding political power. In the USA there is a particular racial dimension to the politics of environmental justice, as there is a strong correlation between being a 'community of colour' and having a disproportionately large share of environmental bads in your neighbourhood. There are a number of published case studies of environmental injustice suffered by African-American communities, such as Center Springs and Forest Grove in Louisiana (Shrader-Frechette, 2002, chapter 4). Similar work has been done for Canada—see, for example, Howard McCurdy's (2001) study of Africville in Nova Scotia. This is correlated with poverty as well, of course, but there is a racial effect even when levels of income are taken into account (Shrader-Frechette, 2002).

The basic goods of environmental justice are those such as clean air and potable water. Below that level of generality, the question of what goods should be goods of environmental *justice*, that people can demand as a right, becomes more complicated. Is, for example, access to open countryside a matter of justice, or just something that would be beneficial to have, but not essential? Then we have the question of what principles should govern the distribution of these goods and bads. The current distribution is highly skewed, and this is reinforced by the fact that when an area is badly affected by environmental bads, those who can afford to move away tend to do so, leaving the area more economically deprived than formerly. Whilst it is difficult to equalize the distribution of environmental goods and bads directly, theoretical attempts to engage with the problem of inequality tend to focus on recognition and participation (Schlosberg, 1999). It is believed that a major driver of the existing skewed distribution of environmental goods and bads is that some communities are relatively 'invisible' to policy-makers, and that if these communities were to gain political recognition, and were able to participate in the democratic process, it would make it harder for government agencies to ignore their environmental concerns.

Work on 'ecological justice' is particularly associated with Brian Baxter (2004). He seeks an answer to the first of the three questions above that will extend the 'community of justice' beyond the human. Whilst we cannot expect non-human nature to be an 'agent' of justice, acting in ways that are concomitant with principles of distribution, we can treat natural objects as recipients of justice, that is, we can view the non-human natural world as having rights against us, even if we cannot expect any reciprocation. This is not straightforward, as any attempt to operationalize ecological justice would need a decision on what features of non-human nature are picked out as suitable recipients of justice—the natural world as a whole, species, or individual organisms? If we see non-human nature as a recipient of justice in this way, we then need an answer to question two, what goods might we be allocating across the species boundary? For Baxter, the important good here is 'ecological space'. Whatever else other species may require for their flourishing, we know they require ecological space in order to live out their natural life cycles, bring the next generation into existence, and continue the process of adaptive evolution. In order to complete this conception of ecological justice, we would require some principles of distribution to allow us to determine how ecological space was to be allocated between humans and the appropriate level of non-human nature.

Ecological justice offers radically different answers to our three questions about justice, when compared with traditional human-centred accounts. Working out a conception of ecological justice along these lines would not be an easy task, but there is no reason to suppose that important political problems must be particularly tractable. It is worth noting that much work on animal rights also seeks to extend our notion of the community of justice, at least to the 'higher' animals such as the great apes.

Green political theory and democracy

On democracy, see also Chapter 21.

We saw earlier in the chapter that the eco-authoritarian writers of the early 1970s despaired of the ability of liberal-democratic institutions to resolve the environmental crisis. Since then, a lot of work in green political theory has examined the relationship between democratic processes and the kinds of policy outcomes that greens want to see. Unfortunately, for anyone seeking guidance on this relationship the answers range from the view that there is no intrinsic relationship at all between democratic values and green values, to the contention that green values are an absolute prerequisite for the achievement of democracy. It is difficult to summarize a very diverse literature succinctly, so instead I will sketch out a few key positions.

The view that there is no connection between green values and democratic values was put most forcefully by Robert Goodin in his *Green Political Thought* (1992). Green values are *substantive* and *outcome-based*. Greens prize the preservation of natural processes and the outcomes of natural history. How something comes to be what it is, that it is 'natural' rather than anthropogenic, is what counts. Democracy on the other hand is a *procedural* value: what matters is *how* political decisions come to be made, not what the substantive outcome is. On this basis greens should be instrumental supporters of democracy only. If democracy is capable of delivering the outcome greens seek then all well and good, but if another political system would be more effective at doing this, then greens have reason to support that system instead. To think that green political thought has an intrinsic relation to democracy is to conflate two very different sets of values.

The opposing view—that there is such a connection—has been articulated in a variety of ways. One version, put forward by John Dryzek (1996), sees environmental values as a necessary precondition for democratic politics. Democratic regimes require sustainable environmental conditions. This may be true, but as has been pointed out by Andrew Dobson (1996), there is nothing special about democracy in this regard. Any form of politics, even authoritarian regimes, requires environmental sustainability for long-term survival. Establishing that there are environmental prerequisites for collective human actions, such as politics, may still be worth pointing out, but this tells democrats that they should be at least minimally 'green', whilst offering no argument to the effect that greens should be democrats.

More mileage in this direction might be gained by exploiting the connection between liberal democracy and the protection of **autonomy** (Eckersley, 1996). Autonomy is most usually associated with 'self-legislation'—the idea of human beings living according to moral precepts that they have freely chosen for themselves, as opposed to an unquestioning obedience to tradition or religious instruction. In developing democracy in a green direction, Robyn Eckersley seeks to adapt the notion of autonomy so that it can be applied across species boundaries. We cannot imagine non-human entities living according to self-chosen moral rules, so instead autonomy is seen as developing or flourishing according to one's own natural inclination. Autonomy now refers to something like following genetic predeterminations without being subjected to human influence, freighting it with meaning that is the very opposite of traditional conceptions (I would hardly be 'autonomous' if I merely followed my natural appetites). If the conceptual move is allowed, then the belief that part of the purpose of liberal democracy is to protect an autonomous sphere for personal development can be extended across the normal species boundary. The protection of autonomy would now also refer to the protection of the ability of non-human entities to flourish in their own way, and in accord with their natural predispositions.

Eckersley's argument is unusual in that it explicitly draws on a notion of liberal democracy. The trend has rather been for greens to look to forms of **'deliberative democracy'** in order to develop a theory that unifies green and democratic thought (Smith, 2003). The main reason for this seems to be that the kind of democratic deliberation envisaged will work to promote the general interest, rather than the interests of factions that may do well under systems that merely aggregate people's existing preferences. Environmental goods are seen as a prime example of something that is in the general interest, but which tends to lose out in the bargaining between competing interests that marks liberal democracy. As bargaining gives way to deliberation, and arguments have to be made in terms of the general good, then we can expect environmental concerns to become more prominent and policy to become more environmentally orientated.

On deliberative democracy, see Chapter 21.

Green political theory and citizenship

Another concept that has come in for green reinvention in recent times is citizenship, and, as with autonomy, we can usefully contrast the traditional view with the 'ecological' view to get a sense of where green theorists are seeking to take it. Traditionally, citizenship has been about the relationship between the individual (the citizen) and the state. The **republican** tradition in particular has put this relationship at the centre of its concerns: what does the individual owe to his or her political community, and what does the community owe to him or her? This relationship is then mapped out across a set of rights and responsibilities—it may be, for example, that one has to be willing to serve one's political community militarily in order to gain the benefits of full citizenship. The work on ecological citizenship by Andrew Dobson (2003) is controversial because it breaks that fundamental link between the citizen and a particular political community. Dobson instead sees the political community as being constructed out of the material interactions that flow between people, wherever in the world they may be. This immediately gives his conception of citizenship a global dimension, as in the contemporary world the material

On citizenship, see also Chapter 20.

flows of economic activity form a worldwide current. Rather as with Baxter's conception of ecological justice, what is owed by citizens is ecological space, although in this context to other human beings, rather than the rest of nature. The duties of ecological citizenship are determined by the size of one's ecological footprint (the area of land that is necessary in order to support one's chosen lifestyle). It is, at least in principle, possible to work out what a global, sustainable, per capita ecological footprint would consist in. This forms the baseline entitlement—to the extent that one's own footprint is in excess of this, one is in the realm of ecological citizenship, and one has a responsibility to reduce one's carbon footprint to the sustainable level, in the process opening up ecological space for those with below-sustainability footprints to increase their own up to the maximum sustainable level.

Dobson's ecological citizenship is an unusual conception of the citizen as well in that it is cast solely in terms of duties, with no corresponding set of rights. The people who are ecological citizens are those, and only those, whose footprints are excessive, and they are under the duty of citizenship to reduce these. However, this is not because those with 'under-size' footprints are also ecological citizens who have a *right* to a fair share. These people are not ecological citizens at all. Dobson explicitly rejects the possibility of pursuing the argument in these terms, passing up what might seem a good set of resources in the more traditional conception of citizenship that may have strengthened his argument (Hayward, 2006).

10.5 Green political theory and global environmental problems: the example of climate change

Environmental problems are no respecters of international boundaries and some of the most pressing concerns we have today, such as climate change, biodiversity loss, and oceanic acidification are intrinsically global in nature. Of these, there is no doubt that climate change has the highest profile and has attracted the most attention from policy-makers around the world. Does green political theory make any direct contribution to discussions about responses to climate change?

The unsurprising answer is 'yes'. There is a rapidly growing literature on the ethics of climate change, with lucid and rigorous work being done by scholars, such as Stephen Gardiner (2006), Dale Jamieson (1996), Simon Caney (2006a), Steve Vanderheiden (2008), and Ed Page (2006). Climate change raises important and difficult questions about responsibility, obligations to distant contemporaries, and obligations to future generations. We will look at each of these in turn.

Responsibility

There is, bar a few outlying voices, now a scientific consensus around the notions that (1) the composition of the atmosphere is changing due to anthropogenic emissions of greenhouse gases, (2) this results in a warming of the earth's climate at a rate unprecedented in the accessible records of previous climatic change, and (3) this warming will have deleterious consequences for most if not all nations on earth, but these impacts will be unevenly distributed. One reasonable question to ask is 'who is responsible for this situation?' The obvious answer is those countries that have the longest history of industrial production, namely the developed Western nations, such as the USA and the European states. These countries have contributed the most to the stock of greenhouse gas in the atmosphere, they have responsibility and (arguably), therefore, they should pay the majority of the costs of making the transition to an environmentally sustainable global economy; this is usually referred to as the 'polluter pays principle'. This is broadly the green position on climate change: we need 'contraction and convergence' toward a sustainable and equitably distributed allocation of greenhouse gas emissions, and developed countries have the biggest responsibility as they have been the largest beneficiaries of previous unsustainable emissions. This view (about 'ecological footprints' more generally, although climate changing emissions are an important part of that) is well-articulated in Dobson's *Environmental Citizenship* discussed above.

The last stage of that chain of argument is complicated, however, by:

- The potential presence of 'excusable ignorance' on the part of past generations of emitters, who did not know (and could not reasonably be expected to have known) that their actions would lead to global climate change.

- The question of whether, anyway, the current generation can be held to be in some way liable for the activities of previous generations, over which they had no influence, even if those generations did know what the consequences of their actions would be.

- The fact that some polluters cannot be made to pay.

Simon Caney considers these problems in his work, and his response is that a 'polluter pays' principle that does target those who can be held responsible for emissions should be supplemented with an 'ability to pay' principle that is not tied to responsibility, but rather to the ability to bear a share of the burden (Caney, 2005b). Thus, a wealthy country that had developed economically without any net contribution to the stock of greenhouse gases in the atmosphere (perhaps by growing a particularly valuable tree species in vast forests) would still be liable to transfer resources to the victims of climate change, by the latter rather than the former principle.

Obligations to distant contemporaries

In addition to questions of responsibility, climate change brings into sharp relief the question of our relationship to distant others, in particular, if we are citizens of an industrialized country, our obligations to inhabitants of the developing world. Again, Andrew Dobson's argument in *Environmental Citizenship* makes a green case for thinking 'we' in developed countries have direct obligations to distant others. Where there is material interaction there is the potential for ecological citizenship, which, simplifying, involves being under an obligation to reduce the size of one's ecological footprint to a sustainable level. Dobson calls his approach 'post-cosmopolitan' as it is intended to have a material, rather than moral basis. Whether he succeeds in this or not, his approach has much in common with cosmopolitan views of global justice in that it accepts responsibilities of justice lie beyond the boundaries of the nation state.

On cosmopolitanism, see Chapter 8.

Green theorists have also challenged conventional ways of thinking about the concept of '**sovereignty**' in international politics. For Robyn Eckersley (2004) the 'two sides' of sovereignty—**self-determination** and non-intervention—can be made to work for democracy and the protection of local ecosystems. For example, 'negative externalities' generated by trans-boundary pollution can be seen as illegitimate interference in self-determination.

Obligations to future generations

A third important justice-related element to the problem of climate change is the obligations of the present generation to future generations. Again the green position is to affirm the responsibility, thus the UK Green Party states that: 'Our actions should take account of the well-being of other nations, other species, and future generations. We should not pursue our well-being to the detriment of theirs'.[1]

As with the question of responsibility, there are complications here that create difficulties for the green view. One very interesting and much discussed difficulty is what has become known as the 'non-identity problem' (Parfit, 1984, chapter 16). This involves a view of identity as being decided by the combination of genetic material that comes together in the matching of egg and spermatozoon. On this view of identity the timing of conception and the identity of the parents is crucial. Take one possible set of matchings, then if different people were to come together or the same people come together at a different time, the identity of their offspring will be different. Why is this a problem for the idea of intergenerational justice with respect to climate change? Because if we had never developed the technology behind climate change, a completely different set of people would now exist in the world (imagine how different a world without the internal combustion engine or electricity generation would be). So, it is not as if *our* lives—the lives of those people currently living on Earth—could have gone better or worse if greenhouse gas emissions had never come about, as *we* would not be here. Similarly, if we take action to curb emissions, we will change the identity of those who will be born (as compared with a 'business as usual' approach). So we do not make people's lives go *better* or *worse* by curbing or not curbing emissions, we just bring a different set of people into existence. This creates a problem if we think our obligations to future generations depend on whether we can harm or benefit them, because when we understand the non-identity problem we see that we can do neither—we just change their identity. Thus, we might conclude, we have no obligations to future generations, as we cannot harm them, and thus we can do as we like. Parfit does not think we should draw this conclusion, however, and he argues instead that we should take the 'no-difference view'—i.e. the non-identity problem should not affect our moral thinking about future generations.

10.6 'Sceptical environmentalism'

In relation to the previous discussion of climate change, there is another position that relates closely to green political thought that is worth discussing, as it casts a sceptical eye over the claims of green political theory. 'Sceptical environmentalism' is almost exclusively

---

[1] See http://www.greenparty.org.uk/about.html

associated with the Danish statistician Bjørn Lomborg, who wrote *The Skeptical Environ-mentalist* (2001). Lomborg's book is subtitled 'Measuring the real state of the world', and the key thesis is that when you examine the best empirical evidence we have, a lot of environmental indicators are getting better, not worse. Where there are genuine global problems, such as with climate change, we need to think carefully about the costs and benefits of the different types of action we might be tempted to take. It would be very easy to talk ourselves into spending far too much in climate change mitigation, given the benefits that it is likely to bring. Lomborg sets the problem up as a dichotomy: we can help the poorest and most vulnerable of the present generation now, or we can devote resources now to helping future generations instead. If we choose the latter course we have to recognize the opportunity costs involved in so doing. The problem with that course of action is that (1) climate change mitigation is expensive for the level of benefit it brings, with net costs after a small reduction in greenhouse gas emissions, and (2) we can expect future generations to be far richer than the present generation, and so you will be assisting the relatively wealthy by depriving the relatively poor. On that basis it would be far more cost-effective to spend resources on benefits for the current global poor, such as providing effective treatment for malaria and HIV/AIDS. We should charge a small tax on carbon to reduce emissions by an efficient amount, but beyond that we should spend the money elsewhere.

It is worth noting that a number of assumptions underpin Lomborg's view and these have been questioned by critics. Lomborg's estimates of the costs and benefits of climate change assume a smooth continuation of existing trends, including the trend for later generations to be wealthier than earlier ones. However, climate change may be marked by abrupt and catastrophic environmental changes, such as the disappearance of thermohaline circulation (for example, the Gulf Stream), massive acceleration of the process of warming through positive feedback loops, or the disintegration of the Greenland or West Antarctic ice sheets, which would add many metres to global sea levels. Any of these events could play havoc with the expected costs and benefits of climate change, and they make it very difficult to model climate change in that way (Broome, 1992).

10.7 Conclusion

As we have seen 'green political theory' as defined here covers a broad range of ideas, prescriptions, and underlying value orientations. A fundamental analytical divide is made between environmentalism, which seeks to address environmental problems within the existing political and economic system, and ecologism, which seeks profound ethical, political, and/or economic transformation. In recent years, work in green political theory has turned from the positing of a comprehensive alternative to existing ways of thinking about ethics, politics, and economics, towards engagement with many existing political concepts, such as justice, democracy, and rights. This does not necessarily imply an abandonment of the transformative ambitions of ecologism, but rather an acceptance of the need to engage other theorists and the broader public in a language that they understand. With respect to ethics and world politics, we see the application of ethical thinking to global problems as a central part of green political theory, and work on the relationship between global justice, intergenerational obligations, and climate change shows this very clearly.

■ QUESTIONS

1. What is the distinction between environmental and ecological political theory?

2. What is supposed to be 'deep' about deep ecology?

3. For social ecologists, what is the meaning of the 'first nature/second nature' distinction?

4. Why did eco-authoritarians argue for the suspension of democratic politics?

5. Why are anarcho-primitivists 'against civilization', and are their arguments convincing?

6. What is the argument for 'ecological justice'?

7. What is unusual about Andrew Dobson's conception of 'ecological citizenship'?

8. What considerations complicate the application of the 'polluter pays principle' with respect to climate change?

9. What is the 'non-identity' problem, and how is it relevant for thinking about climate change?

10. Why is Bjørn Lomborg sceptical of the benefits of climate change mitigation?

■ FURTHER READING

Bookchin, M. (1991) *The Ecology of Freedom: The Emergence and Dissolution of Hierarchy*, rev edn. Montreal: Black Rose Books. This is where Bookchin sets out the basic tenets of social ecology.

Dobson, A. (2003) *Citizenship and the Environment*. Oxford: Oxford University Press. This is where Dobson puts forward his view for a 'post-cosmopolitan' form of ecological citizenship.

Dobson, A. (2007) *Green Political Thought*, 4th edn. London: Routledge. An insightful and comprehensive review of green political theory.

Lomborg, B. (2001) *The Skeptical Environmentalist: Measuring the State of the World*. Cambridge: Cambridge University Press. An iconoclastic view of how we should respond to problems such as climate change.

Naess, A. (1989) *Ecology, Community, and Lifestyle: Outline of an Ecosophy*, transl. D. Rothenberg. Cambridge: Cambridge University Press. A lucid exposition of the principles of deep ecology.

Page, E. (2006) *Climate Change, Justice, and Future Generations*. Cheltenham: Edward Elgar. An analytically sophisticated account of the implications of climate change for what we owe to future generations.

Plumwood, V. (1993) *Feminism and the Mastery of Nature*. London: Routledge. A classic articulation of ecofeminist opposition to patriarchy.

Schlosberg, D. (2007) *Defining Environmental Justice: Theories, Movements, and Nature*. Oxford: Oxford University Press. A thorough discussion of what 'justice' means in the context of ecological politics.

■ WEB LINKS

http://www.ipcc.ch/ The Intergovernmental Panel on Climate Change (IPCC) site is a good place to look for the latest scientific research on climate change.

http://www.unep.org/ The home page of the United Nations Environment Programme.

http://www.envirolink.org/ EnviroLink is a wide-ranging environmental resources site.

http://geography.lancs.ac.uk/EnvJustice/ Lancaster University's Environmental Justice research and resource site, focusing on questions of justice and inequality, especially in the United Kingdom. An American equivalent is based at Clark Atlanta University.

http://www2.etown.edu/vl/globenv.html Extensive links on environmental issues from the WWW Virtual Library.

Visit the Online Resource Centre that accompanies this book to access more learning resources: **www.oxfordtextbooks.co.uk/orc/bell_ethics/**

11 Post-colonial theory

Margaret Kohn

READER'S GUIDE

Post-colonialism is a broad term that refers to a wide range of critical responses to the legacy of colonialism. The intellectual history of this topic dates back to the late nineteenth and early twentieth centuries when intellectuals in the Middle East, India, Latin America, and Africa challenged the cultural and theoretical justifications for European domination. Some argued that European civilization was materialist, individualist, and violent and therefore did not have the moral authority to govern other peoples. Others developed an economic critique of the relationship between countries of the core and the periphery. Contemporary post-colonial theory emerged out of the field of literary studies and emphasizes the relationship between representation, knowledge, and power. The post-colonial critique of 'universalism' has implications for a number of contemporary political issues including global justice and human rights.

11.1 Introduction

In recent years, political theorists have shown a renewed interest in the issue of **colonialism**. They have tended to focus their attention on the treatment of colonialism in the writings of canonical thinkers such as John Locke, Edmund Burke, John Stuart Mill, Denis Diderot, Alexis de Tocqueville, Adam Smith, and Immanuel Kant (Mehta, 1999; Muthu, 2003; Pitts, 2005). This research has made an important contribution to our understanding of a number of themes, including the intellectual history of colonialism, the complexity of these canonical figures, and the relationship between **universalism**, cultural particularity, historical development, and civilization. Strikingly absent from this literature, however, is a detailed analysis of colonialism from the perspective of the colonized. Post-colonialism is a scholarly approach that asks why non-European texts have played such a marginal role in the humanities and social sciences. It also seeks to redress this lacuna by identifying a series of themes, thinkers and movements that illuminate not only our understanding of colonialism and it legacies, but also political power and political change, the core issues of international relations.

Post-colonial theorists have also developed a distinctive approach to ethics. Most academic discussions of 'global justice' start from the perspective of moral universalism and explain why this premise requires that wealthy nations do more to protect **human rights** or provide humanitarian aid to people living in less developed countries. The post-colonial perspective draws attention to two problems with this approach to global justice. First, colonialism itself was often justified as a mechanism for protecting the human rights of native peoples from the cruelty of their own leaders. For example, the Spanish justified their conquest of the Americas as an effort to end cruel practices, such as cannibalism. This history reminds us that ethical arguments are often used to gain support for intervention that actually promotes the military or economic interests of the wealthy countries. Secondly, post-colonial theory also challenges the idea of moral universalism. The key argument is that 'universal' values often reflect the cultural practices and interests of powerful groups.

On the global justice debates, see Chapter 6, 7, 8, and 14.

The study of post-colonialism has developed in different ways in a number of academic disciplines. In literary studies, post-colonial theory has tended to emphasize the relationship between knowledge and power. There has been intense scholarly interest not only in the literary production of former colonies, but also in the theoretical issues raised by academic attempts to represent non-European societies (Ashcroft et al., 1989). The two most influential texts that have framed debates in post-colonial theory are Edward Said's *Orientalism* (1979) and Gayatari Spivak's 'Can the Subaltern Speak' (1994). Marxist-inspired activists and social scientists, on the other hand, have focused on the economic logic of neo-colonialism (Gandhi, 1998). This chapter provides an overview of both of these dimensions and distinguishes them using the labels 'Post-colonial Theory' and 'Theories of Decolonization'.

11.2 Defining concepts

All of the concepts used in this chapter—the West, the Third World, post-colonialism—are themselves highly contested. The issue of naming has been very controversial in post-colonial studies because it is one of the most important acts of representation. For example, the terms 'African-Americans' and 'coloured people' may refer to the same group, but one label is associated with a history of discrimination and the other signals a break with that past. Employing a label not only defines the subject matter in a particular way, but also contains the intended and unintended traces of past meanings. Scholars have debated whether the terms 'Third World' or 'less developed' imply inferiority. Do they make the superiority of Europe and North America seem natural and inevitable? Do the concepts make it more difficult to think critically about what standards should be used for comparing different countries? Mahatma Gandhi raised these questions over 100 years ago in his influential essay 'Hind Swaraj'. At the time, the British Empire defined itself as 'civilized' and the indigenous people of its colonies as 'barbarians'. Gandhi challenged this view and explained that Britain's obsession with material prosperity, competition, and technological innovation brought degradation and ruin (Gandhi, 1993, p. 15). Gandhi defined true civilization as a mode of conduct based on morality and control of the passions (1993, p. 35). He felt that from this perspective, India was more civilized than the European colonial powers.

The terms Western and non-Western are particularly problematic because a lot of post-colonial writing is a hybrid drawn from different sources. Many post-colonial theorists were born in former colonies, but completed their higher education or have teaching positions in Europe or North America. Furthermore, despite the frequent use of the term 'West', it is unclear whether the label refers to a geographical location, a cultural ideal, or a concentration of political power. In the social sciences the terms 'industrialized countries' and 'lesser developed countries' (LDCs) are popular, because they seem to rely on objective economic criteria for constructing categories. The problem with these labels is that economic development is treated as an objective criteria for comparing different countries when, as Gandhi pointed out, some cultures challenge the idea that material prosperity is the most important goal. This chapter uses the terms 'core' and 'periphery' to distinguish between rich, industrialized countries (Europe, Japan, and a number of former settler-colonies), and poorer ones.

Finally, the term post-colonialism itself is the topic of ongoing debate. As Anne McClintock pointed out, it suggests a linear, progressive history that leads from colonialism to post-colonialism. This is misleading in a number of ways. It obscures the way that colonialism varied in different regions and periods. Even if we focus exclusively on modern European colonialism, there is no clear line dividing before from after. There was an early period of colonialism in the Americas (sixteenth and seventeenth centuries) followed by independence movements in the eighteenth and nineteenth centuries. These were successful at the same time that European countries were establishing new colonies in Africa and Asia. Furthermore, some scholars feel that the term post-colonialism implies that colonialism is definitively over, when the legacy of colonialism deeply structures the present (McClintock, 1992). This chapter uses the term post-colonialism as a broad term that describes the period of European domination, the movements for national liberation, and the legacies of colonialism in the contemporary period.

Part of the difficulty of defining post-colonialism comes from the complexity of defining colonialism. Colonialism is a practice of domination, which involves the subjugation of one people to another. There are at least two different forms of modern European colonialism: settler colonies and colonies of exploitation. Settler colonies are places such as the United States, Canada, Mexico, Brazil, South Africa, Australia, and New Zealand, where a significant population of European emigrants settled permanently. The term 'colonies of exploitation' usually refers to places such as India and most of sub-Saharan Africa (excluding South Africa and Kenya), where the small European population was largely made up of government bureaucrats and merchants without permanent roots in the country. Of course, the settler colonies also had very different histories, depending on whether the European population displaced the indigenous population and ultimately became a colonial power itself (e.g. the United States), mixed with the indigenous people (much of South America), or segregated itself while remaining a powerful minority (Algeria, South Africa). While any discussion of post-colonialism must remain attentive to these complexities, the term still captures an important set of commonalities. It identifies the experience of foreign political, cultural, and economic domination as a salient issue and draws attention to the legacies of this history in the present.

11.3 **Post-colonial theory**

Orientalism

Although the field of post-colonial studies is just emerging in political and ethical theory, it is well established in other disciplines in the humanities and social sciences. In literary studies, in particular, scholars have explored the way that the history of colonialism is celebrated, justified, repressed, and contested in works of literature. The seminal text in the interdisciplinary field of post-colonial studies is Edward Said's *Orientalism*, which was originally published in 1978. Drawing upon post-structuralist theory, Said argued that the Orient was the constitutive outside of the West. The term 'constitutive outside' describes the way in which a society takes a series of negative characteristics and projects them onto an excluded group, thereby reinforcing a sense of **cultural identity**. By representing the Orient as irrational, sensual, and violent, **Orientalism** served to establish the superior rationality of the Occident. Thus, according to Said, Orientalism was not just an academic discipline that produced expert knowledge through the study of linguistics, anthropology, literature, and religion, but also a stable and recurring set of images that served to define, dominate, and restructure the Middle East. Ultimately then, Said's original investigation of the concept of Orientalism served to draw attention to the way that knowledge is implicated in power. The supposedly disinterested academic study of the Middle East served to support European colonialism and imperialism both implicitly, as an ideological rationale, and explicitly, as an instrument of power.

On post-structuralism, see Chapter 3.

Said uses the term Orientalism in several different ways. First, Orientalism is a specific field of academic study about the Middle East and Asia, albeit one that Said conceives quite expansively as including history, sociology, literature, anthropology, and especially philology. He also identifies it as a practice that helps define Europe by creating a stable depiction of its other, its constitutive outside. In other words, Orientalism is a way of characterizing Europe by drawing a contrasting image or idea, based on a series of binary oppositions (rational/irrational, mind/body, order/chaos) that manage and displace European anxieties. Finally, Said emphasizes that it is also a mode of exercising authority by organizing and classifying knowledge about the Orient. This discursive approach is distinct both from a materialist assumption that knowledge is simply a reflection of economic interests and from an idealist conviction that scholarship is objective and neutral.

On represen-
tations of
non-Western
societies, see also
Chapter 12.

On Foucault,
see Chapter 3.

Not only did Said draw attention to the deeply racist and demeaning depictions of the Middle East and Islam in European literature and humanist scholarship, he also contributed to broader debates about epistemology. Epistemology is a philosophical term that refers to theories of knowledge. Said reminded his readers that the images, concepts, metaphors, and assumptions that organize the way that we view reality and interpret texts are neither objective nor subjective. Instead, they are deeply influenced by discourses, e.g. informal rules and patterns that structure knowledge in a given period. Said's use of discourse analysis was inspired by the work of the French philosopher Michel Foucault. For both Said and Foucault, knowledge is not only used instrumentally in the service of power but can also itself be a form of power. To clarify the distinction between an instrumental and constitutive use of knowledge, consider the following examples. You know that your little brother likes ice cream and therefore you offer him ice cream as a reward for keeping a secret. This is an instrumental use of knowledge. Now imagine that everyone in your former high school knew that a certain group was popular. This widely shared belief in their superiority—this knowledge—*made* them popular and is, therefore, a constitutive form of power. In *Orientalism*, Said showed that knowledge of the Middle East was a constitutive form of power that facilitated the exercise of European domination.

Debates about orientalism

Orientalism was a very influential and controversial book that inspired debates about the relationship between knowledge and power. *Orientalism* helped scholars and students from a range of disciplines see things that they had not seen before. It inspired numerous theoretical reflections on the problem of representation and subsequent studies of the production of knowledge in particular geographical, disciplinary, and temporal contexts. Despite these achievements, critics have faulted *Orientalism* for failing to suggest a more adequate way of studying the cultural production of Third World countries (Young, 1990b, p. 167). Although Said insists that he does not foreclose the possibility of doing non-Orientalist scholarship on Islam or the Middle East (1979, p. 326), it seems very difficult, given the political and epistemological challenges that he identifies. In *Orientalism*, Said shows that the scholarly study of the Middle East has always been tied to the exercise of political power. Orientalists accompanied military expeditions and later were members of the colonial service or were responsible for training colonial administrators. In *Covering Islam* (1981), Said concludes that this remains virtually unchanged today except the new Orientalists are American social scientists with consulting contracts and institutional and economic links to oil companies, media, and government interests. For example, in the wars in Iraq and Afghanistan, the United States Army introduced the Human Terrain System. The programme was designed to use social science to meet the military's requirements for sociocultural knowledge. According to one Human Terrain Team member, 'One anthropologist can be much more effective than a B-2 bomber—not winning a war, but creating a peace one Afghan at a time' (US Army, 2009).

There is also a deeper epistemological reason that orientalism is difficult to overcome definitively. According to Said's epistemological premises, objectivity is impossible. Orientalism is not just an ideology, but a discourse and, as such, it is a system that governs the production of subsequent knowledge. The extremely stereotypical character of work that passed as scientific study of the Middle East was possible, as Said shows, because it was verified not by fidelity to some true Orient (something which, for Said, cannot exist), but rather because of its consistency with already established 'truths' about the object. Even a traveller or scholar critical of imperialism would almost inevitably take for granted the existence of something called the Orient and see it as fundamentally opposed to the West. The political implications of orientalism cannot be reduced to the bad intentions of its practitioners. Many orientalists had a deep admiration for their object of study and devoted their lives to translating and disseminating works of high culture. Nevertheless, according to Said (1979, p. 2), they are still orientalist because their approach was based on 'an ontological and epistemological distinction made between "the Orient" and (most of the time) "the Occident"'.

In *Orientalism*, Said analyses a wide range of texts from overtly racist and **ethnocentric** invectives to seemingly flattering assessments. Statements in the first category are initially the most shocking and range from religious attacks on Mohammed as a debauched imposter and idolater (1979, pp. 65–6) to straightforward claims to civilizational superiority by British colonial administrators. The sympathetic portraits, however, are more important for Said because they reveal something more interesting than the well-documented existence of ethnocentrism in Western scholarship. Instead, they show that a certain set of assumptions and images cut across texts that were produced by writers with different goals and ideologies. A discourse is distinct from an ideology and is arguably more important because it can influence a range of different political ideologies. Said's brief discussion of Marx's writing on India is particularly important because it dramatically illustrates this point. According to Said, Marx is an orientalist because he invoked the concept of 'oriental despotism' to explain why Indian feudalism was unlikely to achieve a bourgeois revolution on its own and, therefore, needed an external impetus—the British—to transform it.

Aijaz Ahmad criticized Said, insisting that it is wrong to use Marx as an example of orientalism (1992, pp. 159–220). Marx ultimately favoured British imperialism because he thought it ushered in the modernization that was a necessary precondition of socialism, but his defence of the progressive character of British rule differed markedly from the arguments advanced by other apologists, such as John Stuart Mill. Marx argued that progress would not be the result of the Indians' gradual assimilation of markets and good government, but rather it would be a product of nationalist struggle *against* imperialist rule.[1] He also criticized the brutality of British rule in India. In other words, the British did not bring civilization, but the struggle to get of rid of the British (while keeping their technology) might. Marx is the best-known of a number of thinkers who reproduced some aspects of orientalism while challenging or undermining others. While Marx uncritically invoked certain 'facts' about Indian political economy, he also challenged the idea of

---

[1] Even such a staunch defender of Marx as Ahmad admits 'it is doubtless true that (Marx's) image of Asia as an unchanging, "vegetative" place was part of the inherited worldview in nineteenth century Europe' (1992, p. 224). Said is right that despite Marx's unusual defence of British imperialism as the precursor to its own negation does not change the fact that this conclusion was based on a fundamentally flawed understanding of Indian political economy.

British civilizational superiority and advocated Indian nationalism. This debate about whether Marxism is orientalist is particularly contentious because Marx's concepts are the basis of the other major strand of post-colonial thought, the one that emerged out of anti-colonial political movements rather than the halls of the university.

Said's interpretation of Marx is an illustration of what some critics have seen as a kind of essentialism in Said's approach. In order to craft a rhetorically powerful indictment of dominant practices of representation, he emphasizes the features of intellectual and literary works that illustrate orientalism, while minimizing other important features. There are advantages and disadvantages to this approach. Taking numerous examples 'out of context' draws attention to the ubiquity and importance of a theme that was marginalized in existing interpretations and, in effect, this creates a new context, a new way of organizing our thinking about how to group together texts. The disadvantage is that it may involve some distortion and leaves the reader with the pessimistic conclusion that resistance to orientalism was non-existent and therefore, perhaps, impossible. This is especially true of Said's discussion of Dante. He points out that in the *Inferno* a small group of Muslims including Avveroes and Saladin are placed along with Abraham, Socrates, Plato, and Aristotle in the first circle of the Inferno where they suffer minimal and even honourable punishment (1979, p. 69). Nevertheless, Said still identifies Dante's work as an example of orientalism because this cosmology is an illustration of the way in which 'Islam and its designated representatives are creations of Western geographical, historical, and above all, moral apprehension' (1979, p. 69). Formulated in this way, orientalism becomes impossible for any Westerner to avoid. Any study of other cultures involves some kind of comparison that assesses unfamiliar works in terms of existing knowledge and relies on criteria from one's own tradition. If any comparison and evaluation, even a complimentary one, is orientalist, then the only available response is to avoid the study of unfamiliar traditions altogether.

In 'Orientalism Reconsidered' (1985) Said admits that the question of how to represent the Arab world is one of the unresolved questions posed by his book. In response to this line of criticism, he attempts to outline an anti-orientalist methodology and identifies a host of recent studies that have contributed to the project of illuminating a non-orientalist 'East'. Several of these studies thematize the problematic of representation, for example Abdul JanMohamed's *Manichean Aesthetics* (1983), which juxtaposes white and black fictional accounts of Africa. Others, including Peter Gran's *The Islamic Roots of Capitalism* (1979) and the work of the 'subaltern studies' group (Ranajit Guha and collaborators) focus on detailed local histories that disrupt the dominant assumptions of political economy. Said contrasts these local narratives with the world history approach of Fernand Braudel, Immanuel Wallerstein, and Perry Anderson that, despite its explicitly anti-imperialist stance, relies on the same universalistic categories that usually erase local differences. In 'Orientalism Reconsidered' Said emphasizes a broadly post-structuralist methodological orientation as the key to resisting orientalism. The crucial components of this methodology include the following:

- Explicit reflection on the problem of representation.

- Awareness of the way that scholars are also part of networks of power.

- Aversion to universalization and attentiveness to local, marginal, and oppositional forces.

- Resistance to the 'sovereign authority (of) methodological consistency, canonicity, and science'. (Said, 1985, p. 106).

The interdisciplinary field of post-colonial studies has tended to focus on the first of these suggestions. Theoretical reflections on the problematic of representation have been particularly prominent in literary studies. These concerns were intensified with the publication of Gayatri Spivak's essay 'Can the Sublatern Speak?'

The problem of subaltern speech

In 'Can the Subaltern Speak?' Spivak turns the critical perspective of post-colonial studies on itself, arguing that 'the much-publicized critique of the sovereign subject ... actually produces a subject' (1994, p. 66). The term **subaltern**, meaning 'lower rank', is taken from the Italian Marxist Antonio Gramsci. Spivak, like Said, is relying on the post-structuralist notion that power is productive and not simply repressive. In other words, post-colonialism, in a sense, creates the marginal person that it then claims to speak for. Of course, there were always people who were exploited by systems of power such as colonialism or **patriarchy**. Spivak's point is that post-colonialism creates an identity as subaltern that becomes the basis for a new kind of knowledge and power.

Spivak's essay inaugurated the second generation of post-colonial criticism, because it took for granted the reader's familiarity with the type of argument made by Said: the claim that the universal, neutral, Western spectator reproduces his or her own world view and reinforces hierarchical power relations when representing the rest of the world. Instead, Spivak focuses her attention on the problems that emerge when scholars attempt to avoid the pitfalls of representation by, as she puts it, letting the subaltern speak for themselves. This desire to uncover and present the viewpoint of oppressed or marginal people as a strategy for challenging dominant ideologies had broad appeal to those on the political left.

The most startling moment of the essay comes at the end when Spivak states with uncharacteristic directness: 'the subaltern cannot speak' (1994, p. 104). For almost two decades since the essay's original publication, students have struggled with this provocative claim. She clarifies the intent of this statement when she adds, 'Representation has not withered away. The female intellectual as intellectual has a circumscribed task which she must not disown with a flourish'. She is challenging the illusion that the problem of representation, including the risks of distortion, misappropriation, authority, and translation can simply be wished away by letting the subaltern speak for themselves. In demystifying the idea of transparent subaltern speech, she is simply drawing the logical conclusions of Jacques Derrida's idea of iterability, which questioned the notion of an authentic original that is the stable source of meaning for subsequent copies. When well-meaning scholars want to let the subaltern 'speak for themselves' they are assuming that removing the intermediary (the expert, the judge, the imperial administrator, the local elite) opens up the space for some authentic truth based on experience to emerge. However, experience itself is constituted through representation; therefore, denying the problematic of representation does not make it go away, but renders it invisible.

On Derrida, see Chapter 3.

There are two sections in the essay where Spivak explores the issue of representation. The first is an extended reading of Marx's *The Eighteenth Brumaire*. Spivak draws attention to the difference between two German words—*vertretung* and *darstellung*, both of which are translated in English as representation. The term *vertreten* usually refers to political representation and has the connotation of substitution. *Darstellung*, on the other hand, connotes something more akin to 'description'. The difference between the two, she suggests, is similar to the difference between a proxy and a portrait (Spivak, 1994, p. 71). Marx used the two dimensions of representation in order to explain the peasantry's support for Louis Napoleon in the national plebiscite. Having failed to constitute itself as a social class (through *darstellung*) the peasantry imagined its own absent unity through identification with a national leader (*vertreten*). Spivak's point is not to privilege one form of representation over the other, but rather to draw attention to the way that our language obscures these very different processes and this, in turn, makes it easier to substitute one for another.

Spivak returns to this issue of representation at the end of the essay in her discussion of *sati* (the ritual suicide of widows). She notes that under British imperial government, *sati* was defined by two groups that competed to give it very different meanings. For the British, *sati* signified the indigenous barbarity that they were in India to prevent and the essentially moral, uplifting nature of their rule. For the patriarchal elite of Indian nationalists, *sati* was a form of resistance, 'proof of their conformity to older norms at a time when these norms had become shaky within' (Spivak, 1994, p. 94). Spivak suggests the possibility of a third alternative to these two hegemonic representations. She tells the story of a relative, Bhuvaneswari Bhaduri, whose suicide in the 1920s was interpreted as the response to the disgrace of an unwanted pregnancy. Spivak suggests an alternative reading 'of the social text of *sati*-suicide' (Spivak, 1994, p. 104), one that emphasizes Bhaduri's membership in a cell of an armed group struggling for Indian independence. Noting that Bhaduri committed suicide while menstruating, she concludes this was meant to be a legible sign that her actions were motivated by political not romantic disappointments. Nevertheless, the suicide was not interpreted as a political act and this, perhaps, illustrates the problem of eschewing the responsibility of interpretation and naively celebrating the transparency of subaltern speech. In the absence of a set of shared cultural meanings that facilitate intelligibility, there is no guarantee that such speech will be understood. This is the reason why Spivak concludes that the female academic should not evade the responsibility of representation. The problem is not so much that the subaltern cannot speak, but that they cannot be understood. Given the difficulty of Spivak's essay, the two points that the first-time reader usually remembers are the conclusion that 'the subaltern cannot speak' and the critique of the hegemonic (e.g. British and patriarchal) representations of the *sati*-suicide. The key to the essay, however, is that 'representation has not withered away'. Transparency and authenticity are impossible and power is ubiquitous; this means that the messy, political, critical, contested work of interpretation is necessary.

11.4 Theories of decolonization

One of the main criticisms of Spivak's work is that the density of her writing makes it difficult for students and activists to decipher her text. Although her work is widely cited in academic circles, critics have argued that the highly theoretical and abstract character of the analysis makes it irrelevant to contemporary political struggles. Aijaz Ahmad has argued that despite Spivak's claims to be working within the Marxist tradition, her essays exhibit contempt for materialism, rationalism, and progress, the core features of Marxism (Ahmad, 1997). According to Ahmad, Spivak is concerned with narratives of capitalism, rather than the institutional structures and material effects of capitalism as a mode of production. Spivak's sharp criticism of movements that essentialize subaltern subjects can also be read as an attack on the basic premise of Marxist politics, which privileges the proletariat as a group with shared, true interests that are produced by the capitalist system. This debate reflects a tension that runs through the field of post-colonial studies. Although some thinkers draw on both Marxism and post-structuralism, the two theories have different interests, methods, and assumptions. In the humanities, post-colonial theory tends to reflect the influence of post-structuralist thought while theorists of decolonization focus on social history, economics, and political institutions. Whereas post-colonial theory is associated with the issues of **hybridity**, **diaspora**, representation, narrative, and knowledge/power, theories of decolonization are concerned with revolution, economic inequality, violence, and political identity.

Marxism was very influential on anti-colonial movements in the twentieth century. As Said pointed out in *Orientalism*, Marx's own position was somewhat ambivalent. Marx criticized the brutality and exploitative character of the British domination of India, but also concluded that colonialism would help dismantle existing quasi-feudal structures, and facilitate the development of capitalism and feudalism. In later writings on Ireland, however, Marx began to reconsider this position. He noted that the long period of English domination had not fostered economic development. Instead, a class of absentee landlords impoverished Ireland by exporting land rents to England, leaving nothing for local investment and ensuring stagnation. In other words, foreign domination strengthened the colonizer and impoverished the colonized country. This idea became the foundation of contemporary **dependency theory** (Amin, 1976). Twentieth-century Marxist theorists, such as Vladimir Lenin, Karl Kautsky, Nikolai Bukharin, and Rosa Luxemburg, wrote critical analyses of imperialism. Lenin's analysis identified imperialism as a phase of late capitalism that allowed advanced countries to delay economic crises by controlling markets overseas (Lenin & Bukharin, 2009). In the period after the Second World War, a growing number of Third World intellectuals appropriated Marxist concepts and methods to understand the relationship between colonial powers and their colonies. They emphasized the economic exploitation that impoverished the Third World and the class divisions in the colonies that fostered or undermined anti-colonial struggle (Mariátegui, 1988). The most influential of these theorists of decolonization was Frantz Fanon.

Fanon's *Wretched of the Earth*

Frantz Fanon was born in Martinique and trained in Paris as a psychiatrist. He practiced in Algeria during the bloody war of national liberation (1954–62), where he wrote some of the most enduring reflections on the political and psychic dimensions of racism and violence. He was a supporter of the Algerian liberation movement, the FLN, and was deported from Algeria for his political activities. His two most famous works *The Wretched of the Earth* (Fanon, 1963) and *Black Skins, White Masks* (Fanon, 1967) are distinguished

On Fanon, see also Chapter 17.

by their sensitivity to the interrelationship between objective historical conditions and human attitudes towards those conditions. *The Wretched of the Earth* was written in 1961, just months before Fanon died of leukaemia. The book is a theoretical reflection inspired by the anti-colonial struggle in Algeria and the experience of the newly independent nations in Africa. In *The Wretched of the Earth*, Fanon describes the colonial world as a Manichean one, a world divided in two, enforced by violence and marked by racial differ- ence. But instead of reversing and thereby reproducing these terms, he explains how the native bourgeoisie and the elite in newly independent African countries often create neo- colonial structures of domination.

Although Fanon was not an orthodox Marxist, his analysis reflects the influence of Marxist categories, including class analysis and an emphasis on the economic bases of culture. This may be due to the influence of his friend Aimé Césaire, a Marxist theorist and leading political figure from Martinique. Fanon, however, used historical material- ism to come to an original understanding of the post-colonial situation. He also insisted that race is a fundamental category for understanding the colonial situation, which could not be reduced to economic terms. His analysis of the economic structure of colonialism also emphasized its distinctive characteristics. Based on his analysis of Europe, Marx had focused on the leadership of the urban proletariat, whereas Fanon identified the rural peasantry as the most revolutionary class in colonized countries. Since the peasantry was still united by indigenous traditions and did not share any benefits of the colonial system, they were well positioned to fight against colonialism. Fanon recognized that the small number of unionized urban workers in Algeria were not an exploited class, but an elite. He was also very sceptical of the nationalization of industry as a strategy for achiev- ing economic autonomy. He argued that nationalization was the favoured policy of the urban middle-classes because it allowed them to continue to exploit the masses for their own benefit. Nationalization, according to Fanon, was a way of maintaining the institu- tional structure of colonialism, while replacing the colonists with native intermediaries. Essentially, the economic role of the former colony would remain unchanged, but the native bourgeoisie would receive a small percentage of the surplus value that was being extracted. This was their reward for using any means necessary—coercion or consent—to ensure the continued submission of the masses.

Fanon argued that culture played an important role in building the **legitimacy** of the post-colonial state. In a chapter entitled 'The Pitfalls of National Consciousness', he criticized nationalism because he worried that it was primarily a way to encourage the exploited natives to identify with their new post-colonial masters. By celebrating indigenous cultural traditions, the new elites were trying to forge a sense of shared identity that masked their opposed economic interests. According to Fanon, the emphasis on négritude or pan-Africanism was a way that the indigenous bourgeoisie could distinguish themselves from Europeans and justify their monopoly on prestig- ious jobs in education and the civil service. This critique of the post-colonial state influenced African intellectuals such as Ngugi wa Thiong'o. Ngugi is a Kenyan author and cultural theorist. His novel *Petals of Blood* is a literary rendering of Fanon's cri- tique of the parasitic character of the post-colonial urban bourgeoisie, the repressive character of some post-colonial states, and the cultural strategy used to legitimize it (Ngugi, 2005).

In addition to his critique of cultural nationalism, Fanon also exposed the way that universalism is implicated in justifying and legitimizing colonialism. Modern colonialism is beset by a certain fundamental paradox. On the one hand, it is designed to promote the interests of one group over another and, as such, it relies on a strong sense of racial or cultural difference and superiority. On the other hand, one of the major rationales for colonialism was to improve the lives of the indigenous people, providing the benefits of a more advanced civilization, including the rule of law and good government. How was it that universal values such as freedom, rights, and reason could be used to justify domination and exploitation? According to Fanon, the colonial state justified its exclusionary and hierarchal structure by criticizing indigenous values and culture. In other words, the colonizers claimed that the natives could not be granted rights and freedom because they did not understand these values. Thus, the idea of European civilization and its universal values became a way to justify colonialism, rather than to criticize it. That is why, according to Fanon, 'when the native hears a speech about Western culture he pulls out his knife' (1963, p. 43).

On violence

The most controversial aspect of *The Wretched of the Earth* is Fanon's defence of violence. Fanon insisted that violence is a necessary part of the process of decolonization. In *The Wretched of the Earth*, he included a lengthy citation from a poem by Aimé Césaire depicting a slave stabbing his master to death and concluded, 'The colonized man finds his freedom in and through violence' (Fanon, 1963, p. 86). According to Fanon, violence is the only way to achieve decolonization and an inevitable response to the violent character of the colonial state. Moreover, through violence, the native achieves a sense of human dignity and the community builds solidarity. Amilcar Cabral, a leader of the armed liberation struggle against the Portuguese, developed a similar argument that linked violence, revolutionary struggle, and cultural renewal (Young, 2001, pp. 284–5).

For Fanon, the violent character of the struggle for decolonization is a product of the violence of the colonial situation. Colonialism is systematic exploitation and, as such, can only be maintained through force. Dismantling this system is violent because it changes the existing order of the world, which is an inherently chaotic process (Fanon, 1963, p. 36); colonialism is also a system of privilege and those who benefit from it will not give up their privilege without a fierce struggle. The scholarly debate focuses on whether *The Wretched of the Earth* should be read as advocating violence or simply noting the ubiquity of violence.

Fanon's analysis of violence does not focus exclusively on its political and instrumental effects. He notes that the anger experienced by the native is frequently expressed through criminal activity, vendettas, or tribal war. In-group violence is a permitted outlet for the feelings of subordination and humiliation caused by unfair treatment by the racist colonial state. According to Fanon, this destructive cycle can only be cured when violence is externalized and focused on the agents of oppression. Fanon also sees violence as part of a process of psychic transformation and liberation. It is this component that scholars have found most troubling.

Fanon suggests that engaging in violent resistance transforms an individual from a passive victim into a human being with agency. This claim reflects the influence of the German philosopher G. W. F. Hegel (1979), particularly the famous story of the master and slave in the *Phenomenology of Spirit* (1807). Hegel was trying to explain the emergence of personhood, which he believed required the recognition of another person. Each being desires to be recognized while withholding recognition from the other. They enter into a struggle and eventually one decides to accept subordination, rather than risk death. This person becomes the slave and the victor becomes the master. One way of reading this story is to conclude that liberation will occur only when the native ('the slave') is willing to risk his life in order to achieve freedom. Although Fanon does seem to endorse this view, he does not celebrate violence for its own sake. He emphasizes that the violence of colonized people is proportional to the violence exercised by the threatened colonial regime (1963, p. 88). He also reminds his audience that the violent tactics used by the FLN are modest compared with the aerial bombardments employed by the French state. The violence that becomes visible during the anti-colonial struggle, he insists, is really just a more overt manifestation of the sporadic and invisible violence of daily life under colonialism.

The legitimacy and utility of violence was also an important question for Mahatma Gandhi, another participant in the anti-colonial struggle. He also developed his ideas about violence and non-violence while directly participating in the struggle for Indian independence. Of course Gandhi reached very different conclusions about these same issues. He felt that violence violated Hindu religious doctrines. Furthermore, it damaged the individual and undermined his political goal. In addition to developing a theory and practice of non-violence, Gandhi also articulated a strongly worded critique of Western civilization. Despite Gandhi's prominence as a political figure and thinker, his work has been less influential on contemporary theories of decolonization, perhaps because his emphasis on asceticism, spirituality, and non-violence are at odds with modern ideologies.

Gandhi's critique of Western civilization

Gandhi is probably the best-known critic of colonialism and the subject of several excellent books in political theory (e.g. Parekh, 1989). Trained as a barrister in England, he became politically active while living in South Africa. He experienced repeated racial discrimination and, in response to a 1906 law mandating that Indians register with the government, he organized a successful campaign of civil disobedience. After returning to India in 1915, he became interested in the plight of impoverished agricultural workers. He came into conflict with the British colonial state while he was organizing small farmers to protest an onerous tax increase that was imposed during a time of famine. His fame and influence spread and, in 1921, he became the head of the Indian National Congress.

Gandhi's theoretical project was a radicalization and politicization of Hindu moral teaching, developed in the context of anti-imperial struggle and influenced by figures such as Tolstoy, Ruskin, and Thoreau. Even compared with other critics of colonialism, Gandhi advanced a particularly forceful critique of modernization and Western civilization. His critique was first developed in the form of a dialogue published in the newspaper *Indian Opinion* and subsequently anthologized as *Hind Swaraj*. He challenged the position of Indian nationalists who wanted 'English rule without the Englishman' (Gandhi, 1993, p. 12). Gandhi's idea of Indian independence (*swaraj*) involved rejection of the British influence in India, not just the British themselves. Gandhi questioned the basic values of the British, including democracy, materialism, modern education, and technology. He even criticized popular symbols, such as doctors, lawyers, and railroads. For example, he argued that the profession of medicine created illness by providing palliatives that encouraged people to continue to live unhealthy lifestyles and lawyers encouraged conflict, rather than resolving it. Similarly, he felt that technology created new desires, rather than satisfying basic needs, and left people less time for pursuing spiritual obligations. Although he subsequently modified some of the more extreme formulations, throughout his life he continued to criticize materialism, and the economic and political dependency that it fostered. His embrace of tradition and rejection of modernity and materialism were not merely theoretical. He himself engaged in spinning cloth by hand and encouraged his followers do the same in order to achieve *swadeshi* (a kind of communal self-sufficiency).

His most famous theoretical innovation, however, was *satyagraha*. He coined the term to describe his distinctive practice of non-violence. It was a way of harnessing moral power in the service of political change. The term *satyagraha* is often translated as civil disobedience, but Gandhi wanted it to convey a much broader sense of the power of truth, love, and non-violence.

Non-violence (or *ahimsa*) was a doctrine with deep roots in Hindu religious teaching. Hindu thinkers disapproved of violence for several reasons: it violated the sacred character of life; it stirred up negative emotions such as anger and hate; and it corrupted the soul thereby undermining spiritual progress (Parekh, 1989). Gandhi, however, radically reconfigured this traditional doctrine by insisting that not doing harm was not enough. Instead of non-attachment, he advocated an active ethos of responsibility for remedying injustice and suffering in the world.

Gandhi employed the practice of non-violent resistance in the struggle against British colonialism. He led public demonstrations, including the famous salt march, a protest against the British monopoly on and taxation of salt. It was part of his broader strategy of drawing attention to the heavy burden that the British Raj placed on the most vulnerable Indians. In his writings, he expressed confidence that non-violence was not only morally superior, but also more effective at achieving its goals. He insisted that when an oppressor or even a criminal is confronted with love, rather than hate, he is transformed by the encounter and, frequently, the capacity for love is awakened. Violence simply inspires hatred and ushers in a never-ending cycle of revenge.

Fanon and Gandhi are usually seen as emblematic of opposing approaches to decolonization. Fanon saw violence as inevitable and effective in achieving both individual transformation and collective revolutionary consciousness. Gandhi rejected violence, and emphasized both the psychic and tactical benefits of unleashing the moral power of non-violent resistance. Fanon was influence by psychoanalysis and Marxism, while Gandhi drew on Hindu religious doctrine and European romantic anti-capitalism. Despite these important differences, however, there are also more subtle points of convergence. Both Gandhi and Fanon worried that the anti-colonial struggle would be in vain if it meant that the colonists were simply replaced with native people who ran the same institutions and shared the same values (Gandhi, 1998). Both also emphasized that national independence had to lead to positive change in the lives of the rural people, who bore the costs of the colonial state without sharing in any benefits. They both endorsed a decentralized system of semi-autonomous villages to safeguard the democratic character of the new state and prevent the dominance of a new, authoritarian elite. Finally, while Gandhi and Fanon had very different understandings of the psyche, both were very attentive to the relationship between personal transformation and political agency. Their shared concerns about the legitimacy of violence, the revolutionary process, and the challenge of founding a more just polity have structured debates about decolonization.

11.5 **Contemporary issues**

In the academy, 'post-colonial theory' has been more prominent than 'theories of decolonization'. This is probably due to the fact that the political project of decoloniza-tion was largely achieved in the 1960s while the issues of identity and cultural power are not resolved by the transfer of sovereignty from the colonial power to the post-colonial state. Hybridity and diaspora have become important concepts in post-colonial studies. These concepts reflect the influence of Homi Bhabha, who challenged the dichotomy between colonial modernity and tradition that was frequently used as the rhetorical basis for anti-colonial movements. He suggested that invoking tradition as a stable category could unwittingly reinforce the set of binary oppositions (civilized/savage, modern/back-ward, rational/habitual) that legitimized colonialism and other forms of domination. Instead, Bhabha emphasized the subversive effects of **mimicry** (1994). Mimicry or imitation can also be a form of mockery and reconfiguration, rather than simply the assimilation of foreign values. Destabilizing binaries is also a way of destabilizing bounda-ries, which in turn opens up the space to refashion post-colonial identities. The terms hybridity and diaspora have been particularly popular because they describe the experi-ence of many scholars, who were born in post-colonial states, but live and work in the 'metropole'. Situated both within and outside of the geographical and cultural centres of power, these intellectuals have reflected on the cultural dimensions of processes of globalization. Globalization, however, is not just a recent phenomenon. Work in the new field of diaspora studies has drawn attention to the long history of the 'Black Atlantic' (Gilroy, 1993) linking Africa, the Caribbean, and the Americas. Subsequent research has explored the cultural dimensions of globalization and the experience of **transnational** communities (Appadurai, 1996; Ong, 2000).

One of the most important recent works in post-colonial theory is Dipesh Chakrabarty's *Provincializing Europe* (2000), a study that challenges the universal claims of European modernity from the perspective of nineteenth-century Bengal. Chakrabarty not only discusses aspects of colonial history, but also develops a theory of history. He contrasts traditional historical narratives of linear progress, which helped to underpin the Western imperial project, with an alternative model that stresses plurality, nostalgia, and con-testability. He highlights the powerful connections between political projects and how we understand the past. Most post-colonial theorists are not convinced that liberalism lives up to its own self-understanding as universal and inclusive. Some political theorists, however, think that liberalism can be adapted to absorb some of the lessons of post-colonialism, and that in this modified form it provides the best solution to contemporary political problems. In *Postcolonial Liberalism* (2002), for example, Duncan Ivison argues that the values and practices of both indigenous and non-indigenous peoples are best realized in a liberal political order.

The critique of global economic inequality developed by anti-colonial thinkers has also had an impact on contemporary debates about globalization. Some scholars use the term imperialism or neo-imperialism to describe economic domination that is exercised through international institutions, rather than direct political or military control (Harvey, 2005). The term neocolonialism is another way of describing the economic control that colonial powers exercise over their former colonies (Nkrumah, 1966). The danger of neocolonialism was an important theme in Fanon's *Wretched of the Earth*. World systems theory and dependency theory are schools of thought that use neo-Marxist concepts to explain continued global inequalities. Dependency theorists such as former Brazilian President Fernando Cardoso conclude that the international system is structured to redistribute wealth from the periphery (mostly former colonies) to the core. The main idea is that countries that industrialize later are not able to follow the same path as countries like Britain, the United States, France, and Germany, which industrialized in the nineteenth century. Britain, for example, financed its economic expansion using resources extracted from the slave economies in the New World. It also controlled vast natural resources and markets for its products. Newly industrializing countries have none of these advantages and the world system is structured to perpetuate the underdevelopment of peripheral countries. Through finance capital, multinational corporations, technology, trade restrictions, and other mechanisms, the core countries appropriate the vast majority of global wealth. Although world systems theory is a form of economic analysis and not an ethical theory, it is often endorsed by those who also conclude that the continued gap between core and periphery is unjust, and should be remedied.

Post-colonial theory also provides critical insight into contemporary debates about human rights and **humanitarian intervention**. One important debate in the literature of human rights is whether these rights are universal or embedded in the culture and goals of the West. In 'Savages, Victims and Saviors: The Metaphor of Human Rights', Makau Mutua argues that human rights discourse characterizes people from the periphery as either victims or savages (2001). Africans in particular are cast as either brutal violators of human rights or helpless, passive victims. Mutua's claim is that human rights are not just abstract ideas but also a particular kind of story, one in which Western states and non-governmental organizations (NGOs) are portrayed as virtuous moral agents. Ironically, the human rights agenda is based on the Kantian idea of recognizing the dignity of all people, but it is dehumanizing because it reinforces negative stereotypes about Africa and overlooks the important role of indigenous activists who do not describe their own work in the abstract language of rights.

On human rights, see Chapter 13.

11.6 Conclusion

Post-colonialism is a broad term that refers to a wide range of theoretical reflections on the legacy of colonialism. The intellectual history of this topic dates back to the late nineteenth and early twentieth centuries when anti-colonial and anti-imperialist intellectuals in the Middle East, India, Latin America, and Africa challenged the cultural and theoretical justifications for European domination. Some argued that European civilization was materialist, individualist, and violent, and therefore did not have the moral authority to govern other peoples. Others developed an economic critique of the relationship between countries of the core and the periphery. For example, José Mariátegui, the Peruvian socialist, argued that the Latin American ruling class allowed foreign economic interests to exploit natural resources (1988). The profits were mainly exported abroad or used to finance the elite's luxurious lifestyle rather than invested productively. This analysis is similar to world systems theory and dependency theory, approaches which are used to understand the persistence of global inequalities today. The struggles for independence in the post-war period also inspired theoretical reflections on violence, revolution, and the problem of founding a new polity when many of the existing institutions and ideas are deeply implicated in a history of domination.

The term 'post-colonial theory', however, usually refers to the work of university-based intellectuals who began to reflect on the way in which the colonial world was studied and represented in the academy, and in the popular imagination. In his path-breaking book, *Orientalism*, Edward Said argued that the Orient was constituted through the discourse of orientalism and this process served the broader project of political power. For Said, the experience of actual colonial domination was not the key factor; in fact, a number of important countries in the Middle East, such as Iran and Turkey, were never European colonies. Nevertheless, the construction of the Orient as irrational, sensual, exotic, and fanatical legitimized European hegemony. From this perspective, literature, scholarship, and journalism become important sites for the exercise—and potentially also the subversion—of power. Even though this approach has been most influential in the humanities, it has implications for the study of international relations. It casts doubt on the ideal of neutral, objective scholarship. It draws attention to the relationship between knowledge and power, and challenges us to think about whose interests 'truth' serves and what perspective it reflects. Finally, it helps students to think critically about images and narratives that portray people from other parts of the world as violent, irrational, dishonest, greedy, and incapable.

■ QUESTIONS

1. What does Said mean by the term orientalism? What are some of the main criticisms of his argument?

2. What is a discourse and how does it differ from ideology?

3. What are the main features of post-colonial theory? How does it differ from theories of decolonization?

4. What are the main features of the post-colonial critique of human rights?

5. Why does Spivak conclude that the subaltern cannot speak?

6. How does Fanon's theory of decolonization differ from Marxism? How is it similar?

7. Why does Fanon defend violence?

8. What does Fanon mean when he writes, 'when the native hears a speech about Western culture he pulls out his knife …'? What are the implications of this quote for contemporary debates about humanitarian intervention?

9. Given Fanon's doubts about Western culture, why is he sceptical of alternatives like negritude?

10. What does Gandhi think of European civilization?

▓ FURTHER READING

Alcoff, L. (1991) The problem of speaking for others. *Cultural Critique*, 20:5–32. This article is an accessible introduction to some of the issues raised in Spivak's essay 'Can the Subaltern Speak?' It looks at the challenges involved in representing the ideas of subaltern groups.

Brewer, A. (1990) *Marxist Theories of Imperialism: A Critical Survey*. Milton Park: Routledge. This book provides an introduction to dependency theory and world systems theory, as well as a detailed discussion of thinkers such as Marx, Lenin, and Luxemburg.

Doty, R. L. (1997) *Imperial Encounters: The Politics of Representation in North-South Relations*. Minneapolis: University of Minnesota Press. This study shows how theories of representation can illuminate issues in international relations, particularly relations between the north and the south.

Fanon, F. (1963) *The Wretched of the Earth*. New York: Grove Press. This book is one of the seminal works in the field of post-colonial theory. It is an analysis of the psychological and political dimensions of the struggle for independence, as well as the challenges confronted by post-colonial states.

Gandhi, L. (1998) *Postcolonial Theory: A Critical Introduction*. New York: Columbia University Press. This book is a very sophisticated yet still readable summary of the main currents in post-colonial theory. Although written from the perspective of literary studies, it provides a broad overview of different debates in the field.

Mutua, M. (2001) Savages, victims and saviors: the metaphor of human rights. *Harvard International Law Journal*, **42**, 201–34. This article uses the insights of post-colonial theory to challenge the assumptions of human rights discourse.

Said, E. (1979) *Orientalism*. New York: Vintage. This path-breaking study exposed the way that the 'orient' was constituted through the discourse of orientalism.

Young, R. (2001) *Postcolonialism: An Historical Introduction*. Oxford: Blackwell. This book provides the best introduction to theories of decolonization. It covers a wide range of thinkers from Las Casas to Foucault. Young situates the thinkers in both their historical and intellectual context.

▓ WEB LINKS

http://www.postcolonialweb.org/poldiscourse/themes/themes.html This website provides a very useful overview of post-colonial theory from the perspective of literary studies. It defines key terms and introduces students to a range of theoretical issues. It also includes short encyclopaedia entries on key figures in this tradition.

http://www.english.emory.edu/Bahri/ This is a website maintained by the English Department at Emory University. It includes an overview of the field and links to more detailed analyses of important figures.

http://plato.stanford.edu/entries/colonialism/ This encyclopaedia entry provides an overview of colonialism and post-colonialism from the perspective of political theory.

http://www.libraries.iub.edu/index.php?pageId=3511 This is a research guide that focuses on post-colonial theory. It includes an extensive bibliography of key works in the field.

Visit the Online Resource Centre that accompanies this book to access more learning resources: www.oxfordtextbooks.co.uk/orc/bell_ethics/

Comparative political thought: beyond the non-Western

Christopher Goto-Jones

READER'S GUIDE

The field of comparative political thought (CPT) is anxious about its appropriate range of activity. It is a response to accusations that mainstream political theory remains staunchly Eurocentric. CPT aims to broaden the theoretical base of political inquiry by being as culturally inclusive as possible; it seeks to transcend national boundaries and build a body of theory that is somehow 'global'. However, CPT is sensitive to the ways in which 'comparison' can function to separate (rather than include), and thus anxious that it may actually reinforce the problem. This chapter suggests a way of understanding and practicing CPT that resolves the field's anxieties about its 'non-Western' focus. It concludes that for CPT to be a meaningful field it must be concerned with theoretical discontinuities, rather than cultural differences; this will require a radical re-thinking of the dimensions of political thought as a whole.

12.1 Introduction

Unlike some of the other sub-fields of political thought, comparative political thought (CPT) remains rather unstable in its organization and principles. It is a relatively young field and its parameters are still being formed. Part of the reason for its ongoing fluidity is the way in which it provokes such strong reactions from scholars in various fields. In particular, it generates powerful ethical dilemmas. Indeed, the foundational premise of comparative political thought is that the discipline of political theory is essentially **ethnocentric**. This accusation is becoming increasingly difficult to refute, and the fact that the canon of political thought taught in universities all over the world tends to consist almost exclusively of dead, white, 'Western' men is becoming increasingly embarrassing and shameful. Here, 'Western' refers to the loose cultural bloc where political ideas are rooted in European tradition. Hence, in this chapter the terms 'Western' and 'European' are used interchangeably.

However, the stakes are high. Whilst it seems difficult to argue that political theory should not include the non-European, finding ways to include it without completely dismantling the field of political thought and rebuilding it from scratch in a more inclusive way is extremely complicated. Taking the rest of the world seriously might mean exploding current conceptions of political theory altogether. Understandably, there is a reluctance to take this step, not least in purely institutional terms. As a result, comparative political thought risks becoming a ghetto into which the rest of the world is forced: it becomes a way for the mainstream of political theory to ease its conscience about ignoring the world outside of Euro-America without actually having to accept that the world has anything to do with its central concerns. Political theory and CPT subsist as neighbours, rather than as parts of the same territory of knowledge.

This kind of understanding of the role of CPT often leads to its characterization as 'non-Western political thought'. In the earliest days of the field, before the development of a post-colonial consciousness, the most popular form of scholarship in this area was the attempt to bring 'East and West' into dialogue with each other, as though these two fictional realms were so radically different that conversations between them (if realms can have conversations) needed to be mediated in a special way. In the shadows of this enterprise we might hear the words of Rudyard Kipling's *Ballad of East and West*: 'Oh, East is East, and West is West, and never the twain shall meet'.

On post-colonialism, see Chapter 11.

However, even if we can leave aside the troubling ethical issues generated by this stance, this kind of ghettoization does not seem to isolate the core issue: if it is the case that there are political ideas outside of Europe that are so different from those inside of Europe, what is it about those ideas that makes them so different? In order for the answer to this question to fall within the parameters of political theory (rather than geography), the answer cannot be simply 'because they are outside Europe'. Rather the answer must engage with a politico-theoretic issue. Unfortunately, however, many writers in this young field still employ the term 'non-Western' as an answer, at least implicitly. Hidden behind this answer is a better one: some political ideas outside of Europe are so different from some ideas within Europe that they constitute discontinuities in our structures of thinking about politics; they provoke metaphysical and cosmological issues and show how our understanding of politics is deeply and essentially connected to these philosophical questions. Here, 'metaphysics' refers to inquiry into the fundamental nature of being and the world, and 'cosmology' (a branch of metaphysics) refers to the study of the universe in its totality, including humanity's place in it. What is especially exciting about this formulation is that it suggests that not all non-European thought falls into this category (because it is sometimes rather similar to certain Western ideas) and also some European thought will fall into it too (because the history of Western political thought is not smooth or continuous).

That is, CPT is about understanding across philosophical and political discontinuities, and not across the border between 'the West and the Rest'. To rephrase this, CPT is political thought that is conscious of (and engaged in the interrogation of) metaphysical and cosmological issues as politics. If we are sympathetic with those who think of CPT as non-European political thought (Dallmayr, 1999), or even with those who suggest that CPT should really be concerned with inter-religious comparison (March, 2009a), then we must simply assume that this is what they mean. Any focus on origins or attempts to represent particular groups risks derailing both the intellectual and ethical project, as we will see.

12.2 Politics *and* comparative political thought

The field of comparative political science has developed without much reflection on the role or place of theory, and certainly without much anxiety or concern for the origins of the theoretical apparatus deployed. Indeed, scholarship in comparative politics has tended to be 'problem-driven', seeking a range of case-studies from around the world in order to test the universal applicability of a mainstream hypothesis and received problems. Hence, scholars of comparative politics have tended to view theories and methods (often rather eclectically) as tools to help them frame and explain accepted empirical problems (Kohli, 1996). A great deal of the literature is concerned with understanding the conditions under which categories from Western political theory become visible, stable, or viable in places where those categories may not have long-established intellectual histories: Under what conditions can democracy emerge and flourish? What are the necessary conditions for the formation of a modern nation state? The implications of this approach are that 'democracy' and 'nation state' are (or should be) universal categories.

In other words, comparative politics is often comparative in the simplest (and sometimes most violent) sense: it identifies 'comparable' (i.e. similar) data sets and then uses them to validate its starting assumptions. For those critical of this enterprise, comparative politics works in collusion with a form of politically co-opted 'Area Studies' (as institutionalized in the USA after the Second World War) to reduce the 'non-Western' into objects of study for the so-called West, denying the vast majority of the globe its subjectivity and positing it as only a source of data (for the West to analyse in its own terms) and not of innovation or theory (Dutton, 2002; Sakai & Harootunian, 1999). This critique is often tied to opposition against the implicit ethnocentrism of '**modernization theory**', which posits the gradual convergence of all societies around the modern state form of the West and seems to deny the possibility of viable politico-theoretical models that diverge from those of the West.

In more recent years, especially since the end of the Cold War, the ethical dilemmas associated with asserting this kind of theoretical **universalism** have become increasingly difficult to ignore. The liberal triumphalism of the 1990s that led some to proclaim the 'end of history' (Fukuyama, 1992) quickly gave way to an anxious kind of pluralism, as numerous nations began to assert not only their political autonomy, but also their cultural and philosophical traditions. The neat European project of modernity, captured most powerfully by Kant in the idea of a universal and relentless progression towards the ideal republic or cosmopolis—the perfect political organization in which the rational laws of nature (*cosmos*) were in accord with the laws of society (*polis*)—seemed to be unravelling. The relationship between power and this model was revealed as undeniable— the modernity project began to look like an ideology (Latham, 2000)—and, hence, its lauded 'naturalness' was radically challenged.

For some commentators at the turn of the millennium, world politics was being played out in terms of a clash of religious world views—modernity's faith in progressive seculari- zation seemed to have been overthrown (Huntington, 1996). An implication of this was that the field of political thought was recovering the domain of metaphysics, an arena of philosophy that it had self-consciously rejected during the **Enlightenment**. World politics became a pluralistic space of multiple world views and alternative cosmologies— this was the so-called 'politics of uncertainty'. Political thinkers recovered the idea of *cos- mopolitics* to talk about the political stakes involved in the mediation of these competing metaphysical visions (Cheah & Robbins, 1998). Perhaps for the first time, CPT started to appear on the agendas of political thinkers, commentators and even policy-makers. The most high-profile example, especially after 11 September 2001, was the case of Islamic fundamentalism, and a series of important works about Islam have moved perceptions of CPT towards comparative religion (March, 2009b; Euben, 1999). However, also on the agenda in the USA and Europe was the question of the political, ideological, and even cos- mological principles at work in the rapidly maturing Russian Federation and the People's Republic of China. Liberal capitalism no longer seemed natural, inevitable, or progressive for the whole world, and comparative politics could no longer be naive about the political and ethical content of its theoretical and methodological apparatus.

Whilst this story goes some way towards explaining how CPT has recently found its way onto the agendas of more mainstream and conventional research programmes and interest groups, it is important to reflect that this is itself a story of 'Western' political manoeuvring: CPT now begins to look *useful*, in so far as it is focused on attempts to understand (and mitigate against) genuine (or dangerous) political difference in the con- temporary world. However, CPT need not be directed so instrumentally. Indeed, there is a powerful ethical argument to be made regarding the *need* for CPT as a way of confront- ing the parochialism or ethnocentrism of the academic field of political thought (and especially the history of political thought).

In other words, if scholars who profess to be interested in the history of political ideas are not interested in the shape and logic of such ideas outside of the West, then their claims to be interested in political thought per se are disingenuously Eurocentric; what really interests them is a narration of the development of the 'imagined community' of the West via a history of the political concepts that chartered its course. Political thought becomes a sub-field of transatlantic history. If there is a case for the inclusion of the non-European (which I take to be undeniable), then there is also a case to be made for re-labelling nearly every textbook ever written on political thought as 'non-comparative political thought' or simply 'European political thought', although such labels will also be problematic. Consider the classic work by Quentin Skinner, *The Foundations of Modern*

Political Thought (1978), or even the recent volume that revisited its influence and importance, *Rethinking the Foundations of Modern Political Thought* (Brett & Tully, 2006), which makes no mention of any non-European thinkers, but which consciously identifies itself without a geocultural referent. That is, Europe quietly claims universalism—or, perhaps, claims it with such unembarrassed volume that nowhere else can be heard.

12.3 **The politics *of* comparative political thought**

Given that it seems to be almost impossible to make an ethically respectable case for the exclusion of most of the planet from the field of political thought, how is it possible that European political thought can still pretend to be universal, and why is CPT not the dominant trend in the field? For what reasons do political theorists tend to be happy to embrace an anxious oblivion about the notion that peoples outside of Europe have thought about politics in a manner rigorous enough to be called 'political theory'?

One of the reasons has to do with the institutional make-up of the academy in Europe and the USA, where the study of the so-called 'non-Western' has tended to be ghettoized into 'Area Studies' departments and, hence, structurally divorced from the mainstream disciplines, such as political theory. The hegemony of history (and culture) in the various regional sub-fields of Area Studies makes those fields relatively unreceptive to inquiries that are not orientated towards characterizing the areas themselves. That is, scholars in Area Studies may be interested in reading, say, Chinese or Islamic political thought (to cite two non-commensurable categories: a national and a **transnational** tradition), but their main agenda may be to understand what such intellectual traditions tell us about China or Islam, rather than about how this thought can contribute to the discipline of political thought per se.

For a number of influential critics, one of the major problems with Area Studies (that allies with its bias towards instrumentalizing all objects of inquiry into cultural artefacts) is its linguistic fetishism. That is, the faith that acquiring a non-European language, by itself, enables scholars to access and interrogate any kind of material in that language, or the faith that multilingualism is the holy grail of comparative studies, rather than simply part of a box of useful tools that also includes *theories and methods* for interrogation of both original texts and translations (Chow, 2006). In fact, such faith mistakes a *necessary* condition for a *sufficient* one: whilst it is obviously *necessary* for anyone interested in the contribution of, say, Tibetan political thought to be able to read Tibetan texts, it is *also* necessary that such a scholar is theoretically and methodologically prepared to deal with (or even identify) political ideas when they find them. Language is not perfectly transparent and the field of Area Studies, particularly in its more **Orientalist** forms, often faces charges of theoretical and political naivety (or even offensiveness) because of its failure to recognize this. Even worse, the most extreme criticism of Area Studies along these lines is that practitioners are really seeking to *become* their subject matter. Attempts to theorize the politics of translation have been important in confronting this charge (Sakai, 1997).

The tendency for political theorists to ignore the non-European, and the tendency for Area Studies specialists to ignore questions of grand theory, might be seen as mutually reinforcing. Because much of the work that moves towards political thought in Area Studies is conducted by linguists, philologists, or cultural historians, the field of political theory can argue that the regions in question *might* contain thinking about politics, *but* that the representations of these ideas in Area Studies fail to make them recognizable as political theory; conversely, then, scholars in Area Studies have their suspicions about the Eurocentricity of political theory confirmed. The result is mutually agreed isolation, premised on (not unjustified) insecurities on both sides. Some branches of political theory, such as post-structuralism and post-colonialism, are able to engage with this complicated politics of knowledge. However, the mainstream of the history of political thought begins to look like a type of (European) Area Studies itself.

See Chapters 3 and 11.

In some ways, this situation simply reflects the ways in which knowledge is organized and territorialized in universities, and this dilemma represents an implicit call for some kind of educational reform. However, the recognition of the need for reform is, of course, not the same as having a plan for that reform! One thing that seems to characterize the fledgling field of CPT is the tendency to stop at *criticism* of the status quo and not to take the next step into *critique*. That is, there is a clear passion (almost a moral righteousness) in the calls for political theory to open its doors to the non-European, and the ridiculousness of keeping these doors closed is now so blatant that it has become offensive. Unfortunately, as we have seen, the imperfect and often unconvincing attack from Area Studies is not even the attack of David against Goliath (the institutionally peripheral against the central); it lacks the menacing threat and overwhelming power of, say, Commodore Perry's 'black ships' that forced Japan to open its doors to the West (and Western political thought) in the 1850s. However, a single well-placed stone—let's call it the unequivocal charge of parochialism—felled Goliath, and we all know that this was the morally correct result.

For a discussion of the subaltern, see Chapter 11.

However, there is an ethical trap waiting to be sprung here: to say that it is correct that Goliath be felled, or that political theory must open its doors to the non-European, is not at all the same thing as saying that *what comes next is better*. There is an often unspoken missionary element in CPT that seeks not only to make the field inclusive, but actually to *convert*. However, it is not the case that the **subaltern** is always *right*, even if there is an ethical imperative that the subaltern be heard. The confusion of these different assertions can lead into dangerous territories: in order to see the value of their ideas as concepts within political theory, it is not necessary to believe (for instance) that the wartime Japanese Kyoto School's vision of a political system, in which individuals and the state exist in a condition of mutual and absolute self-contradiction, is *better* than liberal democracy (and, hence, that the world would be a better place if Japan had won the Second World War). Such a belief represents a kind of *tenkô* (a Japanese term meaning political/ideological conversion), rather than an engagement in political theory per se. Unfortunately, however, this kind of morally righteous *tenkô* is not uncommon in Area Studies, where a subtext of *becoming* and of *representation* has cast a long shadow. One of the issues with this kind of affective relationship between scholar and material is that it encourages the field to set different critical standards for the interrogation of the material: criticism should be as free, unsentimental and respectful whether the material is 'non-Western' or not.

In the end, it seems possible that the key might be to de-privilege regional appellations altogether, rather than to emphasize them, otherwise the spectres of nationalism, patriotism, fundamentalism, and identity politics seem to warp and swamp everything. Different national or religious traditions should be the occasion, not the focus, of comparative political thought: the focus should be on conceptions of the political, and the geocultural–linguistic–historical location of these conceptions is relevant only to the extent that their context constitutes an aspect of their meaning (the debate on context and meaning in the history of ideas is sophisticated and rich). One might fantasize about a fictional textbook on the history of political thought that deliberately eschews all references to the place or origination of the ideas it discusses. However, in this fictional case, has not the term 'comparative' effectively vanished? Or is there another sense of its meaning that can be preserved?

12.4 What is comparative political thought?

One of the most immediate problems for CPT concerns the meaning and function of the term 'comparative'. As we have seen, this term is generally considered to function as a kind of geocultural 'expander', encouraging the field of political thought to look out beyond the boundaries of the European for sources of theoretical insight. Of course, such a mode immediately pushes the field into some dangerous ethical territory, since it risks establishing itself in terms of the (imperial) expansion of Europe. Resolution of this issue, to which we will return later, hinges at least partially on the specific ways in which the idea of comparison is deployed. Unfortunately, in the words of Rey Chow, comparison is a 'historically over-determined problematic' (Chow, 2006, p. 72). In particular, it is often utilized in ways that render it functionally indistinguishable from allied terms such as 'global', 'international', 'cross-cultural', or more recently 'transnational'. In other words, 'comparison' is frequently used to signify an approach that seeks the transcendence of narrowly nationalistic or even regional perspectives, what Fred Dallmayr (1999) calls 'planetary political thought' or Roland Bleiker (2004) 'global dialogue'.

   This inclusive usage of 'comparative' is commonplace despite the clear (and logically necessary) process of separation and distancing of the 'other' that is required in order to juxtapose two or more artefacts or ideas. In order to compare two entities, you have to start by asserting their separateness, which risks *generating* (rather than dissolving) a 'them' and 'us' outlook. In some ways, the dominant move towards reading 'comparative' as 'inclusive' appears to be an attempt to avoid the ethical and political problems of alienation that juxtaposition necessarily brings. Nonetheless, the tension between inclusion and distancing is an essential anxiety in the field.

   Allied to this problem of distancing is the notion that the project of comparative political thought is to compare a series of peripheral Others with a central, established column of European political theory. In other words, if we are going to take comparison seriously, then it must also operate between those Others (perhaps even to the exclusion of the West) since it is conceivable that there are conceptions of the political that are shared in various traditions, but that are entirely absent (or relatively insignificant) in the West. Such conceptions should not be ignored merely because they cannot be related back to European political theory. It may transpire that the West is actually rather peripheral to many interesting and important concepts and discussions. In the case of Japan, for example, there is a long and well-established tradition of comparative political thought centred around Confucian and Buddhist concepts that are shared and contested between the various national traditions of East Asia.

The inclusive sense of the purpose of comparison owes a great deal to the field of comparative literature, which arguably finds its origins in the German writer Johann Wolfgang Goethe's influential concept of *Weltliteratur* (world literature). In this case, the meaning establishes a trajectory towards a grand utopian vision of global synthesis or underlying commonality. It is explicitly a universalist vision, in which the particularities of specific national traditions are *both* embraced for their own sakes *and* seen together as parts of a transcendent whole. In many ways, this contagious vision of world literature has been an attempt to overcome the boundary-marking salience of political borders and linguistic traditions.

Like CPT, comparative literature is a broad and loosely organized field. It benefits from the existence of a series of 'classic' texts, such as *Theory of Literature* (Wellek & Warren, 1984), which CPT cannot claim. Indeed, scholars of comparative political thought are poorly served when it comes to key texts that can function as focal points for the theoretical and methodological issues of the field. As a result, some of the most interesting and innovative work in this mode has drawn on literary theory for its inspiration and method. Whilst there are good reasons for this interdisciplinary move, the embrace of literary theory as the basis of CPT has not been widely accepted in the mainstream of the discipline of political theory, where there remains a form of allergy regarding the blurring of the boundaries between politics and art. One consequence of this is a form of resistance against CPT as insufficiently informed by political theory itself, locating it instead as a branch of literature (or cultural studies).

To some extent, this strategy of denial parallels that employed against Area Studies more generally, whereby the insights garnered into non-Western political ideas from these fields are denigrated by the mainstream as lacking the necessary rigour to really impact political theory. In the most chauvinistic versions of this denial, the reliance on this kind of interdisciplinarity demonstrates not only that extra-European political thought is inadequately studied, but also that the cultures under analysis simply have no political theory worthy of the name. The retort, of course, increasingly popular in any number of fields, is that interdisciplinarity is an essential feature of the enterprise— indeed, that rigid disciplinarity is an artefact of the intellectual climate and socio-political circumstances of nineteenth-century Europe.

Nonetheless, the problem of the method or practice of 'comparison' itself is seldom considered in a rigorous or critical manner in the literature, and it is rarely pushed beyond a rather fluffy sense of inclusivity. As Chow puts it:

More often than not, it is assumed that comparison occurs as a matter of course whenever we juxtapose two (or more) national languages and literatures, geographical regions, authors, or themes, and rarely do critics stop and ponder what the gesture of comparison consists in, amounts to, indeed realizes and reinforces. (2006, p. 72)

As we will see, part of the problem for political theory in this respect is the difficulty of identifying units or even categories appropriate for comparison. A classic formulation of the problem is Michel Foucault's *The Order of Things* (1970), in which he documents the ways in which the classifications, categories and organizational units of knowledge in the Western academy have developed and, in the process, the 'common ground that once existed among things has purportedly become lost'. Evidently, Foucault's influential study was inspired by his encounter with the 'Chinese encyclopaedia' of Jorge Luis Borges, 'in which all the familiar landmarks and connections of Western thought are disturbed and threatened with collapse' (Chow, 2006, pp. 75–6). The crucial point for us here is the way in which Foucault highlights the contingency of the categories of knowledge that have been (mistakenly) taken as natural in European disciplines, and simultaneously points to the way in which recognition of this contingency could be perceived as threatening and dangerous to the foundations of those disciplines.

On Foucault, see Chapter 3.

From this we must understand that the project of CPT requires a willingness to abandon at least some of the concepts and categories that have defined the disciplinary highways of political theory in Europe—should we really be looking for the state, for rights, for democracy, or even for the nation? Or are there other concepts that may be more useful, for which Europe developed no terms and, hence, for which it does not even know how to look? This implies that we must be willing to read Europe back through a comparative lens and refashion our understanding of its political ideas in new terms—in terms unfamiliar to the traditional canon of political theory. It also implies, however, a chronic methodological dilemma: if we detach comparative political thought from conventional, European understandings of the parameters of the political, what are we actually going to look at? Does not the term 'political' vanish this time?

Accepting the necessarily de-centred foundations of comparison raises a host of other problems, not least because this acceptance appears to be the rejection of foundations altogether. In other words, our inquiries become doubly untethered: if we explore the intellectual traditions of (say) Japan and discover nothing that appears to be a recognizable conception of the political, must we conclude that Japan lacks political thought or that our functional conception of the political is flawed? (Perhaps surprisingly, both of these positions have been forcefully argued in the literature on Japanese intellectual history.) If the latter, then we must balance the possible gains of rendering the political as radically elastic against the risk of it suddenly loosing shape altogether. The alternative appears to be recourse to a kind of quasi-mystical, universal foundation to all things (which may be common to all but is finally explicit and knowable to none), of the kind intimated by the German philosopher Martin Heidegger (1982) in his *Dialogue on Language Between a Japanese and an Inquirer*. This option allows us to ground the political in a universal, but obstructs us from being able to talk about it in anything other than contingent terms (Goto-Jones, 2005a).

12.5 Comparability in comparative political thought

Even if and when we become comfortable with the contours of the problem of the process of comparison, the question of where and how to find comparable entities becomes significant. In practice, it seems that most work in comparative political thought takes this vital step for granted. That is, especially as they emerge from Area Studies, projects tend to *begin* with an intuition about the political importance of the ideas of, say, Gandhi or Confucianism (to cite two incommensurable categories: an individual and a tradition), and *then* lead on to an exposition of how or why they are important in practice. Comparison is then asserted as the most appropriate mode in which to consider their political thought.

To some extent, of course, this moment of intuition is vital to all scholarly endeavours. However, in this case it also serves to leap-frog a vital stage in the development of a methodology for CPT. What is skipped here is a system for understanding *who* might constitute a political thinker in a range of different places and times, and *what* might constitute political theory in a range of different conceptual schemas and even media.

With regard to the question of 'who', under what conditions are so-called 'religious' thinkers to be included? Should we consider artists or poets? Must the thinker be a public intellectual and, hence, a political actor, or are social recluses included? Can we consider groups or movements or even traditions, as well as individuals? In other words, what constitutes a comparable 'whom', and when are these agents actually incomparable? Is it really appropriate or sensible, for instance, to compare Kant with Confucianism or Nietzsche with Zen, both of which are surprisingly common? Can individual European thinkers really be compared with elaborate and diverse intellectual and spiritual traditions with hundreds or thousands of years of debate behind them?

One of the many dangers here is simply vulgarity: the assertion that 'Zen' contains a coherent political theory is silly, since Zen is a broad tradition containing a range of debates and problematics in the sphere of politics and ethics, not an identifiable or singular unit of knowledge. When we attempt to compare Nietzsche with Zen, whom do we take to represent Zen, and which texts do we look at and why? Zen as a whole has no voice or conceptual integrity. In other words, making this kind of comparison appears to be a mistake grounded in an ignorance of the incommensurability of the categories cited; this may simply reflect a merely passing acquaintance with Zen. In terms of the politics of knowledge, this move looks like a kind of violence that denigrates Zen by reducing it to a vulgar (mis)representation. Why not compare Nietzsche and a particular thinker in the Zen tradition, say, Dôgen? Interestingly, when we read comparative texts from the modernizing period in Asia, we sometimes see the same category mistake in reverse, where, say K'ang Yu-wei is compared with (Western) philosophy as a whole or Gandhi is compared with Christianity.

There are similar issues with regard to the question of 'what' can constitute a comparable political idea. Are we looking for ideas and concepts that already resemble those with which we are familiar, such as approximations of the notion of democracy or statehood? Or, if this is our quest, are we simply imposing 'our' political schema on another and ignoring the possibility that there are really different concepts in different contexts—is this merely a process of violence through translation? Interestingly, we see this process in reverse in nineteenth-century China and Japan (and elsewhere), as political thinkers sought to 'assimilate' ideas and concepts from the European tradition by associating them with familiar terms in Chinese or Japanese that seemed to best approximate their meanings (Howland, 2002). This raises an interesting question for us about the boundaries (if we recognize them) between comparison and assimilation.

If we are not looking for other words for or elaborations of political ideas we already have, for what are we looking? Are religious ideas permissible and, if so, under what conditions? When (and where) does metaphysics become interesting for a political theorist? Here we are probing the frontiers of the concept of the political itself: once the 'political' is untethered from the universal aspirations of European categories, how can 'we' be sure that we will know where to look for it or that we will even recognize it when we see it?

More practically: when we are looking for political ideas outside of the European tradition, what kinds of sources should we be looking at? Is political theory always written in the form of an extended philosophical treatise? Should we also be looking at poetry, art, graphics, music, games, or new types of techno-political media (Bleiker, 2001)? Is the technology of political thought culturally determined or universal? Even if these technologies are universal, do we need to be open to the possibility that the treatise is not the only (or even the major) technology and, hence, that we should consider whether alternative media hold important expressive potentials for political ideas that a more 'conventional' treatise cannot express? Hence, should comparison function inter-medially, as well as internationally? Here, we are probing the frontiers of the types of literacies required for different technologies of political theory that may be found in different places at different times (or even in the same places at the same time).

12.6 **Comparison, origination, and discontinuity**

The most obvious and frequent candidates as targets of CPT are thinkers from outside of Europe who are recognizably engaged in the enterprise of philosophy, political theory, or perhaps are simply politically engaged public intellectuals. In practice, of course, there is already a politics of familiarization at play in these kinds of categories, as the comparison here strives to interpret 'comparable' as 'similar', or at least as 'functionally equivalent'.

Whilst this strategy is commendably straightforward, it raises a number of additional problems for the dimensions and meaning of CPT. The most immediate issue concerns modernity. That is, it is often the case that thinkers who fall into this category of comparability, such as the Kyoto School of Philosophy in early twentieth-century Japan, are those who are self-consciously engaging with texts, ideas, and thinkers from Europe as part of an explicit process of national modernization in the face of Western power. In other words, there is an argument to be made that 'we' recognize the Kyoto School as political philosophers not necessarily because of anything 'Japanese' about their ideas, but rather because of the way that their work actually engages with mainstream ideas, concepts, and debates from the European history of political thought. In many respects, they were engaged in political philosophy *in Japan*, not necessarily *Japanese* political philosophy (Goto-Jones, 2005b).

If this argument holds water (and I do not claim to defend it here), then we must ask the question: what is comparative about analysing the Kyoto School? Or, to phrase this question more provocatively: why is it *comparative political thought* when we read the Kyoto

On the Frankfurt School, see Chapter 2.

School and just *political thought* when we read the Frankfurt School? Unless we default to the position that 'political thought' is code for European political thought, in order for the answer to this question to be ethically acceptable we must be able to say something other than 'because the Kyoto School was Japanese'.

In fact, in this concrete case, there are good reasons why the Kyoto School does require the comparative qualification, but these reasons have little to do with Japanese-ness, whatever that might be. However, for now it is important to note how the myth of origination—i.e. that CPT should be primarily about the non-Western—continues to be contagious and powerful in the ascription of 'comparative' to political thought, at least intuitively. The problems of this become even more obvious when we consider the international mobility of scholars, thinkers, and political figures in the modern world—what precisely is it about a thinker that pushes them out of mainstream political thought and into comparative political thought? Is it about names, ethnicities, education, interests, religious affinities, citizenship, or even gender? More than anything, in practice, the issue appears to be the language in which a thinker writes—if they write in a non-European language, then they must be 'compared' to people who write in European languages. We have already seen the potential effects of an emphasis on multilingualism in the politics of knowledge, and also the insidiousness of the idea of a European core against which all political notions should be compared.

In other words, the notion of comparison as tied to origination forces us to think along these problematic and muddled lines, and it seems to be a mistake, or at least not *necessarily* helpful. This is in addition to our earlier concern to ensure that CPT (if it is to be part of political theory rather than Area Studies) should be concerned with political ideas per se and not in itself a lens for the characterization of different cultures.

One way in which this emphasis on origination does open up new avenues for CPT, however, is by revealing that 'comparison' does not designate absolute categories. Indeed, there appear to be 'degrees of comparitivity'. We might pose the question: *to what extent* is it necessary to interrogate the politics of, say, the Kyoto School of philosophy from a comparative standpoint? Comparison becomes a continuum, with a spectrum of possible proximities stretched between things that are radically different and those that are actually similar, and the decision to deploy it becomes both more sophisticated and more political as awareness of this increases.

Hence, rather than between units of differing origination, it is possible that comparison really functions most meaningfully across spaces of distance that we might call *discontinuities*. Of course, the embrace of the discontinuous in the history of philosophy is often associated with Foucault, who famously criticized the disciplines of history and philosophy for what he took to be their reliance on continuities. Indeed, he talks about 'a particular repugnance to conceiving of difference, to describing separations and dispersions, to dissociating the reassuring form of the identical' (Foucault, 1972, p. 12). He argues forcefully that the discontinuous should be recovered as a means of innovative inquiry. To be clear, he does not advocate the abandonment of continuities: they 'must not be rejected definitively of course, but the tranquility with which they are accepted must be disturbed' (Foucault, 1972, p. 25).

In recent years there has been 'an increasing emphasis on the instructive value to be derived from the discontinuities in the history of ideas' (Runciman, 2001, p. 90). In the words of Charles Taylor, the quest for these discontinuities requires 'recovering previous articulations which have been lost' (Taylor, 1984, p. 18). David Runciman concurs that these discontinuities represent 'the discarded options in the history of political thought, the forgotten periods during which people in whom we can recognize something of ourselves construed the predicament in which they found themselves quite differently from the way we construe ours' (Runciman, 2001, p. 90).

If it is true that the idea of discontinuity can help us understand some working parameters for the enterprise of CPT, then one of the issues for us is to what this term might refer to in practice. On the most intuitive level, it appears to correspond merely to difference. However, if this were the case then *all* philosophy or political thought would be comparative, which would make the term meaningless. For Taylor there are two important ways in which a philosopher can be innovative: the first is within the dominant philosophical schema of the day (he suggests that in the modern period this should be characterized as the 'epistemological model', following Descartes), while the second is outside this hegemonic system—it is a discontinuity. Taylor is clear that it is the latter type of innovation that marks out the greatest and most significant thinkers—he cites Hegel and Heidegger as examples in modern times.

Whilst this sense of the discontinuous might seem to provide an excellent opportunity for the comparative project, since it sets out some theoretically coherent parameters to define the borders across which comparison might meaningfully occur, in practice the literature acts quickly to cut off the possibility that the 'discontinuous' and the 'non-European' might (also) coincide. Taylor, for instance, is clear that the kind of discontinuities in which historians of political thought should be interested lie *within* European history, rather than without it. He states quite emphatically that immersion in the European tradition (i.e. a knowledge of the history of European philosophy) is *necessary* for innovation of this second, discontinuous type; without such a grounding in the history of philosophy, new ideas (no matter how innovative they may seem) are not *discontinuous*, but merely *disconnected* (Taylor, 1984, p. 18). In other words, Taylor's sense of discontinuity requires (or privileges) an existing, continuous and essentially static historical narrative from which the discontinuity can diverge. The existing (European) narrative itself is assumed and actually reinforced rather than challenged. I imagine that Foucault would find this a fascinating example of the persistence of a 'repugnance' for discontinuity camouflaged under its apparent embrace.

However, Taylor is certainly not alone in this interpretation, indeed it defines the mainstream of the history of political thought. For example, Lorenz Krüger utilizes the same meaning of 'discontinuity' to explain the innovations of Heidegger, who searched back through the history of (European) philosophy in his quest to find thinkers who could support his endeavours to overthrow the conventions of Western metaphysics. Krüger stresses the importance of Heidegger's immersion in the history of philosophy (in Europe), arguing that it is only there that genuine 'discontinuities' can be found. This is why Heidegger 'does not turn to extra-scientific wisdom of just any kind, say Buddhism, but to the Pre-Socratics' (Krüger, 1984/90, p. 97).

Leaving aside the question of whether Krüger is actually right about the sources of Heidegger's innovations or whether Heidegger was, in fact, a good example of CPT in action (May, 1996), it is obviously sensible to assert that a thinker will only be aware of the significance of their own discontinuities if they are already aware of the narrative from which they diverge. However, *awareness* of innovation and *innovation* itself are not the same thing.

What is needed here is a realization that there is no category differential (difference in kind) between discontinuities within European history (i.e. those between an apparent Cartesian mainstream and other 'lost' schemas) and discontinuities between the European mainstream and non-European schemas. Calling the former a 'discontinuity' and the latter a 'disconnection' appears to be merely a semantic strategy to defend Eurocentricity. Whilst Krüger and Taylor both attempt to assert the contrary, arguing that issues surrounding language erect an insurmountable barrier between 'East and West' in philosophy that leaves us 'without the remotest idea how even to go about arbitrating' between them (Taylor, 1984, p. 30), such an argument is distasteful and unconvincing. Indeed, it is a clear example of the prejudice against non-European languages, and of the confusion of linguistic difference for theoretical difference, which we have already seen. The refusal to see the non-European as *either* communicable with the mainstream of political thought *or* as instances of creative discontinuity amounts to a refusal to see it at all.

To return to our running example: the 'Japanese' Kyoto School of philosophy is a historical example of how the problem of European and non-European languages do not represent an insurmountable barrier for politico-philosophical dialogue. Indeed, this interesting school manages to engage simultaneously with apparently 'disconnected' political ideas drawn from German idealism, Neo-Confucianism from China, and various forms of Buddhism as developed in Japanese history. In other words, the Kyoto School is a good example of a body of work that genuinely attempts to incorporate political ideas from across discontinuities (which are also across national boundaries in this case). It demonstrates that the assertion of a category difference between a discontinuity and a disconnection is false. Kyoto philosophers learnt German, French, and English, as well as Chinese and Japanese in order to be able to read texts in the originals and, hence, pursue their project of bringing discontinuous ethical and political ideas into dialogue with each other. Multilingualism here was simply a tool.

This brings us back to the illustrative question of whether studying the Kyoto School should constitute 'comparative' political thought. Or rather, it rejuvenates the question of the *extent to which* the comparative method is appropriate to the study of the political thought of the Kyoto School. Leaving aside the question of linguistic difference—on the basis that multilingualism is possible and even common, and also noting that translation mitigates against this issue—and also the question of origination per se, the question begins to revolve around the extent to which the Kyoto School represents a discontinuity with 'our' political ideas (whomever we are—and our identity literally takes a central place here). That is, is there a substantial, theoretical boundary between 'them' and 'us' across which comparison can or should be made, where 'us' simply means any school that is not the Kyoto School?

A detailed answer to this question is beyond the scope of this chapter. However, we should note the dimensions of a possible answer: are there aspects of the political thought of the Kyoto School, which are not common to the mainstream of political theory (in Europe) and are these aspects so substantially innovative that they constitute discontinuities in Taylor's sense? In my view, we must answer this question in the affirmative, not because the Kyoto School is Japanese but because of the way in which the thinkers of that school draw on texts and ideas about ethics and politics from a range of different intellectual traditions that rest upon radically different cosmological and metaphysical foundations. They are not within the 'epistemological model' of Descartes. As intimated earlier, the return of metaphysics to the field of political thought is one of the conditions of the possibility of comparative political thought, since metaphysical and cosmological differences cut to the root of what is meant by discontinuity. Cosmopolitics and comparative political thought tend towards each other.

Intriguingly, the Kyoto School's own sense of its discontinuity with what it perceived to be a European tradition of thinking about politics was at least in part based on its own apparent willingness to look beyond the national boundaries of its political and philosophical traditions. That is, one of the aspects that might mark the Kyoto School as discontinuous (and, hence, suitable for comparative study), is the way in which its world view was already inclusive of difference. Ironically then, the Kyoto School seems discontinuous to 'us' precisely because it was already engaged in comparative political thought at a time when Europe appeared to be radically nationalized and parochial about the enterprise of political theory (Goto-Jones, 2009). Understandably, this has made the legacy of the Kyoto School highly controversial; its ideas are closely associated with the ideology of Japanese imperialism.

One of the fascinating and potentially useful consequences of this sense of comparison across discontinuities is the way in which it opens up the field to a whole new range of possibilities. Whilst it takes CPT seriously as a distinct category of inquiry, it avoids the ethnocentric temptation to require that 'comparative' refers simply to non-European (in the sense of language, religion, or origination), and it disrupts tendencies towards vulgar generalizations about continuous traditions. Furthermore, it allows that in a globalized world of constant cultural and intellectual interchange and dialogue, some (if not even most) political thought found outside of Europe is not actually sufficiently discontinuous with the mainstream discipline for it to be privileged (or marginalized) and framed comparatively. That is, mainstream political thought itself should already engage with this material, and political theorists should consider the need to learn the necessary languages to do so, just as many find it essential to read German. The other side of this, however, is that 'comparison' may actually be the most appropriate frame through which to view discontinuities *within* the European history of political thought as well as those found outside of Europe. We might argue, for instance, that Heidegger's attempts to escape from the metaphysical traditions of European philosophy make his work so discontinuous with it that the most suitable terms in which to discuss Heidegger are those of comparative philosophy or comparative political thought. Indeed, many of the grandly innovative discontinuities cited earlier by Foucault, Taylor, Runciman, and Krüger might usefully be seen in this way. Discontinuities from outside of the European tradition should be treated no differently.

12.7 Conclusion

In the end, reading 'comparative' in terms of discontinuity rather than origination enables comparative political thought to avoid many of the ethical problems that have tied it to a sense of 'West versus non-West' and also the ways in which an emphasis on origins has pulled the enterprise into the realms of cultural studies. Instead, deploying comparison around discontinuities re-centres the concern on political ideas per se, rather than on places; CPT remains primarily concerned with political thought.

As intimated earlier, it is important to insist that 'discontinuities' are not defined only in terms of their distance from a central column of European experience—'us' is a relative term. The enterprise of CPT *as* the interrogation of discontinuous political ideas exists in the space between any two (or more) discontinuous models, be that between Hegel and Zhu Xi, or between Nishida Kitarô and Nagarjuna, or even between Heidegger and Aquinas. The field is concerned with this type of relationality in general, not necessarily with the relations between Europe and an other in particular.

An implication of this, of course, is that a range of new questions becomes both possible and interesting: *to what extent* is it appropriate to deploy the comparative method when talking about the political ideas of thinkers A and B, where A and B can be from anywhere and 'anywhen' and use any language? The answers to this question may prove to be surprising and productive, even in (and perhaps especially in) unexpected and previously unexplored areas. We might expect that this type of project will reveal a range of discontinuities where we had previously seen continuities and, hence, that the 'tranquillity' with which Foucault accused us of accepting them will be disturbed. The answers are likely also to confirm our earlier suspicion that there are 'degrees of comparitivity' that correspond to 'degrees of discontinuity'. Whilst it is not necessary to conclude by asserting that all political thought is comparative (since there are clearly lines of *continuity* in certain traditions and schools), it seems likely that comparison will become more central to the overall field than in the past.

Perhaps the most radical implication of this schema, however, is that it requires the acknowledgement that both the enterprises of *political thought* and *comparative political thought* should be globally inclusive. Neither can be organized around geocultural blocks or ethnocentric principles of exclusivity. The sense of comparative political thought as a holistic or transnational project inspired by Goethe's *Weltliteratur,* designed to explode the parochialism of political thought itself, is thus left behind. Indeed, this schema takes it as ethically and intellectually *necessary* for both political thought and CPT to be globally inclusive in this way. Instead, the two sub-fields are distinguished methodologically (and non-exclusively), by methods appropriate for the study of continuity in political ideas, on the one hand, and methods appropriate for the study of discontinuity on the other. Vitally, CPT becomes political thought that is conscious of (and engaged in the interrogation of) metaphysical and cosmological issues *as* politics.

To restate this more provocatively: CPT can no longer be used as a way to ease the consciences of ethnocentric political theorists who might feel that the extra-European world need have nothing to do with them because they are engaged in mainstream political thought and not CPT. The world can no longer be displaced or marginalized into 'comparative'; all political thought *needs* (ethically and intellectually) to be conscious of the world.

QUESTIONS

1. Is comparative political thought the same thing as non-Western political thought?

2. Is 'comparative' necessarily the same as 'inclusive'?

3. Is it possible to define the parameters of the 'political' in comparative political thought?

4. What does 'origination' mean, and how does it function to problematize the project of comparative political thought?

5. What is a theoretical discontinuity?

6. What kinds of discontinuities might justify the enterprise of comparative political thought?

7. Under what circumstances is cosmology a political realm?

8. What does it mean for ideas, thinkers, or traditions to be 'comparable'?

9. If the field of political theory were less Eurocentric, would there still be a need for CPT?

10. Is CPT necessarily interdisciplinary?

FURTHER READING

Bell, D. (2000) *East meets West: Human Rights and Democracy in East Asia*. Princeton: Princeton University Press. An influential attempt to bring various thinkers from European and East Asian traditions into conversation with each other in the field of human rights.

Chakrabarty, D. (2000) *Provincializing Europe: Postcolonial Thought and Historical Difference*. Princeton: Princeton University Press. A classic statement of the problems of dislocating Europe from the centre of narratives about world history.

Chow, R. (2006) *The Age of the World Target: Self-Referentiality in War, Theory, and Comparative Work*. Durham: Duke University Press. A provocative analysis of self-referentiality as a core dilemma of the Euro-American condition in the contemporary period, highlighting the politics of engaging with ideas and literatures from outside this grouping.

Dallmayr, F. (1999) *Border-Crossings: Towards a Comparative Political Theory*. Lanham: Lexington Books. A classic exploration of CPT as a global project.

Euben, R. (1999) *Enemy in the Mirror: Islamic Fundamentalism and the Limits of Modern Rationalism*. Princeton: Princeton University Press. An analysis of the ways that Islam represents a powerful discontinuity from 'Western' rationalism.

Goto-Jones, C. (2005) *Political Philosophy in Japan: Nishida, the Kyoto School and Co-Prosperity*. London: Routledge. A reading of the controversial Kyoto School, seeking to integrate its ideas in the mainstream of political theory.

Jung, H.Y. (ed.) (2002) *Comparative Political Culture in Age of Globalization: An Introductory Anthology*. New York: Lexington Books. A wide cross-section of essays on different aspects of comparative political culture and CPT after the end of the cold war.

WEB LINKS

http://sitemason.vanderbilt.edu/psci/ackerly/comparativepoliticaltheory Enables users to sign up to mailing lists for the Comparative Political Thought Listserv, which is a useful source of information on developments and courses in CPT.

http://plato.standford.edu/entries/comparphil-chiwes/ An example of how the comparison of national traditions (in this case, China) might work in comparative philosophy.

http://plato.standford.edu/entries/cosmopolitanism/ An example of how ideas about cosmopolitanism might relate to questions of CPT.

Visit the Online Resource Centre that accompanies this book to access more learning resources: **www.oxfordtextbooks.co.uk/orc/bell_ethics/**

 PART THREE

Issues

13 Human rights

Duncan Ivison

READER'S GUIDE

In this chapter we explore different ways of understanding and justifying human rights. We begin by identifying certain general features about rights and then distinguish human rights from other kinds of rights. We consider different ways of justifying human rights, taking into consideration objections that have been made regarding their purported universality, the coherence and plausibility of human rights claims, and their political value. In the course of this argument we link human rights to a particular conception of *political* agency. We conclude by asking whether, given this account, there is a human right to democracy.

13.1 Introduction

It is tempting to say that the challenge of **human rights** is not whether they exist, but whether they can be enforced—whether they can be made real. Ask most people what human rights are and they can at least give you an idea of what constitutes a *violation* of human rights: unlawful killing, torture, arbitrary detention, denial of religious freedom, forced migration, enforced starvation, or the withdrawal of medical care. People will also, very likely, associate these kinds of harms with the actions of *states*. It is the abuse of political power by government agencies and officials that seems central to the violation of human rights. The great human rights instruments of recent times (the *Universal*

Declaration of Human Rights and the conventions that followed) are seen as attempts to create a moral and legal bulwark against the atrocities that marked the twentieth century. The worst of those atrocities—including the Holocaust, Pol Pot, and the Rwandan genocide—involved horrific abuses of state power, as well as by other powerful political actors.

Human rights enjoy a pre-eminence in global political discourse they have never previously had. They have become integrated into the rhetoric of just about every global institution, from the United Nations (UN) to the World Bank, and have even been embraced by multinational corporations. However, at the same time the record on the ground is mixed. If we live in an age of human rights, then we live also in an age of human rights *abuses*. This might be considered a kind of progress, just insofar as we now at least pay attention to abuses we did not before. However, critics worry that human rights might be worse than ineffective—they might be part of the problem. One criticism is *conceptual inflation*: just because they are so prominent, anything good or desirable is translated into a human right. However, if that's true, then what real work can the concept do? What distinguishes a human rights claim from other kinds of claims, including other kinds of rights and those to do with **distributive justice**? Another problem is *political*; human rights can end up being used in ways that undermine the very ends for which they are said to exist. They depend on states for their realization (for the foreseeable future) and yet states represent one of the greatest threats to human rights. They are meant to provide a basic threshold of decency in world politics and yet they are invoked to justify military aggression, often cloaked as '**humanitarian intervention**'. They are meant to embody the fundamental equality of human beings, and yet they end up empowering the already powerful insofar as they depend on existing (**statist**) legal systems tilted in favour of those with the resources to access (or block) legal remedies.

On humanitarian intervention, see chapter 18.

Hannah Arendt, in a short section of her book *The Orgins of Totalitarianism*, provides a famous discussion of one of the fundamental paradoxes of human rights. In many ways, she inverts the thought expressed at the beginning of this chapter. Her starting point is the seemingly abysmal *failure* of human rights; namely, the situation faced by stateless persons before, during and after the Second World War:

> Not only did the loss of national rights in all instances entail the loss of human rights; the restoration of human rights, as the recent example of the State of Israel proves, has been achieved so far only through the restoration of national rights. The conception of human rights, based on the assumed existence of a human being as such, broke down at the very moment when those who professed to believe in it were for the first time confronted with people who had indeed lost all other qualities and specific relationships—except that they were still human. The world found nothing sacred in the abstract nakedness of being human. (Arendt, 1973, p. 299)

The paradox for Arendt was that to have a human right seemed to require being a member of a state in which one's basic rights were already protected, but human rights are supposed to be possessed by everyone, whether or not they are already members of a liberal society. What the stateless lack is recognition of what she called their 'right to have rights': the right to belong to some kind of organized community. Human rights must surely be related to this notion, she is suggesting. But what underlies this right, and how best to conceive of it?

Arendt's formulation of the problem and her suggestion about the need to articulate a basic 'right to have rights' provides a useful starting point for our discussion of human rights. In what follows I want to address two basic challenges. First, what distinguishes a human right from other kinds of rights claims? What is the relationship between human rights understood as a *moral* claim and as a *legal* or *political* claim (a distinction Arendt is hinting at in the discussion above)? Secondly, what are the political dimensions of human rights? What is the relationship between human rights and the exercise of various relationships of power? We conclude with a brief case study that brings together these two challenges: Is there a human right to democracy? Can you only enjoy human rights if you live in a democratic political system and, if so, what implication does this have for thinking about the realizability of human rights in the world today?

13.2 Human rights and other kinds of rights

Rights can be distinguished from other kinds of claims—like claims about moral validity per se—in two ways. First, when we say that someone's rights have been violated, we are usually referring to the fact that they have been *wronged* in some specific sense. It's not just that it's too bad, but that some particular kind of wrong has occurred. If someone has a right then they have a *claim* against someone (or institution) and it should be enforceable. This means that rights are closely related to duties and obligations. Philosophers refer to this as the *co-relativity* of rights and duties.[1]

Two general ways of making sense of rights are the '**interest**' and '**choice**' accounts (Hart, 1984; Raz, 1986). On the choice account, a right refers to an uncontested domain of choice or sovereignty on the part of the individual. To be a rights holder is to have control over the duty in question, and be able to demand or waive its performance. For example, if I have a right to walk unimpeded across your land, then you have a correlative duty not to interfere with my progress. However, I might decide not to 'stand' on my right and thereby waive the requirement that you perform your duty. I might do so because we are neighbours and I know you are trying to protect it from over-use. Or we might have come to an agreement about using another footpath. The basic idea, however, is that I have a choice over the matter; I can exercise some degree of sovereignty over my actions. The choice account ties rights closely to the notion of **autonomy** and thus to a powerful vision of liberal political thought. According to the interest account, on the other hand, rights refer to certain important interests I have. To say I have a right to X is to say that others have a duty to perform some act (or forbear from acting) that promotes or protects my interests. Of course, those interests have to be sufficiently weighty to impose the kinds of duties we think follow from a rights claim and, here, the debate is joined. The argument between defenders of these two approaches is ongoing and complex. However, what both approaches make clear is that rights have to be *justified*. In claiming a right I must be claiming something others have good reason to accept they are under a duty to protect or promote. Declaring something a right does not, on its own, transform it into one.

---

[1] The analysis of the correlativity of rights and duties has spawned an extensive philosophical literature. The classic discussion is by Hohfeld (1978).

The link between rights and the harms people suffer is especially important when thinking about human rights. The kind of harms that trigger this co-relation are, as I suggested above, usually associated with the abuse of power: torture, mass killing, racial discrimination, religious persecution, arbitrary detention, etc. These are the kinds of harms that we link almost automatically to the language of human rights. These are also the kinds of harms often inflicted by states and their agencies, but not only them. Non-state actors are capable of violating people's rights too. Moreover, states are also needed to *protect* human rights, by providing the legal and political infrastructure to make them real. Here, we arrive at an uncomfortable truth about the relationship between rights—and especially human rights—and states. States are both part of the problem and part of the solution. The exercise of political power, however worthy the intention lying behind it, is always connected to the potential use of force and violence.[2]

This leads to another aspect of rights claims. Claims about rights are (or at least should be) oriented towards institutional embodiment and enforceability. We want rights to be *enforceable* claims, and this is only possible in some kind of political community. If I have a right to something, then I have an entitlement, and that entitlement imposes obligations on others. However, to realize my entitlement, the claim has to be enforceable in some way—not necessarily immediately, but in some foreseeable, plausible future. This is true of both positive and negative rights. A negative right is a right to non-interference. Property rights are often conceived of in this way: I have a right not to be disturbed in the enjoyment of my property. A positive right, on the other hand, is a right of access to some good that others have a duty to provide me. Socio-economic rights are often understood along these lines. A right to employment, for example, involves a claim for access to employment that the state (among others) has a duty to provide. However, ambiguity abounds in distinctions between negative and positive rights. A negative right often requires not only that others *forbear* from acting, but also that such forbearance is likely to be forthcoming. This may well require all manner of positive action, such as providing an effective rule of law and the means to enforce property rights (Shue, 1996; Holmes & Sunstein, 1999).

Another important distinction is between *moral* and *legal* rights. There is a long and complex history lying behind the idea of 'subjective rights'—that is, the notion of what we think of today as 'individual rights' (Tuck, 1979; Brett, 1997). However, the basic idea is that individuals are said to have certain rights in virtue of their possession of a set of inherent qualities, faculties, or powers; whether it is the 'fact' that they are God's children, or because they are sentient, use language, exercise reason, are equally vulnerable to certain harms, or possess 'dignity'. To have a right, in this sense, is to have a claim that is *prior* to any actually existing legal, cultural, or political system of enforcement. Indeed, such rights are meant to serve as an external threshold against which any legal or political system ought to be measured (this raises an interesting question about the nature of **legitimacy**, which we shall touch on below).

So moral rights are valid in virtue of the moral claims underlying them. Legal rights are valid to the extent that there is a legal system in existence that is legitimate and capable of enforcing them. The problem with moral rights, of course, is that there is enormous

---

[2] For a broader discussion of the relationship between rights and power see Ivison (2008).

disagreement about what morality entails. It has proven difficult to specify exactly which properties or qualities human beings are said to have in virtue of which moral rights should be ascribed. On the other hand, if we suppose that all rights are legal rights—or at least, that the only rights worth talking about are legal rights—then it is hard to make sense of the critical use of rights talk, and especially human rights. For some critics this is a perfectly acceptable price to pay, especially given the conceptual inflation they associate with the rise of human rights discourse (Geuss, 2001). However, for others the price is too high. For them moral rights are indeed genuine rights, even if not immediately enforceable. At the very least, people have rights *claims*, which serve as a critical threshold against which to judge the exercise of political power. So we say that the human rights of refugees living in dreadful conditions in refugee camps are being violated, even if we know that the governments responsible for their plight are unwilling to help and the 'international community' is impotent, because to say otherwise is to deny the fundamental autonomy and dignity of those refugees. We say it because we mean it as a criticism of those governments' impotence and as a means of spurring action. However, it also means accepting that there is probably no single philosophical 'foundation' for human rights claims. There are different ways of justifying human rights, some of which may overlap, but not always or necessarily.

So the challenge of justifying and specifying the relevant features of individuals or groups to which *human* rights refer is a significant one. There is extensive disagreement not only among philosophers about these kinds of questions—between Kantians and **utilitarians**, contractualists and moral realists, etc.—but among the rest of society too, and between different societies. So one strategy has been to try and narrow the range of possible things to which human rights can refer. This make them akin to what philosophers like John Locke called '**natural rights**': those basic rights to life and liberty that are ascribable in virtue of certain features common to all human beings. However, if we turn to the *Universal Declaration of Human Rights* (1948), or the various conventions and treaties that followed, we find appeals to a whole range of things that go well beyond natural rights. Article 23, for example, declares that everyone has the right to the free choice of employment, as well as to 'just and favourable conditions of work and to protection against unemployment'. This presupposes a whole range of social, economic, and legal relationships. Work is undoubtedly an important facet of human well-being, the equal access to which we may well want to protect. However, we will not be able to justify a *right* to 'just and favourable conditions' without appealing to a complex social and economic system in order to make sense of to whom the duties for enabling the right apply, and from where the resources required to fulfil it are to be found. So to go down the road of returning human rights to the scope of 'natural rights', we would have to radically revise our standard lists of human rights. James Griffin puts the general challenge this way:

It is not that the term 'human rights' has no content; it just has far too little for it to be playing the central role that it now does in our moral and political life. There are scarcely any accepted criteria, even among philosophers, for when the term is used correctly and when incorrectly. The language of human rights has become seriously debased (Griffin, 2001, p. 306).

However, if the validity of human rights must await agreement on their philosophical foundations, then we will be waiting for a very long time indeed.

This leads to a different, more *political* conception of human rights. According to this view, there is no chance of settling on any one philosophical foundation for human rights or any single mode of justifying them. Instead, there are a multiplicity of possible foundations and justifications, and the crucial task is to discover those that work best given the circumstances particular agents face in appealing to human rights in the first place. Whatever foundations rights have will lie in what works best in making them real for the people who need them most. This also suggests paying close attention to the existing and emerging practice of not only human rights law, but what we might call human rights political practice.

This political conception of human rights is refreshing, but raises some pressing philosophical questions that cannot be evaded. There has to be *some* kind of philosophical core to the human rights we are appealing to, even given the great diversity of circumstances and uses to which they can be put. If the Chinese government can legitimately claim it is protecting people's human rights by locking them up without trial, and yet at the same time Chinese dissidents are appealing to human rights to criticize those actions, then the concept has lost serious critical purchase in global political discourse.

13.3 **What are human rights for?**

Let's work our way backwards, so to speak, in tackling this problem. What do we need a theory of human rights for? One way of making sense of this idea is to see human rights as emerging out of our participation in what we might call the 'global political structure' (Beitz, 1999, 2001; O'Neill, 2000). By this I mean the set of economic and political institutions—including norms, rules, practices, and processes (the World Trade Organization [WTO], North American Free Trade Association [NAFTA], the World Bank, the IMF, the UN, etc.)—that have a profound effect on the quality of life of people everywhere. As Onora O'Neill has argued, we should see our actions, including our participation in and support of our domestic political arrangements, as having causal and institutional consequences for others well beyond our borders (O'Neill, 2000; see also Pogge, 2008). We have a *collective* responsibility for these consequences since none of us, individually, can act effectively to address the inequalities that are generated by our actions.[3] There are some difficult questions here: are these obligations 'thick' or 'thin'? Do they take precedence over other kinds of obligations we may have, including those tied to our membership in particular political communities? I cannot address the detail here, aside from saying that a theory of justice—domestic or global—will most likely be much more demanding than a theory of human rights. A theory of justice articulates an optimal pattern of the distribution of the benefits and burdens within and/or across societies in such a way that each receives their 'due'. What people are 'due' will be determined according to a substantive account of the relevant values (equality, liberty, etc.). A theory of global justice and a theory of human rights can intersect in various ways, but they remain distinct kinds of theories.

 On theories of justice, see Chapters 1 and 14.

---

[3] At the very least, we have a duty *not* to co-operate with those processes that result in the violation of people's human rights. Thomas Pogge mounts an interesting version of this argument in relation to the justification of human rights in order to overcome typical objections about the difficulty of delivering 'positive' (social, economic) as opposed to 'negative' (civil, political) human rights. See Pogge (2008).

Human rights are not simply the product of philosophizing. They have emerged as much from political struggle and activism (between King and Parliament, workers and capitalists, the stateless and states), as any kind of moral consensus (Bobbio, 2000; Ivison, 2008). Modern human rights play a number of different roles in international politics, but perhaps their most general role is in providing a common standard for evaluating the behaviour of states and other powerful political actors with regard to the vital interests of individuals and groups (Beitz, 2001). This becomes clear when we examine existing human rights instruments, such as the *Universal Declaration* and the two accompanying Covenants. In addition to listing basic rights to do with liberty and the rule of law (e.g. Articles 1–14, 18–19), there are provisions associated with the right to 'nationality' (Article 15), the right to 'take part in the government' of their country (Article 21), and social and economic rights (e.g. Articles 22–26). As common standards they do not necessarily resolve disagreement in themselves, but act as a form of global '**public reason**' that disciplines the discussion about what kind of standards should apply in relation to the protection of the vital interests of individuals everywhere (Beitz, 2001; Cohen, 2004b).

Thus, as I suggested above, human rights are not akin to traditional natural rights. The main human rights instruments today contain clauses and articles that presuppose all manner of social institutions and processes that have not existed everywhere across time. They presuppose the existence of separate legal systems, developed economies and the capacity of states to do all kinds of things—like raise revenue, enforce the rule of law and other norms, as well as provide collective goods (Beitz, 2003, p. 43). As our world changes, so too will the kinds of threat we face and, therefore, so too will our list of human rights (Donnelly, 2003; Shue, 1996). It's no surprise, for example, that many are increasingly concerned about the link between environmental degradation (climate change, drought, etc.) and human rights. Do we have duties to future generations not to pollute the planet? Does unfettered market behaviour actually undermine the human rights of present and future generations by contributing to the destruction of the environment?

On the environment and ethics, see Chapter 10.

However, although Griffin's desire to reduce human rights to as narrow a range as possible is questionable, his challenge is surely a good one. What if we cannot find enough settled uses or paradigm cases, upon which to build up at least a minimally coherent whole? How can an incoherent and indeterminate set of principles or norms guide anything?

If human rights are too vague they are unenforceable and subject to manipulation. If there is confusion about their intellectual coherence then it's not clear how they can attract the reasoned loyalty of people around the world. However, the more determinate we make them, the more we risk drawing on premises that cannot be justified in conditions of deep social and cultural pluralism. If the justification of human rights depends on sorting out large meta-ethical questions first, then the people who need them most will be waiting too long. If they depend on accepting a particular creed of liberalism, then they risk becoming too sectarian. The worry is not that we may offend non-liberal societies, so much as making sense of the different ways and contexts in which the values underlying human rights can be realized. Saudi Arabia is not a liberal society, but there are reformers and activists there who look to human rights for guidance and support. Iran is a theocracy, but it has a long tradition of political and social criticism that draws on various sources, including the language of human rights. The experience of the poor and the oppressed in Sri Lanka or Burma will invariably shape the way activists and reformers there understand and make use of human rights.

13.4 Human rights and urgent interests

If all this is true, then human rights are moral and legal claims relating to a particularly important set of interests human beings share (note that I am adopting the 'interest' approach as opposed to the 'choice' approach to rights more generally). They also refer to interests that are under particular *threat* from the exercise of power, especially by the state and its agencies. They usually presuppose various kinds of social and political arrangements for their conceptualization and realization. However, human rights apply not only to governments and their agencies, as if only government officials have duties not to interfere or undermine the basic interests of persons. Many of the duties to which basic human rights refer impose duties on all of us (see, for example, Articles 1–4 of the *Universal Declaration of Human Rights*). If we accept something along the lines of the existence of a global political structure as suggested above, each of us has a duty not to co-operate (insofar as we can) with the imposition of an institutional order that does not provide secure access to the basic interests referred to by human rights (Pogge, 2008).

Is there something more that can be said about the nature of human rights? Many of the preambles of the most prominent human rights documents include reference to the 'inherent dignity ... of all members of the human family' (*Universal Declaration*), and that all members of this family are 'born free and equal in dignity and rights' (Article 1). The two Covenants refer to the 'inherent dignity' of human persons, from which 'the equal and inalienable rights of all members of the human family ... derive' (Preamble). However, a fully satisfactory conception of what dignity entails, arguably, would come close to a complete conception of morality, and that is not what human rights morality should aspire to, or so it seems to me. Rather, human rights should pick out a particularly important set of human interests. They are not meant to provide an exhaustive list of criteria for the assessment of every situation and specify every entitlement or duty an individual might have, all things considered. Yet we must be able to say *something* about what lies behind the concept of human rights—something about the basic philosophical structure one is appealing to.

There are two broad strategies. First, one can try and appeal to as parsimonious a set of norms or values as possible in order to maximize the opportunity of convergence. Secondly, one can try to find a more comprehensive justification of human rights that offers a richer set of critical standards, but which therefore requires a more robust standard of justification. The first promises flexibility and the accommodation of diversity, but risks diluting critical bite. The second promises more critical bite, but potentially at the cost of widespread acceptability.

On international law, see Chapter 15. The first strategy has its roots in the approach of an influential early modern philosopher who was central to the development of modern international law: Hugo Grotius (1583–1645). His strategy was to try and find a minimal set of propositions which, whatever else one believed, one could accept if any kind of human society was to be possible—a form of 'ethical minimalism' (Tuck, 1994). The belief in the right to self-preservation (and correlative to that, the right to defend oneself), was supposed to be universal in just this sense. This kind of ethical framework was not meant to be a comprehensive account of man's moral life, but rather the basis for 'inter-national or inter-cultural negotiation, by providing the common ground upon which the rival and conflicting cultures could meet' Tuck (1994, p. 167).[4] The thought was that the law of nature and the law of nations could be bridged on the basis of a minimalist core of morality observable by all rational creatures, whatever their cultural or religious background. However, this in itself said nothing about the conduct of such negotiations, or whether or not others would be accorded the appropriate standing, such that they could be said to possess any fundamental rights in the first place. So there are two challenges facing the minimalist approach: first, identifying the relevant 'minimalist' principles and, secondly, specifying in what sense they are minimalist and what work they can actually do.

The elision of nature and culture in rights discourse is also exemplified by the French Assembly's *Déclaration des droits de l'homme* of 1789 (Pagden, 2003). The 'rights of man' *sound* like natural rights—that is, 'natural inalienable and sacred to man'—and yet are declared in the name of a sovereign people by the French National Assembly (the nation is the source of all sovereignty, and no man or group of men is entitled to 'any authority which is not expressly derived from it'). Moreover, the most basic rights in the Declaration are *civil* and *political* rights, and appear to derive from the status of their holders as *citizens*, as members of an already established political community, as opposed to their membership of humanity in general (Pagden, 2003, p. 189). Even Immanuel Kant, who is seen as one of the key forerunners of the modern doctrine of human rights, generally conceived of rights as best protected *within* (republican) states, albeit formed into a global federation of like-minded states (Kant, 1991).

On citizenship, see Chapter 20.

For some historians of human rights the conclusion to be drawn, therefore, is that human rights are actually specific cultural artefacts masquerading as **universal** values. It follows, argues Pagden, that if 'we wish to assert any belief in the universal we have to begin by declaring our willingness to assume, and to defend, at least some of the values of a highly specific way of life'—basically, that of a liberal democratic state (Pagden, 2003, pp. 172–3). This has consequences for thinking about contemporary justifications of human rights. 'A liberal democratic Islamic state is an oxymoron', suggests Pagden, and the changes required to enable religious freedom and equality for women, for example, will only come about from outside of Islam (Pagden, 2003, p. 199). Whatever the merits of Pagden's analysis of Islam, his argument deftly dramatizes the tension between minimalist and comprehensive justifications of human rights. How minimalist can the justification of human rights be without undermining the critical role many see as their *raison d'être* in global politics? How thick can they be without undermining the role they play as genuinely common *global* standards?

---

[4] It is important to distinguish this from the 'actual overlapping consensus' argument defended by Michael Walzer (1994). Walzer's claim is that human rights should be the product of an *actual* overlapping agreement between the existing conventional moralities in the world today. The main problem with this approach is that actual agreement is far too strong a condition to impose on the justification of critical standards. It ties the standards too closely to the *extant* content of people's moral beliefs and practices.

13.5 **Human rights and agency**

The best justification of human rights should aim to make them a *common* standard, but where 'common' falls somewhere between comprehensive and minimalist.[5] Michael Ignatieff argues that human rights have gone global not because they serve the interests of the powerful, but because they managed to 'go local': embedding themselves in the 'soil of cultures and worldviews independent of the West, in order to sustain ordinary people's struggles against unjust states and oppressive social practices' (Ignatieff, 2001, p. 7). Elsewhere he has referred to the emerging language of international human rights as a kind of 'hybridized vernacular', not necessarily cut loose from liberalism, but not as dependent on a specific creed of it as critics often suppose (Ignatieff, 1999, p. 320). Ignatieff intends this as a descriptive claim—and a hopeful one at that—but I think it provides an interesting normative vision too. What are the conditions required for human rights to go local? One thing it suggests is a form of *justificatory minimalism* (Cohen, 2004b, p. 193). Although Ignatieff claims that the best conception of human rights is 'minimalist, negative, prudential and historical', he accepts the scope of contemporary human rights norms, which are anything but minimalist and negative. It is hard to justify rights without saying non-trivial things about substantive—and thus contestable—conceptions of the person, and of the necessary conditions for political legitimacy. So what can we say?

Let us begin with the connection between human rights and agency. Human rights aim to protect certain crucial aspects of human agency, but what are these? Very generally, to be an agent means being capable of *having* a life, one that you can call your own in some way; at the very least, it means not to be dominated to such an extent that my life feels as if it just is not mine, and perhaps could never be. It also means that the choices I have are real, or at least feasible, which entails that I have the capacities to act on them. Having these capacities and being able to pursue your own direction in life also means having the basic material resources required to do so; security from harm, sufficient shelter, health, food, education, property of some kind, and access to some kind of cultural structure and the public goods it brings (language, institutions, norms, etc.). So a degree of autonomy, liberty, and adequate material provision are crucial for agency. These bare notions can be filled out in many different ways.

Note that all of this is consistent with an emphasis on the fundamentally relational nature of agency and an emphasis on our responsibilities as well as our rights. We are all dependent, vulnerable beings. We are also able to reflect on the nature of our dependencies and vulnerabilities.[6] We are dependent on others for our development, security, and well-being (emotional, psychological, and physical), as well as on the material, social, and cultural environments in which we live. We are all vulnerable to various kinds of

---

[5] The idea of a 'common standard' can be found in important papers by Beitz (2001, 2003) and Cohen (2004b). There is a slightly different sense in Tully (1995), where he appeals to a certain model of practical reasoning found in the common law. I draw on all of these here. For more discussion see Ivison (2008).
[6] Which means that certain crucial capacities—such as imagination, empathy, and compassion—are crucial for realizing human rights too. For an interesting discussion of the role of the imagination and empathy in the history of human rights, see Hunt (2007).

afflictions (physical and psychological), and to the abuse of the exercise of power. We have obligations in light of these dependencies and vulnerabilities. However, in order for us to be capable of forming meaningful relationships and fulfilling our obligations in the first place, certain basic conditions are required, including achieving certain basic capabilities and being protected from certain basic harms. Not all of these needs and vulnerabilities are best addressed through human rights, but they can be used to mark out at least one particularly urgent and important set of interests which most human beings share. Understood in this way, promoting human rights enables individuals to fulfil their obligations as much as it protects from unreasonable interference (Bell, 2000; Cohen, 2004b).

So we need a conception of human agency that is rich enough to provide content to the idea of human rights, but not so rich that it embodies a comprehensive view of the good. The scope for reasonable disagreement expands as we think about the global **public sphere**, and borderline cases complicate things. We also need to remain open-minded about exactly who is in or out in relation to the category of 'human' in human rights. Great apes, who share many capabilities with us, are clearly candidates for human rights too, as our views change about the margins of our species (Cavalieri & Singer, 1995). It was not that long ago, after all, that many people struggled with the idea that women or indigenous peoples had the moral standing to claim human rights. Perhaps 'human rights' then should go the way of the 'rights of man', and we should instead talk simply about 'basic rights'.

13.6 **The right to politics**

Recall that we began with a discussion of Hannah Arendt's conception of human rights as involving an appeal to the idea of 'the right to have rights'. Our discussion of agency can help elaborate this idea a bit more fully, and put into sharper focus the notion of a specifically political conception of human rights.

The right to have rights is that basic right—that basic claim—upon which more specific conceptions of rights can be constructed. So the right to have rights is something like a right to *participation*, or a right to *politics*, in the sense that to treat me as someone capable of holding rights in the first place is to see me as entitled to be part of the process of determining the meaning and articulation of those rights (Balibar, 1994; Waldron, 1999). The right to have rights forms the threshold—the condition of possibility—against which to test the construction of various particular rights, and also our judgements about the limits of those rights.

Two candidates for making further sense of this idea are what Rainer Forst calls the 'right to justification', and what Bernard Williams has called the 'basic legitimation demand' or 'BLD' (Forst, 1999; Williams, 2005b). Both of these notions are linked to the idea that what it means to be treated as a human agent involves being treated in a manner for which adequate reasons can be provided. We encountered this idea earlier when pointing out that rights had to be justified and not simply asserted. The idea that Forst and Williams are appealing to is that any legitimate form of political order must be justifiable to those who are subject to it. Might does not make right. The crucial question then concerns the nature of the reasons offered, and Forst and Williams present two interesting ways of thinking about this challenge.

Forst offers an essentially Kantian argument, but tries to sidestep some of the more controversial aspects of Kant's actual moral doctrines. According to Forst, the adequacy of reasons that can serve to legitimate a political order will be determined through processes of 'reciprocal justification'; that is, actual dialogue between culturally and historically situated individuals. However, the validity of any proposed universal norm or rule—including the validity of human rights—does not depend on *literal* agreement, but instead is determined in relation to the outcome of a suitably designed 'communicative procedure'. This is a procedure in which everyone, at least ideally, is able to deliberate collectively over those rules and norms that affect their most important interests. The right to have rights just is this 'right to justification'. Forst is attempting to save a Kantian idea of reasonableness poised in-between a **positivist** story about the validity of human rights (they exist only where they are actually enforceable through law), and a purely rationalist one (human rights as moral rights disclosed through universal reason).

Williams, on the other hand, offers a less Kantian and more historicist account of legitimation that can be used to think about the justification of human rights. Legitimate rule will be that which *would* be acceptable to individuals thinking reflectively about their situation, albeit from an avowedly non-Kantian perspective (Williams, 2005a, pp. 4–7; see also Williams, 1981, pp. 101–13). The less legitimate the system of political rule, the more likely the violation of human rights, but we still need to know if what is acceptable to individuals is not a product of the very relations of power we want the BLD to address. For this Williams turns to the 'critical theory principle': 'the acceptance of a justification does not count if the acceptance itself is produced by the coercive power which is supposedly being justified' (Williams, 2005a, p. 6; also pp. 14, 71–2). The paradigm case of failing to meet the BLD is unmediated coercion; the claim that might makes right. However, the particular answers as to what is acceptable with regard to legitimation can vary. Liberals set higher standards as to what counts as the kind of disadvantages we should care about and which cannot be rationalized by the need for some kind of political order. The state should not become part of the problem for which it is supposedly an answer (i.e. the need for political order). Nor can an existing political order be legitimated simply by reference to its continuing existence; once the legitimacy of a regime is raised, some kind of justification must be forthcoming, and it must be acceptable to those who are subject to it. This is precisely *one* role that human rights can play in global politics—providing a threshold against which the legitimacy of any kind of political regime can be judged.

Williams's account gives us a clear line to some basic human rights—to protection against unlawful killing, torture, arbitrary detention, and the denial of freedom of association and expression. These rights will imply other rights, since one kind of right may require a bundle of other claims to be fulfilled in order to be realized. We have already seen, for example, that Arendt thought that human rights were only meaningful if people also had a right to political membership. A right to participate in democratic decision-making may well require a right to freedom of expression, freedom of movement, and freedom of association, as well as basic socio-economic rights to food, shelter, and employment. So there are complex casual and normative relations between different rights. Minimal or basic human rights spill over and connect up with a range of other claims (Habermas, 1996; Fabre, 2000; Nickel, 2007).

The further we move away from the paradigmatic cases, however, the more difficult the judgements become. As we saw above, it is one thing to say that people are owed certain things as a *right*—that someone would be wronged in a very specific sense in being denied X—and another to say it would be a very good thing if they had X. This problem is often raised in relation to social and economic rights. No one would deny that employment is a valuable good and prolonged, involuntary unemployment a genuine bad. A right to employment, however, requires that the state not only have adequate resources to deliver employment to all but the capacity as well. Full employment might be an appropriate objective for public policy, or as part of the platform of a political party, but can we translate it into a human right? Against whom would the right be held, and to whom (or what) would the duties correlate?

Still, there is no hard line between what is plausible or implausible as a human rights claim. As social, political, and historical circumstances change, so too will our judgements about where to draw the line. Indeed, one important purpose of human rights discourse is to remind us of our duties to work towards a world in which human rights are more likely to be realized than they are now.

Williams's conception of the BLD provides an attractive way of thinking about the kind of justification we need to undergird a self-consciously political theory of human rights. Human rights, on this account, involve claims to distinct forms of political action and to the conditions required for persons to be conceived as properly political agents. These claims, and the rights that accompany them, are also, importantly, indeterminate. First, because aspects of any existing social or political order can always (at least potentially) be put into question, insofar as its institutions and processes require ongoing legitimation. So the mere presence of a particular constitutional or political form cannot, on its own, guarantee human rights. Secondly, because as the world around us changes, so too will the kinds of threats we face and thus the interpretation of what constitutes a threat to our most vital interests. Moreover, if the effectiveness and meaning of rights is shaped by political activism, as I have suggested it is, then by claiming rights they were previously denied, or in putting them to work in new ways, individuals and groups can, in effect, create new rights. Thus, the gap between human rights and civil rights can sometimes be a kind of 'productive failure' (or paradox), despite Arendt's searching critique.

13.7 Case study: is there a human right to democracy?

If human rights are linked to a distinctly *political* form of agency, and if—at a minimum—basic human rights imply or perhaps even require a host of other rights, then what kind of role should they actually play in global politics? I have suggested that they provide a common standard for evaluating and shaping the behaviour of states and other significant political actors in relation to the urgent interests that individuals share.

Does it follow that there is a human right to democracy? Article 21 of the *Universal Declaration* suggests that there is, appealing as it does to a right to 'take part in the government' of your country, and that the 'will of the people' shall be the 'basis of the authority of the government'.

On democracy, see also Chapter 21.

Does this amount to a human right to democracy? The key claim in support of such an argument would be that it is only a democratic society that can provide the conditions required to treat each individual with the dignity and equal respect they are owed, and upon which human rights ultimately rest. There might be prudential reasons for not imposing democracy on others, but the moral case in its favour is clear. Democracy is thus not only *empirically* required to protect or promote human rights (i.e. democratic systems, in practice, are best at protecting human rights), but *morally* required. States that lack democratic political arrangements are thus violating the human rights of their members. It might also follow that democratic arrangements beyond the state are required, if in order to protect the basic interests of individuals, democracy must become increasingly **transnational** and 'de-territorialized' (Bohman, 2007).

Let's test this argument. What it relies on is a close association between the demands imposed by a conception of human rights and a rich conception of democracy. By a 'rich conception' I mean not simply the view that democracy consists in competitive elections in which each individual has the right to vote for the party (or candidate) of their choice, but something much more. According to the richer view, a democratic society is one in which people enjoy equal rights of participation (to vote, to hold office, freedom of association and expression, etc.), and something like an equal opportunity for effective political influence (Cohen, 2001, 2006, pp. 241–2). A democratic *society* is one in which the political system reflects a particular conception of the person as free and equal.

Imagine a state in which a non-democratically elected elite exercises political authority.[7] In order to become a member of the ruling class, one must be properly educated and trained, a process in principle open to all, but which is inevitably restricted to a small segment of the population. The role of this group is to discern, interpret, and implement the general will of the people. As a citizen, you do not have a right to direct political participation, but there are various fora in which you can make your views known, and the regime allows for lively and generally uncensored public communication, including a relatively free press. There are not free elections for membership of the ruling group, but regular referenda are held regarding important public policy decisions, which the ruling group takes seriously. There is an effective system of law, which is enforced in a generally non-arbitrary way. There is reasonable social mobility, at least in relation to non-political domains, and although there is a state-endorsed religion, religious minorities are allowed to practice their beliefs without harassment, and are not officially blocked from becoming part of the ruling group (difficult as that is for everybody). Assume also that women are able to make their views known in the various formal and informal fora to which citizens can contribute, although they often face restrictive social and cultural norms.

Is our imaginary state violating the rights of all its citizens, just insofar as they are not entitled to an equal individual right to political participation? It will depend, of

---

[7] This example is based loosely on Rawls's discussion in (1999) p. 78ff.

course, on what we mean by democracy and what we think the role of a conception of human rights should be.

First of all, we may want to say that it is a condition for enjoying human rights that they be genuinely embedded in the public culture of that society, but what does 'embedded' mean? One way to make sense of it would be to ask if the protections offered are actually based on respect for the basic interests of individuals—on their 'dignity' or equal worth—such that they can be claimed irrespective of the individual's social or cultural standing, and cannot be overridden by other policy considerations? Or are the protections offered only loosely analogous to human rights? That is, they overlap with what we generally think of as human rights, but are actually grounded on other considerations, such as cultural or religious norms. Our imaginary society might well lack a fully liberal conception of equal worth or dignity that underlies many accounts of human rights, but since it would be far too demanding to insist that people accept human rights for the *same reasons* in liberal democratic states, it seems a non-starter to demand it of people living in states with very different political arrangements. However, the crucial issue is the extent to which people's human rights really are protected, whether for the 'right' reasons or not, and this is where the claim about democracy enters the picture.

It matters crucially what we mean by democracy. What if—as in our imaginary society—there were modes of collective **self-determination** that fell short of the rich conception of democracy, but were not simply autocracies either? Return to our example. Members of that society are able to hold their ruling elite accountable in some ways (regular referenda; a relatively free press; participation in deliberative, although non-binding fora). They are able to express their dissent and criticize public decisions, at least to some extent. Now imagine that this results in a society in which people's basic interests are generally protected, but also at least *some* of their political interests too, just because of this limited mode of collective self-determination. It's still not a democratic society in the rich sense. Does that mean the human rights of its members are being violated?

It is important to note that the question is not whether we should tolerate terrible evils like slavery, genocide, enforced starvation, or religious persecution. We should not, and any conception of human rights must make that very clear. The question is whether a society that aimed to protect the human rights of its members must necessarily be a democratic one. The answer will depend on your interpretation of the demands of democracy and the role that human rights should play in global politics. Are the requirements for protecting human rights less demanding than those for realizing a democratic society? I believe they are, but even if so, human rights still set a standard against which (too) many aspects of our world would be found deeply wanting.

13.8 Conclusion

We began by trying to distinguish human rights from other kinds of rights claims. Starting with Arendt's criticism of a purely moral conception of human rights, we went on to consider a distinctly political conception of human rights. A political conception is particularly attuned to the role we expect human rights to play in global politics. That means taking the scope for reasonable disagreement about important political values seriously, but also linking human rights to the protection and promotion of individuals' political agency. We then considered whether or not a democratic political order was a necessary condition of such a conception; in other words, whether there is a human right to democracy. The answer will depend on whether it is possible to distinguish between the demands of democracy and those of human rights. Whatever the ultimate answer, I hope to have shown that human rights can play a vital—albeit always contested—role in global politics today.

QUESTIONS

1. What distinguishes human rights from other kinds of rights?

2. What did Hannah Arendt mean by 'the right to have rights'?

3. Can human rights be justified? Upon what basis should they be justified?

4. What is the difference between human rights understood as 'moral rights' and human rights as 'legal rights'? Which is more plausible and why?

5. Are human rights universal?

6. What should the role of human rights be in global politics?

7. How 'thick' or 'thin' (long or short) should our list of human rights be?

8. Are states necessary for protecting human rights?

9. What is the relationship between human rights and democracy? Can human rights be adequately protected in non-democratic states?

10. Are human rights actually realizable?

FURTHER READING

Beitz, C. (2001) Human rights as a common concern. *American Political Science Review*, 95:269–82. A very clear defence of human rights in relation to contemporary global politics and as distinct from 'natural rights'.

Beitz, C. (2009) *The Idea of Human Rights*. Oxford: Oxford University Press. A lucid account of the role of a common conception of human rights in world politics.

Bobbio, N. (2000) *The Age of Rights*. Cambridge: Polity. An interesting historical treatment of the emergence of rights.

Donnelly, J. (2003) *Universal Human Rights in Theory and Practice*. Ithaca: Cornell University Press. One of the clearest and best discussions of the relationship between theory and practice in the human rights philosophical literature.

Griffin, J. (2008) *On Human Rights*. Oxford: Oxford University Press. A systematic discussion of the philosophical foundations of human rights, with particular attention to the problem of human rights 'inflation'.

Ignatieff, M. (2001) *Human Rights as Politics and Idolatry*. Princeton: Princeton University Press. An interesting defence of a 'minimalist' conception of human rights.

Nickel, J. (2007) *Making Sense of Human Rights*, 2nd edn. Oxford: Blackwell. An excellent philosophical treatment of human rights that discusses many of the philosophical objections and challenges to them.

Pogge, T. (2008) *World Poverty and Human Rights: Cosmopolitan Responsibilities and Reforms*, 2nd edn. Cambridge: Polity. A powerful and distinctive defence of human rights in relation to global justice and especially global poverty.

Shue, H. (1996) *Basic Rights: Subsistence, Affluence and US Foreign Policy*, 2nd edn. Princeton: Princeton University Press. One of the best discussions of the idea of 'basic rights' and the distinction between negative and positive rights and human rights.

◼ WEB LINKS

http://www.un.org/Overview/rights.html The text of the *Universal Declaration of Human Rights*.

http://www.amnesty.org/ Amnesty International is one of the leading organizations promoting and monitoring human rights abuses around the world.

http://www.msf.org/ *Médecins Sans Frontières* is one of the leading humanitarian organizations in the world, providing emergency medical aid in the context of massive natural disasters, famine, civil wars, and other desperate situations.

http://www.hrw.org/ Human Rights Watch takes an active role in monitoring and reporting on human rights abuses around the world.

http://www.oxfam.org/en/about Oxfam International is a confederation of 13 non-governmental organizations working together to address global poverty and injustice.

Visit the Online Resource Centre that accompanies this book to access more learning resources: www.oxfordtextbooks.co.uk/orc/bell_ethics/

14 Poverty and global distributive justice

Kok-Chor Tan

READER'S GUIDE

This chapter surveys the problems of global poverty and global inequality. With regard to global poverty, it assesses two ethical approaches to grounding and specifying the duty of assistance—a utilitarian approach and a deontological (rights-based) approach. With regard to global equality, it provides an overview of some of the challenges surrounding the ideal of global distributive justice. Specifically, it identifies three phases in the development of that ideal: first, that of extending arguments for equality from the domestic to global domains; secondly, that of establishing the priority of global justice over patriotic concern; and thirdly, that of showing that the conditions for distributive equality are not exclusive to the domestic state. It closes with a case study about global distributive justice.

14.1 Introduction

Our current world is marred by stark poverty, and great and increasing economic inequalities between the global well-off and the global poor. Yet global poverty and global inequality are distinct problems, and while most philosophers accept that there is a pressing moral duty to mitigate world poverty, there is profound disagreement over whether global justice includes, in addition to the alleviation of poverty, a further commitment to mitigate economic inequality among individuals in the world. However, the problem of world poverty is not philosophically trivial either, for questions remain regarding the basis and extent of the moral duty to alleviate it. This chapter will survey some philosophical debates surrounding the duty to respond to poverty (section 14.2) before moving on to discuss the problem of global inequality (section 14.3). In the Case study, I will examine the conditions under which global distributive obligations arise.

14.2 **World poverty**

An estimated 1.1 billion people live on less than $1/day (the baseline for extreme poverty), and about 2.6 billion live on less than $2/day (moderate poverty) (United Nations Development Programme, 2008). Although it is deplorable that the international community is responding inadequately to poverty, few philosophers deny that there is a moral duty to provide some form of assistance to the global poor. However, they disagree over the basis of the duty to assist the poor, and consequently the content and demands of such a duty. To the extent that the lack of a concerted effort to respond to poverty is due to actual disagreements over the ground and content of this duty, philosophy has the role of providing conceptual clarification. In this section, I discuss two main ethical approaches to the problem of global poverty—a **utilitarian** approach and a rights-based **deontological** one.

A utilitarian argument

Utilitarianism is a moral theory that holds that the right act is that which maximizes well-being or happiness (broadly construed) for the greatest number of persons. According to utilitarian morality, if the suffering of the global poor can be eliminated by the rich redistributing some of their resources and wealth without significant sacrifice (without, therefore, lowering overall global well-being or utility), it is a failure of morality that the well-off are not contributing to counter world poverty. Peter Singer presents the most famous version of this argument in his essay 'Famine, Affluence and Morality' (1972). He argues that the rich owe those suffering from avoidable misery and impoverishment a duty of assistance or rescue up to the point where further contributions will render the rich as badly off as the people they are assisting. That is, on Singer's utilitarian view, to the extent that the suffering and death of the global poor can be prevented by the rich without their having to make comparable sacrifices, it ought to be prevented.

> On utilitarianism, see also Chapter 4.

Singer's conception of global justice is demanding and, on first reading, given the urgent challenge of global poverty, its 'demandingness' seems appropriate. Yet the 'demandingness' of Singer's theory is, in the eyes of his critics, a fatal flaw (e.g. Fishkin, 1982). On Singer's approach, it is inconsistent with the demands of morality (here, the moral demand to assist the global poor) to pay attention to non-utility maximizing personal pursuits or projects that one might have, when sacrificing these projects can improve the condition of the poor (without rendering the contributor equally or more worse-off). For example, on Singer's account, it is hard for me to justify my life-long goal of climbing Everest, which will require me to commit time and resources to the enterprise, when the money I would spend on this personal project could be deployed to do a lot more global good. Yet this seems in violation of 'commonsense morality' that certain personal projects and pursuits can be morally valuable as well. Singer accepts that his moral ideal is highly demanding, but he insists that if this is what morality demands, then so much the worse for commonsense morality (Singer, 1972, p. 235).

Nonetheless, for practical purposes, Singer is prepared to accept a more modest claim: that persons are to contribute up to the point where further contribution will result in a sacrifice of 'comparable moral significance' (Singer, 1972, p. 238). A morally significant sacrifice will include, presumably, the abandonment of one's educational plans, but not the sacrifice of an extra vacation or a second car. However, is this general criterion still, nonetheless, too demanding? Some critics believe so, especially if some costly non-utility maximizing pursuits that may not pass the test of 'comparable moral significance' are, nonetheless, hugely important for an agent, such as a person's life goal of climbing Everest or pursuing a second graduate degree purely for the sake of learning.[1] The difficulties surrounding Singer's conclusion regarding famine relief stem from general difficulties associated with utilitarianism itself: utilitarianism, given its ultimate objective of maximizing overall utility, seems to be an overly austere moral theory that is unable to tolerate non-utility maximizing **personal prerogatives** and projects that are integral to any meaningful individual life.[2]

A deontological argument

An alternative moral theory to utilitarianism is the deontological approach. Deontological moral theories do not derive the rightness or wrongness of an act simply from the consequences of the act (as in utilitarianism), but from some notion of the (non-consequential) rights and obligations that agents independently have.

One deontological approach to world poverty that is diametrically opposed to utilitarianism takes the respect and protection of basic rights instead of utility maximization as the starting point. Henry Shue, in his groundbreaking *Basic Rights* (1996), makes the case for the basic right to subsistence by arguing that there is no morally significant difference between the right to subsistence and the right to security (which he presumes reasonably that his audience endorses). Like security rights, subsistence rights are basic rights in that they are rights that need to be respected and protected if the rights of persons to other important things are to be exercisable. For example, the right to education cannot be properly exercised if children go to school hungry and malnourished. Shue rejects the traditional distinction that security rights are *negative* rights in the sense that they generate only a duty of non-interference, whereas subsistence rights are *positive* in the sense that they require positive acts of assistance. Rather, Shue argues, security and subsistence rights entail both (negative) duties of non-interference and (positive) duties of protection and assistance (Shue, 1996). For example, proper protection of persons' security rights in

---

[1] Conversely, if we grant that these pursuits qualify as morally significant, then the duty to assist is limited by personal prerogatives of various kinds. Richard Miller (2004) pursues this criticism against Singer further. It is worth noting that in *One World* (2002), Singer recognizes that public policy has to be realistic if it is to be effective and recommends that as a policy he would make an even more modest demand: 'anyone who has enough money to spend on the luxuries and frivolities so common in affluent societies should give at least 1 cent in every dollar of their income to those who have trouble getting enough to eat, clean water to drink, shelter from the elements, and basic health care' (p. 194).
[2] There is an impressive body of literature on how utilitarianism could be reconciled with personal concern and prerogatives (e.g., Scheffler, 1982).

society will require not just that the agents of society refrain from assaulting its members (**negative duty**), but also that they offer protection to them from attack by each other and so on (**positive duty**). Conversely, proper protection of persons' subsistence rights will require not just that society provide the basic conditions necessary for economic production—such as law and order, adequate mechanisms for the distribution of goods, and state support for those who are in need of assistance (positive duty)—but also that it does not, say in complicity with a **transnational** corporation, undermine its citizens' means of subsistence (negative duty).

What is distinctive about the basic rights approach to world poverty compared with the utilitarian account is that there is a reasonable cut-off point for duty bearers: rights generate the duty to protect people against basic needs deprivation, and the duty to assist them when they are deprived of these basic needs. However, unlike the utilitarian view, it does not demand that one contributes up to the point where further contribution will result in decreased overall utility. Once deprivation ceases and protection against potential deprivation is reasonably guaranteed, there is no further duty to contribute based on basic rights. To be sure, it is possible within the basic rights approach that the degree of deprivation is so severe and widespread as to require an immense amount of sacrifice on the part of contributors if they are to fully discharge their obligations to meet the basic needs of the poor. However, this would be a contingent point (and not true of the real world currently) and is not necessitated by the structure of the moral theory itself. A basic rights approach in principle can, and in practice does, avoid the 'overdemandingness' problem that confounds the utilitarian globalist.

One influential deontological alternative to Shue's emphasizes (or rather grants) negative rights and duties across the board. Seeking to avoid the philosophical debate as to whether basic rights are negative or positive (that is, whether there is fundamentally only the negative right not to be interfered with, or whether there is also the positive right to assistance), Thomas Pogge (2002) argues that even if our basic moral duty is the negative one of not doing harm, the fact is that the global rich have harmed, and are continuing to harm, the global poor via the global institutional framework that they are actively helping to sustain. As an example, Pogge refers to the World Trade Organization's (WTO) norms and agreements that are highly disadvantageous to the poor, but highly advantageous to the rich, and that are imposed on the poor by delegates representing the global rich. Thus, since the basic injunction not to do harm has already been violated, and is continuing to be violated, there is a corresponding duty of justice on the part of the wrong-doer to make amends for the harm—to take positive steps to cease harming and, where complete cessation of harm is not possible, to take measures to alleviate the harm being inflicted. Thus, the global rich owe it to the global poor to reform the global economic order, and to provide other forms of protection and aid to the poor to repair the harms they are doing and have done. For Pogge, therefore, the debate is thus a 'factual', rather than a philosophical one (Pogge, 2002, p. 14). Even if the basic moral duty is merely the modest and negative one of not doing harm, if it can be shown that the global rich are, in fact, harming the poor, then they have the 'belated' duty of justice to attend to the harms done. For Pogge then, the problem of world poverty is not to be understood in terms of helping the poor, but in terms of *not harming* the poor.

Pogge's approach is distinctive and has received deserved attention (e.g., Jagger, 2009). However, as some commentators have pointed out, it is not clear if Pogge successfully avoids philosophical contention altogether. The conception of harm that drives his conclusion (that the global order is harmful to the global poor) is itself a philosophical position and needs to be defended. Pogge claims that the global poor are being harmed because the rich impose on them a global order that deprives them of access to basic goods *when* an alternative arrangement is available (e.g., Patten, 2004; Tan, 2010). Pogge needs to understand harm in this comparative way because he needs to be able to say that the present global order is harming the poor even though this order could be better for the poor than nothing at all. It is harming the poor, on Pogge's analysis, because an alternative global order friendlier to the poor *could be* adopted by the rich (2002, pp. 16, 139). However, in this case, Pogge has to explain the basis of the obligation of the rich to choose this alternative global framework over the less friendly framework. A plausible explanation is the assumption of a prior positive duty *to support* a background institutional order of a certain sort, namely one in which people are not denied access to basic goods. In other words, Pogge has to be assuming that we have the duty of justice to choose a global arrangement, where there are alternatives, which at least does not deny anyone the means of subsistence. However, this means that we have not only the negative duty not to harm, but the positive duty to take steps to meet the needs of others. Yet this is at odds with Pogge's own minimalistic moral assumption that there are only negative duties and rights. Pogge's aspiration to derive robust duties to protect the poor from a modest moral starting point is thus arguably unrealized.

While the problem of world poverty is morally urgent and pressing, and while there are different arguments attempting to clarify the basis of the duty of assistance, it is less philosophically contentious than a further question: does global justice also entail a commitment to regulate social and economic inequalities?[3] In other words, even if we are to live in a world in which absolute poverty is non-existent, or a world in which no persons are deprived of basic needs and denied well-ordered societies of their own, do lingering economic inequalities present a problem of global justice? Unlike the consensus that there is a moral duty to counter world poverty, philosophers disagree over whether there is any commitment to global distributive equality. We can call this the problem of *global distributive justice*.

There is, of course, a connection between inequality and poverty in that if inequalities within a capitalist society are great enough, then the comparatively less well-off can find basic goods priced out of their reach. So to the extent that immense inequality can have impoverishing consequences for the disadvantaged, the moral concern with alleviating poverty can generate a concern (albeit indirectly) with inequality. However, the philosophically more challenging question is this: does global justice require mitigating inequality in itself as a direct concern? Is economic inequality, even when it does not impoverish some people absolutely, an injustice? While the morally more urgent task is that of countering global poverty, the philosophical quest of identifying what global justice fully requires is

---

[3] That it is less contentious is due to the early efforts of authors like Singer and Shue. In contrast, see Hardin (1996 [1983]) for an early objection to global assistance. See Aikens and LaFollette (1996) for further discussion on justice and poverty.

not self-indulgent while persons' basic needs remain unmet. Clarifying what global justice fully demands will provide us with the longer-term vision of what an ideal world should look like even as we address more pressing problems, such as severe poverty. This is important as it may matter for how we conceive of and respond to the problem of poverty, and if we conclude that global justice includes some kind of egalitarian distributive concern, we acquire additional reasons for objecting to the present global order.

14.3 Global distributive justice

As noted above, the question of global distributive justice must be distinguished from the problem of poverty. A substantive difference between the duty to eliminate poverty and the duty of distributive justice is that the former is fulfilled once the threshold of poverty is crossed, whereas the latter is continuously in force so long as global inequalities persist (e.g., Rawls, 1999, Part III).

An example of a global distributive principle might be a 'globalized' or cosmopolitan Rawlsian '**difference principle**'. Rawls's difference principle holds that social and economic inequalities can only be justified if they are to 'the greatest benefit of the least-advantaged member of society' (Rawls, 2001a, p. 42). A global difference principle would thus constrain global economic and social inequalities by requiring that the global order be one in which the worst-off person fares best compared with how she would do under alternative arrangements. This principle would remain in force indefinitely, unlike the duty to eliminate poverty, continuously regulating the basic institutions of the social order to ensure that it is to the greatest advantage of the worst-off. Is there a case for a global difference principle or some other principle of egalitarian global distributive justice? In this section, I will use the terms 'global justice' and 'global egalitarianism' to mean 'global distributive justice' unless otherwise stated, and advocates of this ideal will be referred to as 'global egalitarians' or 'cosmopolitans'.

On Rawls's theory of justice, see Chapter 1.

On cosmopolitanism see Chapter 8.

Looking back at debate over the past 30 years, we can identify three phases in the development of this ideal. The first stage involves responding to what I will call the *methodological challenge*. Here, the globalists' quest was to extend arguments for distributive justice, originally conceived for the limited context of the nation state, to the global arena. The particular challenge was to overcome the methodological assumptions found in influential theories of domestic justice—such as, for example, that the state is a closed system of social co-operation and is relatively self-sufficient (e.g., Rawls, 1971, p. 8). The second stage involves addressing the challenge of *patriotic concern*. The challenge is that even if the case for extension could be made, global justice would come into conflict with various local special and personal commitments and concerns individuals ordinarily have. Patriotic commitments—the special concern and duties of justice persons have to their compatriots—present one obvious challenge (Miller, 1995). The mission of the globalists in this stage of the debate was to maintain the priority of global justice in the face of the allegedly opposing demands of patriotic concern. The third and current stage of the debate returns to the fundamental question first addressed in stage one: are there principles of global distributive justice to begin with? Critics suggest that the 'extension

This argument is also discussed in Chapter 8.

project', as I will call it, failed to recognize that arguments for distributive justice apply only under circumstances that obtain within the state, and therefore the methodological assumptions should not have been lifted. We can call this the *limited scope of justice thesis* (Blake, 2001; Nagel, 2005; Sangiovanni, 2007). I will discuss each of these stages in turn, and outline how globalists have responded, or could respond, to the specific challenges raised.

Stage one: the methodological challenge

The most prominent early arguments for global justice attempted to extend Rawls's theory of justice to the global domain (Barry, 1974; Pogge, 1989; Beitz, 1999). In *A Theory of Justice* (1971), Rawls presented a theory conceived for the state and, to that end, he reasonably imposed some simplifying assumptions to get started. The key assumption is that the state is a closed and self-sufficient system of social co-operation (Rawls, 1971, p. 8). Inspired by, but also in reaction to Rawls, globalists like Beitz (1999) and later Pogge (1989) argue that if we lift Rawls's methodological assumptions, as we should if we want to change the subject from *domestic* to *global* justice, then we would effectively arrive at a 'globalized' version of Rawls's theory. That is, Rawls's two principles of justice, including his distributive principle, would apply globally. The argument is that once we reject the assumption of the state as a self-sufficient and closed system, and instead recognize states to be interacting and even engaging in forms of social co-operation with other states, the Rawlsian method of reasoning must necessarily take on a global scope. Therefore, Rawls's principles of justice, including specifically his difference principle, have global application. The difference principle has a role in regulating socio-economic inequalities among persons in the world independently of their state affiliation. These arguments have been further developed by cosmopolitan theorists, such as Simon Caney (2005a) and Darrel Moellendorf (2002).

Thus, the first task in the global justice debate was to show how and why the methodological statist assumptions in arguments for justice can and ought to be dropped, and how, if these assumptions are indeed transcended, arguments for distributive justice are extended to the global domain. The extension project was widely endorsed in the early part of the global justice debate, and many philosophers otherwise sympathetic to Rawls's basic project, such as Thomas Scanlon (1975) and Brian Barry (1974), took the cosmopolitan's side.

Stage two: patriotic concern

In response to the extension argument, a new set of challenges began to emerge. These challenges were not directed at the cosmopolitans extension argument per se. They forward, instead, the argument that global distributive demands are in tension with more local and special commitments that persons ordinarily have. The most poignant of these partial commitments and obligations are demands associated with persons' respective national memberships. As a member of a nation state, it is argued, one has special concerns and commitments to fellow members that one need not have towards strangers and global egalitarianism risks riding roughshod over them. The patriotic challenge replicates a recurring debate within moral philosophy: how can the *impartial* demands of morality be reconciled with the personal and *partial* commitments that typify a complete and valuable human life? Just as it is implausible according to some moral philosophers to presume that there is one ultimate moral value that all moral actions must aim at, so some critics of cosmopolitanism claim that it is implausible to hold that there is one common morality governing our duties to both compatriots and foreigners. For example, how can we plausibly say that one's duties to compatriots and family members are identical to the duties that one owes to persons in general, or that the former duties are secondary to the general duties one owes to persons at large?

Thus, even philosophers like Samuel Scheffler (2001) who find aspects of global justice appealing urge a more modest or 'moderate' understanding of cosmopolitanism to accommodate these partial commitments. However, a more stringent version of the challenge comes from nationalist theorists like David Miller (1995, 2000) and Margaret Moore (2001). They argue that when there is a conflict between different domains or spheres of justice, it is not so straightforward that one domain should be supreme. When the demands of global justice compete with the demands of national justice, one cannot assume that the default is to grant primacy to global demands. To the contrary, there are good special reasons, reasons having to do with the ideal of the nation state, for giving preference to national demands. These arguments point to the special ethical significance of shared nationality for cementing commitments to democratic principles and **social justice** at home.

On nationalism, see Chapter 7.

It is important to appreciate the form of the challenge here. The patriotic challenge does not deny that there are valid global distributive principles. That is, it does not take issue with the extension project. What it puts forward is what we may call a limitation or 'limiting' argument (Jones, 1999a, p. 111), namely, that while there could be good reasons for global distributive obligations, there are also good (if not more important) reasons for other kinds of obligations that conflict with the global ones. The challenge aims to show that at the very least global distributive commitments have to be limited if not generally overridden by patriotic commitments.

Understanding the form of the challenge properly is important because it shows the form an appropriate response could take. Faced with the patriotic challenge (read as a limitation argument), the cosmopolitan need not provide another independent argument for global egalitarianism. That such a commitment could be independently valid is accepted by the patriotic challenge. What the cosmopolitan needs to show is that in cases where global and patriotic principles or commitments compete, global commitments take priority. That is, what is at stake is the *priority*, rather than the *validity*, of global justice. Thus presented, some might think that the patriotic challenge is rather weak since it has already conceded the validity of global justice. However, in fact, as mentioned, the patriotic challenge is an instance of a deep and recurring quest in moral philosophy, that of reconciling valid but competing moral claims. Rather than representing a weak challenge that can be ignored, the patriotic challenge is one expression of an abiding problem of moral philosophy and poses a serious challenge that the globalists must address.

In response, cosmopolitans argue that national and patriotic commitments cannot be *justly* discharged unless the obligations of global justice are met. Just as justice constrains the range of personal pursuits in the domestic context, so too global justice should limit national and patriotic demands. Special co-operatives and interest groups (such as a co-operative business association) within a domestic society may have their own local distributive concerns, but these groups will not know what they are justly entitled to distribute among their own members without reference to what distributive justice for society at large requires of them. A co-operative may have its own internal distributive ideals, but if its internal distribution is to be just, the co-operative must first honour the rightful demands of other co-operatives and non-members generally. In other words, claims of justice regulating external relations *among* groups have priority over claims of justice *within* groups, for members of a group cannot know otherwise if their internal or-ganization is valid with respect to what is owed to non-members. We can call the former 'external justice' and the latter 'internal justice', and hold as a norm that external justice takes precedence over internal justice. Thus, the demands of global justice have priority over the demands of patriotism. Global justice sets the bounds of acceptable patriotic concern, as justice in the domestic setting provides the parameters for acceptable per-sonal pursuits (Tan, 2004; Moellendorf, 2006).

To illustrate the above, consider this question: may a relatively well-off nation devote some of its resources to further improving its already very good health care system, or should it direct these resources to supporting health care efforts in poorer countries? Sup-pose this nation decides that as a matter of justice, its priority is to provide even better care for its citizens. The argument above suggests that if the well-off nation, in fact, is not entitled to these resources, then its priority claim is invalid. Before we can determine whether this nation may use these resources to promote the ends of its members or to serve the cause of domestic justice, we need to ask: from the standpoint of global justice, is that nation entitled to these resources? The answer is 'yes' if these are resources that it has left-over after it has discharged its duties of global distributive justice. It is 'no' if these are resources it is able to retain precisely because it has ignored its duties of global distributive justice. Global justice has priority in this sense: it determines the bounds of permissible national pursuits.

Stage three: the limited scope thesis

Both the patriotic challenge and the globalist response accept the validity of the demands of global justice. This is where the debate enters the third stage. The challenge here de-nies that there are valid global distributive principles. In effect, it says that the extension attempt in the first stage made a fundamental mistake—it wrongly applies reasoning relevant for a particular social context to an inappropriate (global) context. Arguments for distributive justice take hold only when certain conditions obtain, and while these conditions do obtain in the context of the state they are *absent* in the global context. In-deed, the critics argue that attempts to globalize Rawls misunderstood his own arguments about distributive equality (e.g., Freeman, 2006a; Heath, 2006).

Thus, unlike in the previous discussion, the cosmopolitan's task here is not to establish the *priority* of global justice, but to establish its *validity*. The debate revisits the fundamen-tal philosophical question 'Why does equality matter?' and asks whether the reasons for equality transfer to the global arena. I will examine some recent prominent arguments for equality that limits its scope to the state. These are arguments from (1) reciprocity, (2) coercion, (3) shared governance, and (4) social co-operation.

Reciprocity

One argument is that equality matters because of the ideal of reciprocity—that in a social system, members are required to justify to each other the shared arrangement that they are imposing on each other. The argument for equality based on reciprocity is that any common arrangement that allows for arbitrary inequalities would violate the ideal of reciprocity. Therefore, such an arrangement could be reasonably rejected.

Does the argument from reciprocity really limit the scope of distributive equality to the state? In the *Law of Peoples* Rawls explicitly appeals to the ideal of reciprocity in objecting to the globalists. The ideal of reciprocity in the domestic arena requires that the gap between rich and poor cannot be too wide; but in the global arena, Rawls argues, reciprocity can be satisfied without this egalitarian commitment (1999, pp. 113–15). Reciprocity is met when all peoples are willing to assist each other to support decent institutions of their own. That is, while reciprocity generates distributive commitments among members of a liberal state, it does not generate distributive commitments among persons globally.

On Rawls's account, see Chapter 6.

However, why should the *criterion of reciprocity* issue different demands in the domestic and global arenas? One might argue that reciprocity by itself does not present a reason for equality that limits its scope to the nation state. Something more has to be said about the special quality of the state such that reciprocity *among citizens* imposes demands significantly different from demands among persons globally. If it is reciprocity that both grounds distributive equality and limits it to the state, then it has to be reciprocity of a very specific kind and this has to be spelled out (Caney, 2008).

Coercion

To identify the distinctiveness of the state, some commentators have stressed that an important difference between the state and the global arena is that the former is a *legally ongoing coercive order*. That is, the state is an entity that is able to lawfully exercise force over its citizens and has the **authority** to determine their legal rights and entitlements and obligations. It is this fact of lawful coercion that generates egalitarian commitments among members of a nation state; and because there is not a lawful global coercive authority, there is no similar reason for caring about global equality (Miller, 1998b; Blake, 2002).

One important line of argument draws on the idea of **autonomy**: since lawful coercion is in the first instance autonomy restricting, it must be justifiable to those being coerced if the lawful coercion is to be **legitimate** (Blake, 2002). Such an arrangement would be justifiable, on this account, if significant special consideration is given to fellow members. One such special consideration is that of not allowing for arbitrary inequalities among members. That is, a coercive order is acceptable in spite of its restrictions on autonomy, if these restrictions are compensated for by limiting economic inequalities among persons living under it. For example, the civil laws that society enforces—laws that determine contractual rights, ownerships, taxation, and so on—restrict persons' autonomy, and this system of coercion is legitimate only if it can be acceptable to all, in particular to those who are most significantly relatively disadvantaged (Blake, 2002). This means adopting a principle of mitigating the situation of the worst-off under this arrangement through some distributive commitments. It is only when the worst-off see that the coercive arrangement is, nonetheless, on the whole to their advantage that they will also see it as reasonable.

There are a couple of ways to respond to this argument. One is to question the premise that coercion is the necessary condition of egalitarian justice. It might be the case that where there is lawful coercion, some distributive commitments need to be acknowledged to make that arrangement legitimate in the eyes of all subjects. However, it does not follow that coercion must be a necessary condition for distributive justice—it is open to the coercion argument that there are other reasons for limiting inequality besides that of legitimizing coercion, reasons that could obtain globally.

The second response puts pressure on the empirical claim that there is not a coercive global order. Many observers question this premise (Cohen & Sabel, 2006; Abizadeh, 2007). They argue that there is an ongoing coercive global legal order that is both profound and pervasive and hence restricts autonomy. Consider immigration restrictions. These are lawful coercive institutional arrangements, enacted domestically, but sanctioned by the international legal order, which have a profound impact on the autonomy of outsiders who want to gain admission into a country. Thus, if the need to legitimate domestic lawful coercion generates an egalitarian commitment in the domestic setting, then global lawful coercion should similarly generate global egalitarian commitments. Why, otherwise, should the person who is kept out of a rich country by the coercive rules of immigration regard the global system under which such restrictions are permitted as legitimate, especially if their being kept out means considerably restricting their life opportunities?

On immigration, see Chapter 20.

A defender of the coercion argument might say that there is something distinct about those who are coerced *as members* of a state and those who are coerced as non-members, and that a stronger justification is owed to members, but none, or only a weaker one, is owed to non-members. However, a reason for this distinction has to be given; it cannot just be assumed that membership enjoys a priori special moral standing.

Shared-governance

Thomas Nagel's essay 'The Problem of Global Justice' (2005) introduces a second element in addition to coercion to pinpoint the moral difference between coercion among members and coercion against outsiders. If successful, Nagel's account shows why coercive immigration policies need not submit to the test of legitimacy in the eyes of outsiders. This additional element is the notion of 'joint-authorship' of the laws of one's society, or the implication of one's will in a political system in which one participates. Unlike the coerced outsiders wanting to get inside, insiders are not just subject to coercion. Citizens of a state are coerced under a system of which they are also rightly joint-authors. That is, they are living under a shared coercive system whose establishment and maintenance they ought to be able to consent to, and whose legitimacy consequently relies on their acceptance of this arrangement. To put it simply, persons who ought to have a say in the design of socio-political institutions in their society have the right to demand that these institutions treat them in certain ways if the coercive powers of these institutions are to be deemed legitimate. Thus, it is only among joint-authors of a coercive arrangement, Nagel argues, that the demands for legitimacy can be made.

According to Nagel, as in the coercion argument, one necessary condition for gaining legitimacy is that no arbitrary inequalities be allowed, thus triggering the basis for distributive equality. This provides the argument for why distributive justice matters within the state—the state is, after all, a coercive order, but one in which citizens ought to have a voice in how this order is regulated. However, for Nagel, since there is no global coercive order that *is also* regarded as the joint project of all persons, there is no basis for global distributive demands. A system may, indeed, be coercive to some persons, but if it does not also engage their will they cannot ask for any justification of the arrangement. Objections to global inequalities simply do not gain a 'toehold', as Nagel puts it, because the concern for legitimacy in the global sphere does not arise in the same way as in the domestic case. We can call this the 'shared-governance' argument (Macedo, 2010).

Both core premises of the argument, the normative and empirical, need further defending if the shared-governance argument is to succeed. The empirical premise that there is not a global order that implicates the wills of individuals is questionable. The fact that we do challenge some decisions of global institutions because they have ignored the viewpoints of persons affected suggests that we ideally conceive of them as objects of joint authorship (Cohen & Sabel, 2006). So even if we accept that distributive demands can be made not just among persons merely affected by a common social arrangement, but by those who also have the special status as joint-authors of the system, it does not follow indisputably that distributive justice has no global application.

The normative premise can also be questioned. As some commentators have pointed out, it seems a little perverse (Julius, 2006; Tan, 2006; Abizadeh, 2007). It suggests that my coercion of you requires no justification when you have no say at all about what I can do to you, whereas if you are regarded as someone having some decision-making rights, I will need to justify my coercion of you. This curiously removes protection for those who are most vulnerable to my decisions and actions, namely those who are powerless and disenfranchised from my decision-making process. Joint-authors, on the other hand, are by comparison less vulnerable by virtue of their role as collaborators in the design and sustenance of a given lawful system. So the normative premise seems morally untenable—it offers protection against arbitrary threats to members, but removes protection from those who are most vulnerable by virtue of their non-member status.

Moreover, intuitively speaking, why shouldn't someone who is not a joint-author of a system of coercion be in a position to ask for justification when the system impacts them profoundly? Isn't the fact that a non-member is significantly affected by the set of laws we enact a sufficient reason for according them the right to demand some accounting from us? Nagel's joint-condition—that only those who are joint-authors under a coercive arrangement have the standing to demand that the system be made legitimate—seems too stringent.

Social co-operation

Recently, some philosophers have returned to the ideal of reciprocity to defend the limited scope thesis, but this time they argue that the special character of domestic institutions generates a special requirement of reciprocity in the domestic context. This special character is that of *social co-operation*. A democratic society is seen as a society based on fair social co-operation, and this means, among other things, that the terms of social engagement are those that all members can reasonably endorse (Rawls, 2001a, pp. 6, 120). One requirement for reasonable acceptance is that no arbitrary inequalities be permitted in society, thus generating a concern for distributive equality. It is because society is a system of social co-operation that distributive justice commitments take hold, but because there is no scheme of global social co-operation, these commentators argue, there is no global reciprocity of the relevant sort that can generate distributive commitments (Freeman, 2006a; Sangiovanni, 2007).

The argument from social co-operation relies on both a normative premise and an empirical premise, namely, that distributive justice arises only in the context of social co-operation and that there are no global institutions of social co-operation. To respond to this argument, one has to refute either (or both) of these premises. To refute the empirical premise, the globalist has to show that there are, in fact, global institutions based on social co-operation. The premise flatly contradicts the fact of increasing global interaction and co-ordination, and commitments to common global projects and goals (such as environmental protection and a commitment to **human rights**). Therefore, cosmopolitans will challenge the claim that there is not extensive global social co-operation (Beitz, 1999; Buchanan, 2000).

On empirical globalization, see Chapter 4.

The normative premise may also be challenged. It holds that justice kicks in when there is institutionalized social co-operation, but it leaves open the question whether justice itself could demand the establishment of institutions of social co-operation where none existed. In other words, social co-operation may be a sufficient condition for distributive justice, but it need not be a necessary condition. Accordingly, the globalist may respond by arguing that whereas distributive justice demands social co-operation—in the sense that social co-operation is an integral aspect of distributive justice—distributive justice commitments do not presuppose existing social co-operation. Demands of justice could be made among persons *prior to* any co-operative arrangements existing among themselves (Abizadeh, 2007; Caney, 2008). For example, one could argue that in a situation where there is sufficient interaction among agents, these agents have a duty of justice to ensure that this interaction is based on fair terms. If two societies A and B are unavoidably engaged in competition over a moderately scarce resource, it could be said that this fact of unavoidable engagement entails a duty of social co-operation between A and B. That is, why not say that from the point of view of justice, agents have the duty to ensure that they fairly co-operate with each other when interaction is unavoidable? If social co-operation requires certain institutional arrangements to be realized, then why not hold that the relevant agents have the duty of justice to create such institutions?[4] These are plausible alternatives to the position that distributive justice applies only where there *already exist* institutions of social co-operation.

---

[4] For arguments in this spirit see Beitz (1983).

14.4 Case study: the possibility of global distributive justice

To illustrate the above discussion as to whether the fact of pervasive and profound impact can generate distributive egalitarian demands, consider the following scenario. Imagine two self-sustaining and self-sufficient societies—A and B—functioning with minimal co-operation in a what is more or less a global **state of nature**, meaning by this that there are not any substantial background norms or rules regulating their joint conduct. The main point is that A and B have little direct contact with each other. The basic norms of humanitarianism could compel one society to come to the assistance of the other should it face severe difficulties and be unable to provide the basic conditions of a decent life for its members (including meeting their basic needs and the means for sustaining a minimally well-ordered society). Let us also accept that so long as each of these societies is able to support a reasonable standard of life for its members, inequalities in each of their capacities toward this end in themselves do not raise a question of justice under the condition of non-interaction. On this conception of distributive justice, a necessary condition for distributive justice commitments between A and B is that there is some degree of interaction between them.

However, what form must this interaction take? Does it require that A and B actually be engaged in some kind of sustained co-operative venture, or must it require that A and B are engaged in some form of shared governance? While either co-operation or shared governance would certainly generate distributive demands among A and B, it seems that the relevant interaction condition for generating distributive obligations is met whenever either A or B is able to *systematically impact* the other in profound and pervasive ways.

Suppose that A and B live off the same river, with A settled upstream and B downstream. In the absence of any interaction between A and B, one may grant that since each is able to support a decent standard of living for its own members, the fact that they rely on the same resource pool need not generate distributive egalitarian concerns between them. In the state of nature both are equally able to extract resources from the river. Now suppose that in order to increase its yield of fish, A decides to install a net across the river, a policy that will have profound implications for individuals in B. Members of A know that they should not impoverish B—that would violate the accepted norm of basic humanity—so they make sure that the net allows some smaller fish to reach B to harvest. So persons in B are not denied access to their basic resource, but nonetheless their quality of life is impaired. The inhabitants of B now have to work extra hours each day to maintain the same level of production it had prior to A's action.

A's decision to act in this way is not the result of any co-operative arrangement with B. Indeed, it is blatantly unco-operative. Nor was this decision arrived at jointly by A and B. Members of B had no say in the decision. Yet this seems to be a form of interaction that necessarily brings A and B together into a justice-relationship—that is, into a relationship in which B is in a position to demand from A some explanation and justification for what A is doing. Unless A is willing to accept that its decision has no external legitimacy and that B consequently has every right to attempt to destroy its net, it must seek to explain its decision to B's satisfaction. That B is now worse-off than before is not simply a natural fact and neither just nor unjust in itself, but it is due to the impact of A's decision, a decision that A has the obligation of rendering acceptable to B if the new arrangement is to be legitimate from B's perspective.

If this is correct, the justificatory dialogue could perhaps proceed in this way: B could come to accept A's practice only if B also benefits from it. Thus, A may accept an obligation to distribute a portion of its increased yield to B in a way that also improves B's situation in order to render the new arrangement acceptable to B. So B could be willing to let A improve its quality of life on the condition that B, the worse-off society, benefits. We have just stated the general form of Rawls's 'difference principle'—that inequalities admitted under a social arrangement are acceptable if that arrangement benefits the least advantaged most compared with alternative arrangements. The end result does not have to take the form of the Rawlsian difference principle, but this does illustrate how A and B could come together into a justice-relationship that could ground egalitarian distributive commitments between them even in the absence of existing co-operation or shared governance. That societies enact policies and institutions that have profound and pervasive impact on each other seems to be sufficient for triggering forms of inter-societal distributive demands.

Perhaps a more basic point could be brought to the foreground here: so long as there are some accepted common norms that regulate how societies should interact with each other, distributive commitments potentially could arise. Consider another case: imagine two societies, C and D, living on either side of a river, each minimally well-ordered in the way described above. Yet because of the way natural resources are naturally distributed, C, occupying the north-side of the river, is much better off than D, south of the river, which has to make do with harsher natural conditions. Now if C and D are in a state of nature, the fact that D is poorer than C raises no concerns of justice. It is just a natural fact that there are fewer resources south of the river, and this is neither just or unjust in itself. This is compounded by the (also natural) fact that in this state of nature, members of D are free to cross the river and take advantage of the resources on the other side. So in a global state of nature, the uneven distribution of the earth's natural resources presents no challenge of justice because people are also naturally at liberty to roam the surface of the earth and, hence, free to move to where the resources are.

However, imagine that C actually says to people in D: 'No, you may not cross over to our side of the river, because this is our territory, and you ought to respect our borders. We will also respect yours. Indeed, we live in a world order in which each society is expected to respect the territorial boundaries of other societies.' In response, however, it is reasonable for D to ask: 'Why should we respect this border? There is no natural border here but for your saying so and our recognizing it is so. And why should we accept this supposed "world order" that presumes the salience of borders? If you would like us to respect your border, make us an offer and show us why we have reasons to respect your territorial claim as legitimate.' If C recognizes that it needs to legitimate its claim to D on the ground that D would have no reason for respecting that claim otherwise, then C must accept that it falls into a justice-relationship with D. We can imagine the dialogue culminating in some distributive obligations between C and D in the way described above.

This last hypothetical case suggests that the pervasive impact that grounds justice-demands can be present even in the absence of direct interaction where the impact of one on the other is directly the result of the former's action (as in A versus B), but more generally when there are common background norms or institutions mediating the relationship between the relevant parties (as in C versus D). In other words, where there are norms and rules that each society is expected to affirm (such as respecting borders), the presence of these rules and norms brings all affected into a common justice-relationship, for any party disadvantaged under the arrangement could ask those more advantaged: 'Why should we accept the terms of this arrangement?' To render any shared and binding arrangement legitimate in the eyes of the disadvantaged, one response might be to make it the case that this arrangement is one which benefits them most compared with alternative arrangements. Thus, the very presence of a global order, whose norms and rules each society is expected to endorse, could be sufficient to generate the normative requirement that the level of inequalities that this arrangement can allow be regulated by some global distributive principle.

14.5 Conclusion

Philosophers tend to agree that correctable global poverty is unjust. The main problem, then, is a political one: the lack of practical action to address this injustice. In short, one might say that the problem of global poverty is politically urgent though philosophically less controversial. Still, philosophy can help clarify our understanding of why global poverty is an injustice and the extent of our duties in response to it.

The problem of global inequality and distributive justice is of a different kind. Here, there is less agreement among both ordinary persons and philosophers as to whether global inequality itself is unjust. As this chapter suggests, the philosophical debate on this issue continues. One might say that global inequality is philosophically controversial though in itself a less urgent practical matter than that of severe global poverty.

One might think that there has not been a lot of progress over the past 30 years if global egalitarians are simply back to where they started—namely, trying to establish the case for global egalitarianism. However, this is too pessimistic. Along the way, the arguments have become a lot more sophisticated and informed; indeed, as we have seen, the current debate has ignited a series of new discussions about why equality matters. Our understanding of why equality matters has been enriched due to the global justice debate and this is philosophical progress.

The defence of global distributive justice will require continuing engagement with the philosophical question of why distributive equality matters. In addition to showing how dominant accounts of why equality matters (e.g. the arguments from reciprocity, coercion, shared-governance, institutionalism) do not successfully limit the scope of distributive equality, global egalitarians should take the initiative and propose, or revive, alternative accounts of why equality matters that are more straightforwardly extendable to the global domain.

▨ QUESTIONS

1. Are the issues of poverty and inequality conceptually distinct problems of global justice?
2. Why do critics say that the utilitarian approach to world hunger is morally too demanding? Do you agree?

3. Is there a universal right to subsistence? How is a rights-based approach to world hunger different from the utilitarian approach?

4. Is the global order harmful to the poor? Specifically, can we say that it is harmful without presup-
   posing a strong moral claim about what persons owe to each other?

5. Do arguments for why distributive equality matters for a society carry over to the global domain?

6. Do our commitments to compatriots take priority over commitments to foreigners?

7. Is the reason for taking distributive equality seriously within the state due to the need to legitimize the coercive authority of the state? Or are there other reasons why distributive equality
   matters?

8. Do we have duties of global distributive justice only when there is ongoing global economic co-
   operation?

9. From the case study, could one argue that A is obliged only to repair B's condition—that is, to
   make it as well-off as it was before A's action—and not be engaged in an ongoing distributive
   egalitarian arrangement with B?

10. Suppose that we humans discover a severely impoverished colony of human-like creatures in a
    distant galaxy and that we could assist them by sending resources to them without significant
    sacrifice on our part (though still at some costs). Do we have a moral obligation to do so? What
    if this colony is not impoverished, but only not as well-off as we are? Does this make a difference
    to our moral assessment of the situation?

▩ FURTHER READING

Beitz, C. (1999) *Political Theory and International Relations,* 2nd edn. Princeton: Princeton Univer-
    sity Press. A ground-breaking work that bridges normative political theory and international
    relations. Beitz extends Rawls's argument for distributive justice to the global domain.

Caney, S. (2008) Global distributive justice and the state. *Political Studies,* **57**:487–518. A response
    to recent arguments that distributive justice is a form of associative duty confined to the state.

Miller, D. (2007) *National Responsibility and Global Justice.* Oxford: Oxford University Press. A
    defence of a minimalist conception of global justice in light of the prerogatives of national
    responsibility.

Nagel, T. (2005) The problem of global justice. *Philosophy and Public Affairs,* **33**:113–47. Argues
    that distributive justice is a political duty that arises only in the context of the state in which
    citizens are conceived as co-authors of their shared system of law and government.

Nussbaum, M. (1996) *For Love of Country: Debating the Limits of Patriotism,* J. Cohen (ed.). Boston:
    Beacon Press. A discussion of patriotism in light of cosmopolitan ideals, with critical responses
    by other authors.

Pogge, T. (2002) *World Poverty and Human Rights: Cosmopolitan Responsibilities and Reforms.* Cam-
    bridge: Polity Press. An attempt to derive demanding duties to respond to world poverty from
    the morally minimalist principle that persons have the moral duty not to do harm.

Rawls, J. (1999) *The Law of Peoples.* Cambridge. Harvard University Press. A social contractarian
    account of global justice; among other things, it argues that while global justice includes a
    duty of assistance it does not have a duty of distributive justice.

Shue, H. (1996) *Basic Rights: Subsistence, Affluence and US Foreign Policy*, 2nd edn. Princeton: Princeton University Press. An influential defence of the means to subsistence as a basic right.

Wenar, L. (2008) Property rights and the resource curse. *Philosophy & Public Affairs*, 36:2–32. A discussion of how the proper enforcement of property rights can help to respond to global poverty.

▓ WEB LINKS

http://www.undp.org/ The website of the United Nations Development Programme (UNDP) contains information about and analysis of global inequality and poverty. It also links to a range of UN publications, including the annual Human Development Reports.

http://www.un.org/millenniumgoals/ The UN Millennium Development Goals were targets set for the significant reduction of poverty and hunger by 2015. You can check progress here.

http://www.policyinnovations.org/ideas/media/audio/data/000082 An interview with Thomas Pogge on global institutions and the role of resources.

http://www.philosophytalk.org/pastShows/GlobalPovertyandInternationalAid.htm An interview with Peter Singer on global poverty and international aid.

http://plato.stanford.edu/entries/international-justice/ A useful overview of international justice, written by Michael Blake, from the *Stanford Encyclopedia of Philosophy*.

Visit the Online Resource Centre that accompanies this book to access more learning resources: **www.oxfordtextbooks.co.uk/orc/bell_ethics/**

15 International law

Anthony Carty

READER'S GUIDE

International law sits uncomfortably in law departments, for being too political, and politics departments, for being too legalistic. The discipline is torn by fundamental controversy both about its viability and its goals. This chapter provides an elementary survey of the basic elements of the subject of international law that reflects these pressures. Some are confident that international law can grow into a world constitution, whereas others consider that the anxiety of states to hold on to their sovereignty will keep it within modest bounds. The chapter also considers the impact of critical legal studies on these more traditional debates and ends up arguing for a place for a historian's understanding of the hopes and limitations of international law.

15.1 Introduction

International law is the law that governs states and intergovernmental organizations. It has its primary source in the consent of states as expressed in rules of general **customary international law** and in treaties, whether general or bilateral. The sources are authoritatively set out in Article 38 (1) of the Statute of the International Court of Justice, an organ of the United Nations (UN). The UN Charter is itself a multilateral treaty that rests, for its validity, on the customary law rule that treaties are legally binding and must be observed. Much of international law is codified in general treaties, on the law of treaties, of the sea, diplomatic immunities, trade among states (the World Trade Organization), international crimes, and **human rights**. However, customary international law, a kind of law that is inferred from the general practice of states, still provides the overall structure of the international legal system as a whole. Many vital parts of the law are not codified, especially the rules on the birth and extinction of states, and the rules on the use of force. While the jurisdiction of the International Court of Justice rests on the consent of individual states, it can be asked to give advisory opinions by the other organs of the United Nations. In either capacity it enjoys great **authority** as an interpreter of both general customary and treaty law.

International law has become, in the eyes of its practitioners, no longer in need of theoretical grounding. One can look to the discipline through the established sources of the law. These will be, above all, rooted in general customary law—a form of tacit or implicit state consent, treaties or unilateral declarations. Textbooks in international law will typically regard possible value foundations of the subject as meta-legal, beyond the scope of the discipline. Indeed, they will confine their discussion of the sources of international law to commenting on what the International Court of Justice has to say about the practice of states as evidence of customary law (Evans, 2003).

However, this hope for the complete formal autonomy of international law is mistaken. International lawyers have taken refuge in the apparently rigorous legal technique of commenting on judicial decisions to determine what is or is not international law. Yet, formally, international law rests upon the consent of states, in the mainstream view. So it is necessary to look more directly at the actual evidences of state consent in order to see what a reflection upon all of the evidence indicates about the character of international law as a system. To undertake this analysis the concept of paradigm will be used in this chapter. It will be argued that reflections upon the actual practice of states have, particularly since 1989, given rise to quite distinct paradigms of the nature of international law. That is to say, international lawyers are seriously questioning what exactly is their understanding of international society and the relation of international law to it. This questioning has probably led to some misunderstandings in their arguments with one another, because they are, in fact, making judgements about questions of international law based upon different conceptions of the nature of the international legal order.

The dominant Western conception of international law since the 1990s has been that of a world constitutional order, centred on the principles and institutions of the United Nations Charter. The expectation became increasingly strong that a legal order that was still based upon the stability afforded by the de facto established power of states—and for this simple reason dependent upon their consent for law to be created—could come to express a respect for human rights and even a right to democracy in their internal affairs (Fox & Roth, 2000). However, the 'constitutional approach' has provoked a revisionist 'classical' international law response. According to this view, there is no complete, hierarchical international legal order, but merely a formal, horizontal order among states, as meta-juridical entities, with no additional material values permeating this system, other than those precisely located in formally agreed norms (Weil, 1983).

A third paradigm is the critical approach to international law. The primary legal consequence of the critical approach is no more than to juxtapose the other two legal approaches and to suggest that there is no way to resolve the contradictions which they appear to represent. So, in the most well known and accessible version of this theory

Martti Koskenniemi (2006) divides international legal argument into two forms, the apologetic and the utopian. The former alleges that legal argument is about legitimating the **sovereignty** of states, while the utopian is an appeal to objective principles of justice above states. These are not exactly the classical and liberal approaches, but the critical dichotomy does capture the idea of a schizophrenic opposition at the heart of international law.

A final approach is a contextual international law. States do not owe their existence only to an international legal order. They pre-exist it historically. Communities are historically situated, not fully self-reflective and, therefore, not fully conscious of the complexities of their relationships with one another. International law, as consensual commitment, whether explicit or implicit, is only part of ongoing relationships and it can only be preserved if the relationships themselves are preserved.

15.2 International law as a world constitutional order

It is fair to say that the present dominant mainstream approach to international law is constitutionalist. International law as a profession of legal studies or as an approach to international relations, attracts those who wish to move beyond the national state in the study of both law and international society. The starting point of this approach can probably be said to be the impact of the First World War (1914–18) on Western consciousness. This led to a widespread disillusionment with the previously comfortable acceptance of the classical doctrine of the sovereignty of states. Such a doctrine assumed not merely that states were legally free to do as they pleased except to the extent that they had accepted legal obligations, but that an international society based upon so much state freedom was fundamentally viable. The inclusion of a virtually unfettered right to go to war among these freedoms did most to compel an abandonment of the model. The constitution building, first, with the League of Nations in 1919 and then with the UN Charter in 1945, is about the limitation of the right to war and the attempt to monopolize, as far as possible, the right to use force in an international institutional framework. As state monopoly of the use of force is a main characteristic of the modern state, it can fairly be said that these developments point in the direction of the construction of a world state, which holds individual states accountable for the treatment of its individual citizens, the primary subjects of the international community (Fassbender, 1998; Nijman, 2004).

Whatever the drafting defects of the League Covenant, the UN Charter is virtually categorical in giving the UN, through its Security Council, a monopoly on the legitimate use of force. Article 2/4 of the UN Charter is given the interpretation that no threat or use of force whatever against the territorial integrity or political independence of any state is permissible. This is interpreted, in the dominant opinion, to mean not merely that any attempt to annexe a country is illegal, but any use of force directed to change the composition of a government or even to change its policies is contrary to Article 2/4. This is taken to exclude the minority interpretation that any use of force which does not aim to annexe territory or even to overthrow a government does not come within the purview of the prohibition (Gray, 2008).

The same categorical character attaches to the so-called self-defence exception of Article 51 of the UN Charter. This allows the use of force, pending an intervention of the Security Council itself, only in the event of an armed attack by another state. There are disputes about whether the reference in Article 51 to an inherent right to self-defence means that there remain exceptions to the ordinary meaning of Article 51 as allowing self-defence only in the face of an armed attack. However, even those who allow exceptions usually go only so far as permitting an armed response to a *clearly physically imminent attack*. An attack must be so far gone in actual military preparation that only a use of force across the boundary of a state will prevent it. The Israeli attack on the Egyptian air force in June 1967, or the UK attack on the ship *Caroline*, within US territorial waters in 1839, are taken as paradigm examples. **Pre-emptive** attack against a country supposed to have aggressive intentions is excluded, except where approved by the Security Council (Gray, 2008).

 On pre-emption, see also Chapter 16.

Hence, the powers of the Security Council are crucial to the whole constitutionalist perspective on international law. The consent of the Security Council, including the concurring or acquiescing votes of the five permanent members—France, the United Kingdom, Russia, China, and the United States—is essential to the legality of any use of force beyond the terms of the fairly clear Articles 2/4 and 51. This is the lynchpin of most controversy at present about the use of force in international law. The Charter as a constitutional document does not allow any individual states to claim a special authority to use force to protect or enforce human rights or humanitarian standards. There is simply nothing in the constitution permitting it. There is a fundamental principle here that a constitution is a community act and no individual state can undertake to enforce collective values without collective authority.

Equally, the lynchpin of the Charter serves to exclude extensive concepts of self-defence, which would include a right of anticipatory or pre-emptive self-defence. Underlying this prohibition is the exclusion of the discretion for one state to decide that another state, by its general conduct, by its growing geopolitical, economic, or other potential, constitutes a medium- to long-term threat, which a state is entitled to anticipate while it still has the initiative or any other measurable advantage. It can be easily seen that such doctrines undermine the Charter completely as a constitutional document and leave it open to states to exercise a sovereign discretion to use force where they think international order and security require it.

Much of this approach to the Charter as a constitutional document (Fassbender, 1998) would be accepted by the classical and contextual approaches to international law.

However, since the end of the cold war and particularly in Central Europe, the constitutionalist approach has taken on a specifically liberal, anti-nation state view of the international order. Progressive development of the legal order means the transfer of powers from the nation state to regional and international organizations, as well as to specialized, functional bodies, although the concept of world state as such is avoided. These so-called post-national bodies have, and should have, an increasing responsibility for the implementation of a core value system, shared by the whole international community, effectively the whole body of international human rights. An increasingly integrated international legal order makes necessary a political decision-making process where the national and the post-national must complement each other (De Wet, 2006).

On human rights, see Chapter 13.

At the same time, it has to be recognized that Europe is going through an immense process of self-reflection, in which the very idea of constitution, and not only a European constitution, is contested. A sceptical intellectual climate challenges simplistic notions of popular sovereignty in recognition of the complexity of the processes of the government of the modern world. It sees that the search for **legitimacy** in a continent that has experienced so much war and dictatorship is bound to be hesitant. This uncertainty and self-doubt accepts that the classical authority of the state is obviously surpassed by the sociological fact of globalized transboundary networking, but it does not see the international constitutionalist project as any more than a quest for an all-encompassing perspective on a world society, where states are still an unavoidable part of the picture (Klabbers et al., 2009).

Nonetheless, the centrepiece of the idea of an international constitutional order is that the state is not an autonomous, self-creating, or otherwise self-sufficient entity, but that it is no more than one institutional means whereby the international community tries to assure the public welfare of *individuals* within and beyond its jurisdiction. The state is assigned certain competences over its citizens, which it has to exercise within the limits of international law, particularly the wide ranging rules to do with human rights. The International Court of Justice (ICJ) has affirmed in the *Certain Military Activities* against Nicaragua Case (World Court, 1986) that the enforcement mechanisms contained in human rights conventions may not be, as it were, supplemented with a unilateral use of force by an individual state. As will be seen later in the next section, such a doctrine of necessity to justify the use of force, supposedly to uphold international law, plunges the states concerned into a pre-constitutional, classical international law mode, if it does not eject them altogether from the realm of international law.

In the United States some political theorists and international lawyers (Tesón, 1998; Rawls, 1999; Buchanan & Golove, 2002) spot a weak point in the international law account of statehood that legal constitutionalists work with. They notice that states are historical facts, usually the outcome of coercion and often not democratic. Classical international law was merely satisfied with the acquiescence of a population in its government, so as to legitimize a state in international law. These scholars have an agenda for what they call the democratization of international society, which accords rights and privileges '… only to those states that meet the requirements of transnational justice, understood as respect for individual rights' (Buchanan & Golove, 2002, p. 887). This would-be reformist approach to international law risks conflict with constitutionalist international lawyers around the issue of a possible unilateral right of states to bring about regime change. The latter regard the prohibition of the use of force outside the terms of the UN Charter as the lynchpin of legal order, while the former see a contradiction between the democratic ideals of constitutionalism and the actual state with which the lawyers are willing to work (Buchanan, 2004).

Apart from the unresolved question of the nature of the state, the constitutional legal approach has still to consider a rather broad agenda of matters that it recognizes do require to be regulated in any viable legal order. The first concerns the problem of the **failed state** and collective responsibility for state-making. It is possible to look to this instance to see whether the approach is too ambitious, but that may not be fair, because recent examples of purported **state building** were, it could be argued, undertaken outside of the international constitutional law framework. The USA and UK did not have UN authorization for their intervention in Iraq in 2003, and did not seek it for their intervention in Afghanistan in 2001. In both cases, however, Western military activity is covered by wide-ranging UN mandates and so it is legitimate to ask whether the constitutional paradigm is here proving realistic. The dominant European and American view appears to be that state building, preferably through the UN, is unavoidable (Cooper, 2003).

The second issue is whether a concept of global public interest, similar to that which exists in domestic public law, can be made to fill out gaps that exist in a consensual system of international law. States appear to be able to exercise their sovereign discretion without regard to what other states' interests may be, unless they have accepted clear limits on their sovereignty. Nonetheless, international law does not afford a doctrine of abuse of rights. Such a doctrine would mean that an otherwise unobjectionable use of a right would become illegal, because, in some sense, it might be said that the exercise of the right would impose *unreasonable hardship* on another country. The recent and on-going crisis in financial and banking matters shows states exercising a sovereign right to regulate their individual monetary matters as they please, without regard to the financial welfare of other countries. For example, the decisions of the Irish and German governments to give absolute guarantees for the depositors in their banks were taken without regard for the implications this might have for the banks of countries that are not able or willing to give such extensive guarantees (Lowenfeld, 2008). There has been remarkable progress in the sphere of economic law in regulating tariffs and non-tariff barriers, i.e. broadly speaking restricting the use of direct state power to advantage the industrial power of one's own country in competitive trading with other countries. However, there has been no comparable agreement on the development of a global competition law (Lowenfeld, 2008). Broadly speaking, the same considerations apply to the attempt to apply an abuse of rights doctrine to issues of environmental welfare. The general principles of the English common law of nuisance, for instance, are not regarded as politically credible or useful as a mechanism for a failure to agree globally on the complex mechanisms needed to cope with global warming. It is obvious that states have not until now been able to agree on binding legal principles with respect to global warming and climate change (Sands, 2003).

On climate change, see Chapter 10.

Nonetheless, the direction for the constitutionalist is clear. There is simply a need to develop through a consensual form of regulation, in an ever increasing degree, the public space for the international community, always reducing gradually the individual liberty of states. The *Nationality Decrees Issued in Tunis and Morocco* case on nationality law, already in the inter-war period, set out the fundamental constitutionalist doctrine that no matter is essentially within the domestic jurisdiction of any state (World Court, 1923). The scope of individual state freedom remains large, but it is always being further and further eroded. This is seen as a desirable goal. At the same time the doctrine of the *Lotus Case* (World Court, 1927), combined with the absence of a doctrine of abuse of rights in international law, means that even the constitutionalists remain confronted with the anxiety that James Brierly expressed shortly after the end of the First World War, when he and others first expounded the constitutionalist perspective (Nijman, 2004). They saw there were very many matters remaining unregulated in the public interest at the international level, which one would usually expect to be regulated at the national level. The question may then be posed—constitutionalists do not pose it—whether there are so many such matters that the constitutionalist paradigm needs to be reconsidered or at least qualified.

15.3 **Return to a classical international law?**

In International Relations (IR) theory a distinction is made by Martin Hollis and Steve Smith between an exogenous and endogenous view of the place of the state in relation to international society. The latter term expresses the idea that the state creates itself, while the former view would mean that international society constitutes the state (Hollis & Smith, 1990). The essence of the classical opposition to the constitutionalist approach is that the state is a meta-juridical fact, meaning that international law is not able to constitute the state, but merely recognizes the consequences of its firm establishment. This is what underlies the so-called *Montevideo criteria* (1932), which serve as classical benchmarks for the admission of a state into the international legal community (Brownlie, 2009). A state must have a stable government, with control over a definite territory and the acquiescence of the population. The *Island of Palmas Case* (1924) constructs the international law of territory around the concept of the relative effectiveness of the exercises of state sovereignty over the territory by competing states (Carty, 2007; Brownlie, 2009). In other words, the creation of a state is not normally a communally or **socially constructed** event. Already in the 1930s, Hans Morgenthau criticized Hans Kelsen's view that the state as a legal entity owes its existence to the international legal order, in the sense that its legal authority is delegated to it by the international legal order (Carty, 1998). In fact, he argued that the concentration of power within the state cannot be penetrated by the international order, except through its acquiescence. Morgenthau objects that there is no evidence of an international social order having any compelling domestic impact.

It is arguable that once the meta-juridical character of the state is realized, then large parts of a complete international legal order may unravel. The security trouble spots on the earth, especially Israel/Palestine, Kashmir, Taiwan, the Indian-Chinese border, and the whole series of failed or quasi-failed states, such as Afghanistan, Somalia, Iraq, the Congo, and Pakistan appear to show the relative impotence of the international community either to impose or to facilitate/mediate order within states. The reason is that the *international* is not strong enough to impose itself upon, or otherwise to constitute, the *national*.

On humanitarian intervention, see Chapter 18.

This is the socio-political context in which to reflect for a second time on the place of human rights and doctrines of **humanitarian intervention**. The assumption of the classical approach is that, as a matter of fact, the international is too weak to impose itself upon the national or domestic. Human rights are effective, if at all, only at the domestic level. Beyond that implementation will depend upon the relative power of individual states. In this context the notion of humanitarian intervention, as a mechanism for ensuring a minimum conduct by states towards their citizens, is problematic, because it *can only be* put into practice by stronger alliances of states against weaker ones. Innovative ideas about a right of the people to democracy or to **self-determination** will also come up against the absence of any regular, institutional mechanism which can specify when the right applies and how it is to be enforced.

Another aspect of the meta-juridical nature of the state is that there is no public international law of territory. That is to say, no positive law norms assign particular territories to particular states, despite the role of general peace treaties in the history of Europe. While principles of legitimacy (and later democratic legitimacy) have been worked out between rulers and their subjects, the growth of European and later world public order has not been accompanied by clear public law rules for relations of princes, rulers or governments with one another. The so-called law of territory does not have a public or vertical character, except for the recent prohibition of the use of force, which brings with it the rule against the acquisition of territory through the illegal use of force. Instead, adjudication of territorial disputes is a matter of assessing bilateral, competing claims to territory, based upon relative levels of intensity or effectiveness of activity of a limited number of particular states. Indeed, virtually all such adjudications have taken place in a colonial or post-colonial context and always assume the legitimacy of the title of whatever colonial state had primacy (Carty, 1986).

A restatement of the classical position has been made as a conscious questioning of liberal constitutionalism (Weil, 1983). Prosper Weil argues that states relate to one another legally in purely horizontal relations. On this view, because there is no international community, there is no public interest and relations are determined by treaties as expressions of the will of states. From a legal perspective the state, juridically, is a formal entity, i.e. an addressee of international legal norms that are, in principle, almost entirely the product of state will, in which the participation of the particular state will usually be indispensible.

This classical approach to international law recognizes only whatever treaty limitations have actually been agreed. So, in principle, individual human rights questions are a matter for the domestic jurisdiction of states, since no human rights treaty gives either states or international organizations the legal right to intervene coercively in the internal affairs of a state. As for the collective rights of minorities or the question of the self-determination of peoples, these can hardly be posed in legal terms as against the sovereignty of the state. States will not accept a legal duty that in certain defined circumstances, they must accept dismemberment. The idea is inconceivable (Crawford, 2006).

A concept of public legal interest is very difficult to imagine if the major part of international law is contractual or delictual (i.e. private law terms for treaty law or the law of state responsibility). So this approach does not, obviously, deny the legal character of a fundamental treaty, such as the Genocide Convention, for those states that are parties to it, but it does not understand a concept of **obligations *erga omnes*** (a duty owed by one state to all members of the legal community) apart from the duties accepted by states as parties to particular multilateral treaties, which contain explicitly the idea of general obligation. Therefore, international law does not understand the idea of a state being guilty of a criminal offence—that is, a wrongful act that it can be said to have perpetrated against the international community as a whole as distinct from a legal wrong it has done to a particular state. There can be no concept of ***ius cogens***, an international legal public policy, if by that is meant a norm that does not have its origin in the wills of individual states and can be abrogated by them at any time. Indeed, the state is legally free to entrench itself in its auto-interpretation of its legal obligations, unless it has committed itself to international adjudication (Weil, 1983).

Finally, and most fundamentally, the concept of *lacuna* in the law is central to the classical approach. It will often be the case, as a matter of fact, that the will of states has not regulated a particular matter between them. As a formal system of law, international law cannot then have recourse to general values of 'civilization', whether nineteenth-century Christian civilization or late-twentieth-century Western liberal democracy and the rule of law, to 'fill the gap'. There is no material unity of values underlying the world as a whole, which remains a pluralistic forum, in which law, as the free expression of the wills of states, remains a neutral instrument (Weil, 1983). Even less could there be a doctrine of *abuse of rights*. The idea that there could be an unsocial use of an admitted right, e.g. the use of the water resources of one's own territory (an international river) to the disadvantage of an upper riparian state is not legally acceptable. This does not exclude, indeed it makes it all the more desirable, that there should be an effective international regulation of a common river by the states directly affected. Until this happens, the proponent of the classical approach argues that the principle of territorial sovereignty applies within each territory, come what may.

On realism, see Chapter 5.

In conclusion one might observe that the classical approach resembles **realism** in one very specific respect. Raymond Aron, a leading classical realist, rejected the first-wave constitutionalist agendas of James Brierly, George Scelle, and Hersch Lauterpacht, saying that he preferred as more close to the facts the nineteenth century classical doctrine that state sovereignty preceded international law, to their view that it was specifically the international legal order which accorded personality to states (Aron, 1966). As already noted above, it was Morgenthau who rejected Kelsen's doctrine of delegation by the international order to states for the same reason.

15.4 Critical approaches to international law

The basic tenet of the critical approach is the failure of legal norms to provide clear directions to states. Logical and grammatical interpretations of norms still leave decision-makers to have recourse to subjective and, therefore, political choices, instead of knowing that the norms have unambiguously limited the sovereignty of the state. Every opposition of argument in adjudication, but also in diplomatic exchanges, depends upon two types of argument clashing. The first is an appeal to a standard of objective justice to which states should submit as something standing above them in authority, above their subjectivity and their freedom. The second is an appeal to the freedom of states, to their right to freedom of action, an apology for their behaviour, which starts from the 'on the ground' level, concrete behaviour of states. Critical legal studies is primarily negative in outcome because it robs the progressive, constitutionalist project of any objective foundations, reducing the claims or pretentions of each side to equivalences of subjective preference.

However, the critical approach is not intended to be predominantly conservative. Effectively, it will deny the conservatives their most prized possession, their so-called legal rigour, a reflection of what they believe is the realism with which they face the meagreness of international law's progress. Critical legal studies delights in showing that the sovereign freedom of the state is usually replicated in a clashing freedom of another state, so that the judicial choice made between them is *fully* arbitrary. Therefore, critical legal studies rob the classical approach of the consolation of rule-abidingness which it thinks it shares with the liberal approach.

Critical legal studies try to argue for the existential responsibility of the lawyer for the choices he or she advocates, that these are essentially political, in the sense that the norm does not determine the decision. However, if that is true, the legal foundations for a society governed by the rule of law and by human rights have disappeared. While the conscious rejection of the liberal project is certainly not accompanied by the equally conscious adoption of the classical project, nonetheless the treatment of all discourse as subjectivized and politicized—including legal discourse—means the same in the end as the classical approach, digging one's heels in behind one's own arbitrarily held opinion, which is the same as what is achieved by state sovereignty.

The critical approach is already present, in epistemological terms, in the work of Vattel (1758). For him, the sovereignty of the state meant that princes could not challenge one another's judgements, since each had to presume the other made choices in good conscience. At present critical international legal studies joins forces with post-structuralism in that it considers the signifier and the signified to be inseparable. Translated into the language of international law this means the constitutionalist is precluded from appealing to international community core values that stand above the subjectivity of states. Legal arguments merely express the subjective projections of individuals about how they would like the world to be ruled. They are inherently imperialist in so far as they are implemented without consensus.

On post-structuralism, see Chapter 3.

However, the classical belief in a wide measure of sovereignty remaining for states and vindicated by an objectively verifiable practice based on their consent, is regarded as illusory. In the critical view all states claim freedoms that inevitably clash. There is no clear guidance for states coming from customary practice, only contradiction.

A crucial additional dimension of post-structuralism in this critical international law approach is the binary opposition of the pseudo-objective and the pseudo-subjective approaches. They always go together in a dialectic of a negative pair. Legal arguments, in the jurisprudence of the World Court, vacillate between the two positions, giving the appearance of painful and, therefore, impartial deliberation. However, all the World Court is doing thereby is to hide the fact that it has no authoritative legal answer and is merely making political choices, devoid of legal authority (Kennedy, 1978; Koskenniemi, 1989).

Critical international legal studies are based upon a profound and very close criticism of the jurisprudence of the two courts, the Permanent Court of International Justice (PCIJ) and the International Court of Justice (ICJ) (Kennedy, 1987; Koskenniemi, 2006). For this reason the approach carries great weight in the mainstream of the discipline as an effectively disturbing challenge. For instance the *Lotus Case* (World Court, 1987) can be represented as a triumph for the freedom of Turkey to prosecute a negligent French ship captain for a collision on the High Seas, in the absence of a rule prohibiting it from exercising jurisdiction over a French national for an action outside Turkish jurisdiction, if the person comes within its, i.e. Turkish, jurisdiction. This can ensure that a state that has an interest can contribute to maintaining order beyond state boundaries. However, the critical approach would claim that the French could equally argue that the Turkish action is an interference with a French freedom to control the possibly criminal conduct of its own nationals when they are not within the jurisdiction of any other state. Other states which stand equal to France have no authority over its nationals.

Another favourite case is the *Nuclear Tests* (World Court, 1974). Here, there was a dispute between France and Australia and New Zealand about French nuclear tests in seas near their coasts. The French government gave a declaration that it was ceasing tests. This was a unilateral undertaking of an informal kind, but the Court chose to regard it as a formal legal commitment, so that it, the Court, no longer had any case to hear. The critical argument is that the choice of the ICJ to regard the French statement as binding on them was arbitrary. Indeed, all discoveries of the will of states, the classical source of international law par excellence, are regarded as capricious and wilful by the critical school, a projection of the political prejudices of the judges. This is a fateful critique to make of the rigour of the classical approach to international law.

More recently, there has developed a colonialist and even post-colonialist critique of international law from within the critical school. The colonial history approach may be Marxist or socialist in its concern to use historical methods to demonstrate objective contradictions in the application of the principle of legal equality to states, peoples and individuals (Koskenniemi, 2004; Anghie, 2004; Carty, 2004). The argument goes so far as to say that the unresolved issue of Western responsibility for **colonialism** means the inevitability of reproducing patterns of inequality at present, especially in international economic institutions and treaty relationships. This approach to international law does not say that conceptually it is born of colonialism, but it has always displayed colonial characteristics and aspects of it continue to be marred by colonialism, e.g. especially the law of territory (as discussed earlier).

On post-colonialism, see Chapter 11.

An alternative post-colonial approach to international law treats of international law as part of the imagination of the colonizers and colonized. It comes closer to the spirit of the critical approach in so far as it subjectivizes both sides of the frame and relativizes them in relation to one another. There is no 'truth' of a once and for all colonial injustice, but there is a continuing fear of the other which dominates international relations and has its roots in cultural difference (Berman, 1999). This approach to international law has in common with the classical and contextual approaches the merit of facing directly the character of the collective entities that occupy international society and reflects directly on their consciousness. While not offering a narrative of diplomatic history, it relies heavily on past documentation of the behaviour of countries, through literature, art, and popular media as evidence of their legal understanding of colonial and post-colonial experience (Berman, 1999).

15.5 International law contextualized

There is room for a modified version of the classical approach to international law, which also accepts some aspects of the critical approach. The contextualized approach, which I favour, accepts, with the classical approach, that international law as a system is not hierarchical, but horizontal. It insists the approach has to be contextual, precisely because law, as such, does not exhaustively define the state for the simple reason that international law does not create the state. Therefore, the meta-legal aspect of the state has to be taken into account to assure the viability of what law there is. However, this approach also does not simply accept the 'factual' nature of the state, a blank 'thereness', but endeavours to recognize the components of this 'thereness' especially in terms of culture, understood, above all, anthropologically and historically (Carty, 2007). States are historically constituted, as well as being conscious, deliberating communities. They are, finally, communities that make voluntary, deliberate, and therefore legal commitments, which reduce the scope of unconscious habit in their relations with one another. However, there is always the possibility that the very conclusion of agreements entails misunderstandings, which can auger badly for their future.

There is no global representative order, no 'becoming' world state. According to the contextual view, the liberal paradigm that authority must be found somewhere to enforce global and universal standards must be rejected as structurally bound to produce the contradiction of a small number of states claiming this authority on behalf of the world community. Instead, the development of normativity is necessarily a dialogic, ongoing process. Critical legal theory is correct that there is no automatic, objective interpretative standard that can provide unambiguous accounts of norms. However, critical theory does not offer an account of the state. It vacillates between the classical and the liberal concepts of the state, appearing to accept these two as exclusive alternatives, a binary opposition, without critical theory itself engaging with a theory of subjectivity that has any prospect of participating in norm creation and norm application. In fact, there is nothing to distinguish the critical theory of the state from the classical **positivist** theory that a state is a subject of international law simply and only in the sense that rules of international law are addressed to it (Cassese, 2005). Both theories of international law suppose the existence of abstracted, so-called 'willing entities' that, in the classical view, produce self-addressing norms, and in the critical view, norms that signify the 'willing' of binary and interminable contradictions. The contextual approach, as a modified classical and critical approach, accepts that the agenda for international law is actually historically and presently concretely located in relations among particular communities. It is necessary not only to understand the agreements, but also how the parties continue to interact, considering their relations as a whole.

So, for instance, the Israeli and Kashmiri conflicts—among the most destabilizing of 'inter-ethnic' conflicts—reflect gaps in the liberal approach to world society. A global constitution should have a ready-made, fully packaged solution to such state creation or failed state creation situations, which could be effectively imposed. Instead, the world community is impotent to play the midwife at the birth of states. International society's security frontier is replete with such virtual stillbirths in, for example, the divided Korea, Sri Lanka, the Sudan, and Georgia-South Ossetia.

These cases are so serious as to threaten to marginalize international law as a discipline, because its definition of the state as a meta-juridical fact merely presents an intellectual vacuum, which neither classical nor critical lawyers will fill. The latter may celebrate the contradictions between, for instance, the Israeli desire for territorial integrity and security, and the Palestinian desire for autonomy and self-determination. Such polarized dichotomies reflect an unwillingness, equal to the classical lawyers, to engage with the intricacies of contemporary collective conflicts. One may well speculate that the reason for such reluctance is that the critical scholar shares with the liberal the belief that, while there may be no absolute way to ground the value of the individual, still the individual is the only 'reality' and that they should be left to wallow in their own ambiguity or even 'despair'.

The most serious controversies in international law can usually be attributed either to the failure to confront the stillbirths of so many would-be states or to confront their potential disintegration. However, the fragility of states is usually also a function of the pathology of the relationships that other states have with them. Hence, their difficulties are not a clarion call for a supposed detached international community to 'come to the rescue'. Supposed 'rescuers' are usually part of the problem.

On humanitarian intervention, see Chapter 18.

For instance, take the popular question of whether there is a right of humanitarian intervention. The question usually arises where there is a profound crisis within a particular state, possibly a break up, as in the Sudan or the Congo, but not necessarily, as the government may itself be viewed as pathological, as in Iraq. Liberal constitutionalists will be inclined to suppose that the human rights obligations of individual states may be enforced *erga omnes* by individual states, if necessary, *but on behalf of the global community*. The classicists will react that no individual legal interest of a state goes so far and, most certainly, it has no global representative function or authority. Equally, in effect, the critical school will say that some states claim an objective standard of justice—which would stand above states and could justify intervention—while others will appeal to the sovereign freedom of individual states to stand upon their freedom and their right to resist community interference in the absence of their own proven consent, which alone can provide overriding normative legitimacy—a rehash of the liberal-classical contradiction.

These contradictions can be multiplied across the whole spectrum of international relations that might be, should be, or are thought to be regulated by law. These include the present financial chaos, runaway pollution, nuclear proliferation, energy waste, and exploitation—all occasions where a public interest constitutional lawyer and a national judiciary would assert the existence of general principles of law to reign in the abusive use of state sovereignty by large states. In legal terms, given the liberal, constitutionalist paradigm, such arguments cannot be said to be 'wrong'. However, from a classical perspective they are not realistic and no significant state is going to accept such arguments in diplomatic legal exchanges or submit to an arbitration that might enforce such general principles. The classicist can try to trump general principles of law through an absence of state practice, i.e. actual concrete evidence that states have accepted such standards in their relations with one another. Of course, the critical school will point to the moral confusion and ambiguity of it all.

A contextual approach is empirical and concrete both about the extent of international law, its textual rigour or lack of it, as well as being empirical about the meta-legal context in which rules have evolved. The fundamental point to remember is quite simply that all states are substantially if not fundamentally meta-legal in character. Some, such as Germany at present, owe their status to a series of multilateral treaties. Others owe their existence to mutually agreed compacts between two or three states, which happen to interest no one else, e.g. the Czech and Slovak Republics, and the status of Northern Ireland. However, most states are communities simply accepted into the international community, whether decades or centuries ago, because they appear to be internally viable e.g. China, Russia, the United States, Iran, and many others. This is what makes up the classical law of recognition (Lauterpacht, 1947).

The states have usually had immensely close and often pathological relationships with other states (Buzan, 1983). To say of relationships that they have become pathological or are only beginning to work their way out of pathology, is to say that relationships among collective, organized communities of peoples quite simply have a troubled history. At various times these relationships have been unequal, exploitative, and remain unresolved in some respects. While the ideal may be harmony and equality, the essential prerequisites for stability in and the developing complexity of legal relationships—i.e. quite simply, deepening categorical, conscious (legal) commitments to one another—are not necessarily attained. There is no agreement on who has been exploiting whom or what the true nature of previous relationships actually was. On no issue does diplomatic history guarantee agreement. It merely presents the variety of understandings that exist. This may frustrate the liberal, ground complacency in the classicist, or call for a disillusioned pessimism in the critical scholar. For the contextualist it is simply *work to be done, the task ahead*. The context explains not only why there are obstacles to legal development, but also their exact nature and the possibilities for legal development.

Contextualism is, of course, not a technique or mechanism to produce legal development and progress, but merely a setting of the agenda, in which a partnership between law and diplomatic history—in the widest cultural and geopolitical sense—has to play an integral part. However, in contrast to the critical and classical approaches to international law, the contextualist identifies the concrete historical communities that confront one another and tries to understand how they have got to where they are. It then understands the possibilities of legal normative developments in the wider context of other forms of normative development, remembering always that the normal national form of development of law through the legislature and judiciary are always neither fully present nor fully absent in the ambiguous world of inter-state relations and quasi-international organization.

15.6 Case study: international law, the use of force, and the war in Afghanistan

Since the 9/11 events and the invasion of Afghanistan by the US and the UK in the autumn of 2001, this conflict has gradually become the most pressing in contemporary international affairs. The war began in self-defence because it was alleged that Afghanistan was giving harbour to Al-Qaeda terrorists. It expanded, under UN Security Council resolutions, to full-scale state-building in Afghanistan and has now extended to include extensive US military operations in Pakistan.

This case study poses a test case for the foundations of international law because it can be taken as an expression of the constitutionalist view that the international order can and should strive to construct states which have certain characteristics of liberalism, democracy, and the rule of law (Cooper, 2003). Since this exercise has formal UN authorization, one might say that the Security Council functions effectively as the Executive organ of institutionalized international society. It is difficult to fault this interpretation completely, as the construction of a new government in Afghanistan has goals to protect the rule of law, democracy, human rights and the suppression of criminal activities such as **terrorism** and the drugs trade, at least in the terms of the relevant Security Council Resolutions (Gray, 2008). The weak link is the nature of the governmental construction that is going on, whether it is significantly indigenous, whether it is effective or whether it is actually a Western construction that, even with continuous Western backing, is folding up (Rashid, 2009).

The case study also allows for a classical interpretation. This starts from the customary international law position that the US could argue that the harbouring of Al-Qaeda was a violation of the duty of Afghanistan under the 1970 Declaration of the Principles of Friendly Relations Among States not to allow its territory to be used in such a way as to constitute a threat to other states, i.e. by allowing it to be a launching ground for the organization of armed attacks abroad. The USA and the UK claimed a right of self-defence without recourse to the UN Security Council for authorization. They could rely upon the terms of Article 51 of the UN Charter, which provides that nothing in the Charter takes away the inalienable right of a state to defend itself against an armed attack. The classical approach then invites arguments about whether such a response to 9/11 is really a response to an armed attack, but it is possible to argue that under classical law, it was reasonable to take measured steps to be assured that a particular type of attack would not be repeated. Arguments could also be brought to show that the Taliban Afghan government was not itself directly liable for the aggression of Al-Qaeda, but only indirectly responsible for the consequences of what happened on its territory. On this basis, the classical paradigm is stretched to breaking point if the USA and the UK go so far as to bring about regime change, in order to install a government with even the limited objective of assuring that there would be a government in the country that would prevent further Al-Qaeda operations against them (Gray, 2008).

It is reasonable for the critical approach to international law to point out how serious are the gaps in the norms which international law has to interpret. It can again draw a dichotomy between the constitutionalist and classical approaches, arguing that each can be played off against the other. It is true that the Security Council provides a cover for NATO actions in constitutionalist terms, but this is to accept a regime change already put in place. It is also possible to argue that the military action in Afghanistan has some cover from the traditional law of self-defence, depending on how hard one wishes to push doctrines of defence against armed attack to include defence against imminent attack, to extend that even to an anticipatory right of self-defence. The difficulty is that no clear state practice is emerging to confirm such extensions and one is left with a sense of a vacuum of normativity in international law, which the critical school would use to show the dangerous malleability and core ambiguity which lies at the heart of the contradictions between the constitutionalist and classical approaches to the international law on the use of force.

However, the contextual approach insists upon the need directly to confront the history of Afghanistan and the nature of its relationships with its neighbours, especially Pakistan, the USA, and the UK. This means asking the difficult empirical question of how far the parties actually engaged in the conflict understand or misunderstand one another. This is the context in which to ask whether the regime in Afghanistan is capable of surviving on its own without the support of external powers. This is a question that is, in effect, borrowed from classical international law, which forbade interventions in civil wars where the two sides were evenly matched, although there was some tolerance for the idea that assistance could be provided to an established government where it was merely suppressing disorder. Now a question may be whether outside powers are engaged with what amounts to the virtual recreation of the whole being of a state. However, such criteria are arguably too vague without the explicitly evaluative analysis as to whether the governing structures of Afghanistan are being predominantly shaped from within or without Afghan society (Rashid, 2009).

The fundamental difficulty is whether, given the longer historical view, it is possible to say that the government of Afghanistan reflects a relationship of equality and mutual autonomy with its neighbours, whether geographically proximate or further afield. In the contextualist view it is not useful to ask more detailed questions about, for example, either the law of self-defence under the UN Charter or a reasonable exercise of the powers of the Security Council, unless one has a wider and concretely detailed picture of whether Afghanistan's relationships with other states are harmonious or pathological. This investigation must include not only the history of external interventions, e.g. previous UK interventions in the region, but also a close analysis of the day-to-day management of the country to see whether its actual running leaves any real autonomy to what can be characterized as Afghan authorities (Rashid, 2009).

None of this is to deny the technical integrity of the international law on the use of force or the law of international organization as it affects the operations of the Security Council. It is simply to insist that the surrounding environment that international law needs to support it has to include a close reading of the communities which make up international society. The classical view of states, their creation and their dissolution as meta-legal facts, reflects realism about the ability of states to shape one another's existence. In this view, it is more realistic than the constitutionalist perspective, which believes that the strength of the international community, as reflected in the Security Council, is such that it can shape national societies. The contextual approach, without denying the integrity of the rules and institutions of international law, recognizes that international law rests upon the possibility of relations among peoples—the Afghans and others—which are marked by a continuing practice of mutual respect, free from mutual fear (Carty, 2007). Without an understanding of the pathologies that lead some nations to compensate their own internal anxieties by projecting them onto others it is inevitable that the rules of law so far developed among states will be prey to manipulations and sheer contradictions, which will rob the law of any credibility—this is clearly the case at present in Afghanistan.

15.7 **Conclusion**

The main feature of arguments about international law at present is that clashes are usually rooted not merely in the technical detail of particular paradigms of the discipline, but actually in clashing paradigms. Some international lawyers use the UN Charter or what they call the 'law of the Charter' to support constitutionalist perspectives, while others refer to material norms of the Charter, especially Article 51, to revert to classical pre-Charter international law. Contradictions abound and one whole school, the critical school, treats these contradictions as the hallmark of the subject at the present time. In fact, the most prudent way to proceed is to recognize that those who advocate and rely upon international law in contemporary international society may well be starting from quite different theoretical foundations. One needs to be alert to the presence of conflicting paradigms. The final counsel is to recognize that international legal norms do play a significant role, but that other types of normative considerations also apply. These norms come into play most of all when diplomats are striving to maintain strong and balanced relationships among states that have themselves to be understood largely in their meta-legal aspect, as creations of history and culture, only malleable to a limited degree through the voluntarist techniques of legal commitment, i.e. agreements in the form of treaties, unilateral, or multilateral declarations. In fact, the contextualist way to describe the progressive development of international law over and against the dead weight of culture and history is to observe and facilitate new achievements in the law as the conscious reflection of the increased maturity of the relations of states with one another.

QUESTIONS

1. What is the place of the UN Charter in the contemporary international legal order?

2. What are the fundamental rules of international law at present concerning the use of force by states?

3. Does international law have a clear legal definition of the state?

4. Does international law aspire to incorporate a set of liberal, constitutional legal values in international society?

5. Are there affinities between what international lawyers call a classical approach to international law and the realist school of international relations?

6. Is the UN Security Council the effective arbitrator of legality in contemporary international society?

7. Could it be argued that individual states have a right to use force to prevent grave violations of human rights by other states against their own citizens?

8. Does international law have rules and principles adequate to regulate virtually every difficulty that could arise in international society, or should one accept that there are serious lacunae in the international legal order?

9. Should international law be regarded as an autonomous legal order or is it in need of the support of other disciplines, such as history, anthropology, or philosophy?

10. Is it true that one single paradigm of international law is significantly stronger than the others, even if it cannot exclude them entirely?

▓ FURTHER READING

Anghie, A. (2004) *Imperialism, Sovereignty and the Making of International Law*. Cambridge: Cambridge University Press. Sets out the fullest case that colonialism shaped the origins of, and continues to shape, international law.

Carty, A. (2007) *Philosophy of International Law*. Edinburgh: Edinburgh University Press. Sets out a case for the contextualist paradigm of international law.

Cassese, A. (2005) *International Law*, 2nd edn. Oxford: Oxford University Press. An interdisciplinary account of mainstream international law.

De Wet, E. (2006) The international constitutional order. *International and Comparative Law Quarterly*, **55**:53–76. A succinct statement of the constitutionalist project.

Fassbender, B. (1998) The United Nations Charter as the Constitution of the International Community. *Columbia Journal of Transnational Law*, **36**: 529–619. The seminal article on the constitutionalist approach.

Fox, G., & Roth, B. (2000) *Democratic Governance and International Law*. Cambridge: Cambridge University Press. Debates the undemocratic character of the classical idea of the state in international law.

Gray, C. (2008) *International Law and the Use of Force*, 3rd edn. Oxford: Oxford University Press. International law discussions about recent questions of the use of force.

Koskenniemi, M. (2006) *From Apology to Utopia: The Structure of International Legal Argument*, 2nd edn. Cambridge: Cambridge University Press. The canonical text of the critical approach to international law.

Nijman, J. (2004) *The Concept of International Legal Personality, An Inquiry into the History and Theory of International Law*. The Hague: Asser Press. Provides a historical and philosophical foundation for the constitutionalist paradigm.

Weil, P. (1983) Towards relative normativity in international law. *American Journal of International Law*, **77**:413–42. The classicist reaction to the constitutionalist paradigm.

▓ WEB LINKS

http://www.un.org This site contains the records of meetings and resolutions of the UN Security Council, as well as the decisions and advisory opinions of the International Court of Justice.

http://www.ejil.org The website of the *European Journal of International Law*, which contains numerous articles and special issues covering most fully the debates in this chapter.

http://www.journals.cambridge.org/action/displayJournal?jid=LJL The website of the *Leiden Journal of International Law*, one of the leading periodicals in the field.

Visit the Online Resource Centre that accompanies this book to access more learning resources: **www.oxfordtextbooks.co.uk/orc/bell_ethics/**

16 The ethics of war: the just war tradition

Nicholas Rengger

READER'S GUIDE

This chapter offers an account of the historical development of the just war tradition, its major conceptual claims in the contemporary context, current debates within it—for example whether the traditional distinction between the *jus ad bellum* and the *jus in bello* is valid—and some possible criticisms of it. It concludes with a discussion of how the tradition has been deployed in the context of the post 9/11 so-called 'war on terror'.

16.1 Introduction

It is a truism that almost all the political communities of which we have any record have used coercive force. It has been used to manage conflict and division within societies, and also in asserting the interests and desires of societies against each other. This fact of the human political condition has remained true across time and place, in many different cultural settings, and in the context of many different political and institutional forms. However, the use of such coercive force, as has also long been recognized, creates profound ethical dilemmas. This is true even in domestic contexts—over what kind of force may be used to uphold the law, for example—but it is perhaps especially acute when societies use coercive force, and especially violent coercive force, against other societies. The questions are many and subtle: Is a society permitted to use *any* force to secure its interests, defend its integrity and/or uphold, or even spread, its values? What conditions or contexts, if any, permit the use of such force? Should we expect the use of such force to be governed by the normal rules governing force? And so on.

These questions have long been a staple of the philosophical discussion of politics, and in the wake of the attacks of 11 September 2001 they remain both vital and highly controversial. In the context of European thought, at least, and from Antiquity onwards, consideration of such questions has essentially been constructed around three 'ideal' positions: (1) that war is *never* legitimate; (2) that in war *everything* is legitimate; and, finally, (3) that in war some sorts of restraint, both on what we can legitimately fight for and on how we may legitimately fight, are morally required.

The first view, usually known as pacifism, was virtually unheard of prior to the coming of Christianity, but has been a persistent, if minority, position ever since, both within the Christian tradition and outside it. The second view has come in many forms, but its various modern versions have usually been allied to the evolution of the European states-system, in particular to traditions such as *raison d'état* and *Machtpolitik*. It has often been seen as complementary to a 'realist' position in international relations, although whether this is an appropriate way of seeing '**realism**' is, of course, another matter.

 On pacifism, see Chapter 17.

 On realism, see Chapter 5.

The **just war** tradition is a version of the last view—the dominant version it has taken (in Europe and later the United States) over the last thousand or so years. The key work establishing and refining the tradition was done roughly between the fifth and the seventeenth centuries, at which point a broad consensus on claims the tradition makes had been reached. However, after that period the tradition went into a partial eclipse, until it was reinvigorated by the movements to control war that gave birth to the codification of the laws of war in the nineteenth century. That was followed by a great burst of intellectual activity after the Second World War, which has created a renaissance of writing and thinking about the just war tradition unparalleled since the seventeenth century (Bellamy, 2006).

The just war tradition has thus displayed great longevity and huge intellectual power. However, its character is often misunderstood. It is often seen as a kind of 'moral calculus' that allows politicians or citizens to do a quick calculation and work out whether this or that instance of the use of force is 'just'. In fact, such a view profoundly misconceives the nature of the tradition. As the theologian Oliver O'Donovan argues:

> … it is very often supposed that just war theory undertakes to *validate or invalidate particular wars*. That would be an impossible undertaking. *History knows of no just wars, as it knows of no just peoples* … one may justify or criticize acts of statesman, acts of generals, acts of common soldiers or of civilians, provided one does so from the point of view of those who performed them, i.e., without moralistic hindsight; but wars as such, like most large scale historical phenomena, present only a question mark, a continual invitation to reflect further. (O'Donovan, 2003, p. 13, emphasis added)

This needs to be borne in mind as we explore the just war tradition. This chapter is structured as follows. I first offer a brief account of the historical development of the tradition. The second section then lays out the way that what I will term the 'classical' just war tradition understood its central claims and contrast that with the way modern writers have reconfigured the tradition. A third section then considers some of the major criticisms that have been made of the notion of a just war and where we stand now in relation to thinking about it. In the case study, I consider the events of the post-9/11 world as an example of how the tradition functions in the contemporary context.

16.2 History of the tradition

Normative attitudes about what it is permissible to do in war are features of virtually every culture and time period. The Ancient Greek practice of war, for example, operated under a series of conventions that were, for the most part, adhered to and which, when violated, brought genuine opprobrium, and sometimes worse, on the heads of the violators. The ransom of prisoners, the possibility of burying the dead who had fallen on the battlefield, the honouring of certain sacred truces (such as those celebrating the Olympic games): these were conventions that had the effective force of law. When they were violated, the shock and anger was heartfelt, as Thucydides makes clear in his celebrated account of the Peloponnesian war between Athens and Sparta. The Romans, by contrast, while they also had complex conventions concerning war—indeed, in Rome the whole process of going to war was heavily formalized—had few constraints at hand once a war was itself deemed legitimate. This led to some medieval writers inventing a class or type of war—the *bellum Romanum*; a war without limits or restraints (Coppieters & Fotion, 2002).

The just war tradition itself emerges out of the encounter of such general practices of war fighting and legitimation with specifically Christian concerns about the legitimacy of fighting at all. Early Christian communities were largely pacifistic and, although this generally held while Christianity was a persecuted and minority sect, it became a great problem after Christianity became an official religion of the Roman Empire. Christian leaders rapidly became involved in the internal politics of the Empire and, thus, the question as to how they could square the teachings of Jesus with the responsibilities of political office became increasingly acute.

This led influential church leaders such as Ambrose, Bishop of Milan (ACE 340–397) and even more importantly Augustine, the Bishop of Hippo (ACE 354–430) to sketch out a framework that permitted Christians to undertake, in certain contexts, military action in defence of the Empire. Essentially, Augustine argued that human beings were all 'fallen', that is to say sinful and, thus, subject to many conflicting desires, some noble, but many not. The result is that conflict, and thus war, are inevitable aspects of the fallen condition of humankind. In his major work *The City of God*, Augustine is unsparing in his analysis of the follies and stupidities of war, and it is clear that he shares much of the early Christian fathers hostility to it and to the 'martial virtues' that perpetuated it. However, he also thought that under some very specific circumstances a Christian should fight, if called upon to do so by a legitimate ruler. He is clear that the sin inherent in this action (which will after all result in the death and injury of others) will fall on the ruler, not the dutiful Christian solider, but also insists that Christians must fight with the right attitude. They must not hate and give themselves up to the frenzy of battle, but rather fight regretfully and with humility. In these remarks about war, scattered through works like *The City of God*, and many sermons and pastoral letters, Augustine provided some of the intellectual foundations for what becomes—much later—the organized body of doctrine we can call 'the just war tradition'.

It is not until Thomas Aquinas (1225–74) that we see the tradition as it is later understood begin to emerge. Aquinas shared with Augustine the view that war was the consequence of sin, but he differed from him in thinking that all war is sinful. Rather, following Aristotle, Aquinas saw government and politics as a trust wherein rulers are responsible for the common good and that, to fulfil this responsibility, they may sometimes—and rightly—have to use lethal force. However, it is also true that force can be directed towards evil ends as well as good ones and, thus, the decision to use force, as well as how it is used, needs to be carefully considered. Aquinas argued that force is morally legitimate if three conditions have been met. First, it must be waged by and through a legitimate public authority (not, in other words, by 'private' groups or individuals or by illegitimate authority). The second condition is that there must be a 'just cause', which for Aquinas essentially meant that the party attacked must be guilty of some wrongdoing. Finally, the third condition is that those prosecuting a just war should have a 'rightful intention'. Here, Aquinas is picking up on Augustine's point about the Christian fighting with the correct moral attitude, but he generalizes it to suggest that both the reason for which the force is used and the way in which it is used must intend 'the advancement of good and the avoidance of evil' (Brown et al., 2002, p. 214).

It is in the work of the scholastic philosopher Aquinas, then, that the lineaments of the just war tradition were first outlined. However, as James Turner Johnson has put it, to all intents and purposes:

… there is no just war doctrine, in the classic form as we know it today, in either Augustine or the theologians or canonists of the high Middle ages. This doctrine, in its classic form, does not exist before the end of the Middle Ages. Conservatively, it is incorrect to speak of classic just war doctrine existing before about 1500. (Johnson, 1974, pp. 7–8)

Crucial to the development of what Johnson calls 'classical just war doctrine' were the writings of a group of theologians and philosophers often referred to as the 'School of Salamanca' (after the University in Spain where many of them were trained or based). One writer in particular was central: Francisco de Vitoria (1492–1546). His lectures, on a wide variety of subjects, became central to the revival of scholastic and Thomistic philosophy both in his own day and for several centuries afterwards.[1] Vitoria lectured many times on topics connected with war, including on conquest and the laws of war, but the issues that occasioned his most influential reflections on the topic were all connected with the Spanish conquest of America and its treatment of the native inhabitants living there, which Vitoria found to be appalling.

In his celebrated lecture *De Indis* (*On the Indians*) Vitoria is straightforward: 'Difference of religion', he says, 'is not a cause of just war.' Following Aquinas, he argues that the only justification for war is a wrong done or received, and the only way of identifying this and, therefore, identifying whether a war is just or not is through the application of the natural

---

[1] Thomism is the name of the movement that took its philosophical and theological inspiration from the writings of (Saint Thomas) Aquinas.

law, common to all, Christian and non-Christian alike. It was this claim that led him to state, controversially in his own day, that the Spanish crown was not justified in using force against the non-Christian inhabitants of its new world colonies in order to deprive them of their property. However, in advancing this argument, Vitoria tackles a topic of huge significance for the evolution of the just war tradition; Johnson calls it 'the problem of simultaneous ostensible justice' (Rengger, 2008a).

The standard view, in earlier just war thinkers, was that it is incoherent to talk of a war being 'just on both sides'. Aquinas, for example, is usually read as insisting that a just war is one fought in response to some fault, a view we have seen Vitoria agreeing with. Yet if this *is* the case, then clearly there cannot be *justice* on both sides, though there certainly can be—and very often will be—injustice on both sides. 'In the case of each of the prospective belligerent's having a claim on something in dispute, there must be no war, and if one occurs, it is not just but unjust on both sides at once' (Johnson, 1974, p. 186).

Vitoria then suggests that this presents us with an ethical *dilemma*: 'if each side is just, neither side may kill anyone from the other and therefore such a war both may and may not be fought' (quoted in Johnson, 1974, p. 187). However, he goes on to argue that the resolution of this dilemma can be found in the recognition of a distinction between *genuine* just cause and *believed* just cause, or what he calls, 'invincible ignorance'. The point he emphasizes here is that people fighting a war should assume that those opposing them are guilty of ignorance, rather than genuine wrong doing; in other words, it emphasizes that while *in truth* (i.e. in the sight of God) there is no such thing as a war just on both sides, human knowledge is incapable of judging this with any degree of accuracy. The obvious implication is that in fighting a war, one should develop as many restraints as possible, given that those who oppose you may not be guilty of genuine fault, but merely of invincible ignorance.

It is this insight that gradually separates out the two aspects of the tradition that have become canonical:

- The *jus ad bellum* (justice of war)—this relates to why and for what reason force can be used.
- The *jus in bello* (justice in war)—this relates to what can be done in war itself, who can be targeted, and what amount of force might be used.

Working from the position established by the school of Salamanca, the tradition develops in leaps and bounds in the ensuing period, although hardly in a linear fashion.

It is these assumptions that have generated what I will term, following Johnson, 'classic' just war arguments, but they have been supplemented since the late eighteenth century by what we might call the growing 'juridicalization' of the just war (Rengger, 2002). The growing significance of formal international law in the years after 1860 became central to the changing character of the *jus in bello*. Another significant departure was the issuing of general regulations to established armies, the most celebrated example being the General Orders No. 100—*The Instructions for the Government of Armies of the United States in the Field*—prepared and mainly written by Francis Lieber at the invitation of General Henry Wager Halleck, during the American Civil War (1861–65). In both cases the concern springs initially from the problem of distinguishing combatants from non-combatants. Civil wars require a treatment of irregular warfare that had previously not been discussed (except in the occasional accounts of the ethics of siege craft in medieval writing on the just war) and which gave rise to a considered discussion of duties owed to prisoners of war, a subject only cursorily treated by earlier theorists. At roughly the same time, the gradual process of the codification of international law—indeed, what one might call the 'project' of international law itself—begins to take shape and this has pronounced affects on the *jus in bello*, including the formal adoption of agreements limiting and banning certain classes of weapons or particular types of action (for a recent example, think of the Mine Ban Treaty, outlawing the use of landmines).[2] Much of this has been embedded in the operation of international institutions, e.g. the United Nations (UN) system and the creation of the **International Criminal Court** (ICC) in 1998.

On international law, see Chapter 15.

16.3 **The classical just war and the modern just war**

The positions I identify in this section are composites drawn from a variety of different writers; not all of them can be found in every just war advocate. Nonetheless, there are broad positions one can characterize as 'classic' and 'modern' just war accounts, and it is worth emphasizing both their similarities—they are after all part of an ongoing tradition of thought—and their differences.

So how should we characterize the general ethical position of the 'classic' just war writers? Essentially, as I remarked above, the tradition was seen as having two parts, the *jus ad bellum* and the *jus in bello*. The *jus ad bellum* coalesced around a set of seven principles, which are still often cited as central to modern invocations of the tradition. These are:

- *Just cause*: we have seen the evolution of this in both Aquinas and Vitoria; for classic just war theory it meant response to a wrong done.

- Right authority: as above, but this emphasizes the public aspect of legitimate resort to force. War must be made by a legitimate public authority.

- Right intent: perhaps the oldest strand in classic just war theorizing, traceable to Augustine, it usually implies the correct attitude to both the fact of war and to waging it (not with hate or out of a desire for vengeance).

- Proportionality of ends: this follows from the previous three criteria—the ends sought must be proportionate to the damage inflicted and the harm done.

- *Last resort*: this criterion is also logically entailed by the others. If the end is proportional, in that the just cause is righting a wrong and if you are waging it with right intent, the use of force must be the 'last resort'. Everything short of war should be tried first.

- Reasonable hope of success: war should not be undertaken, according to classic just war doctrine, if there is not a reasonable hope of its succeeding in its proportionate ends.

---

[2] This is formally known as the Convention on the Prohibition of the Use, Stockpiling, Production and Transfer of Anti-Personnel Mines and on their Destruction. However, it has not yet been ratified by a number of major countries, including the United States, China, and Russia.

For, of course, the harm you do in war is legitimate if, and only if, it reverses or responds to greater illegitimate harm, and if there is no realistic prospect of success, this will not be the case.

- *The aim of peace*: among the central claims, from Augustine onwards, is that all use of force must have as its stated aim the end of returning to a peaceful, settled world. Only for that end is force justifiable at all.

The *jus in bello*, meanwhile, had come to revolve around two central principles:

- *Proportionality of means*: again this is a logical entailment. If you are subject to an irritating but largely insignificant border skirmish, it is not proportionate to the damage done to (for example) use the full weight of your military to destroy the enemy capital city. You must make the means you use proportionate to the means that are used against you.

- *Non-combatant immunity*: this is the flowering of Vitoria's notion of 'invincible ignorance'. Because you have to assume false belief, rather than malevolent will, on the part of your adversaries you must put the maximum restraints in place and this means you must heavily restrict who counts as legitimate targets. Essentially only 'combatants'—those actively engaged in prosecuting the war—can be legitimate targets, and that means that (for example) those enemy soldiers who have surrendered cannot be targeted as they are no longer active in prosecuting the war and nor, of course, could enemy civilians. This generates very difficult questions in an age of so-called 'weapons of mass destruction'. The cold war, for example, raised for many the prospect of Western policy being predicated upon something—the system of nuclear deterrence—that was, by definition, morally wrong. For some just war advocates even the threat of nuclear use was immoral and should be abandoned as it violated this criterion of the just war tradition (e.g. Anscombe, 1981).

In the context of classic just war theorizing there is perhaps one other topic that needs to be mentioned, since it is a widely cited aspect of traditional just war thinking, and has come to play an important—and heavily contested—role in modern just war thought: this is what is usually called the 'doctrine of **double effect**'. One can find the origin of this idea in Aquinas's discussion of individual defence against armed attack (Brown et al., 2002, pp. 184–5). Aquinas holds that it is permissible (i.e. not sinful) to kill in self-defence on condition that the aim you have is to save your life and is not, in itself, to aim at the death of your attacker. *If* their death was an unintended by-product of their attack on you, then you have killed without sin. It is the effect of your self-defence, but not its intention, hence there is a 'double effect' to your act.

On the doctrine of double effect see also Chapters 17 and 19.

The application of this idea to the just war is fairly straightforward. It has been used to claim that an attacking force can target a military installation (say a munitions factory) even if the likelihood is that targeting the installation will also kill many civilians who would normally be considered 'non-combatants' and, hence, beyond the scope of legitimate attack. Many contemporary just war thinkers have developed this logic (e.g. Walzer, 1977, pp. 151–9), but others have argued that it is a complete misreading of Aquinas' point. G. E. M. Anscombe (1981), for example, referred scathingly to what she saw as 'double think about double effect'. We will return to this debate later.

How does modern just war theorizing differ from the 'classic' doctrine? This is a complex story, but there are two points that need to be made about the transition from the one to the other. The first is the obvious point that the just war tradition in its classic mode evolved against the background of the medieval and Renaissance worlds. The forms of political community were shifting and fluid, and the nature of politics was very different from the modern world. In particular, the evolution of the modern state and, by the mid-eighteenth century at least, of the system of states, started to reshape aspects of the tradition. Once it became commonplace, for example, to assume that states had a right to pursue their interests by the use of force then the *jus ad bellum* becomes far more attenuated, since its central concern—under what circumstances may force be used—is already answered. It is significant that it was really the *jus in bello* that remained the active part of the tradition until well after the Second World War, since it is this that dovetails most obviously with the institutionalization and legalization that marked international relations in the nineteenth and twentieth centuries (Rengger, 2008a).

The second point, of course, is that the revival of the just war tradition after the Second World War, brought about as it was by a range of both intellectual and political events—for example, the creation of the UN, and the adoption of the Universal Declaration on Human Rights and the Genocide Convention, on the one hand, and the US trauma in Vietnam on the other—raises again the questions that lay at the heart of the *jus ad bellum*. States could no longer simply assume a right to use force whenever they felt like it, yet the world was still composed largely of states. This produced many ambiguities in modern versions of the tradition.

Thus, for example, 'just cause' in the traditional just war setting ranged from the defence of the innocent against armed attack, through the retaking of persons, property, or values unjustly taken, to the punishment of perceived evil. In the modern context, however—at least until very recently—it shrunk to national self-defence against armed attack or, perhaps, retaliation for armed attack (Johnson, 1984).

These developments have unquestionably shaped a good deal of contemporary just war theorizing. Initially, it was largely in the areas of religious thinking on questions of war and peace that the tradition was most obviously and most consciously rethought. Protestant theologians, notably Paul Ramsay, and then later James Turner Johnson and Oliver O'Donovan, have refined the traditional inherited categories and sought to deploy them in modern contexts (Ramsay, 1968; Johnson, 1974, 1981, 1984; O'Donovan, 2003). However, in Catholic social thought too, the tradition was revived and discussed at length (e.g. Grisez, Boyle, & Finnis, 1987). Perhaps most influentially in this vein, the political theorist Jean Bethke Elshtain has developed an important body of work on the just war drawing on many theological sources, but also engaging with the secular realities of the modern period (Elshtain, 1987, 1992, 2003, 2008).

Among the most significant developments, however, have been attempts to develop a *secular* version of the concepts and categories of the just war tradition. For the most part, this has been done through putting the classic just war criteria listed above into dialogue with aspects of the contemporary international system, international law, and political philosophy. The paradigm case of 'secular' just war theorizing is Michael Walzer's book

Just and Unjust Wars (1977).[3] In a symposium published to mark the twenty-fifth anniversary of the publication of *Just and Unjust Wars*, Michael Joseph Smith made the point that 'since its appearance the book has been a standard text at universities throughout the world—as well as at military academies including West Point' and adds that 'I would … name it without hesitation as the indispensable modern classic in the field. Most of the people I know who teach in this area would agree' (Smith, 1997, pp. 3–4).

It is, of course, impossible in a short survey such as this to do justice to the complex argument Walzer develops in the book, but given its significance a few comments are appropriate. After an opening section where he establishes (against the 'realist'[4] position I mentioned above) what he terms 'The Moral Reality of War' he turns to what he calls 'The Theory of Aggression' (essentially his version of the *jus ad bellum*). In the first place he adopts, almost casually, and from the beginning, the assumption that the principal agents of war are states and he thus structures the 'legalist paradigm' around his treatment of the rights of political communities. These rights, Walzer tells us, are merely the collective form of individual rights. This way of thinking generates, he argues, the 'legalist paradigm' that, however it might be slightly modified or reworked in practice (and he accepts that it would be), is the basic way we should ground and frame the just war tradition. 'It is', he tells us, 'our baseline, our model, the fundamental structure for the moral comprehension of war' (Walzer, 2000, p. 61).

What this claim does, of course, is to set up the just war as fundamentally state-based and connect it with the language of rights as it has developed within the modern states system. This then generates in its turn what Walzer terms the 'War Convention' (his version of the *jus in bello*), in the course of which he discusses many of the most difficult issues of the *jus in bello* (for example, non-combatant immunity versus military necessity, war against civilians, guerrilla war, terrorism, and reprisals). He then deals with some major contemporary dilemmas of war. Some of these, such as neutrality, are clearly influenced by the cold war setting in which he first wrote the book, but others, for example, nuclear deterrence and 'Supreme Emergency'—on which more in a moment—have permanent and even some very stark contemporary resonances. He closes the book with a discussion of the responsibility of political and military leaders and of non-violence.

On the ethics of responsibility, see Chapter 5.

Given that the so-called 'war on terror' is often seen as a 'Supreme Emergency'—an existential threat to one or more political communities—it is worth spending some time on the idea. Walzer suggests that the idea of Supreme Emergency is, in fact, a compound of two conditions, both of which must be present if it is to be (justifiably) invoked: danger and imminence.

> [Supreme Emergency] is defined by two criteria, which correspond to the two levels on which the concept of necessity works: the first has to do with the imminence of the danger and the second with its nature. The two criteria must both be applied. Neither one by itself is sufficient as an account of extremity or as a defence of the extraordinary measures extremity is thought to require …

---

[3] Other editions were published in 1991, 2000, and 2008. For some of Walzer's other writings on the use of force, see Walzer (2004). For a recent important secular defence of the just war tradition, see Coady (2008b).

[4] I use quotation marks to indicate that this may not be a very good way of conceptualizing 'Realism' (see Chapter 5), but it is Walzer's usage so I will let it stand here.

can a supreme emergency be constituted by a particular threat—by a threat of enslavement or extermination directed against a single nation? Can soldiers and statesmen override the rights of innocent people for the sake of their own political community? I am inclined to answer this question affirmatively, though not without hesitation and worry ... (but) danger makes only half the argument; imminence makes the other half. (Walzer, 1977, pp. 252–5)

Walzer illustrates this thesis with two detailed examples, both cases where the central principle of the *jus in bello*—non-combatant immunity—was intentionally violated. The first is the strategic bombing of German cities by the British between 1940 and 1943, which he argues could be seen as a context in which Supreme Emergency was legitimately deployed because both danger and imminence were present. The British state faced catastrophic defeat. The second is the decision to drop the Atomic Bomb on Japan in August 1945. Walzer argues that because the United States was not facing defeat, this did not represent a case of Supreme Emergency, and that therefore the bombing was doubly a crime, because neither of the necessary conditions was present (see also Rengger, 2008b).

Walzer's book has had, as we noted, a profound impact in its own right but it has also helped to generate a renaissance in just war writing. Taken together, this body of work ties in current reflections on the just war with contemporary political, legal and institutional issues, such as **humanitarian intervention**, **terrorism** and the so-called 'war on terror' (as we shall see in the case study). However, it also has to be said that in the process the shape and content of the tradition has changed a good deal. Traditions do change, of course, and one might say that the just war tradition has of necessity been very good at changing over the years, otherwise it is hard to see how a body of thought originating in the late antique world could continue to be of relevance in the twenty-first century, as the just war tradition most certainly is. However, there are questions as to just how the tradition has changed and whether it has changed for the better.

See Chapters 18 and 19.

Perhaps the most radical *contemporary* change is the attempt to construct a 'cosmopolitan' just war theory. This is associated with the more general development of a 'cosmopolitan turn' in contemporary political philosophy. While cosmopolitanism has a number of different meanings, in contemporary **analytic political theory** it usually refers to a morally universalistic claim that individual human beings are the source and proper recipient of moral worth, and that (for example) political communities only have derivative moral value, when they have such value at all. In the context of the just war tradition, cosmopolitan political theory—represented by scholars such as Simon Caney (2005a), David Rodin (2002), and Cécile Fabre (2008)—has launched an attack on much of the traditional apparatus of the just war. It has challenged, for example, state-centric notions of the just war (as found in Walzer) and even the idea of just cause itself, as well as the distinction between the *jus ad bellum* and the *jus in bello*.[5] Ironically, in this respect at least, they are harking back to pre-sixteenth-century understandings, when the distinction was far less clear.

On cosmopolitanism, see Chapter 8.

We can perhaps most usefully close this section with a brief summary of how and in what way the modern just war differs from its 'classic' precursor.

---

[5] Jeff McMahan (2009), for example, challenges the distinction between *jus ad bellum* and *jus in bello* by arguing that it is wrong to fight in a war that lacks a just cause. Another important recent challenge to traditional just war categories can be found in May (2007).

- The modern just war takes its starting point from the state system and assumes—at least as a working hypothesis and notwithstanding the recent emergence of an attempt to create a 'cosmopolitan' just war theory—that the principal units of analysis are states and their militaries. The classic just war tradition made no such assumption.

- While there has been much excellent modern just war writing from within theology, the most significant development within the tradition is the emergence of a broadly secular body of writing working within the general assumptions of the tradition.

- The classic just war was a largely *casuistic* tradition—that is to say a tradition of moral reasoning that took specific cases seriously and sought to generalize *from* them, rather than impose principles *upon* them—which drew on legal theory, as well as philosophical and theological ideas. The modern just war tradition is far more obviously **universalistic** in its orientation—taking moral rules and applying them to war—and also much more legalistic.

- Some contemporary just war thinkers have been keen to add a third category to the *jus ad bellum* and *jus in bello*. This is usually referred to as *jus post bellum* and it is held to apply to the circumstances that obtain after wars (Orend, 2002; Bass, 2004; Kleffner & Stahn, 2008). It draws attention to the obvious fact that the use of force in any context has effects that last long after the fighting is over and that there is no point in prosecuting a 'just war' if the resulting post-war situation is unjust. There is much to this argument, the only question being whether a separate category is needed to account for it. Some would claim it is already covered by such notions as last resort, proportionality, and reasonable prospect of success. Nonetheless, this certainly is an important area in contemporary just war thinking.

- The modern just war has tended to drop or de-emphasize some central just war ideas (e.g. the notion of right intent and the idea of punishment) and changed the character of others (e.g. just cause). It is both narrower and, at least arguably, more permissive. For example, in the context of just cause, in much contemporary just war writing this has become almost equivalent to the idea of 'defence against attack'. This is how Walzer largely understands it. However, this was most emphatically not how (say) Vitoria understood it. From this perspective, a defensive war may be just, but only if other criteria are met as well and, moreover, non-defensive wars, such as those to punish wrong doing, might themselves be just.

This latter point is one that is taken up in a good deal of still more recent writing, particularly on humanitarian intervention and on notions of **preventive** war. The idea of humanitarian intervention has been one of the most important areas of debate in the 1990s and early twenty-first century. Since Chapter 18 has a full discussion of it we will not dwell on that here, except to say that this also changes aspects of traditional just war criteria; specifically notions of right authority. Does an intervention that is being launched for humanitarian purposes have to be authorized by a body other than a given state? For example, the UN Security Council, the body charged with the maintenance of international peace and security. As we shall see, such claims were both made and hotly disputed in the context of the 2003 invasion of Iraq.

However, this point can be extended beyond the simple fact of the direct use of military force to 'intervene to save lives' (as, arguably, in Kosovo in 1999). In 2002, the United

States published a new and heavily revamped National Security Strategy (US Government, 2002). In this document the US government made plain that, in keeping with what President George W. Bush had said at various points in the previous 18 months, it intended not merely to respond to attacks, but to pre-empt them. As the Strategy stated:

The gravest danger our Nation faces lies at the crossroads of radicalism and technology. Our enemies have openly declared that they are seeking weapons of mass destruction, and evidence indicates that they are doing so with determination. The United States will not allow these efforts to succeed. We will build defenses against ballistic missiles and other means of delivery. We will cooperate with other nations to deny, contain, and curtail our enemies' efforts to acquire dangerous technologies. *And, as a matter of common sense and self-defense, America will act against such emerging threats before they are fully formed.* (Emphasis added).

This document touches on one of the more ambiguous areas of the just war tradition: the distinction between *pre-emption* and *prevention*. Pre-emption is usually understood as an attack conducted by actor A in anticipation of an *imminent* attack against A by the forces of actor B. Prevention, on the other hand, is understood as acting in advance of a 'threat being fully formed'—that is to say in advance of any clear capability or deliberate intent to attack. The just war traditionally permits pre-emption where the danger of imminent attack is real; it does not allow preventive war at all. If we think for a moment, it is clear why this is so. A preventive war could (at best) be a war launched in anticipation of harm to come—but there has been no harm as yet, so no wrong done, so no just cause. Obviously, a preventive war could hardly be a last resort and it is very hard to see how it could be proportionate, for one would have to ask, proportionate to what, no harm having been done? Among the most important debates ongoing in the just war tradition today is between those who think some form of preventive war is necessitated by contemporary conditions and those who do not (Rengger, 2008b; Doyle, 2008; Luban, 2004).

16.4 **Criticisms of the tradition**

Of course, any tradition that has been in existence for as long as the just war tradition will have picked up its fair share of critics. Let me take four general criticisms in turn.

One of the longest standing criticisms of the just war tradition as a whole is that it simply encourages, rather than discourages, the use of force; that it is, effectively, complicit with a ruinously expensive (in both material and moral senses) war system. This kind of complaint goes back at least to the Christian humanist Erasmus (1469–1536) who wrote an eloquent attack on the tradition in his 1519 tract *The Complaint of Peace*. A more theoretically inclined (though very different) version of a nonetheless similar argument was developed by the German jurist and political thinker Carl Schmitt (1890–1985) in his celebrated book *The Nomos of the Earth* (2003). Erasmus' attack was motivated by a Christian hostility to the idea of war as such (similar to that of the early Church fathers); Schmitt's by a belief that by 'moralizing' war, the just war tradition made it more likely that people would regard war as a sacred duty, which would lead them to make holy war, rather than the limited wars of material self-interest that characterized the European

For further criticisms, see Chapters 17 and 19.

states system in its heyday. However, neither of these arguments is especially persuasive. Many just war thinkers (for example, Augustine) are every bit as hostile to war as Erasmus is, even though they make allowance for war in certain very specific circumstances and, furthermore, it seems unlikely (to put it mildly) that the use of force by states or other agents will cease, whether or not there is a just war tradition, and so it can hardly be said that the tradition 'encourages' a practice that seems fairly ingrained anyway. The use of force for political ends hardly needs the just war tradition to 'encourage' it or make it more prevalent than it already is.

A second criticism often made with respect to the evolution of the laws of war since the middle of the nineteenth century at least, and by extension of many of the 'secular' just war thinkers who rely upon them, is that they are effectively a sliding scale, constantly playing a game of catch up with new developments in military technology. The role of submarines in both the First and Second World Wars is an example that has been often discussed in this context (e.g. Walzer, 1977, chapter 9). Sinking merchant shipping was deemed to be against the laws of war and yet no punishment was visited on the perpetrators, and the rules were not basically changed. There is something to this criticism, although it might be added that the requirements of framing particular instances of law may often also run this risk since the very specificity necessary will require close attention to the particularities of whatever is involved (a type of weapon, for example). However, it is certainly also true that some successes seem to have been had in (for example) banning certain classes of weapons pretty effectively (chemical weapons, landmines) even if there are some violations of such agreements. So it would seem that, while this is a danger and it should be guarded against, it is by no means inevitable and so cannot be held to invalidate the tradition.

A third area of criticism points to the inherently ambiguous character of the *jus in bello*. It claims to restrain war, for example, but acknowledges rules like military necessity that permit the overcoming of such restraints. The nub of this criticism is that to all intents and purposes the just war tradition is like trying to repair an amputated limb with sticking plaster. In the event of a clash, military necessity always triumphs and so the rules are only obeyed when there is no real cost to obeying them, which suggests that they are not really *rules* at all. This is the criticism that Anscombe (1981) levels at many of those modern just war thinkers who try and use 'double effect' to justify (for example) bombing raids that killed many thousands of non-combatants.[6]

At one level this criticism merely points out the inherent difficulty of restraint in an environment of extremes—which few, if any, just war theorists would deny—and it is surely the case that the fact that such judgements are inherently difficult and often messy does not imply that they cannot or should not be made at all.

A final criticism that can be made has much more force. This is simply the claim that, while it may well be the case that all political communities have moral frameworks for the adjudication of questions surrounding the ethics of force, the just war tradition has a very clear Christian point of origin and was framed, for much of its life, in explicitly Christian terms. Is it possible then simply to 'secularize' it and retain the power that the overall framework of the tradition has? This is perhaps one of the major areas of debate

---

[6] I should emphasize that Anscombe is arguing from within the just war tradition; from, in fact, a very conservative (and religiously inspired) version of the classic just war doctrine.

and contestation in the contemporary tradition, and one cannot, of course, settle it here. It is worth merely observing that the question of the grounding of ethical rules for the restraint of force has been a permanent question (although how it is understood clearly changes over time) and is with us still.

16.5 Case study: the just war after 9/11

The attacks on Washington and New York on 11 September 2001 came as an enormous shock and created immediate calls for the USA to retaliate. The question initially was who to strike back at. Fairly quickly, however, the finger of blame pointed at Al-Qaeda (literally 'the base'), the Islamic group which had originated in the Afghan war against the Soviet Union during the 1980s, but which had subsequently become increasingly critical of the USA in particular and the West in general (as well, indeed, of so-called 'apostate' Arab or Muslim regimes that sided with the West). By the late 1990s they were claiming to be at war. Al-Qaeda had attacked the twin towers in New York before (in 1993) and evidence was garnered from many other sources that pointed in their general direction (Wright, 2007).

The problem, of course, was that Al-Qaeda was not a state and had no 'territory' to attack. However, it was known to be based in Afghanistan and had, intelligence suggested, run many training camps there. The Afghan regime of the time was the Taliban, a group originally based on an Islamist student organization, which was dedicated to a particularly virulent form of ascetic, Sunni Islam, and had already made itself hugely unpopular both inside and outside Afghanistan by (for example) dismantling education for women, insisting on a very conservative interpretation of Islamic legal codes and destroying shrines to other religions. Thus, the US administration of George W. Bush decided that it would strike Al-Qaeda there. However, initially it demanded that the Taliban government surrender Osama Bin-Laden (the leader of Al-Qaeda) and his chief deputies, and close down all their operations in Afghanistan. When this was refused the US and its allies, together with the Northern Alliance (a group of former Mujahedeen long hostile to the Taliban) attacked both the Taliban and Al-Qaeda in Afghanistan.

How might we see this sequence of events in terms of the just war tradition? Most contemporary just war thinkers were of the view that an attack on the perpetrators of the 9/11 attacks was, in itself, justified—that it would constitute a morally legitimate act of war. Some, indeed, went further, and suggested that a punitive attack—to right the wrong done—would also be acceptable, and this marked a distinct change of tone for the modern just war tradition (Lang, 2008), although this was certainly a minority position. Most also agreed that the attack on the Afghan government was legitimate since the government had played host to Al-Qaeda while it was planning the assault and had been given a chance to hand over the alleged perpetrators after the attacks and had failed to do so. Here, the crucial criteria being met were:

• *Just cause*—it was a legitimate act of defence against attack.
• *Right authority*—the United States, as a well-ordered polity, has a right to defend itself against external attack.

- *Last resort*—the attacks were not launched until the Taliban had been given a chance to hand over those responsible.

- *Reasonable prospect of success*—given the weight of US and allied military power, plus very general political support across the globe, plus allies on the ground.

- *Proportionality of ends and the end of peace*—the response was an attack to remove the possibility of further attacks and to bring the perpetrators to justice, thus restoring peace.

In terms of the *jus in bello*, the war in Afghanistan for the most part seemed to be guided by the two governing principles, *proportionality of means* and *non-combatant immunity*, although there was (and is) a worryingly high incidence of deaths caused by so-called 'friendly fire' and the messiness of any actual combat operation always has to be born in mind.

So, while it is certainly the case that one can query some aspects of both the decision to use force and the manner in which force was used, in the Afghan case one can say that a good case can be made that the criteria of the just war tradition were in large part met. Of course, recalling Oliver O'Donovan's remark quoted at the beginning of this chapter this does not mean we can neatly tick all the boxes and say 'this was a just war' and move on. That is not how the tradition works; rather one makes ethical evaluations of the decisions made in the context of specified instances of the use of force.

Let us now turn to the next major instance of the use of force in the so-called 'war on terror'—the US-led invasion of Iraq in 2003. Here, on the just war criteria, there is far more room for criticism, both of the decision to use force and of the manner in which force was used. To begin with, the justifications offered for the war by the US and its allies are far more ambiguous in terms of the criteria than was the case in Afghanistan. Whatever the state of US-Iraqi relations in 2001, no convincing evidence had been uncovered to link Iraq with any involvement in the 9/11 attacks and, however recalcitrant Saddam Hussein had and was being in fulfilling his obligations under the 1991 Gulf War ceasefire agreement, he had obviously not attacked the United States. So it cannot be contended with any plausibility that the 2003 invasion was a response to a direct wrong done against the US. The public justification was thus largely predicated on Saddam's allegedly maintaining a Weapons of Mass Destruction (WMD) programme, in violation of the ceasefire, but even had that proven to be true, it is very unlikely that, on just war criteria, this alone could serve as a plausible justification for the use of force. It is not the case that mere possession of WMD constitutes an attack, or a wrong done, to the US (else all other possessors of WMD would also be guilty) and absent that, it is not clear how the possession of WMD by itself would constitute a just cause.

Moreover, the attack was clearly not, in this instance, a last resort, even in the context of WMD—as the international inspectors, led by Hans Blix, made very clear. It is also certainly arguable that the ends were disproportionate to any harm done. Nor was it conducted unambiguously by the right authority since in this case—without an actual attack, which did, of course, occur in the previous case—the question of what form the 'right authority' actually takes is far more problematic, for as we remarked above for many people only the UN Security Council could authorize such a move. There was thus much discussion at the time of the need for a resolution—or a second resolution—at the UN to legitimate military action. The point in this context is not to argue over whether those who made this claim were right, but merely to point out that in the Iraq context it is an important question which cannot simply be answered by seeing the US as a well-ordered polity and thus a 'right authority' in terms of the just war tradition.

On top of this there is a great deal that might be said about the manner in which the war was prosecuted. While the military campaign itself seemed broadly to be proportionate and there were no egregious examples of the violation of non-combatant immunity, after the actual collapse of Saddam's power things became far murkier. It is a reasonable question to ask whether enough thought was given to the elements of *jus post bellum*, whether one wants to see them in the light of traditional just war criteria or in the more modern sense that the term evokes.

16.6 Conclusion

In conclusion, it is worth simply remarking again on the longevity of the tradition and on the centrality of the categories that it has evolved for thinking about the ethics of the use of force in world politics. Their relevance, as the case study showed, is central to contemporary discussions as it is to much older ones. That does not prove the tradition to be correct, of course, but it does perhaps suggest the permanence of the questions with which the tradition deals. As long as human beings and the political structures they create remain much as they are and have been, it is unlikely that the ethical dilemmas surrounding the use of force will go away. In that context the continuously evolving answers to those dilemmas offered by the just war tradition will remain one of the most powerful, complex and thoughtful responses to them.

▓ QUESTIONS

1. What kinds of ethical dilemmas does the existence of force in the world reveal?

2. Why would resort to force have been problematic for the early Church?

3. Trace the evolution of the central ideas of the modern just war from the fifth to the sixteenth century.

4. Assess the validity of the traditional just war criteria for the *jus ad bellum* and the *jus in bello*.

5. How persuasive is the idea of collapsing the just war into *jus ad bellum* and *jus in bello* in the first place?

6. Do we need a separate notion of the *jus post-bellum*?

7. What are the main criticisms of the just war tradition and how might you respond to them?

8. Is the just war tradition necessarily founded on religious principles or can we ground it successfully on a secular basis?

9. Is Walzer right to suppose that there are 'supreme emergencies' that require us to 'set the rules aside'?

10. How real is the distinction between pre-emption and prevention? What do you make of the claim that we now need a legitimate doctrine of justifiable preventive war?

▓ FURTHER READING

Doyle, M. (2008) *Striking First: Pre-emption and Prevention in International Conflict.* Princeton: Princeton University Press. The best single-volume treatment advocating a limited doctrine of justified preventive war.

Elshtain, J.B. (1987) *Women and War.* New York: Basic Books. A path-breaking interrogation of the just war from a leading contemporary political theorist.

Johnson, J.T. (1975) *Ideology, Reason and the Limitation of War: Religious and Secular Concepts, 1200–1740.* Princeton: Princeton University Press. One of the best general historical treatments of the evolution of the just war tradition.

Johnson, J.T. (1981) *Just War Tradition and the Restraint of War: A Moral and Historical Inquiry.* Princeton: Princeton University Press. Sequel to the above and again a superb historical treatment.

McMahan, J. (2009) *Killing in War.* Oxford: Oxford University Press. A powerful challenge to existing just war categories, including the distinction between *jus ad bellum* and *jus in bello*.

O'Donovan, O. (2003) *The Just War Revisited.* Oxford: Oxford University Press. An important study by a leading theologian and interpreter of the just war tradition.

Rodin, D. (2002) *War and Self Defence.* Oxford: Oxford University Press. An important argument criticizing the common modern analogy between individual and collective self-defence and a harbinger of the new 'cosmopolitan' just war theory.

Walzer, M. (1977) *Just and Unjust Wars: A Moral Argument with Historical Illustrations.* New York: Basic Books. The classic discussion of the modern secular just war tradition and a magnificent study.

▓ WEB LINKS

http://www.globalsecurity.org/military/library/policy/national/nss-020920.pdf The text of the US National Security Strategy of 2002.

http://www.justwartheory.com/ This site contains a very useful range of materials on the just war tradition.

http://www.cceia.org The site of the Carnegie Council for Ethics in International Affairs contains resources devoted to understanding a wide range of ethical dilemmas in international affairs, and especially the use of armed force.

http://www.tandf.co.uk/journals/titles/15027570.asp *The Journal of Military Ethics* is an academic publication dedicated to discussion of the ethical dimensions of modern conflict.

Visit the Online Resource Centre that accompanies this book to access more learning resources: **www.oxfordtextbooks.co.uk/orc/bell_ethics/**

17

The ethics of war: critical alternatives

Patricia Owens

READER'S GUIDE

The 'just war' is not the only tradition that has thought deeply about the moral and ethical context of the use of organized violence. This chapter offers an account of some of the critical alternative approaches to the ethics of war. These are pacifism and strategic non-violence, realism, feminism, and post-colonial theory. Each of the approaches reject a number of the underlying assumptions about politics and ethics found in the just war tradition; it cannot act as a meaningful arbiter of political and military ethics because it misconstrues the fundamental nature of both. The chapter also offers a case study of the effort to defend 'preventive war', military action to avert a future harm before it actually materializes, and the attempt by liberal institutionalists to loosen the just war tradition's prohibition on such wars.

17.1 Introduction

Destroying things, and killing and tormenting people for political ends. This makes war one of the most morally problematic of all human endeavours. War is so awful that it often exceeds the normal bounds of comprehension. Some aspects of the activity do not fit into ordinary patterns of thought. In his book, *The Natural History of Destruction*, W. G. Sebald describes the aftermath of a fire bombing campaign in 1943. He writes:

Horribly disfigured corpses lay everywhere ... doubled up in pools of their own melted fat, which had sometimes already congealed. The central death zone was declared off-limits in the next few days. When punishment labour gangs and camp inmates could begin clearing it ..., after the rubble had cooled down, they found people still sitting at tables or up against walls where they had been overcome by monoxide gas. Elsewhere, clumps of flesh and bone or whole heaps of bodies had cooked in the water gushing from bursting boilers. (Sebald, 2003, p. 28)

The Allies' intention was to destroy civilian residential districts in Hamburg and other cities so as to break Germany's will, to bring about the total defeat of the Nazi regime at whatever cost. Later Sebald quotes a passage from the diary of a survivor, one of the one-and-a-quarter million civilians who were internally displaced as a result of the firestorms. He recalls a hoard of refugees scrambling onto a train in Upper Bavaria. A suitcase made of cardboard:

... falls on the platform, bursts open, and spills its contents. Toys, a manicure case, singed underwear. And last of all, the roasted corpse of a child, shrunk like a mummy, which its half-deranged mother has been carrying about with her, the relic of a past that was still intact a few days ago. (Sebald, 2003, p. 29)

'War is hell' is perhaps the most succinct expression of its often arbitrary cruelty. It was coined in 1864 by General William Sherman upon the destruction of Atlanta during the American Civil War. War is hell. However, does this mean that it is never permissible? The very declaration may serve as a justification for some of war's worst excesses. If it is in the nature of war to be hellish, then once it begins those involved can hardly be blamed for its misery and destruction. On this view, wars that are necessary are just and necessity is determined by the exigencies of the prevailing political order. As the ancient historian Thucydides (*c.*460–395 BCE) famously had the Athenian generals say to the defeated and soon to be massacred islanders of Melos 'the strong do what they will and the weak suffer what they must'. We may condemn the 'atrocities' of our enemies. But deep down aren't such condemnations the stuff of hypocrisy and propaganda? Wouldn't we all do the same if necessity demanded it, if war itself conditioned us into doing what we must to win or survive?

On the just war tradition, see Chapter 16. Earlier chapters in this book have suggested that the laws of war, and the moral and ethical systems that underpin them, above all the **just war** tradition, hold that the answer to this charge of wartime moral hypocrisy is 'no' (Walzer, 1977). Legal and ethical codes exist that seek to determine when it is permissible to make war and what it is right—and wrong—to do in any given wartime context. On this view, partisans in violent conflict have a right to protest, and even seek recompense when the laws and ethics of war are breached. This does not mean that law and morality are always successful in reining in the worst excesses of war or that all are in fact treated equally; only that we are in possession of a moral language and a system of prohibitions that can have (some say increasingly have) the effect of constraining otherwise untrammelled and ever-escalating violence.

The basic language most often used in the West to discuss the permissibility of war largely derives from the tradition of the just war, as discussed by Nicholas Rengger in Chapter 16. For just war thinkers, war is not recognized as simply the required instrumental decision to achieve a specific political end. They wish to imagine the decision to go to war as an *ethical* choice in itself. In some circumstances, war is the *right thing to do*. Rather than a definitive set of principles or overarching theory about war, the notion of the just war is continually evolving and is behind some of the most important legal innovations in the regulation of armed force. Yet it is prudent to question the assumptions about politics and war underpinning the just war tradition. This chapter offers an account of some of the critical alternative approaches. These are pacifism and strategic non-violence, **realism, feminism**, and post-colonial theory. They suggest that the just war tradition cannot act as a meaningful arbiter of political and military ethics because it misconstrues the fundamental nature of both.

17.2 **Pacifism and strategic non-violence**

Although one may accept the principles of the just war from a secular position, it is worth recalling that the tradition was first formulated as a Christian doctrine. Christian writers realized that to be politically relevant the Church needed to say something practical about war, to make the wars of the Roman Empire more compatible with the 'moral' teachings of the Church. The result was a list of conditions under which war could be sanctioned by the Christian hierarchy. Until that time, the Church had been influenced by Jesus Christ's pacifist teachings. In the Sermon on the Mount, Jesus stated that one should 'not resist an evildoer' and articulated what might be called his 'turn the other cheek' philosophy. In Christ's words,

If anyone strikes you on the right cheek, turn the other also; and if anyone wants to sue you and take your coat, give your cloak as well ... Love your enemies, do good to those who hate you, bless those who curse you, pray for those who abuse you. (Matthew, Chapter 5, verses 38–42)

Not all Christians are pacifists. The Salvation Army view themselves as soldiers for Christ. ('Onward, Christian soldiers'). Nonetheless, there are strong religious and secular forms of pacifist thought. Pacifism is the principled opposition to all forms of violence. It can never be morally legitimate to wage war, to willingly kill people. There are no political values that are proportionate to the loss of human life and the perpetuation of the cycle of violence at the origin of war. We know that the just war tradition also usually begins with a strong assertion of the fundamental rights of individuals. However, its proponents argue that wars in defence of fundamental rights may be justified. The problem with this position from a pacifist perspective is that given the nature of war itself the notion that there are fundamental rights that must not be breached should lead to the renunciation of violence. The fact is that war inevitably involves the death of innocents who are by definition non-culpable; they are not deserving of blame or punishment. However, to engage in war is to participate in the realm of uncertainty and chance. One can never know the full consequences of one's actions, but what is certain in war is that the fundamental right to life of some innocent individuals will be destroyed.

For pacifists this is a formidable problem that the just war tradition has always failed to overcome. Even if a war is aimed solely at those culpable of gross rights violations and the intention is that no individual who is not directly responsible for the wrong should be killed, this cannot be guaranteed. The just war tradition's 'doctrine of double effect'

On the doctrine of double effect, see Chapter 16.

is insufficient. This doctrine holds that the accidental killing of civilians is defensible as long as the intention of any particular military strike is not to kill civilians and efforts have been made to minimize losses. For most pacifists, the sanctity of human life is an absolute principle; there are no exceptions to the dictum that one must never knowingly take another human life, even if 'accidentally'. As such, one ought to refuse all participation in war and work toward dismantling the war system. This does not mean that one must be passive in the sense of taking no action to resist gross injustice. Mohandas K. Gandi (1869–1948), the leader of Indian independence from British colonial rule, argued that resistance to such oppression could be achieved through non-violent actions, including massive demonstrations and civil disobedience.

On Gandi, see Chapter 11.

The previous chapter discussed why just war theorists refuse to rule out violence in principle—the consequences of *not* using violence can sometimes be too much to bear. In a position closer to realism, which we discuss momentarily, the necessity of preventing and resisting evil may mean that the rights of some individuals can knowingly and willingly be overridden. After all, non-violence can have its own moral and practical costs. 'If you are not prepared to take a life', George Orwell wrote in his reflections on Gandhi, 'you must often be prepared for lives to be lost in some other way' (1994, p. 464). 'Just warriors' reject the pacifist conclusion that the nature of war is so awful that there can be no honourable course to take. They step back from this because, unlike realists, they want war to be more than an instrumental means to a political end. They want war, on occasion, to be the noble thing to do. But perhaps the choice is not always between embracing pacifism and accepting the just war tradition in which violence may be ruled out in practice, but not in principle.

Pacificism is the general opposition to war *unless* in the absolute last resort war might further the cause of peace (Ceadal, 1987). Also falling somewhere between pacifism and the just war tradition is a position known as strategic non-violence. Advocates of strategic non-violence are not necessarily pacifist but hold that in certain circumstances the use of force is less likely to achieve political goals and is therefore in some sense 'less strategic'. (The aim of strategy is to win the overall war in a manner consistent with the political goals being pursued, to make war useful for politics.) Sometimes non-violence can be more reliable than violence. Supporters point to the success of strategic non-violence throughout history by means of non-co-operation with repressive authorities, boycotts, refusals to collaborate, symbolic protests, civil disobedience, and the establishment of alternative institutions (Sharp, 2005; Arendt, 1972). History is filled with examples of non-violent action and resistance by the materially less powerful but the numerically superior. The assumption underlying much writing on strategic non-violence is that government power is only possible through the co-operation of large numbers of people. If those people withhold their consent then through protest and persuasion the established system can be disrupted and transformed. What can emerge is 'an almost irresistible power' and 'one of the most active and efficient ways of action ever devised, because it cannot be countered by fighting' (Arendt, 1958, pp. 200–1). Note, however, that the opposition to organized violence among advocates of strategic non-violence is pragmatic, rather than strongly grounded in ethics. Yet it is an approach with enormous ethical implications in that, if successfully tried, it can substantially reduce the loss of human life that often accompanies revolutionary political action.

17.3 **War and realist ethics**

As Duncan Bell observed in Chapter 5, political realists are sometimes caricatured as immoral advocates of nothing but a crude form of power politics. In fact, writers associated with this tradition are deeply concerned with ethics (Bell, 2009a). Based on their perception of the historical record and the reality of war, they simply observe a different ethical and political world to those associated with the just war tradition. For realists, political actors cannot escape doing evil in politics; the best we can do is choose the lesser evil. War cannot—and should not—be made noble. Before explaining why this might be so it is important to address a number of misconceptions about the place of ethics within realist thinking about war and highlight the diversity of realist positions.

Michael Walzer (1977) set out his defence of the just war tradition in opposition to a very narrow version of realism. He took as his primary targets of attack Thucydides and Carl von Clausewitz, the Prussian general and pre-eminent theorist of war. As already noted, in his *History of the Peloponnesian War*, Thucydides had the Athenian generals suggest that might (brute force) determined what is right—the strong do as they will and the weak accept what they must. Walzer also attacked Clausewitz because he hardly touched on the laws and norms that were already regulating the wars of his day. 'We can never introduce a modifying principle into the philosophy of war', Clausewitz wrote in *On War*, 'without committing an absurdity' (Clausewitz, 1976, p. 76). However, are realist accounts of war really this simplistic? Surely this tradition possesses a more sophisticated understanding of war, politics, and the relationship between them.

What is war? For Clausewitz, war is an act of force to compel an enemy to submit to one's will. Its essence is violent combat. He believed that there was nothing in the idea of violent combat itself that necessarily imposed limits on its reach. The natural tendency was for both sides to escalate the level of violence until the other must give in. This was why, in the abstract idea of war, there was no logical limit to the application of force. Of course, Clausewitz knew that this could not be true in reality. There are limitations to the violence one side inflicts on the other. Things go wrong in the day-to-day of war; plans cannot always be executed. However, above all, war is a creation of politics. Restraint on the battlefield is a product of *political* command and direction. Political groups go to war to protect their interests. Any limitations and restraints on war are also political. They should not be confused with the idea that there is some external moral code at work.

Not all realists are as categorical as Clausewitz, who after all viewed war from the perspective of a military strategist. There is an important strand of classical realist thought that is more subtle on the subject of organized violence and ethics. For the German sociologist, Max Weber (1864–1920), politics is competition for control over legitimate violence. To be truly political is not to always use violence, but be ready to do so when necessary. This means that there is always a risk of doing evil. The only consolation is that the amount of evil done is less than would otherwise have been. Weber's (1946) influential 'ethic of responsibility' is an ethic of the lesser evil—do evil to reduce or remove a greater evil. Realism does not begin with the assumption that there are real and objective moral truths; even if they exist they are politically irrelevant. On this view, war is permissible if it is judged to be a response to a greater evil. The choice of political end for which a war is fought is ultimately arbitrary and historically contingent.

For realists, the choice to use violence in any given circumstance should never be accompanied by self-aggrandisement or appeals to high-minded principles. They are sceptical of the idea of a 'just' war because they are fearful of what happens when humans become possessed by political passions and commitments, such as the belief that one is fighting for ultimate ends such as justice, freedom and democracy. For this reason the classical realist Hans Morgenthau (1904–80) preferred order over unrealizable international justice. He advocated political action for narrowly defined national interests, not abstract ideals, and he viewed this as a deeply ethical position that might restrain imperial hubris. To pursue the national interest, nothing more and nothing less (and respect the right of others to do so), is the best chance to reduce the amount of political violence. Politics is the realm of tragedy. What was good today could be evil tomorrow. Excessive moral talk, what Weber called 'bigoted self-righteousness' (1946, p. 118), is self-serving hypocrisy that demonizes the enemy and justifies military escalation. In a similar vein, but with a different understanding of politics and power, Hannah Arendt (1906–75) criticized political moralism. For her, violence could be justified and was rational only for short-term ends, not abstract ideals. 'The practice of violence, like all action', she noted, 'changes the world, but the most probable change is to a more violent world' (Arendt, 1969, p. 80).

In a far more polemical tone than Weber, Morgenthau, and Arendt, Carl Schmitt (1888–1985) set out a series of objections to the idea of a just war that are, in effect, realist. For Schmitt, killing could only be politically, not morally, justified. As part of his broad criticism of liberal political categories, he wrote that, 'The justification of war does not reside in its being fought for ideals or norms of justice, but in its being fought against a real enemy' (Schmitt, 1996, p. 49). The real enemy is an existential adversary that threatens the way of life of the political community. To use violence against such an opponent is justified on non-moral grounds since there is no universally accepted ethical system on which to base claims of justice. In *Theory of the Partisan* (2004), Schmitt gives the example of groups fighting in a civil war. He argued that just conduct in war (*jus in bello*) is only possible if the idea of a just cause (*jus ad bellum*) is abandoned. Both sides must recognize the right of the other, the legitimate enemy, to engage in war for concrete and limited ends. The historical evidence Schmitt cites to support this is the rules established by European states after the **Treaty of Westphalia** (1648). War was defined as the legitimate activity of states in pursuit of state interest. Above all, for realists, strong moral justifications for war encourage self-righteousness, self-delusion, and a tendency to justify escalation (also see Booth, 2001).

On the *jus ad bellum* and *jus in bello*, see Chapter 16.

17.4 Feminisms and the ethics of war

On feminist ethics, see Chapter 9.

Feminism is both a political movement seeking to end the gender-based subordination of women and men, as well as being comprised of a number of diverse approaches to the study of politics, society and economy. The latter group of feminists uncover the gendered relations of power which sustain the conditions necessary for war preparation and war-fighting. Like pacifists, but unlike realists and 'just warriors', many feminists do not assume that war is an inevitable part of political life. They do not accept the necessity of violence as the basic starting point for ethical analysis. Rather they show that the **social construction** of hierarchical difference between 'men' and 'women' helps to make war possible and perpetuate its supposed legitimacy (Enloe, 2000). Some feminists have taken this to mean that if **patriarchal** social structures can be transformed then it may be possible to change or even eliminate war. If gendered social relations are a cause of war, that is, if militarism requires men and women to behave in gender stereotypical ways, then important elements of the war system might be undone by transforming gendered social relations.

Feminists define gender as the social construction of difference between 'men' and 'women'. 'Gender is not a synonym for women' (Carver, 1996). When feminists investigate the relationship between war and gender, they are not just looking at the question of women and war, but men and masculinity as well. Both men and women can be feminists. Gender relations of power hurt men as well as women. This is especially evident in wartime and the effort to produce certain kinds of soldiers. The **disciplinary power** exerted on the minds and bodies of men during military socialization has often been achieved through reinforcing misogyny, homophobia, and racism. This does not mean that all men and all soldiers are misogynists, homophobic, and racist, or that all soldiers are men. Rather, that a common part of military training, most often in a homosocial environment (a social relationship between members of the same sex) has been to prey on the most vulnerable and insecure elements of young men's sense of their own masculinity.

Some feminist activists are strongly anti-militarist, arguing for the ethical superiority of peace-making activities and the repugnance of war, and that women can make a distinctive contribution to **peace-building**. They hold that women are naturally more peaceful than men and feminists ought to be committed to non-violence. In a similar form of gender stereotyping, Francis Fukuyama (1998) claimed that Western democracies are allegedly more peaceful than other regime types partly because they enjoy a higher level of women's political participation. This is a problem, he suggested, since most of the rest of the world has been slower to integrate women into the political process and, therefore, has a greater propensity for aggressive foreign policies. Because male aggressiveness is assumed to be rooted in biology, 'feminized' policies could be a danger for the West (see Boer & Hudson, 2002).

Most feminists point to the huge problems with such crude ideas, not least the supposed biological link between male sexuality and aggression and female nurturing practices and peace (Tickner, 1999; see also Bell, 2006). The notion that men are by nature more aggressive than women, and that matriarchies are less conflict-prone and more co-operative than patriarchies, is one of the misleading stereotypes held about the implications of feminist ethics. The actual evidence is extremely weak. One important and wide-ranging study has found that there is no connection between a 'distinctly male genetic code' and war; evidence linking testosterone levels to war are 'vague' and 'nebulous'. None of these factors are 'strong enough to explain much about gendered war roles' (Goldstein, 2001, p. 182). For example, there is clear evidence of aggressive maternal behaviour. Women have been active participants in countless military struggles, especially in guerrilla wars and insurgencies, which are the most common form of war. That women choose to engage in acts of violence is no more pathological than it is for men. Women combatants are not behaving 'like men'. Women are agents, motivated by political causes in much the same way that men are. Nonetheless, one of the ways that women are subordinated is through presenting their violence as somehow different to men's violence. As Laura Sjoberg and Caron Gentry put it, 'Women who commit violence are often identified not as terrorists or war criminals, but as *women* terrorists and *women* war criminals' (2008, p. 7).

For some feminists, the just war tradition has been an important part of the ideological 'war system'. They have criticized this tradition for simultaneously failing to account for the way war tends to impact on the lives of men and women differently, and that women are also combatants in armed struggle. The direct impact of war on women includes casualties, a greater number of women war refugees, sexual violence against women, prostitution around military bases, and domestic violence (Lorentzen & Turpin, 1998). Despite these deliberate and contingent effects of war, the traditional narrative of the just war tradition constructs women as innocent and 'beautiful souls' to be defended and protected by manly 'just warriors' (Elshtain, 1995). The related 'protection myth', the notion that wars are fought by men to protect the innocent ('womenandchildren'), obscures the reality of systematic violence against women in wartime and a variety of other forms of gender essentialism.

There is certainly enormous diversity among feminist scholars, including fierce disagreements about how war as a social and political practice should be understood. Unsurprisingly, this means that there is not one feminist approach to the ethics of war or normative evaluation of political violence. We have noted the existence of a feminist peace politics that rejects political violence outright. But there are also feminist reformulations of the 'just war'. On this view, distinctly feminist values relating to empathetic co-operation can provide the basis for an alternative and more robust theoretical underpinning for the tradition (Sjoberg, 2006). However, feminists are perhaps less likely than 'just warriors' to offer legitimation for particular wars, but, as Kimberly Hutchings points out, this is not due to a feminist peace politics that essentializes gender roles, 'but from the contingent fact that few instances of the use of violence do anything but sustain, or at the very least, leave unaltered, gendered relations of power in the world as it is' (Hutchings, 2000, p. 125). War is based on the subordination of women to such an extent that only a radical transformation of the 'war system' can lead to the achievement of gender equality.

17.5 Post-colonialism and the ethics of war

On post-colonialism, see Chapter 11

Just as some scholars have supported certain wars on feminist grounds, others have defended the right of colonized peoples to take up arms against their oppressors. Post-colonialism highlights the continuity and persistence of colonial forms of power in contemporary world politics, including the way force is organized and justified, and seeks to understand, rather than simply condemn, expressions of force that respond to various forms of imperial domination. The theoretical premises underpinning the post-colonial approach to the ethics of war overlap with a number of the other approaches addressed in this book, including feminism and post-structuralism. It rejects the universalizing and totalizing claims of European social and political thought, suggesting that the just war tradition has never been neutral in terms of race, gender, and class, but has helped secure the domination of the Western world over the global South.

An important method of post-colonial research is to take apart the building blocks of dominant patterns of thought to reveal how they evolved in the colonial encounter between the West and the third world. Several of the treasured theoretical concepts of Western thought, such as science, reason, and the laws of war, attained their particular meaning as part of the effort to distinguish Europe from the non-European world and establish the superiority of the former (Anghie, 2004). As Sankaran Krishna puts it, Europe 'reserved for itself the attributes of civilization, culture, religiosity, science, rationality, private property, and humanity, and attributed to the other the precise opposites—barbarity, a lack of history, superstition, lack of private property, and inferiority' (Krishna, 2001, p. 408). This cultural process, known as '**Orientalism**', occurred at the same time as Europe was embarking on its world changing mission to control, dominate and physically occupy much of the planet for its own enrichment (Said, 1979). These representations have been absolutely crucial to the success of the economic and military subordination of the global South by the North and the construction of identities in both. In particular, Orientalist representations of an inferior and violent 'other' have made it easier for Western states to dehumanize those who have sought to resist, justify war against them, and thereby reinforce hierarchical power relationships in world politics (Stanski, 2009).

How have the dominant approaches to the history, theory and ethics of war obscured the legitimacy of non-Western expressions of force, that is, uses of force by the weak? Recall how in the 'Melian Dialogue' as reported by Thucydides the conquering Athenian generals inform the lowly islanders of Melos that they must submit to the will of the strong. This is the implicit (and sometimes explicit) message of much Western writing on warfare, a quintessentially Athenian subject (Barkawi & Laffey, 2006). Western literature on the history and theory of war, including the just war tradition, advances the interests of the political communities in which the writing is conducted. For example, criteria for a 'just war', such as the idea that war must be waged by a 'legitimate authority', privileges state power and violence at the expense of non-state actors. We see this in the different response by much of the 'international community' to Israel's use of force and groups in Palestine who use force to resist the occupation of their land. The distinction between regular wars among states, and irregular wars between states and other groups, was reflected in the emerging system of the laws of war from which non-Christian 'barbarians' were excluded. As a post-colonial scholar has put it, one of the consequences is that 'the loss of lives during encounters between states and non-sovereign entities is of no consequence' and while 'the overwhelming number of these casualties [are] either brown or black ... sovereignty remains lily-white' (Krishna, 2001, p. 406).

Even though the legitimacy of anti-colonial struggles after the Second World War was eventually incorporated into the laws of war, there is still uncertainty and much hypocrisy surrounding whether to introduce legal protection to unconventional combatants, those that do not wear uniforms, carry their weapons openly, and perhaps break a number of the conventions established by Western states. Post-colonial writers point to the double standards that permit atrocities conducted by states but condemns out of hand such actions by non-state actors (Barkawi, 2006). Colonial and post-colonial fighting is represented in Western commentary in a far more overtly political and polemical language, of civilization and barbarism (Shy & Collier, 1986). Often there is slippage between the language of 'just' wars and that of 'civilized' wars, between describing a war as 'unjust' and then 'barbaric'.

This is significant for post-colonial scholars because discourses of civilization and barbarism have always tended to accompany Western uses of force in the non-Western world. In the contemporary period, this manifests itself in the notion of '**humanitarian intervention**', in which the West defines itself as the principle site of ethics and much of the rest of the world as an object to be 'saved' by its benevolence (see also Vitalis, 2000). Post-colonial scholars point out that the West has been far too quick to associate ethical practice with apparent compliance with the laws of war written by Western states for Western states. Possession of sophisticated weaponry, better able to distinguish between combatants and civilians, does not mean one is fighting on the side of justice and right. In the context of a violent struggle, political groups will use whatever means are available to them and should not be automatically condemned for doing so, even though we may wish to make ethical judgements about particular acts in particular contexts (Asad, 2007). This strand of post-colonial thought has much in common with realist criticisms of moralism in the political realm.

On humanitarian intervention, see Chapter 18.

Given that it is the West that has violently subjugated much of the rest of the world, claims about the 'humanitarian' character of Western force have often been greeted with disdain. As Frantz Fanon (1925–61) put it,

On Fanon, see also Chapter 11.

when the native hears a speech about Western culture he pulls out his knife—or at least he makes sure it is within reach … Leave this Europe where they are never done talking of Man, yet murder men everywhere they find them … in all corners of the globe. (Fanon, 1963, pp. 43, 311)

Fanon was a psychiatrist and a revolutionary during the Algerian independence struggles against France. He identified what he saw as the inherent violence in struggles for decolonization and the possibility that anti-colonial violence might contribute to a new more humanistic order of global freedom. In his words,

… for the colonized people this violence … invests their characters with positive and creative qualities. The practice of violence binds them together as a whole, since each individual forms a link in the great chain, a part of the great organism of violence which has surged upward in reaction to the settler's violence in the beginning. (Fanon, 1963, p. 93)

This is not only an argument for the necessity of armed struggle to rid the colonized of their oppressors. Violence is understood as a 'cleansing force' for the body and productive of new forms of knowledge about the world. Through violent resistance the colonized might 'understand social truths' (Fanon, 1963, p. 147). Above all, as an approach to the ethics of war, post-colonialism points to the double standards of the West's ethical evaluations of its own violence. It suggests that much of the terminology of the just war tradition fails to correspond to the realities of imperial violence as experienced in the non-Western world, that is, for most of the people of the world. Moreover, its Eurocentrism hinders our ability to understand the character and legitimacy of non-Western expressions of armed force.

17.6 Case study: can preventive war be justified if we institutionalize the 'just war'?

After the 9/11 attacks, then US President George W. Bush declared that the United States would engage in what he called wars of 'pre-emption' against the nation's new and more dangerous enemies—terrorists and rogue states armed with weapons of mass destruction. The 'Bush Doctrine', which was outlined in the 2002 National Security Strategy document, holds that the USA is justified in going to war to avert a future harm before it fully materializes. It also maintained that the protections afforded to enemy combatants, such as the legal rights associated with prisoner of war status, were outdated. On this view, members of Al-Qaeda and other terrorist networks are not soldiers fighting for a recognizable cause. They are evil men undeserving of legal protections. War needed to be made more usable and conduct in war less constrained. Existing legal and ethical prohibitions needed to be softened.

The Bush doctrine was clearly a deliberate challenge to what many saw as the prevailing norm in international politics and the bedrock of just war theory, that war was a last resort to be used only in self-defence or (more controversially) to prevent or end genocide. Defenders of the Bush doctrine argued that under new global conditions, with enemies that could not be deterred and who might strike with weapons of mass destruction against civilians in the US homeland, the concept of 'self-defence' needed to be redefined. In the just war tradition, war is only permissible in response to an actual or imminent attack. For Bush, it can be justified to avert a future harm. As David Luban has put it, many

believe that in the current era a double standard is appropriate, in which the United States is simply not bound by rules of general applicability across all states. The United States gets to do things, like launch preventive wars or insist on its own military pre-eminence, that other states do not get to do. (2004, p. 210)

How should we think about these developments? The first point to note is that the Bush administration's use of the term 'pre-emption' was unfortunate. What Bush really meant to assert was a right to *preventive* war. Preventive war is the launching of an attack in anticipation of a future loss of power and/or security. This should not be confused with pre-emption, which is an early tactical strike aimed at achieving a specific military advantage. Preventive war is in the realm of grand strategy. Pre-emption is a military tactic. It's what is done on the battlefield. Nonetheless, should we accept the Bush Doctrine? If not, could the principle of preventive war somehow be revised and updated to make it compatible with the just war? Liberal institutionalists have begun to argue that we do not have to choose between the traditional view of preventive war or the just war prohibition. The just war tradition has paid too little attention to the possibilities of fundamental changes to the architecture of international governance. It may be possible to create new institutions to regulate the use of force in the new era of 'global terrorism' (Buchanan & Keohane, 2004). New international institutions, innovation in the global governance structure, create 'new moral possibilities' (Buchanan, 2007).

If we accept the Bush doctrine's direst interpretation of the new global context—terrorist networks that cannot be deterred from using weapons of mass destruction—then perhaps a blanket prohibition on the use of preventive force in self-defence is untenable. If so, then the question becomes one of determining the circumstances under which it is acceptable (Doyle, 2008). For liberal institutionalists, we cannot decide whether to reject the principle of preventive war without looking at possible institutional solutions to some of its dangers. Multilateral institutional safeguards could reduce the chances of powerful states abusing 'preventive self-defence' to pursue other (imperial) interests. They could root out misrepresentations of facts and the existence of ulterior motives for war such as oil or strategic influence. States wishing to embark on preventive war could pre-commit to a post-intervention impartial evaluation of their actions and should be willing to accept significant sanctions if they were found to have acted in bad faith (that is, for reasons other than responding to a real threat). With full access to the post-invasion occupied territory, the multilateral body could punish the warmongers by making them pay the financial costs of the war and excluding them from decisions about how post-war reconstruction should proceed. Because all this might be possible, liberal institutionalists suggest we should not dismiss the possibility of a just preventive war (Buchanan & Keohane, 2005; Buchanan, 2007).

Pacifists, of course, reject the very idea of using violence for political ends and so would not be persuaded by this most recent effort of the just war tradition to appeal to the powers that be. It does not become morally legitimate to wage war, to willingly breach fundamental **human rights** by killing people, because it is sanctioned by an international institution. Some pacifists might go further in condemning this updating of the 'just war' by pointing out that, once again, its advocates have been co-opted by the powerful. Supporters of strategic non-violence could point to alternative forms of revolutionary political action short of full-scale war. Given that war is the realm of uncertainty and chance, there is no guarantee that 'preventive' war will make the world a more secure place. Some uses of force are counter-productive. There is certainly disagreement over whether the 2003 invasion and occupation of Iraq increased or decreased the threat to the West from **transnational** terrorist groups. We do know that thousands of civilians have been killed and no weapons of mass destruction were found. For some, preventive war is a different name for imperial aggression and should never be condoned.

Some feminists are more likely than pacifists to consider the possibility of revising the just war tradition to take account of what many see as the new realities of world politics after 9/11. Influential feminist Jean Bethke Elshtain (2003) controversially supported the Bush administration's decision to invade Iraq and did not view this to be in tension with her feminist principles. On the contrary, she argued that in the post-9/11 debate 'We underestimate the centrality of the gender question at our peril' (2003, p. 38). However, other feminists were highly critical of the Bush administration's effort to adopt the plight of 'womenandchildren' as part of the justification for the invasion of Afghanistan. For Zillah Eisenstein, 'First Lady Laura Bush along with the rest of President Bush's women helpmates … took the post September 11 moment and appropriated the language of women's rights for a right-wing and neoliberal imperial agenda' (Eisenstein, 2004, p. 148).

The effort to create multilateral safeguards in cases of preventive war is a clear challenge to the conventional realist position that global institutions have a negligible effect on matters of national security. The conventional realist response is to point to the fact that existing global institutional resources for constraining war are weak. In the foreseeable future it is simply not feasible to suppose that multilateral forums will come into being in which meaningful checks and balances could work. No such arrangements could be sufficient to avoid abuse by powerful states because international institutions are the product of powerful states. To be sure, institutions are important for facilitating inter-state co-operation, but in the process of institutional design some participants always have a disproportionate influence. The long-term effect is to advantage the interests and values of some states, rather than others. For example, the United States might self-bind in institutions as a way to reassure other states given the power imbalances and practice strategic restraint in relation to other great powers (Ikenberry, 2001). However, in rela-tion to weaker states, precisely those most likely to be objects of preventive war, this is not the case and never will be. Any new framework seeking to regulate military power will maintain, rather than challenge, the current political, military and economic order (Crawford, 2007).

Liberals tend to understand institutions in terms of their role in constraining pre-existing power. With so-called preventive war, global deliberative forums are supposed to constrain the ability of powerful states to claim they are acting in self-defence when, in reality, they are not. Post-colonial theorists point out that institutions do more than just regulate or constrain behaviour. They also produce new forms of power. On this view, lib-eral institutionalists (and conventional realists) are unable to account for the truly subtle ways that institutional power operates. All institutions are 'determined by and grounded in mechanisms of disciplinary coercion' (Foucault, 1984, p. 219). International institu-tions are also disciplinary apparatuses that help to produce what world power demands, that is, obedient, productive, and loyal client states in the global South. It is difficult to imagine the United States even consulting with developing countries in an institutional forum about whether and when it can use preventive force, let alone anything remotely approximating joint decision-making or mutual deliberation. Sustained questioning of the very assumptions that underpin recent arguments in favour of preventive war, which are crucial from a post-colonial perspective, is not in the interests of the powerful.

17.7 Conclusion

Strategy is the art of realizing political goals through war or the threat of war. It is the link between politics and the use of armed force in any specific context. Some strategic think-ers present their ideas (and strategic policy discourse) as if they had very little to do with ethical considerations. In the words of Colin Gray,

Ethics, as a distinctive source of constraint or encouragement bearing upon strategic behaviour, remain of trivial significance ... [A]lthough a library of philosophical and psychological specula-tion has been written about ethics and modern war ... no sound strategic history of the twentieth century would spend many pages on ethics as an independent shaper of strategic behaviour. Sub-ject to the admittedly proliferating laws of war, soldiers and strategists have been inclined to view the claims of justice as translated by the perceived needs of their particular polity, civilization, or ideology, and as mediated by the political-military necessities of the moment. (Gray, 1999, p. 69)

Rather than serving as a clear argument about the problem with existing accounts of the ethics of war, this provocative statement illustrates the poverty of much contemporary strategic thought. Gray admits that ethical beliefs are important, but that canonical work in strategic studies ought to ignore them because some soldiers and strategists happen to not see their daily activities as shaped by ethical structures.

Ideas about strategy and politics reflect and are embedded in a whole series of assumptions, both stated and unstated, about which community is to be secured through force and who it is that may be killed. The fact that politicians, commanders, and combatants often act unethically is not a sufficient reason to neglect the underlying normative and ethical structures that shape war-preparation and war-fighting. In the end, we may conclude that these underlying structures do not correspond with how they are set out in the just war tradition. This chapter has shown that there are a number of strong criticisms of the political/strategic mindset of just war and that there are a series of critical and compelling alternatives to it. Most moral talk about war may, indeed, be spurious hypocrisy. But not all of it is. Good students of ethics and world politics must try to distinguish between them.

▓ QUESTIONS

1. Why do pacifists reject war?

2. What are the advantages of strategic non-violence?

3. Does realism lack ethics? Relate this to the question of war.

4. Do you agree that 'might makes right'? How might this shape our understanding of the ethics of war?

5. Why do most feminists reject the notion that women are more peaceful than men?

6. What is the 'protection myth'?

7. What is Orientalism and how does is illuminate the way some forms of organized violence are considered just and others are not?

8. What's wrong with the just war tradition?

9. Which of the main approaches surveyed in this chapter is the most convincing and why?

10. Should we think of these approaches as mutually exclusive, or can some of them be combined to provide a more compelling account of the ethics of war than found in the just war tradition?

▓ FURTHER READING

Arendt, H. (1969) *On Violence*. New York: Harcourt. This short book sets out to undo the glorification of violence that swept across radical social and political movements during the 1960s.

Elshtain, J. B. (1995) *Women and War*. Chicago: University of Chicago Press. This is an important feminist study of the myth that men are 'just warriors' and women are the 'beautiful souls' to be saved.

Fanon, F. (1963) *The Wretched of the Earth*. New York: Grove Press. This is the canonical work of one of the most important thinkers in the post-colonial tradition.

Schmitt, C. (2004) *The Theory of the Partisan: A Commentary/Remark on the Concept of the Political*, trans. A. C. Goodson. East Lansing: Michigan State University Press. In this lesser known of Schmitt's works he sets out an historical and philosophical critique of liberal efforts to introduce legal regulation of partisan warfare.

Sharp, G. (2005) *Waging Nonviolent Struggle: 20th Century Practice and 21st Century Potential*. Manchester: Extending Horizons Books. In this book, a well-known scholar of strategic nonviolence outlines how acute conflicts can be waged without using violence.

Shue, H., & Rodin, D. (eds) (2007) *Preemption: Military Action and Moral Justification*. Oxford: Oxford University Press. This is a good collection of essays written by moral philosophers and political scientists on the issues raised by pre-emptive and preventive military action.

Teichman, J. (1986) *Pacifism and the Just War: A Philosophical Examination*. Oxford: Blackwell. This is a good in-depth discussion of the philosophical roots and historical evolution of pacifism in comparison to the just war tradition.

■ WEB LINKS

http://www.justwartheory.com/ This is a 'non-profit, critically annotated aid to philosophical studies of warfare', with an emphasis on the just war tradition.

http://www.ppu.org.uk/pacifism/ This is the website for the Peace Pledge Union, a London-based organization that pledges to 'renounce war and never again to support another'.

http://athome.harvard.edu/programs/iwz/panel.html A website with a series of useful discussions about how gender 'matters in the war zone' run out of Harvard University.

http://classics.mit.edu/Thucydides/pelopwar.html Here is a link to Thucydides' famous account of the Melian Dialogue, an important source in some realist accounts of wartime ethics.

http://www.marxists.org/subject/africa/fanon/conclusion.htm This is the short conclusion of Franz Fanon's powerful defence of anti-colonial violence.

Visit the Online Resource Centre that accompanies this book to access more learning resources: **www.oxfordtextbooks.co.uk/orc/bell_ethics/**

READER'S GUIDE

This chapter examines the ethical dimensions of humanitarian intervention. It points to the inherently ethical meaning of humanitarian intervention, suggesting that it cannot be understood without attention to the ethical dilemmas surrounding it. At the same time, the chapter argues that ethics alone does not give us the full meaning of the challenges of humanitarian intervention, pointing to the need for a combined ethical, legal, and political assessment. The chapter reviews a range of theories from philosophy, political theory, and international relations to understand humanitarian intervention. It explores the debates arising from the 'Responsibility to Protect' doctrine and concludes with an examination of the Sudan crisis as revealing some of the complexities of humanitarian intervention.

18.1 Introduction

Humanitarian intervention raises profound questions about ethics and world politics. What level of suffering or rights violation justifies military intervention? Should the goal of an intervention be feeding people, arresting those who violate rights, or the recreation of a broken political society? What responsibilities do individual states, the United Nations, and the international community more broadly defined have in such situations? In order to understand interventions in places as diverse as Somalia (1992), Kosovo (1999), and Sudan (2009), it is important to understand the ethical imperatives that shape the discourse surrounding these events.

This chapter makes three arguments. First, at the heart of humanitarian intervention (HI) is an ethical dilemma concerning international order: It violates one core norm (**sovereignty**) in order to uphold another (**human rights** and/or **human security**). In the balance between these norms, interventions can tip the scales from one side to the other. Decisions and debates about HI are inherently ethical; that is, they force us to make choices about how to balance order and justice.

Secondly, over time, these decisions and debates shape the global political system. Each intervention and non-intervention constructs the international system. For instance, the evolution of HI from Somalia to Sudan points to how the international order has evolved, from one in which feeding starving people was a justified reason for action to one in which arresting a sovereign head of state who is violating human rights may be justified. This evolution results from and shapes the international order. Other actions and debates play an important role in shaping the system, but HI exists at the intersection of some of the most important norms in the international system. Combined with the first point, this leads to the conclusion that an inherently ethical issue is at the core of internal relationships.

Thirdly, while ethical assessments are at the heart of an issue like HI, such assessments cannot avoid the centrality of politics and history for a full understanding. This does not mean that the pursuit of power is more important than seeking to do the right thing. Rather, those who call for intervention on the basis of moral claims need to keep in mind important political questions such as agency (i.e. who can and should intervene) and **authority** (i.e. who has the **legitimacy** to determine when and how interventions take place). Moreover, calls for a universal ethical framework within which HI makes sense must be attentive to historical contingencies and contexts in which a call for HI may be interpreted by some as a new form of **colonialism**.

The chapter proceeds as follows: the first section demonstrates the inherently ethical nature of HI by arguing that its very meaning is structured by normative assumptions. The second section explores a set of normative theories concerning HI—**realism**, liberal internationalism, **cosmopolitanism**, constructivism, international society, international law, and **just war**—in terms of how they understand HI. The third section examines the development of the Responsibility to Protect, from its origins in United Nations **peace-keeping** doctrines, through to a more robust form of peace enforcement. The case study then examines the debate over intervention in Sudan.

18.2 Defining humanitarian intervention

Humanitarian intervention is difficult to define. This is because the very concept is both descriptive and normative, i.e. it simultaneously identifies a phenomenon and evaluates it. This dual descriptive and evaluative element of the concept means that it must be understood through the contexts in which it is employed. As the philosopher Ludwig Wittgenstein argued, meaning comes through the use of terms, not through a simple linking of a term to reality (Wittgenstein, 1958). This does not imply that the meaning of HI is impossible to pinpoint or that it varies in each specific historical instance. Rather, the point is that calling a particular action a HI does not make sense outside of specific political contexts. Importantly, as these contexts shift, what counts as an HI also shifts.

While the context helps to establish the meaning of a term like HI, some basic ideas can provide a foundation. Intervention has a meaning outside of international affairs—in interpersonal relationships, for example, it means involvement in the affairs of someone else without their consent. This basic definition can have both positive and negative valences; positive if intervention is designed to help and negative if it is undertaken to harm. Dilemmas at the interpersonal level arise when an intervention designed to help an individual is not necessarily the kind of help they want. So, for instance, a family may 'intervene' with someone who is an alcoholic to change their behaviour, an intervention they may resist. At the same time, such interventions may result from reasons that are not purely altruistic, such as embarrassment about that individual.

When it comes to international affairs, the concept of an HI parallels this interpersonal understanding. HIs are undertaken by states in the affairs of other states in situations where the target state does not seem capable of performing the functions required for governance. What those functions are and what constitutes the threshold of when an HI is justified creates the difficulty of making choices about different situations.

One commonly accepted definition of intervention is 'the exercise of authority by one state within the jurisdiction of another state, but without its permission'. Intervention is humanitarian when 'its aim is to protect innocent people who are not nationals of the intervening state from violence perpetrated or permitted by the government of the target state' (Nardin, 2006, p. 1). While this definition may sound right to us today, in fact, intervention as a distinct practice in international affairs did not exist until there was a state into which military troops could be interjected (Lang, 2003, pp. 1–10). This means that HI makes little sense prior to the emergence of the sovereign state system, or **Westphalian** order, that emerged in the late seventeenth century.

A political context in which HI might be considered a reality, a situation in which defined territorial entities responsible for governance emerged, did begin to develop in the late medieval period. As it did, theorists of war and peace began to write about the contexts in which force might be used for what we would today consider humanitarian purposes. For instance, the fifteenth-century theologian Francisco Vitoria argued that kings might use military force in order to punish other kings who had violated the rights of their subjects (Vitoria, 1991). The seventeenth-century theologian and lawyer Hugo Grotius argued that military force can be used to defend the helpless and punish those who violate the rights of others (Grotius, 2005). Neither theorist used the word 'intervention' to explain these actions, much less 'humanitarian', but they were analysing situations that have some parallel with modern debates about HI.

As the sovereign state system developed, however, intervention of any kind, including HI, came to be understood as more of a problem than as a way to help the suffering of others. In the eighteenth and nineteenth centuries, positivist international law grew in importance, creating an international normative order that privileged the state as the vehicle most centrally concerned with the good life. **Positivism** is the idea that law arises from what the sovereign says it to be, rather than from a correspondence between law and ethics. At the international level, where there exists no clearly defined sovereign, positivism came to mean law as embodied in treaties and explicit agreements among states, rather than vague appeals to customs, ethics, or religious values. In accordance with this positivist assumption, then, state leaders did not subject themselves to potential interventions because they controlled the agreements and treaties. Thus, as international law developed during the nineteenth century, intervention became progressively illegal, for to violate the boundaries of the sovereign state was to violate the international order (Vincent, 1974). Even more importantly, non-intervention came to be a defining feature of the international order.

John Stuart Mill, the nineteenth-century philosopher, captures how this emerging moral and political order was sustained by the principle of non-intervention. In 'A Few Words on Non-Intervention', published originally in 1859, Mill critiques the claim that intervention should only be undertaken for national self-interest (Mill, 1984). One might therefore assume that he supported HI, but instead he argued that intervention is only allowed if it is in response to an already ongoing intervention by a more powerful entity, i.e. when a state was subject to 'foreign' intervention. Mill was writing at a moment when the idea of 'foreign' and 'domestic' had solidified in the minds of European intellectuals and political actors. To intervene in this context meant undermining the normative structure of the European order, making the idea of HI largely irrelevant here. Instead, there was only intervention, which violated the norms of the European society of states.

Yet, this was not the only context within which intervention took place during the time of Mill's writing. Although he concludes that interventions should not take place among 'Christian' nations, Mill is quite clear that intervention is necessary between imperial powers and their dominions. Allowing intervention in this imperial context while forbidding it in the European context resulted from the different international societies that were in existence at this time, a difference defined in large part by assumptions about moral progress and race:

On colonialism, see Chapter 110.

> To suppose that the same international customs, and the same international rules of morality, can obtain between one civilized nation and another and between civilized nations and barbarians, is a grave error into which no statesman can fall into ... [Barbarians] cannot be depended on for observing any rules. Their minds are not capable of so great an effort ... (Mill, 1984)

This distinction between barbarians and civilized nations informed Mill's view that intervention might well be necessary in some contexts, such as in places like India, where Mill himself had played a role as a colonial administrator (Bell, 2010).

The difference between a European context in which non-intervention defined the political order and the colonial one in which intervention was necessary for sustaining that context demonstrates the constitutive nature of intervention. As is explored in more detail below, to say that a practice constitutes something means that through its repeated iterations, the action in question begins to shape the core ideas and principles of a particular order. What is interesting in the case of intervention is how it played a role in shaping two global contexts: in the European one, intervention is a form of interference; those against whom it is undertaken consider themselves to be agents who can make decisions about their political future. In the imperial one, intervention is necessary to keeping in place an order in which Europeans can justify their continued political dominance. Intervention plays a key role in constituting this bifurcated nineteenth-century political order, one in which Europe is a place of international legal order and the remainder of the world is a place of imperial conquest and control.

The constitutive nature of HI can still be seen today. During the 1990s, HI evolved into a more central part of international security. Undertaking what seem to be missions of rescue has begun to constitute a particular type of international system, one that perhaps echoes the system that Mill unconsciously identified. Anne Orford has recently examined HI in the context of the Australian-led intervention in East Timor in 1999, and she concludes that HI has constructed an international order in which some states control the system by drawing on discourses of '**failed states**' (Orford, 2003). This new political order allows for **peace-building** and/or **state-building** exercises in which elites from the UN and other international organizations step in to govern a political community. Interventions in Cambodia in 1993 and Afghanistan in 2002 provide examples of this more assertive UN role. Some have pointed to the parallels of these new UN led interventions as evidence of a neo-trusteeship emerging in the international order (Bain, 2003). As these military-led state-building interventions have increased in frequency and, in particular after the Bush Administration claimed that US-led interventions in Afghanistan and Iraq were partly humanitarian, their positive moral valance has been increasingly questioned (Bellamy & Wheeler, 2007).

It is important to keep in mind how the meaning of HI arises from and is shaped by a wider set of political and moral dynamics that shape the international system as a whole (Finnemore, 2003). The point to emphasize is that while we can move toward clearer meanings about intervention and HI, we should not forget that these definitions are constituted by the international order from which they arise.

18.3 Normative theories of humanitarian intervention

Theories tend to be either explanatory or normative.[1] This chapter focuses on normative theories; that is, theories that present arguments concerning whether or not HI should take place, what its goals should be, and how it should be conducted. Such theories are not simply ethical ones, but range across ethics, religion, law, and politics. The theories surveyed here certainly do not exhaust the possible approaches to the subject, but they at least capture some of the complexity and difficulty about making normative claims in a world that includes a wide range of agents and value systems.

Realism

On realism, see Chapter 5.

Realism begins with certain assumptions about human nature and politics. For many realists, human nature is inherently power-seeking and self-interested (Morgenthau, 1948). In the political realm, this basic human nature results in the pursuit of power above all else. Power is not simply material, but can be psychological as well. For realists, then, human action in the political realm can be explained through the concept of power.

---

[1] In point of fact, most theories about the social and political world have some combination of explanation and evaluation. For heuristic purposes, this chapter will emphasize the normative side of such theories, while keeping in mind that such theories will often assume explanations about the social and political realm. For more on this issue, see the discussions by Duncan Bell in the introduction, and Andrew Gamble in Chapter 4.

Realists couple this basic assumption about human nature with a second key assumption: without any clear authority with the power to coerce, what they call an **anarchic** political order, individuals will focus primarily on protecting themselves and/or the community in which they live. Because international relations is precisely this kind of a system, realists argue that almost every action in international relations can be traced back to the pursuit of power designed to provide security for the state. As a result, realists tend to view intervention as a tool for increasing the power of the intervening state. Such a motivation for action would run counter to the idea of an intervention being undertaken to help protect human rights. Hence, according to realists, in a system of anarchy, an HI generally cloaks the interests of the most powerful states. As an example, Noam Chomsky (who may not describe himself as a realist) has long argued that the use of military force by the United States is motivated by its economic needs in the international order. His critique of the NATO intervention in Kosovo provides one of the clearest expressions of this position (Chomsky, 1999).

Realists argue that if we wish to understand HI, we need to focus on motivations and the anarchic international system that allows the most powerful agents to control the world. However, if we start to think more carefully about motives, this crass variant of realism becomes somewhat problematic. For instance, classical realists understand that concerns outside of the pursuit of power motivate people at times (Williams, 2007; Bell, 2009a). Hans Morgenthau argued that foreign policy is not only about the pursuit of power but also about the fulfilment of a national purpose (Morgenthau, 1962). Such a purpose might include the protection of rights. For instance, Canadians may contribute to peacekeeping missions because they see their presence in the broader international order as supportive of the UN and multilateral security structures.

Nicholas Wheeler has demonstrated that a fixation on motives hides more than it reveals about HI (Wheeler, 2000), and he argues that interventions should be defined not by the motives that prompt them but by the consequences they produce. If an intervention results in the protection of human rights or an increase in human security, it should be classified as an HI. For example, he argues that the Vietnamese intervention in Cambodia in 1978 was an HI, a claim that runs counter to what the Vietnamese government of the day claimed. They argued that the intervention was for their own protection, yet it toppled the genocidal regime of the Khmer Rouge. So, although the state undertaking the intervention claimed it was for realist reasons, the consequences suggest it was humanitarian.

While realism is an important theory of IR, certain versions of it rely too heavily on assumptions about human nature and motive. To better understand the ethics of HI, it is important to be more critical about these assumptions (Lang, 2009).

Liberal internationalism

Liberal political theory emphasizes rights first and foremost. These rights tend to be primarily civil and political rights, or what are sometimes called 'negative rights'. These include the right to life, speech, religious worship, and association. As a distinct set of protections, these rights arose in the seventeenth century in the work of such thinkers as John Locke (Locke, 1980). However, these are not the only rights that liberals claim as central. With the

On theories of right, see Chapter 13.

Industrial Revolution and the influence of various forms of socialism, social and economic rights emerged as similarly important. These rights include the right to employment, health care, and education, what some have called 'positive rights'. Liberalism as a political theory tends to emphasize the first set of rights, although most liberals today see the importance of social and economic rights as central for the ability to exercise the first set of rights. Liberal political theory also assumes that protection of these rights works best within defined political communities; liberal internationalism, in turn, can be seen as a form of liberalism that assumes the existence of an international order defined by sovereign states.

One theorist who takes a liberal position on HI is Fernando Tesón (2003). Tesón claims that HI is justified to stop tyranny in a state, for a tyranny prevents individuals from realizing their life pursuits. For Tesón and other liberal internationalists, the protection of rights requires the reconstruction of sovereign states, even if this requires violating their sovereignty to create a liberal political order. Other liberals have made similar arguments (Smith, 1989; Ignatieff, 1994; Rieff, 2005).

A version of liberalism informed a certain type of HI as it emerged in the early twentieth century. Sometimes called **Wilsonianism**, this general approach to foreign policy made the case for the protection of individuals from unjust governments. Under President Woodrow Wilson, the US intervened in Mexico, Central America and Bolshevik Russia in support of what Wilson claimed were universal rights to democracy (Lang, 2002). There are obviously important questions to raise about whether or not these interventions were truly 'humanitarian', but they certainly embodied a form of liberalism as their underlying justification. At the same time, the fact that a state with particular interests undertook the intervention made many sceptical of whether or not such actions were intended to create a more liberal order, rather than simply reinforcing American power.

This kind of intervention leads us to the second type of liberalism, which speaks more directly to the dilemma of who should undertake HI. This liberalism, more common in International Relations (IR), focuses on how international institutions can mitigate some of the more negative elements of the anarchic system identified by the realists and, perhaps, undertake HIs in ways that conform to a more just international order. Primarily, these liberals focus on how the UN and other international organizations can protect human rights (Doyle, 1997).

The primary institution through which such efforts have been undertaken is the UN Security Council, especially in the post-cold war era during which the idea of peacekeeping was transformed into one of peace enforcement. UN Secretary General Boutros Boutros-Ghali helped to formulate this shift to a more aggressive form of HI in his *Agenda for Peace* (Boutros-Ghali, 1992). In this seminal document, he first presented the traditional conception of peacekeeping, which focuses on the idea that international forces can be used to monitor a ceasefire in certain types of conflict zone, but only if the two sides have agreed to allow such forces to enter. This model first appeared in 1956, when then Canadian Foreign Minister Lester Pearson proposed a force be placed in the Sinai Peninsula between the warring Israeli and Egyptian forces (MacQueen, 2006). Boutros-Ghali argues that while such forces remain important, stronger modes of peace enforcement are necessary as well. Such forces will not always be accepted by both sides in a conflict, but may be necessary to ensure security through aggressive military actions in support of human rights or human security.

Liberalism sees the evolution of peacekeeping to peace enforcement as a positive development in the international system. Yet, as evidenced by the failed intervention in Somalia in 1992–93, the increasing role of UN peacekeepers in the international order did not necessarily bode well for peace and security. As one of the warlords in Somalia, General Mohammed Farah Aideed, increased his power during the intervention, he came to see the UN forces as a hindrance to his ability to control the country. As a result, he attacked UN peacekeepers in June 1993, which led the UN and Boutros-Ghali to advocate aggressive military action in response. This eventually led to a US force coming under fire in October 1993, resulting in the deaths of 19 US soldiers (Bowden, 1999). While the October firefight and deaths should not be blamed on the UN or Boutros-Ghali, it did result in part from an overall mission shift to a more aggressive mode of peace enforcement.

While co-operation among powerful actors in pursuit of HIs can sometimes lead to an increased level of human security, it can also lead to greater conflict when local actors refuse to co-operate with the wishes of the powerful. IR liberalism focuses primarily on why and how powerful states co-operate in pursuit of human security, but such co-operation often does not include the interests of those against whom interventions are being undertaken. An ethical perspective on HI needs to not simply call for rescue and multilateralism, but also consider the political needs of those on the ground (Lang, 2002).

Cosmopolitanism

Realism and liberal internationalism assume a world of sovereign states in which those states protect and define the rights of individuals. Yet, ironically, it is states that are the most persistent violators of the rights of citizens, a fact which gives rise to the need for HI in the first place. One theoretical perspective asks whether or not the world ought to be organized around the sovereign state system, especially if rights and security are not protected by states. This theory has become known as cosmopolitanism. On cosmopolitanism, see Chapter 8.

Cosmopolitanism comes in many forms, not all of which speak directly to the question of HI. Cosmopolitanism finds its roots in ancient Stoicism, the Greek philosophical movement that argued individuals are not citizens of any single community but part of a world community. Cosmopolitanism is at its core a liberal political theory, but differs from the liberal internationalist theory by refusing to accept that rights should be protected by the sovereign state (Caney, 2005a; Brock, 2009).

Cosmopolitan theorists recognize that we are not in such a world at the present, but some argue that we can move in the direction of such a world order. Patrick Hayden, for instance, proposes a 'realist cosmopolitanism', one that finds in various practices of the international system signs of an emerging cosmopolitan society but does not presume that we have reached such a stage yet (Hayden, 2005).

On one level, cosmopolitan theory in the ideal sense would have nothing to say about HI, for if there were a world order without states there would be no need to intervene. But, of course, cosmopolitan theorists recognize that this is not the world in which we live, so they develop what might be called non-ideal theory concerning questions of war and peace. Simon Caney, for instance, argues that HI can be justified in accordance with some basic principles of cosmopolitanism, particularly those that focus on the defence of human rights. He argues in response to objections from those who wish to defend the sovereignty of the state that such concerns reflect an alternative principle than that of rights—what might be called stability or order. These concerns, while important, may not necessarily undermine the centrality of protecting rights. Instead, Caney argues that various kinds of communal rights (including state sovereignty) are only justifiable insofar as they do not undermine or conflict with individual human rights. If human rights are being overridden, not only does the international community have a right to intervene, it has a duty.[2] This kind of argument demonstrates how the political theory of cosmopolitanism generates a more permissive justification of HI than many other approaches (Caney 2005: 226–262; see also Brock 2009: 172–189).

Interestingly, these accounts often draw heavily on the just war tradition as a theoretical framework for developing their account of HI. This tradition is explored in more detail below, but it may say something about the difficulties of making cosmopolitan claims about HI that theorists need to turn to an alternative approach. The difficult issue, hinted at above, is that HI is an ethical dilemma in a world of sovereign states. If we move outside of that world, as cosmopolitans suggest we ought, then there is no longer an ethical dilemma. HI simply becomes a police action designed to ensure the protection of rights. It would no longer be HI, but something different.

Constructivism

Constructivism is an IR theory that has both explanatory and normative dimensions. Constructivists argue that our ideas about the world help constitute that world. For instance, there is nothing we can point to and identify clearly as a 'state'. Rather, states exist only because we have shared ideas about politics, collectives, and territory. The fact that these ideas help to construct our world does not make that world any less 'real'; instead, it only points to how ideas play a role in creating that world.

Social constructivists argue that our shared ideas constitute the reality of the international system. This assumption applies to those concepts that are at the very heart of international relations, such as anarchy and sovereignty (Wendt, 1999; Philpott, 2001).[3] This form of constructivism uses the idea of norms, which are principles, ideas and assumptions about identity and behaviour (Katzenstein, 1996). Constructivist research in this vein seeks to identify norms that play a key role in shaping the international political order and tease out how those norms may or may not lead to particular types of outcomes (Goldstein & Keohane, 1993).

HI has been a staple topic for constructivist scholarship. One interesting strand seeks to explain why HIs do not happen when it appears they should. Martha Finnemore has argued that to understand intervention, we must understand even more core ideas such as what it means to be a human being deserving of rescue (Finnemore, 1996). She points

---

[2] Note that Caney qualifies this argument in various ways by drawing on categories from the just war tradition, including proportionality, legitimate authority, and last resort.

[3] There are various kinds of constructivism. For other variants, see Kratochwil (1989); Onuf (1989). Post-structuralists also focus on the constitutive character of language and norms (Campbell, 1992; Walker, 1993).

out that in the nineteenth century, there was a shift in European conceptions of what it means to 'count' as being worthy of rescue, a shift that started to transform the two worlds identified in John Stuart Mill's arguments against intervention.

Michael Barnett has explored one of the most troubling cases of non-intervention, that of Rwanda in 1994. When violent conflict broke out between Tutsi and Hutu groups in Rwanda in early 1994, neither the UN nor any of the great powers undertook an HI. As the conflict escalated, it soon became clear that this was genocide, with the resulting death toll reaching in the hundreds of thousands (Des Forges, 1999). During the geno- cide, Barnett was working in the UN Department of Peacekeeping (Barnett, 2002). He witnessed decisions concerning Rwanda, particularly the way in which the bureaucracy of the UN chose to classify events in Rwanda as 'civil war', rather than genocide, leading them to be more wary of advocating an HI. Barnett argues that the choice not to inter- vene resulted from the way in which the bureaucratic culture had constructed a world in which certain types of conflicts deserve HI and others do not. Of course, it is not only the UN that constructed the conflict in a way that prevented intervention; a constructivist might make similar arguments about why the US and other great powers did not act on their own. Nevertheless, the indictment of the UN here is important for understanding how and why what seem like obvious needs are not met in the international realm.

Constructivism thus provides a useful way of seeing why HI may or may not take place in certain contexts. Because it focuses on norms and rules, it verges toward an ethical ap- proach to the subject. Yet, while it addresses the way in which norms and rules function, it is not quite the same as an ethical approach. For instance, many constructivists try to avoid ethical arguments about what choices *should* be made when faced with situations like Rwanda or Kosovo. There is nothing inherently wrong with such an approach, but because many constructivists veer toward liberal tendencies, they may smuggle in their normative assumptions about the way the world should be without engaging in clear ethi- cal argument.

International society

Another theory that arises from IR is International Society, which is sometimes called the **English School** (Dunne, 1998). This approach to international relations assumes that there is a society of states that constitute the international system. Within this society, certain norms function to keep order and advance the interests of those within it. Inter- national society theorists argue that states are not completely self-interested, but share certain ideas about what constitutes proper behaviour. This society was originally Europe beginning in the seventeenth century, but has progressively expanded to include the entire globe (Bull & Watson, 1984).

On interna- tional society, see Chapter 6

International society is defined first and foremost by the protection of sovereignty. The sovereign state, especially as it emerged in the European context of post-Westphalia, is constituted by principles such as international law, diplomatic practice, and, importantly, non-intervention. However, as international society has evolved in the last 50 years to highlight the centrality of human rights, the importance of sovereignty has been called into question. The trajectory of works by R.J. Vincent, an important theorist in this tra- dition, demonstrates this shift. In his first book, Vincent argued that non-intervention was a central principle of the international order (Vincent, 1974). His next book, however, argued that human rights have become an increasingly important principle of international order, and that this challenges the centrality of the norm of non-intervention (Vincent, 1986).

This dilemma leads to a division between 'pluralist' and 'solidarist' approaches to international order and justice (Coicaud & Wheeler, 2008). The pluralist believes that each state has a right and responsibility to ensure that its own citizens are protected, and that their security is ensured. The solidarist believes that there is a single global normative framework, shaped by a shared set of norms revolving around human rights. The difference between these two positions is fundamental to the ethical dilemma at the heart of HI (Bull, 1984). A pluralist would generally argue that non-intervention should remain the core principle of the international order, for each community is responsible for its own citizens' rights. A solidarist would take an opposing position and argue that individuals deserve protection no matter what community they live in. If rights are being violated, the international society as a whole, usually through some co-operative security structure, but perhaps by leading states acting alone, should undertake an HI to protect them. Some have tried to reconcile these two different positions (Wheeler, 2000), but their seeming incompatibility is a challenge to English School theorists. More importantly, as the international system has been subject to the forces of globalization, assumptions about sovereign states being able to provide security and protect the rights of their citizens have been increasingly called into question (Buzan, 2004). Some from the pluralist tradition have been much more sceptical of intervention, arguing that it violates the core norm of the system, the idea that states are its principal members (Jackson, 2000).

On Rawls's law of peoples, see Chapter 6.

John Rawls, a major liberal political theorist, made an argument about intervention that was much closer to the international society approach than liberal internationalism. In *The Law of Peoples* (1999), Rawls employed a version of his **veil of ignorance** to argue that individuals choosing principles to guide international society would choose those that map onto a pluralist approach. Rather than construct an argument that focuses on a shared notion of rights, Rawls concluded that individuals in such a starting point would focus on the importance of sovereign equality, adherence to treaties, and global action in realms where it is possible to do so. He also argued that HI would be rare unless there was a major violation of rights taking place, meaning that 'well-ordered' societies that were not necessarily liberal might well be able to conduct their politics without interference.

International law

On international law, see also Chapter 15.

International law is not a theory of international relations, but a set of rules about how states and other agents in the international order should conduct their affairs. The international law dealing with HI has evolved over the past 20 years, although there does not yet exist any consensus on what those laws mean. The traditional legal account privileges state sovereignty, making any form of intervention a serious wrong.

The Charter of the United Nations includes a strongly worded statement against intervention in Article 2(4): 'All Members shall refrain in their international relations from the threat or use of force against the territorial integrity or political independence of any state, or in any other manner inconsistent with the Purposes of the United Nations'. After the end of the Second World War, the prohibition on intervention increased in strength, as communities that had previously been colonies achieved statehood and zealously sought to protect their hard fought gains. Some have argued that those states are not truly sovereign, but only 'quasi-states' (Jackson, 1990), an argument that suggests that they should be liable to intervention if they fail in their duties of governance. At the same time, as these newly decolonized states increased in numbers in the 1960s and 1970s, they asserted their power through the UN General Assembly, where they became the majority. In 1965, the General Assembly passed Resolution 2131 that stated decisively

No State has the right to intervene, directly or indirectly, for any reason whatever, in the internal or external affairs of any other State. Consequently, armed intervention and all other forms of interference or attempted threats against the personality of the State or against its political, economic and cultural elements, are condemned.

This was followed by the Declaration on Friendly Relations Among Nations (GA Res 2625), which clearly stated that intervention was illegal. While UN GA resolutions are not legally binding, this, along with other resolutions passed in years following, did firmly establish a sense in the international community that intervention should never be allowed.

At the same time, this firm defence of sovereignty was countered by the rise in legal instruments affirming the protection of civil, political, social and economic rights (embodied in the two covenants on human rights, drafted in 1966). Furthermore, the Convention on the Prevention and Punishment of Genocide, which came into force in 1948, gives a strong justification for intervention to either stop genocide or even arrest those responsible for conducting one in order that they may be tried before the **International Criminal Court**. The increasing importance of protecting human rights and ensuring human security has, in other words, begun to challenge the norm outlawing intervention and support justifications for HI. Because there exists no clearly defined and legally binding treaty justifying HI, this evolution of human rights norms as a grounding for HI is better understood as a **customary international law**, one that some would argue is weaker than treaty-based laws such as those found in the Charter of the UN and GA resolutions (Byers, 1999).

One of the most difficult challenges to the international legal norms concerning HI came with the Kosovo intervention in 1999. In 1998, leaders in the US and UK began to argue that the Serb government of Yugoslavia was abusing the constitutional rights of Kosovar Albanians. These abuses became progressively more extreme and, as a result, the US government asserted that it would take military action if they did not stop. US leaders soon realized that the UN Security Council, which would be the legal institution best placed to authorize such a military action, would not support intervention, with both Russia and China refusing to agree to an intervention. Knowing that they could not get a resolution in the Security Council, the Clinton administration and Blair government turned to NATO as a regional organization through which they could undertake such action. After an air war that lasted approximately three months, the government of Slobadan Milosevic agreed to the conditions of the NATO forces and relinquished de facto control of Kosovo. While the intervention was clearly not legal, even UN Secretary General Kofi Anan suggested it was morally justified.

The Kosovo case demonstrated the continuing tensions between a legal regime based on non-intervention and a legal structure that supports human rights. The problem of what to do when the official public authorities of the UN will not act, yet when abuses are taking place, poses the ethical dilemma of HI starkly. While customary international law may well be moving toward support for HI, it does not seem that treaty based law is moving that way.

The just war tradition

On the Just War tradition, see Chapter 16.

The core of the just war tradition rests on the idea that not all ends justify the use of force and that even when ends are accepted as just, not all means are justified to achieve these ends. The tradition, therefore, proposes certain legitimate reasons to go to war *(jus ad bellum)* and criteria of acceptable behaviour during war *(jus in bello)*. In recent years, a third category of ethical reflection has been added, *jus post-bellum*, or the norms, rules, and laws that should guide the way a post-conflict situation is handled. It is important to keep in mind that the just war tradition is a framework for evaluating the use of force and 'not a weapon to be used to justify a political conclusion or a set of mechanical criteria that automatically yields a simple answer, but a way of moral reasoning to discern the ethical limits of action' (United States Conference of Catholic Bishops, 1993, p. 6).

Just war provides a way to avoid the dilemmas of HI as they exist within international law. Instead of slavishly accepting the modern sovereign state system as the only guiding principle for considering when to use force, the just war tradition includes a much wider set of criteria that must be taken into account when deciding whether or not to use force. These include a just cause, right authority, right intention, last resort, proportionality, discrimination, and probability of success. In order for any use of military force to be just, each of these criteria needs to be taken into account. When it comes to HI, international law in its more traditional formulation focuses primarily on the question of right authority or who is authorized to undertake such actions. According to the just war tradition, however, while a right authority is important, it must be connected to these other criteria as well. The importance of just cause is, in fact, paramount. So, if there is an egregious violation of human rights or human security taking place, an HI may well be justified (Johnson, 1999; May, 2008).

While the just war tradition provides categories through which ethical assessment of HI can take place, it does not decisively determine whether or not a situation demands an intervention. Some have taken the just war tradition and turned it into a checklist of sorts, by which we can tick off boxes that seem to justify an intervention. The intersection of politics and ethics is never that simple, however, and to conceive of the just war tradition as providing such an easy answer would be an injustice to those who have written within it. For some, the tradition actually serves to legitimate uses of force that create an international system more permissive when it comes to violence (Booth, 2001). If we understand the tradition instead as a tool for helping make judgements, then it may help train all those engaged in decisions about the use of force to more critically assess their options (O'Donovan, 2003; Rengger, 2002).

18.4 **The responsibility to protect**

The previous sections reviewed both the inherently ethical nature of HI and some different theoretical approaches to understanding it. This section provides a brief overview of how HI evolved from peacekeeping to the doctrine of the Responsibility to Protect (R2P). This doctrine arose from a wide array of sources, but can most clearly be identified as a product of frustrations with the international legal order and UN peacekeeping culture that prevented more robust efforts to protect human rights and security.

As noted above, in 1994 the UN, and the international community more generally, failed to respond to genocide in Rwanda. In the course of only two months, over 800,000 people were murdered in an ongoing ethnic conflict between Tutsi and Hutus. What made this catastrophe even worse was that the leader of the UN peacekeepers already positioned in the country had warned of the dangers of an impending genocide (Dallaire, 2004). A second failure occurred in 1995 when over 10,000 Muslim men and boys were slaughtered by Serb forces in Srebrenica while UN peacekeepers stood by. When Kofi Annan, who had served as the head of the Department of Peacekeeping in the UN system during both these episodes, became Secretary General of the UN in 1996, he authorized reports on both tragedies (United Nations 1999a,b). These reports and the Kosovo campaign were then followed by a 2000 report that recommended substantial revisions to the Department of Peacekeeping Operations (DPKO) within the UN bureaucracy (United Nations, 2000). Commonly known as the Brahimi Report, it reinforced the traditional UN idea of peacekeeping that relied on the consent of the parties in a conflict. This suggestion moved away from the more aggressive peace enforcement ideas found in Boutros-Ghali's *Agenda for Peace*. At the same time, cognizant of failures in Rwanda and Srebrenica, it recommended that if individuals were in danger of being harmed, UN peacekeeping forces should be able to step in and use force. This report led to a major restructuring of the DPKO and the call for clearer criteria about when an intervention can take place.

This move toward providing clear criteria for when an intervention can take place culminated the next year in an important statement on HI. In December 2001, the International Commission on Intervention and State Sovereignty, funded by the Canadian Government, issued *The Responsibility to Protect*, a report that sought to shift the discourse of international humanitarian action and international security more broadly away from debates on the right to intervene toward a discourse surrounding the 'responsibility' of various actors to provide for human security. It arose, at least in part, from the frustration of many that while a serious humanitarian disaster was developing in Kosovo, the UN Security Council would not authorize military action.

The report's most important contribution to the idea of HI is to shift the discourse surrounding HI to one of responsibilities, rather than rights. It begins with the principle that states have a responsibility to protect rights and security, but when they fail in that responsibility, the international community must take up the mantle. Reacting to the Kosovo tragedy, it argues that the Security Council should be the first source of authority, but, at times, regional organizations may need to come forward in response to failures in state responsibility.

The report is an interesting mix of international law and just war. It is framed in the same way as traditional international law, beginning with the principle of non-intervention. It then goes on to suggest that at times this rule can be overridden (International Commission on Intervention and State Sovereignty, 2001, pp. 31–2). Judgements about how to override the rule result from a framework that is very much like the just war tradition, with considerations of just cause, authority, intention, and proportionality all playing important roles. There has been an exponential increase in interest in the Responsibility to Protect, one that reflects its power and importance in an international system struggling to come to terms with the new challenges to international security and ethics (Bellamy, 2009).

The evolution of peacekeeping to more forceful modes of HI as embodied in the responsibility to protect idea reflects a shift from a purely moral hope to concrete political objectives. This is not to say that these objectives will be achieved any time soon; rather, the point is that there is a reflection in this evolution of a need to address the full range of ethical and political dimensions of HI. The case of Sudan demonstrates that this evolution has now progressed to the point of enforcing human rights and human security through more punitive modes of intervention.

The Responsibility to Protect is perhaps one of the most important theoretical and practical innovations in HI since the creation of the UN system. The report has become central not only to scholars but to the UN as an institution, as reflected in the appointment of a Special Advisor on the Responsibility to Protect in July 2008. Rather than being premised on the assumption that sovereign states have sole responsibility for their affairs, responsibility for human welfare has moved to the international community as a whole. The report retains the centrality of the UN Security Council as the authority charged with making that responsibility concrete in crisis situations. By challenging the centrality of state sovereignty and moving attention to the UN Security Council, the report may well presage a significant shift in our shared understandings of HI.

18.5 Case study: Sudan

HI can be evaluated in a wide range of ways, as demonstrated by the previous sections. As the Responsibility to Protect brings some of these together, many believed it would provide more concrete answers to the dilemma of when to intervene. Despite these hopes, there remain areas of clear human rights violations and perhaps even genocide where the international community does not seem to be responding with military force. One of the most pressing is Sudan, where first a civil war and what appears to be genocide has been at the forefront of debates about HI. To understand the difficulties in responding to rights and security violations through an HI, this case study examines what the international community has done and failed to do in Sudan.

Two distinct UN missions are operating in the Sudan: UNMIS and UNAMID.[4] These two missions have different mandates, although they seek to co-operate. The first, UNMIS, was authorized in March 2005 by Security Council Resolution 1590. Its mandate is to facilitate the implementation of a peace agreement signed in January 2005 between the

---

[4] Details on the missions come from the UN website, specifically the UNMIS site at http://www.un.org/Depts/dpko/missions/unmis/ and the UNAMID site http://www.un.org/Depts/dpko/missions/unamid/.

Government of Sudan (GOS) and the main rebel group in the South, the Sudan People's Liberation Movement/Army (SPLM/A). The Security Council authorized 10,000 troops and 715 police officers. The goal is to help those who have already agreed to peace make it happen rather than a more aggressive peace enforcement policy.

The second mission in Sudan, UMAMID, was authorized to deal with the situation in Darfur, a region in the west of the country. In the summer of 2004, the African Union authorized a small peacekeeping force designed to monitor the N'Djamena cease-fire, an agreement between the GOS and rebel groups in Darfur, particularly the Justice and Equality Movement (JEM), which aligned itself with the SPLM/A. On 31 July 2007, the UN Security Council finally approved its own mission to Darfur with Resolution 1769. This created what has become known as a hybrid UN-AU mission, entitled UNAMID. Although authorized to have almost 20,000 troops, its strength has yet to achieve this level due to both budgetary and political delays. Unlike UNMIS, its mandate includes the obligation to protect the civilian population against attacks from the militia forces. While its overall responsibility is to implement the Darfur peace agreement, its more robust capacity to protect civilians differentiates it from the UNMIS mission. Although it is officially mandated to do this, there has been little evidence that it has effectively been able to stop much of the main violence.

At the same time, the term genocide has been used to describe the activities of various militias against the citizens of Darfur. In September 2004, US Secretary of State Colin Powell admitted before the UN Security Council that genocide was taking place in Darfur, but in violation of the spirit of the Genocide Convention, denied that the international community had the obligation to use military forces to stop it. Parallel with this, the newly created International Criminal Court (ICC) began to investigate various actors in the Darfur region and the GOS for possible indictments for the crime of genocide. In March 2005, the UN Security Council referred the situation in Sudan to the ICC for consideration by means of Resolution 1593. In July 2007, the ICC Prosecutor issued warrants for the arrest of top officials in the GOS for genocide in Darfur. In July 2008, the Prosecutor requested an arrest warrant for the President of Sudan, Omar Bashir, and in March 2009 the judges of the court agreed with the prosecutor and issued that warrant.

Some important questions about Sudan remain to be answered. First, once the ICC became involved and demanded the arrest of the President, has this changed from an HI to something we might call a punitive intervention (Lang, 2008, pp. 58–77)? The UN has not sent troops to arrest President Bashir, but will this warrant change the dynamics of the UN missions currently operating in Sudan? Would this mean a radical change in the meaning of HI? As noted in the first section, the meaning of this concept has helped constitute the international system at key points; perhaps this shift to a more punitive ethos suggests something about a shift in our understandings of international politics and ethics.

Secondly, many have argued that the Responsibility to Protect doctrine is tailor-made for exactly this kind of situation. There is a government failing in its responsibility to protect its citizens so the automatic rule for the international community is to intervene. Indeed, the R2P NGO has issued its own declaration stating exactly this.[5] At the same time, others are pointing out that this move to an automatic rule-like application of

---

[5] See http://www.responsibilitytoprotect.org/index.php/pages/6

criteria may not be advancing the interests of the international community as a whole or the people in Darfur. Alex Bellamy, a strong proponent of the R2P idea, has argued that it should not be an automatic set of criteria for intervention. Bellamy suggests disassociating intervention from the R2P criteria, and instead using them as a means to develop more sustained and long-term reforms of the international political structure (Bellamy, 2009), but if the R2P does not provide us with criteria for what to do in Sudan, what good will it do us?

Thirdly, is it possible to address issues like Sudan and, indeed, the wider issue of HI through a purely ethical lens? The response to the arrest warrant of President Bashir in the Arab world has been extremely hostile. This is not because Arabs are somehow incapable of considering the ethical dimensions of international affairs; rather, they have asserted that such actions feed into an international system in which powerful states determine the rules by which weaker states live. More importantly, the indictment of President Bashir ignores the political side of these kinds of conflicts. By placing the conflict into the ICC ambit, the difficult task of peacemaking will be undercut. No Sudanese government agency will be willing to undertake peace negotiations with UN representatives if they are seen to be in collusion with the ICC.

18.6 Conclusion

What the discussion in this chapter perhaps suggests is that international ethics can only take us so far in seeking to bring about peace and justice. It may well be that greater consideration needs to be given to the political side of international affairs, which includes issues such as authority, power, and history. When combined with international ethics, such considerations give us a wider picture of what can and cannot be accomplished in an international order still resting between forms of global authority and conflicts arising from global anarchy.

▓ QUESTIONS

1. How does humanitarian intervention 'constitute' the international order?

2. Should the goal of an intervention be feeding people, arresting those who violate rights, or the recreation of a broken political society?

3. Which agents—individual states, regional organizations, or international organizations—are responsible for undertaking humanitarian interventions?

4. Is humanitarian intervention a new form of colonialism?

5. Why would sovereign states in an anarchic system undertake a humanitarian intervention?

6. Do liberal internationalists or liberal cosmopolitans have stronger ethical arguments about humanitarian intervention?

7. What kinds of military tactics and strategies are justified when undertaking a humanitarian intervention?

8. Can humanitarian intervention undertaken without UN authorization be legal?

9. Has the Responsibility to Protect radically changed the international system?

10. Should humanitarian intervention be used in the pursuit of international criminal justice in cases where state leaders are violating human rights?

▓ FURTHER READING

Barnett, M. (2002) *Eyewitness to Genocide: The United Nations and Rwanda*. Ithaca: Cornell University Press. A first-hand account by a scholar who worked in the UN Office of Peacekeeping during the Rwandan genocide.

Boutros-Ghali, B. (1992) *An Agenda for Peace*. New York: UN Publications. An argument by the then Secretary General of the United Nations that peacekeeping needed to become more robust.

Finnemore, M. (2003) *The Purpose of Intervention: Changing Beliefs about the Use of Force*. Ithaca: Cornell University Press. A constructivist account that traces the changing justifications for humanitarian intervention.

Holzgrefe, J., & Keohane, R. (eds) (2003) *Humanitarian Intervention: Ethical, Legal and Political Dilemmas*. Cambridge: Cambridge University Press. A collection of articles that bring together philosophers, political theorists, and lawyers to confront the dilemmas raised by humanitarian intervention.

Lang, A., Jr. (2002) *Agency and Ethics: The Politics of Military Intervention*. Albany: SUNY Press. A constructivist account of the political and ethical dilemmas surrounding humanitarian intervention.

Tesón, F. (1989) *Humanitarian Intervention: An Inquiry into Law and Morality*. Dobbs Ferry: Transnational Publishers. A strong liberal internationalist justification for intervention by an international lawyer.

Vincent, J. (1974) *Non-Intervention and International Order*. Princeton: Princeton University Press. A clear statement about why intervention can undermine an international society of states.

Wheeler, N. (2000) *Saving Strangers: Humanitarian Intervention in International Society*. Oxford: Oxford University Press. An argument for humanitarian intervention that focuses on consequences, rather than on the intentions of the intervening states.

▓ WEB LINKS

http://www.un.org/Depts/dpko/dpko/index.asp The United Nations Department of Peacekeeping manages UN peacekeeping operations around the world.

http://www.responsibilitytoprotect.org/index.php A website that promotes the idea of the responsibility to protect within civil society groups around the world.

http://www.cceia.org The Carnegie Council for Ethics in International Affairs is an American non-profit organization that has a vast array of resources devoted to understanding the ethical dilemmas surrounding humanitarian intervention (and many other issues as well).

http://www.elac.ox.ac.uk/ The Oxford Institute for Ethics, Law, and Armed Conflict is a multidisciplinary institute that provides resources on humanitarian intervention and a range of other issues in armed conflict.

http://www.genocideintervention.net/ The website of the Genocide Intervention Network combines a range of NGOs working to stop genocide through humanitarian intervention.

Visit the Online Resource Centre that accompanies this book to access more learning resources: www.oxfordtextbooks.co.uk/orc/bell_ethics/

19 Terrorism

Virginia Held

READER'S GUIDE

The chapter shows how terrorism is an important issue for ethics and world politics. It briefly reviews some relevant historical examples of terrorism from ancient times to the present, and considers what is or is not successful in reducing it. The chapter then examines possible definitions of 'terrorism' and the difficulties encountered with many of them. Arguments concerning the unjustifiability or not of terrorism are considered. The points of view of dissident groups and dominated peoples are discussed, together with those of established states and their governments. Finally, the chapter explores various grounds for moral judgements concerning terrorism, and it suggests guidelines for reducing the use of all forms of political violence.

19.1 Introduction

The occurrence of **terrorism** illustrates the inescapability of ethics in world politics. There is little doubt that terrorism will usually be judged on moral grounds and that judgements about it affect world events. It is clear that propaganda about terrorism is pervasive and that impartial moral assessments of terrorism are needed for thoughtful persons to understand their responsibilities. There is also little doubt that terrorism is an important issue about which states must formulate policies and citizens must judge their governments' positions. All persons should assess the moral justifiability of the actions of the groups with which they identify as they engage in or deal with political violence, including terrorism and counter-terrorism.

Terrorists often believe they are acting to liberate people from foreign occupation and oppression. The compatriots of those attacked by terrorism often demand that their leaders use massive military force to respond to or prevent terrorism, thus widening the violence. These and other forms of political violence need to be judged on moral grounds, as well as for efficacy. Different groups that use the weapon of terrorism can have very different political objectives, as can states that go to war. It is a mistake to think of all terrorists as alike.

19.2 **A brief history of terrorism**

Terrorism, including suicide terrorism, is not a new phenomenon and should not be associated with any particular religion. Early examples include the Jewish Zealots (or Sicarri) of the first century AD who engaged in terrorist campaigns against the Romans in Judea and against Jews who collaborated with the Romans. They infiltrated cities controlled by the Romans, and killed Jewish collaborators and Roman legionnaires with a dagger (or *sica*). They kidnapped Temple Guard staff for ransom and they poisoned their victims (Bloom, 2007). Another early example is that of the Hindu Thugs whose organization, the longest lasting terrorist group in history, survived from the fifth-century BCE until the nineteenth century. The Thugs strangled their victims and buried rather than cremated them in order, they thought, to supply the Goddess Kali with blood to keep the world balanced (Bloom, 2007). There are many other examples.

The term 'terrorist' derives from 'The Terror' of 1793–94 at the time of the French Revolution. It referred not to the insurgents to whom the term is now usually applied, but to the terror imposed by the new state on the enemies of the revolution (Richardson, 2006).

For an example of suicide terrorism prior to the suicide attacks of the twenty-first century one can point to the Liberation Tigers in Sri Lanka fighting to achieve independence for their Tamil ethnic minority. By 2001 they had carried out about 220 suicide attacks, killing a Sri Lankan president, a former Indian prime minister, various government ministers, and mayors. In these attacks, hundreds and perhaps thousands of civilians died 'though civilians were never their explicit target' (Waldman, 2003). According to S. Thamilchelvam, the Tigers' political leader, suicide bombings were used to make up for the Tamils' numerical disadvantage; the goal was 'to ensure maximum damage done with minimum loss of life' (Waldman, 2003).

Terrorists are routinely portrayed as exceptionally irrational and exceptionally immoral. Many scholars who study terrorism reject such views. Concerning rationality, political scientist Martha Crenshaw concluded some time ago that 'terrorism has been an important part of successful struggles for independence from foreign domination' and that it is only rational that others learn from this experience (Crenshaw, 1983, p. 7). Mia Bloom, in her useful study of suicide terrorism, reaches a comparable conclusion. She observes that:

... although the individual bombers might be inspired by several—sometimes complementary—motives, the organizations that send the bombers ... are rationally motivated and use violence to achieve their goals. The operations are carefully calculated and aimed at ending a foreign occupation, increasing the prestige of the organization that uses them, and leading to regional autonomy and/or independence. (Bloom, 2007, p. 3)

Bruce Hoffman defended a similar view.

All terrorism involves the quest for power ... to effect fundamental political change. ... Terrorists [are] convinced that only through violence can their cause triumph and their long-term political aims be attained. Terrorists therefore plan their operations in a manner that will shock, impress, and intimidate. (Hoffman, 1998a, p. 183)

Louise Richardson, another political scientist, concludes that terrorists are almost never the psychopaths or one-dimensional evildoers they are portrayed to be. They are often angry 'young idealists wanting to do their part' for their country or group and are 'motivated by a desire to right wrongs and do their best' for what they consider a noble political cause (Richardson, 2006, p. xv).

The objectives of terrorists and their supporters may be morally abhorrent, as many would think those of the Taliban are, or they may be justifiable. Judging the means used should not be substituted for evaluating the goals themselves. Both are necessary. Whether the acts that terrorists commit are exceptionally wrong or comparable with other kinds of political violence will be discussed later.

There have been claims that the West is currently faced with a 'new kind of terrorism', such that no lessons of the past are relevant. Such views served to support the misguided 'war on terrorism' of the administration of US President George W. Bush, but have been effectively refuted (Crenshaw, 2008). Richardson argues that the US government's failure to understand terrorism or learn from previous experience with it has been disastrous. 'We cannot defeat terrorism by smashing every terrorist movement', she writes.

An effort to do so will only generate more terrorists, as has happened repeatedly in the past. We should never have declared a global war on terrorism, knowing that such a war can never be won ... Rather, we should pursue the more modest and attainable goal of containing terrorist recruitment and constraining the resort to the tactic of terrorism. (Richardson, 2006, p. xix)

The lessons of the past, in case after case, are that military responses alone are ineffective in curbing terrorism. Although military attacks may be politically popular, and are often demanded by a public seeking 'action', terrorism has actually been ended when those resorting to it have found, and been enabled to use, other means to pursue their goals.

Robert Pape, supporting his view with a vast amount of empirical data, shows that the primary goals of nearly all terrorists are to expel military forces from the lands of the groups they identify with (Pape, 2005). This should certainly be considered in weighing arguments for using military force to deal with terrorism. That launching a war to crush a terrorist threat produces large numbers of new recruits for terrorism is entirely foreseeable. Since terrorist organizations cannot exist without a continual supply of new recruits, a more effective as well as more morally defensible policy to confront the problem of terrorism, in the view of many who are knowledgeable about it, is to undermine the appeal of terrorist organizations to potential recruits. Terrorists use criminal acts in pursuit of their political goals and can be responded to in the short term with the apprehension, trial, and punishment of those involved in ways that minimize the appeal of such violence. Security in the form of police protection may often be useful, but responding with wider war magnifies not only the violence, with all its moral costs, but also the sympathy felt for the war's victims and the terrorist groups who claim to fight for them. In the longer term, responses need to involve diplomatic, political, social, and economic measures.

19.3 Questions about definitions

How should 'terrorism' be defined? It is a highly contested concept even among scholars. In the political realm, the word is almost always applied to the acts of opponents, almost never to similar acts carried out by the speakers' government or group. A 'terrorist' is usually thought to carry out acts that are unjustified, in contrast with the acts of combatants of whose cause a speaker approves and whose acts, although violent, are considered justified. How 'terrorism' is defined thus deeply affects the moral judgements that ought to be reached concerning it. In the discussion that follows, a definition that makes terrorism equivalent to murder and thus wrong by definition will be avoided, since we ought to be able to ask questions about whether this form of political violence can or cannot ever be justified.

Governments usually define terrorism as something only their opponents engage in. Many in government and the press apply the term 'terrorist' only to those who seek to change policies or to attack a given political system or the status quo. The definition used by the US State Department has included the claim that it is carried out by 'subnational groups or clandestine agents' (US Department of State, 1998, p. vi). International law has seemed to concur (Fullinwider, 2003). If the armed forces of states perform similar acts, these are often described as military action or some such violence, but not 'terrorism'.

However, the members of groups seeking to oppose the military forces of occupying or colonial powers often consider their own violence to be justified resistance, and the violence used by the governments they see as oppressing them as violence that terrorizes them. Opponents within a state ruled by an unacceptable regime can hold a similar view. When in the 1970s and 80s the military rulers of Argentina caused thousands of their suspected opponents to 'disappear' in order to spread fear among other potential dissidents, an impartial view might conclude that this was state terrorism. Israeli and US political scientists Neve Gordon and George López contend that: 'Israel's practice of state-sanctioned torture [against Palestinians] also qualifies as ... political terrorism. It is well known that torture is not only used to extract information or to control the victim; it is also used to control the population as a whole'. They conclude persuasively 'that states can terrorize and can use soldiers, airplanes, and tanks to do so. ... Terror should not be reduced to the difference between non-state and state action. (Gordon & Lopez, 2000, p. 110).

We can also discern state-sponsored terrorism when the government of one state funds and supports terrorism carried out by members of groups or states not under its control. The United States routinely lists a number of countries (e.g. Iran and Syria) that, it claims, support terrorist groups elsewhere. In that case, US support in the 1980s for the government-backed 'Contras' in Nicaragua, who spread fear of what would happen to people if they joined or supported the Sandinista rebels, also falls into this category. Most states identify this type of activity as aiding terrorism when their adversaries engage in it, but not when they themselves do so.

Most scholars, if not all, agree that governments, as well as opposing non-state groups, can engage in what they would call 'terrorism'. They are often divided, however, on what distinguishes terrorism from other forms of violence. Terrorism is certainly violence and it is political in character. War is also political violence on a larger scale, as is guerrilla war, and civil war and revolutionary war. Political violence can also be more limited than most terrorism, as in the assassination of a particular political leader. Terrorism usually seeks to terrorize—to spread fear among a wider group than those directly harmed or killed (Kapitan, 2003), and it very often attacks members of an opposing group other than those who compose its armed forces.

An important definitional question is whether the targeting of civilians must be part of the definition of terrorism. Many of those who write about the subject make the targeting of civilians the defining feature of terrorism (Walzer, 2002; Coady, 2004; Primoratz, 2004). Others, however, see problems with this definition. If 'the deliberate killing of innocent people', as Michael Walzer puts it (2002, p. 130), is to be the central characteristic of terrorism or what distinguishes it from other kinds of political violence and war, terrorism becomes, by definition, morally unjustifiable in the same way that murder is. It then is often thought unnecessary to consider the justifiability of the political aims of those who resort to this kind of political violence, and progress in understanding how best to reduce and to counter terrorism can be undermined.

The descriptive implications are also problematic. As Walter Laqueur writes, 'most terrorist groups in the contemporary world' use terrorism as part of larger campaigns that attack many targets, such as 'the military, the police, and the civilian population'. A definition focused on targeting civilians then 'may not be very helpful in the real world' (Laqueur, 2003, p. 233). Robert Goodin argues persuasively against viewing terrorism within the framework of '**just war** theory' and its moral conditions and assessments. He thinks that doing so puts the emphasis on the killing of non-combatants and fails to appreciate what makes terrorism distinctive from other forms of violence—its intent to spread terror (Goodin, 2006).

On just war theory, see Chapter 16.

If targeting civilians must be part of terrorism, then blowing up the United States Marine Corps barracks in Lebanon in 1983 and killing hundreds of marines, and blasting a hole in the US Navy destroyer *Cole* and killing 17 sailors in Yemen in October 2000, would not count as instances of terrorism, and yet they are routinely offered as examples of it. The Irish Republican Army (IRA) used terrorism in its campaign to gain independence for Northern Ireland, attacking British soldiers, as well as civilians. Much Palestinian violence that is considered terrorism is directed at Israeli soldiers. Although we might say that such descriptions are simply wrong, we might do better to find a definition of 'terrorism' that includes them.

Even more awkward for the definition that makes the killing of civilians the key feature of terrorism is that we would have to make a sharp distinction between the 11 September 2001 attack on the World Trade Center by the terrorist group Al-Qaeda, which seems to have been as clear an example of terrorism as any, and the attack on the Pentagon that same day with entirely similar means and by the same group. Although some civilians work at the Pentagon, it is primarily a military target. On this definition the attack on it would not then be counted as terrorism, and this seems unpersuasive.

If one tries with this definition to include such cases as instances of terrorism on the grounds that only those presently engaged in combat should count as legitimate targets, one ignores the distinctions underlying the rule that in armed conflict, non-combatants should not be targeted. As Robert Fullinwider writes, 'combatants are first of all those in a warring country's military service. They are ... fair targets of lethal response ... even when they are in areas to the rear of active fighting and even when they are sleeping' (Fullinwider, 2003, p. 22). What counts is whether they are members of the armed forces or a fighting group. Another problem with holding that members of the armed forces working at the Pentagon should be thought of as civilians is that it puts the burden of being 'legitimate targets' on the lowest levels of the armed forces and exempts those who give them their orders, send them into combat, and make them instruments of violence.

Moreover, if attacking civilians is the defining characteristic of terrorism, a great many actions that are typically not called terrorism would have to be redesignated: the bombings of London, Dresden, Hiroshima, and Nagasaki during the Second World War, for instance. The bombings of all those other places where civilians live and become targets, as well as where the aim to spread fear and demoralization among wider groups was surely present, would all be examples of terrorism. A prime example would be the US bombing campaign in the Vietnam War. Perhaps we should accustom ourselves to calling all of these 'acts of terrorism'. On the other hand, a definition of terrorism that does not require such massive rewriting of history might be more appropriate. There is something fundamentally persuasive about the minimal definition of terrorism used by the Brazilian revolutionary Carlos Marighela. In his 1969 handbook of urban guerrilla warfare, he means by terrorism 'the use of bomb attacks' (Marighela, 1971, p. 89).

Of course, what many discussions of terrorism try to do is to formulate a definition such that what *they* do is terrorism and *unjustified,* whereas what *we* and our friends do is not terrorism, but justified self-defence or 'response'. Building the targeting of civilians into the definition can be aimed at accomplishing this since 'intentionally killing innocent people' seems by definition wrong and unjustified. However, to avoid an indefensible double standard, the judgement should then be applied not only to those usually thought of as terrorists, but also to many actions of our own and our allies' governments. Walzer does not escape a judgement of bias when he argues that terrorism is never justified, even in a just cause, because it deliberately kills innocents, but that the allied bombing of German cities in the early years of the Second World War was justified even though many innocent civilians were deliberately killed (Walzer, 2000, chapter 16).

A definition of terrorism can recognize that terrorism very frequently targets non-combatants without making this a defining feature of terrorism. Terrorism is political violence that usually spreads fear beyond those attacked, as others recognize themselves as potential targets, but this is also true of much warfare. In short, terrorism seems to be on a continuum with other forms of political violence, rather than to be uniquely atrocious.

19.4 Terrorism and justification

It is often argued that terrorism *intentionally* targets civilians, while the violence of governments seeking to suppress or prevent it causes civilian casualties only incidentally, or as a by-product, and that this is of great moral importance. The argument relies on

⇄ On the 'Doctrine of Double Effect' see also Chapter 16.

the so-called 'Doctrine of **Double Effect'** according to which an act that aims at good results, but that also has bad results, may be morally acceptable if the bad results are not intended. An example from discussions of war is that the bombing by a state engaged in a just war of a factory producing weapons for an opponent's army can be morally acceptable even if nearby civilians are killed because such deaths are unintended. It can well be argued that this argument cannot bear the weight it has been assigned in discussions of political violence.

The distinction between targeting civilians intentionally and only killing them foreseeably as collateral damage means little to those who identify with the dead. Conventional warfare may proclaim an intent to spare civilians, then yield to 'military necessity', killing everyone in a given area. Or, as weapons become more precise, states may target specific persons and facilities, and only kill civilians inadvertently, but in far greater numbers than those killed by terrorism. Over many years, the deaths of Palestinian children have been approximately eight times the deaths of Israeli children resulting from the conflict (Kristof, 2008). With the Israeli assault on Gaza in January 2009 this disparity greatly increased. David Rodin argues against the view that intention makes all the difference. He points out that non-combatants have the right to not be harmed by violence when force is used recklessly or negligently, as well as when it is used intentionally, and that the former is common in conventional warfare (Rodin, 2004).

When the US responded with military force in Iraq to what was claimed to be a terrorist threat posed by Saddam Hussein, it caused the deaths of some 10,000 civilians in just the initial invasion (Massing, 2007, p. 87). Since then, the war has led to the deaths of many tens of thousands and perhaps hundreds of thousands of civilians (Altman & Oppel, 2008). Terrorism, in comparison, has killed relatively small numbers. In conventional war, the killing of civilians often becomes routine and overlooked. Certainly, some terrorists commit atrocities that are absolutely horrendous. So do some members of the armed forces in the course of fighting wars. The goals of some terrorists are, without doubt, morally indefensible. So are the goals of some who use ordinary military power. If, however, the objectives for which they are used are justifiable, the weapon of terrorism and how it is used are not necessarily more immoral than the weapon of conventional military force and how it is used.

Those who use terrorism often believe they have no other way to resist unjust oppression and sometimes this judgement may be correct. To the opponents of those with vastly superior power, terrorism is often seen as self-defence, or reprisal against attacks they have suffered, attacks by the strong on the weak. What is initial provocation and what is 'response' is often highly contentious. Mia Bloom observes that 'Israel has responded to every ceasefire of Palestinian suicide attacks with targeted assassination thus unleashing a new round of reprisals and counter attacks.' The reasoning has been that assassinating their operatives saps the effectiveness of terrorist organizations. However, it has not worked: the organizations 'are fully capable of replacing operatives as fast as Israel … eliminates them' (Bloom, 2007, pp. 190, 38).

If it is sincerely believed that only force rather than argument will move an opponent, and that one's position and aim are clearly just, force applied through terrorism may be on a par with force applied through conventional arms in being resorted to in the first place. Sheikh Ahmad Yassin, a founder of Hamas who was assassinated by Israel in March

2004, said that 'Once we have warplanes and missiles, then we can think of changing our means of legitimate self-defense, but right now, we can only tackle the fire with our bare hands and sacrifice ourselves' (Bloom, 2007, pp. 3–4). The Secretary-General of Palestinian Islamic Jihad, as summarized by Ehud Sprinzac, has said:

Our enemy possesses the most sophisticated weapons in the world and its army is trained to a very high standard ... We have nothing with which to repel killing and thuggery against us except the weapon of martyrdom ... [H]uman bombs cannot be defeated. (Bloom, 2007, pp. 89–90)

In assessing the justifiability of the means used in violent conflict, the demand that opponents of states with armed forces and sophisticated weaponry fight the way such states do amounts to an argument that opponents should meet a powerful state on the latter's own ground so that the powerful state can defeat them. From the point of view of a militarily weak opponent, it would be irrational, as well as impossible to do this. Terrorism is a weapon that helps to neutralize the enormous military power possessed by some states. Using this weapon can be the rational course of action for such states' opponents, and not clearly more immoral than war, which many consider capable of being just. Robert Fullinwider observes that 'since the United States is a country founded on violent rebellion against lawful authority, we can hardly endorse a blanket disavowal of the right by others violently to rebel against their own oppressors' (Fullinwider, 2003, p. 24).

It is not inherently better to use force or violence to maintain an existing political situation or territorial boundary than to use force or violence to change them. Stability has definite value, if it can be maintained without the undue use of force or violence. When it becomes sufficiently intolerable to enough people for it to be maintained only with severe repression, however, the use of force or violence to change the political situation or territorial boundary may be less unjustifiable than using them to maintain the intolerable situation. The better alternative in all such cases is to observe guidelines to achieve such change through peaceful means, for example, by negotiations, international judicial decisions, or referenda. However, when the power resisting change refuses to employ such means, violence to change the situation may be better than violence to maintain it, if the new situation will be more just.

Only governments with highly sophisticated weaponry can afford to be extremely selective in their targets. The Allied powers in the Second World War could not afford to be, and even the 'smart bombs' of recent years often make mistakes. In the wars of the 1990s, 75–90% of all deaths were of civilians, making it hard to accept that terrorism is morally far worse than war (Hedges, 2003). The relevant comparison with respect to civilians seems to be which side—in the pursuit of its political goals—is causing the greater loss of civilian life. Then, in a political conflict in which at least one side uses terrorism, if the deaths caused by both sides are roughly equivalent, the argument may appropriately focus especially on the justice, or lack of it, of the political goals involved.

That civilians are to be spared in military conflict, while the members of armed forces are 'legitimate targets' is widely accepted, in principle if not in practice. It is a fundamental law of war, resting on the assumption that civilians are 'innocent'. The applicability of this principle to conflicts involving non-state groups is problematic. We can perhaps agree that small children are innocent, but beyond this, there is little moral clarity (Honderich, 2002). First of all, many members of the armed forces are conscripts who have no choice but to be combatants. Many others have been pressed into service by economic necessity and social oppression. It is unclear why they should be seen as legitimate targets while those who send them into battle are exempt. Many civilians may have demanded of their governments the very policies that opponents are resisting, sometimes using terrorism to do so. Unfortunately, terrorism that kills civilians to oppose a government's policies does not distinguish between those who support that government and those who do not. But neither does counterterrorism that kills civilians distinguish between those who support terrorist groups and those who do not.

Governments try hard to portray terrorist groups as those who cause violence that would otherwise not exist and to depict their own efforts to suppress that violence, however violently they do so, as a justified response to provocation. However, if the governments agreed to what the groups seek—independence, for instance—the terrorists' brutal acts would often not take place. Thus, the violence used to suppress terrorism is the price paid to maintain a given political arrangement, just as the violence used by the dissatisfied group is the price of pursuing its goal. From a moral point of view, it is entirely appropriate to compare these levels of violence. The status quo is not, in itself, morally superior; it may include grievous violations of rights or denials of legitimate aims. Whether the goals of a dissatisfied group are morally defensible needs to be examined, as does whether a government's refusal to accede to these goals is morally defensible. From a moral point of view, using violent actions to bring about change is not inherently worse than doing so to prevent such change. The costs of stability, as well as of change, need to be assessed.

19.5 Reducing violence

More promising arguments against terrorism are that it does not achieve its perpetrators' objectives and that other means are not only more justifiable, but also more successful. However, then the burden of making them more successful falls on governments and those with power. When non-violent protest is met with bloodshed and consistently fails to change the offending policies even when they are unjustifiable, it is hard to argue that non-violence works, whereas terrorism does not. Terrorist Leila Khaled said about the Palestinian airliner hijackings of the 1970s that they were used as a kind of struggle to put the question—who are the Palestinians—before the world. Before we were dealt with as refugees. We yelled and screamed, but the whole world answered with more tents and did nothing. (Nasr, 1997, p. 57)

Terrorists often feel, mistakenly or not, that violence is the only course of action open to them to advance their political goals. It is the responsibility of those who are able to do so to make this assessment untrue.

As many have noted, one of the most effective ways to reduce the appeal of terrorism to the disaffected is to enable them to participate in the political processes that concern them. Democracy is more effective than counter-terrorism, although bringing it about can be extremely difficult and it certainly cannot be imposed by outsiders. As Benjamin Barber writes,

violence is not the instrument of choice even under tyrannical governments because confrontations based on force usually favor the powerful ... But it can become the choice of those so disempowered by a political order (or a political disorder) that they have no other options. ... To create a just and inclusive world in which all citizens are stakeholders is the first objective of a rational strategy against terrorism. (Barber, 2003, pp. 77, 88)

One may have grave doubts about whether the criteria offered by just war theory can *ever* be satisfied, especially in the case of conflicts fought with contemporary weaponry. One can doubt that just war theory, developed for conflicts between the armed forces of states, is applicable to conflicts involving non-state groups. One can still agree that some wars, tactics, and purposes are *more unjustifiable* than others. Then, *if* war can be justified, as many believe, it would seem that some terrorism can be also. Andrew Valls argues that 'if just war theory can justify violence committed by states, then terrorism committed by non-state actors can also, under certain circumstances, be justified by it as well' (Valls, 2000, p. 66). Other sources of moral assessment may offer even stronger grounds than just war theory for claiming that terrorism is at least not more unjustifiable than war.

For other criticisms of just war theory, see Chapter 17.

No form of violence can be justified unless other means of achieving a legitimate political objective have failed, but this is *also* a moral requirement on the governments that oppose change and seek to suppress terrorism. Additionally, those with more power have a greater obligation to avoid violence and to pursue other means of obtaining political goals since alternative courses of action are more open to them.

There are also some quite different principles than those invoked in just war theory that need to be considered with respect to terrorism. For instance, *do not capitulate to injustice by accepting it*. This advocates resistance, in some form, toward injustice, although it leaves open what form resistance should take. If a liberation struggle involves long years of peaceful protest availing no progress, although provoking harsh repression, it may then, justifiably we may think, turn to attacking property, but not persons. If this is then met with nothing but still harsher repression, the movement may conclude that it needs to move to violence against persons as a last resort. Conscientious persons may conclude that such resistance—in some form—may be less unjustified than is the repression (for an example, see the Case study at the end of this chapter).

Another principle relevant to evaluating political violence is: *do not bargain from a position of extreme weakness*. This is not a moral principle, but if the goal of a group is just and if we think it is justified in pursuing it, the advice can become a moral guideline in figuring out what the group ought to do to further its goal. If a group seeking fundamental political change such as liberation from an oppressive occupation has no power to exert, no leverage against the occupying power, but is admonished to renounce violence prior to negotiations, this may amount to capitulation. If we then make a moral evaluation of such capitulation, we might find it to be unjustifiable capitulation to injustice. Gandhi, surely a champion of non-violence, nevertheless thought that 'it is better to resist oppression by violent means than to submit' (McAllister, 1982, p. vi).

To understand how to reduce terrorism and its appeal to new supporters, one ought to pay attention to the motives of terrorists. In 1986, Benjamin Netanyahu, later a prime minister of Israel, described the terrorist as 'a new breed of man which takes humanity back to prehistoric times, to the times when morality was not yet born' (Netanyahu, 1986, pp. 29–30). In 2002 he repeated nearly the same words, calling terrorists 'an enemy that knows no boundaries' and saying that 'we are at the beginning of a war of worlds'— Israel and other democracies against 'a world of fanatic murder[ers] trying to throw on us inhuman terror, to take us back to the worst days of history' (Wines, 2002, A9).

Such views imply that there is no justification for considering terrorists' arguments: they do not function within the same realm of discourse or circle of humanity. Many who talk with and study terrorists disagree, finding them articulate and rational (Hoffman, 1998a; Richardson, 2006; Bloom, 2007). Those who support terrorism may often be misguided, but they are not necessarily more morally depraved than many members of the armed forces of established states and their civilian supporters who calculate the costs in weaponry and personnel of military gains, or who look forward to obliterating their opponents. Both sides may be characterized by a gross lack of feeling for the victims of their violence or what feelings they have may be overridden by the calculations of necessity.

To prevent terrorism, much more might be achieved by engaging in moral argument with its potential recruits than by declaring that terrorists and their supporters are so far beyond the moral pale that discussion with them is either pointless or wrong. Sometimes, trying to understand terrorism is equated with excusing it. This is a grave mistake. We need to distinguish between causal explanations and normative evaluations, and we are all in need of both sorts of inquiries. In order to reduce all forms of political violence we need to understand the way those who use it think and feel and the arguments they find persuasive.

19.6 Forms of moral discourse

Moral arguments concerning terrorism and other political violence can appeal to a variety of moral approaches. One is rights-based. It sees rights as near absolute constraints on actions to achieve desired results. It recognizes the rights persons have to life and personal safety, and provides grounds for condemning terrorism as violating the rights of its victims (Primoratz, 1997). However, such arguments are not conclusive since persons also have rights to be free of oppression, and if terrorism to liberate a population follows from respect for these rights, it may be less unjustifiable than is their denial.

Another moral approach on which arguments concerning terrorism are based is **consequentialist**. It condemns terrorism if it produces consequences that are more bad than good (Honderich, 2002). This moral approach does not provide an absolute condemnation of terrorism or of any other political violence. Its judgments depend on whether such violence actually brings about a greater good, such as liberation from oppression, or greater bad consequences, such as death and suffering. It is usually taken to conclude, for instance, that some revolutions have been worth the costs in terms of lives lost and suffering endured. It can condemn both terrorism and counter-terrorism, or it can justify them, depending on their actual outcomes. Such outcomes are often very difficult to predict, hence this approach may fail to offer adequate moral guidelines for what we ought to choose to do.

A much newer approach is offered by a feminist **ethics of care** (Held, 2006). It has been developed through the experience of caring for others and being cared for. Such experience is truly universal since no person can survive into adulthood without having received a great deal of care. The ethics of care attends to, and appreciates the values involved in, the labour of care. In contrast with the cluster of values associated with justice—impartiality, equality, fairness—it emphasizes a different cluster of values—responsiveness

On feminism, see also Chapter 9.

to need, sensitivity, empathy, and trust. It evaluates existing practices of care and shows how they need to be improved. It sees persons as relational, rather than as self-sufficient individuals, and it especially values caring relationships. It has been developed as a moral approach suitable for evaluating issues not only in the realms of family and friendship where its applicability is most clear, but also in the world beyond. The ethics of care can offer guidance for political life and international affairs (Tronto, 1993; Robinson, 1999; Held, 2006).

The ethics of care provides strong grounding for valuing non-violence over violence in political conflict. Violence damages and destroys what care labours to create. Care instructs us to establish the means to curb, contain, prevent, and head off the violence that characteristically leads to more violent behaviour. In bringing up children, this requires a long process of nurturing and education in order to cultivate non-violent feelings, self-restraint, appropriate trust, and an understanding of the better alternatives to aggressive conflict. In interactions with others at some distance, the primary institutions with which to prevent and deal with violence are political and legal, and care can recommend acceptance of these institutions when appropriate even as it recognizes their limits. Moreover, it can suggest alternative ways of interacting that may prove more satisfactory, and these understandings can be matched at the international level.

With the guidance of the ethics of care, we would acknowledge that violence is an aspect of human reality that must be expected, but that we can successfully work to contain it. With care, we can decrease violence and the suffering and damage it brings about. Guided by the values of care, we would restrain rather than destroy those who become violent, we would inhibit violence as non-violently as possible, and we would especially work to prevent violence, rather than wipe out violent persons.

Carol Gould argues that terrorism exemplifies a failure to care. Of the 11 September 2001 attacks on the World Trade Center towers she says 'there was not only the violation of rights but also what we might call a wholesale lack of human fellow-feeling, an absence of caring about or empathy with the potential victims on the part of the terrorists' (Gould, 2004, p. 350). We can agree and still note that this is true of most violence, especially war. Violence inherently disregards its victims, war supremely so in the extent of its destruction and the numbers of its victims. Some individual participants in terrorism as in war or other violence may mourn the victims they produce; many will not. Terrorism may fail in its absence of empathy less brutally than the war with which many think it should be answered.

The ethics of care can help us to empathize with the victims of violence, whatever the kind of violence. It also asks us, as Gould notes, to better understand those who turn to violence. We need to be aware of the combination of humiliation and deprivation that leads people to support and sometimes to engage in terrorist acts, and how policies damage and oppress others. Understanding how to draw potential recruits away from the path of violence is crucial. The key, in Mia Bloom's view, 'is to reduce [terrorists'] motivations for suicide bombings rather than their capabilities to carry them out … There are no military solutions to terrorism' (Bloom, 2007, pp. 39–40). Answering terrorism with wider war is among the least successful, as well as most uncaring of responses, multiplying both new victims and new recruits. The lesson that has already been taught many times is that states cannot translate overwhelming military force into victory over terrorists.

➡ For feminist criticism of the just war, see also Chapter 17.

Robin May Schott argues effectively against the just war tradition on which many base a strict moral divide between terrorism and war. She finds that the just war tradition all too easily normalizes war, suggesting that as long as certain limits are observed, war is morally acceptable (Schott, 2008). She uses the German philosopher Immanuel Kant to argue that war is never morally acceptable, but an ethics of care might even more reliably keep us from forgetting that war is always atrocious, even if sometimes better than its alternatives. Which terms one uses to make the distinction between war being sometimes necessary or better than its alternatives but never morally acceptable is somewhat arbitrary. The point to remember is that it should always have been prevented, averted, avoided. If it has become better than capitulation against an aggressor or abdication of responsibility in the face of genocide, the situation already represents a massive moral failure. Similar arguments apply to terrorism and other forms of political violence.

The ethics of care can accept the underlying norms of the just war tradition, such as the requirement that one's cause be just and that the violence used must be proportional. It is better able to keep in mind the overriding context of caring relations between human beings that are so obviously shattered by war and other violence.

The ethics of care can help us to listen to the views of others and try to understand their points of view. Care inherently involves attentiveness to others and responding to needs, and its values prepare us to do what is needed to reduce and undermine trends toward violence. Those motivated by care will be open to the evidence that terrorism is not defeated by greater violence, but by promoting other means through which those resorting to violence can pursue their political objectives. It will promote persuasion where those objectives are unjustifiable and should be changed.

We should constantly and insistently remind ourselves and others that violence is often or usually counterproductive, and that there are nearly always better and more effective non-violent ways of pursuing political objectives. Yet there are good reasons to not rule out as always unjustifiable all uses of violence, as the ethics of care would agree. Some violence is usually thought defensible in the enforcement of justifiable law. Yet education, treatment, and negotiation can usually preclude much of the need for violent law enforcement. Protest that may become violent is often thought better than acquiescence in morally indefensible repression. However, civil actions of various kinds, such as protests, demonstrations, and disobedience, together with clever and creative uses of the media, can often shame repressive opponents. Non-violent opposition often has more chance of success than the violence that invites greater violence or repression that, though ineffective, can be politically popular.

The ethics of care would direct us to counter-terrorism with policies that will not only be more caring in the ways that they themselves minimize violence but also more effective in undermining the violence of those opposing us.

19.7 Case study: the fight against apartheid in South Africa

Let us consider the thinking of Nelson Mandela and Oliver Tambo in the struggle to overcome apartheid in South Africa. Most philosophers would have no trouble agreeing that their goal was just. Perhaps most would also agree that if non-violence was producing no progress toward ending apartheid over a long period of time, the movement to liberate non-white South Africans was less unjustified in considering violence than the government that opposed such progress was in using violent repression.

Nelson Mandela explained the carefully considered progression that occurred from peaceful protest to violent struggle in the movement to liberate black South Africans from white oppression. He wrote:

... the hard facts were that fifty years of nonviolence had brought the African people nothing but more and more repressive legislation, and fewer and fewer rights ... [I]n May and June of 1961, it could not be denied that our policy to achieve a nonracial state by nonviolence had achieved nothing and that our followers were beginning to lose confidence in this policy ... Each disturbance pointed clearly to the inevitable growth among Africans of the belief that violence was the only way out—it showed that a government which uses force to maintain its rule teaches the oppressed to use force to oppose it. (Johns & Davis, 1991, pp. 119–20)

Mandela recounted how he and some colleagues concluded that since violence was inevitable, since the threat of civil war loomed and should especially be avoided, 'the decision was made to embark on violent forms of political struggle'. He felt 'morally obliged' to do what he did as the government's repression 'had left us with no other choice' (Johns & Davis, 1991, p. 120). Mandela argued that 'Four forms of violence are possible. There is sabotage, there is guerrilla warfare, there is terrorism, and there is open revolution.' At this stage, he recounts, 'we chose to adopt the first method [sabotage] and to exhaust it before taking any other decision' (Johns & Davis, 1991, p. 121).

In subsequent decades, violence increased. Repression became more brutal and the movement to end apartheid moved to guerrilla activity. By 1985, Oliver Tambo defended the use of violence in the struggle for black liberation with analogies to the Second World War:

We recognized that if the struggle is intensified beyond the levels that we had maintained for 20 fruitless years of selected sabotage ... it was inevitable that life would then be lost. Even in the course of attacking military establishments, the army, the police, there would be bloodshed ... the innocent would be hit ... We would be fighting an intense struggle with arms, and it was unavoidable. This is what we decided ... (Johns & Davis, 1991, p. 246)

Tambo went on to emphasize the violence used by the government against black South Africans and he expressed understanding of their reaction:

There has been such an onslaught on our people by the Pretoria regime, there has been so much killing and shooting—shooting of children who ... are killed because they are ... throwing a stone ... This enrages the people and ... we can understand that they can go to excesses in the way that they respond to this unbridled violence of apartheid. (Johns & Davis, 1991, p. 246)

When asked to condemn African National Congress attacks and bombings, he said:

In 1982 ... there was this mounting offensive against the ANC ... we were the victims of assassinations, of massacres ... An armed struggle is an armed struggle. People die ... [W]e cannot condemn [the bombings]. That is part of the struggle. The enemy is the enemy ... How many children were ... killed when the RAF was bombing away in Germany and other places? ... The other liberation movements have taken up arms and intensified their struggles and won their independence on our borders ... A war is a war. We have delayed it, but we cannot delay it indefinitely. Apartheid is a crime against humanity ... We have got to fight it. We will fight it as resolutely as the British people fought Nazi Germany. (Johns & Davis, 1991, p. 248)

In South Africa, violence was limited and apartheid was ended without civil war, but if white South Africans had been more adamant and united about preserving apartheid, and if F. W. deKlerk had not come into power, and released Mandela and lifted the ban on the ANC, could Mandela or Tambo have been justified in resorting to terrorism? If they were still not justified in resorting to terrorism because there are always further non-violent means that can be tried, and effective leadership might have persuaded others to remain patient and not resort to revolution that would have caused much greater loss of life, would their terrorism at least have been less unjustified than the even greater violence used by the South African government to suppress the movement to end apartheid?

The applicability of such questions to the struggle of the Palestinians for a state of their own may be considered. Questions such as these can lead us to reconsider moral principles and to improve our moral understanding.

19.8 **Conclusion**

Terrorism is not a new phenomenon in human history and should not be associated with any particular religion or group. Terrorism is a form of political violence, as is war on a much larger scale. Terrorism frequently or usually targets civilians. This violates the laws of war developed for conflicts between states with armed forces. However, relatively powerless groups use terrorism because it undercuts the superior power of established states. Terrorism is not uniquely atrocious. If the cause for which a group uses violence is just, violence used against it may be more unjustifiable than the violence, including terrorism, used by the group in pursuit of that cause. Violence in all cases, however, should nearly always be avoided. The ethics of care may be a more reliable source than many other moral approaches for moral judgements counselling against the use of violence, especially war. Military violence in response to terrorism is nearly always ineffective as well as morally unjustified.

▣ QUESTIONS

1. Should the term 'terrorism' be understood as violence that always targets civilians?
2. Why is terrorism called a weapon of the weak?
3. Why do some theorists think that war can be justified, but terrorism cannot?
4. What was and was not unique about 9/11?
5. What are some of the main values emphasized by the ethics of care?
6. Has military strength been effective in fighting terrorism?
7. Can states engage in terrorism or can only non-state groups and individual persons do so?
8. Is terrorism ever a rational strategy to employ?
9. Why is it important to consider when and where the word 'terrorism' was first used?
10. What is the principle of double effect?

FURTHER READING

Bloom, M. (2007) *Dying To Kill: The Allure Of Suicide Terror*. New York: Columbia University Press. Highly informative and balanced analysis of suicide terrorism and of the groups that use it.

Gehring, V. (ed.) (2003) *War after September 11*. Lanham: Rowman & Littlefield. A useful collection of essays by philosophers, social scientists, and legal theorists.

Goodin, R. (2006) *What's Wrong with Terrorism?* Cambridge: Polity. Examines the weapon of fear used by terrorist groups and by states.

Held, V. (2008) *How Terrorism Is Wrong: Morality and Political Violence*. New York: Oxford University Press. Essays evaluating forms of political violence and the grounds on which such judgements can be made.

Jaggar, A. M. (2005) What is terrorism, why is it wrong, and could it ever be morally permissible? *Journal of Social Philosophy*, **36**:202–17. Discusses issues of justification in various contexts.

Kapitan, T. (2003) The terrorism of 'terrorism'. In: James P. Sterba (ed.) *Terrorism and International Justice*. New York: Oxford University Press, pp. 47–66. Analyses the rhetoric surrounding terrorism, especially in the Israeli-Palestinian conflict.

McPherson, L. (2007) Is terrorism distinctively wrong? *Ethics*, **117**:524–46. A philosophical exploration of definitional problems and implications.

Primoratz, I. (ed.) (2004) *Terrorism: The Philosophical Issues*. New York: Palgrave. An excellent collection that deals with questions of definition and justification, and that discusses a number of cases.

Richardson, L. (2006) *What Terrorists Want: Understanding the Enemy, Containing the Threat*. New York: Random House. One of the best accounts of what works and what does not in countering terrorism.

WEB LINKS

http://www.cfr.org/issue/135/terrorism The Council on Foreign Relations provides articles, documents, and information on many aspects of terrorism.

http://www.isn.ethz.ch The International Relations and Security Network, a Swiss information service, offers a wide range of views on terrorism in context.

http://www.jjay.cuny.edu/terrorism The database and information on programmes of the Center on Terrorism at John Jay College of the City University of New York.

http://www.st-andrews.ac.uk/~cstpv/programmes/programmes.html The Centre for the Study of Terrorism and Political Violence at the University of St Andrews, UK, is one of the leading European institutes studying terrorism.

Visit the Online Resource Centre that accompanies this book to access more learning resources: www.oxfordtextbooks.co.uk/orc/bell_ethics/

Citizenship, immigration, and boundaries

Arash Abizadeh

READER'S GUIDE

This chapter treats two major questions: 'Do liberal democratic polities have an obligation to keep their borders open to foreigners?' and 'Who has the right to determine a polity's border policies (citizens only, or foreigners as well)?' We treat these questions in light of the fundamental normative principle on which liberal democracy is founded: that the state's exercise of political power is legitimate only if the state recognizes everyone *subject* to its power as equal *citizens*. We examine the following arguments: that the values of *liberty* and *equality* (or *justice*) require open borders and free movement; that closed borders are necessary to protect the social, cultural, and political prerequisites of democracy; that the principle of democratic self-determination implies that a political community has the right to determine its own boundary laws; and that, because foreigners are subject to border laws, they must be granted a say in determining them.

20.1 Introduction

It is estimated that, in 2008, there were over 200 million inter-state migrants worldwide—over 3% of the world's population. The contemporary causes of inter-state migration are a matter of great complexity and controversy. Beyond enabling factors such as the collapse of the Soviet Union, the opening up of China, and advanced technologies of transport and communication, researchers have identified several more direct forces:

- Significant cross-country disparities in income and employment opportunities.
- A growing global demographic imbalance, with industrialized countries facing labour shortages (because of ageing and shrinking populations), and poorer countries home to large numbers of young workers seeking opportunities abroad.
- The liberalization of flows of goods, capital, and services.
- Increasing demand for low-skilled services in industrialized countries.
- Periodic declines in labour demand in developing countries (International Organization for Migration (IOM), 2008; United Nations Department of Economic and Social Affairs (UN DESA), 2006, 2007).

Interstate migration raises a host of ethical and policy questions, concerning, for example, the implication of migration for economic development and productivity, domestic security, social integration, national identity, and global justice. Here we are concerned primarily with the question of the **legitimacy** of the state's exercise of power. Over the past century, almost all states have sought to regulate the conditions under which individuals could leave and/or enter their territory. The passport has become a ubiquitous instrument of state power, along with visa policies, immigration, residency and citizenship laws, check points, border patrols, detention centres, and forced deportation. It is true, of course, that many migrants cross state boundaries in accordance with legal procedures authorized and enforced by states, but others—an estimated 10–15% of inter-state migrants—are *extralegal migrants* whose status is in violation of the visa laws or regulations imposed by the state of destination (IOM, 2008). Still others attempt (or simply wish) to migrate, but are prevented by state controls. Some are motivated to migrate by fear of persecution, famine, destitution, or ecological disaster, others for economic or work-related purposes, some for study or training, and others to join family abroad. Whatever their reasons, anyone attempting to cross a state boundary in today's world will find themselves subject to the instruments of state power. Our question is whether and under what conditions this exercise of state power—particularly by industrialized liberal democratic states—is legitimate.

20.2 Citizen versus subject

One of the central questions of political philosophy is if and how the exercise of political power could be legitimated. Political philosophers have traditionally asked: 'What gives political rulers their **authority**?' and 'What obligations do subjects owe their rulers?' One answer popular in early modern Europe was that legitimate authority simply arises from the effective exercise of political power. According to the ideology of absolute state **sovereignty**, the point of legal and political institutions is simply to keep the peace. Whoever is able to impose order and offer protection from attack, therefore rules legitimately and ought to be obeyed. The emphasis here was on the *obligations* owed to the state by those subjected to its power.

This model of the individual as a mere *subject* of power was challenged from early on. Beginning with the assumption that human beings are by nature free and equal, **social contract** theorists concluded that a legitimate political society or state could arise only from the consent of those subject to its authority. Since few persons could be said actually to have consented to the founding of their political society, in practice these social contract theorists gravitated towards a principle of *hypothetical* consent, according to which the state's political authority is legitimated by reference to the terms to which persons *would* agree, if given the opportunity to choose. However, since individuals would agree only to terms that protect their fundamental interests, those subject to political power not only have obligations, but also enjoy rights as members of the political society.[1] Not merely subjects, they must also be *citizens*.

Civil and social rights: liberalism

The rights of citizenship emphasized by the 'classical' *liberal* strand of the social contract tradition were civil rights, which protect a citizen's freedom, as a private person, from interference by the state and others in society, and enable each to undertake contracts. The later, 'social' strand of liberalism suggested that civil rights must be supplemented by social (or socio-economic) rights, guaranteeing some minimum level of economic welfare. Other social liberals went even further, arguing that social rights must realize a comprehensive scheme of **distributive justice** that equalizes socio-economic opportunities and minimizes socio-economic inequalities. (Social rights also became central to the socialist tradition.) Such rights, whether civil or social, imply significant constraints on state sovereignty: Political power must be exercised according to laws containing institutionalized protections for citizens. Hence the association of liberalism with the constitutional state, that is, a state whose executive and legislative discretion is constrained by institutionalized constitutional principles.

Political rights: democratic republicanism

However, the *democratic-republican* strand of the tradition suggested that consent is necessary not only for legitimating the establishment of the state, but also, on an ongoing basis, in the formulation of law. Democratic republicans argued that the 'people' subjected to political power must also be the author of the laws through which power is exercised: that legitimacy derives not from state sovereignty, but from *popular* sovereignty.[2] Hence, beyond the state sovereignty model of the individual as subject, and the liberal model of the citizen as a bearer of civil (and social) rights, there also developed a democratic-republican model, which portrayed the citizen not merely as protected by the law, but as actively engaged in formulating it. The rights emphasized by this model of active citizenship were thus political rights of participation.[3]

---

[1] A classic example is John Locke (1690), *Second Treatise on Government*.
[2] A classic example is Jean-Jacques Rousseau (1762), *On the Social Contract*.
[3] For the three kinds of rights, see Marshall (1950). For the two models of citizenship, see Walzer (1989); Leydet (2006).

Membership

Indeed, some democratic republicans, typically called civic republicans, argued that in addition to political rights, active participation requires civic virtues and a willingness to sacrifice for the common good; this public spirit, in turn, must be motivated by a strong sense of patriotic identification with one's polity and fellow citizens. Hence, citizenship has been associated, in the history of political thought, with at least four elements: it denotes, first and at a bare minimum, the legal *status* of membership in a political society; secondly, the set of *rights* attached to that status; thirdly, active political *participation* and the civic *responsibilities* and *virtues* corresponding to it; and fourth, a sense of *identification* (Bosniak, 2006).

As the state sovereignty model of the individual-as-subject makes clear, there is no conceptual link between the first two elements; one of the most significant political achievements of the modern national state was to fuse the status of political membership and equal rights together in the single category of national citizenship. Prior to the French Revolution of 1789, for example, rights and privileges in France were attached primarily to class membership, rather than political membership: Neither did French subjects enjoy equal rights, nor were foreigners necessarily denied privileges. The Revolution fused together political membership and equal rights (Brubaker, 1992).

20.3 Citizen versus foreigner

Two major ideological impetuses behind this fusion were the liberal model of the rights-bearing citizen, and the democratic-republican model of the active citizen and popular sovereignty. Yet implicit in these models, and their demand that subjects also be citizens, was not only a claim about what goes along with being a citizen, namely a set of equal rights, and a claim about the collective source of sovereignty, namely the people, but also about who *ought* to be a member of the people, namely all those subject to the state's exercise of political power. In practice, exceptions and inequalities of course remained; the exclusion of women and colonized persons have been glaring examples. However, future demands for further inclusion could always be made, by asking whether the currently constituted boundaries of citizenship were legitimate according to the normative aspirations internal to liberal or democratic theory itself, i.e. whether the equation of subject and citizen had been fully realized in practice.

The fusion of political membership and equal rights in the status of citizenship ostensibly created a new domestic realm of inclusion and equality. Ironically, in so doing, the modern state simultaneously also created an external realm of exclusion and inequality: the citizen was defined not only in contrast to the mere subject, but also in contrast to the foreigner, whose non-membership was supposed to justify unequal treatment by the state.

There are, therefore, potentially three distinct problems of legitimation:

- How to legitimate the *state* and its constitution.
- How to legitimate the *law*, through which the modern state exercises power.
- How to legitimate political boundaries, whether *territorial* or *civic*.

While the first two legitimacy questions have been routinely treated in the history of modern political thought, the question of the legitimacy of the people and its boundaries in relation to foreigners has often been overlooked (Näsström, 2007). To some extent, this neglect has reflected the assumption that the territorial boundaries of the state contained everyone subject to its exercise of political power. On this assumption, the state could satisfy the demand that everyone subject to its power be equal citizens by recognizing as citizens everyone within its territorial boundaries. This assumption in fact held a great deal of plausibility as long as territorial boundaries existed, but were not coercively regulated by the state against foreigners. Except for in times of emergency, such as war, early states did not routinely regulate their boundaries against foreigners. They did not need to: there existed many other barriers to cross-border migration, such as brute physical geography and distance, as well as social and political barriers to emigration within would-be migrants' countries of origin. (Many states frequently imposed *emigration*, rather than immigration, restrictions on their own populations.) However, once states began to regulate their territorial boundaries coercively against foreigners, the assumption lost its plausibility. Indeed, the civic boundary of citizenship, which the state also claimed legitimately to enforce, became the basis for policing territorial boundaries: For the first time, during the First World War, states began issuing passports and using them on a permanent and normalized basis to police on a massive scale the movement of people into their territory (Torpey, 2000).

The problem for the liberal and democratic-republican models, and so for states that aspire to be constitutional democracies, is that, in one crucial respect, the state's enforcement of boundaries is different from any other instance of its exercise of political power. If the state exercises power over, and enforces its laws against, only those persons within its own territory, then at least in principle it can confine the scope of its power to its own citizens, by recognizing the entire subject population as equal citizens. However, this is not possible, even in principle, if the state seeks coercively to enforce its territorial and civic boundaries against foreigners, i.e. to regulate if and how foreigners can come to its territory (immigration) and/or become citizens (naturalization). This is a unique conceptual feature of boundaries: constituting and enforcing them always necessarily subjects both insiders and outsiders to the exercise of political power. The question, from the perspective of the two models that demand that subjects also be citizens, is how to legitimate such an exercise of power over those whom the civic boundary simultaneously constitutes as non-citizens deprived of the rights of citizenship.

20.4 The state sovereignty model

A second reason for the neglect of the question of the legitimacy of the people, and the citizen/foreigner boundary, has been the influence, in inter-state affairs and law, of the ideology of state sovereignty. If sovereignty lay with the state, the legitimacy of which was grounded in its capacity to impose social order and protect its population from attack, then its boundaries could be equated with the territory effectively controlled and protected by the state. The development of the modern state thus saw a shift in the nature of legal and political jurisdiction: Whereas earlier, in feudal Europe, overlapping and cross-cutting political jurisdictions had been based on personal status, the modern centralized state asserted jurisdiction primarily over its bounded *territory*. Jurisdiction over persons became derivative: Anyone present in the state's territory was its subject (Brubaker, 1992; Pangalangan, 2001).

Since the primary boundaries were territorial, the sovereign territorial state was naturally thought to have authority to dictate who may enter and exit its territory and under what conditions. The ideology of state sovereignty thus did not merely help account for the location of territorial boundaries, namely as far as effective control reached (McCorquodale, 2001). It also helped explain the state's right coercively to regulate *civic*, as well as territorial boundaries, according to the requirements of security. The primary concern of the state sovereignty model, after all, is the peace, order, security, and preservation of the state and its population. While champions of the liberal model believed that there exist moral constraints on how the state could legitimately treat its subjects, defenders of state sovereignty argued that moral considerations could arise—if at all—only *after* the state, and its capacity to keep the peace, had already been firmly secured.[4] The natural, pre-political human condition, on this view, is fragile and insecure, and moral relationships amongst human beings are a luxury made possible only by an already established background context of security. Without security, there can be no morality. It is precisely the function of the sovereign state to provide this background context, in order to *make* moral relations amongst members possible. State sovereignty consequently cannot be restricted by moral considerations that threaten the state's capacity effectively to keep the peace. Least of all can state sovereignty be restricted by moral constraints on its treatment of outsiders, particularly since moral relations arise only amongst members of a single political society (Hailbronner, 1989).

This ideology is reflected in modern international law and the legal norms of most states, even would-be constitutional democracies: according to a widely cited United States legal maxim, for example, every state has the authority 'inherent in sovereignty, and essential to self-preservation, to forbid the entrance of foreigners within its dominions, or to admit them only in such cases and upon such conditions as it may see fit to prescribe'.[5] Boundary control, including of immigration and naturalization, is essentially regarded here as the functional equivalent of war, and the state's authority to determine and enforce border policy as unrestricted as its supposed authority to wage war (Scanlan & Kent, 1988).

The state sovereignty model thus provides answers to two questions about regimes of border control. The first question is: who has the legitimate political authority to legislate and implement border policy? This *procedural-political* question about authority asks who has a right of representation (and/or participation) in the decision-making process: members of a political society only, or foreigners as well? The second question is: what moral reasons or norms, if any, must inform the political authority (whoever it is) and constrain it in setting border policy? This *substantive-moral* question about discretion asks whether

---

[4]The most distinguished branch of this argument stems from a tradition that includes Niccolò Machiavelli, Thomas Hobbes, and Carl Schmitt: the tradition of *raison d'état*.
[5]*Nishimura Ekiu v United States*, 142 US 651, 659 (1892), cited in (Hendrickson, 1992).

legislating and coercively enforcing the closure of boundaries against some persons is morally *permissible*, *required*, or *forbidden*. Closure is permissible if the decision-making authority has the moral right to close the borders or leave them open, required if it has a duty to close them, and forbidden if it has a duty to keep them open. To the first question, the ideology of state sovereignty answers that the legitimate decision-making authority is the state itself (acting on behalf of its own population only); to the second question it answers that the state is not constrained by any moral considerations.

The question is whether, and on what grounds, the liberal and democratic-republican models might challenge these answers.

20.5 The liberal model

One way the liberal model challenged state sovereignty was by placing moral constraints on how the state could legitimately treat its own population. A second way was to impute obligations to the state in its treatment of foreigners. After all, the model began with a conception of each human being as free and equal. Domestically, the state must be constrained by the terms to which free and equal persons would agree. Hence the specific rights of citizens. Yet although these rights arise by virtue of membership in political society, the moral status of freedom and equality giving rise to them was imputed to human beings as such. This suggested that persons enjoyed certain '**human rights**', and were owed certain obligations, either simply by virtue of their humanity, or by virtue of relationships that human beings share apart from membership in a common political society (Beitz, 2004).

On human rights, see Chapter 13.

The liberal doctrine of human rights has produced one of the most significant challenges to the state sovereignty model, not merely in international law, but in the domestic law of many constitutional states as well. Since the Second World War, international law and even many states have come to recognize rights constraining the state's boundary sovereignty. The two most obvious such constraints correspond to the right of any person freely to leave a state's territory and the right of a citizen freely to return to it. The liberal strand of social contract theory has seen the right of exit as absolutely crucial for legitimating the state's exercise of power, on the grounds that, without it, a state's population could not be understood to have consented to its rule. (They would effectively be its prisoners.) Such a right was not, however, legally recognized by most states or international law until well into the twentieth century (Hendrickson, 1992). Article 13 of the 1948 Universal Declaration of Human Rights thus marked a departure from tradition when it proclaimed that every person 'has the right to leave any country, including his own, and to return to his country'.

A more far-reaching constraint concerns states' obligations to refugees, i.e. to persons who flee their home and fear returning because of a threat to their life or some basic liberty. Many liberals have argued that states are morally required to permit such persons entry to their territory. It is true, of course, that neither current international law nor state practice has fully recognized such a duty. The Convention and Protocol Relating to the Status of Refugees (1951, 1967) only recognize as refugees those fleeing social and political persecution (but not those fleeing famine, economic destitution, ecological disaster, war, or gender-based persecution). Furthermore, the Convention and Protocol do not oblige states to permit refugees to *enter* their territory. Rather, they simply oblige states not to *return* refugees, who have *already* entered, back to the territory where their lives or freedoms are threatened (the obligation of 'non-refoulement'). It is thus only the refugee's presence within the *territory* of the state that gives rise to any legal obligations. In practice, even aspiring constitutional democracies have routinely flouted this minimal principle and have exercised their considerable powers to ensure that refugees cannot reach their territory in the first place. Hence, current state practice and legal norms fall well short of what liberal commitments seemingly require (Dummett, 2001; McCorquodale, 2001). Despite these important qualifications, it nonetheless remains true that today both international law and many domestic legal systems do impose institutionalized restrictions on the state's discretion to regulate its own boundaries. (Many states grant refugees who have reached their territory legal rights and standing in judicial proceedings concerning their asylum claims.)

The putative obligation to keep borders open to refugees concerns only one particular class of foreigners. Yet the basis for this obligation is the liberal assumption that *all* humans are free and equal beings, of equal moral worth. Recently, some liberals have accordingly argued that the freedom and equality of each human being oblige the state to leave its borders open to *everyone*. They argue for a universal right of immigration, not just emigration.

Liberal arguments for open borders

Liberals who argue for a strong presumption in favour of open borders advance two main arguments, one appealing to the value of *freedom*, the other to *equality* or *justice*. Both arguments begin with the empirical observation that when the state closes its borders it uses coercion, which inherently restricts persons' freedom. The second argument makes the further observation that, in a world with extreme levels of material poverty and inequality, when a prosperous state closes its borders, it effectively uses coercion to protect the prosperity of its own citizens by depriving the worst off from opportunities to share in it. These observations are important because to say that all human beings are free and equal is implicitly to question all coercively enforced boundaries restricting freedom and entrenching inequality.

The liberty argument

Classical liberals focus exclusively on the first observation. Liberals typically argue that there are some basic liberties so fundamental to a free life that they can only be legitimately restricted for the sake of the basic liberties themselves. These are the liberties that civil rights are designed to protect above all, such as freedom of expression. **Freedom of movement** is often thought to be one of these basic liberties, because without it individuals would not be able to pursue their own choices and projects about how to live; it is not only an important liberty in its own right, but a prerequisite to guaranteeing other basic liberties (Rawls, 1971). This is in part why liberal democracies typically recognize a civil right to free movement *within* their own territory. Hence, the first main liberal argument for a strong presumption in favour of open borders is that the same considerations justify a basic human right to free movement across state boundaries. Because a basic liberty is at stake, states have a prima facie duty to keep their borders open to everyone; the only way border coercion could be justified is if it were for the sake of enhancing basic liberties themselves (Carens, 1987, 1992).

Let us grant, for the moment, that freedom of movement is a basic liberty, and that states have a corresponding prima facie duty to keep their borders open to all. (A prima facie duty is one that may be overridden by other duties). Then the obvious way to resist the conclusion that states have an *all-things-considered* duty is to show that closing borders to some persons is necessary for protecting some other basic liberties. So, for example, even domestically the civil right to free movement does not mean that a person can go just *anywhere* on the state's territory. For the sake of public order, which is necessary to protect basic liberties and civil rights, movement may be legitimately restricted (e.g. by traffic regulations). For the sake of protecting freedom of association, or property rights, or private contracts, free movement may also legitimately be restricted (e.g. you cannot enter my home without my permission). Similarly, it may be permissible (or even required) for some states to close their borders to some people for the sake of protecting basic liberties. Given current levels of global economic inequality, if prosperous states were to open their borders to everyone, they might experience a massive, speedy rise in population levels, which in turn might lead to chaos and a general breakdown of public order. First, the sheer numbers may overwhelm the state's capacity to maintain security and protect civil rights in its territory (Carens, 1987, 1992); secondly, the great number of poor immigrants could instigate a collapse of the domestic economy, and in turn lead to chaos (Isbister, 2000); and, thirdly, the sheer numbers and cultural diversity of the new arrivals could overwhelm the society's capacity to integrate them, leading to social collapse (Kymlicka, 2001). The debate therefore turns on the empirical question of what levels of immigration the state could handle before nearing this threshold of collapse; advocates of open borders typically respond that today's states can afford vastly more open borders than is their current practice. A similar, but more controversial argument points not to the numbers, but to potentially illiberal or subversive immigrants, who might destroy liberal state institutions—the most extreme example is immigrants intent on **terrorism**. The argument is more controversial because, typically, liberals believe that the state cannot legitimately curtail basic liberties based merely on its evaluation of a person's character or future intentions (Cole, 2000).

Critics of open borders, however, often go further, and simply deny that inter-state free movement is a basic liberty at all. Some argue that the right to free movement only arises within a particular institutional context: the state must recognize free movement domestically as a basic liberty in order to justify its imposition of a coercive legal system on free and equal persons within its territory. Since the state does not coercively impose its legal system on outsiders, however, it has no duty to recognize their freedom of movement into its own territory (Blake, 2003, 2006). The difficulty with this account lies in explaining why, if what triggers the requirement of justification is state coercion, border coercion should be any different (Abizadeh, 2007). Others critics pursue a different strategy. A powerful justification for recognizing free movement as a basic liberty, after all, is that it is necessary for protecting individuals' freedom to pursue their own life projects, from amongst an adequate range of valuable options. Many critics argue, however, that except for cases where one's state of origin fails to provide these options (such as in the case of refugees and failed or tyrannical states), free movement *within* one's own state is sufficient to protect such options (Perry, 1995; Miller, 2005). The difficulty with this argument arises from the fact that much of world's population live in states that *do* systematically fail to provide these options, an observation pointing to the second main argument for open borders.

The equality/justice argument

The second argument is made by social liberals who appeal to the values of equality and justice. Granting that interstate movement may not be a basic liberty, they nonetheless insist that, given the massive levels of global poverty and inequality, and the failure of many states to provide their populations with an adequate range of valuable life options, prosperous liberal states have a duty to keep their borders open to the global poor. Justice either imposes a duty of humanitarian assistance in the face of great (and desperate) need, or a duty to redress global inequalities. The duty arises because, according to the liberal model, the state must recognize the equal moral worth of each person: the coercive restriction of individuals' freedom by the state requires a justification recognizing the inherent freedom and equality of all. Therefore, insofar as border coercion protects and entrenches global poverty and inequality, it is illegitimate (Carens, 1987, 1992).

It might be asked whether migration is an effective means for combating global poverty or inequality. Some argue that migration may in some respects be more effective than direct foreign aid, because it avoids the potential for bureaucratic inefficiencies or corruption associated with aid (Perry, 1995). Others argue that open borders would fail to help those most in need, because migrating is possible only for those with the financial means (Woodward, 1992). It is even possible that, because of the 'brain drain' phenomenon, open borders would be positively detrimental to those left behind in impoverished countries. Others argue, however, that the brain drain phenomenon and the possibility of emigration thanks to education, simply increases incentives for education in countries of origin, and that any losses are offset by the phenomenon of family remittances (see Faini, 2007). The World Bank estimates that officially recorded remittance flows to developing countries totalled 265 billion USD or 2% of GDP in 2007 (Ratha et al., 2008).

Another way to challenge this second argument for open borders is to reject the assumption that states and/or their citizens are obliged (to foreigners) to reduce global poverty or inequality in the first place. According to many liberals, the point of principles of distributive justice is to regulate shared socio-political institutions. Therefore, unless persons share such institutions, they cannot have duties of justice to each other. Critics of global justice then simply deny that the earth's population shares the relevant institutions; only citizens (and residents) of a single state do. For example, some argue that the point of principles of justice is to legitimate coercive political institutions; that duties of justice consequently arise only between persons whose lives are regulated by shared coercive institutions; and that, since there is no global state, there are no global duties of justice (Blake, 2001; Nagel, 2005). Again, the challenge for these critics is to show why the inter-state system of border coercion does not qualify as the relevant kind of coercive institution, especially since a key *function* of such coercion is to defend global inequalities. Alternatively, many argue that the point of principles of distributive justice is to regulate the distribution of goods jointly produced by social co-operation; that social co-operation only truly exists when there are shared socio-political institutions regulating the fundamental terms of co-operation; and that such institutions are normally confined to within states (Freeman, 2006a,b). However, 'social co-operation' either refers to mere social *interaction* or, more strongly, it exists only when people interact on the basis of fair principles of reciprocity or justice. On the one hand, the challenge for these critics is that if social co-operation means mere social interaction, then today's levels of globalization seem enough to give rise to demands of justice (Beitz, 1999; Buchanan, 2000). On the other hand, if social co-operation means that people *already* are fulfilling their duties of justice to each other, then it seems that these critics are perversely implying that duties of justice arise only between people who are already fulfilling their duties to each other (Abizadeh, 2007)!

For more on this topic, see Chapters 6, 7, 8, and 14.

Most liberal critics of global justice are, in any case, willing to grant that all human beings have a social right to minimum levels of material subsistence and that, consequently, citizens of affluent states have a duty to reduce extreme *poverty* abroad. Often they simply wish to deny that citizens of affluent states have a duty to reduce *inequality* (Miller, 1998a). Yet given the appalling levels of global destitution today, even this concession would seem enough to carry the second argument for open borders. States would have a prima facie duty to open their borders, not just to socio-political refugees, but to all *potential* economic refugees—a rather enormous number. Critics of open borders would then need to show that such prima facie duties to foreigners, whether to reduce poverty or inequality, are overridden by other considerations.

Liberal arguments for closed borders

For social liberals, the most important such consideration is the welfare state and the social rights it is meant to protect. At least three potential arguments for closed borders, grounded in welfare considerations, have been suggested. First, given the enormous levels of current global inequality, open borders may permit such massive levels of migration to prosperous states that, as a result, their economies would collapse. Secondly, even if prosperous states' economies survived, their capacity to sustain a welfare state may still collapse, or at least come under so much strain so as to compromise the state's capacity to fulfil putative special responsibilities to its own current citizens (and perhaps residents). Thirdly, as long as there is no global state, open borders may unfairly disadvantage citizens of states who finance welfare schemes more generous than the global norm. Finally, some liberals point beyond welfare considerations, and towards the state's role in protecting its citizens' culture.

Economic collapse

Most liberals would agree that no state has a duty to adopt policies leading to economic collapse. If open borders would lead to economic collapse, even the coercive exclusion of impoverished foreigners could be justified, consistently with the equal moral worth of all, because otherwise not only would native citizens suffer, but impoverished immigrants would find no relief either. Moreover, if opening borders would lead to the welfare state's collapse, then even if the duties of distributive justice were global in scope, closing borders could be justified to foreigners on the grounds that the long-term prospects for global justice depend on the consolidation (not destruction) and gradual expansion of existing welfare institutions and social rights. Critics argue that these justifications for closing borders would be consistent with respecting the freedom and equality of foreigners only if the states invoking them also discharge their obligations of global justice by other means, such as foreign aid (Bader, 2005). Others, in any case, argue that, as a matter of empirical fact, prosperous liberal states can afford to open their borders to vastly greater numbers of immigrants than they currently do, without collapse (Chang, 1997). Indeed, many argue that, given their ageing populations, the continuing prosperity of the industrialized economies in the North, and their capacity to sustain the welfare state, actually *depends* on permitting greater numbers of immigrant workers (UN DESA, 2001).

Welfare strain and special obligations

Rather than arguing that open borders would lead to the complete *collapse* of the economy, a weaker claim is that open borders would harm prosperous countries' impoverished native citizens. Poor immigrants would *strain* the welfare state's social services, or wage competition with immigrants would push wages of poor domestic workers down (Woodward, 1992; Macedo, 2007). If true, these harms to the domestic poor might justify closing borders, but only if the state had special obligations for the welfare of its current citizens. Moreover, these special obligations would have to be strong enough to override more general obligations of global justice. (Special obligations arise from particular actions, such as promises, or relationships, such as friendship; some think that citizens have special obligations to each other and the state to its own citizens, thanks to special relations between citizens.) The problem is that, according to many philosophers, special obligations are compatible with the freedom and equality of all only if they do not serve—especially via coercion—to reinforce inequalities between insiders and outsiders (Scheffler, 2001; Abizadeh & Gilabert, 2008).

Fairness to contributors

The welfare state is usually only able to recognize social rights and provide benefits, such as free universal healthcare or old age pensions, thanks to mandatory taxes paid by citizens (and residents). This is why welfare states directly tie the social rights of citizenship to its obligations: citizens wishing an extensive welfare state must necessarily accept the collective burden of financing it. These obligations, moreover, are usually spread throughout the entire life-cycle of a citizen: a young adult, for example, usually pays taxes at a rate much higher than warranted by the healthcare benefits she presently receives, but later in life as a senior citizen will receive health services much greater than the taxes she will pay. Annual contributions, in other words, do not directly 'pay' for the services enjoyed that year. The fusion of social rights and obligations in the status of citizenship, and the fact that the rights/obligations ratio varies greatly from one life-stage to another, present a fundamental problem for open borders. If different polities adopted different tax and welfare regimes, open borders would create incentives for people to live their healthy and productive working years in polities with low taxes and minimal welfare services, and migrate to a high-tax state with generous welfare programmes in their hospital-prone and non-working years. In other words, without a global state to enforce a global taxation regime, productive citizens living in states with generous welfare regimes risk becoming 'suckers' open to inter-state exploitation. Hence the third social liberal argument for closed borders: that, without a global state, open borders would be *unfair* to productive native citizens, because their lifetime contributions would be susceptible to exploitation by immigrants who benefit from the welfare state, without having contributed their fair share (Heath, 1997). To work as an argument for closing borders to the global poor, however, one must assume that justice requires that social benefits be distributed only to those who have contributed to making them possible. This is a controversial assumption. Many argue that justice requires extending benefits to persons in dire need, even if they have not made any earlier contributions (Gilabert, 2007).

Protecting culture

For more on this argument, see Chapter 7.

Some liberals also argue that the state has a right (if not duty) to close its borders to foreigners to protect the integrity of its citizens' *culture*. The argument is that meaningful freedom or **autonomy** requires an adequate range of valuable options and that a person's culture is the 'context of choice' providing it. A culture is the source of beliefs about what is valuable and offers options corresponding to those beliefs. Therefore, closing borders is justified as the necessary means for protecting citizens' cultural 'context of choice' from being submerged or destroyed by immigration (Kymlicka, 1995, 2001; Heath, 1997). The difficulty with this argument is its very limited application. Cultural change is only a risk to autonomy if the culture that provided a person with valuable options is eroded *and* they are unable to assimilate to the new cultural forms replacing it, in the sense that they are unable to see the new cultural options as having value (Patten, 1999). This disorientating form of assimilation generally occurs only in cases of very rapid assimilation or of assimilation through oppression. The argument, therefore, does not justify protecting citizens' culture from immigration-induced change per se, but only from rapid and disorienting, or oppressively imposed, change (Perry, 1995; Bader, 2005). Some argue that the only circumstance in which high levels of immigration might submerge a native culture in this way is when a political society is colonized or subjected to the rule of oppressive invaders—and never simply because of open borders (Dummett, 2001).

20.6 The democratic-republican model

Like liberals, democratic-republican critics of the state sovereignty model have demanded that those *subject* to state power be recognized as *citizens*. Not the state, but the people, is sovereign in this view: The coercive exercise of political power is legitimate only insofar as the people subjected to it can, in some sense, see themselves as the author of the laws through which it is exercised. Despite their critique of state sovereignty, however, democratic republicans have typically sided *against* liberals who argue, on moral grounds, for a duty to open borders. Two arguments are typically provided: that closed borders are *instrumentally* necessary for ensuring the empirical preconditions of viable democratic practice; and that the democratic principle of **self-determination** *intrinsically* entails the unilateral right to control one's own borders, including the moral permission to close it to foreigners. Recently, however, some have argued that the democratic principle of popular sovereignty demands that foreigners have political rights to participate in determining the laws that govern immigration and naturalization.

Prerequisites of democracy: a community of character

Many authors claim that viable democratic practice instrumentally requires a 'community of character' with a strong sense of patriotic identification, or shared national public culture, that would be undermined by open borders (Walzer, 1983). Civic republicans in particular argue that democratic institutions can only thrive amongst citizens whose strong sense of patriotism inspires sacrifice and a vigilant defence of their institutions. Others argue that a shared national public culture is necessary to effect social integration democratically, to ensure the social trust necessary for democratic deliberation, or to ground a shared identity necessary for democratic projects (Miller, 1995). These empirical claims remain controversial, however. Some argue that democratic motivation and social integration, social trust, and shared identity do not depend on a single national public culture, and that well-designed institutions are able to integrate, foster social trust, and even foster shared identity in contexts of diversity (Abizadeh, 2002; Pevnick, 2009). On this view, open borders are compatible with patriotism and social integration, especially because immigrants are usually highly motivated in their wish to belong. If there is a problem, it is not open borders, but the marginalization of immigrants by the host society.

The self-determination argument

The intrinsic argument appeals to the democratic principle of self-determination. To say that the people is sovereign is, in part, to say that it has the right to decide how to run its own affairs and determine the public character of its community, without the interference of outsiders. Since who counts as a member of the political community and who is permitted to live in its territory are matters that certainly affect the polity's character, it has often been argued that a democratic people has the right to determine its own admission laws (Walzer, 1983; Whelan, 1988). This is a powerful argument. Although it is not an argument for closed borders, it is an argument for a democratic polity's unilateral right to close its borders. As such, it is an argument against any putative duty to open one's borders.

Transnational political rights

There is a potential difficulty with the self-determination argument, however. The principle of self-determination takes for granted that we know beforehand who legitimately comprises the collective 'self' with the right of self-determination. It presupposes that the 'self' of self-determination are those who are *already* citizens. Yet the democratic principle of popular sovereignty does not start by taking who is a citizen for granted. When under South African apartheid, for example, only whites were recognized as full citizens, the principle of popular sovereignty did not imply that these citizens had the right (of self-determination) to decide whether to permit blacks to acquire full citizenship. The principle *demanded*, rather, that all those subject to the exercise of political power be recognized as citizens, with rights of democratic participation in determining the laws through which that power is exercised over them. If such political rights are attached solely to the status of citizenship, then all subjects of political power should be recognized as citizens.

This is why the state's enforcement of the boundaries of citizenship poses a unique problem. On the one hand, it is an intrinsic feature of civic boundaries that they distinguish between citizens and non-citizens. Insofar as the rights of political participation are attached to the status of citizenship, such boundaries tell us who enjoys and who is deprived of such rights. On the other hand, enforcing boundaries is one of the most significant ways in which the state exercises political power over both insiders and outsiders, i.e. over citizens *and* foreigners. If only citizens can participate in determining the laws, and if boundary laws govern both citizens and non-citizens, then it appears that some people are subject to the exercise of political power without any say over how that power is exercised over them. Yet this would violate the democratic principle of legitimation. It is for this reason that some have argued that, in the case of boundary laws, rights of political participation must be detached from the status of citizenship: they argue that according to the democratic principle of popular sovereignty, foreigners should be granted political rights to participate in determining the laws governing immigration and naturalization (Abizadeh, 2008). One difficulty with this lies in precisely what the institutional implications would be and exactly how such institutions could realistically arise in a world where states jealously guard their sovereignty. Others, moreover, have argued that being subject to political power is not sufficient to motivate the demand for political rights. Pointing to the example of tourists, who are also subject to a state's laws, they have argued that political rights of participation need only be granted to those with a significant 'stake' in the polity's future, for example only if one's autonomy or well-being depends on its political institutions in the long run (Bauböck, 2007a,b). This would presumably imply that only *some* foreigners have a legitimate claim to participate in determining a polity's boundary laws.

20.7 Case study: fortress Europe?

Today, most countries are, to varying degrees, simultaneously countries of origin, transit, and destination for interstate migrants. This contrasts with half a century ago, when most countries of origin were European, and only a small number of industrialized countries—such as Australia, Canada, and the United States—were countries of destination. Whereas for several centuries Europeans systematically migrated, whether as colonists, immigrants, or refugees, to the Earth's four corners, today the tide has reversed—Europe has become a major destination for inter-state migrants. By 2005, Europe was home to an estimated 64 million inter-state migrants—over a third of inter-state migrants worldwide, and almost nine per cent of the European population (IOM, 2008; UN DESA, 2006, 2007).

The phenomenon of in-migration has, in recent decades, faced contradictory imperatives in the 15 (primarily west European) states that comprised the European Union until 2004. On one hand, economic and demographic imperatives have pushed EU-15 countries towards greater openness. Economic integration within the EU has itself favoured increased labour mobility. EU-15 states also face a rapidly ageing (and potentially shrinking) population that jeopardizes their welfare state's tax base and labour force, and domestic labour shortages have, in turn, compromised the ability of several EU-15 states to compete in the global market. As a result, many have actively sought economic or labour migrants (Favell & Hansen, 2002). Finally, the ideological self-image of the EU as a progressive world actor, respectful of its international obligations, has pushed EU states at least to pay lip-service to the recognized rights of refugees under current international law.

On the other hand, since the 1980s, west European states have witnessed ever-increasing public hostility to migrants and the consequent rise of far-right anti-immigrant parties. Public debate has reflected anxieties over migrants' supposed threat to the welfare state, job opportunities for citizens, social integration, national identity, liberal democratic values, the rule of law, and security. Moreover, fears in some EU-15 states over their failure to integrate substantial domestic Muslim populations have been grafted onto fears about migrants. Particularly since the terrorist attacks of 11 September 2001, European public and governmental discourse has inextricably linked migration to concerns about security and crime. This has combined with another major development: the legalization of inter-state migration. While the great waves of European emigration were undertaken largely without a framework of migration laws, the past century has witnessed increasing attempts by states legally to regulate migration. This has also made migration's 'illegalization' possible: by the twenty-first century, publics and governments have routinely come to view administrative visa violations as akin to criminal violations, rightly subjected to measures normally reserved for criminal law. For these reasons, scholars speak of the '**securitization**' and 'criminalization' of migration in Europe (Karyotis, 2007; Dauvergne, 2008).

Hostility has been particularly strong against asylum-seekers claiming to be refugees and extra-legal migrants. In part, anxiety about asylum-seekers has been fuelled by the public's difficulty in distinguishing refugees, as defined by international law, from extra-legal economic migrants. Asylum-seekers frequently enter a state without authorization and so strictly speaking are extra-legal. Furthermore, because international law does not recognize those fleeing economic destitution as refugees, many extra-legal economic migrants, fleeing a genuine deprivation of basic liberties, nonetheless present themselves as fleeing socio-political persecution. Hence the increasing perception and treatment of asylum-seekers as 'criminals', both before and after they have crossed inter-state borders.

This set of contradictory imperatives has produced paradoxical results for the regulation of inter-state migration both *within* and *to* Europe. The most dramatic change over the past half century, namely the gradual establishment and eastward expansion of the EU itself, reflects this paradox. On one hand, EU institutions have significantly lowered the barriers to intra-EU migration. Today almost all EU states are part of the Schengen Area, within which border controls have been almost wholly eliminated. Moreover, EU law today recognizes free movement by citizens of the EU as a 'fundamental freedom', comprising the freedom to move, take up employment, and establish oneself and one's family in any EU state, along with the right to equal treatment in employment, public housing, and tax and social advantages, regardless of state citizenship (Meloni, 2006; Guild, 2007; European Commission, 2008).

This trend towards open borders received its most dramatic impetus recently with the eastward expansion of the EU, from 15 member states to 25 in 2004, and then to 27 in 2007. The prospect of expansion created considerable consternation within pre-2004 EU-15 states.

Many feared that, because of lower wages and higher unemployment in the new central and eastern European member states, lifting migration controls would trigger massive labour migration to the more prosperous western European states. As such, the treaties of accession permitted temporarily maintaining some restrictions against workers from states acceding in 2004 and 2007. Although most EU-15 states initially opted for transitional restrictions, some, facing labour shortages, did not, and by 2009 only four maintained them against the 2004 acceding states. The empirical evidence suggests that the ensuing labour migration had largely positive effects for EU-15 economies, and that in any case there was considerably less migration than anticipated. There was little evidence of an expansion-induced surge in workers or welfare expenditures (Barrell et al., 2007; European Commission, 2008).

On the other hand, this very opening *within* the EU has placed tremendous pressure on EU states to adopt a common set of external border controls and policies to regulate migration *into* the EU. The Amsterdam Treaty brought visas, asylum, immigration, and free internal movement under common EU jurisdiction,[6] and since then the EU has taken steps towards a common asylum system and immigration policy. There is now a European Border Agency, and the Schengen Area's expansion has been accompanied by common rules on external border controls, policing, and information sharing.

The result is what some call 'Fortress Europe': a realm whose internal borders are open, but whose external borders are strenuously policed to keep out unwanted migrants. In part because under current international law a state's legal obligations to refugees arise only if they are already on its territory, EU states have undertaken drastic policing measures to prevent asylum seekers from ever reaching their soil in the first place. Already, new EU member states have had to adopt new border controls on their eastern frontiers, restricting mobility from countries with which they previously had relatively open borders. The direct human cost of attempting to seal Europe's borders, which of course involves a massive deployment of state-sanctioned violence, has been very high. According to one press review, over 13,000 persons have died since 1988 along European frontiers, including over 5000 missing at sea (Fortress Europe Blogspot, 2009). The increased security and criminalization of migration have also witnessed the establishment of several hundred detention centres, where extra-legal migrants (including asylum seekers) who have reached European soil are held in prisons and other facilities while their cases are processed. Conditions at these 'camps' vary considerably by country, and have been routinely denounced by human rights organizations (Raj, 2006; Dauvergne, 2008).

Many critics argue that it is a mistake to conflate security issues, however real, with migration. Others ask whether, after centuries of migrating to other regions in search of prosperity or refuge, Europeans are not obliged to reciprocate, now that migration flows have reversed. Moreover, migration into the EU is arguably inevitable, no matter how tight border controls are: Persons fleeing destitution, war, and persecution will continue to risk their lives in search of refuge. Refusing legal migration places thousands of lives at risk, and forces thousands more to reside within the EU, but outside the law. The effect within the EU itself is to create a vulnerable, legally unprotected workforce exploited by European industries for profit. Many ask whether this state of affairs is compatible with the EU's aspirations to be a just, liberal democratic society.

---

[6] The exceptions are Denmark, the UK, and Ireland.

20.8 **Conclusion**

The history of political thought has witnessed at least three models of the individual's relationship to political society: the state sovereignty model of passive subject; the liberal model of rights-bearing citizen, protected by the laws; and the democratic-republican model of active citizen, who participates in creating the laws. Both citizenship models have demanded that the state's exercise of political power be legitimated by recognizing all subjects of state power as equal citizens. Yet the citizen has been defined not only in contrast to a mere *subject*, but the *foreigner* as well, and once the state attempted to close its territorial and civic boundaries to foreigners, the citizenship models gave rise to a legitimation problem: border coercion subjects individuals who inherently are *not* citizens to the state's political power. Two questions arise: is there an obligation to keep the state's borders open? And, who has the right to set a state's border policy?

We have examined, from a liberal perspective, the *liberty* argument, according to which free movement is a basic human right, and the *equality* or *justice* argument, according to which open borders are necessary to reduce global poverty and inequality. We also considered, in favour of closed borders, arguments arising from concerns about the domestic economy, the welfare state, and cultural protection. Furthermore, in favour of allowing citizens unilaterally to determine their own border policies, we considered the democratic principle of self-determination; and in favour of granting foreigners some democratic say over immigration and naturalization laws, we considered concerns about the exercise of arbitrary power over voiceless foreigners. While we have not definitively settled any of the debates, one thing is clear—immigration and border control go to the heart of one of political philosophy's most fundamental questions, namely, how to legitimate the exercise of political power by some human beings over others.

■ QUESTIONS

1. What are three major models of the relationship between the individual and state power?

2. Is citizenship an institution of inclusion or exclusion?

3. Is there a right to free movement across state boundaries?

4. Would open borders trigger massive migration and economic collapse?

5. Would open borders erode the institution of citizenship?

6. Does a constitutional democracy have the right unilaterally to control its own borders?

7. How can a state's exercise of power over foreigners be legitimated?

8. Is liberal democracy compatible with closed borders?

9. Under what circumstances and for what reasons could a state close its borders to foreigners?

10. Does Europeans' previous history of emigration oblige them to open their borders to migrants today?

■ FURTHER READING

Barry, B., & Goodin, R. (eds) (1992) *Free Movement: Ethical Issues in the Transnational Migration of People and of Money*. University Park: Pennsylvania State University Press. A collection of articles on the ethics of migration, from liberal egalitarian, libertarian, Marxist, natural law, and realist perspectives.

Dauvergne, C. (2008) *Making People Illegal: What Globalization Means for Migration and Law*. Cambridge: Cambridge University Press. Argues that the recent rise in the 'illegalization' of migration represents an attempt by states to re-assert their sovereignty in the face of globalization.

Dummett, M. (2001) *On Immigration and Refugees*. London: Routledge. An informed and impassioned plea for open borders, with a focus on the British case. Links efforts to control migration with the history of racism.

Ethics and Economics, 2007; **4**(1). Available at: http://ethique-economique.net/Volume-4-Numero-1.html. A collection of short articles on the ethics of migration.

Gibney, M. (ed.) (1988) *Open Borders? Closed Societies? The Ethical and Political Issues*. New York: Greenwood Press. A useful collection of articles on the ethics of migration.

Miller, D., & Hashmi, S. (eds) (2001) *Boundaries and Justice: Diverse Ethical Perspectives*. Princeton: Princeton University Press. Articles on the role of boundaries in delimiting property and political rights, from religious and secular perspectives.

Schwartz, W. (ed.) (1995) *Justice in Immigration*. Cambridge: Cambridge University Press. Articles by economists, political scientists, and philosophers about the moral bases of immigration policy.

Swain, C. (ed.) (2007) *Debating Immigration*. New York: Cambridge University Press. A collection of essays on the ethics of migration in Europe and the USA, including discussion of law, policy, economics, demographics, and race.

Torpey, J. (2000) *The Invention of the Passport: Surveillance, Citizenship, and the State*. Cambridge: Cambridge University Press. Focusing on the US and western Europe, Torpey documents the twentieth century rise of the state's attempt to control migration across its borders.

■ WEB LINKS

http://www.iom.int/ The website of the International Organization for Migration. An indispensable, up-to-date source for data about global migration trends.

http://www.imldb.iom.int/ The International Migration Law Database contains a vast amount of authoritative material about international laws concerning migration, as well as the legal regimes of different countries.

http://www.migrationpolicy.org/ The Migration Policy Institute is a think tank dedicated to the study of migration.

http://www.migreurop.org/ Migreurop is a militant European pro-migrant group. The site includes documentation of anti-migrant abuses and migration detention centres in Europe.

http://www.unhcr.org/ The United Nations High Commissioner for Refugees. The site provides up-to-date information about refugees and internally displaced persons around the world.

Visit the Online Resource Centre that accompanies this book to access more learning resources: **www.oxfordtextbooks.co.uk/orc/bell_ethics/**

21 Democracy and world politics

James Bohman

READER'S GUIDE

Globalization and other facts about the increasing scale and interdependence of modern societies have given rise to new 'circumstances of politics'. In the eighteenth century, the new circumstances of war and political violence led thinkers such as Immanuel Kant, among others, to argue for an ever expanding confederation of republics. While most people reject the idea of a world state, today more and more political problems are dealt with by international institutions. Furthermore, political institutions have emerged beyond the state, such as the European Union (EU). This chapter discusses the lively debates about whether democracy can be achieved beyond the state, and how rule by the people could be institutionally organized. As a case study, discussion concerning the 'democratic deficit' in the EU helps to illuminate the requirements of democracy across borders.

21.1 Introduction

Debates in democratic theory are often presented as recurring struggles among great schools or 'isms'. A prominent example of this would be the debates between liberalism, with its emphasis on rights that protect individuals from state interference, and **republicanism**, with its very different concern with status and non-domination (Held, 2006).

This mode of presentation often obscures the differing assumptions that underlie many theoretical disputes, especially when they take place during periods of historical change and uncertainty. Ours is such a period. For example, while announcements about the 'end of the nation state' may well be premature, there is good social scientific evidence to suggest that the democratic character of this political form may well be declining, or at least at risk (Held et al., 1999). If the changes taking place are great enough, the difficulty in making such assessments may in part have to do with long-held assumptions about what democracy is. Perhaps it is not democracy as such that is threatened, but rather an important and widely accepted interpretation of it. Indeed, the assumptions about democracy that we make are far more historically specific than we realize; the burgeoning discussion of cosmopolitan, **supranational**, and **transnational** alternatives to the nation state has again revealed just how difficult it is to talk about a transformation in democracy without implicitly assuming too much of our inherited ways of thinking.

Disputes about the future of democracy within and beyond the state, especially the question of whether we have already experienced its historically best realization, depend less on differences in diagnoses of its current problems than on normative issues involving debates about differing interpretations of the meaning of democracy in the global era. However much they differ in their theoretical justifications and institutional proposals, those who argue for the need for greater democracy at the global level must ultimately share very similar diagnoses of the problems with the current international system. Given that democracies have worked together to produce the international system as it currently exists, the prior question is more of what *sort* of democracy? The current transformation of democracy is not historically unique. It has already undergone at least two transformations: first, the ancient democracy of assembled citizens and, secondly, modern representative democracy. Now, with the increasing significance of globalization and the emergence of the European Union (EU) and other robust transnational institutions, it is reasonable to think that democracy may be undergoing yet another transformation. As Robert Dahl asks (1989, p. 224), 'Given the limits and possibilities of our world, is a third transformation of democracy a realistic possibility?'

Democracy has long played a role in discussion of world politics. The first task is to discuss the terms of the debate about modern democracy. Democracy is defined in different ways in different contexts, but the underlying idea that most conceptions of democracy share is the ideal of self-rule: in a democracy, the people govern themselves. Given this definition, in this chapter I discuss some of the ways in which self-rule is increasingly challenged by forces beyond the borders of the state. First, the limits of state capacity have become particularly salient, with the emergence of globalization, with new forms of interdependence and institutions beyond the state. Secondly, modern democracies have always seen themselves as playing an important role in implementing peace and security. Indeed, cosmopolitans such as Immanuel Kant who believe in a world legal and political order have long hoped that democracies would form the basis of international peace. However, the discussion has shifted from such instrumental benefits of democracy as peace and security to more substantive discussions of cosmopolitan or transnational democracy. Democracy across and beyond borders cannot be the same as democracy within a delimited political community. Few defend a world state, but if the differences among societies are too great, how can we talk about a cosmopolitan or transnational democracy? To date, there are many transnational institutions, but none are really democratic in the sense of self-rule. Finally, we turn to the EU, which provides a good case study of the problems with and prospects for the emergence of a new democratic political order.

21.2 Democracy: a great transformation?

Democracy is ascendant across the globe, but in a particular and familiar form: constitutional democracy with a protected set of basic rights, the separation of powers, and universal suffrage of adult citizens. There are now and always have been many competing interpretations of the ideals of democracy. Nonetheless, it can still be said that the core of any such interpretation is some idea of self-rule, which can be continuous (as in the form of the ancient Athenian assembly) or merely periodic (as in the brief minutes in which we cast our ballots). Even with this conceptual core, there are also significant disagreements about the requirements for self-rule. The growing size and complexity of modern societies has sometimes been thought to challenge the very idea of self-rule. Jean-Jacques Rousseau thought that a self-governing people could only number a few thousand; however, one contemporary democracy, India, has over a billion or so members. While some democracies, such as France, aspire to create a shared political culture, others, such as Canada, have embraced **multiculturalism** and a political culture based on heterogeneity, rather than prior conditions of commonality. Some argue, then, that democracy can only be realized on a small scale and in a shared community, while others see size and heterogeneity as enabling conditions of democracy, rather than as constraints.

Democracy in the modern state is rife with these tensions. None is perhaps more disputed than the question of *who* belongs to the political community and has the status of a member. The idea of a self-ruling people—of citizens ruling and being ruled in return—necessarily requires a bounded political community, consisting of all those and *only* those who are full citizens. This delimitation makes it possible for all citizens to be *both* authors *and* subjects of the law, so that they need only obey those laws that they themselves have made. The liberal perspective on the history of the modern state optimistically asserts that once the connection between universal **human rights** and the principle of democracy is made, only effective international law and its enforcement stands in the way of the solution to the gap in the scope of democracy. While the constitutions of modern states typically do list basic human rights, the gap has not been closed, especially when one thinks of political rights for non-citizens.

On citizenship, see Chapter 20.

On human rights, see Chapter 13.

Even this tension fails to give us the full picture of the limits of universality inherent in the form of modern democracies. As Jürgen Habermas puts it, the natural law theory espoused by most founders of modern constitutional orders requires that the political community consists of 'a determinate group of persons, united by the decision to grant to each other precisely those rights that are necessary for the legitimate ordering of their collective existence by means of positive law' (Habermas, 2001c, p. 63). One might think that these limitations on democracy are just an historical accident. Instead, Habermas is expressing the idea that boundaries are essential to democracy itself. Thus, while human rights are moral rights that apply to all persons, the political right to be the author of the law is limited to a specific group of people. Thus, the fundamental difference is between the positive status of being a citizen *within* a political community and the negative status of merely being a bearer of human rights. Citizens are empowered to make the laws that they want, without considering the legitimate claims to justice that everyone can make in virtue of having human rights.

Legal cosmopolitans such as Kant sought to extend the scope of the juridical status to all persons, seeing the creation of a global legal community as the solution to the problem of increased interdependence. This would mean that citizenship ought to be extended, where everyone who has human rights is also a member of humanity or a 'citizen of the world'. This claim is sometimes criticized (Brown, 1995; Barry, 1982). However, the solution only goes so far, creating institutions that see human rights as juridical statuses that supplement political membership in a state, but these statuses are not sufficient for non-domination, whatever the achievements of the current human rights regime, since they say nothing directly about *who* makes the laws. Without an accompanying political status, the real possibility of legal domination cannot be avoided. Within a political community, such legal statuses add to the powers of free and equal individuals; they have a right to petition a court to hear their claims, just as they have various rights that make it possible for these same petitioners to initiate deliberation about the fairness of these procedures. Thus, universal legal status cannot simply be realized in being protected by judges or courts, but by having a status as a citizen to resist limitations on one's freedom and well-being. However, this difficulty raises the question of whether democracies are necessarily delimited political communities, in which people are both authors and subjects of the laws.

This issue also concerns the *how* question of democracy: how do the people rule themselves in a democratic manner? While there are certainly many different answers to this question, two are particularly salient. The first is **aggregative** and relies on voting as a means for selecting representatives, who make the laws together in the name of 'the people'. This is the most common form of nation state democracy today. Some who support the aggregative conception argue that voting provides the basis for the people to select among elites and vote them out of office when they act consistently against the common interest (Schumpeter, 1947). The second conception is **deliberative**, where decisions are democratic to the extent that citizens reason together publicly on matters of common concern. Broadly defined, a deliberative conception of democracy includes any one of a family of views, according to which public deliberation of free and equal citizens is the core of legitimate political decision-making and self-government. This conception is most generally conceived in opposition to the aggregative conception of social choice and decision-making, which it argues fails to capture how citizens have an equal say in decisions that affect them. Beyond this fundamental agreement, however, each of the terms of this definition is hotly debated among deliberative democrats (Gutmann & Thompson, 2004; Bohman & Rehg, 1997; Rosenberg, 2007). Various institutional and non-institutional locations for deliberation have been proposed and debated, as have various attempts to determine their feasibility. At the core of deliberative democracy, in any of its forms, is the idea that deliberation essentially involves publicly giving reasons to justify decisions, policies or laws, all of which are the means by which citizens constitute and regulate their common life together. Democracy on this view, then, consists in reasoning together with fellow citizens about issues that affect them and, where possible, coming to an agreement or at least a compromise that all can accept.

The aggregative conception of democracy is certainly more familiar and is the product of the last great transformation of democracy in the modern period. Most modern democracies have two major features: voting, now based on universal suffrage of all competent adult citizens; and elections, which serve primarily to choose representatives in the legislature. While the legislative bodies often deliberate, fundamental decisions are also made by voting. When the political community gets large enough, most people think that representation is the only way to keep the idea that the people should rule themselves, if only indirectly (Runciman & Brito Vieira, 2008). Since the people delegate their sovereign powers to their representatives who make decisions within a legislative assembly, these representatives can also delegate popular **authority** to some other institution, such as the EU. While allowing for scale that is much larger than the Athenian assembly, aggregative democracy can be easily scaled up beyond the state. Multi-nation states that employ this form of democracy, however, do not incorporate delegation so easily, especially when there are conflicts among relatively equal national minorities, as in Belgium. In this case, it is unclear how representatives are supposed to assemble as a unitary, self-legislating people. Canada, for example, thinks of itself as composed of peoples, rather than forming 'We, the People'. Moreover, even if that problem were solved by shared constitutional principles based on patriotism, the devices of representation become more tenuous as the community grows larger and multilevelled, and generally the **legitimacy** of international institutions is borrowed from the democracy within the states that delegate authority to them. Most administrative bodies in the EU are justified in this way, but that hardly makes them democratic. Such institutions are not the expression of self-rule, and often may even be sources of domination for weaker democratic states. Because of this problem, Dahl and others argue that international institutions based on delegated authority alone cannot become democratic (Dahl, 1999, pp. 19–37).

Although the exact scope of any of these conceptions is a matter of debate, for our purposes it is important that the democratic ideal has to be one that could apply at various levels, from the local to the national to the transnational. Democracy based on voting and representation favours a particular ideal of self-rule that seems to require a delimited political community in which people are both the authors and the subjects of the laws. Since the EU cannot make this sort of claim about its laws, it is hard for many to see it as democratic at all. It seems to be increasingly the case that many people who are subject to the laws are now no longer their authors, either because subjects of the law are not citizens or, if they are, because they are excluded and thus not represented. Deliberative democracy, by contrast, provides a normative ideal for self-rule that is broadly applicable in many different contexts.

Sociologically inspired scepticism about democracy usually points to various social facts and trends in modern society in order to show that the preconditions for democracy as self-legislation of a people no longer exist. Certain conditions make initiating and sustaining deliberation possible, and in their absence it would be hard to call the deliberation in various institutional locations either public or democratic. These conditions seem to include:

- The existence of formal institutions of some kind to organize opportunities for influence over decisions, such as a parliament or a citizens' assembly.

- The existence of **civil society** as the domain of free association and political activity.

- A **public sphere** that permits communication across these various political units.

Such conditions do hold in a transnational context, as formal institutions are now expanding. For this reason, deliberative democracy seems to have significant advantages over the aggregative conception in discussing democracy beyond the state.

The possibility of domination from actors and institutions outside the state suggests new 'circumstances of politics' (Weale, 1999, pp. 8–13; Waldron, 1999, pp. 114–17). Globalization may be thought of optimistically as the creation of a shared condition, so that we all belong to a shared 'community of fate' as many have thought of nation states. Rather than a common space or a singular and uniform condition, however, global interdependence is more often than not highly stratified with 'differential interconnectedness in different domains' (Held et al., 1999, p. 27). Here, we may think of global warming as an example. While it is a problem for all people, those who live on islands are much more immediately affected by climate change. Thus, decisions made in one place can affect the life prospects of many others who have no voice or vote. In many domains, social activities and processes 'cross boundaries in one direction only' (Dobson, 2003, pp. 12–21), as when resources exit and no wealth returns for the common good. In some domains, such as global financial markets, globalization is profoundly uneven and reinforces already-existing hierarchies. Inequalities in political access to international rule-making institutions or in the ability to control globalization processes may reflect older patterns of subordination and order, even while the processes exclude some communities from financial markets entirely and make others more vulnerable to its increased volatility. This range of social activities and the organizations that plan and carry them out are thus changing the 'circumstances of politics'.

On the environment and political theory, see Chapter 10.

If we accept that many social actions have this kind of intended or unintended influence, then we cannot choose those with whom we must co-operate, and in the absence of such a choice, the existing scheme of co-operation must be open for negotiation and deliberation. Interdependence without voluntary co-operation will often mean that we are effectively included in many social and economic consequences without having any choice in the matter (O'Neill, 1996, p. 119). Inclusion in such plans that are carried out for the sake of others who benefit from them (such as the shareholders of some corporation or the citizens of another state) is itself a form of domination. When the International Monetary Fund (IMF) loans money to poorer states, these governments are required to adopt particular policies, such as adjusting the percentage of their gross national product (GNP) used by governments for social welfare. In these cases, the new circumstances of politics present a profound challenge to self-rule, so that being a citizen of a democracy is no longer by itself sufficient for non-domination. Moreover, even democracy within states cannot be thought to be so unified, given the rise of pluralism and complexity. Many decisions are now made by experts and legislatures have little ability to check their powers. Moreover, nation states can no longer exercise full control over economic decisions such as standard setting about environmental policies that directly affect their economic well-being. Whether aggregative or deliberative, democratic politics is embedded in the 'context of large and complex social processes the whole of which cannot come into view, let alone under decision-making control' (Young, 2002, p. 46). Pluralism—the growing heterogeneity of people in any relatively open democracy—challenges the very legitimacy of the traditional democratic idea of a 'people', which is now both culturally diverse and no longer based on shared status as citizens come to live with many non-citizens in their midst.

These new forms of domination are not necessarily concerned only with states and state actors. Early in the modern period, Kant and others became concerned with one of the new international circumstances of politics: the increasing capacity for state violence. Through their willingness to engage in multilateral negotiations, democracies might be thought to be motivated to act in such a way as to avoid the forms of domination inherent in the new circumstances of politics. This idea came to be thought of in terms of the 'democratic peace' hypothesis—that is, the proposition that democracies are less likely to go to war than other kinds of states and even less likely to go to war with each other (Doyle, 1983; Russett, 1993). Democracy understood as constitutional government should be able to check state violence and domination. However, it is also true that democracies that engage in war and the preparations for war become less democratic. The favoured option in the modern period, that of a sovereign state exercising non-domination at home and domination abroad, has become increasingly less tenable.

21.3 Challenges to democracy within states: war, peace and global governance

Traditionally, the state has been involved in domination through its capacity to engage in organized violence or war. Democracies do go to war against non-democracies, although 'almost never' against other democracies (Russett, 1993). Many explanations have been offered for why this is the case, such as the ability of democratic citizens to defend their rational self-interests or the likelihood that citizens in one democracy will trust the citizens of another democracy. Democracy might reasonably be thought to have this effect precisely because it gives citizens the freedoms and powers that provide means by which to avoid the ills of war. The political ills of war, however, are revealed even in wars with non-democracies, measured not just in terms of the human suffering and domination of non-citizens, but also the costs to citizens' powers and freedoms. In times of peace, these freedoms and powers are more likely to flourish and entrench more robustly democratic practice.

However, the institutionally embedded deliberative powers of citizens are no longer sufficient to check the institutional powers of states to initiate wars, and these arrangements have left citizens vulnerable to expanding militarization that has correspondingly weakened these same entitlements. The effects of the Iraq war on civil liberties in the United States show this democracy-undermining tendency. Liberal democracies have not only restricted some civil rights, but have become human rights violators, with the use of extralegal detention centres in Guantanamo, 'extraordinary rendition' to third party countries, and the use of torture in order to achieve security (Mayer, 2008). As such, they might be said to have become less democratic, certainly in the active sense of creating enabling conditions for challenging the use of force. If democracy permits citizens to seek peace, then decreasing the powers of citizens to influence decisions would make war more likely. Thus, the institutional capability to wage war increases along with the heightening of executive and administrative powers within the state on matters of security, for this often bypasses democratic mechanisms of deliberation and accountability, and thus works against democratization (where this is understood precisely as the widening and deepening of the institutional powers of citizens to initiate deliberation and participate effectively in it). This is not true only of war and war-making powers, but other institutions that have taken on many tasks of government formerly confined to states.

These examples show that under the new circumstances of politics the old republican formula that 'to be free is to be a citizen of a free state' is no longer sufficient for non-domination (Deudney, 2007). Because of this lack of congruence between decision-takers and decision-makers, one aim of global democratic politics should be to permit those affected to give their voluntary consent to international policies. For example, the IMF has the capacity to dominate many developing countries by imposing terms of co-operation upon them that extend to all areas of economic policy. This is true of private actors as well, as when global corporations extract resources such as oil and give the funds directly to dictators who control and dominate their own citizens.

These facts lead to the conclusion that the absence of democracy makes it more difficult to achieve important goals of social life, such as self-development. Among its many instrumental benefits, democracy helps people avoid great harms, including famines as well as war (Sen, 1982; Doyle, 1983). For my purposes here, however, the constitutive elements of justice have greater prominence: a practice is just only if it treats participants as free and equal, and unjust to the extent that it does not. Ultimately, democracy promotes justice precisely because it enables citizens to *demand* to be treated justly. I take it as uncontroversial that the current global system, characterized by extreme destitution, sweatshops and other forms of tyranny and domination, is neither fully just nor fully democratic nor able to realize basic human rights and freedoms. Achieving non-domination requires more than simple governance institutions. It requires access to influence for individuals when they are affected by potentially dominating actions and actors. This is the primary virtue of democratic institutions, but what sort of democratic institutions? To answer this question, we need a clearer idea of the feasible alternative conceptions of democracy beyond the state.

21.4 **Cosmopolitanism and democracy: debating the alternatives**

In this section, I outline and assess current cosmopolitan and transnational theories in developing an adequate account of democracy beyond the nation state. As I suggested in the previous section, this would mean that the international system was not just orientated to states, but must also include individuals as citizens of the world, so that they can make claims to democratic transnational institutions. The dominant theories can be compared on five axes. They may be:

- Political or social.
- Institutional or non-institutional.
- Democratic or non-democratic.
- Transnational or cosmopolitan.
- Bottom-up or top-down.

All of these theories are informed by often implicit background assumptions about the scope of political obligation, whether it is moral to the extent that it is concerned with individuals and their life opportunities, social to the extent that it makes associations and institutions central, or political to the extent that it focuses on specifically legal and political institutions, including citizenship.

Democratic minimalism: Allen Buchanan

The best place to begin is to consider the most minimalist account of international democracy, which is offered by Allen Buchanan. Like Rawls, Buchanan thinks that 'peoples' are the basic units of a global order. Rawls proposes that we should determine the **basic structure** of institutions that peoples (not individuals) would agree to in the **original position**—in which people hypothetically deliberate without knowing their final position in the global order—while tempering the scope of these institutions through toleration required by the fact of pluralism. This assumption leaves no room for genuinely political and democratic institutions, precisely because states are thought to organize a 'people' who share a common culture and are 'decent' to the extent that they protect a subset of the most basic human rights. Even though Buchanan begins by endorsing this moral minimalism about basic rights, he disagrees with Rawls and others about 'how minimal this minimum is' (Buchanan, 2004, p. 176). The next step for Buchanan is to argue that it is democracy that best protects 'basic' human rights through the 'right combination' of representative institutions; these institutions are said to 'most reliably achieve the accountability necessary for protecting basic human rights', understood as basic interests that are essential to leading a decent human life (2004, p. 189). Thus, Buchanan is a political cosmopolitan who endorses political rights and democratic institutions because they are necessary for the accountability of any institution, including international ones.

On Rawls's international theory, see Chapter 6.

It is arguable that such an instrumental justification is insufficient on its own terms. If we take seriously Buchanan's claim that political rights are to be included among human rights, so that there is a right to democracy, then he does not go far enough. For example, despite the fact that democracy is the best means to protect human rights, Buchanan accepts trade-offs between 'the capacity to protect basic human rights and building the capacity for democratic governance'. This contradicts the right to democracy. Nor can democracy truly protect human rights unless it protects rights, such as freedom of association, participation, and expression, among many others. The justification of democracy in terms of human rights is thus unavoidably intrinsic, as well as instrumental; that is, the one cannot be realized without the other.

Post-national democracy: Jürgen Habermas

On Habermas, see also Chapter 2.

The second conception is associated with the work of Habermas and is more strongly democratic, to the extent that it is guided by a particular ideal of a self-determining people who govern themselves by acts of legislation. Democracy on the nation state model connects three central ideas:

- That the proper political community is a bounded one.
- That it possesses ultimate political authority.
- That this authority enables political autonomy, so that citizens may 'choose freely the conditions of their own association' (Held, 1995a, p. 45).

The normative core of this conception of democracy is the conception of freedom articulated in the third condition: that the subject of the constraints of law is free precisely in being the author of the laws. Habermas recognizes that the conditions under which democracy operates are changing. Yet, when discussing 'post-national' legitimacy, Habermas clearly makes **self-determination** by a singular *demos* (people), the fundamental normative core of the democratic ideal, and thus cannot account for the new circumstances of politics.

In both *The Postnational Constellation* and more recent essays on the EU, Habermas seeks to expand his view of an international order to accommodate more institutions that can create effective global governance (Habermas, 2001b, pp. 132–5). One weakness of this strategy is that Habermas wants to have it both ways. When considering new institutions of governance instead of government, he describes them in non-democratic terms, as a 'negotiating system' governed by fair bargaining within policy networks (see also Slaughter, 2004). This is because he clearly, and perhaps surprisingly, accepts that democracy can only be had within states, leaving only negotiation *between* democracies as the fundamental form of political activity at the transnational level. Without a common ethical basis for a shared form of life, effective institutions beyond the state must look to a 'less demanding basis for legitimacy in the organizational forms of an international negotiation system' (Habermas, 2001b, pp. 135–8). This position is transnational to the extent that publics and civil society should be able to have some influence over such a system. The stronger criteria for democracy, such as deliberation and self-rule, are not applied outside the nation state, where governance is left to policy networks. The sole remaining important democratic role of international order is legal: they establish and protect basic human rights for everyone. Like Kant before him, cosmopolitan law becomes the basis for the achievement of human rights.

Cosmopolitan democracy: David Held

David Held's work on cosmopolitan democracy provides a more complete account than the previous two more minimalist positions. It is also more closely tied to an empirical examination of the impact of globalization than Habermas's conceptual claims about the limits of the democratic community. Not only does Held show how international society is already thickly institutionalized well beyond the systems of negotiation that Habermas makes central, he further recognizes that 'individuals increasingly have complex and multilayered identities, corresponding to the globalization of economic forces and the reconfiguration of political power' (Held & McGrew, 2002, p. 95). For example, many citizens do not live out their lives in their country of birth, but rather acquire many different social roles and political statuses. As economic interdependence expands, cross-border associations form to protect shared interests. New international courts may be called on to adjudicate conflicts and violations of human rights. Such potentially overlapping identities are the basis for participation in global civil society, in non-governmental organizations (NGOs), and in other transnational civil associations, movements, and agencies that create opportunities for political participation at the global level. The potential advantages of Held's approach over the other two approaches are thus threefold:

- An emphasis on a variety of institutions.
- A multiplicity of levels and sites for common democratic activity.
- A focus on the need for organized political actors in international civil society to play an important role in a system of global democracy.

Despite these advantages, the self-legislating *demos* reappears in Held's explicitly Lockean insistence that 'the artificial person at the centre of the modern state must be reconceived in terms of cosmopolitan public law' (Held, 1995a, p. 234). According to this view, democracy is not manifested in individual legislative acts, but in making the global political framework itself the subject of the popular will and consent. Once legitimated, this political subject emerges within a 'common structure for political action' that enables individuals and groups to pursue their individual and collective projects, but where cosmopolitan law demands the subordination of regional, national and local sovereignties to an overarching legal framework.

Held's demand for democratic control over 'the overarching general legal framework' creates a fundamental continuity between democracy within and beyond the nation state, but it arguably does so at a high cost. First, it removes many decisions from democratic institutions and puts them in the courts. While courts are forums for deliberation, their decisions settle issues in ways that democratic deliberation does not. This introduces a fundamental disanalogy with other cases of democratic self-determination. Law is not necessarily linked to self-determination. In a word, in a period when even democracy in the state is disaggregated and decentred, the cosmopolitan conception of democracy risks increasing rather than decreasing the problems of domination. I return to this theme below when discussing the EU.

Transnational democracy: John Dryzek

The fourth and final position can be called 'transnational', rather than cosmopolitan, precisely because it rejects the traditional state model for a 'bottom-up' strategy that promotes a robust transnational civil society and public spheres as the basis for an alternative to the subordination of citizens to a common framework of public law. This account rejects the analogy to democracy in the nation state, seeing its development as one of an ever-declining democracy, rather than a threshold to be met by international institutions. According to John Dryzek, its leading proponent, 'there are imperatives that all states must meet' that are located in the core areas of its functioning, including economic growth, social control, and legitimation. These imperatives impose 'structural limitations' on the state's public orientation in matters of policy (Dryzek, 2002, p. 93). In the international arena, Dryzek's approach is further supported by the increasing importance of NGOs and the emergence of transnational public spheres, consisting primarily of informal networks of association and communication (Dryzek, 2006, p. vii). It is also supported by the emergence of various international 'regimes'—that is, agreements about the rules and decision-making procedures that regulate specific activities or domains, including commercial whaling, the rights of children, nuclear accidents, and so on.

As with Held's insistence on an 'overarching framework', one possible weakness is that this shift to informal networks and weak publics comes at a high price for democracy. The complementary weakness to Held's juridical model derives from the fact that on Dryzek's account transnational democracy can only be 'contestatory'—democracy, on this view, consists in challenging decisions that have already been made by other forms of authority, such as international arbitration boards that defend free trade. Dryzek thus ends up with a kind of institutional minimalism that also leaves out the dimension of active and empowered citizenship. This is most evident in the following sort of claim: 'Most of the government that does exist (in the form of organizations such as the UN, WTO or the EU) is not at all democratic, which suggests that transnational democrats might usefully focus their efforts on governance' in which civil society already has a largely contestatory, but informal role (Dryzek, 2002, p. 133). Lacking any clear account of such success remains insufficient. Effective contestation assumes that no one is dominated within the institutional order and that those who exercise the power to make decisions are open to influence. The same is true of Held's more maximalist account since the kind of institutional framework that he develops, while differentiated and multilevelled, does not address the issue of the appropriate active powers of citizenship sufficient for democratization in the international sphere.

A possible synthesis

These criticisms of the range of possible theories of democracy beyond the state suggest a fifth alternative: it must be institutional, political, democratic, and transnational. The first two features are necessary for the theory to be of the appropriate type, minimal or not. The first question is then: should these institutions be cosmopolitan or transnational in scope? It is arguable that cosmopolitan theories do not transform democracy enough, because they assume a top-down account of fundamentally legal global institutions. In this respect, transnational democracy seems to be the preferred alternative from the perspective of establishing deliberative democracy. At the same time, Dryzek's bottom-up version does not make any distinctive form of transnational citizenship very important and, thus, does not envision that citizens will make decisions themselves rather than challenge them after the fact. A normatively richer alternative is to reject both bottom-up and top-down approaches to the fifth axis in favour of an approach that emphasizes vigorous interactions between publics and institutions as the ongoing source of democratic change and institutional innovation. Here, deliberation replaces contestation as the proper democratizing activity. An adequate theory must in this respect be more like Held's cosmopolitanism, with its well-articulated multilevelled institutional structure. While I defend a different way of developing this basic sort of institutional structure (Bohman, 2007), it is hard to see how any conception of transnational democracy can avoid using its general structural features. In this way, the account of transnational democracy offered here will preserve the best features of these other conceptions, while overcoming their weaknesses.

Such an interactive and deliberative approach can also appeal to some actually existing institutions to test its feasibility and adequacy. Indeed, the EU exhibits this kind of structure rather well, to the extent that it includes novel ways of organizing public deliberation across borders. In particular, Joshua Cohen and Charles Sabel (2004) have discussed interactions between publics and institutions that facilitate citizens' influence over dispersed, but empowered decision-making processes, such as the Open Method of Coordination (OMC). The goal of the OMC is to form policies across the countries of the EU, but without assuming uniformity from the outset. Each country deliberates about its policy, say in the area of employment, but with the exchange of information and arguments across various sites of deliberation. This exchange of information will then bring about a new phase of deliberation, where each considers the arguments and policies of the other group in light of their own goals and objectives. After this phase is over, the countries monitor each other's performance, allowing them to modify their own policies in light of the best practices. This process is democratic in a deliberative sense; it also produces better knowledge about all the available alternatives, allowing for fruitful revisions based on comparison to other practices.

Even if such processes are still in need of further democratization, they exhibit two core institutional features lacking in Dryzek's transnational conception: they are both deliberative and reflexive, that is, they see democracy as the means by which democracy can be changed when the conditions demand it. Cohen and Sabel call such a process 'directly deliberative polyarchy' (Cohen & Sabel, 1997). It is 'direct' since all those affected participate in deliberation, citizens as well as officials. It is a 'polyarchy' because each group is empowered to make decisions on its own, in light of their own deliberation and the deliberation of the others. Such possible democratizing processes embody just the sorts of interactions among publics and institutions that, as John Dewey once put it, 'break existing political forms' (1988, p. 244). This kind of deliberative polyarchy exemplifies the possibilities inherent in the transnational account. It also suggests how they can transform and reform democratic practices so that they can become more democratic. This capacity to use democracy for the sake of improving democracy has not yet been fully achieved by the EU.

21.5 Case study: a 'democratic deficit' in the European Union?

While certainly the most successful of all existing transnational institutional forms, the EU is not a democracy, at least not yet. The EU is for this reason perhaps best described as a 'polity in the making', and as such needs more democracy for its increasing authority to be legitimate. Without such democratic legitimacy, the citizens of various Member States may find that some decisions are impervious to citizen influence and popular control, no matter how much those institutional structures resemble a parliamentary form. This issue of democratic legitimacy comes to the fore, perhaps most especially, whenever the EU attempts to engage in democratic reform. Citizens may feel that they cannot influence policies and decisions in the EU, or worse yet, may not even know how to do so because of poor links between the governors and the governed (MacCormick, 1996, p. 130). Such a perceived 'democratic deficit' may lead to the result that it is very difficult for such a polity to create the means and ends necessary for achieving its own democratization. In short, the EU would fail to meet the conditions of democracy that it requires for its Member States.

Different possibilities for democratization beyond the nation state remain open to the EU, each of which depends on a different understanding of the type of political body the EU is supposed to be. In part, they depend on making European citizenship in some way comparable to the rich array of rights and opportunities associated with national citizenship that have emerged from long historical struggles for democratic reform within states (Shaw, 1999). The democratic deficit thus applies to a recurrent problem of transnational institutions, and it would be a singular achievement if the EU could become the first to achieve legitimate and democratic reform (Schmitter, 1998, pp. 13–36).

This difficulty has become even more entrenched for the EU, since there is no 'People' that it is supposed to organize into a subject. Instead, the more modest goal is that of 'bringing the peoples of Europe together in an ever closer Union'. The 'peoples' that were to ratify the constitutional treaty of 2004 were the national publics, not the citizens of Europe. When the citizens of EU member states were asked to put the proposal to a vote, the publics of France and the Netherlands rejected the democratic legitimacy of the constitution as a means to democratic reform. One main purpose of this democratic reform would be to address the issue of the potential losses of freedom and accountability. Some may think that the EU can never be a democracy, unless it created a parliament in which representatives, rather than the leaders of states, actually made the law. Yet the EU has no legislative body, since its Parliament does not have the authority to enact the law directly. Even if it did, would the deficit be solved?

The only solution is, as Henry Richardson has put it, to look for a way in which 'the processes that form the popular will can be distributed across the various parts of the constitutional structure' (Richardson, 2002, p. 70). The difficulty here is that in the case of the EU, it is the executive power of the Council, consisting of the prime minister (or executive) from each state, as empowered in the 2001 Laeken Declaration, that has the legitimate right to make such a proposal, independently of any exercise of the popular will. But if citizens are to be engaged both as citizens of Europe and of the member states, their will must be engaged at various stages and locations in the process. The challenge of democratic reform is that citizens have to have the democratic authority to create those institutions that constitute such authority in the first place. In order to do this, citizens must be able to deliberate about the democratic deficit and have their deliberation influence attempts at democratic reform. However, rather than a general 'democratic deficit', the difficulty of reform is more properly a 'deliberation deficit' that also leads to a 'popular deficit'.

The democratic deficit in the EU is instructive in another respect. It shows democratization outside the nation state is different from democratization within it. For example, law may have different roles in different types of institutions. In the EU, law-making is less tied to political processes of contestation and accountability, especially given the diminished role of the European Parliament (EP) relative to national governments. In this way, law is less subject to political influence and may lead to a distinctive form of domination through emerging forms of legal authority. An increasingly larger proportion of legal policy comes from directives and decisions made by intergovernmental bodies. The same is true for the WTO or the North American Free Trade Agreement (NAFTA). While the result of agreement among states, these sorts of bodies are authoritative in ways that can bypass the democratic mechanisms that check state power.

There are positive features of the EU which favour democratization. This potential can be seen in the way that the 1950 European Convention for the Protection of Human Rights and the recent 2000 Charter of Fundamental Rights of the European Union entrench human rights and grant to individuals the right of petition. In this way there are (at least in the juridical dimension) multiple new institutions and memberships that can be invoked in making claims about human rights. The Charter functions in just this transnational way, not as a binding document, but as grounded in the constitutional traditions of the member states (Habermas, 2001b, pp. 5–6). In this way, the protection of human rights at various levels empowers citizens in ways that would not be available in the state institutions that monopolize legal authority at a single level.

How could the EU become better at being an agent for democratization? It is unclear whether it would be sufficient to create a more effective and empowered EP, perhaps with two chambers. The point here is not to see the EP as some privileged source of democratic legitimacy, but as just one of the locations for distributing deliberative and popular powers. The EU also has some interesting institutional designs that could promote public deliberation in a more direct way. As Cohen and Sabel have argued, a 'directly deliberative' design in many ways incorporates the capacity for learning and innovation typical of economic organizations (Cohen & Sabel, 2004, pp. 370–5). In such practices, various bodies collaborate in deliberation to produce policies that are more responsive to issues at the local and regional levels, especially if they involve citizens directly. This kind of process would have more legitimacy than popular referenda, in which citizens can express their approval or disapproval in a yes/no vote. Directly deliberative designs of this type are already used in various states, such as the British

Columbia Citizens' Assembly, in which ordinary citizens met to reform electoral laws that were widely seen as inadequate. Here, we might think that what is needed is not just parliamentary representation, but also citizen representation on important occasions for public deliberation about basic issues of democracy. However, since only a small number of citizens can actually participate in any given decision-making process, they cannot really be acting for themselves alone, but are clearly deciding for and representing other citizens and not merely themselves. To use Mark Warren's term, they are acting in the role of 'citizen representative' (Warren, 2008, p. 50). In this way, citizens can be involved in decisions about the nature of democracy in the EU, without leaving these issues only to public officials or to the vagaries of public referenda, both of which tend to be democratically arbitrary. For this to work, there would have to be a European-wide public sphere organized around newspapers, the media, and the Internet, as well as the empowered participation of citizens acting as representatives of other citizens in deliberation about the nature and form of European democracy and its deficits (Fung, 2003; Bohman, 2007). Such innovations, should they be tried, could help to establish greater deliberative and popular legitimacy, two areas in which traditional forms of democratic citizenship, participation and representation do not currently work so well in the EU. These same innovations could help improve democracy within states as well.

21.6 Conclusion

Democracy fundamentally demands self-rule. Many features of contemporary society seem to work against this ideal, including pluralism, complexity, and the increasing influence of global forces. However, often what seems to be an obstacle to democracy is also an opportunity for its transformation. Given the new circumstances of politics, new transnational forms of self-rule are needed. Rousseau thought that a robust democracy could not have more than a few thousand citizens; today India alone is nearly one billion people. The emergence of new and more flexible practices, such as those of deliberative democracy and citizen representatives, shows the possibility that a properly organized, large-scale global or regional democracy does not need to sacrifice self-rule. However, the process of creating democracy beyond and across nation states is a difficult one, as the example of the EU shows. For many, the most important practical question is whether or not there is any real alternative, especially now that humanity faces challenges such as global warming and deepening economic inequality. At the same time, the worldwide demand for equal and effective political rights and emerging innovative forms of democracy give us reason to believe that expanding democracy will be part of the solution.

▥ QUESTIONS

1. Why does globalization challenge the effectiveness of current forms of democracy?

2. What is meant by the term, 'the circumstances of politics'? How might they change our expectations about democracy?

3. Can international institutions become democratic, or do they derive their legitimacy only from member states?

4. What is the difference between an intrinsic and an instrumental justification of democracy? How might they be combined?

5. Is deliberative democracy more applicable than aggregative democracy to international institutions?

6. What does Allen Buchanan think is the most important achievement of democracy? Does he think that democracy can be promoted by international institutions?

7. What does Jürgen Habermas think is essential to democracy? Can the people be both 'the authors and the subjects of the laws' if there is more than one people or demos in the same institution?

8. What are the strengths and weakness of cosmopolitan democracy? Is the idea of a world parliament a plausible one?

9. Compare and contrast the two main approaches to transnational democracy. Can democracy work only informally in the public sphere or should citizen deliberation influence ultimate decisions? How is this different from cosmopolitan democracy?

10. What is the 'democratic deficit' of the European Union? How might it be corrected?

▨ FURTHER READINGS

Beitz, C. (1979) *Political Theory and International Relations*. Princeton: Princeton University Press. One of the first works to defend a cosmopolitan political order based on equal respect for individuals.

Bohman, J. (2007) *Democracy Across Borders: From Demos to Demoi*. Cambridge: MIT Press. The focus here is on the main arguments for transnational democracy.

Buchanan, A. (2004) *Justice, Legitimacy and Self-Determination: Moral Foundations for International Law*. Oxford: Oxford University Press. Buchanan offers an instrumental defence of global democracy as a means to achieve human rights.

Deudney, D. (2007) *Bounding Power: Republican Security Theory from the Polis to the Global Village*. Princeton: Princeton University Press. This important study rethinks security in terms of the republican, democratic tradition.

Dryzek, J. (2006) *Deliberative Global Politics: Discourse and Democracy in a Divided World*. Cambridge: Polity Press. This book offers one of the main defences of deliberative democracy at the global level.

Habermas, J. (2006) The constitutionalization of international law. In: J. Habermas, *The Divided West*. Cambridge: Polity Press, pp. 115–93. This lengthy essay is Habermas's best statement of his conception of democracy and international law.

Held, D. (2006) *Models of Democracy*, 3rd edn. Cambridge: Polity. An excellent introduction to democratic theory.

Held, D. (1995) *Democracy and the Global Order: From the Modern State to Cosmopolitan Governance*, Cambridge: Polity. Held offers one of the first and most influential statements of the idea of cosmopolitan democracy.

Held, D., McGrew, A., Goldblatt, D., & Perraton, J. (1999) *Global Transformations: Politics, Economics, and Culture*. Cambridge: Polity. This work discusses the complex social science of globalization.

Weiler, J.H.H. (1999) *The Constitution of Europe*. Cambridge: Cambridge University Press. Weiler offers the most complete discussion of issues of constitutionalization and democracy in the European Union.

▓ WEB LINKS

http://www.opendemocracy.net A popular and wide-ranging website dedicated to the discussion (and promotion) of democracy at all levels (local, national, regional, global). It contains news links, in-depth articles, book reviews, podcasts, and much more.

http://www.idea.int The International Institute for Democracy and Electoral Assistance is an intergovernmental organization that promotes democratic reform around the world.

http://www.globalpolicy.org/globalization Useful links and other online resources on globalization hosted by the Global Policy Forum, a non-profit organization based in New York.

http://www.europa.eu The website of the European Union. It contains a vast amount of information about the aims, institutions, and policies of the European Union, as well as links to relevant sites.

http://www.arena.uio.no/ Arena is an institute for the study of democracy and governance in the EU based at the University of Oslo.

Visit the Online Resource Centre that accompanies this book to access more learning resources: www.oxfordtextbooks.co.uk/orc/bell_ethics/

GLOSSARY

aggregative democracy A conception of democracy according to which the main feature of democratic decision-making is the aggregation of individual preferences on policy options, or on candidates for political office, by voting, selecting winners preferably by majority rule.

analytic philosophy The dominant current in twentieth-century Anglophone philosophy, which regarded the task of philosophy as mainly that of analysing questions of language, meaning, and logic, and largely excluded questions of metaphysics and ethics/morality. Earlier analytic philosophy aimed at replacing ordinary language, for the purposes of (natural) scientific enquiry, with a perfectly defined and precise artificial language. Later analytic philosophy abandoned this project in favour of a rigorous analysis of ordinary language itself.

analytic political theory/philosophy A label for contemporary Anglophone political philosophy in the wake of John Rawls's *A Theory of Justice*. It shares similarities of style with **analytic philosophy** (clarity and precision of expression), but does not primarily aim at analysing political concepts, but at developing normative recommendations for social and political behaviour, and accords centrality to ethical and moral concepts, such as justice, rights, autonomy, and virtue.

anarchy Literally 'without rulers'. In international relations theory anarchy is a condition in which the actions of states are shaped by the need for security in an international system that lacks a higher political or legal authority (such as a global state).

authority The power to issue commands that are, or ought to be, obeyed because of whom they issue from.

autonomy An individual has autonomy to the extent that he or she rationally chooses his or her acts and omissions in accord with his or her own judgement and inclinations—where 'rationality' implies at least a minimal capacity to understand and foresee the probable consequences of those acts and omissions.

basic structure A technical term employed by John Rawls to refer to a set of major social institutions that distribute rights and duties between individuals, and which exert a profound influence on motivations and life prospects.

biopower/biopolitics A conception of power advocated by Michel Foucault that emphasizes the ways social power is exerted upon the human body as such, including public health programmes and population control.

capability approach An approach to the interpersonal comparison of advantage under which an individual's level of advantage depends on their capacity to function or to act in certain listed ways, e.g. to be well nourished, mobile, and literate.

choice theory of rights A theory of rights that holds that the purpose of a moral right is to guarantee its bearer a protected domain of choice, in which they might act as they see fit, and is not subject to interference by other agents.

civil society The collection of voluntary associations in political societies that help to mediate between the state and the citizens.

coercion The forcing of someone to do something by threatening them with an unpleasant outcome if they do not comply. Some theorists think that the threatened outcome must also be wrongful in order for the threat to count as coercive. The term is sometimes used more widely to refer to the use of force, both threatened and actual, to achieve some aim.

collective action problem A problem that arises when there is a benefit to be had from people joining together to provide a good, but where individuals also face a cost for providing that good that they might hope to avoid (by 'free-riding' on the actions of others). For example, a group of ship owners may collectively decide to construct a lighthouse (which is a 'public good'), but if one can avoid paying their share of the costs they cannot be prevented from benefiting from the light house.

colonialism This is characterized by two main related practices. Settler colonies arose when European peoples appropriated the land of indigenous peoples in the 'new' world (e.g. Australia). Colonies of exploitation are based on the extraction of resources and the control of populations through colonial administrations (e.g. India).

communitarianism A position that originally arose as a critique of liberal theories of social justice. It objects to liberalism's perceived excessive focus on individual goods, and emphasizes the importance of more collective ways of life, often informed by traditional cultural practices. In the debate on global justice, communitarians are opposed to cosmopolitan conceptions of justice, and stress the right of communities (national and otherwise) to **self-determination**.

conception of the good This refers either to (1) a person's full set of persisting and stable preferences, or (2) the package of substantive commitments (that include beliefs, preferences, and habits) relating to how to live life well.

consequentialism A moral theory that bases the rightness or wrongness of conduct solely on the extent to which it maximizes good consequences and minimizes bad consequences. Usually contrasted with **deontology**.

cosmopolitanism Cosmopolitans see themselves as citizens of the world—as members of a global community of human beings, with robust responsibilities to others in the global community. Cosmopolitans believe that all individual human beings have equal moral worth and that the strength of our moral obligations to others is not diminished by national borders.

cultural identity This refers to an individual's sense of belonging to a cultural or ethnic group. The term is most often used to describe the content of that individual's identity – for example, 'wearing the veil is part of my cultural identity'.

cultural relativism The view that either (a) what is right or wrong is entirely a matter for cultural determination and/or (b) that there is no basis for saying that the values of one culture are better than those of another.

customary international law International law derived from the actual practice of states. Along with general principles of law and treaties customary practice is a primary source of international law.

deconstruction A philosophical approach particularly associated with Jacques Derrida, which uses close textual analysis to reveal the variety of meanings of a given text, while also challenging the idea of authoritative interpretation.

deliberative democracy A form of collective decision-making, whereby laws and policies are legitimate to the extent that they are publicly justified to the citizens of the community. Public justification is justification to each citizen as a result of free and reasoned debate among equals.

dependency theory A Marxist-influenced social science theory based on analysis of international economic dependence, in which wealthy states in the core of the world system exploit weaker and poorer states in the periphery. Dependency theory suggests that international trade leads to the lasting dependency of the periphery upon the core.

deontology A theory is deontological in form if it grounds morality in imperatives that lay down moral

obligations that are independent of the consequences of their being followed. This is contrasted with **consequentialism**.

diaspora The movement of populations sharing common ethnic identity to a new territory, specifically the permanent settlement of such communities in far removed areas. Diasporas are often associated with political efforts to retain cultural identity.

différance A term developed by Jacques Derrida that exploits a double meaning in French, implying both 'difference' and 'deference'. This idea illustrates the instability and contextual nature of meaning.

difference principle A principle of social justice advocated by Rawls, which prohibits inequalities in income and wealth that are detrimental to the least advantaged.

dirty hands (the problem of) This refers to the ethical dilemma that, sometimes, a particular political action will be wrong according to regular codes of morality, but might, nevertheless, be necessary or permissible for the promotion of overriding political goals.

disciplinary power An idea developed by Michel Foucault that focuses on the use of power to control (to discipline) the activities of individuals across many spheres of social life.

discourse ethics An approach to moral theory associated with Jürgen Habermas, which focuses on the moral significance of the norms of discourse intended to achieve common understanding.

distributive justice The consideration of the proper distribution of benefits, wealth, and other goods between individuals or communities. This can be examined at the domestic, international, or global level.

double effect A doctrine of moral philosophy that has its origins in medieval scholastic philosophy. It holds that the quality of the intention of the perpetrator of a morally bad (or unjust) action makes an irreducible difference to the moral quality of the action itself, independently of its outcome. For example, deliberate killing is generally regarded as worse than avoidably and foreseeably causing someone's death.

duty, negative A duty that requires abstaining from an action, in particular from an action that would violate a right of another person. In traditional moral philosophy, negative duties are often regarded as the core duties of justice. See **duty, positive**.

duty, positive A duty to undertake a certain action, either because it is required by the rights of other people and, hence, by justice (for example, the duty to pay taxes in order to sustain a functioning police service) or because it is required in order to fulfil obligations that are not matched by corresponding rights of other people (such as the duty to engage in charitable activity). See **duty, negative**.

English School A school of international relations theory that focuses on the existence of a society of states (or 'international society'), characterized by a variety of norms and institutions that structure international politics despite the lack of higher authority in the international system. International society is structured by the institutions of war, diplomacy, the balance of power, international law, and sovereignty.

Enlightenment (the) A historical period, ranging from the late-seventeenth and through the eighteenth century, which was characterized by a critique of authority, an increasing trust in the power of reason and a focus on the individual.

ethics of care An approach to normative ethics developed by a strand of feminism in the second half of the twentieth century, which centres on values such as responsiveness to need, sensitivity, empathy, and trust, and is put forward as a rival conception to **consequentialism** and **deontology**.

ethics of principled conviction A term coined by the German sociologist Max Weber. It refers to an approach to ethics that relies on unconditional ethical prescriptions and regards the intention to abide by these as the main characteristic of a moral action, independently of the consequences that it may produce (see **deontology**). Weber argued that the ethics of principled conviction is generally unsuitable for politicians (see **ethics of responsibility**).

ethics of responsibility A term coined by the German sociologist Max Weber. According to the ethics of responsibility, the moral task of the politician is not to act in accordance with unconditional ethical prescriptions (see **ethics of principled conviction**), but to combine political conviction with an awareness of the behaviour of others and good strategic judgement. This requires, in particular, the capacity to strike compromises.

ethnocentrism The view that one's own ethnic group or culture is superior to another based on some qualities inherent in that ethnicity or culture. This can often be expressed in an unconscious manner importantly affecting the study of both ethics and politics.

failed state Refers to states that have, or are perceived to have, failed to uphold the basic responsibilities of sovereign government. This includes the inability to control territory, to exert legitimate authority, to provide public services or to uphold fundamental responsibilities in the international community.

fascism An extreme right-wing variant of **authoritarianism** that (among other things) celebrates the superiority of a particular ethnic group or nationality, first used to describe the regime of Mussolini in Italy from 1922 to 1943, and also applied to Nazi Germany (1933–1945). See also **totalitarianism**.

feminism Both a political movement and an intellectual perspective that focuses on the unequal treatment of women and the importance of gender awareness.

foundationalism (ethical) A view that seeks to deliver a rational foundation for ethics/morality by externally grounding it on non-moral considerations, such as self-interest, and, hence, to provide an answer to the sceptical question 'why be moral?' (as opposed to the question 'what does morality demand?').

freedom of movement This refers to the freedom to move within or between political communities without any other obstacles than those imposed by other basic liberties. It is generally defended as a precondition of individual **autonomy**. Domestic freedom of movement is uncontroversially acknowledged as a basic liberty; the question whether freedom of movement across state borders is also a basic liberty is hotly contested.

full compliance, theory of A theory that discusses the norms that justice or morality requires, on the assumption that those norms would be respected by all agents subject to them. It is also sometimes referred to as **ideal theory**.

gender mainstreaming A strategy for encouraging gender equality that seeks to make gender awareness and the development of gender equality part of all of the activities of an organization. Gender mainstreaming has been particularly important in international organizations such as the United Nations, where it has been included in policy development, research, advocacy, legislation, as well as planning, implementation, and monitoring.

governmentality An idea developed by Michel Foucault that identifies both the ways in which sovereign power seeks to control the development of individuals in accordance with government policies and the specific practices through which individuals are governed.

human rights These refer to moral rights that belong to all human beings by virtue of their humanity, which override or generally outweigh other moral considerations. Human rights correlate with the duties of all human beings—and especially all governments—to respect, protect, and promote the interests identified by these rights.

human security An alternative approach to the study of security in international relations, it replaces the focus on national security with a focus on global vulnerabilities and the protection of human individuals.

humanitarian intervention Intervention, often but not only employing military force, in the affairs of another political community intended to accomplish a humanitarian purpose (such as addressing gross violations of human rights).

hybridity In post-colonial theory, hybridity refers to the interaction, mixing, and transformation of cultures. It is intended to replace static and cohesive notions of culture, and emphasizes the dynamic and pluralizing effects of cultural interaction.

ideal theory For the technical sense of the term, coined by John Rawls, see **full compliance, theory of**. In a wider sense, ideal theory seeks to answer the question of which principles of justice or morality ought to govern an ideal community or society.

interest theory of rights A theory of rights that locates the basis of a moral right in an interest of its bearer that is important enough, and of the right kind, to hold other agents under a duty to respect or promote it.

International Criminal Court An international court set up by the Rome Statute in 1998, which has the power to try individuals and heads of state for war crimes, crimes against humanity, genocide, and the crime of aggression.

ius cogens (Latin for 'compelling law') A term used in international law for legal norms from which no derogation by declaration or treaty is permissible. All norms of *ius cogens* impose **obligations *erga omnes***. There is no consensus in international law on which norms count as *ius cogens* (uncontroversial examples include the prohibition to engage in genocide or aggressive war), nor on how a norm comes to acquire this status.

just war An influential tradition of ethical thought that considers the legitimacy of declaring (*jus ad bellum*) and fighting (*jus in bello*) war, as well as, more recently, conditions after war (*jus post-bellum*). The tradition is Christian in origin, but has been adapted for secular purposes.

law of peoples A term from the philosophy of John Rawls, it refers to law governing relations between liberal and non-liberal peoples of the world. For Rawls, this law consists of principles acknowledging peoples' independence, their equality, their right to self-defence, and their duties of non-intervention, to observe treaties, to honour a limited set of rights, to conduct themselves appropriately in war, and to provide limited assistance for peoples living in certain kinds of unfavourable conditions.

legitimacy (empirical and normative) In the empirical sense, coined by the sociologist Max Weber, a political authority enjoys legitimacy if there is widespread belief among those subject to its power that it has the right to govern. In the normative sense, an authority is legitimate if it fulfils the moral conditions necessary for possessing this right.

libertarian This refers to an ideology that celebrates freedom and is suspicious of government. The term was originally associated, and in some circles is still associated with the anarchist vision of a non-coercive, egalitarian society, based on social co-operation. Its more common usage in contemporary political theory is to refer to a conservative ideology that advocates, for both economic and moral reasons, a minimal role for government and a maximal role for the market in economic affairs. It is sometimes also referred to as 'classical liberalism'.

liberty An individual has liberty in a purely descriptive sense in relation to a given domain of acts and omissions if, and only if, they can do as they wish within that domain. If the individual chooses whatever act or omission they like, then it follows that other people are not preventing that individual from acting, or omitting to act, as they choose. The domain of conduct in relation to which an individual has liberty may be extensive or narrow, depending on context. As long as they can choose even a single act or omission, however, that individual is at liberty in relation to that particular act or omission. It is a separate question whether the individual's liberty has value in a given context.

mimicry In post-colonial theory mimicry refers to the adoption of colonial ideas, attitudes, and discourses by subjects of colonialism. This mimicry has a subversive and destabilizing element as neither the repeated discourse nor the colonized subject are legitimate representations of the original colonizing discourse and subject.

minimal state Introduced by Robert Nozick, the term refers to a state that restricts itself to enforcing basic property rights and rights against harm. A minimal state exercises sole **authority** in a given territory to arbitrate in judicial matters and enforce its judgments. Its protection is afforded to all who live within that territory. See also **libertarian**

modernization theory A theory of socio-economic development in which traditional societies are assumed to evolve through a predictable series of stages towards a modern social order, including particular economic and political structures, generally associated with the contemporary capitalist nation-state.

multiculturalism This term can refer to the fact of cultural diversity in countries ranging from the former Yugoslavia to the USA, and may also describe the coexistence of different kinds of cultural group within a country.

natural rights These are rights that exist in nature independently of any actual human laws or customs.

neo-liberalism An approach to politics that minimizes the scope of the **authority** of the state and turns most decisions over to the market or voluntary organization's. See also **libertarian.**

non-ideal theory In Rawlsian terms, a theory that seeks to identify the norms of justice or morality agents have to follow when **full compliance** cannot be assured. In a wider sense, a theory that takes as its starting point the non-ideal conditions of existing societies or communities, in order to indicate desirable and feasible paths for improvement. See also **ideal theory**.

obligations *erga omnes* (Latin for 'toward all') A term used in international law to refer to legal obligations that all subjects of international law hold towards all other subjects, as opposed to obligations that only hold between certain parties (such as those imposed by bilateral treaties). An example is the obligation of states not to engage in aggressive war. Obligations *erga omnes* are generally also part of international *ius cogens*.

Orientalism In post-colonial theory Orientalism refers to the way that the Western tradition, in thought and art, expresses hostile and deprecatory views of the East, particularly though the prior construct of 'Eastern' societies as possessing essentialist and demeaning characteristics.

original position A hypothetical situation employed by Rawls to compare competing principles of social justice by asking which would be chosen by rational individuals were they to be situated behind a **veil of ignorance** that deprives them of knowledge of their fortunes in the social and natural lottery, as well as of their conception of well-being.

patriarchy This literally means 'rule of the father'. It is used in feminist philosophy to mean a society that is structured according to sexual inequality, with men being advantaged and women disadvantaged. Patriarchies, in this feminist sense, need not have male political leaders, although men usually occupy more positions of political power than do women.

peace-building The processes and activities necessary to resolve violent conflict and establish sustainable peace; this includes conflict transformation, reconciliation efforts, economic development, and political reform.

peacekeeping An effort to help countries involved in conflict or war with conditions necessary for peace; this generally involves diplomatic intervention and the placing of neutral troops between warring parties.

personal prerogative A term used in contemporary political philosophy to refer to a permission to ascribe greater moral weight to one's own personal projects than to those of other people. The extent of a personal prerogative is delineated by one's duties of justice.

pluralism (in international relations) A term coined by Hedley Bull. Pluralists hold that international society (as a society of states) should limit itself to recognizing and complying with the minimal rules necessary for its own continuance. See also **solidarism** and **English School**.

positivism, legal The view that rights are creations of positive law or conventional social norms that set out what is acceptable behaviour in particular societies. Positivists hold that these rights are subject to evaluation, criticism, and moral legitimation, but contend that this is a matter of deciding whether rights serve important human values and interests, rather than of acquiring knowledge of pre-existing natural or moral rights.

pre-emptive war In the **just war** tradition, and international law generally, pre-emptive wars are wars of self-defence in which the threatened party is able to respond to an *imminent* threat or aggression.

preventive war Preventative war is often confused, or rhetorically conflated, with **pre-emptive war**. The key distinction is that preventative wars are fought to prevent a threat from developing in the first place or to change the international balance of power. Unlike pre-emptive wars, they are not a response to an *imminent* threat.

primary good A good that any rational person would want, whatever else they might want.

private sphere This refers to areas of life, such as the family, that are thought, in classical liberalism, to be separate from political influence and interference. Feminists have criticized the idea that the private sphere is immune from political consideration. See also **public sphere**.

proportionality In the ethics of war, and the **just war** tradition in particular, proportionality refers to the need to ensure that excessive force is not used to obtain military objectives.

public reason The common reason that all citizens in a pluralistic democracy use to advance their justifications of public policies.

public sphere Defined in contrast to the **private sphere**. The public sphere refers to areas of life that are properly subject to political interference, or which serve as spaces for political discussion and the formation of public opinion. The public sphere is sometimes referred to as the 'political sphere'. This concept has been applied at the global level and the idea of a global public sphere is commonly used now.

realpolitik This refers to international politics and diplomacy based on considerations of power and other practical matters, rather than ideological considerations, such as ideals, morals, and principles.

realism An approach to politics that focuses on the centrality of power, conflict, and violence. The position is politically indeterminate—it can either defend the status quo or be used to challenge it. In international relations theory, realism emphasizes state power, security, and the national interest, making use of notions of self-interest and the constraints placed on states acting in an **anarchical** international system.

republicanism A tradition of political theory going back to antiquity that emphasizes the values of non-domination, and the political participation and vigilance of the citizenry, and which accords centrality to citizenship virtues, such as a willingness to make sacrifices for the common good, and identification with one's political community.

secession This describes the process in which a portion of a political community divorces itself from the rest of the community to form its own state—that is, a group's act of breaking away from a larger nation to establish its own system of government. For example, the Basques wish for secession from Spain's rule, because they see themselves as culturally distinct from the Spanish.

securitization The political process by which a particular issue (say immigration of HIV/AIDS) is constructed as a national security threat or as an existential threat to the security of the political body.

self-determination The view that each people or nation should have its own set of political institutions to enable it to decide collectively on matters that are of primary concern for its members.

social construction This refers to the process by which **social norms** affect our lives, either by shaping the options that are available to or appropriate for us, or by affecting the way in which we interpret society, understand ourselves, and form preferences.

social contract theory The view that political **authority** and obligation is justified, because citizens have formed a contract with each other to obey the law. The theory usually does not claim that contemporary citizens give their actual or tacit consent to obey the law, being more commonly used in relation to hypothetical consent (consent that *would* be given in some imagined world, if certain conditions hold).

social justice, principles of These refer to norms that provide uncompromising, or especially weighty, moral standards for resolving individuals' competing claims on the design of influential social and political institutions.

social norms These are informal rules about how people ought to behave in a society. Examples of social norms include rules of etiquette, clothing, and social interaction. Social norms can become internalized, such that people prefer to comply with them.

solidarism (in international relations) A term coined by Hedley Bull. Solidarists argue that it is desirable and possible for states as members of international society to unite in the pursuit of shared goals over and above that of securing their own coexistence (such as, for example, the pursuit of **human rights**). See also **pluralism** and **English School**.

sovereignty The power to issue laws and regulations that cannot be contested or revoked by any other authority applying to a given geographical territory. State sovereignty refers to the position of the state as the supreme authority within a given territory. Historically, this was emphasized by the doctrine of absolute state sovereignty, according to which the authority of the state is not subject to any rules enforceable by any other agent. Popular sovereignty, meanwhile, is a doctrine that the people are the supreme authority in a given geographical territory.

state-building The attempt to build, or re-build, the institutions of weak, post-conflict and failed states, by either foreign countries that have intervened in the state in question or as a commitment of the international community as a whole to vulnerable states.

state of nature This term refers to a condition of human life in which there is no society larger than the family grouping, or, if there is a larger society, no government or positive laws.

statism A view of society that supports the concentration of economic and political power in the state.

subaltern Refers to those that are from areas or groups excluded from dominant power structures, including colonial subjects, minorities, and women. One can speak of a subaltern perspective or of the views of the subaltern.

sufficiency principles These are moral principles, assuming there are non-instrumentally morally relevant thresholds. They are often employed to claim that, when evaluating distributions, what matters is whether individuals have enough to escape absolute deprivation or to live above some critical threshold.

supranational A term that is most commonly used to describe international associations (most notably the EU) that have regulatory and enforcement powers over their member states that were traditionally regarded as part of state **sovereignty**, and whose decision-making mechanisms are not based on a veto power of each member state, as under traditional international law, but at least partly on majoritarian procedures.

terrorism A notoriously contested concept that is more often used to condemn a particular form of political violence than to describe it. Attempts at definition emphasize the terrorists' intention to spread fear among a group wider than that of the victims of direct attack; more contested definitional proposals contend that it has to be carried out by non-state agents, must be used to destabilize and challenge (rather than stabilize) an existing status quo or regime, or must target civilians.

totalitarianism A form of **authoritarian** government that demands complete subservience to the state and in which the government penetrates all spheres of life. Usually applied to Nazi Germany, Fascist Italy, and the Soviet Union.

transnational A term that is often used as simply synonymous with 'international' or 'multinational', but may also refer to an arrangement, policy, or organization, that applies, or operates across, national boundaries, without being either controlled by states or by a **supranational** institution, e.g. the Catholic Church.

universalism A term that may either be used substantively, to refer to a normative theory that issues principles and rules that are supposed to apply to all persons regardless of context, or methodologically, referring to a theory that accepts that principles and rules may differ according to context, but only because of reasons that are universally acceptable.

utilitarianism The doctrine, of which there are many versions, that social institutions and practices should be organized so as to maximize general welfare or common good as the sole ultimate ethical value, and that individual actions ought also to aim at this end.

veil of ignorance A phrase coined by Rawls to refer to the limited knowledge of characteristics—for example, sex, race, and class—that can be (dis)advantaging in the real world, but which ought not to be (dis)advantaging in the just society.

virtue ethics A tradition in ethical philosophy inspired by Aristotle in particular, which eschews a focus on duty or consequences in favour of a concern for ethical excellence attained through the development of specific virtues, such as courage, sympathy, or temperance.

Westphalia, Treaty of (Peace of Westphalia) Refers to two treaties signed in 1648 (the treaties of Osnabrück and Münster) that ended the Thirty Years' War and the Eighty Years' War. The peace of Westphalia initiated a new European order based on state sovereignty, which provided the basis for the contemporary international order.

Wilsonianism Describes an ideological approach to foreign policy, derived from Woodrow Wilson, which emphasizes the need to ensure world peace through self-determination, democracy, and capitalism. The distinction between hard and soft Wilsonianism refers to the role that military power should play in securing peace.

■ REFERENCES

Abizadeh, A. (2002) Does liberal democracy presuppose a cultural nation? Four arguments. *American Political Science Review*, 96:495–509.

Abizadeh, A. (2007) Cooperation, pervasive impact, and coercion: on the scope (not site) of distributive justice. *Philosophy & Public Affairs*, 35:318–58.

Abizadeh, A. (2008) Democratic theory and border coercion: no right to unilaterally control your own borders. *Political Theory*, 35:37–65.

Abizadeh, A., & Gilabert, P. (2008) Is there a genuine tension between cosmopolitan egalitarianism and special responsibilities? *Philosophical Studies*, 138:348–65.

Acharya, A., & Buzan, B. (eds) (2009) *Non-Western International Relations Theory*. London: Routledge.

Adorno, T. (1996) *Aesthetic Theory*. Minneapolis: University of Minnesota Press.

Adorno, T. (2001) *The Culture Industry*. London: Routledge.

Adorno, T., Frenkel-Brunswik, E., & Levinson, D. (1993) *The Authoritarian Personality*. New York: Norton.

Ahmad, A. (1992) *In Theory: Classes, Nations, Literatures*. London: Verso.

Ahmad, A. (1997) Postcolonial theory and the post-condition. *Socialist Register*, 33:353–82.

Aikens, W., & LaFollette, H. (eds) (1996) *World Hunger and Morality*. New Jersey: Prentice Hall.

Alexander, L., & Beitz, C. (eds) (1985) *International Ethics: A 'Philosophy and Public Affairs' Reader*. Princeton: Princeton University Press.

Allen, A. (2008) *The Politics of Our Selves: Power, Autonomy and Gender in Contemporary Critical Theory*. New York: Columbia University Press.

Almeida, J.M. (2003) Pluralists, solidarists and the issues of diversity, justice and humanitarianism in world politics. *International Journal of Human Rights*, 7:144–63.

Almeida, J.M. (2006) Hedley Bull, 'embedded cosmopolitanism', and the pluralist-solidarist debate. In: R. Little & J. Williams (eds), *The Anarchical Society in a Globalized World*. Basingstoke: Palgrave, pp. 51–72.

Altman, L., & Oppel, R., Jr (2008) W.H.O. says Iraq civilian death toll higher than cited. *New York Times*, Jan. 10:A14.

Amin, S. (1976) *Unequal Development: An Essay on the Social Formations of Peripheral Capitalism*, transl. B. Pearce. New York: Monthly Review.

Anderson, E. (1999) What is the point of equality. *Ethics*, 109:287–337.

Anghie, A. (2004) *Imperialism, Sovereignty and the Making of International Law*. Cambridge: Cambridge University Press.

Ankersmit, F. (2002) *Political Representation*. Stanford: Stanford University Press.

Anscombe, G.E.M (1981) *Collected Philosophical Papers*, Vol. 3. Cambridge: Cambridge University Press.

Appadurai, A. (1996) *Modernity at Large: Cultural Dimensions of Globalization*. Minneapolis: University of Minnesota Press.

Appiah, K.W. (2006) *Cosmopolitanism: Ethics in a World of Strangers*. New York: Norton.

Archibugi, D. (2008) *The Global Commonwealth of Citizens: Toward Cosmopolitan Democracy*. Princeton: Princeton University Press.

Archibugi, D., & Held, D. (eds) (1995) *Cosmopolitan Democracy: An Agenda for a New World Order*. Cambridge: Polity.

Archibugi, D., Held, D., & Köhler, M. (eds) (1998) *Re-imagining Political Community: Studies in Cosmopolitan Democracy*. Cambridge: Polity.

Arendt, H. (1958) *The Human Condition*. Chicago: University of Chicago Press.

Arendt, H. (1969) *On Violence*. New York: Harcourt.

Arendt, H. (1972) Civil disobedience. In: H. Arendt, *Crises of the Republic*. New York: Harcourt, pp. 49–103.

Arendt, H. (1973 [1951]) *The Origins of Totalitarianism*. New York: Harcourt Brace Jovanovich.

Armitage, D. (2000) *The Ideological Origins of the British Empire*. Cambridge: Cambridge University Press.

Arneson, R. (1997) Equality and equal opportunity for welfare. In: L. Pojman & R. Westmoreland (eds), *Equality: Selected Readings*. Oxford: Oxford University Press, pp. 229–41.

Arneson, R. (1999) Equality of opportunity for welfare defended and recanted. *Journal of Political Philosophy*, 7(4):88–97.

Aron, R. (1966) *Peace and War: A Theory of International Relations*, transl. R. Howard & A. Baker Fox. Garden City: Doubleday.

Asad, T. (2007) *On Suicide Bombing*. New York: Columbia University Press.

Ashcroft, B., Griffiths, G., & Tiffin, H. (1989) *The Empire Writes Back: Theory and Practice in Postcolonial Literatures*. London: Routledge.

Audi, R., & Wolterstorff, N. (1997) *Religion in the Public Square*. Lanham: Rowman & Littlefield.

Aurelius, M. (1998) *The Meditations of Marcus Aurelius Antoninus*, transl. A. S. L. Farquharson. Oxford: Oxford University Press.

Austin, J.L. (1961) *Philosophical Papers*. Oxford: Oxford University Press.

Austin, J.L. (1962) *Sense and Sensibilia*. Oxford: Oxford University Press.

Ayer, A.J. (1946) *Language, Truth and Logic*, 2nd edn. London: Victor Gollancz.

Bader, V. (2005) The ethics of immigration. *Constellations*, 12:331–61.

Baert, P. (2005) *Philosophy of the Social Sciences: Towards Pragmatism*. Cambridge: Polity.

Bain, W. (2003) *Between Anarchy and Society: Trusteeship and the Obligations of Power*. Oxford: Oxford University Press.

Balibar, E. (1994) *We, the People of Europe? Reflections on Transnational Citizenship*, transl. J. Swenson. Princeton: Princeton University Press.

Barber, B.R. (1989) *The Conquest of Politics: Liberal Philosophy in Democratic Times*. Princeton: Princeton University Press.

Barber, B.R. (2003) The war of all against all. In: V. Gehring (ed.), *War after September 11*. Lanham: Rowman & Littlefield, pp. 51–91.

Barkawi, T. (2006) *Globalization and War*. Lanham: Rowman & Littlefield.

Barkawi, T., & Laffey, M. (2006) The postcolonial moment in security studies. *Review of International Studies*, 32(2):329–52.

Barnett, M. (2002) *Eyewitness to a Genocide: The United Nations and Rwanda*. Ithaca: Cornell University Press.

Barrell, R., FitzGerald, J., & Riley, R. (2007) *EU Enlargement and Migration: Assessing the Macroeconomic Impacts*, NIESR Discussion Paper No. 29 (March). Available at: http://www.niesr.ac.uk/pubs/DPS/dp292.pdf (accessed August 2009).

Barry, B. (1965) *Political Argument*. London: Routledge.

Barry, B. (1974) *A Liberal Theory of Justice*. Oxford: Oxford University Press.

Barry, B. (1982) Humanity and justice in global perspective. In: J. R. Pennock & J. W. Chapman (eds), *Ethics, Economics and the Law*. New York: NYU Press, pp. 219–52.

Bartelson, J. (1995) *A Genealogy of Sovereignty*. Cambridge: Cambridge University Press.

Bass, G. (2004) *Jus post bellum*. *Philosophy & Public Affairs*, 32:384–412.

Basu, A., & McGrory, C.E. (eds) (1995) *The Challenge of Local Feminisms: Women's Movements in Global Perspective*. Boulder: Westview Press.

Bauböck, R. (2007a) Political ethics of external citizenship, paper presented at *American Political Science Association Annual Conference*, Chicago.

Bauböck, R. (2007b) stakeholder citizenship and transnational political participation: a normative evaluation of external voting. *Fordham Law Review*, 75:2393–447.

Baxter, B. (2004) *A Theory of Ecological Justice*. London: Routledge.

Beck, U. (2006) *The Cosmopolitan Vision*, transl. C. Cronin. Cambridge: Polity.

Beetham, D. (1991) *The Legitimation of Power*. London: Macmillan.

Beitz, C. (1979) *Political Theory and International Relations*. Princeton: Princeton University Press.

Beitz, C. (1983) Cosmopolitan ideals and national sentiment. *Journal of Philosophy*, 80(10): 591–600.

Beitz, C. (1994) Cosmopolitan liberalism and the states system. In: C. Brown (ed.), *Political Restructuring in Europe: Ethical Perspectives*. London: Routledge, pp. 123–36.

Beitz, C. (1999) *Political Theory and International Relations*, 2nd edn. Princeton: Princeton University Press.

Beitz, C. (2001) Human rights as a common concern. *American Political Science Review*, 95:269–82.

Beitz, C. (2003) What human rights mean. *Daedalus*, 132:36–46.

Beitz, C. (2004) Human rights and the law of peoples. In: D. K. Chatterjee (ed.), *The Ethics of Assistance: Morality and the Distant Needy*. Cambridge: Cambridge University Press, pp. 193–216.

Bell, D. A. (1993) *Communitarianism and Its Critics*. Oxford: Oxford University Press.

Bell, D. A. (2000) *East Meets West: Human Rights and Democracy in East Asia*. Princeton: Princeton University Press.

Bell, D. (2006) Beware of false prophets: biology, human nature, and the future of international relations theory. *International Affairs*, 81: 479–96.

Bell, D. (ed.) (2007) *Victorian Visions of Global Order: Empire and International Relations in Nineteenth Century Political Thought*. Cambridge: Cambridge University Press.

Bell, D. (ed.) (2009a) *Political Thought and International Relations: Variations on a Realist Theme*. Oxford: Oxford University Press.

Bell, D. (2009b) Writing the world: disciplinary history and beyond. *International Affairs*, 85:3–23.

Bell, D. (2010) Empire and imperialism. In: G. Claeys & G. Stedman Jones (eds) *The Cambridge History of Nineteenth Century Political Thought*. Cambridge: Cambridge University Press.

Bell, D., & Sylvest, C. (2006) International society in Victorian political thought: T. H. Green, Herbert Spencer, and Henry Sidgwick. *Modern Intellectual History*, 3(2):1–32.

Bellamy, A. (ed.) (2005) *International Society and its Critics*. Oxford: Oxford University Press.

Bellamy, A. (2006) *Just Wars: From Cicero To Iraq*, Cambridge: Polity Press.

Bellamy, A. (2009) *Responsibility to Protect: The Global Effort to End Mass Atrocities*. Cambridge: Polity Press.

Bellamy, A., & Wheeler, N. (2007) Humanitarian intervention in world politics. In: J. Baylis, S. Smith, & P. Owens (eds), *Globalization and World Politics*. Oxford: Oxford University Press, pp. 523–39.

Benhabib, S. (1992) *Situating the Self: Gender, Community and Postmodernism in Contemporary Ethics*. London: Routledge.

Benhabib, S. (2002) *The Claims of Culture: Equality and Diversity in a Global Era*. Princeton: Princeton University Press.

Benhabib, S. (2004) *The Rights of Others: Aliens, Residents, and Citizens*. Cambridge: Cambridge University Press.

Benhabib, S. (2006) *Another Cosmopolitanism: Hospitality, Sovereignty, and Democratic Iterations*. Oxford: Oxford University Press.

Benn, S., & Peters, R.S. (1959) *Social Principles and the Democratic State*. London: Allen & Unwin.

Bentham, J. (1843a [1786–1789]) Objects of international law. In: J. Bowring (ed.), *Essay I of Principles of International Law* in *The Works of Jeremy Bentham: Volume Two*. Edinburgh: William Tait, pp. 537–40.

Bentham, J. (1843b [1786–1789]) A plan for an universal and perpetual peace. In: J. Bowring (ed.), *Essay IV* of *Principles of International Law* in *The Works of Jeremy Bentham: Volume Two*. Edinburgh: William Tait, pp. 546–60.

Bergo, B. (2007) Emmanuel Levinas. *Stanford Encyclopedia of Philosophy*. Available at: http://plato.stanford.edu/entries/levinas (accessed August 2009).

Berlin, I. (1969) *Four Essays on Liberty*. Oxford: Oxford University Press.

Berman, N. (1999) In the wake of empire. *American University International Law Review*, 14:1521–54.

Bernstein, J. (2002) *Radical Evil: A Philosophical Interrogation*. Cambridge: Polity.

Bernstein, J. (2005) *The Abuse of Evil: The Corruption of Politics and Religion since 9/11*. Cambridge: Polity.

Bhabha, H. (1994) *The Location of Culture*. London: Routledge.

Blackburn, S. (2001) Relativism. In: H. LaFollette (ed.), *The Blackwell Guide to Ethical Theory*. Oxford: Blackwell, pp. 38–52.

Blake, M. (2002) Distributive justice, state coercion, and autonomy. *Philosophy & Public Affairs*, 30:257–96.

Blake, M. (2003) Immigration. In: R. G. Frey & C.H. Wellman (eds), *A Companion to Applied Ethics*. Oxford: Blackwell, pp. 224–38.

Blake, M. (2006) Universal and qualified rights to immigration. *Ethics and Economics*, 4:1–6.

Bleiker, R. (2001) The aesthetic turn in international political theory. *Millennium*, 30:509–33.

Bleiker, R. (2004) Globalizing political theory. In: S. White & J. Moon (eds), *What is Political Theory?* London: Sage Publications, pp. 124–45

Bloom, M. (2007) *Dying To Kill: The Allure of Suicide Terror*. New York: Columbia University Press.

Bobbio, N. (2000) *The Age of Rights*. Cambridge: Polity.

Boer, A.M., den, & Hudson, M. (2002) A surplus of men, a deficit of peace: security and sex ratios in Asia's largest states. *International Security*, 26(4):5–38.

Bohman, J. (2007) *Democracy Across Borders: From Demos to Demoi*. Cambridge: MIT Press.

Bohman, J., & Rehg, W. (eds) (1997) *Deliberative Democracy: Essays on Reason and Politics*. Cambridge: MIT Press.

Bookchin, M. (1995) *From Urbanization to Cities: Towards a New Politics of Citizenship*, rev. edn. London: Cassell.

Bookchin, M. (1996) *The Philosophy of Social Ecology: Essays on Dialectical Naturalism*. Montreal: Black Rose Books.

Booth, K. (2001) Ten flaws of just war. In K. Booth (ed.), *The Kosovo Tragedy: The Human Rights Dimension*. Portland: Frank Cass, pp. 314–24.

Borradori, G. (2003) *Philosophy in a Time of Terror: Dialogues with Jürgen Habermas and Jacques Derrida*. Chicago: University of Chicago Press.

Bosniak, L. (2006) *The Citizen and the Alien: Dilemmas of Contemporary Membership*. Princeton: Princeton University Press.

Boucher, D. (1998) *Political Theories of International Relations: From Thucydides to the Present*. Oxford: Oxford University Press.

Boutros-Ghali, B. (1992) *An Agenda for Peace*. New York: UN Publications.

Bowden, M. (1999) *Black Hawk Down: A Story of Modern War*. New York: Atlantic Monthly Press.

Brecher, B. (2007) *Torture and the Ticking Bomb*. Oxford: Blackwell.

Brett, A. (1997) *Liberty, Right and Nature: Individual Rights in Later Scholastic Thought*. Cambridge: Cambridge University Press.

Brett, A., & Tully, J. (2006) *Rethinking the Foundations of Modern Political Thought*. Cambridge: Cambridge University Press.

Brock, G. (2009) *Global Justice: A Cosmopolitan Account*. Oxford: Oxford University Press.

Broome, J. (1992) *Counting the Cost of Global Warming*. Cambridge: White Horse Press.

Brown, C. (1995) International political theory and the idea of world community. In: K. Booth & S. Smith (eds), *International Relations Theory Today*. Cambridge: Polity, pp. 90–110.

Brown, C., Nardin, T., & Rengger, N. (eds) (2002) *International Relations in Political Thought: Texts from the Ancient Greeks to the First World War*. Cambridge: Cambridge University Press.

Browning-Cole, E., & Coutrap-McQuin, S. (eds) (1992) *Explorations of Feminist Ethics: Theory and Practice*. Indianapolis: Indiana University Press.

Brownlie, I. (2009) *Principles of Public International Law*. Oxford: Oxford University Press.

Brubaker, R. (1992) *Citizenship and Nationhood in France and Germany*. Cambridge: Harvard University Press.

Buchanan, A. (2000) Rawls's Law of Peoples: rules for a vanished Westphalian world. *Ethics*, 110:697–721.

Buchanan, A. (2004) *Justice, Legitimacy, and Self-Determination: Moral Foundations of International Law*. Oxford: Oxford University Press.

Buchanan, A. (2006) Taking the human out of human rights. In: R. Martin & D. Reidy (eds) *Rawls's Law of Peoples: A Realistic Utopia?* Oxford: Blackwell, pp. 150–68.

Buchanan, A. (2007) Justifying preventive war. In: H. Shue & D. Rodin (eds) *Preemption: Military Action and Moral Justification*. Oxford: Oxford University Press, pp. 126–42.

Buchanan, A., & Golove, D. (2002) Philosophy of international law. In J. Coleman & I. Shapiro (eds) *The Oxford Handbook of Jurisprudence and Philosophy of Law*. Oxford: Oxford University Press, pp. 868–934.

Buchanan, A., & Keohane, R. (2004) The preventive use of force: a cosmopolitan institutionalist perspective. *Ethics and International Affairs*, 18:1–22.

Buchanan, A., & Keohane, R. (2005) Justifying preventive force: reply to Steven Lee. *Ethics and International Affairs*, 19:109–12.

Bull, H. (1966) The Grotian conception of international society. In: H. Butterfield & M. Wight (eds), *Diplomatic Investigations*. London: Allen & Unwin, pp. 51–73.

Bull, H. (1984) *Justice in International Relations: The Hagey Lectures*. Waterloo, Ontario: University of Waterloo.

Bull, H. (2002) *The Anarchical Society: A Study of Order in World Politics*, 3rd edn. Basingstoke: Palgrave.

Bull, H., & Watson, A. (eds) (1984) *The Expansion of International Society*. Oxford: Clarendon Press.

Bulley, D. (2009) *Ethics as Foreign Policy: Britain, the EU, and the Other*. New York: Routledge.

Burchell, G., Gordon, C., & Miller, P. (eds) (1991) *The Foucault Effect: Studies in Governmentality*. Chicago: University of Chicago Press.

Burchill, S. (2005) *The National Interest in International Relations Theory*. Basingstoke: Palgrave.

Burchill, S., et al. (eds) (2009) *Theories of International Relations*, 4th edn. Basingstoke: Palgrave.

Burke, A. (2008) Postmodernism. In: C. Reus-Smit & D. Snidal (eds) *The Oxford Handbook of International Relations*. Oxford: Oxford University Press, pp. 359–78.

Butler, J. (2004a) *Undoing Gender*. New York: Routledge.

Butler, J. (2004b) *Precarious Life: The Powers of Mourning and Violence*. London: Verso.

Buzan, B. (1983) *People, States and Fear: The National Security Problem in International Relations*. Brighton: Harvester Press.

Buzan, B. (1996) The timeless wisdom of realism. In: K. Booth, S. Smith, & M. Zalewski (eds), *International Theory: Positivism and Beyond*. Cambridge: Cambridge University Press, pp. 47–65.

Buzan, B. (2004) *From International to World Society? English School Theory and the Social Structure of Globalisation*. Cambridge: Cambridge University Press.

Byers, M. (1999) *Custom, Power, and the Power of Rules: International Relations and Customary International Law*. Cambridge: Cambridge University Press.

Campbell, D. (1992) *Writing Security: United States Foreign Policy and the Politics of Identity*. Minneapolis: University of Minnesota Press.

Campbell, D. (1999) The deterritorialization of responsibility: Levinas, Derrida, and ethics after the end of philosophy. In: D. Campbell & M. J. Shapiro (eds) *Moral Spaces: Rethinking Ethics and World Politics*. Minneapolis: University of Minnesota Press, pp. 29–57.

Campbell, D. (1998a) *National Deconstruction: Violence, Identity, and Justice in Bosnia*. Minneapolis: University of Minnesota Press.

Campbell, D. (1998b) *Writing Security: United States Foreign Policy and the Politics of Identity*, rev. edn. Minneapolis: University of Minnesota Press.

Campbell, D. and Shapiro, M. (eds) (1999) *Moral Spaces: Rethinking Ethics and World Politics*. Minneapolis: University of Minnesota Press.

Caney, S. (2001) Cosmopolitan justice and equalizing opportunities. *Metaphilosophy*, 32:113–34.

Caney, S. (2005a) *Justice Beyond Borders: A Global Political Theory*. Oxford: Oxford University Press.

Caney, S. (2005b) Cosmopolitan justice, responsibility, and global climate change. *Leiden Journal of International Law*, 18:747–75.

Caney, S. (2006a) Cosmopolitan justice, rights, and global climate change. *Canadian Journal of Law and Jurisprudence*, 19:255–78.

Caney, S. (2006b) Global justice: from theory to practice. *Globalizations*, 3:121–37.

Caney, S. (2008) Global distributive justice and the state. *Political Studies*, 56:487–518.

Caney, S. (2009) Cosmopolitanism, culture and well-being: a cosmopolitan perspective on multiculturalism. In: N. Holtug, S. Laegaard, & K. Lippert-Rasmussen (eds), *Nationalism and Multiculturalism in a World of Immigration*. Basingstoke: Palgrave, pp. 21–52.

Card, C. (ed.) (1991) *Feminist Ethics*. Lawrence: University Press of Kansas.

Carens, J. (1987) Aliens and citizens: the case for open borders. *Review of Politics*, 49:251–73.

Carens, J. (1992) Migration and morality: a liberal egalitarian perspective. In: B. Barry & R. E. Goodin (eds) *Free Movement: Ethical Issues in the Transnational Migration of People and of Money*. University Park: Pennsylvania State University Press, pp. 25–47.

Carr, E.H. (1939) *The Twenty Years' Crisis 1919–1939: An Introduction to the Study of International Relations*. London: Macmillan.

Carson, R. (1962) *Silent Spring*. London: Penguin.

Carty, A. (1986) *The Decay of International Law*. Manchester: Manchester University Press.

Carty, A. (1998) The continuing influence of Kelsen on the general perception of the discipline of international law. *European Journal of International Law*, 9:344–54.

Carty, A. (2004) Marxism and international law – perspectives for the American (twenty-first) century. *Leiden Journal of International Law*, 17:1–24.

Carty, A. (2007) *Philosophy of International Law*. Edinburgh: Edinburgh University Press.

Carver, T. (1996) *Gender is not a Synonym for Women*, Boulder: Lynne Rienner.

Cassese, A. (2005) *International Law*, 2nd edn. Oxford: Oxford University Press.

Cavalieri, P., & Singer, P. (eds) (1995) *The Great Ape Project: Equality Beyond Humanity*. New York: St. Martins.

Ceadel, M. (1987) *Thinking about Peace and War*. Oxford: Oxford University Press.

Chakrabarty, D. (2000) *Provincializing Europe: Postcolonial Thought and Historical Difference*. Princeton: Princeton University Press.

Chan, J. (2000) Legitimacy, unanimity and perfectionism. *Philosophy & Public Affairs*, 30(3):257–96.

Chang, H. (1997) Liberalized immigration as free trade: economic welfare and the optimal immigration policy. *University of Pennsylvania Law Review*, 145:1147–244.

Charvet, J. (1998) International society from a contractarian perspective. In: D. Mapel & T. Nardin (eds), *International Society: Diverse Ethical Perspectives*. Princeton: Princeton University Press, pp. 114–31.

Cheah, P., & Robbins, B. (eds) (1998) *Cosmopolitics: Thinking and Feeling Beyond the Nation*. Minneapolis: University of Minnesota Press.

Chomsky, N. (1999) *The New Military Humanism: Lessons from Kosovo*. London: Pluto Press.

Chow, R. (2006) *The Age of the World Target: Self-Referentiality in War, Theory, and Comparative Work*. Durham: Duke University Press.

Clausewitz, C., von (1976) *On War*, M. Howard and P. Paret (eds). Princeton: Princeton University Press.

Coady, C. A. J. (2003) War for humanity: a critique. In: D. Chatterjee & D. Scheid (eds), *Ethics and Foreign Intervention*. Cambridge: Cambridge University Press, pp. 274–95.

Coady, C.A.J. (2004) Terrorism and innocence. *Journal of Ethics*, 8(11):37–58.

Coady, C.A.J. (2008a) *Messy Morality: The Challenge of Politics*. Oxford: Oxford University Press.

Coady, C.A.J. (2008b) *Morality and Political Violence*. Cambridge: Cambridge University Press.

Cohen, G.A. (2001) *If You' an Egalitarian, How come you' so Rich?* Cambridge: Harvard University Press.

Cohen, G.A. (2003) Facts and principles. *Philosophy & Public Affairs*, 31(3):211–45.

Cohen, G.A. (2008) *Rescuing Justice and Equality*. Cambridge: Harvard University Press.

Cohen, G.A. (1989) On the currency of egalitarian justice. *Ethics*, 99:906–44.

Cochran, M. (2008) The ethics of the English school. In: C. Reus-Smit, & D. Snidal (eds) *The Oxford Handbook of International Relations*. Oxford: Oxford University Press, pp. 286–97.

Cochran, M. (2009) Charting the ethics of the English school: what 'good' is there in a middle-ground ethics? *International Studies Quarterly*, 53:203–25.

Cohen, J. (2004a) Whose sovereignty? Empire versus international law. *Ethics and International Affairs*, 18(3):1–24.

Cohen, J. (2004b) Minimalism about human rights: the most we can hope for?', *Journal of Political Philosophy*, 12(3):190-213.

Cohen, J. (2006) Is there a human right to democracy? In: C. Sypnowich (ed.), *The Egalitarian Conscience: Essays in Honour of G. A. Cohen*. Oxford: Oxford University Press, pp. 226–48.

Cohen, J., & Sabel, C. (1997) Directly deliberative democracy. *European Law Review*, 3:313–42.

Cohen, J., & Sabel, C. (2004) Sovereignty and solidarity: EU and US. In: J. Zeitlin & D. Trubek (eds), *Governing Work and Welfare in a New Economy: European and American Experiments*. Oxford: Oxford University Press, pp. 345–75.

Cohen, J., & Sabel, C. (2006) Extra republican nulla justitia? *Philosophy & Public Affairs*, 34(4):147–75.

Cohen, M. (1985) Moral skepticism and international relations. In: C. Beitz, M. Cohen, & A. J. Simmons (eds), *International Ethics*. Princeton: Princeton University Press, pp. 3–51.

Coicaud, J-M., & Wheeler, N. (eds) (2008) *National Interest and International Solidarity: Particular and Universal Ethics in International Life*. Tokyo: UN University Press.

Cole, P. (2000) *Philosophies of Exclusion: Liberal Political Theory and Immigration*. Edinburgh: Edinburgh University Press.

Commoner, B. (1971) *The Closing Circle: Nature, Man and Technology*. New York: Alfred Knopf.

Connell, R. (2008) *Southern Theory: Social Science and the Global Dynamics of Knowledge*. Cambridge: Polity.

Connolly, W.E. (1995) *Identity/Difference*. Minneapolis: University of Minnesota Press.

Connolly, W.E. (2000) *Why I Am Not a Secularist*. Minneapolis: University of Minnesota Press.

Constant, B. (1988) The liberty of the ancients as compared to the moderns [1819]. In: B. Constant. *Political Writings* B. Fontana (ed.) Cambridge: Cambridge University Press, pp. 308–29.

Cooper, R. (2003) *The Breaking of Nations: Order and Chaos in the Twenty-first Century*. London: Atlantic Books.

Coppieters, B., & Fotion, N. (eds) (2002) *Moral Constraints of War: Principles and Cases*. New York: Lexington Books.

Cox, R. (1981) Social forces, states, and world orders: beyond international relations theory. *Millennium*, 10:126–55.

Craig, C. (2003) *Glimmer of a New Leviathan: Total War in the Realism of Niebuhr, Morgenthau, and Waltz*. New York: Columbia University Press.

Crawford, N. (2002) *Argument and Change in World Politics: Ethics, Decolonization, and Humanitarian Intervention*. Cambridge: Cambridge University Press.

Crawford, J. (2006) *The Creation of States in International Law*, 2nd edn. Oxford: Clarendon.

Crawford, J. (2007) The false promise of preventive war: the 'new security consensus' and a more insecure world. In: H. Shue & D. Rodin (eds) *Preemption: Military Action and Moral Justification*. Oxford: Oxford University Press, pp. 89–125.

Crenshaw, M. (1983) Introduction. In: M. Crenshaw (ed.), *Terrorism, Legitimacy, and Power*. Middletown: Wesleyan University Press.

Crenshaw, M. (2008) The debate over 'new' vs. 'old' terrorism. In: I. A. Karawan, W. McCormack, & S. Reynolds (eds), *Values and Violence: Intangible Aspects of Terrorism*. Heidelberg: Springer, pp. 117–37.

Dahl, R. (1989) *Democracy and its Critics*. New Haven: Yale University Press.

Dahl, R. (1999) Can international organizations be democratic? A skeptic's view. In: C. Hacker-Cordon & I. Shapiro (eds), *Democracy's Edges*. Cambridge: Cambridge University Press, pp. 19–37.

Dallaire, R. (2004) *Shake Hands with the Devil: The Failure of Humanity in Rwanda*. London: Arrow.

Dallmayr, F. (1999) *Border-Crossings: Towards a Comparative Political Theory*. Lanham: Lexington Books.

Dauvergne, C. (2008) *Making People Illegal: What Globalization Means for Migration and Law*. Cambridge: Cambridge University Press.

Davion, V. (1994) Is ecofeminism feminist? In: K. Warren (ed.), *Ecological Feminism*. London: Routledge, pp. 8–28.

De Wet, E. (2006) The international constitutional order, *International and Comparative Law Quarterly*, 55:53-76.

Der Derian, J., & Shapiro, M. (ed.) (1989) *International/Intertextual Relations: Postmodern Readings of World Politics*. Lanham: Lexington Books.

Derrida, J. (1981) *Dissemination*, transl. B. Johnson. Chicago: University of Chicago Press.

Derrida, J. (1982) Différance. In: J. Derrida *Margins of Philosophy*, transl. A. Bass. Chicago: University of Chicago Press.

Derrida, J. (1989–1990) The force of law: the 'mystical foundation of authority'. *Cardozo Law Review*, 11:921–1045.

Derrida, J. (1994) *Specters of Marx: The State of the Debt, the Work of Mourning, and the New International*, transl. P. Kamuf, New York: Routledge.

Derrida, J. (1998) *Of Grammatology*, transl. G. Spivak. Baltimore: Johns Hopkins University Press.

Derrida, J. (1999) Marx and sons. In: J. Derrida, T. Eagleton, F. Jameson, A. Negri et al. (eds) *Ghostly Demarcations: A Symposium on Jacques Derrida's Specters of Marx*. London: Verso, pp. 213–69.

Derrida, J. (2005) *Rogues: Two Essays on Reason*, transl. P.-A. Brault and M. Naas, Stanford: Stanford University Press.

Derrida, J. (2008) *The Gift of Death and Literature in Secret*, 2nd edn, transl. D. Wills. Chicago: University of Chicago Press.

Des Forges, A. (1999) *Leave None to Tell the Story: Genocide in Rwanda*. New York: Human Rights Watch.

Deudney, D. (2007) *Bounding Power: Republican Security Theory from the Polis to the Global Village.* Princeton: Princeton University Press.

Dewey, J. (1988) The public and its problems. In: J. A. Boydston (ed.) *The Later Works, 1925–1937, Vol. 2.* Carbondale: Southern Illinois University Press, pp. 235–72.

Diderot, D. (1754) Cosmopolitan, or cosmopolite. In: D. Diderot & J. le Rond D'Alembert (eds), *Encyclopédie, ou dictionnaire raisonné des sciences, des arts et des métiers* (1751–1772), vol. 4. Chicago: University of Chicago, ARTFL Encyclopédie Projet, R. Morrissey (project ed.). Available at: http://encyclopedie.uchicago.edu/ (accessed August 2009).

Dillon, M., & Neal, A. (eds) (2008) *Foucault on Politics, Security and War.* New York: Palgrave.

Dillon, M., & Reid, J. (2007) *The Liberal Way of War: Killing to Make Life Live.* New York: Routledge.

Dobson, A. (1996) Democratising green theory: preconditions and principles. In: B. Doherty & M. de Geus (eds), *Democracy and Green Political Thought: Sustainability, Rights, and Citizenship.* London: Routledge, pp. 132–50.

Dobson, A. (2003) *Citizenship and the Environment.* Oxford: Oxford University Press.

Dobson, A. (2007) *Green Political Thought,* 4th edn. London: Routledge.

Donnelly, J (2000) *Realism and International Relations.* Cambridge: Cambridge University Press.

Donnelly, J (2003) *Universal Human Rights in Theory and Practice.* Ithaca: Cornell University Press.

Donnelly, J (2008) The ethics of realism. In: C. Reus-Smit, & D. Snidal (eds) *The Oxford Handbook of International Relations.* Oxford: Oxford University Press, pp. 151–62.

Doyle, M. (1983) Kant, liberal legacies and foreign affairs, Parts I and II. *Philosophy & Public Affairs,* 12:205–35.

Doyle, M. (1997) *Ways of War and Peace: Realism, Liberalism and Socialism.* New York: W.W. Norton.

Doyle, M. (2008) *Striking First: Preemption and Prevention in International Conflict.* Princeton: Princeton University Press.

Dryzek, J. (1996) Political and ecological communication. In: F. Mathews (ed.), *Ecology and Democracy.* London: Frank Cass, pp. 13–30.

Dryzek, J. (2002) *Deliberative Democracy and Beyond: Liberals, Critics, Contestations.* Oxford: Oxford University Press.

Dryzek, J. (2006) *Deliberative Global Politics: Discourse and Democracy in a Divided World.* Cambridge: Polity Press.

Dummett, M. (2001) *On Immigration and Refugees.* London: Routledge.

Dunn, J. (1990) *Interpreting Political Responsibility: Essays, 1981–1989.* Cambridge: Polity.

Dunne, T. (1998) *Inventing International Society: A History of the English School.* Basingstoke: Macmillan.

Dunne, T., Kurki, M., & Smith, S. (eds) (2007) *International Relations Theories: Discipline and Diversity.* Oxford: Oxford University Press.

Dutton, M. (2002) Lead us not into translation: notes toward a theoretical foundation for Asian studies. *Neplanta: Views from South,* 3:495–537.

Dworkin, R. (2000) *Sovereign Virtue: The Theory and Practice of Virtue.* Cambridge: Harvard University Press.

Eckersley, R. (1996) Greening liberal democracy: the rights discourse revisited. In: B. Doherty & M. de Geus (eds), *Democracy and Green Political Thought.* London: Routledge, pp. 212–36.

Eckersley, R. (2004) *The Green State: Rethinking Democracy and Sovereignty.* Cambridge: MIT Press.

Edkins, J. (1999) *Poststructuralism and International Relations: Bringing the Political Back In.* Boulder: Lynne Rienner.

Edkins, J. (2000) *Whose Hunger? Concepts of Famine, Practices of Aid.* Minneapolis: University of Minnesota Press.

Ehrlich, P. (1968) *The Population Bomb.* New York: Ballantine.

Ehrman, J. (1995) *The Rise of Neoconservatism: Intellectuals and Foreign Affairs, 1945–1994.* New Haven: Yale University Press.

Eisenstein, Z. (2004) *Against Empire: Feminisms, Racism, and the West.* London: Zed Press.

Elman, C. (2010) *Recovering Realism.* London: Routledge.

Elshtain, J.B. (1987) *Women and War.* New York: Basic Books.

Elshtain, J.B. (1992) (ed.) *Just War Theory.* Oxford: Blackwell.

Elshtain, J.B. (1995) *Women and War.* Chicago: University of Chicago Press.

Elshtain, J.B. (2003) *Just War against Terror: The Burden of American Power in a Violent World*. New York: Basic Books.

Elshtain, J.B. (2008) *Sovereignty: God, State, and Self*. New York: Basic Books.

Engle Merry, S. (2006) *Human Rights and Gender Violence: Translating International Law into Local Justice*. Chicago: University of Chicago Press.

Enloe, C. (2000) *Manoeuvres: The International Politics of Militarizing Women's Lives*. Berkeley: University of California Press.

Estlund, D. (2008) *Democratic Authority: A Philosophical Framework*. Princeton: Princeton University Press.

Euben, R. (1999) *Enemy in the Mirror: Islamic Fundamentalism and the Limits of Modern Rationalism*. Princeton: Princeton University Press.

European Commission (2008) *COM(2008) 765: The Impact of Free Movement of Workers in the Context of EU Enlargement*. Brussels: Commission of the European Communities. Available at: http://ec.europa.eu/social/main.jsp?catId=508&langId=en (accessed August 2009).

Evans, M. (ed.) (2003) *International Law*. Oxford: Oxford University Press.

Fabre, C. (2000) *Social Rights under the Constitution*. Oxford: Oxford University Press.

Fabre, C. (2008) Cosmopolitanism, legitimate authority and the just war. *International Affairs*, 84:963–76.

Faini, R. (2007) Remittances and the brain drain: do more skilled migrants remit more? *World Bank Economic Review*, 21:177–91.

Fanon, F. (1963) *The Wretched of the Earth*. New York: Grove Press.

Fanon, F. (1967) *Black Skins, White Masks*. New York: Grove Press.

Fassbender, B. (1998) The United Nations Charter as the constitution of the international community. *Columbia Journal of Transnational Law*, 36:529–619.

Favell, A., & Hansen, R. (2002) Markets against politics: migration, EU enlargement, and the idea of Europe. *Journal of Ethnic and Migration Studies*, 28:581–601.

Ferguson, J. (1994) *The Anti-Politics Machine: 'Development', Depoliticization, and Bureaucratic Power in Lesotho*. Minneapolis: University of Minnesota Press.

Finnemore, M. (1996) Constructing norms of humanitarian intervention. In: P. Katzenstein (ed.), *The Culture of National Security: Norms and Identity in World Politics*. New York: Columbia University Press, pp. 153–85.

Finnemore, M. (2003) *The Purpose of Intervention: Changing Beliefs about the Use of Force*. Ithaca: Cornell University Press.

Finnis, J., Boyle, J., & Grisez, G. (eds) (1987) *Nuclear Deterrence, Morality, and Realism*. Oxford: Clarendon.

Fishkin, J. (1982) *The Limits of Obligation*. New Haven: Yale University Press.

Flyvbjerg, B. (2001) *Making Social Science Matter: Why Social Inquiry Fails and How it Can Succeed Again*, transl. S. Sampson. Cambridge: Cambridge University Press.

Forst, R. (1999) The basic right to justification. *Constellations*, 6:35–60.

Fortress Europe Blogspot (2009) *Immigrants Dead at the Frontiers of Europe*. Available from http://fortresseurope.blogspot.com/. (accessed January 20 2009).

Foucault, M. (1970) *The Order of Things*. New York: Random House.

Foucault, M. (1972) *The Archaeology of Knowledge*, transl. A. Sheridan. New York: Pantheon Books.

Foucault, M. (1977) *Discipline and Punish: The Birth of the Prison*, transl. A. Sheridan. New York: Vintage.

Foucault, M. (1978) *The History of Sexuality, Volume 1: An Introduction*, transl. R. Hurley. New York: Vintage.

Foucault, M. (1983) Afterword: the subject and power. In: H. Dreyfus & P. Rabinow (eds), *Michel Foucault: Beyond Structuralism and Hermeneutics*, 2nd edn. Chicago: University of Chicago Press, pp. 208–29.

Foucault, M. (1984) The juridical apparatus. In: W. Connolly (ed.), *Legitimacy and the State*. Oxford: Blackwell, pp. 201–22.

Foucault, M. (1985) *The Use of Pleasure: Volume 2 of the History of Sexuality*, transl. R. Hurley. New York: Vintage.

Foucault, M. (1993) About the beginnings of the hermeneutics of the self: two lectures at Dartmouth. *Political Theory*, 21:198–227.

Foucault, M. (1997a) On the genealogy of ethics: an overview of work in progress. In: P. Rabinow (ed.), *Ethics: Subjectivity and Truth: Volume 1 of*

The Essential Works of Michel Foucault. New York: New Press, pp. 253–80.

Foucault, M. (1997b) What is enlightenment? In: P. Rabinow (ed.), *Ethics: Subjectivity and Truth: Volume 1 of The Essential Works of Michel Foucault*. New York: New Press, pp. 303–19.

Foucault, M. (2000) 'Omnes et Singulatim': toward a critique of political reason. In: P. Rabinow (ed.), *Power: Volume 3 of The Essential Works of Michel Foucault*. New York: New Press, pp. 180–201.

Foucault, M. (2003) *Society Must be Defended: Lectures at the Collège de France 1975–1976*, M. Bertani & A. Fontana (eds), transl. D. Macey. New York: Picador Press.

Foucault, M. (2007) *Security, Territory, Population: Lectures at the Collège de France 1977–1978*, M. Senellart (ed.), transl. G. Burchell. New York: Palgrave.

Fox, G.H., & Roth, B. (2000) *Democratic Governance and International Law*. Cambridge: Cambridge University Press.

Fox, W. (1995) *Toward a Transpersonal Ecology*. Totnes: Green Books.

Franco, P. (2004) *Michael Oakeshott: An Introduction*. New Haven: Yale University Press.

Frankfurt, H. (1988) Equality as a moral ideal. In: H. Frankfurt, *The Importance of What we Care About*. Cambridge: Cambridge University Press, pp. 134–59.

Fraser, N. (1989) *Unruly Practices: Power, Discourse, and Gender in Contemporary Social Theory*. Minneapolis: University of Minnesota Press.

Fraser, N. (2008) *Scales of Justice: Reimagining Political Space in a Globalized World*. New York: Columbia University Press.

Freedom House (2009) *Freedom in the World*. Lanham: Rowman & Littlefield.

Freeman, S. (2001) Illiberal libertarianism: why libertarianism is not a liberal view. *Philosophy & Public Affairs*, 30:105–51.

Freeman, S. (2006a) Distributive justice and *The Law of Peoples*. In: R. Martin & D. Reidy (eds), *Rawls's Law of Peoples: A Realistic Utopia?* Oxford: Blackwell, pp. 243–62.

Freeman, S. (2006b) The law of peoples, social cooperation, human rights, and distributive justice. *Social Philosophy & Policy*, 23:29–68.

Freeman, S. (2007) *Justice and the Social Contract: Essays on Rawlsian Political Philosophy*. Oxford: Oxford University Press.

Friedman, M. (2006) *The Neoconservative Revolution: Jewish Intellectuals and the Shaping of Public Policy*. Cambridge: Cambridge University Press.

Frost, M. (1996) *Ethics in International Relations: A Constitutive Theory*. Cambridge: Cambridge University Press.

Frost, M. (2009) *Global Ethics: Anarchy, Freedom and International Relations*. London: Routledge.

Fukuyama, F. (1992) *The End of History and the Last Man*. London: Penguin.

Fukuyama, F. (1998) Women and the evolution of world politics. *Foreign Affairs*, 77(5):24–40.

Fukuyama, F. (2006) *America at the Crossroads: Democracy, Power, and the Neo-Conservative Legacy*. New Haven: Yale University Press.

Fullinwider, R. (2003) Terrorism, innocence, and war. In: V. Gehring (ed.), *War after September 11*. Lanham: Rowman & Littlefield, pp. 21–33.

Fung, A. (2003) Recipes for public spheres. *Journal of Political Philosophy*, 11:338–367.

Gamble, A. (1996) *Hayek: The Iron Cage of Liberty*. Cambridge: Polity.

Gamble, A. (2009) *The Spectre at the Feast: Capitalist Crisis and the Politics of Recession*. Basingstoke: Palgrave.

Gandhi, L. (1998) *Postcolonial Theory: A Critical Introduction*. New York: Columbia University Press.

Gandhi, M. (1993) *The Penguin Gandhi Reader*, R. Mukherjee (ed.). New York: Penguin.

Gardiner, S. (2006) A perfect moral storm: climate change, intergenerational ethics, and the problem of moral corruption. *Environmental Values*, 15:397–413.

Gardner, L. (1976) *Imperial America: American Foreign Policy since 1898*. New York: Harcourt.

Gauthier, D. (1986) *Morals by Agreement*. Oxford: Oxford University Press.

Gellner, E. (1983) *Nations and Nationalism*. Ithaca: Cornell University Press.

Geuss, R. (1980) *The Idea of a Critical Theory: Habermas and the Frankfurt School*. Cambridge: Cambridge University Press.

Geuss, R. (2001) *History and Illusion in Politics*. Cambridge: Cambridge University Press.

Geuss, R. (2008) *Philosophy and Real Politics*. Princeton: Princeton University Press.

Gilabert, P. (2007) Contractualism and poverty relief. *Social Theory and Practice*, 33:277–310.

Gilligan, C. (1982) *In a Different Voice: Psychological Theory and Women's Development*. Cambridge: Cambridge University Press.

Gilroy, P. (1993) *The Black Atlantic: Modernity and Double-Consciousness*. London: Verso.

Glock, H-J. (2008) *What is Analytic Philosophy?* Cambridge: Cambridge University Press.

Goldstein, J. (2001) *War and Gender: How Gender Shapes the War System and Vice Versa*. Cambridge: Cambridge University Press.

Goldstein, J., & Keohane, R. (eds) (1993) *Ideas and Foreign Policy: Beliefs, Institutions and Political Change*. Ithaca: Cornell University Press.

Goodin, R. (1988) What is so special about our fellow countrymen? *Ethics*, 98:663–86.

Goodin, R. (1992) *Green Political Thought*. Cambridge: Polity Press.

Goodin, R. (1995) *Utilitarianism as a Public Philosophy*. Cambridge: Cambridge University Press.

Goodin, R. (2006) *What's Wrong with Terrorism?* Cambridge: Polity.

Gordon, N., & López, G. (2000) Terrorism in the Arab-Israeli conflict. In: A. Valls, (ed.) *Ethics in International Affairs: Theories and Cases*. Lanham: Rowman & Littlefield, pp. 99–113.

Goto-Jones, C. (2005a) If the past is a different country, are different countries in the past? On the place of the non-European in the history of philosophy. *Philosophy*, 80:29–51.

Goto-Jones, C. (2005b) *Political Philosophy in Japan: Nishida, the Kyoto School and Co-Prosperity*. London: Routledge.

Goto-Jones, C. (2009) The Kyoto School, the Cambridge School, and the history of political philosophy in wartime Japan. *Positions: East Asia Cultures Critique*, 17:13–42.

Gould, C. (2004) *Globalizing Democracy and Human Rights*. New York: Cambridge University Press.

Gran, P. (1979) *The Islamic Roots of Capitalism: Egypt, 1760–1840*. Austin: University of Texas Press.

Gray, C. (2008) *International Law and the Use of Force*, 3rd edn. Oxford: Oxford University Press.

Gray, C.S. (1999) *Modern Strategy*. Oxford: Oxford University Press.

Green, L. (1990) *The Authority of the State*. Oxford: Oxford University Press.

Green, D., & Shapiro, I. (1994) *Pathologies of Rational Choice Theory: A Critique of Applications in Political Science*. New Haven: Yale University Press.

Greenleaf, W.H. (1966) *Oakeshott's Philosophical Politics*. London: Longmans.

Griffin, J. (2001) First steps in an account of human rights. *European Journal of Philosophy*, 9:306–27.

Grisez, G., Boyle, J., & Finnis, J. (1987) *Nuclear Deterrence, Morality and Realism*. Oxford: Oxford University Press.

Grotius, H. (2005) *The Rights of War and Peace*, R. Tuck (ed.). Indianapolis: Liberty Fund.

Guild, E. (2007) Citizens without a constitution, borders without a state: EU free movement of persons. In: A. Baldaccini, E. Guild, & H. Toner (eds), *Whose Freedom, Security and Justice? EU Immigration and Asylum Law and Policy*. Oxford: Hart Publishing, pp. 25–56.

Gutmann, A. (1985) Communitarian critics of liberalism. *Philosophy & Public Affairs*, 14:308–22.

Gutmann, A. (ed.) (1994) *Multiculturalism: Examining the Politics of Recognition*. Princeton: Princeton University Press.

Gutmann, A., & Thompson, D. (2004) *Why Deliberative Democracy?* Princeton: Princeton University Press.

Guzzini, S. (1993) Structural power: the limits of neorealist power analysis. *International Organization*, 47:443–78.

Guzzini, S. (2004) The enduring dilemmas of realism in international relations. *European Journal of International Relations*, 10:533–68.

Habermas, J. (1984–7) *The Theory of Communicative Action*, transl. W. McCarthy. Cambridge: Polity.

Habermas, J. (1987/1990) *The Philosophical Discourse of Modernity: Twelve Lectures*, transl. F. G. Lawrence. Cambridge: MIT Press.

Habermas, J. (1989) *The New Conservatism: Cultural Criticism and the Historian's Debate*, transl. S. W. Nicholson. Cambridge: MIT Press.

Habermas, J. (1992) *The Structural Transformation of the Public Sphere*. Cambridge: MIT Press.

Habermas, J. (1996) *Between Facts and Norms: Contributions to a Discourse Theory of Law and Democracy*, transl. W. Rehg. Cambridge: Polity.

Habermas, J. (2000) *The Inclusion of the Other.* Cambridge: MIT Press.

Habermas, J. (2001a) *Moral Consciousness and Communicative Action.* Cambridge: MIT Press.

Habermas, J. (2001b) *The Postnational Constellation: Political Essays.* Cambridge: MIT Press.

Habermas, J. (2001c) Why Europe needs a constitution. *New Left Review,* 11:5–26.

Habermas, J. (2006a) The constitutionalization of international law. In: J. Habermas, *The Divided West,* C. Cronin (ed.), Cambridge: Polity Press, pp. 115–93.

Habermas, J., & Derrida, J. (2003) February 15, or what binds Europeans together: a plea for a common foreign policy, beginning in the core of Europe. *Constellations,* 10:291–7.

Hacker, P.M.S. (2006) Soames' history of analytic philosophy. *Philosophical Quarterly,* 56(222):121–31.

Hacking, I. (1990) *The Taming of Chance.* Cambridge: Cambridge University Press.

Hailbronner, K. (1989) Citizenship and nationhood in Germany. In: W. R. Brubaker (ed.), *Immigration and the Politics of Citizenship in Europe and North America.* Lanham: University Press of America, pp. 67–79.

Hall, I. (2006) *The International Political Thought of Martin Wight.* Basingstoke: Palgrave.

Halper, S., & Clarke, J. (2004) *America Alone: The Neo-Conservatives and the Global Order.* Cambridge: Cambridge University Press.

Hardin, G. (1968) The tragedy of the commons. *Science,* 162:1243–8.

Hardin, G. (1996) Lifeboat ethics: the case against helping the poor. In: Aikens, W., & LaFollette, H. (eds), *World Hunger and Morality.* New Jersey: Prentice Hall, pp. 5–25.

Hart, H.L.A. (1961) *The Concept of Law.* Oxford: Oxford University Press.

Hart, H.L.A. (1963) *Law, Liberty, and Morality.* Stanford: Stanford University Press.

Hart, H.L.A. (1968) *Punishment and Responsibility: Essays in the Philosophy of Law.* Oxford: Oxford University Press.

Hart, H.L.A. (1984) Are there any natural rights? In: J. Waldron (ed.), *Theories of Rights.* Oxford: Oxford University Press, pp. 77–90.

Harvey, D. (2005) *The New Imperialism.* Oxford: Oxford University Press.

Haslam, J. (2002) *No Virtue Like Necessity: Realist Thought in International Relations since Machiavelli.* New Haven: Yale University Press.

Haugaard, M. (ed.) (2002) *Power: A Reader.* Manchester: Manchester University Press.

Hayden, P. (2005) *Cosmopolitan Global Politics.* Aldershot: Ashgate.

Hayek, F.A. (1960) *The Constitution of Liberty.* London: Routledge.

Hayek, F.A. (1983) *Knowledge, Evolution, and Society.* London: ASI Research.

Hayward, T. (2006) Ecological citizenship: justice, rights and the virtue of resourcefulness. *Environmental Politics,* 15:435–46.

Heath, J. (1997) Immigration, multiculturalism, and the social contract. *Canadian Journal of Law and Jurisprudence,* 10:343–61.

Heath, J. (2006) Rawls on global distributive justice. *Canadian Journal of Philosophy,* Supplement, 31:193–226.

Hedges, C. (2003) *What Every Person Should Know about War.* New York: Free Press.

Hegel, G.W.F. (1979) *Phenomenology of Spirit* (1807), transl. A. Miller. Oxford: Clarendon.

Heidegger, M. (1982) A dialogue on language between a Japanese and an inquirer. In: M. Heidegger, *On the Way to Language.* New York: Harper & Row, pp. 1–54.

Heilbroner, R. (1974) *An Inquiry into the Human Prospect.* London: Calder & Boyars.

Held, D. (1980) *Introduction to Critical Theory: Horkheimer to Habermas.* Cambridge: Polity.

Held, D. (1995a) *Democracy and the Global Order: From the Modern State to Cosmopolitan Governance.* Cambridge: Polity.

Held, D. (2004) *Global Covenant: The Social Democratic Alternative to the Washington Consensus.* Cambridge: Polity.

Held, D., McGrew, A., Goldblatt, D., & Perraton, J. (1999) *Global Transformations: Politics, Economics, and Culture.* Cambridge: Polity.

Held, D., & McGrew, A. (2002) *Globalization/ Antiglobalization.* Cambridge: Polity.

Held, D., & McGrew, A. (2007) *Globalisation/Anti-Globalisation: Beyond the Great Divide,* 2nd edn. Cambridge: Polity.

Held, V. (1993) *Feminist Morality: Transforming Culture, Society and Politics.* Chicago: University of Chicago Press.

Held, V. (ed.) (1995b) *Justice and Care: Essential Readings in Feminist Ethics*. Boulder: Westview Press.

Held, V. (2006) *The Ethics of Care: Personal, Political, and Global*. New York: Oxford University Press.

Hendrickson, D. (1992) Migration in law and ethics: a realist perspective. In: B. Barry & R. E. Goodin (eds), *Free Movement: Ethical Issues in the Transnational Migration of People and of Money*. University Park: Pennsylvania State University Press, pp. 213–31.

Herz, J. (1951) *Political Realism and Political Idealism: A Study in Theories and Realities*. Chicago: University of Chicago Press.

Herz, J. (1981) Political realism revisited: response. *International Studies Quarterly*, 25:201–3.

Hobsbawm, E.J. (1990) *Nations and Nationalism since 1780*. Cambridge: Cambridge University Press.

Hobsbawm, E.J. (1994) *Age of Extremes: The Short Twentieth Century, 1914–1991*. London: Abacus.

Hoffman, B. (1998a) *Inside Terrorism*. New York: Columbia University Press.

Hoffmann, S. (1981) *Duties Beyond Borders: On the Limits and Possibilities of Ethical International Relations*. Syracuse: Syracuse University Press.

Hoffmann, S. (1998b) *World Disorders: Troubled Peace in the Post-Cold War Era*. Boulder: Rowman & Littlefield.

Hohfeld, L. (1978) *Fundamental Legal Conceptions as Applied to Judicial Reasoning*. New York: Greenwood Publishing.

Holland, N. (ed.) (1997) *Feminist Interpretations of Jacques Derrida*. University Park: Penn State University Press.

Hollinger, D. (2000) *Postethnic America: Beyond Multiculturalism*. New York: Basic Books.

Hollis, M. (1982) 'Dirty hands'. *British Journal of Political Science,* 12(4):385–98.

Hollis, M. (1994) *The Philosophy of Social Science: An Introduction*. Cambridge: Cambridge University Press.

Hollis, M., & Smith, S. (1990) *Explaining and Understanding International Relations*. Oxford: Oxford University Press.

Holmes, S. (2007) *The Matador's Cape: America's Reckless Response to Terror*. Cambridge: Cambridge University Press.

Holmes, S., & Sunstein, C. (1999) *The Cost of Rights: Why Liberty Depends on Taxes*. New York: Norton.

Honderich, T. (2002) *After the Terror*. Edinburgh: Edinburgh University Press.

Honig, B. (1996) *Political Theory and the Displacement of Politics*. Ithaca: Cornell University Press.

Honneth, A. (2007) *Disrespect: The Normative Foundations of Critical Theory*. Cambridge: Polity.

Honneth, A. (2009) *Pathologies of Reason: On the Legacy of Critical Theory*. New York: Columbia University Press.

Hont, I. (2005) *Jealousy of Trade: International Competition and the Nation-State in Historical Context*. Cambridge: Harvard University Press.

hooks, b. (1982) *Ain't I A Woman: Black Women and Feminism*. London: Pluto Press.

Horkheimer, M. (1972) *Critical Theory: Selected Essays*. New York: Continuum.

Horkheimer, M., & Adorno, T. (2002 [1944]) *Dialectic of Enlightenment*. Stanford: Stanford University Press.

Howland, D. (2002) *Translating the West: Language and Political Reason in Nineteenth Century Japan*. Honolulu: University of Hawaii Press.

Humphrey, M. (2007) *Ecological Politics and Democratic Theory: The Challenge to the Deliberative Ideal*. London: Routledge.

Hunt, L. (2007) *Inventing Human Rights: A History*. New York: Norton.

Huntington, S. (1996) *The Clash of Civilizations and the Remaking of World Order*. New York: Simon & Schuster.

Hurrell, A. (2007) *On Global Order: Power, Values, and the Constitution of International Society*. Oxford: Oxford University Press.

Hutchings, K. (2000) Towards a feminist international ethics. *Review of International Studies*, 26(5):111–30.

Hutchings, K. (2004) From morality to politics and back again: feminist international ethics and the civil-society argument. *Alternatives*, 29:239–64.

Hutchings, K. (2007a) Feminist perspectives on a planetary ethic. In: W. M. Sullivan & W. Kymlicka (eds), *The Globalization of Ethics: Religious and Secular Perspectives*. Cambridge: Cambridge University Press, pp. 171–190.

Hutchings, K. (2007b) Feminist ethics and political violence. *International Politics*, 44(3):90–106.

Ignatieff, M. (1994) *The Needs of Strangers*. London: Vintage.

Ignatieff, M. (1999) Human rights. In: R. Post et al. (eds), *Human Rights in Transition: Gettysburg to Bosnia*. New York: Zone Books, pp. 313–24.

Ignatieff, M. (2001) *Human Rights as Politics and Idolatry*. Princeton: Princeton University Press.

Ikenberry, J. (2001) *After Victory: Institutions, Strategic Restraint, and the Rebuilding of Order after Major Wars*. Princeton: Princeton University Press.

Ikenberry, J., & Kupchan, C.A. (2004) Liberal realism: the foundations of a democratic foreign policy. *National Interest*, 77:38–49.

International Commission on Intervention and State Sovereignty (2001) *The Responsibility to Protect*. Ottawa: International Development Research Centre.

International Organization for Migration (2008) *World Migration 2008: Managing Labour Mobility in the Evolving Global Economy*. Geneva: IOM.

Isbister, J. (2000) A liberal argument for border controls: reply to Carens. *International Migration Review*, 34:629–35.

Ivison, D. (2002) *Postcolonial Liberalism*. Cambridge: Cambridge University Press.

Ivison, D. (2008) *Rights*. Stocksfield: Acumen.

Jabri, V. (1999) Explorations of difference in normative international relations. In V. Jabri & E. O'Gorman (eds), *Women, Culture and International Relations*. Boulder: Lynne Rienner, pp. 39–61.

Jackson, P.T. (2010) *An Introduction to Philosophy and International Relations*. London: Routledge.

Jackson, R. (1990) *Quasi-States: Sovereignty, International Relations and the Third World*. Cambridge: Cambridge University Press.

Jackson, R. (2000) *The Global Covenant: Human Relations in a World of States*. Oxford: Oxford University Press.

Jaggar, A. (2005) 'Saving Amina': global justice for women and intercultural dialogue. In: A. Follesdal & T. Pogge (eds), *Real World Justice*. Dordrecht: Springer, pp. 37–63.

Jagger, A. (ed.) (2009) *Pogge and His Critics*. Cambridge: Polity.

Jamieson, D. (1996) Ethics and intentional climate change. *Climatic Change*, 33:323–36.

JanMohamed, A. (1983) *Manichean Aesthetics: The Politics of Literature in Colonial Africa*. Amherst: University of Massachusetts Press.

Jay, M. (1996) *The Dialectical Imagination: A History of the Frankfurt School and the Institute of Social Research 1923–1950*. Berkeley: University of California Press.

Jeffrey, R. (ed.) (2008a) *Confronting Evil in International Relations: Ethical Responses to Problems of Moral Agency*. Basingstoke: Palgrave.

Jeffery, R. (2008b) *Evil and International Relations: Human Suffering in an Age of Terror*. Basingstoke: Palgrave.

Johns, S., & Davis, R.H., Jr (eds) (1991) *Mandela, Tambo, and the African National Congress: The Struggle Against Apartheid 1948–1990: A Documentary Survey*. New York: Oxford University Press.

Johnson, J.T. (1974) *Ideology, Reason and the Limitation of War: Religious and Secular Concepts 1200–1740*. Princeton: Princeton University Press.

Johnson, J.T. (1981) *Just War Tradition and the Restraint of War: A Moral and Historical Inquiry*. Princeton: Princeton University Press.

Johnson, J.T. (1984) *Can Modern War Be Just?* New Haven: Yale University Press.

Johnson, J.T. (1999) *Morality and Contemporary Warfare*. New Haven: Yale University Press.

Jones, C. (1999a) *Global Justice: Defending Cosmopolitanism*. Oxford: Oxford University Press.

Jones, P. (1999b) Human rights, group rights, and peoples' rights. *Human Rights Quarterly*, 21:80–107.

Julius, A.J. (2006) Nagel's atlas. *Philosophy & Public Affairs*, 34:176–92.

Kant, I. (1991) Perpetual peace: a philosophical sketch [1795]. In: *Kant: Political Writings*. Cambridge: Cambridge University Press, H. Reiss (ed.), pp. 93–125.

Kapitan, T. (2003) The terrorism of 'terrorism'. In: James P. Sterba (ed.) *Terrorism and International Justice*. New York: Oxford University Press, pp. 47–66.

Karyotis, G. (2007) European migration policy in the aftermath of September 11: the security-migration nexus. *Innovation*, 20:1–17.

Katzenstein, P. (ed.) (1996) *The Culture of National Security: Norms and Identity in World Politics*. New York: Columbia University Press.

Keene, E. (2005) *International Political Thought: An Historical Introduction*. Cambridge: Polity.

Kellner, D. (1989) *Critical Theory, Marxism, and Modernity*. Baltimore: Johns Hopkins University Press.

Kelly, D. (2003) *The State of the Political: Conceptions of Politics and the State in the Thought of Max Weber, Carl Schmitt, and Franz Neumann*. Oxford: Oxford University Press.

Kennedy, D. (1987) *International Legal Structures*. Baden-Baden: Nomos Verlag.

Keohane, R. (2009) Political science as a vocation. *PS: Political Science and Politics*, 42:359–63.

Kim, S.H. (2004) *Max Weber's Politics of Civil Society*. Cambridge: Cambridge University Press.

Kissinger, H. (1994) *Diplomacy*. New York: Simon & Schuster.

Klabbers, J., Peters A., & Ulfstein, G. (2009) *The Constitutionalisation of International Law*. Oxford: Oxford University Press.

Kleffner, J. K., & Stahn, C. (eds) (2008) *Jus Post Bellum: Towards a Law of Transition from Conflict to Peace*. Cambridge: Cambridge University Press.

Klosko, G. (1992) *The Principle of Fairness and Political Obligation*. Lanham: Rowman & Littlefield.

Klosko, G. (2005) *Political Obligations*. Oxford: Oxford University Press.

Kohli, A. (1996) The role of theory in comparative politics: a symposium. *World Politics*, 48:1–49.

Kolers, A. (2004) Valuing land and distributing territory. In: R. Lee & D. M. Smith (eds), *Geographies and Moralities*. Oxford: Blackwell, pp. 135–48.

Kolers, A. (2009) *Land, Conflict and Justice: A Political Theory of Territory*. Cambridge: Cambridge University Press.

Koskenniemi, M. (2004) *The Gentle Civilizer of Nations: The Rise and Fall of International Law, 1870–1960*. Cambridge: Cambridge University Press.

Koskenniemi, M. (2006) *From Apology to Utopia: The Structure of International Legal Argument*, 2nd edn. Cambridge: Cambridge University Press.

Krasner, S. (1999) *Sovereignty: Organized Hypocrisy*. Princeton: Princeton University Press.

Kratochwil, F. (1989) *Rules, Norms and Decisions: On the Conditions of Practical and Legal Reasoning in International Relations and Domestic Affairs*. Cambridge: Cambridge University Press.

Krishna, S. (2001) Race, amnesia and the education of international relations. *Alternatives*, 26:401–24.

Kristof, N. (2008) Tough love for Israel? *New York Times*, July 24, Op-ed page.

Krüger, L. (1984) Why do we study the history of philosophy. In: R. Rorty, J. Schneewind, & Q. Skinner (eds), *Philosophy in History: Ideas in Context*. Cambridge: Cambridge University Press, pp. 77–101.

Kuklick, B. (2006) *Blind Oracles: Intellectuals and War from Kennan to Kissinger*. Princeton: Princeton University Press.

Kymlicka, W. (1991) *Liberalism, Community and Culture*. Oxford: Oxford University Press.

Kymlicka, W. (1995) *Multicultural Citizenship: A Liberal Theory of Minority Rights*. Oxford: Clarendon Press.

Kymlicka, W. (2001) Territorial boundaries: a liberal egalitarian perspective. In: D. Miller & S. Hashmi (eds) *Boundaries and Justice: Diverse Ethical Perspectives*. Princeton: Princeton University Press, pp. 249–275.

Kymlicka, W. (2002) *An Introduction to Contemporary Political Philosophy*, 2nd edn. Oxford: Oxford University.

Kymlicka, W., & Sullivan, W.M. (eds). *The Globalization of Ethics: Religious and Secular Perspectives*. Cambridge: Cambridge University Press.

Laërtius, D. (2005) Diogenes. In: R. Hicks (ed.) *Lives of Eminent Philosophers: Volume II*. Cambridge: Harvard University Press, pp. 22–85.

Lang, A. (2002) *Agency and Ethics: The Politics of Military Intervention*. Albany: SUNY Press.

Lang, A. (2003) Introduction. In: A. Lang (ed.), *Just Intervention*. Washington DC: Georgetown University Press, pp. 1–10.

Lang, A. (2008) *Punishment, Justice and International Relations: Ethics and Order After the Cold War*. London: Routledge.

Lang, A. (2009) Humanitarian intervention. In: P. Hayden (ed.), *The Ashgate Research Companion to Ethics and International Affairs*. Aldershot: Ashgate, pp. 133–150.

Lacquer, W. (2003) *No End to War: Terrorism in the Twenty First Century*. London: Continuum.

Latham, M.E. (2000) *Modernization as Ideology: American Social Science and 'Nation Building' in the Kennedy Era*. Chapel Hill: University of North Carolina Press.

Lauterpacht, H. (1947) *Recognition in International Law*. Cambridge: Cambridge University Press.

Lawlor, L. (2006) Jacques Derrida. *Stanford Encyclopedia of Philosophy*. Available at: http://plato.stanford.edu/entries/derrida.

Lebow, R.N. (2003) *The Tragic Vision of Politics: Ethics, Interests, Orders*. Cambridge: Cambridge University Press.

Lebow, R.N. (2007) *Coercion, Cooperation, and Ethics in International Relations*. London: Routledge.

Leitenberg, M. (2006) Deaths in wars and conflicts in the twentieth century. *Cornell University Peace Studies Program*, Occasional Paper 29. Available at: http://www.cissm.umd.edu/papers/files/deathswarsconflictsjune52006.pdf (accessed August 2009).

Lenin, V.I., & Bukharin, N. (2009) *Imperialism and War: Classic Writings by V.I. Lenin and Nikolai Bukharin*, P. Gasper (ed.). Chicago: Haymarket Books.

Leydet, D. (2006) Citizenship. *Stanford Encyclopaedia of Philosophy*. Available at: http://plato.stanford.edu/entries/citizenship/ (accessed August 2009).

Lieven, A., & Hulsman, J. (2006) *Ethical Realism: A Vision for America's Role in the World*. New York: Pantheon.

Linklater, A. (1990) *Beyond Realism and Marxism: Critical Theory and International Relations*. London: Macmillan.

Linklater, A. (1998) *The Transformation of Political Community: Ethical Foundations of the Post-Westphalian Era*. Cambridge: Polity.

Linklater, A., & Suganami, H. (2006) *The English School of International Relations: A Contemporary Reassessment*. Cambridge: Cambridge University Press.

Little, R., & Williams, J. (eds) (2006) *The Anarchical Society in a Globalized World*. Basingstoke: Palgrave.

Locke, J. (1690/1980) *Second Treatise on Government*. ed. C. B. MacPherson. Indianapolis: Hacket Publishers.

Lomasky, L. (1986) *Persons, Rights and the Moral Community*. Oxford: Oxford University Press.

Lomborg, B. (2001) *The Skeptical Environmentalist: Measuring the State of the World*. Cambridge: Cambridge University Press.

Long, D., & Wilson, P. (eds) (1995) *Thinkers of the Twenty Years' Crisis: Interwar Idealism Re-Assessed*. Oxford: Clarendon.

Lorentzen, L.A., & Turpin, J. (eds) (1998) *The Women and War Reader*. New York: NYU Press.

Lowenfeld, A. (2008) *International Economic Law*, 2nd edn. Oxford: Oxford University Press.

Lu, C. (2006) World government. *Stanford Encyclopaedia of Philosophy*. Available at: http://plato.stanford.edu/entries/world-government/ (accessed August 2009).

Luban, D. (2004) Preventive war. *Philosophy & Public Affairs*, 32(3):207–48.

Lukács, G. (1972) *History and Class Consciousness*. Cambridge: MIT Press.

Lukes, S. (2005) *Power: A Radical View*, 2nd edn. London: Macmillan.

Lukes, S. (2009) *Moral Relativism*. London: Profile.

Lynn Doty, R. (1996) *Imperial Encounters: The Politics of Representation in North-South Relations*. Minneapolis: University of Minnesota Press.

MacCormick, J. (1996) *The European Union: Politics and Policies*. Boulder: Westview Press.

Macedo, S. (2007) The moral dilemma of U.S. immigration policy: open borders versus social justice? In: C. M. Swain (ed.), *Debating Immigration*. New York: Cambridge University Press, pp. 63–84.

Macedo, S. (2010) When and why should liberal democracies restrict immigration. In: R. Smith et al. (eds) *Citizens, Borders, and Human Needs*. Philadelphia: University of Pennsylvania Press.

Machiavelli, N. (1513) *The Prince*, R. Price & Q. Skinner (eds). Cambridge: Cambridge University Press.

MacIntyre, A. (1981) *After Virtue*. London: Duckworth.

MacKinnon, C. (2006) *Are Women Human? And Other International Dialogues*. Cambridge: Harvard University Press.

Macleod, A. (2006) Rawls's narrow doctrine of human rights. In: R. Martin & D. Reidy (eds) *Rawls's Law of Peoples: A Realistic Utopia?* Oxford: Blackwell, pp. 134–49.

MacQueen, N. (2006) *Peacekeeping and the International System*. London: Routledge.

Mahmood, S. (2005) *The Politics of Piety: The Islamic Revival and the Feminist Subject*. Princeton: Princeton University Press.

March, A. (2009a) What is comparative political theory? *Review of Politics*, 71(4):531–65.

March, A. (2009b) *Islam and Liberal Citizenship: The Search for an Overlapping Consensus*. Oxford: Oxford University Press.

Margalit, A., & Raz, J. (1990) National self-determination. *Journal of Philosophy*, 87(9):439–61.

Mariátegui, J. (1988) *Seven Interpretive Essays on Peruvian Reality*. Austin: University of Texas Press.

Marighela, C. (1971) Handbook of urban guerrilla warfare. In: C. Marighela (ed.) *For the Liberation of Brazil*, transl. J. Butt & R. Sheed. Harmondsworth: Penguin.

Marshall, T.H. (1950) Citizenship and social class. In: T.H. Marshall (ed.) *Citizenship and Social Class and Other Essays*. Cambridge: Cambridge University Press.

Martin, R., & Reidy, D. (eds) (2006) *Rawls's Law of Peoples: A Realistic Utopia?* Oxford: Blackwell.

Marx, K. (1981[1859]) *A Contribution to the Critique of Political Economy*. London: Lawrence & Wishart.

Marx, K. (1998) *The German Ideology Including Theses on Feuerbach*. New York: Prometheus Books.

Marx, K. (2002) *The Communist Manifesto*, ed. G. Stedman Jones. London: Penguin.

Mason, A. (2004) Just constraints. *British Journal of Political Science*, 34:251–68.

Massing, M. (2007) Iraq: the hidden human costs. *New York Review*, Dec. 20:82–7.

May, L. (2007) *War Crimes and Just War*. Cambridge: Cambridge University Press.

May, L. (2008) *Aggression and Crimes against Peace*. Cambridge: Cambridge University Press.

May, R. (1996) *Heidegger's Hidden Sources: East Asian Influences on His Work*, transl. G. Parkes. London: Routledge.

Mayall, J. (2000) *World Politics: Progress and its Limits*. Cambridge: Polity.

Mayer, J. (2008) *The Dark Side: The Inside Story of How the War on Terror Turned into a War on American Ideals*. New York: Doubleday.

McAllister, P. (1982) Introduction. In: P. McAllister (ed.), *Reweaving the Web of Life: Feminism and Nonviolence*. Philadelphia: New Society, pp. i–vii.

McCarthy, T. (1991) *Ideals and Illusions: On Reconstruction and Deconstruction in Contemporary Critical Theory*. Cambridge: MIT Press.

McClintock, A. (1992) The angel of progress: pitfalls of the term 'post-colonialism'. *Social Text*, 31(2):1–15.

McCorquodale, R. (2001) International law, boundaries, and imagination. In: D. Miller and S.H. Hashmi (eds), *Boundaries and Justice: Diverse Ethical Perspectives*. Princeton: Princeton University Press, pp. 136–173.

McCurdy, H. (2001) Africville: environmental racism. In: L. Westra and B. Lawson (ed.) *Faces of Environmental Racism: Confronting Issues of Global Justice*. Lanham: Rowman & Littlefield, pp. 95–112.

McMahan, J. (2009) *Killing in War*. Oxford: Oxford University Press.

Meadows, D., Randers, J., & Behrens, W. (1972) *The Limits to Growth: A Report for the Club of Rome's Project on the Predicament of Mankind*. London: Pan.

Mearsheimer, J. (2001) *The Tragedy of Great Power Politics*. New York: Norton.

Mehta, U.S. (1999) *Liberalism and Empire: A Study in Nineteenth-Century British Liberal Thought*. Chicago: University of Chicago Press.

Meinecke, F. (1957) *Machiavellianism: The Doctrine of 'Raison d'Etat' and its Place in Modern History*, transl. D. Scott. London: Routledge.

Meisels, T. (2008) Torture and the problem of dirty hands. *Canadian Journal of Law and Jurisprudence*, 21:149–73.

Meloni, A. (2006) *Visa Policy within the European Union Structure*. Heidelberg: Springer.

Mill, J.S. (1866) *Principles of Political Economy with some of their Applications to Social Philosophy*. London: Longmans.

Mill, J.S. (1984 [1859]) A few words on non-intervention. In: J. Robson (ed.) *The Collected Works of John Stuart Mill*, Vol. 21. Toronto: University of Toronto Press, pp. 109–24.

Miller, D. (1995) *On Nationality*. Oxford: Oxford University Press.

Miller, D. (1998a) The limits of cosmopolitan justice. In: D. Mapel & T. Nardin (eds) *International Society: Diverse Ethical Perspectives*. Princeton: Princeton University Press, pp. 164–82.

Miller, D. (2000) *Citizenship and National Identity*. Cambridge: Polity Press.

Miller, D. (2005) Immigration: the case for limits. In: A. I. Cohen & C. H. Wellman (eds), *Contemporary Debates in Applied Ethics*. Oxford: Blackwell, pp. 193–206.

Miller, D. (2007) *National Responsibility and Global Justice*. Oxford: Oxford University Press.

Miller, D., & Hashmi, S. H. (eds) (2001) *Boundaries and Justice: Diverse Ethical Perspectives*. Princeton: Princeton University Press.

Miller, R. (1998b) Cosmopolitan respect and patriotic concern. *Philosophy & Public Affairs*, 27(3):202–24.

Miller, R. (2004) Beneficence, duty and distance. *Philosophy & Public Affairs*, 32(4):357–83.

Mills, C., & Pateman, C. (2007) *Contract and Domination*. Cambridge: Polity.

Mills, C. (2005) 'Ideal theory' as ideology. *Hypatia*, 20(3):165–84.

Moellendorf, D. (2002) *Cosmopolitan Justice*. Boulder: Westview Press.

Moellendorf, D. (2006) Equal respect and global egalitarianism. *Social Theory and Practice*, 32:601–16.

Mohanty, C.T. (2003) *Feminism without Borders: Decolonizing Theory, Practicing Solidarity*. Durham: Duke University Press.

Mohanty, C.T., Russo, A., and Lourdes T. (eds) (1991) *Third World Women and the Politics of Feminism*. Indianapolis: Indiana University Press.

Mol, A., & Sonnenfeld, A. (2000) Ecological modernisation around the world: an introduction. *Environmental Politics*, 9(Special Issue):1–14.

Mommsen, W. (1984) *Max Weber and German Politics, 1980–1920*, transl. M. Steinberg. Chicago: University of Chicago Press.

Moore, G.E. (1925) A defence of common sense. In: J. H. Muirhead (eds), *Contemporary British Philosophy*, 2nd series. New York: Macmillan, pp. 191–225.

Moore, M. (2001) *The Ethics of Nationalism*, Oxford: Oxford University Press.

Morgenthau, H. (1946) *Scientific Man versus Power Politics*. Chicago: University of Chicago Press.

Morgenthau, H. (1948) *Politics among Nations: The Search for Power and Peace*. New York: Knopf.

Morgenthau, H. (1952) *In Defense of the National Interest*. London: Methuen.

Morgenthau, H. (1962) *The Purpose of American Politics*. New York: Knopf.

Morgenthau, H. (1978) An intellectual autobiography. *Society*, 15:63–8.

Morgenthau, H. (1985) *Politics among Nations: The Struggle for Power and Peace*, 6th edn. New York: Knopf.

Mouffe, C. (1999) Deliberative democracy or agonistic pluralism. *Social Research*, 66:745–58.

Mueller-Doohm, S. (2004) *Adorno: A Biography*. Cambridge: Polity Press.

Murphy, C. (2001) Critical theory and the democratic impulse: understanding a century-old tradition. In: R. Wyn Jones (ed.), *Critical Theory and World Politics*. Boulder: Lynne Rienner, pp. 61–78.

Muthu, S. (2003) *Enlightenment Against Empire*. Princeton: Princeton University Press.

Mutua, M. (2001) Savages, victims and saviors: the metaphor of human rights. *Harvard International Law Journal*, 42: 201–34.

Nabulsi, K. (1999) *Traditions of War: Occupation, Resistance, and the Law*. Oxford: Oxford University Press.

Naess, A. (1973) The shallow and the deep, long-range ecology movement: a summary. *Inquiry*, 16:95–100.

Nagel, T. (2005) The problem of global justice. *Philosophy & Public Affairs*, 33:113–47.

Nagel, T., Cohen, M., & Scanlon, T. (eds) (1985) *Equality and Preferential Treatment*. Princeton: Princeton University Press.

Nardin, T. (1983) *Law, Morality and the Relations of States*. Princeton: Princeton University Press.

Nardin, T. (2005) Justice and coercion. In: A. Bellamy (ed.), *International Society and its Critics*. Oxford: Oxford University Press, pp. 247–63.

Nardin, T. (2006) Introduction. In: T. Nardin & M. Williams (eds), *Humanitarian Intervention*. New York: NYU Press, pp. 1–4.

Nasr, K. (1997) *Arab and Israeli Terrorism*. Jefferson: McFarland.

Näsström, S. (2007) The legitimacy of the people. *Political Theory*, 35:624–58.

Neiman, S. (2002) *Evil in Modern Thought: An Alternative History of Philosophy*. Princeton: Princeton University Press.

Netanyahu, B. (ed.) (1986) *Terrorism: How the West Can Win*. New York: Farrar, Straus, and Giroux.

Ngugi wa'Thiong'o (2005) *Petals of Blood*. New York: Penguin Classics.

Nickel, J. (2007) *Making Sense of Human Rights*. Oxford: Blackwell.

Nietzsche, F. (1989) *Beyond Good and Evil: Prelude to a Philosophy of the Future*. New York: Vintage.

Nijman, J. (2004) *The Concept of International Legal Personality: An Inquiry into the History and Theory of International Law*. The Hague: Asser Press.

Nkrumah, K. (1966) *Neo-Colonialism: The Last Stage of Imperialism*. New York: International Publishers.

Noddings, N. (1984) *Caring: A Feminine Approach to Ethics and Moral Education*. Berkeley: University of California Press.

Nozick, R. (1974) *Anarchy, State and Utopia*. New York: Basic Books.

Nussbaum, M. (1997) *Cultivating Humanity: A Classical Defense of Reform in Liberal Education*. Cambridge: Harvard University Press.

Nussbaum, M. (2000) *Women and Human Development*. Cambridge: Cambridge University Press.

Nussbaum, M. (2006) *The Frontiers of Justice: Disability, Nationality, Species Membership*. Cambridge: Harvard University Press.

Nussbaum, M. et al. (1996) *For Love of Country*, J. Cohen ed. Boston: Beacon Press.

Oakeshott, M. (1962) *Rationalism in Politics*. London: Methuen.

O'Connor, J. (1998) *Natural Causes: Essays in Ecological Marxism*. New York: Guilford Press.

O'Donovan, O. (2003) *The Just War Revisited*. Cambridge: Cambridge University Press.

Odysseos, L., & Petito, F. (eds) (2007) *The International Political Thought of Carl Schmitt: Terror, Liberal War and the Crisis of Global Order*. London: Routledge.

Okin, S. (1989) *Justice, Gender and the Family*. New York: Basic Books.

Okin, S. (1994) Gender inequality and cultural differences. *Political Theory*, 22:5–24.

Oksala, J. (2005) *Foucault on Freedom*. Cambridge: Cambridge University Press.

O'Neill, O. (1986) *Faces of Hunger: An Essay on Poverty, Justice, and Development*. London: Allen & Unwin.

O'Neill, O. (1996) *Towards Justice and Virtue: A Constructive Account of Practical Reasoning*. Cambridge: Cambridge University Press.

O'Neill, O. (2000) *Bounds of Justice*. Cambridge: Cambridge University Press.

Ong, A. (2000) *Flexible Citizenship: The Cultural Logics of Transnationality*. Durham: Duke University Press.

Onuf, N. (1989) *World of Our Making: Rules and Rule in Social Theory and International Relations*. Columbus: University of South Carolina Press.

Ophuls, W. (1977) *Ecology and the Politics of Scarcity*. San Francisco: W. H. Freeman.

Orend, B. (2002) Justice after war. *Ethics and International Affairs*, 16:43–56.

Orford, A. (2003) *Reading Humanitarian Intervention: Human Rights and the Use of Force in International Law*. Cambridge: Cambridge University Press.

Orwell, G. (1994) *Essays*. London: Penguin.

Osborn, R. (2009) Noam Chomsky and the realist tradition. *Review of International Studies*, 35:351–70.

Pagden, A. (2003) Human rights, natural rights and Europe's imperial legacy. *Political Theory*, 31:171–99.

Page, E. (2006) *Climate Change, Justice, and Future Generations*. Cheltenham: Edward Elgar.

Pangalangan, R. (2001) Territorial sovereignty: command, title, and the expanding claims of the commons. In D. Miller & S. H. Hashmi (eds) *Boundaries and Justice: Diverse Ethical Perspectives*. Princeton: Princeton University Press, pp. 164–82.

Pape, R. (2005) *Dying to Win: The Strategic Logic of Suicide Terrorism*, New York: Random House.

Parekh, B. (1989) *Ghandi's Political Philosophy: A Critical Examination*. Basingstoke: Macmillan.

Parekh, B. (1990) *Colonialism, Tradition, and Reform: An Analysis of Gandhi's Political Discourse*. New Delhi: Sage Publications.

Parekh, B. (1996) Political theory: traditions in political philosophy. In: R. Goodin & H-D. Klingemann (eds), *A New Handbook of Political Science*. Oxford: Oxford University Press, pp. 503–19.

Parfit, D. (1984) *Reasons and Persons*. Oxford: Oxford University Press.

Parfit, D. (1997) Equality and partiality. *Ratio*, 10(3):202–21.

Parrish, J. (2007) *Paradoxes of Political Ethics: From Dirty Hands to the Invisible Hand*. Cambridge: Cambridge University Press.

Pateman, C. (1988) *The Sexual Contract*. Stanford: Stanford University Press.

Patten, A. (1999) The autonomy argument for liberal nationalism. *Nations and Nationalism*, 5:1–17.

Patten, A. (2004) Should we stop thinking about poverty in terms of helping the poor? *Ethics & International Affairs*, 19:9–27.

Payne, R. (2007) Neorealists as critical theorists: the purpose of foreign policy debate. *Perspectives on Politics*, 5:503–14.

Perry, S. (1995) Immigration, justice, and culture. In: W. F. Schwartz (ed.), *Justice in Immigration*. Cambridge: Cambridge University Press, pp. 94–135.

Peterson, V.S. (1990) Whose rights? A critique of the 'givens' in human rights discourse. *Alternatives*, 15:303–44.

Pettit, P. (1997) *Republicanism: A Theory of Freedom and Government*. Oxford: Clarendon Press.

Pettit, P. (2010) A republican law of peoples. *European Journal of Political Theory*, 9(1):70–94 .

Pevnick, R. (2008a) Political coercion and the scope of distributive justice. *Political Studies*, 56:399–413.

Pevnick, R. (2009) Social trust and the ethics of immigration policy. *Journal of Political Philosophy*, 17:146–67.

Philpott, D. (2001) *Revolutions in Sovereignty: How Ideas Shaped Modern International Relations*. Princeton: Princeton University Press.

Pitts, J. (2005) *A Turn To Empire: The Rise of Imperial Liberalism in Britain and France*. Princeton: Princeton University Press.

Plant, J. (1991) Women and nature. In: A. Dobson (ed.), *The Green Reader*. London: André Deutsch, pp. 100–3.

Plutarch (2000) On exile. In: P. H. de Lacy & B. Einarson (eds), *Moralia: Volume VII*. Cambridge: Harvard University Press, pp. 511–71.

Pogge, T. (1989) *Realizing Rawls*. Ithaca: Cornell University Press.

Pogge, T. (1992) Cosmopolitanism and sovereignty. *Ethics*, 103:48–75.

Pogge, T. (2002) *World Poverty and Human Rights*. Cambridge: Polity Press.

Pogge, T. (2008) *World Poverty and Human Rights: Cosmopolitan Responsibilities and Reforms*, 2nd edn. Cambridge: Polity.

Price, R. (ed.) (2008) *Moral Limit and Possibility in World Politics*. Cambridge: Cambridge University Press.

Primoratz, I (1997) The morality of terrorism. *Journal of Applied Philosophy*, 14(33):221–33.

Primoratz, I (ed.) (2004) *Terrorism: The Philosophical Issues*. New York: Palgrave.

Quinton, A. (1989) *Utilitarian Ethics,* 2nd edn. London: Duckworth.

Radkau, J. (2009) *Max Weber: A Biography*. Cambridge: Polity.

Raj, K.V. (2006) Paradoxes on the borders of Europe. *International Feminist Journal of Politics*, 8:512–34.

Ramsey, P. (2002) [1968] *The Just War: Force and Political Responsibility*. Lanham: Rowman & Littlefield.

Rashid, A. (2009) *Descent into Chaos: The United States and the Failure of Nation Building in Pakistan, Afghanistan, and Central Asia*. London: Penguin.

Ratha, D., Mohapatra, S., & Xu, Z (2008) Outlook for remittance flows 2008–2010. *Migration and Development Brief* 8 (Nov 11). Available at: http://siteresources.worldbank.org/INTPROSPECTS/Resources/334934-1110315015165/MD_Brief8.pdf (accessed August 2009).

Rawls, J. (1971) *A Theory of Justice*. Oxford: Oxford University Press.

Rawls, J. (1975/2009) The independence of moral theory. In S. Freeman (ed.), *Rawls (1999) Collected Papers*. Cambridge: Harvard University Press, pp. 286–302.

Rawls, J. (1993) *Political Liberalism*. New York: Columbia University Press.

Rawls, J. (1999) *The Law of Peoples*. Cambridge: Harvard University Press.

Rawls, J. (2001a) In: E. Kelly (ed.), *Justice as Fairness: A Restatement*. Cambridge: Belknap Press.

Rawls, J. (2001b) *The Law of Peoples with 'The Idea of Public Reason Revisited'*. Cambridge: Harvard University Press.

Raz, J. (1986) *The Morality of Freedom*. Oxford: Oxford University Press.

Rejali, D. (2008) *Torture and Democracy*. Princeton: Princeton University Press.

Rengger, N. (2002) On the just war tradition in the twenty-first century. *International Affairs*, 78:353–63.

Rengger, N. (2008a) The *jus in bello* in philosophical and historical perspective. In: L. May (ed.), *War: Essays in Political Philosophy*. Cambridge: Cambridge University Press.

Rengger, N. (2008b) The great treason? On the subtle temptations of preventive war. *International Affairs*, 84:949–61.

Reus-Smit, C., & Snidal, D. (2008b) Between Utopia and reality: the practical discourses of international relations. In: C. Reus-Smit & D. Snidal (eds), *The Oxford Handbook of International Relations*. Oxford: Oxford University Press, pp. 3–40.

Richardson, H. (2002) *Democratic Autonomy: Public Reasoning and the Ends of Policy*. Oxford: Oxford University Press.

Richardson, L. (2006) *What Terrorists Want: Understanding the Enemy, Containing the Threat*. New York: Random House.

Rieff, D. (2005) *At the Point of a Gun: Democratic Dreams and Armed Intervention*. New York: Simon & Schuster.

Risse, M. (2005a) What we owe the global poor. *Journal of Ethics*, 9:81–117.

Risse, M. (2005b) How does the global order harm the poor? *Philosophy & Public Affairs*, 33(4):349–76.

Roberson, B. (ed.) (1998) *International Society and the Development of International Relations Theory*. London: Pinter.

Robinson, F. (1999) *Globalizing Care: Ethics, Feminist Theory, and International Affairs*. Boulder: Westview Press.

Robinson, F. (2003) Human rights and the global politics of resistance: feminist perspectives. *Review of International Studies*, Special Issue, 29:161–80.

Rodin, D. (2002) *War and Self Defence*. Oxford: Oxford University Press.

Rodin, D. (2004) Terrorism without intention. *Ethics*, 114:752–71.

Rose, N., O'Malley, P., & Valverde, M. (2006) Governmentality. *Annual Review of Law and Social Science*, 2:83–104.

Rosen, F. (2006) *Classical Utilitarianism from Hume to Mill*. London: Routledge.

Rosenberg, S. (ed.) (2007) *Deliberation, Participation and Democracy: Can the People Govern?* Basingstoke: Palgrave.

Rosenthal, J. (1991) *Righteous Realists: Political Realism, Responsible Power, and American Culture in the Nuclear Age*. Baton Rouge: Louisiana State University Press.

Rothbard, M. (1977) Robert Nozick and the immaculate conception of the state. *Journal of Libertarian Studies*, 1:45–57.

Rousseau, J-J. (1762) *The Social Contract and Other Later Political Writings*, Victor Gourevitch (ed.). Cambridge: Cambridge University Press.

Ruddick, S. (1989) *Maternal Thinking: Towards a Politics of Peace*. London: Women's Press.

Ruddick, S. (1993) Notes towards a feminist peace politics. In: M. Cooke & A. Wollacott (eds), *Gendering War Talk*. Princeton: Princeton University Press, pp. 109–27.

Runciman, D. (2001) The history of political thought: the state of the discipline. *British Journal of Politics and International Relations*, 3(4):84–104.

Runciman, D. (2006) *The Politics of Good Intentions: History, Fear, and Hypocrisy in the New World Order*. Princeton: Princeton University Press.

Runciman, D., & Brito Vieira, M. (2008) *Representation*. Cambridge: Polity.

Russett, B. (1993) *Grasping the Democratic Peace: Principles for a Post-Cold War World*. Princeton: Princeton University Press.

Ryle, G. (1949) *The Concept of Mind*. London: Hutchinson.

Rynard, P., & Shugarman, D. (eds) (2000) *Cruelty and Deception: The Controversy over Dirty Hands in Politics*. Peterborough, Ontario: Broadview Press.

Said, E. (1979) *Orientalism*. New York: Vintage.

Said, E. (1981) *Covering Islam: How the Media and the Experts Determine How We See the Rest of the World*. New York: Vintage.

Said, E. (1985) Orientalism reconsidered. *Race and Class*, 27(2):1–16.

Sakai, N. (1997) *Translation and Subjectivity: On Japan and Cultural Nationalism*. Minneapolis: University of Minnesota Press.

Sakai, N., & Harootunian, H. (1999) Japan studies and cultural studies. *Positions: East Asia Cultures Critique*, 7:593–647.

Sandel, M. (1982) *Liberalism and the Limits of Justice*. Cambridge: Cambridge University Press.

Sands, P. (2003) *Principles of International Environmental Law*. Cambridge: Cambridge University Press.

Sands, P. (2008) *Torture Team: Rumsfeld's Memo and the Betrayal of American Values*. New York: Palgrave.

Sangiovanni, A. (2007) Global justice, reciprocity, and the state. *Philosophy & Public Affairs*, 35:3–39.

Sangiovanni, A. (2009) Normative political theory: a flight from reality? In: D. Bell (ed.), *Political Thought and International Relations: Variations on a Realist Theme*. Oxford: Oxford University Press, pp. 219–40.

Scanlan, J., & Kent, O. (1988) The force of moral arguments for a just immigration policy in a Hobbesian universe: the contemporary American example. In: M. Gibney (ed.), *Open Borders? Closed Societies? The Ethical and Political Issues*. New York: Greenwood Press, pp. 61–107.

Scanlon, T.M. (1975) Rawls's theory of justice. In: N. Daniels (ed.), *Reading Rawls*. New York: Basic Books, pp. 169–205.

Scheffler, S. (1982) *The Rejection of Consequentialism: A Philosophical Investigation of the Considerations Underlying Rival Moral Conceptions*. Oxford: Oxford University Press.

Scheffler, S. (ed.) (1988) *Consequentialism and its Critics*. Oxford: Oxford University Press.

Scheffler, S. (2001) *Boundaries and Allegiances: Problems of Justice and Responsibility in Liberal Thought*. Oxford: Oxford University Press.

Scheuerman, W. (2009) *Morgenthau*. Cambridge: Polity.

Schlereth, T. J. (1977) *The Cosmopolitan Ideal in Enlightenment Thought: Its Form and Function in the Ideas of Franklin, Hume, and Voltaire 1694–1790*. South Bend: University of Notre Dame Press.

Schlosberg, D. (1999) *Environmental Justice and the New Pluralism: The Challenge of Difference for Environmentalism*. Oxford: Oxford University Press.

Schmidt, B. (1998) *The Political Discourse of Anarchy: A Disciplinary History of International Relations*. Albany: SUNY Press.

Schmidt, B., & Williams, M. (2008) The Bush doctrine and the Iraq war: neoconservatives versus realists. *Security Studies*, 17:191–220.

Schmitt, C. (1996) *The Concept of the Political*, transl. J. H. Lomax. Chicago: University of Chicago Press.

Schmitt, C. (2003) *The Nomos of the Earth in the International Law of the Jus Publicum Europaeum*, transl. G. L. Ulmen. New York: Telos.

Schmitt, C. (2004) *The Theory of the Partisan: A Commentary/Remark on the Concept of the Political*, transl. A. C. Goodson. East Lansing: MSU Press.

Schmitter, P. (1998) Is it possible to democratize the Europolity? In: A. Follesdal & P. Koslowski (eds), *Democracy and the European Union*. Berlin: Springer Verlag, pp. 13–36.

Schofield, P. (2006) *Utility and Democracy: The Political Thought of Jeremy Bentham*. Oxford: Oxford University Press.

Schott, R.M. (2008) Just war and the problem of evil. *Hypatia*, 23:122–40.

Schumpeter, J. (1947) *Capitalism, Socialism and Democracy*. New York: Harper Collins.

Sebald, W.G. (2003) *On the Natural History of Destruction*. New York: Random House.

Sen, A., (1981) Equality of what? In: S. M. McMurrin (ed.), *The Tanner Lectures on Human Values*. Salt Lake City: University of Utah Press, pp. 197–220.

Sen, A.A. (1982) *Poverty and Famines: An Essay on Entitlement and Deprivation*. Oxford: Oxford University Press.

Sen, A. (2009) *The Idea of Justice*. Cambridge: Harvard University Press.

Seneca, L.A. (2001a) On leisure. In: *Moral Essays: Volume II*, transl. J. Basore. Cambridge: Harvard University Press, pp. 180–201.

Seneca, L.A. (2001b) To Helvia his mother on consolation. In: *Moral Essays: Volume II*, transl. John W. Basore. Cambridge: Harvard University Press, pp. 416–89.

Shapiro, I. (2007) *Containment: Rebuilding a Strategy Against Global Terror*. Princeton: Princeton University Press.

Sharp, G. (2005) *Waging Nonviolent Struggle: 20th Century Practice and 21st Century Potential*. Manchester: Extending Horizons Books.

Shaw, J. (1999) The interpretation of European citizenship. *Modern Law Review*, 40:293–318.

Shearmur, J. (1996) *Hayek and After: Hayekian Liberalism as a Research Programme*. London: Routledge.

Sher, G. (1997) *Beyond Neutrality: Perfectionism and Politics*. Cambridge: Cambridge University Press.

Shklar, J. (1989) The liberalism of fear. In: N. Rosenblum (ed.), *Liberalism and the Moral Life*. Cambridge: Harvard University Press, pp. 21–38.

Shrader-Frechette, K. (2002) *Environmental Justice: Creating Equality, Reclaiming Democracy*. Oxford: Oxford University Press.

Shue, H. (1980) *Basic Rights: Subsistence, Affluence, and U.S. Foreign Policy*. Princeton: Princeton University Press.

Shue, H. (1996) *Basic Rights: Subsistence, Affluence and U.S. Foreign Policy*, 2nd edn. Princeton: Princeton University Press.

Shy, J., & Collier, T.W. (1986) Revolutionary war. In: P. Paret (ed.), *Makers of Modern Strategy: From Machiavelli to the Nuclear Age*. Princeton: Princeton University Press, pp. 815–62.

Simmons, A.J. (1979) *Moral Principles and Political Obligation*. Princeton: Princeton University Press.

Simmons, A.J. (2007) *Political Philosophy*. Oxford: Oxford University Press.

Simmons, A.J. et al. (1995) *Punishment*. Princeton: Princeton University Press.

Simpson, G. (2004) *Great Powers and Outlaw States*. Cambridge: Cambridge University Press.

Singer, P. (1972) Famine, affluence, and morality. *Philosophy & Public Affairs*, 1:229–43

Singer, P. (2002) *One World: The Ethics of Globalization*. New Haven: Yale University Press.

Sjoberg, L. (2006) *Gender, Justice and the Wars in Iraq: A Feminist Reformulation of Just War Theory*. Lanham: Rowman & Littlefield.

Sjoberg, L., & Gentry, C. (2008) Reduced to bad sex: narratives of violent women from the Bible to the war on terror. *International Relations*, 22:5–23.

Skinner, Q. (1978) *The Foundations of Modern Political Thought*, 2 vols. Cambridge: Cambridge University Press.

Slater, J., & Nardin, T. (1986) Nonintervention and human rights. *Journal of Politics*, 48:86–96.

Slaughter, A-M. (2004) *A New World Order*. Princeton: Princeton University Press.

Smith, G. (2003) *Deliberative Democracy and the Environment*. London: Routledge.

Smith, M.J. (1986) *Realist Thought from Weber to Kissinger*. Baton Rouge: Louisiana State University Press.

Smith, M.J. (1989) Ethics and intervention. *Ethics & International Affairs*, 3:1–26.

Smith, M.J. (1997) Growing up with *Just and Unjust Wars*: an appreciation. *Ethics and International Affairs,* 11:3–18.

Smith, S. (2007) Diversity and disciplinarity in international relations theory. In: T. Dunne, M. Kurki, & S. Smith, S. (eds), *International Relations Theories: Discipline and Diversity*. Oxford: Oxford University Press, pp. 1–13.

Snyder, A.C. (2003) *Setting the Agenda for Global Peace: Conflict and Consensus Building*. Aldershot: Ashgate.

Snyder, J., & Vinjamuri, L. (2004) Trials and errors: principles and pragmatism in strategies of international justice. *International Security*, 28(3):5–44.

Soames, S. (2003) *Philosophical Analysis in the Twentieth Century*. Princeton: Princeton University Press.

Spinner-Halev, J. (2007) From historic to enduring injustice. *Political Theory*, 35:574–97.

Spivak, G. (1994) Can the subaltern speak? In: P. Williams & L. Chrisman (eds), *Colonial Discourse and Post-Colonial Theory*. New York: Columbia University Press, pp. 66–112.

Spivak, G. (1999) *A Critique of Postcolonial Reason: Towards a History of the Vanishing Present*. Cambridge: Harvard University Press.

Stanski, K. (2009) 'So these folks are aggressive': an orientalist reading of US conceptions of 'Afghan warlords'. *Security Dialogue*, 40:73–94.

Stears, M. (2005) The vocation of political theory: principles, empirical inquiry and the politics of opportunity. *European Journal of Political Theory*, 4(4):325–50.

Sterling-Folker, J. (2005) *Making Sense of International Relations Theory*. Boulder: Lynne Rienner.

Stevenson, S.L. (1944) *Ethics and Language*. New Haven: Yale University Press.

Swift, A., & White, S. (2008) Political science, social science and real politics. In: D. Leopold & M. Stears (eds) *Political Theory: Methods and Approaches*. Oxford: Oxford University Press, pp. 49–69.

Sylvest, C. (2009) *British Liberal Internationalism, 1880–1930: Making Progress?* Manchester: Manchester University Press.

Tan, K-C. (2004) *Justice without Borders, Cosmopolitanism, Nationalism and Patriotism*. Cambridge: Cambridge University Press.

Tan, K-C. (2006) The boundary of justice, and the justice of boundaries. *Canadian Journal of Law and Jurisprudence*, 19:319–44.

Tan, K-C. (2010) Rights, institutions, and global justice. In A. Jagger (ed.), *Pogge and His Critics*. Cambridge: Polity.

Tasioulas, J. (2002) From Utopia to Kazanistan: John Rawls and the Law of Peoples, *Oxford Journal of Legal Studies*, 22:367–96.

Taylor, C. (1984) Philosophy and its history. In: R. Rorty, J. Schneewind, & Q. Skinner (eds), *Philosophy in History*. Cambridge: Cambridge University Press, pp. 17–30.

Taylor, C. (1985) Atomism. In: C. Taylor (ed.), *Philosophical Papers II*. Cambridge: Cambridge University Press, pp. 187–211.

Taylor, C. (1995) Cross-purposes: the liberal-communitarian debate. In: C. Taylor (ed.), *Philosophical Arguments*. Cambridge: Harvard University Press, pp. 181–204.

Taylor, C. (2007) *A Secular Age*. Cambridge: Harvard University Press.

Temkin, L. (2002) *Inequality*. Oxford: Oxford University Press.

Tesón, F. (1998) *A Philosophy of International Law*. Boulder: Westview Press.

Tesón, F. (2003) The liberal case for humanitarian intervention. In: J. Holzgrefe & R. Keohane (eds), *Humanitarian Intervention: Ethical, Legal and Political Dilemmas*. Cambridge: Cambridge University Press, pp. 93–129.

Tickner, J.A. (1999) Why women can't run the world: international politics according to Francis Fukuyama. *International Studies Review*, 1(3):3–11.

Tickner, A.B., & Waever, O. (eds) (2009) *International Relations Scholarship Around the World*. London: Routledge.

Tjalve, V.S. (2008) *Realist Strategies of Republican Peace: Niebuhr, Morgenthau, and the Politics of Patriotic Dissent*. Basingstoke: Palgrave.

Torpey, J. (2000) *The Invention of the Passport: Surveillance, Citizenship, and the State*. Cambridge: Cambridge University Press.

Tremain, S. (ed.) (2005) *Foucault and the Government of Disability*. Ann Arbor: University of Michigan Press.

Tronto, J. (1993) *Moral Boundaries: A Political Argument for an Ethic of Care*. New York: Routledge.

Tuck, R. (1979) *Natural Rights Theories: Their Origin and Development*. Cambridge: Cambridge University Press.

Tuck, R. (1994) Rights and pluralism. In: J. Tully (ed.), *Philosophy in an Age of Pluralism*. Cambridge: Cambridge University Press, pp. 159–70.

Tuck, R. (1998) *The Rights of War and Peace: Political Thought and the International Order from Grotius to Kant*. Oxford: Oxford University Press.

Tully, J. (1995) *Strange Multiplicity: Constitutionalism in an Age of Diversity*. Cambridge: Cambridge University Press.

Turner, R. (2008) *Neo-Liberalism: History Concepts and Policies*. Edinburgh: Edinburgh University Press.

Turner, S. (2009) Hans J. Morgenthau and the legacy of Max Weber. In: D. Bell (ed.), *Political Thought and International Relations: Variations on a Realist Theme*. Oxford: Oxford University Press, pp. 63–83.

United Nations (1987) *Report of the World Commission on Environment and Development*. New York: United Nations.

United Nations (1999a) *Report of the Independent Inquiry into the Actions of the United Nations during the 1994 Genocide in Rwanda*, United Nations Security Council Report S/1999/1257. New York: United Nations. Available at: http://daccessdds.un.org/doc/UNDOC/GEN/N99/395/47/IMG/N9939547.pdf?OpenElement (accessed August 2009).

United Nations (1999b) *Report of the Secretary General Pursuant to General Assembly Resolution 53/35*, United Nations General Assembly Report A/54/549. New York: United Nations. Available at: http://daccessdds.un.org/doc/UNDOC/GEN/N99/348/76/IMG/N9934876.pdf?OpenElement (accessed August 2009).

United Nations (2000) *Report of the Panel on United Nations Peace Operations*. New York: United Nations. Available at: http://www.un.org/peace/reports/peace_operations/ (accessed August 2009).

United Nations Department of Economic and Social Affairs (2001) *Replacement Migration: Is it a Solution to Declining and Ageing Populations?* New York: UN DESA, Population Division. Available at: http://www.un.org/esa/population/publications/migration/migration.htm (accessed August 2009).

United Nations Department of Economic and Social Affairs (2006) *Trends in Total Migrant Stock: The 2005 Revision*. New York: United Nations Department of Economic and Social Affairs, Population Division. Available at: http://esa.un.org/migration/ (accessed August 2009).

United Nations Department of Economic and Social Affairs (2007) *World Population Prospects: The 2006 Revision*. New York: United Nations Department of Economic and Social Affairs, Population Division. Available at: http://esa.un.org/unpp/

United Nations Development Programme (UNDP) (2008) *2008 Human Development Report: Fighting*

Climate Change: Human Solidarity in a Divided World. New York: UNDP.

United States Conference of Catholic Bishops (1993) *The Harvest of Peace is Sown in Justice*. Washington DC: USCCB Publishing.

Universal Declaration of Human Rights (1948) Available at: http://www.un.org/Overview/rights.html (accessed August 2009).

US Army (2009) *Human Terrain System*. Available at: http://humanterrainsystem.army.mil/overview.html (accessed August 2009).

US Department of State (1998) *Patterns of Global Terrorism: 1997*, Department of State Publication10321. Washington, DC: US Department of State.

US Government (2002) *National Security Strategy of the United States of America*. Available at: http://merln.ndu.edu/whitepapers/USnss2002.pdf (accessed August 2009).

Valls, A. (ed.) (2000) *Ethics in International Affairs: Theories and Cases*. Lanham: Rowman & Littlefield.

Vanderheiden, S. (2008) *Atmospheric Justice: A Political Theory of Climate Change*. Oxford: Oxford University Press.

Vattel, E., de (1758/2000) *The Law of Nations*, B. Kapossy & R. Whatmore (eds). Indianapolis: Liberty Fund.

Vincent, R. (1974) *Nonintervention in International Order*. Princeton: Princeton University Press.

Vincent, R. (1986) *Human Rights and International Relations*. Cambridge: Cambridge University Press.

Vitalis, R. (2000) The graceful and generous liberal gesture: making racism invisible in American international relations. *Millennium*, 29:331–56.

Vitoria, F., de (1991) *Political Writings* A. Pagden (ed.), Cambridge: Cambridge University Press.

Waldman, A. (2003) Masters of suicide bombing: Tamil guerrillas of Sri Lanka. *New York Times*, January 14, A16.

Waldron, J. (1992) Minority cultures and the cosmopolitan alternative. *University of Michigan Journal of Law Reform*, 25(3–4):751–93.

Waldron, J. (1999) *Law and Disagreement*. Oxford: Oxford University Press.

Waldron, J. (2000) What is cosmopolitanism? *Journal of Political Philosophy*, 8:227–43.

Walker, R.B.J. (1993) *Inside/Outside: International Relations as Political Theory*. Cambridge: Cambridge University Press.

Wall, D. (ed.) (1994) *Green History: A Reader in Environmental Literature, Philosophy, and Politics*. New York: Routledge.

Wall, S. (1998) *Liberalism, Perfectionism and Restraint*. Cambridge: Cambridge University Press.

Waltz, K. (1979) *Theory of International Politics*. Reading: Addison-Wesley.

Waltz, K. (2008) *Realism and International Politics*. London: Routledge.

Walzer, M. (1977) *Just and Unjust Wars: A Moral Argument with Historical Illustrations*. New York: Basic Books.

Walzer, M. (1980) The moral standing of states: a response to four critics. *Philosophy & Public Affairs*, 9(3):209–29.

Walzer, M. (1983) *Spheres of Justice: A Defense of Pluralism and Equality*. New York: Basic Books.

Walzer, M. (1987) *Interpretation and Social Criticism*. Cambridge: Harvard University Press.

Walzer, M. (1988) Emergency ethics. In: M. Walzer, *Arguing About War*. London: Yale University Press, pp. 33–51.

Walzer, M. (1989) Citizenship. In: T. Ball, J. Farr, & R. L. Hanson (eds), *Political Innovation and Conceptual Change*. Cambridge: Cambridge University Press, pp. 211–20.

Walzer, M. (1994) *Thick and Thin: Moral Argument at Home and Abroad*. Notre Dame: Notre Dame University Press.

Walzer, M. (2000) *Just and Unjust Wars: A Moral Argument with Historical Illustrations*, 3rd edn. New York: Basic Books.

Walzer, M. (2002) After 9/11: five questions about terrorism. In: M. Walzer, *Arguing About War*. London: Yale University Press, pp. 130–42.

Walzer, M. (2004) *Arguing about War*. London: Yale University Press.

Walzer, M. (2005) Emergency ethics. In: M. Walzer (ed.), *Arguing About War*. London: Yale University Press, pp. 33–51.

Walzer, M. (2007) Political action: the problem of dirty hands. In: M. Walzer, *Thinking Politically: Essays in Political Theory*, D. Miller (ed.). New Haven: Yale University Press, pp. 278–96.

Warren, M. (2008) Citizen representatives. In: M. Warren & H. Pearse (eds), *Designing Deliberative*

Democracy: The British Columbia Citizens' Assembly. Cambridge: Cambridge University Press, pp. 50–70.

Weale, A. (1999) *Democracy*. London: St. Martin's.

Weber, M. (1919/1984) The profession and vocation of politics. In: P. Lassman & R. Speirs (eds), *Political Writings*. Cambridge: Cambridge University Press, pp. 309–70.

Weber, M. (1919/1946) Politics as a vocation. In: H. H. Gerth and C. Wright Mills (eds), *From Max Weber: Essays in Sociology*. Oxford: Oxford University Press, pp. 77–128.

Weber, M. (1993) *The Protestant Ethic and the Spirit of Capitalism*. London: Routledge.

Weil, P. (1983) Towards relative normativity in international law. *American Journal of International Law*, 77:413–42.

Weldon, T.D. (1953) *The Vocabulary of Politics*. London: Penguin.

Wellek, R., & Warren, A. (1984) *Theory of Literature*. New York: Harcourt Brace.

Wellman, C.H. (2005) *A Theory of Secession: The Case for Political Self-Determination*. Cambridge: Cambridge University Press.

Wendt, A. (1999) *Social Theory of International Politics*. Cambridge: Cambridge University Press.

Westra, L. (1998) *Living in Integrity: A Global Ethic to Restore a Fragmented Earth*. Lanham: Rowman & Littlefield.

Wheeler, N. (2000) *Saving Strangers: Humanitarian Intervention in International Society*. Oxford: Oxford University Press.

Wheeler, N., & Dunne, T. (1996) Hedley Bull's pluralism of the intellect and solidarism of the will. *International Affairs*, 72:91–107.

Whelan, F. (1988) Citizenship and freedom of movement: an open admission policy? In: M. Gibney (ed.) *Open Borders? Closed Societies? The Ethical and Political Issues*. New York: Greenwood Press.

Wiggershaus, R. (1994) *The Frankfurt School: Its History, Theories, and Political Significance*. Cambridge: MIT Press.

Wight, M. (1966) Why is there no international theory. In: H. Butterfield & M. Wight (eds), *Diplomatic Investigations: Essays in the Theory of International Politics*. London: Allen & Unwin, pp. 17–34.

Williams, B. (1981) Internal and external reasons. In: B. Williams, *Moral Luck: Philosophical Papers 1973–80*, Cambridge: Cambridge University Press, pp. 101–13.

Williams, B. (2005a) *In the Beginning Was the Deed*, G. Hawthorn (ed.). Princeton: Princeton University Press.

Williams, B. (2005b) The liberalism of fear. *In the Beginning was the Deed*, G. Hawthorn (ed.). Princeton: Princeton University Press, pp. 52–62.

Williams, J. (2002) Territorial borders, toleration and the English School. *Review of International Studies*, 28:737–58.

Williams, M.C. (2005c) *The Realist Tradition and the Limits of International Relations*. Cambridge: Cambridge University Press.

Williams, M.C. (2005d) What is the national interest? The neoconservative challenge in international relations. *European Journal of International Relations*, 11:307–37.

Williams, M.C. (ed.) (2007) *Reconsidering Realism: The Legacy of Hans J. Morgenthau in International Relations*. Oxford: Oxford University Press.

Williamson, T. (2005) Past the linguistic turn. In: B. Leiter (ed.), *The Future for Philosophy*. Oxford: Oxford University Press, pp. 106–29.

Wines, M. (2002) Mourners at Israeli boys' funeral lament a conflict with no bounds. *New York Times*, December 2, A9.

Wittgenstein, L. (1958) *Philosophical Investigations*, transl. G. E. M. Anscombe. Oxford: Basil Blackwell.

Wohlforth, W. (2008) Realism. In: In: C. Reus-Smit & D. Snidal (eds), *The Oxford Handbook of International Relations*. Oxford: Oxford University Press, pp. 131–50.

Wolff, R. (1970) *In Defense of Anarchism*. New York: Harper.

Wolin, S. (2004) *Politics and Vision: Continuity and Innovation in Western Political Thought*, expanded edn. Princeton: Princeton University Press.

Wollstonecraft, M. (1992 [1792]) *A Vindication of the Rights of Woman*. Harmondsworth: Penguin.

Woodward, J. (1992) Commentary: liberalism and migration. In: B. Barry & R. E. Goodin (eds), *Free Movement: Ethical Issues in the Transnational*

Migration of People and of Money. University Park: Pennsylvania State University Press, pp. 59–84.

World Health Organization (WHO) (2003) *Climate Change and Human Health—Risks and Responses,* A.J. McMichaele et al. (eds). Geneva: WHO.

World Health Organization (WHO) (2005) *Climate and Health: Fact Sheet,* July 2005. Geneva: WHO. Available at: http://www.who.int/global-change/news/fsclimandhealth/en/index.html (accessed August 2009).

Worster, D. (1994) *Nature's Economy: A History of Ecological Ideas.* Cambridge: Cambridge University Press.

Wright, L. (2007) *The Looming Tower: Al Qaeda's Road to 9/11.* New York: Allen Lane.

Young, I.M. (1990a) *Justice and the Politics of Difference.* Princeton: Princeton University Press.

Young, I.M. (2002) *Inclusion and Democracy.* Oxford: Oxford University Press.

Young, I.M. (2007) *Global Challenges: War, Self-Determination and Responsibility for Justice.* Cambridge: Polity Press.

Young, R. (1990b) *White Mythologies: Writing History and the West.* London: Routledge.

Young, R. (2001) *Postcolonialism: An Historical Introduction.* Oxford: Blackwell.

Zehfuss, M. (2002) *Constructivism in International Relations: The Politics of Reality.* Cambridge: Cambridge University Press.

Zehfuss, M. (2007) *Wounds of Memory: The Politics of War in Germany.* Cambridge: Cambridge University Press.

Zerzan, J. (ed.) (2005) *Against Civilization: Readings and Reflections.* Los Angeles: Feral House.

■ INDEX

North Atlantic Treaty
    Organization (NATO)
    intervention in Kosovo 329,
    335–6
Northern Alliance 305
Northern Ireland
    status of 286
Nozick, Robert [1938–2002] 27,
    76–7, 80
nuclear deterrence 300
Nuclear tests case (ICJ) (1974) 284
nuclear weapons 20, 95
Nussbaum, Martha 153, 157,
    170–1, 177–8

O

Oakeshott, Michael Joseph
    [1901–90] 80, 82, 119
obligations erga omnes 281
O'Donovan, Oliver 293, 299,
    306
Okin, Susan Moller 169
O'Neill, Onora 152, 244
open borders 30
    critics of 366
    cultural change 370
    democratic
        republicanism 370–2
    economic collapse and 368–9
    liberal arguments for 365–8
    self-determination 370
    social rights 369–70
    welfare strain 369
Open Method of Coordination
    (OMC) 389
Operation Desert Storm 97
Ophuls, William 184
Orford, Anne 328
Orientalism 203–7, 317
original position (Rawls) 23, 31,
    47, 121, 139, 169
Owens, Patricia 14

P

pacifism 165, 173, 177, 293,
    294, 311–2
Page, Ed 194
Paine, Thomas [1737–1809] 147
Pakistan 280
Palestine 280, 348, 350
passports 359, 362
Pateman, Carole 10
patriarchy 170, 174, 188, 207,
    208,315

patriotism 2, 123, 136, 225,
    261–4, 361, 371, 381
peace building 167, 328
    women and 315
peacekeeping 329–31
Pearson, Lester Bowles
    [1897–1972] 330
Peloponnesian War 294
peoples
    basic unit of global order
        386
    Rawls' law of 121–4
perfectionism 29
performative contradiction 69
Permanent Court of International
    Justice (PCIJ) 283
Plato [BC 428/427–348/347] 20,
    63, 73
pluralism 46, 118–21, 334, 383
Plutarch [46–120] 147, 156
Pogge, Thomas 9, 146, 149, 153,
    158, 244, 259–60
Pol Pot [1928–98] 240
political violence
    terrorism distinguished 346
    understanding 81–4
polluter pays principle 195
post-colonialism 7, 56, 60, 95,
    200–16, 224
    contemporary issues 214–5
    definition 202
    international law 284
    nomenclature 201–2
    war and 316–8
post-structuralism 5, 24, 48,
    54–70, 95, 105, 165, 175–8,
    203, 206, 209, 224, 283, 317,
    332
    structuralism distinguished
        55
poverty 1, 4, 125–7, 256–71
    alleviation of 2, 30
    causes of 125
    extreme 257
pre-emption
    prevention distinguished 303
pre-emptive attacks 277
prevention
    pre-emption distinguished 303
preventive war 302
    just war and 319–21
prioritarianism 27, 141
problem of dirty hands 95
prostitution 316
psychoanalysis 54
Pythagoreans 62

Q

quasi-failed states 280
Quebec 134

R

racism 10, 204, 242, 315
radical feminism 167
raison d'etat 293 see also realism
Ramsey, Paul [1913–88] 299
rational choice 47, 80
Rawls, John Bordley [1921–2002]
    5, 8, 10, 13, 22–3, 50, 74–8,
    82, 115–6, 125–6, 131–3,
    152–3, 169, 261–2, 264,
    385
    difference principle 25, 125,
        132, 152, 261, 270
    humanitarian intervention 334
    ideal/non-ideal theory 8, 10,
        40, 75
    law of peoples 78, 121–7,
        132–3, 153–4, 265, 334
    liberal political theory
        of 36
    non-foundationalism 23–6
    original position 23, 25–6, 31,
        47, 385
    political philosophy
        after 26–33
    realistic utopia 75, 115
    reflective equilibrium 26
    sense of justice 23–6
    social primary goods 25
    theory of justice 22–3, 47,
        131–2, 169, 171
    veil of ignorance 23, 47, 77,
        125, 334
realism 13, 50, 51, 75, 81–4,
    93–111, 114, 115, 127, 159,
    160, 165, 173, 293
    as radical critique 104–5
    as social science 96–8
    historical perspective 94–5
    humanitarian intervention 325,
        328–9
    international law and 282
    liberal 103–4
    structure of ethical
        argument 101–3
    varieties of 103–5
    war and 293, 300, 312, 313–4,
        318, 320, 321, 328–9
realist cosmopolitanism 331